Plate 1 (*Frontispiece*)

DEPARTMENT OF EDUCATION AND SCIENCE

Children and their Primary Schools

*A Report of the Central Advisory Council
for Education (England)*

VOLUME 1: THE REPORT

LONDON
HER MAJESTY'S STATIONERY OFFICE
1967

First Published 1967
Fifth impression 1969

In August 1963 the Central Advisory Council for Education (England) were asked by Sir Edward Boyle, the then Minister of Education, to consider the whole subject of primary education and the transition to secondary education.

Their Report is now published and everyone—not only those professionally concerned with education, but parents and the general public—must be grateful for the thoroughness with which they have carried out their task.

Primary education is the base on which all other education has to be built. Its importance cannot be overestimated.

The many recommendations in the Report, some of far-reaching significance, will be studied with the greatest care by the Government and, I am sure, by all the other interests concerned. There can be no doubt that the work done by the Council, with so much diligence and public spirit, will enable decisions to be reached on a more informed basis by those who are charged with securing the best development of English education within the resources available. I most warmly thank Lady Plowden and her colleagues for this valuable Report.

ANTHONY CROSLAND

November 1966.

28th October, 1966

Dear Secretary of State,

In August 1963, the then Minister of Education, Sir Edward Boyle, asked the Central Advisory Council for Education (England) "to consider primary education in all its aspects, and the transition to secondary education". I now have much pleasure in submitting the Report of the Council.

The Central Advisory Council for Education (Wales) were given identical terms of reference and we understand that they, too, will report soon. We have been able to keep in touch with their work through the members appointed jointly to both Councils.

Yours sincerely,

BRIDGET PLOWDEN

(*Chairman*)

The Rt. Hon. Anthony Crosland, P.C., M.P.,
Secretary of State for Education and Science

MEMBERSHIP OF THE
CENTRAL ADVISORY COUNCIL FOR EDUCATION (ENGLAND)

Lady Plowden, J.P. (Chairman).

Sir John Newsom, C.B.E., (Deputy Chairman), Chairman, Public Schools Commission; Director, Longmans Green & Co. Ltd.

Mr. H. G. Armstrong, Educational Psychologist, West Riding.

Professor A. J. Ayer, F.B.A., Wykeham Professor of Logic, University of Oxford.

Miss M. F. M. Bailey, Headmistress, Skerton Girls' County Secondary School, Lancaster. (Appointed January 1964).

Mrs. M. Bannister, Housewife and Parent.

Miss M. Brearley, C.B.E., Principal, Froebel Institute College of Education, Roehampton.

Dr. I. C.R. Byatt, Lecturer in Economics, London School of Economics and Political Science. (Appointed February 1965).

The Hon. Mrs. J. Campbell, Housewife and Parent; Hon. Secretary, Richmond upon Thames Association for the Advancement of State Education.

Professor D. V. Donnison, Professor of Social Administration, London School of Economics and Political Science; Vice-Chairman, Public Schools Commission.

Miss Z. E. Dix, Head Teacher, Field End Infants' School, Middlesex.

Professor C. E. Gittins, Professor of Education, University College of Swansea; formerly Chief Education Officer, Monmouthshire; Chairman, Central Advisory Council for Education (Wales).

Miss S. E. Grey, Organiser for Infant Education, Glamorgan; Member of Central Advisory Council for Education (Wales).

Mr. E. W. Hawkins, Director, Language Teaching Centre, University of York; formerly, Headmaster, Calday Grange County Grammar School for Boys, Hoylake, Cheshire.

Miss E. M. Parry, Inspector of Schools, Bristol; Vice-Chairman, National Nursery Examination Board.

Mr. A. Puckey, Deputy Head Teacher, The Elms Junior Mixed School, Nottingham.

Mr. T. H. F. Raison, Editor of "New Society".

Alderman Mrs. E. V. Smith, J.P., Member and former Chairman, Birmingham Education Committee.

Mr. R. T. Smith, Headmaster, Bampton C. of E. Junior Mixed and Infants' School, Oxfordshire.

Professor J. M. Tanner, Professor in Child Health and Growth, University of London, Institute of Child Health.

Brigadier L. L. Thwaytes, D.L., Vice-Chairman, West Sussex County Council; formerly Chairman, West Sussex Education Committee. (Appointed January 1964).

Mr. T. H. Tunn, Director of Education, Sheffield.

Mr. Martin Wilson, C.B.E., Formerly Secretary for Education, Shropshire.

Mr. F. M. White, Headmaster, St. Faith's School, Cambridge. (Appointed January 1964).

Dr. M. Young, Chairman, Advisory Centre for Education; Chairman, Social Science Research Council; Director, Institute of Community Studies.

The Council were appointed in August 1963 and began work under their present terms of reference in October 1963.

Mr. P. Mursell resigned from membership of the Council in January 1964 and Mr. H. B. Rose in February 1965.

The following members of the Department and H.M. Inspectorate assisted the Council (but see also Note on Our Methods of Work and Acknowledgements at end of Chapter 32 and Annex B):

Miss S. M. C. Duncan, H.M.I.

Miss N. L. Goddard, Inspector of Schools, Inner London Education Committee (seconded to Department).

Mr. D. T. Jones, O.B.E., H.M.I.

Mr. J. E. H. Blackie, C.B., H.M.I., Assessor.

Mr. D. H. Leadbetter, C.B., Assessor.

Miss E. M. McDougall, H.M.I., Assessor.

Miss M. E. Nicholls, H.M.I., Assessor.

Secretaries

Mr. M. Kogan (Secretary).

Mr. N. Summers (Assistant Secretary until March 1965.)

Miss C. K. Burke (Assistant Secretary from January 1964).

The estimated cost of the production of the Report is £120,699 of which £38,225 represents the estimated cost of printing and publication £67,637 the estimated cost of research commissioned on behalf of the council and £14,837 the travelling and subsistence costs of members.

Table of Contents

VOLUME 1

Paragraphs

PART ONE

INTRODUCTION

CHAPTER 1 **Introduction**   1–8

PART TWO

THE GROWTH OF THE CHILD

CHAPTER 2 **The Children: Their Growth and Development** ..   9–75

Physical Growth from Birth to Adolescence ..   12 & 13

Individual Differences in Rates of Maturing ..   14–20

The Growth of the Brain   21–23

Critical or Sensitive Periods ..   24–28

The Interaction of Heredity and Environment   29–32

Environmental Factors Affecting Physical

Growth   33–38

The Trend Towards Earlier Physical Maturity..   39–41

The Development of Behaviour   42–52

Language   53–55

The Measurement of Intelligence and its Bearing

on Educational Decisions   56–64

The Emotional Development of the Child ..   65–74

Implications   75

PART THREE

THE HOME, SCHOOL AND NEIGHBOURHOOD

CHAPTER 3 **The Children and Their Environment**   76–101

A Pool of Ability .. ..   83 & 84

Prospects for Improvement .. .. ..   85 & 86

The National Survey   87–89

The Findings of the Survey .. .. ..   90 & 90

Importance of Parental Attitudes   92–101

Paragraphs

CHAPTER 4 **Participation by Parents** **102–130**

    Co-operation with Parents 107–110

    Parent-Teacher Associations 111

    A Minimum Programme 112

    Visiting the Homes 113–118

    A Policy for Each Local Education Authority 119 & 120

    The Community School 121–123

    The Way Ahead 124–126

    Interesting Parents Early 127–129

    Recommendations 130

CHAPTER 5 **Educational Priority Areas** **131–177**

    The Educational Needs of Deprived Areas .. 136 & 137

    Hope for the Future .. .. 138 & 139

    Educational Assumptions and Policies.. .. 140–146

    The Distribution of Resources 147–150

    Educational Priority Areas 151–154

    Special Groups 155–157

    More Teachers 158–162

    Colleges of Education 163

    Buildings 164

    Nursery Education 165

    Other Priorities .. .. 166 & 167

    First Steps.. 168–170

    A Continuing Policy .. .. 171 & 172

    Conclusion 173

    Recommendations 174–177

CHAPTER 6 **Children of Immigrants** **178–199**

    Numbers .. .. 181 & 182

    Educational Problems 183–186

    The Curriculum 187–198

    Recommendations 199

CHAPTER 7 **The Health and Social Services and the School
Child** **200–255**

    The Health of the School Child 202

    The School Health and Dental Service and the
Health Visitors 203–207

    Medical Examinations 208–210

    Child Guidance, School Psychological and
Speech Therapy Services.. 211–214

Paragraphs

Recommendations 215
The Education Welfare Officers 216–220
The Child Care and Probation Services .. 221–223
Voluntary Services 224
Social Work and Related Services 225–227
Organisation and Deployment of Services .. 228 & 229
Co-ordination 230–233
Training and Recruitment 234
The Schools and the Social Services 235–241
Conclusions 242–254
Summary 255
Forms of Report Involving Parents Pages 93–94

PART FOUR

THE STRUCTURE OF PRIMARY EDUCATION

CHAPTER 8 **Primary Education in the 1960s: Its Organisation
and Effectiveness** **256–290**
The Legal Position 257
Reorganisation of Primary and Secondary
Education 258
Changes within Primary Education 259–265
Some Other Features .. .. 265 & 266
Assessments of Primary Education 267–276
Description of Schools 277–289
Recommendation 290
CHAPTER 9 **Providing for Children Before Compulsory Education** **291–343**
I. *The Present Position..* 292–308
The Case for Nursery Education 296–304
Mothers at Work: The Economic Argument .. 305
Arguments against Nursery Education .. 306–308
II. *Our Recommendations: Future Patterns of Nursery
Education* 309–326
Nursery Groups and Day Nurseries: A Unified
Service 313–315
The Age Range of Nursery Education .. 316
Part-Time Nursery Education 317
The Encouragement of Attendance .. .. 318 & 319
Nursery Education and Parents 320–322
The Future of Voluntary Nursery Groups .. 323–325

Paragraphs

Siting of Nurseries   326

III. *The Expansion of Nursery Education: The Places*
     Needed, Their Staffing and Accommodation   ..   327–343

     The Number of Places Needed   328
     Full-Time Attendance for a Minority   ..   329 & 330
     Places Needed   331
     Staffing the Nurseries   ..   ..   ..   332 & 333
     The Numbers Needed: Teachers   ..   ..   334 & 335
     The Numbers Needed: Nursery Assistants   ..   336–338
     Buildings ..   ..   339 & 340
     Conclusion   ..   ..   341 & 342
     Recommendations   343

CHAPTER 10 **The Ages and Stages of Primary Education**   ..   **344–407**
     When Should Primary Education Begin?   ..   344–346
     Disadvantages of Termly Entry..   347–351
     Chronological Versus Developmental Age   ..   352
     Easing Entry to School   353–356
     Age of Entry   357–359
     The Length of the Infant School Course   ..   360–364
     Should the Age of Transfer to Secondary Educa-
     tion be Raised?   365–378
     12 or 13?   379–387
     Provision for Exceptional Cases   388–392
     The Need for a National Policy   393–394
     Making the Changes   395–398
     An Emergency Plan for Infant Schools   ..   399–405
     Conclusion: A Change of Name   406
     Recommendations   407

CHAPTER 11 **Selection for Secondary Education** **408–423**
     Impact of Selection Procedures   ..   ..   411 & 412
     Selection Procedures   413–422
     Recommendations   423

CHAPTER 12 **Continuity and Consistency Between the Stages of**
     Education **424–448**
     Home to School ..   ..   424 & 425
     Separate or Combined Schools   426
     Avoiding Strain at Time of Transfer   427–430
     Contacts Between Teachers in Successive Stages
     of Education   ..   ..   431 & 432

Paragraphs

Interchange of Knowledge of Pupils 433–437
Introducing Pupils to New Schools .. .. 438 & 439
Support from Parents .. .. 440 & 441
Consistency in Work and Organisation .. 442–445
Content of Curriculum .. .. .. 446 & 447
Recommendations 448

CHAPTER 13 **The Size of Primary Schools** **449–467**
The Existing Situation 450
Suitable Sizes of Schools for Primary Children.. 451–456
Economic Arguments 457–459
Staffing Costs in Manpower and Money .. 460
Transport Costs 461
Foreign Practice 462
Conclusions 463–466
Recommendations 467

CHAPTER 14 **Education in Rural Areas** **468–492**
School Closures .. .. 469 & 470
Changing Social Conditions .. .. .. 471 & 472
Rural Schools: The Premises .. .. .. 473 & 474
Staffing 475–477
Children and the Schools .. .. .. 478 & 479
Size and Age Range of Rural Schools .. 470–483
Help for Rural Schools 484–491
Recommendations 492

PART FIVE

THE CHILDREN IN THE SCHOOLS: CURRICULUM AND INTERNAL

ORGANISATION

CHAPTER 15 **The Aims of Primary Education** **493–507**
CHAPTER 16 **Children Learning in School**.. .. .. .. **508–554**
Towards Freedom of Curriculum 508–517
Research on Children's Learning 518–522
Aspects of Children's Learning 523–535
The Time-Table .. .. 536 & 537
Flexibility in the Curriculum 538–542
Use of the Environment 543–548
Discovery .. .. 549 & 550
Evaluation of Children's Progress 551–553
Recommendations 554

Paragraphs

CHAPTER 17 **Aspects of the Curriculum** **555–721**

    (A) *Religious Education* 558–577

        Teachers' Attitudes 563–566

        Difficulties of the Present Position .. 567

        The School Community .. .. .. 568 & 569

        The Act of Worship .. .. .. 570 & 571

        Religious Education 572

        The Agreed Syllabus 573–576

        Recommendations 577

    (B) *English* 578–613

        Speech 580–582

        Teaching Children to Read .. .. 583 & 584

        Standards of Reading 585–590

        A Range of Books 591–596

        Poetry 597–599

        Drama 600

        Children's Writing 601–613

    (C) *Modern Languages* 614–619

    (D) *History* 620–634

    (E) *Geography* 635–646

    (F) *Mathematics* 647–662

    (G) *Science* 663–675

    (H) *Art and Craft* 676–685

    (I) *Music* 686–696

    (J) *Physical Education* 697–713

    (K) *Sex Education* 714–721

CHAPTER 18 **Aids to Learning and to Teaching** **722–733**

    Programmed Learning 728–733

CHAPTER 19 **The Child in the School Community** **734–751**

    Relationships in Primary Schools 736–742

    Punishment 743–750

    Recommendations 751

CHAPTER 20 **How Primary Schools are Organised** **752–833**

    I. *Developments in the Class Teacher System* .. 752–777

      Individual, Group and Class Learning.. .. 754–760

      Team Teaching 761–768

      The Class Teacher 769–771

      Conclusions 772–777

    II. *The Size of Class* 778–788

Paragraphs

Conclusions   786–788

III. *The Composition of a Class*   789–825

     Infant Schools and Classes   792–794

     Junior Schools and Classes   795–797

     Age   798

     "Vertical Classification"   799–804

     Classes Including Less Than a Year Group   ..   805

     Classification by Attainment or Ability (Stream-

     ing)   806–817

     Conclusions   818–825

IV. *The Length of the School Day and Term*   ..   826–832

     Recommendations   833

CHAPTER 21 **Handicapped Children in Ordinary Schools**   ..   **834–860**

     Parents   ..   ..   843 & 844

     The Handicapped Child in the Ordinary School   845–848

     Slow Learners   849–853

     The Teachers   854–859

     Recommendations   860

CHAPTER 22 **The Education of Gifted Children** **861–872**

     Recommendation   872

PART SIX

THE ADULTS IN THE SCHOOLS

     Introduction: The Role of the Teacher   873–878

CHAPTER 23 **The Staffing of Schools** **879–902**

     Men and Women Teachers   ..   ..   ..   881 & 882

     Full-Time and Part-Time Teachers   883

     Unqualified Teachers   ..   ..   884 & 885

     Ratio of Teachers to Pupils   ..   ..   ..   886 & 887

     Distribution of Teachers   ..   ..   ..   888 & 889

     Ancillary Helpers   890–893

     The Future   894–898

     Primary and Secondary School Staffing   ..   899–901

     Recommendations   902

CHAPTER 24 **The Deployment of Staff** **903–948**

     The Proportion of Men and Women Teachers

     in Primary Schools   903–905

     The Criteria for Staffing Schools   906–911

		Paragraphs
	The Recruitment and Use of Part-Time Teachers	912–917
	Various Kinds of Ancillary Help and Helpers ..	918–921
	Teachers' Aides	922–928
	The Head Teacher and His Staff	929–940
	Advice and Inspection	941–947
	Recommendations	948
CHAPTER 25	**The Training of Primary School Teachers** ..	**949–1028**
	The Present Position: A Factual Summary ..	952–957
	The Structure of Training	958–960
	The Students in Training for Primary Work ..	961–998
	Admission of Students	961 & 962
	Proportion of Men and Women Students ..	963
	Mature Students	964
	Graduates	965–969
	The Courses in Colleges of Education and University Departments of Education	970–980
	Main Courses	972
	Education Course and Teaching Practice ..	973
	Curriculum Courses	974
	Staffing of Colleges of Education	975–977
	B.Ed. Courses	978 & 979
	Other Graduate Courses	980
	Some General Points about Students' Life and Work	981–983
	The Relationship between Schools and Teachers in Training Institutions	984–1027
	Teaching Practice	985–990
	Our Views	991
	Other Aspects of the Relationship Between Schools and Teacher Training Institutions ..	992–998
	The Probationary Year	999–1012
	In-Service Training	1013–1027
	Present Provision of Courses and Plans for Expansion	1014–1025
	Courses for Returning Teachers	1026 & 1027
	Recommendations	1028
CHAPTER 26	**The Training of Nursery Assistants and Teachers' Aides**	**1029–1055**
	Existing Schemes of Training	1029–1033

Paragraphs

Other Training Schemes 1034
Our Proposals 1035
Similarities of Training and Recruitment .. 1036 & 1037
Entry Qualifications .. .. 1038 & 1039
The Nature of the Courses 1040–1044
Length of Courses .. .. 1045 & 1046
Status and Salaries of Trainees 1047
Part-Time Training 1048
Location and Staffing of Training 1049
Award of Qualifications 1050
Career Prospects 1051
Probation 1052
Build-Up of Recruitment .. .. .. 1053 & 1054
Recommendations 1055

PART SEVEN

INDEPENDENT SCHOOLS

CHAPTER 27 **Independent Primary Schools** **1056–1079**
Summary of Conclusions and Recommendations 1079

PART EIGHT

PRIMARY SCHOOL BUILDINGS AND EQUIPMENT;
STATUS; AND RESEARCH

CHAPTER 28 **Primary School Buildings and Equipment** .. **1080–1113**
I. *Primary School Building* 1081–1101
The Present State of Primary Buildings .. 1081–1083
School Building Since 1945: Number of Places
and Costs .. .. 1084 & 1085
The Improvement of Old Buildings 1086–1091
Developments in School Building Since 1945 .. 1092 & 1093
Developments Since 1956 1094–1097
Some Design and Planning Implications of Our
Report 1098
Cost Limits 1099
Educational Furniture and Equipment .. 1100 & 1101
II. *Equipment Allowances for Primary Schools* .. 1102–1112
Choices Open to Schools 1107–1110
Assistance for Schools in Special Need .. 1111
Disparity in Local Practice 1112
Recommendations 1113

Paragraphs

CHAPTER 29 **The Status and Government of Primary Education**   **1114–1150**

Some of the Evidence   1116–1117

Standing of Teachers in the Community   1118

The Standing of Primary Teachers Compared with that of Secondary School Teachers   ..   1119–1126

The Standing of Primary School Teachers in their Dealings with Local Education Authorities   1127–1130

Management of Schools   1131–1138

Appointment of Staff   1139–1141

Powers of Head Teachers   1142–1146

Relationships of Heads and Assistant Staff   ..   1147–1148

General   1149

Recommendations   1150

Annex: A Note on the Method of Calculating Unit Totals   ..   ..   Page (421)

CHAPTER 30 **Research, Innovation and the Dissemination of Information** **1151–1166**

Further Studies   ..   ..   1165 & 1166

PART NINE

CONCLUSIONS AND RECOMMENDATIONS

CHAPTER 31 **The Costs and Priorities of Our Recommendations**   **1167–1204**

I. *The Present Position*..   1168–1170

The Economic Yield of Primary Education   ..   1171–1176

II. *The Availability of Resources*   1177–1184

Overall Resources   ..   ..   1177 & 1178

Teachers   ..   ..   1179 & 1180

Aides and Assistants   1181–1183

Priorities   1184

III. *Our Principal Proposals, Their Priority and Timing*   1185–1204

Educational Priority Areas   ..   ..   ..   1186 & 1187

Improvement of Staffing Elsewhere: Teachers   1188

Staffing: Aides and Assistants   1189

Building   1190–1196

Other Proposals   1197–1200

The Order of Priorities ..   ..   1201 & 1202

Costs and Benefits   1203

The Total Costs   1204

Annex A: Factors Affecting Recruitment of Assistants and Aides   1205–1218

Paragraphs

Annex B: Offsets to the Costs of Nursery Provision and the Use of Teachers' Aides: An Estimate of the Output of Mothers who Return to Work ..   1219–1228

CHAPTER 32 **Recommendations and Conclusions** **1229–1252**

    I. *The Changing Direction*   1229–1241

    II. *Recommendations and Conclusions*   ..   .. 1242 & 1243

    III. *A Note on Our Methods of Work, and Acknowledgements*   1244–1252

NOTES OF RESERVATION   *Page*

Note of Reservation on Nursery Education by Mrs. M. Bannister ..   486

Note of Reservation on the Organisation of Services for Under Fives by Professor D. V. Donnison, Sir John Newsom and Dr. M. Young..   487

Note of Reservation on Parental Contribution to the Costs of Nursery Education by Professor A. J. Ayer, Dr. I. C. R. Byatt, Professor D. V. Donnison, Mr. E. W. Hawkins, Lady Plowden, Mr. T. H. F. Raison, Brigadier L. L. Thwaytes and Dr. M. Young   487

Note of Reservation on Religious Education by Professor A. J. Ayer, Dr. I. C. R. Byatt, Professor D. V. Donnison, Mrs. E. V. Smith, Professor J. M. Tanner and Dr. M. Young   489

Note of Reservation on Religious Education by Mr. E. W. Hawkins and Mr. M. Wilson   492

Note of Reservation on Corporal Punishment by Miss M. F. M. Bailey   493

A Suggestion on the Supply and Training of Teachers by Professor A. J. Ayer, Dr. I. C. R. Byatt, Mr. E. W. Hawkins, Sir John Newsom, Lady Plowden and Mr. T. H. F. Raison   493

Annex A: A Questionnaire to Witnesses   499

Annex B: List of Witnesses   504

Annex C: Visits Made   522

Glossary   537

Index   545

No general bibliography is provided but references to printed sources are listed at the end of each chapter.

Figures in the tables throughout the Report are rounded up.

List of Tables, Diagrams and Photographs

Tables   *Page*

1   Percentage Contribution of Parental Attitudes, Home Circum-
    stances and State of School to Variation in Educational
    Performance   33

2   Numbers of Children from Certain Commonwealth Countries
    in English Schools (1966): (Primary and Secondary Schools) ..   70

3   Main Causes and Numbers of Deaths in Children Under 15.
    1931 and 1963   76

4   Provision in England for Children Under Five: 1932 Compared
    to 1965   108

5   Pre-School Provision in England: Information from Depart-
    ment of Education and Science, Ministry of Health and Home
    Office   109

6   English Primary Education: January, 1965   112

7   Children Aged 5-11 in Different Types of School: England   ..   113

8   Maintained Primary Schools: England. Number of Schools
    or Departments According to Numbers of Pupils on the
    Register: January 1965   114

9   Maintained Primary Schools or Departments by Denomination
    January 1965: England   115

10 Nursery Education: Numbers of Full-Time Equivalent Places
    Needed   128

11 Compulsory Education in Infant Schools Under Present
    Arrangements   135

12 Interim Plan for Entry to First Schools   150

13 Cost Limits for Different Sizes of Primary Schools (June 1966)   169

14 Distribution of Pupil/Teacher Ratios by Size of School:
    January 1965: England   170

15 Number of Small Schools in England: 1962-65   173

16 Size of Primary Class, England: January 1965   280

17 Numbers of Handicapped Pupils Receiving and Awaiting
    Special Education (in Special Schools, Classes, Units, in
    Hospitals and at Home) and Prevalence per 10,000 of the
    School Population in England and Wales, 1961 and 1966   ..   299

18 Primary School Staffing, 1947-1965. England   316

19 Number of Classes of Different Sizes in Primary Schools,   316
    1947-65: England   ..   ..

20 Numbers of Primary Pupils Per Full-Time Teacher, January   317
    1965: England   ..   ..

Tables   *Page*

21 Numbers of Primary Pupils Per Full-Time Teacher (Total Full-
    Time and Full-Time Equivalent of Part-Time), January 1965:
    England   317

22 Average Sizes of Class, January 1965: England   317

23 Ancillary Help Employed in Primary Schools, 1965 (England
    and Wales)   318

24 Primary School Staffing: England   320

25 Qualifications of Students Admitted to General, Housecraft,
    P.E. and Shortened Courses in Colleges of Education in the
    Years 1960–61, 1961–62 and 1965–66 (England and Wales) ..   364

26 Total Number of Students in Initial Non-Graduate Courses in
    Colleges of Education by Type of Course and Years (England
    and Wales)   366

27 Number of General and Specialist Colleges Offering Different
    Types of Courses   367

28 Annual Intake of Students to Non-Graduate Courses in General
    Colleges of Education (England and Wales)   367

29 Age of Primary and Secondary School Buildings (England
    1962)   389

30 Specified Defects in Primary School Accommodation (England
    1962)   392

31 Cost of Remedying Defects in School Accommodation (Eng-
    land)   393

32 Equipment and Capitation Allowances: Numbers of L.E.As.
    and Amounts Available at Different Stages of Primary
    Education (1963)   406

33 Salary Scales for Head Teachers   421

34 Deputy Head Teachers and Graded Posts   422

35 The Effects on Overall Staffing Standards of More Favourable
    Staffing Ratios in Educational Priority Areas   443

36 Educational Priority Areas: Teachers, Teachers' Aides and
    Nursery Assistants   444

37 Build-up of Recruitment of Nursery Assistants and Teachers'
    Aides (Including Those Needed for Educational Priority
    Areas)   445

38 Chart Illustrating Possible Expansion of Nursery Provision in
    the Educational Priority Areas and Introduction of Single
    Date of Entry   446

39 Additional Capital Building Costs of Recommendations in the
    Report (Excluding Additions for Increased Numbers, Rehous-
    ing and Replacements)   447

40 Additional Running Costs of Recommendations in the Report   448

41 The Financial Cost of Proposed Nursery Provision   449

Tables   *Page*

42   Public Authorities' Expenditure on Maintained Primary and
     Nursery Schools: England   449

43   Past and Projected Costs of Maintained Primary Schools on
     Present Policies, 1960/61–1978/79: England   450

44   Projected Costs of Maintained Primary Schools and Additional
     Costs Resulting from the Adoption of Our Proposals: England   451

45   Projected Costs of Maintained Primary and Nursery Schools
     and the Additional Costs of Our Proposals: England..   ..   452

46   Assumed Annual Recruitment of School Leavers for Training
     as Nursery Assistants and Teachers' Aides   454

Diagrams

1A   Height of Average Boy and Girl from Birth to Maturity..   8

1B   Rate of Growth in Height ("Height Velocity") of "Aver-
     age" Boy and Girl from Birth to Maturity..   8

2   Year of Menarche   16

3   Proportion of Pupils Aged 13 in All-Age Schools   ..   98

4   Proportion of Pupils Aged Nine in Mixed Primary Schools   98

5   Small Schools in England: Primary (Including All-Age)..   107

6   Numbers of Children in Maintained Primary Schools
     Aged 5 to 11 in 1947–1965, England   111

7   Infant and Junior Classes   280

8   A School for 50 Pupils Aged 5 to 11 Years at Finmere,
     Oxfordshire   396

9   School for 320 Pupils Aged 3½ to 9 Years. Eveline Lowe
     Primary School, Rolls Road, London, S.E.1   400

10   Extension to Convert Existing Infants' School for 240
     Pupils of 5 to 7 Years into School for 320 Pupils of 5 to 8
     Years   401

11   Extensions to Convert Existing Junior Schools for 480
     Pupils of 7 to 11 Years into Schools for 480 Pupils of 8 to
     12 Years   402

12 A & B A Middle School for Pupils of 8 to 12 Years   403 and 404

Plates (between pages 264 and 265).

1   Frontispiece

2   Children at Work 1937

3   and 1966

4   Listening to a Story

Plates

5   Experimenting with Clay

6   Care in Building

7   An Incentive to Read

8 & 9   Looking Forward to Adult Life

10   Living Things

11   A Record of the Past

12   Reading

13   and Writing

14   Concentration

15   Work or Play?

16   Freedom to Move

17   Dramatic Encounter

18   A School in its Environment

19 & 20   The Environment the same School Creates

21   School in a Congested Suburb

22   A Suburban Infant School Without Traffic Dangers

23   Primary Schools in the Centre of a City

24   Primary School and Clinic adjacent to a Secondary School

25   Junior Children Are Most Agile

26   Expression in Movement

27   Finding Out the Properties of Things

28   —and Numbers

29 & 30   Mathematical Problems arise from Real Life

31   Weather Station

32   Comparing Temperatures in a Puddle

33 & 34   Using Mechanical Aids in Small Groups

35 & 36   Learning about Colour and Design

37   Imagination and Accuracy in Reconstructing the Past: Top Juniors

38   Lifting Weights with Pulleys

39 & 40   Differences between Art and Crafts for Boys and Girls are disappearing

41 & 42   Following individual Interest

43   Inventiveness with Materials

44   Individual and Group Work

45 & 46   The Beginning of Life-Long Interests

Copyright

We are grateful to the following copyright holders for permission to reproduce photographs:

Aerofilms Ltd.
Miss E. E. Biggs, H.M.I.
Bristol County Council
Miss E. Davies, H.M.I.
Devon County Council
Mr. D. G. S. Dickson
Essex County Council
Fairy Surveys Ltd.
James Galt and Co. Ltd.
Mr. J. Howard
Mr. K. E. Hoy
Inner London Education Authority
Mr. T. R. Jones
Mr. E. Pearson, H.M.I.
Scholastic Souvenir Company Ltd.
S.G. Photography
Teachers' World
The Times
Universal Studios: by E. W. Williamson, A.R.P.S., A.I.B.P.
Miss J. R. Warner, H.M.I.
Mrs. D. E. Whittaker
Yorkshire (West Riding) County Council

We are grateful to the schools whose work is illustrated in some of the photographs.

Part One

Introduction

CHAPTER 1

Introduction

1. When the Minister of Education asked us "to consider primary education in all its aspects and the transition to secondary education", he was in effect inviting us to tell him how far the intentions of Sir Henry Hadow and his committee had been carried out and how well they had stood the test of time. Hadow, if any man, has the right to be considered the architect of the English educational system as we know it. The three reports of the Consultative Committee under his chairmanship, the Education of the Adolescent (1926), the Primary School (1931) and Infant and Nursery Schools (1933), virtually laid the foundation of what exists today. The purpose to be achieved, and the test by which its success can be recognised, he defined in 1931 in these words "What a wise and good parent will desire for his own children, a nation must desire for all children". Of course, equality of opportunity, even when it means weighting the scales to reduce inequalities, still results in unequal achievements. But, coupled with a commitment to the highest educational standards, it is the touchstone to apply.

2. Underlying all educational questions is the nature of the child himself. Are children of today at the same stage of development as children of the same age were in 1926? Ought all, or nearly all, children of the same age to be able to do the same things? How great are the differences between boys and girls, and do they vary with age? If a child's "intelligence" is tested at the age of eight or eleven, will the results hold good five or six years later? What is the relationship between environmental and genetic factors in the shaping of human ability? We know more than was known a generation ago about physical, intellectual and emotional development in children. Though nobody would suppose that we have now reached final truth, we are in a position to look again at some of the conclusions drawn by the Hadow reports. We do so in Part II of the Report.

3. In recent years a growing awareness has developed of the importance to the individual of his family and social background. The last three reports of the Council, and the Robbins report on higher education, have shown how closely associated are home and social circumstances and academic achievement. Is this just one of those given facts about which schools, and the community, can do nothing? To try to answer this question, we set on foot a National Survey which is included with other surveys of the same nature in Volume 2. Increasing numbers of parents are asking, and we are glad they are asking, how they can help to get the schools their children deserve. Part III of the Report is devoted to these questions of home, neighbourhood and school. It is in part about especially difficult districts or peculiarly awkward circumstances such as how to teach children who do not speak English at home. Most of Part III is about the school round any corner, the schools in which over nine-tenths of our young children are educated.

4. We have studied the structure of primary education and give our conclusions in Part IV. We have dealt with the provision which might be made for

1

nursery education; we have discussed the length of primary school life. All this we could hardly have avoided doing since we were asked to deal with "all aspects of primary education". We have considered not only what is desirable, but whether what is desirable is feasible. One aspect of our enquiry has been made especially difficult and that is a matter on which our advice was specifically asked—the age of transfer to secondary education. In July 1965 the Department of Education and Science asked local education authorities to prepare detailed plans for the development of comprehensive education in their areas before our recommendations were known. The shape of secondary schools, and the accommodation they will require, depend on the age at which primary education ends. It would have been better if the momentous changes in the overall structure of education—the raising of the school leaving age and the associated changes in the age of transfer and secondary school organisation—could have been considered together. We hope that our arguments in favour of a new age of transfer will be taken into account when building programmes and teacher training are planned for the 1970s.

5. The growth of comprehensive education is altering the context in which the primary schools work. In 1963, when we started work, the "11 plus" and all that went before was a major item on our agenda. Should it be retained? This proved to be a question we did not have to answer, though we may say that we welcome the disappearance of transfer examinations. We were left with another question to discuss. In the past many primary schools have "worked to" the 11 plus. If it has not been their Bible, it has often been a taskmaster. It set up minimum standards for the abler children, often in our view the wrong ones, and distorting in their effects on the curriculum. But at least they were standards. The teachers and parents had some yardstick by which to measure their pupils' work. Now it is going. How are they to know what to expect of children? These are among the problems which we discuss in Part V.

6. Part V, "The Children in the Schools", is the heart of the Report. Is there any genuine conflict between education based on children as they are, and education thought of primarily as a preparation for the future? Has "finding out" proved to be better than "being told"? Have methods been worked out through which discovery can be stimulated and guided, and children develop from it a coherent body of knowledge? Has the emphasis which the Hadow Report placed on individual progress been justified by its results? How can head teachers and class teachers arrange the internal working of each school and each class to meet the different needs of the highly gifted boys and girls, of slow learning pupils, and of all the infinite varieties of talent and interest that lie between ? Do children learn more through active co-operation than by passive obedience? In seeking answers to such questions we draw attention to the best practices we have found as a pointer to the direction in which all schools should move. To help children to learn there are 140,000 primary school teachers: they form the subject of Part VI. In this Part, too, the present shortage of teachers is discussed, their training, their use and the support that can best be given to them both inside and outside the school.

7. English primary education has long had a high reputation. We heard repeatedly that English infant schools are the admiration of the world. Were

they resting on past laurels? Ought we to be learning by the experiments other countries were trying? We went to see. Between us, we paid visits, though they had to be brief, to many primary schools in Denmark, France, Sweden, Poland, U.S.A. and the U.S.S.R. Our journeyings are set out in Annex C. Our hosts were worried about many of the same things as we were. They were looking critically at curriculum and methods. They were concerned with such questions as how to provide for children of differing abilities, how to help most effectively children from poor circumstances, and how to recruit and make good use of teachers.

8. Finally, since another full scale enquiry into primary education is unlikely to be made for many years, we have thought it our duty in Part IX to give as close an estimate as we can of the cost of our proposals and to indicate an order of priority.

Part Two

The Growth of the Child

CHAPTER 2

The Children: Their Growth and Development

9. At the heart of the educational process lies the child. No advances in policy, no acquisitions of new equipment have their desired effect unless they are in harmony with the nature of the child, unless they are fundamentally acceptable to him. We know a little about what happens to the child who is deprived of the stimuli of pictures, books and spoken words; we know much less about what happens to a child who is exposed to stimuli which are perceptually, intellectually or emotionally inappropriate to his age, his state of development, or the sort of individual he is. We are still far from knowing how best to identify in an individual child the first flicker of a new intellectual or emotional awareness, the first readiness to embrace new sets of concepts or to enter into new relations.

10. Knowledge of the manner in which children develop, therefore, is of prime importance, both in avoiding educationally harmful practices and in introducing effective ones. In the last 50 years much work has been done on the physical, emotional and intellectual growth of children. There is a vast array of facts, and a number of general principles have been established. This chapter is confined to those facts which have greatest educational significance and those principles which have a direct bearing on educational practice and planning.

11. Among the relevant facts are the early growth of the brain, compared with most of the rest of the body; the earlier development of girls compared with boys; the enormously wide variability in physical and intellectual maturity amongst children of the same age, particularly at adolescence, and the tendency nowadays for children to mature physically earlier than they used to. Among the principles are present-day concepts about critical or sensitive periods, about developmental "sequence" (that is, events which are fixed in their order but varying in the age at which the sequence begins); about the poorer resilience of boys than girls under adverse conditions; and, above all, about the complex and continuous interaction between the developing organism and its environment. Under this last rather cumbersome phrase lies the coffin of the old nature-versus-nurture controversy. A better understanding of genetics and human biology has ended the general argument, and provided a clearer picture of what is implied when we talk of changes in measured intelligence during a child's development.

Physical Growth from Birth to Adolescence

12. The manner in which the skeleton, the muscles and most of the internal organs grow is shown in the curves of height at successive ages of the typical boy and girl. In Diagram 1A the height at each age is plotted; in Diagram 1B, the rate of growth, or velocity. This velocity curve shows that children are growing faster at birth than at any time during post-natal life (they grow fastest before birth) and that the growth rate decreases quite steadily until puberty is reached. From about the age of six to puberty the rate is nearly

7

Diagram 1A

Height of 'Average' Boy and Girl from Birth to Maturity: From 'Standards from Birth to Maturity, for Height, Weight, Height Velocity and Weight Velocity: British Children, 1965'. By J. M. Tanner, R. H. Whitehouse and M. Takaishi. 'Archives of Diseases in Childhood'. 1966.

Children are measured lying down until the age of two but are measured standing after that age. The break in curves represent the differences between these two measurements.

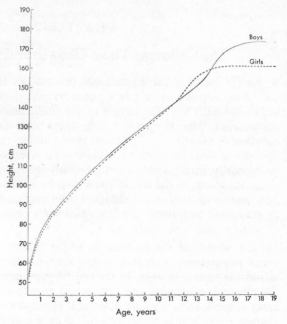

Diagram 1B

Rate of Growth in Height ('Height Velocity') of 'Average' Boy and Girl from Birth to Maturity: From 'Standards from Birth to Maturity, for Height, Weight, Height Velocity and Weight Velocity : British Children, 1965'. By J. M. Tanner, R. H. Whitehouse and M. Takaishi. 'Archives of Diseases in Childhood'. 1966.

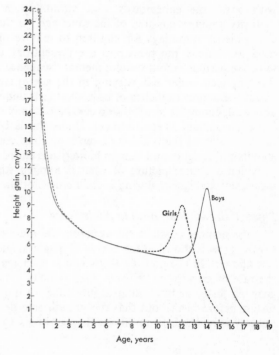

constant. At puberty a spurt occurs, and for a year or two the child grows again at about the rate experienced at the age of two to three.

13. The diagrams show the considerable differences between typical girls and boys. Boys are slightly larger at birth, and grow slightly faster for the first six to nine months. Then the girls' rate becomes greater, and because of this they gradually catch up in size. By six years of age there is little difference between boys and girls in height or weight or other body dimensions except for the head, which in boys is always larger. Girls begin puberty on average two years earlier than boys; hence from about 11 to 14 they are likely to be taller and heavier than boys, and probably stronger too. This simple fact has implications for co-education, especially as at this time girls have acquired the beginning of their sexual characteristics while most boys are still entirely pre-pubescent. Eventually, as the girls' adolescent growth spurt is dying away, the boys' begins. The boys' spurt is more marked than the girls' and is accompanied by a great increase in muscular strength, which does not occur in girls.

Individual Differences in Rates of Maturing.

14. What the diagrams do not show, however, is the wide variations in rate of growth found in any group of normal boys and girls. As a convenient example we may take the age at which menarche, the first menstrual period, occurs. On average this is just over 13·0 years in England at present; but the normal range, comprising 95 per cent of all girls, runs from 10·0 to 15·0 years; for 99 per cent of girls it is from 9·0 to 16·0 years. In practice this means that in a group of 11 or 12 year old girls there will be some whose puberty has not started, others who have full development of the breasts and are menstruating, and a few who are potentially fertile. The same principle applies to boys, though the age at which the pubertal variation between individuals is greatest comes later, at 13 to 14 years. The physical differences between the pre-pubertal and the post-pubertal are even greater in boys than in girls.

15. This individual variation in stage of development can be most dramatically seen at puberty and in relation to physical growth. But it is of cardinal importance to realise that a similar variation exists at earlier ages and in all aspects of growth and development. Thus the notion of developmental age, as opposed to chronological age, has arisen. By developmental age we simply mean the degree to which a child has advanced along the road from birth to full maturity. In the study of physical growth, several methods are used for estimating developmental age. The commonest is by measuring the maturity of the skeleton, especially of the bones of the hand and wrist. From birth onwards the appearances of these bones undergo a sequence of changes, easily seen in an X-ray. The sequence is practically the same in everybody, but the age at which any stage of the sequence is reached varies widely both between the sexes and between individual boys and girls. At birth the average girl is already some weeks ahead of the average boy in "bone age" and she gradually comes to be more and more ahead until at puberty the difference is two years. Among boys of the same chronological age there is a wide range of bone age which, for eight year olds, stretches from six to ten "years".

16. Similar considerations apply to tests of motor development, and it is highly probable they also apply to emotional and intellectual development. Long term studies of the measured intelligence of individual children through-

B

out the whole growing period make it seem likely that children differ in their rates of attaining their adult ability just as they do in attaining their adult height. Conventional tests given on a single occasion are unable to distinguish between acceleration and ability; that is, they do not distinguish a child whose ability will eventually be average, but who is accelerated in his intellectual development, from a child of above average ability who is proceeding at the average rate of intellectual development. Only by repeated longitudinal study can the distribution be inferred.

17. Some of the effects of this variability on the child are obvious enough, especially in relation to physical growth at the older ages. Both the excessively late and the excessively early developer, in physical terms, tend to feel estranged from the general group of children. The isolation of the late developer lasts longer and may lead to serious disturbances of behaviour. Some of the effects are already seen in nursery school; the early maturing child tends to be ahead of the others in motor skill and hence to have a degree of social advantage.

18. It is clearly important to know whether there is any overall "general-factor" of advancement, that is, a significant tendency for all physiological and psychological developments to be advanced together, or whether we have to hold in mind always a whole series of unrelated or only slightly related developmental ages; for example in bone age, in sexual maturity, in motor skill, in measured intelligence and in emotional reactions. The latter seems to be nearer the truth. The age of menarche, and the age of reaching full adult height can both, it is true, be predicted with much greater accuracy from bone age than from chronological age. But the relation between measured intelligence and skeletal age is small.

19. The picture of the growing child emerges as one in which each of a number of facets of physical, intellectual and emotional behaviour is developing slowly or fast, according to the individual and his circumstances. The various facets may only be linked loosely one with another. Thus a 12 year old boy may be beginning puberty, be amongst the strongest of his contemporaries and be skilful at games; but he may still be behind his contemporaries in certain intellectual attainments, not necessarily because he will eventually have little ability in this direction, but because he is developing slowly in these respects.

20. Clearly such a situation makes great demands upon the teacher. The emotional needs and the social interests of a 12 year old entering adolescence will certainly be different from those of a 12 year old whose adolescence is yet to come, whatever intellectual development each may have reached. This individual variability makes itself felt in any group of children and presents the teacher with a complex situation. Much of the variability arises from the biological nature of children; hence it will be with us for the foreseeable future. This demands that teachers should be adaptable in their approach to individuals, and that the educational system itself should be as flexible as possible. A system on the apple sorting model does not square with the nature of the biological material. We need rather to envisage a kind of cats' cradle of opportunity, providing a multitude of differently developing talents with their own appropriate times and degrees of achievement.

The Growth of the Brain

21. The curve of brain growth differs considerably from that of stature illustrated in diagrams 1A and B. From early foetal life onwards, the brain, in terms of its gross weight, is nearer to its adult size than any other organ, except the eyes. At birth the brain is 25 per cent of its adult weight, at six months 50 per cent and at five years 90 per cent. At this last age a child has reached only 40 per cent of his adult stature, and the reproductive organs are barely ten per cent of their adult size. In consequence of its early maturing the brain has a very slight pubertal growth spurt, if any at all.

22. We know distressingly little about the development of the cells and the organisation of the brain. It seems, from the work of Conel[1], that the notion of sequence established so clearly in other areas of development applies here also. Within certain areas of the cerebral cortex there is considerable localisation of functions, certain parts being necessary for vision, others for movement and so on. Around these primary motor, sensory, visual and auditory areas are association areas concerned with the integration of the information arriving at the corresponding primary area. Conel has shown that these primary areas mature in regular sequence; first the motor area, then the sensory, then the visual, then the auditory. Gradually the waves of development, as it were, spread out from the primary areas into the surrounding association areas. There is another gradient of maturity also: within the motor and sensory areas there is strict localisation of function to a part of the body. Cells near the top of the areas, for example, serve the leg; those in the middle, the hand; and those at the bottom, the tongue and mouth. These cells develop in the same sequence as the corresponding parts of the body. The arm cells, for instance, are ahead of the leg cells, just as a baby's arms are more advanced in growth than his legs.

23. There is plenty of evidence that, up to two years of age, brain functions appear when particular structures mature and not before. We know practically nothing, however, about the development of the brain beyond that age, but there is no particular reason to suppose that this generalisation suddenly ceases to be true at 2 or 3 or 13. On the contrary, it is more probable that the higher intellectual abilities also appear only as maturation of certain structures occurs. These structures must be units of organisation widespread through the cerebral cortex, rather than localised areas. Piaget and Inhelder[2] have described the emergence of mental structures in a manner strongly reminiscent of developing brain or body structures; the mental stages follow in a sequence, for example, which may be advanced or delayed, but not altered. There seems good reason to suppose that Piaget's successive stages depend on progressive maturation or at least progressive organisation of the cerebral cortex. For the cognitive stage to emerge, brain maturation is probably necessary, though not, of course, sufficient. Without at least some degree of social stimulus the latent abilities may never be exercised, and indeed the requisite cells may go undeveloped.

Critical or Sensitive Periods

24. We have no exact knowledge about this in relation to higher brain function, but we may at least speculatively extrapolate from experiments by Hubel and Wiesel[3] on simpler systems. Particular cells in the cortex of the

brain of the kitten respond to particular, simple light patterns shone into the eye. This response is functional even before kittens open their eyes. It comes into play as soon as the kittens begin to have visual experience. When, however, kittens' eyes were stitched closed at birth for two or three months and only then opened, these cells failed to function. It seems that experience is necessary to put the finishing touches on these cells, or to prevent them falling back into an atrophy of disuse. Once they have gained experience, the cells can then go on without it, at least for a considerable time. Stitching the eyes of adult cats for several months did not destroy the cells' function.

25. These experiments with cats also provide an example of another general characteristic in development—the critical period. By a critical period is meant a certain stage of limited duration during which a particular influence either from another area of the developing organism, or from the environment, evokes a particular response. The response may be beneficial, indeed perhaps essential to normal development, or it may be pathological (as in the cases of lesions of the foetus caused by the presence of German measles virus, or of thalidomide in the mother at a particular time in pregnancy).

26. A second example of a critical period is seen in the development of the rat. During the first few days after birth the testes of the male rat secrete a substance which passes to the brain and in some way alters the structure of the part called the hypothalamus. Once this has occurred the rat behaves at puberty as a male; the information as to maleness has been implanted into the hypothalamus irreversibly for the remainder of the rat's life. But if the transfer of information be prevented until five days after birth, then the sex of the rat will be indeterminate however much of the substance is administered later. These first few days are therefore a critical period for this development.

27. It is becoming clear that critical periods also exist for stimuli from the environment. Naturally, such an intimate interaction between the animal and its environment can only operate if the environment can be relied on to provide the right stimulus at the right time. Animals, in this sense, are born into "expected" environments, indeed into "required" environments. A duckling will follow the first large object seen at a certain time after hatching. This is usually the mother; but if it happens to be Professor Konrad Lorenz the duckling follows him and remains pathologically attached to humans for the remainder of its life[4].

28. We do not yet know to what extent such critical periods occur in the development of children. Psychologists feel fairly sure that in early infancy, and even longer, the baby "expects" cuddling, and that if he does not receive it, he may become, after a while, pathological in his behaviour, perhaps irreversibly so. Clinical experience with deaf children indicates that the facility for discriminating speech sounds, and therefore for understanding speech and learning to speak, may diminish after early childhood[5]. It would be surprising if at later ages limited periods at least of maximum receptivity did not occur for many skills and emotional developments. A critical period is only the extreme example of a more general class of sensitive periods. It is likely that, in the sphere of learning, periods of maximum sensitivity rather than of critical now-or-never-ness exist. More knowledge of the occurrence and nature of such periods from nursery school age onwards would be invaluable for the teacher and the subject is therefore an important one for educational research.

The Interaction of Heredity and Environment

29. Biologists are now much clearer than they were 30 years ago about the manner in which hereditary and environmental factors interact to produce a characteristic, be that characteristic stature or the score in an intelligence test. What is inherited are the genes. Except in very special instances, such as the blood groups and a few diseases, the chemical substance that any given gene causes to be produced is not directly related to any characteristic of a child or an adult. All characteristics have a history of continuous developmental interactions, first of gene products with other gene products, then of more complex molecules with other molecules, then of cells with cells, of tissues with the environment of the mother's uterus, and finally of a whole complex organism with an equally complex environment during the whole of growth after birth. It is now believed that all characteristics are developed in this way; none is inherited. And none can develop without the necessary genetic endowment to provide the basis, a basis as essential for characteristics which are learned as for those which are apparently not learned. The effect of this new biological outlook is of particular importance when we come to consider the question of changes in measured intelligence.

30. From an educational point of view the characteristics which have most importance such as intelligence are those which vary in degree in a population rather than being simply present or absent. Stature is a similar example related to physical characteristics. One cannot meaningfully talk of genes for tallness nor of genes for high intelligence. What we can say about such characteristics is that in a given population, growing up under given environmental circumstances, x per cent of the variability in height or intelligence can be attributed to inherited factors (the genotype), y per cent to environmental ones, and z per cent to genotype-environment interaction. The point is that hereditability is not a quantity that belongs to a characteristic but to a population in its environment. Accordingly it varies with the population and the environment. The more uniform the environment, the greater the proportion of variability due to genotype. In England, for example, the differences in height between adults are largely due to hereditary causes, for most children have had enough to eat. But in many underdeveloped countries, where starvation and disease are rife, more of the adult variation will be environmental in origin and a smaller proportion genetic.

31. The interaction of genes and environment may not be additive; for example, bettering the nutrition by a given amount may not produce a ten per cent increase in height in each person in a population irrespective of his genetic constitution. There may be genotype-environment interaction. Some people may have a rise of 12 per cent, others of eight per cent, depending on whether they carry genes making them react favourably to this new environmental circumstance. A particular environment, in other words, may be highly suitable for a child with certain genes, but highly unsuitable for a child with others. We do not know if such interactions occur in the genesis, for example, of the variations in measured intelligence in our population. If they do, and in principle this seems likely, it would follow that giving everybody the maximum educational opportunity may mean creating individual educational environments for different children. In the same way deprivation would not necessarily mean the same thing for one child as for another.

32. Genetic factors operate throughout the whole period of growth. Not all genes are active at birth; some only begin to exert their influence after a period of time. Probably this phased effect accounts for the fact that, physically, and perhaps in other respects, children resemble their parents increasingly as they grow older. Some environmental factors, too, may produce little apparent effect when they are most obviously operative, but a larger effect at some later time. This is known as the "sleeper" effect.

Environmental Factors Affecting Physical Growth

33. Adverse environmental conditions may slow down physical growth, and throw the child off his "programmed" curve, that is, off the curve that would be followed by someone of his genotype under optimal environmental conditions. But children possess a great capacity to return to or towards their curves if the environmental circumstances are made better. After temporary disease or starvation, for example, a child may resume growth at twice or three times the normal rate until he has caught up all that he had previously lost. Whether complete catching up is possible, depends on the age at which the child experiences the adverse environment, and the length of time for which he does so. The earlier the adversity and the longer its duration the more lasting its effects. The degree to which similar considerations apply to intellectual and emotional development is unknown and a subject requiring more research.

34. Girls' growth is less affected by adverse circumstances than boys' (see, for example, Appendix 10 for recent evidence collected by the National Child Development Study). This seems to be a general phenomenon as it is true of the females and males of several other mammalian species. It may be due entirely to the earlier physiological maturity of girls, or there may be other causes. Boys are more prone to certain disorders such as epilepsy. They predominate in schools for the educationally subnormal and in child guidance clinics. They have more enuresis, more neurological impairments and more reading difficulties. Possibly these are related to worse regulation of growth in the uterus. There is no definite knowledge yet about this.

35. Children in different socio-economic groups differ in average body size at all ages, those from the better-off groups being larger[6,7]. The difference at present between children in upper middle class homes and unskilled workers' homes amounts to about one inch in height at the age of five rising to $1\frac{1}{2}$ or $1\frac{3}{4}$ inches at adolescence. It is not clear whether height and socio-economic status are as closely associated as they were 30 years ago; but, if there has been any change, it has not been great. Part of the height differential persists in adults and it is not therefore simply a reflection of acceleration or retardation of growth. Indeed, menarche now occurs at approximately the same age in different socio-economic classes. Thirty years ago it was earlier in the well off.

36. The number of children in the family is significantly associated with the rate of growth[8,9]. Children with many brothers and sisters are smaller than those with few. London boys aged five with no siblings are on an average $1\frac{1}{4}$ inches taller than those with four or more siblings[10]. The difference is not confined to height but occurs also in other bodily measurements, and in visual and auditory acuity. A similar relationship has also been shown in tests of mental ability, though whether this persists at older ages is not yet clear[11].

A relationship has been found between the number of children in a family and the age of onset of puberty[12]; few children in the family is associated with early puberty and many children with late puberty. The difference in physical development is at least partly nutritional in origin. The National Food Surveys have shown that families with many children spend appreciably less on food per head than families with few children. Abel-Smith and Townsend[13] have shown that the great majority of the children growing up in families they describe as economically "poor" belong to families with four or more children.

37. Environmental and hereditary factors interact inextricably to produce these differences between socio-economic classes. One set of factors tends to reinforce, not cancel out, the other. Socio-economic classes are heterogeneous and artificial, and it is not so much the family's occupation or income that is operative here as its attitudes and traditions of child care, its child centredness, its whole cultural outlook[14,15]. As the more intelligent and forward looking parent moves up the social scale, so his children's conditions improve: the less intelligent, less ambitious and more passive parent creates conditions which give less stimulation and support to the child's physical development. Similar considerations apply to intellectual development. Intelligent parents, who have themselves gained educational and social advantages, tend to make effective use of the educational, social and medical provision for their children. There is a strong association between the circumstances which affect the nutritional conditions underlying progress in physical development and those other conditions which nourish, as it were, intellectual and emotional growth. The significance of these facts for education lies largely in the light they throw on the progress, or lack of it, made towards equalising even the simple circumstances of life between children of different social classes.

38. There is a small positive correlation between a child's size at any age and his score on tests of measured intelligence. Children in grammar schools, for example, are on an average larger than children of the same age in secondary modern schools. The available evidence makes it seem likely that part at least of the correlation persists into adult life.

The Trend Towards Earlier Physical Maturity

39. During the last 50 years or more there has been a trend towards earlier maturation and greater size at all ages in children. Thus London five year olds in 1959 were on average nearly three inches taller than London five year olds in 1910, and London 13 year olds were nearly four inches taller. Adults, too, have been getting taller during this century but only to a much smaller degree. Most of the increase in height of children is caused by their earlier maturity. At the turn of the century most English boys probably stopped growing at about 22; nowadays they usually stop at 17 or 18.

40. This trend is most clearly seen in age at menarche, illustrated in Diagram 2. The statistics for Great Britain before the late 1940s are less satisfactory than those for other European countries, but the general tendency in this country evidently is in line with others. At present the average age of menarche in Southern England is 13·0 years and probably a month or two later in Northern England. The tendency has been for menarche to commence earlier by an average of about four months per decade. Probably this tendency is

now becoming less as an ultimate threshold is approached. It seems likely, however, that the average menarcheal age will decrease at least to about 12 years 6 months during the next 20 to 30 years.

41. The reasons for this trend are not fully understood, but it seems probable that better standards of nutrition and home conditions, particularly in infancy, are chiefly responsible. The reduction of illness in childhood may also have played a part. The trend has been greater in the worse off sections of the community though not confined to them.

Diagram 2

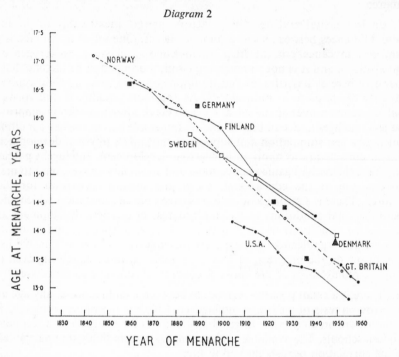

YEAR OF MENARCHE

Secular trend in age at menarche 1830–1960. Values are plotted at year in which the average menarche took place, i.e. in 'recollected-age' data if average menarche of 40-year-olds interrogated in 1900 was 15 years, this is plotted at 1875. This places old data on same age scale as modern probit data. Where age of interrogation is not recorded an estimated amount has been subtracted according to nature of population studied (primiparae, etc.). Grouping errors have been corrected where necessary (i.e. '13-year-olds' centred at 13·5 years, not 13, as in some of the older literature). Sources of data as quoted in original. (From Tanner, *Growth at Adolescence*, Blackwell Sci. Publ.: Oxford.)

The Development of Behaviour

42. Each event in a child's behaviour results from the interaction of his inheritance, his history and his immediate situation. Very few of the child's responses are wholly innate (as are many responses in young birds, for example); most require learning, though the basis on which learning can take place is inborn. The baby depends on environmental stimuli for his development, and these need to be varied and complex if the full range of normal behaviour is to be developed. It is the function of the educational process to provide these stimuli from the moment of birth onwards.

43. The smiling response is one example of the manner in which basic behavioural patterns are elaborated and remoulded by the environment and society during the course of development. During the first two to eight months after birth any object with some resemblance to the pattern of eyes in a human face may elicit a smile from the baby. This behaviour appears to be virtually unlearned and serves to evoke maternal behaviour in the mother or other adult. Gradually learning takes place so that the child distinguishes his own mother from other adults, and for a time smiles only at her. Much later the child or adult uses the same response elaborated and codified to show sympathy with others.

44. The persistence of early responses and particularly of unconscious emotional attitudes towards other people has been stressed especially by the psychoanalysts. Children "identify" with parents and others, imitate them and assume their attitudes. They also project on to them many of their own infantile thoughts and wishes. As they grow up they may transfer these attitudes to others in their environment. Thus the child may re-enact this parental relationship with his teacher; a teacher may partly re-enact with colleagues his own earlier relationships with parents or siblings. Such identification, and the formation of strong emotional bonds between child and teacher, can be valuable educationally if the bonds are positive ones.

45. The child appears to have a strong drive, which shows itself at a very early age, towards activity and the exploration of the environment. He also displays curiosity especially about novel and unexpected features of his experience. As far as can be judged, this behaviour is autonomous since it occurs when there is no obvious external motivation such as hunger.

46. There seems to be a pressure in the young child towards the emergence of sensori-motor skills. He needs opportunity for movement. Even in totally limbless children, this drive towards physical experience finds expression, at first through total body movement, and later, when crawling would normally occur, through locomotion of the trunk alone. But the drive needs support from the environment and such children need to be fitted with artificial limbs at or before the time when they would normally use their arms and legs. In short, the child displays a drive towards mastery of his environment, and tends to adopt a style of behaviour and response which provides a technique for achieving mastery. This technique comes by repetition of experience, and the physical and conceptual skills required to handle experience are then practised without any obvious incentive.

47. Individual differences between children in level of ability, sensitivity, vigour and tempo of response appear very early in life[18]. Different children, even within the same family, often have different temperaments from birth. Parental personality, attitudes and modes of child rearing interact with the child's temperament, reinforcing or conflicting with the ways in which he prefers to respond. It is important that early learning should take into account the child's style of response. Little is known, however, of the way in which the different personalities of parent or teacher and child interact, or of how different attitudes to or modes of rearing affect children of varying endowments. Much more research in this area is needed.

48. In the early stages of the learning process, neuro-motor, perceptual and emotional operations are inextricably bound together. When a child enters

school his success in learning is bound up with the development of emotional control and satisfactory relations with the adults about him. If he does not succeed in this, there is a danger that he may refuse to learn. Intellectual processes in a child will not function fully unless some emotional incentive or interest is present. Freedom from severe emotional disturbance is also a necessary condition of learning.

49. Like the growth of the body, the development of behaviour is a continuous process. The concept of clear cut stages is too crude to describe adequately the subtleties of development though it may at times be useful as a working model. According to Piaget, mental structures appear in a sequence as coherent and regular as many aspects of physical growth, and all people, whatever their variation in pace and final level, pass through the same sequence.

50. Piaget distinguishes four stages in intellectual development, which follow in sequence: "sensori-motor", "intuitive thought", "concrete operations" and "formal operations".* But a child does not switch suddenly from one stage to another, just as he does not suddenly walk. At first he supports himself for brief periods and mostly crawls; then he walks half the time and, later still, he walks as his principal mode of progression. So also with learning to think and to feel. The stages, too, are not irreversible; though a child (or an adult) may operate most of the time in the stage of concrete operations or formal operations, he may relapse into an earlier mode of behaviour in play, or regress into it in confusion or under stress.

51. Just as a child cannot learn to walk before he has learned to stand, in cognitive development the reaching of successive phases depends upon an adequate level of development in the earlier phase. A child cannot learn to read, for example, without having learned to discriminate shapes. Not all individuals reach the same level of development. Mentally sub-normal individuals never fully attain the later stages or may do so only long after the average child. The creative and powerful thinkers in our society go far beyond the stage reached by the average adult.

52. There is the same wide variation in the speed and efficiency with which neuro-muscular skills are acquired as there is in the growth in height or the development of the skeleton. Some children by the age of five have fine hand control and can cut with scissors and draw straight lines and circles; others are clumsy at these activities for several further years. Advancement or retardation of these skills is the result of the interaction of a hereditary tendency and environmental factors such as encouragement or discouragement, training and practice or the lack of it, but in what proportion is not clear. The "self fulfilling prophecy" may operate here as throughout so much

---

*Sensori-motor phase—the child moves from apparently unco-ordinated reflex responses to successively more complex patterns of activity and establishes a rudimentary sense of the persistence of permanent objects, inanimate and human.
Phase of intuitive thought—a transitional phase when children may perceive only one relationship at a time, actions are not reversible, judgments are often based on intuition and dominated by perception.
Phase of concrete operations—a prolonged phase during which children become able to perceive stable and reversible relationships in concrete situations.
Phase of formal operations—children become capable of logical thought, based on symbolic and abstract material.

of the educational process. The advanced and well controlled children may be given the most interesting and demanding tasks, and may claim more of the teacher's time. They thus advance even further. Meanwhile a clumsy child may sit neglected, falling farther and farther behind. It is as though we made a point of giving tall children better food and starving the short children. If we did this, we would certainly see a greater variation in height in the adult population than was necessary on purely genetic grounds.

Language

53. Communication of feeling and attitude between parent and child, child and child, and teacher and child can often take place by non-verbal means such as facial expression, gesture or bodily movement. These are fundamental forms of expression and attention to them is particularly valuable for understanding young children. Experience and feeling may also be communicated through play, through expressive and creative response to media such as paint and clay, and through the re-enactment of emotion in movement, mime and spontaneous dramatisation.

54. Spoken language plays a central role in learning. Parents in talking to their children help them to find words to express, as much to themselves as to others, their needs, feelings and experiences. Through language children can transform their active, questing response to the environment into a more precise form and learn to manipulate it more economically and effectively. The complex perceptual-motor skills of reading and writing are based in their first stages upon speech, and the wealth and variety of experience from which effective language develops. Language originates as a means of expressing feeling, establishing contact with others and bringing about desired responses from them[19]; these remain as fundamental functions of language, even at a more mature level. Language develops through the stages of speech, of repeating the commands and prohibitions of others, to become finally part of the child's internal equipment for thinking. Language increasingly serves as a means of organising and controlling experience and the child's own responses to it[20].

55. The development of language is, therefore, central to the educational process. Children who are brought up in a home background where the forms of speech are restricted are at a considerable disadvantage when they first go to school[21] and may need to have considerable compensatory opportunities for talking if they are to develop verbal skills and form concepts. The child's active vocabulary grows at a dramatic rate between two and five years, reaching an average of over 2,000 words. It has been estimated that a child needs to understand about 3,000 words to begin reading[22]. By four or five years children should be articulating sounds about 90 per cent correctly. Most children can make sentences by the time they go to school and are able to understand simple instructions given by unfamiliar people. Nevertheless, there will be a proportion who, because of difficulties in development or unfavourable backgrounds, are likely to lack fluency or have difficulty in making themselves understood. The psychological trauma of placing a child without adequate powers of communication in a new social situation can be serious.

The Measurement of Intelligence and its Bearing on Educational Decisions

56. The results of tests of intelligence or general ability are usually expressed as an "intelligence quotient" (or I.Q.) and define a child's standing relative to other children. Everything that has been said above about the interaction of hereditary and environmental factors in controlling the development of adult characteristics applies to the scores achieved in those tests. Thus any I.Q. score represents an interaction between hereditary endowment and environmental circumstances, both past and present, including, of course, the influence of parents or teachers. Furthermore it shows how the particular environmental circumstances, past and present, suit the particular genetic endowment of the individual in question.

57. The importance of genetic factors and of very early environment, or both, is shown by the fact that I.Q. remains fairly stable throughout development in most children while varying greatly from one child to another. This also indicates that circumstances rarely change so much for the worse as seriously to lower the I.Q. But the benefits that can occasionally accrue from an improvement in environment, effected perhaps by a transfer from one school to another or by a change of home, are indicated by the large gains, of up to 25 points, made in a short space of time by some children.

58. Large short term changes must be distinguished from longer-term trends. Long term gradual trends may signify a gradual betterment or worsening of a child's environment; but they may alternatively proceed from largely genetic factors if the child is a late or an early developer. Just as some children at the age of five are shorter than most other children of the same age but reach average height by the time they are 15, so some children have a higher rate of gain in intellectual ability than others and so register an increasing I.Q. in successive tests. Brain maturation is not complete until the end of adolescence at the earliest but it is not known whether a spurt in mental growth occurs during adolescence or not. If a spurt does occur the evidence indicates that it can only be a slight one.

59. Investigations by Husen[23] in Sweden and Burt[24] in England record correlations of 0·7 and 0·8 respectively between I.Q.s of boys and girls as ascertained in tests separated by an interval of about ten years. This implies that about ten per cent of the children moved from the lower half to the upper half of the distribution and that a corresponding number moved the other way. Thus if the I.Q. had been made the single criterion at nine or ten for sorting the children into sheep and goats, and if the same criterion had been used again at 19, it would have been found that a mistake had been made in 20 per cent of the cases.

60. Thus the notion of the constancy of the I.Q. is biologically self-exploding as well as educationally explosive. The description of the causes of I.Q. variation given above shows that strict constancy of the I.Q. could not be achieved under any circumstances. The nearer the approach to the ideal state in which each person's environment became perfect for him throughout his whole growth, the nearer, it is true, would be the approach to constancy. But, even then, the long term gains and losses due to the different rates of intellectual development would remain. The I.Q. has indeed its educational uses, but these can only be properly evaluated if we have a clear, not over

simplified idea of what I.Q. test scores represent, on what they are based, by how much they vary, and for what reason.

61. There are also shorter term variations in I.Q. test results attributable to transient effects in the environment. The child on the day of the test may be unhappy, preoccupied, or about to go down with 'flu. He may simply dislike the tester, or he may have his attention wholly concentrated on a football game that afternoon. According to temperament, a child may do better when tested individually by a psychologist than in the impersonal situation of a group test. He may, or may not, have been coached in the type of test used. It has not proved possible to construct tests in which practice does not lead to improvement. Recent figures suggest that a single practice results in an average gain of about five points, while serious coaching might be worth up to 15 points[25,26]. Even the smaller gain would be sufficient to give a considerable advantage to a child on the borderline, who had an even chance of a grammar school place, since with the usual 11 plus borderline, this would be equivalent to a rise of ten percentile ranks. Many group tests have a practice test incorporated in them. Yet variation between primary schools in the amount of coaching given is known from enquiries made by H.M. Inspectors to be one of the reasons why children from some primary schools do better at the secondary stage, and others worse, than their tested intelligence at 11 would suggest.

62. The genetic background against which intellectual ability develops is similar to the genetic background to stature. There are a large number of genes each contributing to this background; in consequence the correlations between twins, between siblings and between children and parents resemble the equivalent correlations for stature, though they are not quite so high, because the direct environmental effect on I.Q. is greater than that on stature. There is also, as with height, a well marked correlation between children's I.Q. and parental occupation. The children of professional parents have an average I.Q. of about 115, and at the other extreme the children of unskilled workers average about 93, although there is considerable overlap between individuals in different socio-economic classes[27].

63. This correlation of test with parents' occupation has sometimes been said to make the use of the tests socially unjust. But in fact the I.Q. scores are not so highly correlated with parental occupation as are the scores in attainment tests or probably as are teachers' ratings. Consequently, in the right circumstances, and in these only, the I.Q. test may serve to pick out a child of ability who would be passed over by an attainment test or a teacher's rating because his home background is poor and his success at school less good than that of more favourably placed pupils.

64. The fact that there are no very precise criteria for determining what constitutes the exercise of intelligence is not an obstacle to the use of intelligence tests, though it creates some difficulty over their interpretation. The tests have been designed to sample a child's powers over a wide field. For example, one of the most used tests, the Wechsler Intelligence Scale for Children (W.I.S.C.), comprises 12 sub-sets called information, comprehension, arithmetic, similarities, vocabulary, digit span, picture completion, picture arrangement, block design, object assembly, coding and mazes. But there are certainly areas of the child's thinking which remain unsampled. Efforts have

been made in the past to devise "culture free" tests, that is, presumably, tests which reflect only genetical endowment and are independent of environment. Such efforts are worth making, but can have only limited success, in view of the analysis of the causes of test scores given above. What we would like to know is just how much more ability could be uncovered in the population if everyone was given the most suitable home and educational environment. We can never know this completely but we can discover more about it. As it is, the tests now being devised try to be "culture fair" rather than "culture free", so that they are not considered suitable if they do not match reasonably well the group for whom they are standardised. Rightly used, the intelligence test can assist us in these efforts: wrongly used, it can frustrate them. Hebb has made a distinction between Intelligence A, genetic potential, and Intelligence B, the ability which can be observed in daily life and sampled by intelligence tests. Most psychologists agree that there is no sharp distinction between measured intelligence and educational attainments. Both are the product of genetic and environmental factors; both are learned. Intelligence refers to generalised thinking powers which have developed from experience in and out of school: attainments are more directly influenced by the school curriculum.

The Emotional Development of the Child

65. The emotional aspects of the child's development, like the intellectual, follow a regular sequence based on the interaction between maturation and biological factors on the one hand and experience and learning within the cultural setting on the other. Emotional, social and intellectual aspects are closely intertwined in mental growth: the child is a total personality. Emotional life provides the spur and in many ways gives meaning to experience. There are widely differing points of view on the importance of innate factors in emotional development. In the Freudian scheme, emotional development is thought of as taking place in a fixed sequence of stages based on instinctual drives which interact with such demands as those imposed by weaning or toilet training. This interaction creates individual personality and affects individual ways of growth. But anthropological and social studies suggest that there may be differences in "basic personality" caused by different ways of upbringing and cultural expectations. Individual personality development, however, depends very much on learning from the expectations and practices derived from the family relationship.

66. In any society the child moves through successive levels of development and encounters crises stemming from the demands made on him by society. The effectiveness with which he has been helped to come to terms with these crises is of lasting importance to him. Failure to master one stage will affect the next, leading to later difficulty or failure to adjust fully as a person and member of society. Emotional life becomes increasingly structured and complex as the child grows and learns. The expression and control of emotional response or feeling develop from a diffuse, total response of comfort or discomfort, sleep or wakefulness in the very young child, involving the whole body and nervous system. At a very early stage there appear more specific responses differentiated by the end of the second year into the emotions of anger, love, fear, jealousy and the like. The child is vulnerable to his emotions, not so much experiencing them as being swept by them. Even the five year old,

despite his apparent balance and control, remains subject to overpowering impulses and fears and is still dependent on those close to him for guidance and control. Common observation as well as the study of the development of brain rhythms in young children suggest that attention and learning are readily affected by discomfort or bodily needs, such as a full bladder, or by emotional upset or tension, and that any emotional disturbance reverberates for a long time. The emotional life of the child of two to five is intimately bound up with his relationships with those who care for and are close to him. Emotional development is related to intellectual development as well as to increasing maturity and experience. In the first year, fears centre around the unknown or sudden changes. Then children begin to show fear of more specific objects and situations, noises, or animals, and readily acquire "conditioned" fears. With capacity for thought and imagination, children come to fear unseen and unknown things emerging from their fantasy life. At a later stage, in the primary school, more fears appear which are related to experience, or are connected with the sense of personal adequacy and need to succeed and be accepted.

67. The child is at first dominated by his needs and impulses. Much early learning is concerned with helping him to live with others, accept delays, deal with frustrations and build up inner controls. Learning theory provides many examples of how this training, within a context of parental and social expectations, occurs. The child is not just "trained" but learns to handle his feelings and drives in constructive ways which have been succinctly described as "the mechanisms of defence". Reasonably phased experiences of delay, frustration and control help to establish the sense of separation between himself and the environment. In play the child masters reality by imitating and acting out situations he has experienced.

68. Aggression is one example of the emotions that the child must learn to handle and express. Some aggressiveness is not only part of the individual's response to difficulties and frustration, but is necessary in social life, to allow the individual to assert his identity and ensure that he gets within reason what he should. Normal progress in transforming aggressive impulses into more mature forms can be seen in the development from the tantrums or the tussling for possession of the two year old to the brief and desultory quarrel of the nursery school child and so to the verbal insults, arguments and discussion of the older junior school child. A major role of the school is to help the child to come to terms with these feelings and not to suppress them, but to understand them and thus to discover how to deal acceptably with them. His experiences with other children give him essential experience in handling relationships.

69. One of the most important aspects of the child's early learning is his dependence on the adults around him. His anxiety over the deprivation or punishment which he experiences in the course of social training leads to an avoidance of the disapproval of the adults who care for him and a seeking for their approval. This is one of the most powerful motives for emotional and other learning, at home, in school, and in social relationships in general. Consistency of handling, too, is an important factor in helping the child to pick his way through the confusion of acceptable and forbidden types of behaviour which, at the time of learning, he cannot fully understand. The

quality of the care and security provided by a child's home during the early years of his life are of extreme importance for his later emotional development. The emotional climate of the home, parental attitudes, values and expectations, whether personal or derived from their social and cultural background, appear more important than specific techniques of child rearing. Maladjustment may result from tensions in the family rather than from an illness in the child himself.

70. The emotional effects of being deprived at an early age of a consistent and warm maternal relationship have become well known through the work of Bowlby and others[28,29]. Cultural deprivation can also have disastrous results. A child brought up in a family which, because of poverty, missing parents, or the low intelligence of parents, cannot provide security or sufficient emotional and intellectual stimulation, may miss a significant stage in his early social development. Children who have been reared in this way often find difficulty in handling their impulses and needs. They may find it hard, too, to make the transition to later learning, since they cannot cope constructively with materials or concentrate. We do not know at what age, and to what extent, this process is reversible by suitable experience or treatment. Left untreated, it may persist in continued ineffectiveness, and in lack of motive for learning in school. It can result in the creation of adults who are feckless, tough and without real feelings, and without any personal identity outside their immediate family group.

71. A child develops from complete dependence on his mother to independence. One major crisis for the child is the separation required of him when he goes to nursery or school. He becomes less dependent on his family and other relations close to him, and experiences increasing inter-dependence with others as he learns social skills, finds new roles and establishes more firmly his own identity. There are strong urges towards growth, maturity and independence, but there are also factors which tend to make the child wish to remain protected and dependent. Family situations, or maternal attitudes, which foster this can cause emotional difficulties in the child, and it has been suggested that over dependency may be one reason for difficulty in independent learning, particularly in reading.

72. The child moves through distinguishable stages in social behaviour. At 15 to 18 months, he recognises and responds to other children. Between two and three and a half he plays for the most part as an individual and not with others. Even at four and five social interaction is loosely structured, and the dependence of the children on adult support is shown by the fact that a nursery group playing together quite effectively will disintegrate when the teacher moves away. In the primary school years, especially from 8 to 12, the child moves increasingly into social groups composed of children of the same age and maturity. In this "peer" group, he learns how to play and live in co-operation and competition, how to control his feelings, establish roles and social techniques, and become accepted for what he is and can do, outside the close relationships of his family on the one hand, and the more formalised relationships and values of the school on the other. Group membership in work and play within the school fosters this social and emotional development, the process of defining oneself as an individual through the reflected appraisal of the group.

73. Moral development is closely associated with emotional and social development. The child forms his sense of personal worth and his moral sense from early experiences of acceptance, approval, and disapproval. Out of an externally imposed rule of what is permitted arises a sense of what ought to be done and an internal system of control: in everyday terms, a conscience. The very young child, limited in understanding, acts according to strict rules, even though he often breaks them. What is right and wrong relates closely to what his parents say and to the situation arising in the home. Later, as the child develops intellectually and lives with others, his sense of right and wrong derives from a wider circle and becomes more qualified; the rules of a game are seen to be arrived at by a consensus, and therefore modifiable by common agreement. Even so, the 11 year old still has a fairly crude and concrete sense of justice. It appears doubtful whether an autonomous conscience is established before adolescence.

74. Although much work has been done on physical growth during puberty, little study has been made of the progress towards emotional maturity and stability. The subject is important not only because it might be relevant to the age of transfer from primary to secondary education, but also because of the increasing number of children who begin to enter puberty before they leave the primary school. Psychological changes at adolescence centre on the search for personal identity, for independence arising out of increasing competence and self-esteem, and on the development of maturer sexual attitudes and behaviour. The emotional changeability of some adolescent children is well recognised, and may sometimes lead to quite bewildering and contradictory behaviour. But opinion differs widely as to whether it is the majority or a minority of adolescents who behave in this way[30]. Both biological and cultural factors affect adolescent behaviour, and physical and phsycological changes do not necessarily coincide. There is also conflicting evidence as to whether the transition from primary to secondary school, selective or unselective, is a cause of distress[31]. What seems most likely is that it brings to the surface psychological difficulties in vulnerable children.

Implications

75. This chapter has been concerned with some aspects of the growth and development of children on which sound educational theory and practice must be built. We have taken them into account in making our recommendations on the issues discussed in the Report. It is not possible to summarise further this material but the more obvious implications of it can be stated baldly as follows:

(a) Individual differences between children of the same age are so great that any class, however homogeneous it seems, must always be treated as a body of children needing individual and different attention.

(b) Until a child is ready to take a particular step forward, it is a waste of time to try to teach him to take it.

(c) Even at the ages with which we are concerned, boys and girls develop at different rates and react in different ways—a fact which needs particular attention because we have co-educational schools. Boys are more vulnerable to adverse environmental circumstances than girls. Both reach maturity earlier than they did.

(d) Though I.Q. scores are a useful rough indication of potential ability, they should not be treated as infallible predictors. Judgments which determine careers should be deferred as long as possible.

(e) Since a child grows up intellectually, emotionally and physically at different rates, his teachers need to know and take account of his "developmental age" in all three respects. The child's physique, personality, and capacity to learn develop as a result of continuous interaction between his environmental and genetical inheritance. Unlike the genetic factors, the environmental factors are, or ought to be, largely within our control.

REFERENCES

[1] Conel, J. L. The Postnatal development of the human cerebral cortex, Vols. I–VI 1939–1959, Cambridge: Harvard University Press.

[2] Inhelder, B. and Piaget, J. The Growth of Logical Thinking from Childhood to Adolescence. 1958, London, Kegan Paul.

[3] Hubel, D. H. and Wiesel, T. N., J. Neuro. physiol, 1963, Vol. 26, 996.

[4] Lorenz, K. The Companion in the bird's world, 1937, Auk 54, 245–273.

[5] Ed. Loring, J. Teaching the Cerebral Palsied Child, 1965, London, Heinemann.

[6] Tanner, J. M. Education and Physical Growth, 1961, University of London Press.

[7] Douglas, J. W. B. 1964, Papers prepared at the request of the Central Advisory Council.

[8] Social Implications of the 1947 Scottish Mental Survey, Report of Scottish Council for Research in Education 1953, University of London Press.

[9] See (7) above.

[10] Scott, J. A. London County Council: Report on Heights and Weights of School Pupils in the County of London in 1959, 1961.

[11] Benech, A. Mathieu, B. and Schreider, Dimensions de la famille et caracteres biologiques des enfants, Biotypologie 21, 4–36, 1960.

[12] See (7) above.

[13] Abel-Smith, B. and Townsend, P., The Poor and the Poorest, Occasional Papers on Social Administration, W.17, Bell, 1965.

[14] Swift, D. F., Social Class and Achievement Motivation, Educational Research VIII (2) 1966.

[15] Davis, A., Social Class Influences on Learning, 1948. Cambridge: Harvard University Press.

[16] Tanner, J. M., Growth at Adolescence, 2nd. Ed, 1962. Blackwell Scientific Publications, Oxford.

[17] Ed. Foss, B. M. Determinants of Infant Behaviour, 1961. Methuen.

[18] Ausubel, D. P. Theory and Problems of Child Development, 1959. Grune and Stratton.

[19] Lewis, M. M. Language, Thought and Personality in Infancy and Childhood, 1963. Harrap.

[20] Luria, A. R., The Role of Speech in the Regulation of Normal and Abnormal Behaviour, 1961. London Pergamon Press.

[21] Bernstein, B., Social Class and Linguistic Development: in Education, Economy and Society, Ed. Halsey, A. H., 1961. New York Free Press.

[22] McCarthy, D. Manual of Child Psychology, Ed. Carmichael, L, New York, Wiley.

[23] Husen, T., The Influence of Schooling upon I.Q. Theoria, 17, 61–68, 1951.

[24] Burt, C., Age, Ability and Aptitude, University of London, Institute of Education, 1954, Evans.

[25] Vernon, P. E., Intelligence Testing, 1952, London: Times Publishing Co.

[26] Vernon, P. E., Intelligence and Attainment Tests, 1960, University of London Press.

[27] See (8).

[28] Bowlby, J., 1951, Maternal Care and Mental Health, Geneva, W.H.O. Monograph Series No. 2, 2nd Ed., 1952.

[29] Deprivation of Maternal Care, 1962, W.H.O. Public Health Papers No. 14, Geneva.

[30] Evidence submitted by Dr. W. Warren and Dr. D. Odlum; 'Journey Through Adolescence' by Dr. D. Odlum, 1957, Delisle Ltd.

[31] P. E. Vernon (Ed.), 'Secondary School Selection', A British Psychological Society Inquiry, 1957.

Part Three

The Home, School and Neighbourhood

CHAPTER 3

The Children and their Environment

76. One of the main themes of Chapter 2 is the interaction between a child's inheritance and his environment. In this chapter we single out the evidence of research—and in particular of our National Survey*—on how much parents influence children's achievement at school and how their influence operates.

77. The Hadow Report on the Primary School[1] acknowledged the good fortune of children who enter school "with the foundations of education . . . well laid" and who, as they grow older, acquire "almost as much general knowledge in the home as . . . in the school, and . . . almost as much information about the world and its way during leisure hours . . . as from the formal lessons in the classroom". The report contrasted the plight of the child from the poor home; "his vocabulary is limited, his general knowledge is narrow; he has little opportunity for reading and his power of expressing himself . . . is inadequate". Despite this acceptance of the importance of the home, the Hadow Report did not give any prominence to it. The main reference occurs in a sub-section on environment which was tacked on to a chapter on mental development.

78. Why then do we devote so much attention to this subject? The power of environment is more obvious than it was then. The progress made since 1931 testifies to it. The rise in educational standards is due to improvements in the schools themselves; but it is also due to changes in the homes from which the children come, and, beyond the homes, to changes in the wider society of which the children and their parents are members. Unemployment has been almost non-existent since the war except in some areas and for a small minority of workers. Incomes have risen, nutrition has improved, housing is better, the health service and the rest of the social services have brought help where it is needed. Some of these changes stand out from a summary of parental circumstances based on interviews with parents of children in primary schools, included in the National Survey (Appendix 3). Parents from all walks of life use these schools. They are more and more a cross-section of the nation. Fathers of children included in the National Survey Sample belong to occupational groups in the same proportions as those which characterise all married men in the country as judged by the 1961 Census. We are nearer, it seems, to the ideal of the Hadow Committee "the primary school, the common school of the whole population"[2].

79. It is apparent that most of the children are now physically healthy, vigorous, curious and alert. Though many primary school buildings date back to 1931 and long before, few children have the pinched faces or poor clothes often seen in photographs of 30 years ago. Yet some children and some parents tail far behind. Twelve per cent of the families in the National Survey had a net income from all sources of £12 10 0d a week or less. The difficulties of children in families such as these are discussed in Chapter 5.

*The whole Survey appears as Appendices 3, 4, 5, 6 and 7 in Volume 2. Its full title is the '1964 National Survey of Parental Attitudes and Circumstances Related to School and Pupil Characteristics'. It is described in the main report as the National Survey.

80. If all goes well, progress in material standards will continue, and over the next 30 years the schools will continue to benefit. But educators are not just the beneficiaries of progress; they are its makers too. Our argument in this and the following chapters is that educational policy should explicitly recognise the power of the environment upon the school and of the school upon the environment. Teachers are linked to parents by the children for whom they are both responsible. The triangle should be completed and a more direct relationship established between teachers and parents. They should be partners in more than name; their responsibility become joint instead of several.

81. The need for this is apparent from the results of the National Survey. This enquiry has taken further the investigations undertaken for the Council in connexion with each of its three last reports.

82. Early Leaving (1954)[3], the first of the three reports, answered a very practical question; why did so many children drop out before completing the grammar school course? It was no surprise that the children of manual workers did less well academically than other children and more often left school at the minimum age. Surely they failed because they were less clever? The surprise, at the time, was that this was far from being the only reason. The enquiry showed that the children of semi-skilled and unskilled manual workers, who were in the top flight of the grammar school intake at the age of 11, had as a group by the end of their secondary school life been overtaken by the children of professional families who had initially been placed below them. Our predecessors summed up their conclusion on the issue as follows:

"In our analysis we have been concerned only with broad classifications, and we are well aware that many individual children of well-to-do parents find little support at home for hard work at school and academic ambition, while many children from very poor homes have parents who know the worth of the education they themselves missed. Still it is beyond doubt that a boy whose father is of professional or managerial standing is more likely to find his home circumstances favourable to the demands of grammar school work than one whose father is an unskilled or semi-skilled worker. The latter is handicapped".

The Newsom Report[4] showed that this handicap was still there about ten years later, but suggested that it might be lessening, at least in the grammar schools. In these schools, the improvement among children from the lower occupational groups was greater than among children from the higher ones.

A Pool of Ability

83. The Crowther Report (1959) dealt with the same theme. Young men were given intelligence tests after they had left school, on recruitment to the Army and the R.A.F. The length of their education was found to be related more closely to the occupation of their parents and to the size of their families than to their intelligence scores. Among the sons of manual workers who left school yearly, there were many of high ability. It was clear that children of high academic promise were not benefiting fully from their education. "It may well be that there is a pool of ability that imposes an upper limit on what can be done by education at any given time. But if so it is sufficiently clear

that the limit has not been reached and will not even be approached without much more in the way of inducement and opportunity".[5]

84. Other research has shown a marked association between parental occupation and measured intelligence, although it has of course always been clear that exceptionally able children, dull children and children who are failing to realise their potential are to be found in each occupational group. There is some evidence that the gap between the measured intelligence of the children of manual workers and of middle class parents begins to widen at a very early age and that the causes are both genetic, as might be supposed from the argument in Chapter 2, and environmental. Hindley found evidence for the widening gap, admittedly on a small sample, in the pre-school years[6]. The polarisation continues, according to Douglas, at the primary stage. At 11 the scores and achievement of children from the different classes are further apart than they were at eight[7]. This growing apart did not occur in Scotland[8]. In England, the process persists in the secondary school. The Robbins Report on higher education referred to the evidence about primary and secondary schools, and concluded that the handicaps imposed on the children of manual workers throughout the years at school did not seem to have been getting less. When the classes were compared, "it looks as if the relative chances of reaching higher education have changed little in recent years".[9]

Prospects for Improvement

85. The research and surveys cited, and much else to the same effect, suggest that we are far from realising the potential abilities of our children. To reveal the influence of parental occupation is a criticism of society; but it is also an opportunity for reform. There must always be a great diversity of parental occupations; but they need not continue to have their present severe discriminatory effect on children's educational prospects. The grosser deprivations arising from poverty can be removed. More parents can be brought to understand what education can do for their children, and how they can work with the schools. The educational disadvantage of being born the child of an unskilled worker is both financial and psychological. Neither handicap is as severe as it was. Both are more severe than they need be. Educational equality cannot be achieved by the schools alone: but the schools can make a major contribution towards ensuring (as Sir Edward Boyle wrote in his foreword to the Newsom Report) "that all children should have an equal opportunity of acquiring intelligence".

86. The last three reports of the Council drew attention to the numerous exceptions to the rule that they established. They pointed to the homes and the schools which produce good or even brilliant results in spite of adverse circumstances. Our own enquiries have been directed to throwing light on the reasons for these exceptions. If we can pinpoint the factors which make good work possible in apparently unlikely circumstances, we may see what most needs to be done to enlarge the numbers of those who succeed. What is it about the home that matters so much? That was the main question we wished to have explored.

The National Survey

87. For our survey a sample of schools was drawn, stratified by size and type. In the first instance the sample included 107 junior and junior mixed and infant

schools but, when the separate infant schools contributing to the junior schools in the sample were added, the total number of schools included came to 173. A sample of about 3,000 children within these schools was then drawn from the oldest infant, first year junior and fourth year junior classes, and the Government Social Survey conducted interviews with their mothers (or, very occasionally, their fathers). The questions asked are listed in Appendix 3 which describes the survey of parental attitudes and its findings in detail.

88. At about the same time that the interviews were held, information was being collected from the 173 head teachers about their schools, the ways in which they were organised and staffed, and their relationships with parents. Class teachers added information about the children in the sample. The attainments of the children were assessed by reading comprehension tests, and a picture intelligence test was also given to top infants. For comparison of the attainment of children within schools, pupils were arranged in rank order by teachers. The opportunity was taken to test the whole top junior group (not only those children in the sample) in reading comprehension, so that comparisons could be made with earlier reading standards. (See Appendix 7). H.M.Is. visited the schools, described the methods used and assessed the teaching. The questions asked of head teachers, teachers and H.M.Is. are included in the annexes to the National Survey (Volume 2). Many references are also made to this data in the text of our report.

89. The main purpose of the survey was to relate what we could learn about home and school to the attainment of the children. For the summarised table in this chapter, the variables used are grouped into three categories. What is included in each category is shown in detail in Appendix 4 (Tables 1 and 3). The first category is broadly called "Parental Attitudes". These attitudes were assessed by parents' answers to such questions as the age at which they wanted children to leave school and the secondary school they preferred. The initiative shown by parents in visiting the school, in talking to heads and class teachers and asking for work for children to do at home was also taken into account. Parents were asked about the time they spent with children in the evening and whether they helped children with school work. There was also an assessment of the literacy of the home as judged by what parents and children read, whether they belonged to a library and the number of books in the home. The second category is "Home Circumstances", including the physical amenities of the home, or lack of them, the occupation and income of the father, the size of family, the length of parents' education and the qualifications they had obtained. The third category is the "State of the School". It covers facts about school organisations such as size of school, size of class and the ways children were put into classes. It also includes facts provided by the head about the experience of the staff and their attendance at short courses, and judgments by H.M.I.s on the quality of the school and the competence of teachers.

The Findings of the Survey

90. The analyses made are more complex than those in previous C.A.C. reports. Not only has more information been gathered about various in-

fluences on attainment; it has been possible to explore more fully the inter-relationship between these influences. The detailed tables in Appendix 4 consequently show not only the simple correlations between individual variables and attainment but also their correlations when the influence of all other variables is taken into account. We can thus show the extent to which each variable "explains" variations in attainment. Size of family, for example, has long been known to be correlated with performance, children from smaller families doing better on the whole than those from larger. But when the effects of other variables are eliminated, family size does not explain the children's test performance as effectively as the attitude of their parents. On the whole, in large families, parents tend to be lower in aspiration, literacy and interest than in small families, and there are obvious reasons why this should be so. But in families of each size—one child, two children and so forth—the difference between the performance of the children varies even more according to the attitudes of the parents.

91. The figures given in Table 1 show, for different ages, the percentage of the variation in performance which can be accounted for by the three main categories of variable. For each age group the comparisons made in the table are of two kinds, between pupils *within* schools and *between* schools. The object of this division was to bring out the extent to which a school's situation depends on the neighbourhood it serves. For comparisons between schools the unit of analysis was the school, and the variables were based on the average for each school of the original variables. For comparisons within schools the variables were the deviations of each pupil from the school average. If

Table 1 Percentage Contribution of Parental Attitudes, Home Circumstances and State of School to Variation in Educational Performance.

	Infants	Between Schools Lower Juniors	Top Juniors	All Pupils
Parental Attitudes	24	20	39	28
Home Circumstances	16	25	17	20
State of School	20	22	12	17
*Unexplained	40	33	32	35
	100	100	100	100
	Infants	Within Schools Lower Juniors	Top Juniors	All Pupils
Parental Attitudes	16	15	29	20
Home Circumstances	9	9	7	9
State of School	14	15	22	17
*Unexplained	61	61	42	54
	100	100	100	100

*The unexplained variation is due to differences between children which have not been covered by our variables, and also to errors in measurement. That so much variation has been explained—the amount in the between-schools analysis is remarkable for an enquiry of this kind—is due in part to the comparatively simple nature of the criterion variable, a reading comprehension test.

neighbourhood were unimportant, and the parents, pupils and teachers in each school were merely random samples of the general population, the two kinds of analysis would give the same result. In fact, they do not; the comparisons between schools account for more variation than those within schools. This is because pupils, parents and teachers in the same school and neighbourhood resemble one another more than they resemble pupils, parents and teachers in general, just as apples growing on the same tree resemble one another more than they resemble apples in general. The apples on a tree in a good situation will do better than those on a tree in a poor situation, unless the latter receives special attention—an implication that is pursued in later chapters.

Importance of Parental Attitudes

92. The most striking feature of both these sets of comparisons is the large part played by parental attitudes, and the fact that it tends to be greater among the older than the younger children. Not surprisingly, there are changes of emphasis within the attitudes of parents as children grow older. Parents' interest is likely to be greater in the children's early years at school when, as the interviewers found, they were more confident about helping children in their work, because they understood it better. It yields some ground to parental aspiration as the children reach the top of the junior school. By that time the children's very success or failure in school work may increase or weaken parental aspiration.

93. The influence of the home has always been known to be important, and the importance of parental attitudes began to emerge in earlier studies such as those of Fraser[10], Floud, Halsey and Martin[11], but now its importance can be better understood. Broadly the same results stand out from other surveys made for us by Professor Wiseman in Manchester on a small group of children, and by those responsible for the National Child Development Study which deals with a national sample, considerably larger than ours, of children born in one week in 1958. Their reports, based mainly on simple correlations, appear in Appendices 9 and 10.

94. Everything that can be learned from the survey about parents and their relation to the schools is therefore important as a signpost for action. First, the interest shown by parents in the enquiry itself is highly encouraging. Only three per cent refused an interview and interviews were carried out with 95 per cent of the sample, a remarkably high response. Over half the interviews lasted for an hour or longer because parents were anxious to talk about their children. More than half the parents had left school at 14, yet three quarters wanted their children to stay at school beyond the minimum age. There was little difference in the number of evenings when parents from different socio-economic groups could spend some time with their children; but it is rather disconcerting to find that only about half the mothers did things with their children for some part of most evenings. Similarly, there was little distinction between the proportion of parents in each occupational group who said they wanted the schools to give their children work to do at home. Yet a far smaller proportion of manual workers than of those in other occupations were in fact given work to do at home by their schools. A quarter of all parents, irrespective of the kind of work done by the fathers, were disinclined to visit schools unless they were specially invited.

95. So far the emphasis has been on respects in which parents thought alike irrespective of their occupational backgrounds. But there were also marked contrasts between manual and non-manual workers, and even more between those in professional and managerial occupations, and semi-skilled and unskilled workers. Perhaps the most noticeable difference was in the part played by fathers in children's education. Over two-fifths of the manual workers had left the choice of school entirely to their wives, as compared with less than a quarter of the non-manual workers. Almost half the manual workers, as compared with less than a quarter of non-manual workers, had not been to their child's present school at all. Less than a quarter had talked to the head.

96. What is particularly true of manual workers is true in somewhat smaller measure of their wives. The higher the socio-economic group, the more parents attended open days, concerts and parent-teacher association meetings, and the more often they talked with heads and class teachers about how their children were getting on. Manual workers and their wives were more likely to feel, when they had visited the schools, that they had learnt nothing fresh about their children, or that teachers should have asked them more. Not surprisingly, less help with school work was given at home to children of manual workers. Considerably lower proportions of parents from manual worker homes bought, for use at home, copies of some of the books children were using at school. Two thirds of unskilled workers had five books or fewer in the home, apart from children's books and magazines, as contrasted with one-twentieth of professional workers.

97. In view of the fact that 29 per cent of all homes have five books or less, the schools are successful in encouraging children to read. About half of the children borrowed books from school to read at home and four-fifths borrowed books either from the school or from public libraries. Only among the children of unskilled workers was there rather less borrowing of books from school, though a substantially bigger proportion of non-manual than of manual workers' children borrowed from public libraries. It looks as though, despite the good work done, the schools need to provide still more books for home use for the children of manual workers.

98. Some explanation may be needed about the relatively low weight which attaches to two of the three variables in Table 1. Some readers may be surprised at what they suppose to be the comparatively small influence of the school. To feel thus is to misunderstand the table. What emerged as important about the schools was the experience and competence of teachers. Most teachers have had a similar education and training, and differ less from one another than parents. The parents have usually had their children in their care for their whole lives, whereas most of the class teachers about whom information was collected had been with the children only for the best part of one school year. It must, therefore, be expected that differences between parents will explain more of the variation in children than differences between schools. It is obvious, too, that parental attitudes may themselves be affected by children's performance at school and by the contacts parents have with schools.

99. Other readers may be surprised that home circumstances at first sight seem less influential than previous enquiries suggested. But this, too, would

be a misunderstanding. The occupational classification used in the Council's earlier surveys was adopted because it was relatively precise, easily ascertainable and known to be associated with what in this survey we have described as "parental attitudes". It should astonish no one to find that, when these attitudes can be assessed separately from socio-economic class, they emerge as more important than occupation taken by itself.

100. A third point that will occur to readers is whether the differences in circumstances account for the differences in attitudes. Our evidence (see Appendix 4) suggests that parents' occupation, material circumstances and education explain only about a quarter of the variation in attitudes, leaving three-quarters or more not accounted for. This implies that attitudes could be affected in other ways, and altered by persuasion.

101. Our findings can give hope to the school, to interested parents, and to those responsible for educational policy. Parental attitudes appear as a separate influence because they are not monopolised by any one class. Many manual workers and their wives already encourage and support their children's efforts to learn. If there are many now, there can be even more later. Schools can exercise their influence not only directly upon children but also indirectly through their relationships with parents.

REFERENCES

[1] Report of the Consultative Committee on the Primary School (Hadow), H.M.S.O., 1931, reprinted 1959, paragraph 48.

[2] See (1), page XXIV.

[3] Early Leaving, Report of the Central Advisory Council for Education (England), H.M S.O., 1954, paragraph 44.

[4] Half Our Future (Newsom), Report of the Central Advisory Council for Education (England), H.M.S.O., 1963.

[5] 15 to 18 (Crowther), Report of the Central Advisory Council for Education (England), H.M.S.O., 1959, Vol. 2, page 206.

[6] Hindley, C. B., 'Social Class Influences on the Development of Ability in the First Five Years'. Child Education, Ed. Skard, A. G., and Husen, T., Copenhagen, Munksgaard, 1962.

[7] Douglas, J. W. B., The Home and the School, MacGibbon and Kee, 1964, page 115.

[8] Douglas, J. W. B., and Ross, J. M. (Medical Research Council Unit) and Maxwell, S. M. M., and Walker, D. A. (The Scottish Council for Research in Education), 'Differences in Test Score and in the Gaining of Selective Places for Scottish Children and those in England and Wales', British Journal of Educational Psychology, June 1966, Vol. XXXVI, Part 2.

[9] Higher Education (Robbins), H.M.S.O., 1963, Appendix One, Part II, paragraph 27, page 52.

[10] Fraser, E., 'Home Environment and the School', University of London Press, 1959.

[11] Floud, J., Halsey, A. H. and Martin, F. M., Social Class and Educational Opportunity, Ed. J. Floud, 1956.

CHAPTER 4

Participation by Parents

102. The National Survey pointed to the influence upon educational performance of parental attitudes. It follows that one of the essentials for educational advance is a closer partnership between the two parties to every child's education. Surveys of this kind do not establish causes, only associations. There is certainly an association between parental encouragement and educational performance. This does not tell us which way round the relationship is. Is performance better where parents encourage more? Do parents encourage more where performance is better? Common sense suggests that each factor is related to the other, and both are related to the work of the school itself. Homes and schools interact continuously. An improvement in school may raise the level of parental interest, and that in its turn may lead to further improvement in school—or deterioration may also be cumulative, as seems often to have happened with the children of manual workers. The movement may start in the home. A strengthening of parental encouragement may produce better performance in school, and thus stimulate the parents to encourage more; or discouragement in the home may initiate a vicious downward circle.

103. Schools exist to foster virtuous circles. They do this most obviously through their direct influence upon children. Where teachers help children to grow, intellectually and emotionally, their very success is likely to evoke a response from the parents. Some schools are already working at the same time from the other end, by influencing parents directly, and the children indirectly through the parents. Can more schools do so and on a bigger scale? Only experience, sieved by discussion and research, will show how effective it can be.

104. Progress will not be easy. There are obstacles on both sides. On the average, schools in the National Survey arranged between six and seven occasions each year when parents could visit. This is creditable enough, but there were not many opportunities to discuss school policy and practice. Though the returns do not make this absolutely clear, it is doubtful whether parents could discuss their children individually with class teachers in the general run of schools (Appendix 3). In the course of our visits to schools, we were almost invariably told by heads that "we have very good relations with parents", however rudimentary the arrangements made. It seems that teachers may be too readily satisfied with the social occasions which accounted for half the times when parents could visit the schools in the National Survey. (Appendix 5, Table 3).

105. There was also little evidence of dissatisfaction on the part of parents. The Social Survey interviews (Appendix 3) found that few parents made criticisms: "Only 11 per cent were not completely satisfied about the arrangements for seeing the head or class teacher. Nine per cent felt that it was not easy to see the teachers whenever they wanted to, seven per cent did not feel that the teachers seemed very pleased when they went to the schools and

seven per cent that the teachers would prefer to keep parents out of the school." (Section 3: paragraph 25). About half of the parents said they would have liked to be told more about how their children were getting on at school. Almost a third thought that the teachers should have asked them more about their children. Even so, the great majority were generally satisfied. (Section 3: paragraph 32).

106. This may only be evidence of their low expectations. People tend to accept what they know and do not demand things they have not experienced. When special efforts have been made in a school, the response from parents, whether or not they were "satisfied" beforehand, has often been striking. Parents, irrespective of social class, took more interest in their children's work in those schools in the National Survey which arranged as many as nine or ten meetings a year at times when fathers could come (Appendix 5, Table 4).

Co-operation with Parents

107. A number of schools were selected for us by H.M.Is as having outstandingly good relationships with parents. They made a practice of involving parents in all sorts of ways, small as well as large. The small ways were many. One of the heads said that she gave children examples of work which they had found difficult, so that they could take them home if they wished, to show to their mothers. "Sometimes a child will say to me, 'I could understand when Mummy explained it'." Other schools write to parents when their children first enter school and suggest ways in which they can help—such as by reading to them and hearing them read.

108. At one infant school, parents are invited to attend school assembly on each Friday and many accept. Afterwards children take their younger brothers and sisters for a quarter of an hour to their classrooms while the head talks to mothers. Sometimes all the children, including the younger ones from home stay in the "hall" (a dining hut) while mothers visit the classrooms to talk to the teachers. During parents' evenings, mothers have used the practical number equipment, so that they can find out how and why their child should use it. They sew and make equipment for the school and help at all school functions. Fathers make corner screens, bookcases and hutches, and repair equipment. Mothers have become so interested that in the last three years four of them have helped the staff when qualified teachers were unobtainable. All have since gone for training as mature students to a day training college.

109. In another school fathers, more than mothers, have been the driving force in the almost 100 per cent strong P.T.A. They raised £8,000, partly through a summer fete attended by 1,000 people. Fathers, mothers and children scoured the beach for cockles to sell on a giant stall. They then built with their own labour a swimming pool, which is open in the evenings, at week ends and in holidays to all children and parents. The building team consisted of fathers who included surveyors, building foremen, lorry drivers, draughtsmen, metal workers, carpenters, painters, electricians and a foreman concrete mixer "as strong as an ox". The P.T.A. pays volunteer teachers to supervise the pool out of school hours. A large green-house has since been built where the children raise flowers for the school and to take round to old age pensioners in the district. There is an annual summer school for parents,

divided for the most part into groups for study of methods used in the school for teaching arithmetic, reading and so forth.

110. Another school was, if anything, even more ambitious. Under the auspices of the P.T.A., about 40 mothers and ten fathers formed a "money raising force", which organised a series of fairs at which articles made by mothers were sold. The proceeds were handed over to a "technical labour force", almost entirely composed of fathers in unskilled occupations who, under the guidance of a few skilled men, learnt to use tools they had never handled before. An information centre was built in the school grounds, and while it was being erected the children were writing hundreds of letters to obtain materials and data for display. A museum centre came next, for exhibits portraying local history, man-made and natural. Later came a children's theatre, which has been used for a drama club, country dancing club, choir and films. Display units, book racks and book cases, base boards for models and handwork trollies were built, along with a nature laboratory and two play houses. A garden was made where before there had been concrete. At every stage the children helped by drawing up plans and preparing costings as part of their arithmetic lessons. As a result of all this, "The pattern of home-school relationships began to change. Instead of only meeting parents who had chips on shoulders, my staff found much smoother and more positive relationships for us all to work with". In schools where parents give practical help of this kind, discussion with teachers about methods used in the school often arises informally over the job and enables parents to understand how the schools work and how to help their children more effectively.

Parent-Teacher Associations

111. Many, but not all, of these exceptional schools had active P.T.As. But the parents did not "run" the school, or attempt to do so. They had suggestions to make and questions to ask about the school and its work: it is one of the purposes of a P.T.A. to stimulate and answer such questions. The head and the teachers had complete control where professional matters were concerned. Some who have given evidence to us expressed the fear that P.T.A.s might interfere in the school, and referred expressly to American experience, where P.T.A.s in one form or another are almost universal. All we can say is that we have received little evidence of this actually happening, on either side of the Atlantic. In our visits to American schools we asked repeatedly for instances where P.T.A.s "ran" the schools. Though we could not explore so difficult a question in any depth on a brief tour we were unable to find such instances, and in general the high quality of parent-teacher relations impressed us as much as any aspect of education we saw in the United States. Yet we do not think that P.T.A.s are necessarily the best means of fostering close relationships between home and school. They can be of the greatest value where good leadership is given by the head. They may do harm if they get into the hands of a small group. It is significant that, according to the Social Survey interviews, a smaller proportion of manual workers attended P.T.A. meetings than any other type of function. (Appendix 3, Table 53). Seventeen per cent of the schools in the National Sample had P.T.A.s (Appendix 5, paragraph 5). They are least common in nursery schools where relations between mothers and teachers are usually very intimate,

rather more common in infant schools and most frequently found in junior and junior mixed and infant schools. It may be that the smaller the school, the less the need for a formal association. Heads have to take account of what they must do directly for children as well as indirectly through their parents. In some schools, at some moments of their history, particularly if heads cannot delegate to others the administrative work of running a P.T.A., it may absorb too much of their attention. What matters most are the attitudes of teachers to parents and parents to teachers—whether there is genuine mutual respect, whether parents understand what the schools are doing for their individual children and teachers realise how dependent they are on parental support.

A Minimum Programme

112. Attitudes best declare themselves by actions and we think that the arrangements of all schools should, as a minimum, cover certain essential relationships, though the ways through which they find expression may differ. Beyond the minimum, all kinds of experiments are desirable. We make the following suggestions:

(i) *Welcome to the School*

A child and his parents need to be welcomed when he is first admitted to school, or when his parents have moved into the district and he has to attend a new school. Each parent should be invited to an interview with the head, to meet the class teacher and see at work the class into which the child is to go, as well as to see the school generally and to hear about its organisation. Unless this interview takes place by appointment, it is unlikely to be leisurely enough. If a single date of entry is introduced and children have a medical examination before, arrangements can then be made for parents and children to visit the school later. Over a third of the parents in the National Survey did not see the head before their children started school. (Appendix 4, Section 3: paragraph 15). Less than half the children in the special group of infant starters visited their class before admission. (Appendix 6, Table 5).

(ii) *Meetings with Teachers*

Parents need more than anything else a chance of regular private talks with the teacher mainly responsible for their child. Heads and class teachers should make themselves accessible to parents for informal exchanges, so that, as one parent said, parents know their children's teachers at least as well as they know the milkman. They will then feel confident in entrusting their children to them. Head and class teachers should make a point of being about in the class room or playground when parents fetch their children. It may help parents and busy teachers if there are known times each week when teachers are available, though if parents turn up in an emergency head teachers should make every effort to see them. There could also be somewhat more formal arrangements for individual interviews, preferably twice during the year, once in the first term so that the parents can give information to the class teacher, and once in the third term to hear about the child's progress. There should be occasions when talks can last at least a quarter of an hour. Some, but not all, of these private talks can be arranged in conjunction with an open day or evening when a single class is "at home" to parents. The head teacher can then relieve the class teacher so that parents can have personal interviews, and at the same time parents can see their children's classroom and the rest of the school. Certainly some meetings between parents and teachers should take place when fathers are available. The evidence of the National Survey shows that this is least common in schools where many parents are semi-skilled or unskilled workers. (Appendix 5, paragraph 6). The best time to see fathers must depend on the individual school, particularly since some fathers are on shift work. We were encouraged to hear from one school in the National Survey that fathers were willing to lose pay in order to visit the school during working hours: we had noted in Poland that parents were paid for time spent in this way. In some schools, open days take place on "occasional holidays"; evening sessions, whether for individual interviews or other purposes, occur in the teacher's free time. It has always been recognised that teachers should give as much time out of school as is required for the efficient carrying out of their duties. It might be well for local authorities and heads to make this clear. It should sometimes be possible to modify the school timetable so that parents can talk privately with teachers.

(iii) *Open Days*

Some teachers are sceptical about open days because they may become such formal occasions that they dominate and distort the children's work. Yet children and their parents enjoy an occasion when it is possible to see the work of the school systematically, and it should be possible to keep preparation within reasonable bounds. Parents who may be shy of an individual interview may find it easier to come with others. Teachers can take the opportunity to make appointments for talks with individual parents. Open days ought to be so timed that both fathers and mothers can be present, which ordinarily means repeating the occasion in the daytime and in the evening. Particularly in villages and small towns, invitations can be extended to the community as a whole, and the result, if not the intention, may be to recruit voluntary help for the school.

(iv) *Information for Parents*

Parents need information not only about their own children's progress but also of a general kind about what goes on in the school. The local education authority might suggest that schools prepare a booklet, giving parents the basic facts about their organisation, the size of classes, whether they are streamed, and how to get in touch with the teachers. It could also include a brief account of the school's educational objectives and methods. Parents wish children to do school work at home (Appendix 3, Section 2: paragraphs 30–32). The booklet could advise parents on the kind of work children can profitably do at home, tell them about arrangements for home reading of library books and ask for parents' co-operation. Parents would in effect receive a prospectus, as in an independent school. It would help them both to choose a school for

c

their children and to work with the school once the choice was made. In addition, every school should give an opportunity, through meetings and informal discussions, for parents to hear about the methods of teaching in use. Homework should be a matter for discussion and agreement between home and school and the school should give thought to the form of homework most suitable to children's varying circumstances. Few other social institutions have changed their attitudes and techniques as quickly and as fundamentally as the primary school. Sometimes there has been little short of a revolution, since the parents were at school themselves. They may hear about these changes in a garbled way from other parents or perhaps from the mass media, before they learn about them from the school. The school should explain them so that parents can take an informed interest in what their children are doing. Parents will not understand unless they are told.

(v) *Reports for Parents*

Written reports in the past have often been a waste of time since they were so conventional that they conveyed nothing to parents. There is a genuine problem; parents need to know how their children are getting on, yet some may fail to distinguish between effort and achievement or be wounded by the truth and discourage their children. Useful reports are difficult to write and take time. They are much more helpful if the teacher knows the parent for whom he is writing. On balance, we think it would be helpful if parents were given a written comment at least once a year. On pages 93 and 94 is an example of a fairly conventional report which is better than many because it puts some emphasis on general development and invites comment from parents. We also reproduce examples of letters which might be sent by head or class teachers to parents. Written comment would supplement discussion with parents about children's progress. In Chapter 12 we suggest that this discussion should be based on children's individual records or folders.

Visiting the Homes

113. However many and pressing the invitations from school, some parents will not respond, and amongst them will be some of those whose children most need help. Should they be sought out? It would be a policy of despair to do nothing about them. One possibility would be for teachers to ask parents if they would be willing to be visited at home, and if they were, to do so. This is a fairly general practice in Sweden and has been tried in England too. One infant school head told us that she visited the homes of all new entrants in the holiday before they were admitted. J. B. Mays has described how home visiting on the part of teachers made for good relations between homes and schools, and others have had similar experience[1]. But it cannot be recommended as a universal recipe. Not all teachers will be willing, nor all parents, and even if they were it would not always be right. The children's interests should be paramount, and if there is any reason to think that they do not want their teachers to visit their homes, it may be best to wait until they are willing. If teachers do not go, someone should. Every parent who does not come near the school should be visited once a year by an education welfare officer, if only to see if any groundless fears about the school have arisen which can easily be removed.

114. We have two main reasons for making these suggestions. Parents have a right to know what goes on in their children's schools, and the right to any guidance they can be given about the support they can offer the school. The second, and more important reason, is the one implied by the results of the National Survey—by involving the parents, the children may be helped.

115. How well such proposals work depends upon the skill and tact with which schools approach the task, and choose from the array of methods open to them. Many different approaches are needed. Whenever possible, an attempt should be made to measure the outcome in terms of children's performance. To show the kind of thing that might be done by teachers to influence parental attitudes a small scale demonstration of this kind was made at our request with the co-operation of the Institute of Community Studies in a three form entry junior school. Most of the fathers were manual workers. The trial project is being fully reported elsewhere[2].

116. The action taken was rather similar to that which we have recommended —all parents were, for instance, invited during the year to a private talk with their child's class teacher; meetings were held for parents at which teaching methods were explained and discussed; and leaflets were circulated giving information about the school and about the methods used in it. The educational performance of the children, as judged by tests of verbal and non-verbal intelligence, of ability at reading and arithmetic, was measured in September, 1965, near the beginning of the school year, before the attempts to involve the parents more closely, and again in May, 1966, to be in time for this Report. Appropriate age allowances were made.

117. On the whole, both parents and teachers appreciated what was done. Most parents considered they knew more about the school towards the end of the year than they had at the beginning, and teachers that they understood the children somewhat better for knowing more about their home backgrounds. One of the unexpected outcomes of the discussion meetings was that teachers learnt, as well as parents, from hearing their colleagues explain their methods. As one teacher said "You could see how the other teachers teach— it was a sort of refresher course for me". There was some improvement over the period in the children's performance, particularly in arithmetic. This improvement was most marked amongst the least able children. The private talks with teachers and the discussion meetings appeared to have the most impact. Many of the parents, when questioned at the beginning of the year, said they were puzzled about modern teaching methods. These seemed to be so different from the ones in use many years ago when they were themselves children at school that they often did not know what to say when their children asked them for help. "When I try to help him he says we don't do it that way. They have to learn words in a block—you know, bits of words. Then they also learn words in a piece all at once". The discussion meetings gave such parents the first chance they had had to find out what today's teaching methods are like. As a result, they could understand better what their children were doing, take more interest in their school work and give them more effective help. Quite a number of parents stopped worrying about their children's apparent lack of progress in the 3Rs when they began to appreciate the approach of a modern primary school. The performance of their children benefited.

118. The growing interest of parents in informed help on educational matters is shown by the response to an Advisory Centre which publishes a magazine every two months and answers enquiries by post. It is used by highly educated parents[3]. If they have a need for advice it seems obvious that less knowledgeable parents have a greater need. To meet the demand an Advice Bureau was run for seven days in a department store in a large town. Although nearly half the enquiries came from parents in professional and managerial occupations, a quarter of those who wanted advice were skilled manual workers. The experiment was thought to be justified by the interest and enthusiasm of the questioners, their frequent ignorance of the way the educational system worked and the relief they showed at receiving support for their ambitions, or reassurance that their problem was not unusual or insoluble.

A Policy for each Local Education Authority

119. All the proposals made so far are for individual schools, and of a kind that could be acted on by any head who both wishes and is able to carry his staff with him. Other proposals call for policy decisions by administrative authority. The first of these concerns the Department of Education: we hope they will issue a booklet containing more extensive examples of good practice in parent-teacher relations than we have room for here. It would also be helpful to issue a circular to local authorities asking them to let the Department know what steps they have taken to inform parents about the schools, what special efforts are being made to foster good parent-teacher relations in the schools and what success is being achieved.

120. The second proposal is about choice of primary school. How far should parents be given a choice? Section 76 of the Education Act gives it to them quite specifically—"and so far as is compatible with the provision of efficient instruction and training and the avoidance of unreasonable public expenditure, pupils are to be educated in accordance with the wishes of their parents"—and we would not want that changed. In practice the freedom is often nominal, and has to be where there is only one school in a neighbourhood or where one favoured school would burst its walls without some form of zoning. About half the county schools in the National Survey were not zoned. (Appendix 5, paragraph 4). We realise that choice is more often exercised by middle class parents. But we are sure that parents must be given some choice whenever this is possible and they should have information on which to base it. They are more likely to support a school they have freely chosen, and to give it the loyalty which is so essential if their children are to do the same. Whenever a school is unpopular that should be an indication to the authority to find out why and make it better.

The Community School

121. Our third general proposal is about the "community school". By this we mean a school which is open beyond the ordinary school hours for the use of children, their parents and, exceptionally, for other members of the community.

122. The 1944 Education Act recognised in Section 7 that local education authorities have a responsibility to contribute "to the spiritual, mental and physical development of the community"; and this responsibility is one that

is as relevant to primary as to secondary schools or to any other branch of the education system. Both before and after 1944 there have been many experiments designed to make fuller use of school buildings. The Cambridgeshire Village Colleges inspired by Henry Morris are famous throughout the world and have spread far beyond the county boundaries. They were, and are, "establishments planned as a community centre for young people and adults in such a way as to accommodate, in addition to further education activities, a secondary school"[4]. A voluntary body, supported by the London County Council, pioneered play centres in primary school premises, open for local children when the ordinary schools are closed, and other cities followed suit. Some play centres are open only after school hours and some also in the holidays. In other places swimming pools, adventure playgrounds and play parks have been built in school grounds or parks and thrown open to the community. We have also heard of several primary schools in town and country which run after-school clubs meeting as often as once every school day. In one school in the National Survey "there is after-school activity on almost every evening during the year when groups of children meet voluntarily for pottery, drama, recorder playing, gardening, rural science (partly in the surrounding district), football, athletics, jumping and agility work." Parents are welcome. Many come to help and take the opportunity of talking informally with the staff about their children. We have also heard of schools which have organised clubs in the long summer holidays. In spite of these successful enterprises, recreational provision for primary school children by local authorities, voluntary bodies and schools is very uneven. Some heads cannot run after-school clubs because their buildings are used each evening by outside organisations. Only four per cent of the parents interviewed in the National Survey said that they had any indoor recreational and play centres available. 32 per cent were anxious for swimming pools to be provided and 27 per cent wanted outdoor playgrounds and indoor recreational centres. (Appendix 3, Section 2, paragraphs 57, 59). Virtually none of the recommendations made by the Council's second report in 1948 on out of school activities has been acted on.

123. The impression of members of the Council who made visits abroad was that in recent years more progress has been achieved in other countries. In the United States, for instance, community schools of one kind or another are now common. We visited one in New Haven, Connecticut. Its centre was an elementary school but in addition there were two extra sessions daily as well as weekend and holiday sessions, all in the charge of a Vice Principal directly responsible to the Principal (or head) of the school. The first of the out of school daily sessions was from 3–5 p.m. and was for pupils from the ordinary school. The second was from 7–9 p.m. and was for high school pupils and adults. These were the kind of classes that were organised in the afternoon session of one particular day:

Class	Tutor
English class for Spanish-speaking children	University student, paid
Modern dance	Professional dance teacher, paid
Children's theatre	Actress, unpaid
Woodworking	Teacher, paid

Special tutoring for backward children	University student, unpaid
Girls' Club	Two housewives, unpaid
Science class	Teacher, paid
Reading circle	Individual help from 18 specially trained parents.

In the Soviet Union and in Poland many schools have extended hours. These are used in part for teaching, especially for the most and least able children, and in part to encourage individual initiative and hobbies, which often result in achievements of a high standard. Pioneer palaces provide exceptionally good facilities and skilled help for some children. In Denmark there are leisure time houses which arrange recreational activity for school children and others. They have lending libraries of toys as well as books.

The Way Ahead

124. School buildings and grounds represent an immense capital investment which has been provided by the community; the community should have such access to them as is compatible with their effective day time use. For adult and youth education in general, secondary schools, with their specialised equipment, are the most suitable. Primary schools are the obvious place for out of school activities for children and also for experiments in collaboration with parents. They have the advantage that they are more genuinely neighbourhood schools than are schools for older pupils. Parents do not have far to travel to them. An N.U.T. survey[5] showed that more than half of all primary schools are used outside school hours. The more they are used by parents who understand what the schools are trying to do, and by the children themselves, the less interference there should be with day-time use.

125. There are, of course, difficulties which increase when buildings are modern and designed for children, and learning methods are informal. Rooms lead from one into another and it may not be easy to keep individual rooms out of use; paintings and clay models are carefully displayed; mathematical and scientific experiments must be left up until they are completed. A satisfactory solution might be to reserve the classrooms for school and after-school use by children, and to provide adequate storage for community purposes. A hut in the playground can be valuable. An additional parent-community room has already been built in some schools by parents and designed so that it is suitable for use both by adults and children. The hall and playing field can often be used by children and adults without difficulty. Evening use should not be allowed to disturb the day-time work of the school, and the school should have priority at least for part of the week for evening activities associated with it. It would be sensible to give the head teacher, as in some of the schools we saw in the U.S.A., and as in the Cambridgeshire village colleges, an overall responsibility for the school in the day and in the evening. It could be exercised, in schools which were heavily used outside school hours, by deputy heads, one primarily responsible for the day time, and one for out of school activities. This arrangement would call for modification of the Burnham scale, which allows for only one deputy head for primary schools. At the least, the head should have some voice in the evening use of his school, and managing bodies should interest themselves in it and represent the school's needs to the local education authority.

126. We, therefore, hope that attempts of many different kinds will be made to use primary schools out of ordinary hours. Activities should be mainly devoted to children and families associated with the school rather than the community at large, save, for example, in a village which has no hall. Children can be given opportunities during a late afternoon session, and in the day time during holidays, for carrying on their hobbies, and for expression in the arts and for games. Parents can be invited to the school in the evenings to learn about its ways and to make things that will be useful for the school. Parents and others in the community should help to organise activities and staff the school during its late afternoon session, just as they have rallied to provide play groups and to support youth clubs. We know of an authority which launched a carefully planned campaign to recruit youth workers by large scale publicity, by organising a meeting of those interested, confronting them with the work which needed doing, and then providing some training. In this way they solved part of their staffing problem in this sector of education. Local education authorities, heads and school managers might run a similar campaign for helpers for out of school activities and a list could be kept of those who could give regular or occasional help. But a community school could not exist without some additional professional staff, including teachers ready to work for a third session, and they would cost money. We envisage that parents themselves would make a financial contribution towards the cost of out of school activities as they have already done in some schools and play centres. We have heard of out of school clubs now functioning where some play leaders are paid by the local authority and some are volunteers. This arrangement does not produce insuperable difficulties any more than it does in youth work. The local authority's contribution to costs would vary from district to district. In what we later describe as "educational priority areas" it would have to be heavy. In many of these areas, as we heard from the children in one of them, "there is nowhere to play and we can't do anything without getting into trouble with somebody". An experiment is already being tried in one of these areas of appointing a teacher who gives one day-time session to the school and one to a play centre in the school. We hope that the biggest effort to develop community schools will be made in educational priority areas.

Interesting Parents Early

127. We are interested to hear of one school which made a point of arranging evening functions for parents two or three years before their children were old enough to attend school. Displays of picture books and toys were arranged and informal discussions were held about ways of bringing up young children. Though psychologists emphasise the great importance of early years in children's education, we have lagged behind some other countries in providing guidance for parents. From the first, health visitors have done much in their individual visits to homes to guide mothers, and this is still the most important aspect of their work in parent education. Health visitors are also encouraged to set up mothers' clubs in connection with welfare clinics, and these clubs are increasing in number especially in clinics which have their own premises, and where health visitors have ancillary help in routine matters.

128. Women's magazines and television can play a useful part in drawing parents' attention to their children's needs, particularly if they do not adopt too much of a middle class approach. A recent experiment in group viewing in schools and technical colleges, and subsequent discussion of a television programme on Growth and Play, met with some success. One viewing group in a college of further education led to a course for parents in the following session. In this college a parents' club is to be formed. Most of those who took part in the group viewing had had no previous connection with a parent-teacher association or a technical college. Contact was usually made with them through circulars to parents in the primary schools. More extensive publicity for opportunities of this kind is needed since few young parents whose children had not reached school age and whose need may well have been greatest, attended the groups. Some technical colleges which have developed N.N.E.B. courses are becoming known as centres for work in child development and are receiving requests for discussion courses from parents, as well as from women who hope to work professionally with children. Many opportunities for parent education, formal and informal, occur in community centres and other forms of adult education. Together with others such as health visitors, teachers could become an important source of guidance for parents on what to do with children out of school.

129. Much depends on the teachers. Every chapter could end thus—but perhaps it is even more apt here than elsewhere. Teachers are already hard pressed, and nowhere more so than in the very districts where the co-operation of parents is most needed and hardest to win. We are aware that in asking them to take on new burdens we are asking what will sometimes be next to impossible. Forty children will seem enough to many, without adding 80 fathers and mothers. Yet we are convinced that to make the effort will not only add depth to their understanding of their children but will also bring out that support from the home which is still often latent. It has long been recognised that education is concerned with the whole man; henceforth it must be concerned with the whole family.

Recommendations

130. (i) All schools should have a programme for contact with children's homes to include:

(a) a regular system for the head and class teacher to meet parents before the child enters.

(b) arrangements for more formal private talks, preferably twice a year.

(c) open days to be held at times chosen to enable parents to attend.

(d) parents to be given booklets prepared by the schools to inform them in their choice of children's schools and as to how they are being educated.

(e) written reports on children to be made at least once a year; the child's work should be seen by parents.

(f) special efforts to make contact with parents who do not visit the schools.

(ii) The Department of Education and Science should issue a booklet containing examples of good practices in parent-teacher relations. The Department should inform themselves of the steps taken by authorities to encourage schools to foster good relations.

(iii) Parents should be allowed to choose their children's primary school whenever this is possible. Authorities should take steps to improve schools which are shown to be consistently unpopular with parents.

(iv) Primary schools should be used as fully as possible out of ordinary hours.

(v) Heads should have a say in the evening use of their buildings. When buildings are heavily used two deputy head teachers should be appointed, one responsible for out of school activities. This would involve a modification of the Burnham provisions.

(vi) Parents and other adults should be invited to help the school with its out of school activities. Parents might contribute towards the cost of out of school activities, to supplement the costs borne by the local education authority.

(vii) Community schools should be developed in all areas but especially in educational priority areas.

REFERENCES

[1] J. B. Mays, Education and the Urban Child, Liverpool University Press, 1962.
[2] M. Young and P. McGeeney. 'A Junior School and its Parents', forthcoming. Routledge, Kegan and Paul.
[3] Lindsey March. 'The "Education Shop" Report on a Social Experiment',
[4] Ministry of Education. Further Education. H.M.S.O., 1947.
[5] The State of Our Schools. N.U.T. 1962, Part 1, paragraphs 28.

CHAPTER 5

Educational Priority Areas

131. In Chapter 3 we tried to disentangle some of the principal influences that shape the educational opportunities of children, and to assess and compare their importance. The task of abstracting them and measuring the impact made by each when "all other things are equal" is the continuing concern of research workers. But policy makers and administrators must act in a world where other things never are equal; this, too, is the world in which the children grow up, where everything influences everything else, where nothing succeeds like success and nothing fails like failure. The outlook and aspirations of their own parents; the opportunities and handicaps of the neighbourhood in which they live; the skill of their teachers and the resources of the schools they go to; their genetic inheritance; and other factors still unmeasured or unknown surround the children with a seamless web of circumstance.

132. In a neighbourhood where the jobs people do and the status they hold owe little to their education it is natural for children as they grow older to regard school as a brief prelude to work rather than an avenue to future opportunities. Some of these neighbourhoods have for generations been starved of new schools, new houses and new investment of every kind. Everyone knows this; but for year after year priority has been given to the new towns and new suburbs, because if new schools do not keep pace with the new houses some children will be unable to go to school at all. The continually rising proportion of children staying on at school beyond the minimum age has led some authorities to build secondary schools and postpone the rebuilding of older primary schools. Not surprisingly, many teachers are unwilling to work in a neighbourhood where the schools are old, where housing of the sort they want is unobtainable, and where education does not attain the standards they expect for their own children. From some neighbourhoods, urban and rural, there has been a continuing outflow of the more successful young people. The loss of their enterprise and skill makes things worse for those left behind. Thus the vicious circle may turn from generation to generation and the schools play a central part in the process, both causing and suffering cumulative deprivation.

133. We have ourselves seen schools caught in such vicious circles and read accounts of many more. They are quite untypical of schools in the rest of the country. We noted the grim approaches; incessant traffic noise in narrow streets; parked vehicles hemming in the pavement; rubbish dumps on waste land nearby; the absence of green playing spaces on or near the school sites; tiny play grounds; gaunt looking buildings; often poor decorative conditions inside; narrow passages; dark rooms; unheated and cramped cloakrooms; unroofed outside lavatories; tiny staff rooms; inadequate storage space with consequent restriction on teaching materials and therefore methods; inadequate space for movement and P.E.; meals in classrooms; art on desks; music only to the discomfort of others in an echoing building; non-soundproof

partitions between classes; lack of smaller rooms for group work; lack of spare room for tuition of small groups; insufficient display space; attractive books kept unseen in cupboards for lack of space to lay them out; no privacy for parents waiting to see the head; sometimes the head and his secretary sharing the same room; and, sometimes all around, the ingrained grime of generations.

134. We heard from local education authorities of growing difficulty in replacing heads with successors of similar calibre. It is becoming particularly hard to find good heads of infant or deputy heads of junior schools. We are not surprised to hear of the rapid turnover of staff, of vacancies sometimes unfilled or filled with a succession of temporary and supply teachers of one kind or another. Probationary teachers are trained by heads to meet the needs of their schools but then pass on to others where strains are not so great. Many teachers able to do a decent job in an ordinary school are defeated by these conditions. Some become dispirited by long journeys to decaying buildings to see each morning children among whom some seem to have learned only how not to learn. Heads rely on the faithful, devoted and hard working regulars. There may be one or two in any school, or they may be as many as half the staff, who have so much to do in keeping the school running that they are sometimes too tired even to enjoy their own holidays.

135. We saw admission registers whose pages of new names with so many rapid crossings out told their own story of a migratory population. In one school 111 out of 150 pupils were recent newcomers. We heard heads explain, as they looked down the lines, that many of those who had gone were good pupils, while a high proportion of those who had been long in the school came from crowded, down-at-heel homes.

The Educational Needs of Deprived Areas

136. What these deprived areas need most are perfectly normal, good primary schools alive with experience from which children of all kinds can benefit. What we say elsewhere about primary school work generally applies equally to these difficult areas. The best schools already there show that it is absurd to say, as one used to hear, "it may be all very well in a nice suburb, but it won't work here". But, of course, there are special and additional demands on teachers who work in deprived areas with deprived children. They meet special challenges. Teachers must be constantly aware that ideas, values and relationships within the school may conflict with those of the home, and that the world assumed by teachers and school books may be unreal to the children. There will have to be constant communication between parents and the schools if the aims of the schools are to be fully understood. The child from a really impoverished background may well have had a normal, satisfactory emotional life. What he often lacks is the opportunity to develop intellectual interests. This shows in his poor command of language. It is not, however, with vocabulary that teaching can begin. The primary school must first supply experiences and establish relationships which enable children to discriminate, to reason and to express themselves. Placing such children in the right stance for further learning is a very skilled operation. But those who have done remedial work will be aware of the astonishing rapidity of the progress which can be achieved, particularly in extending vocabulary, once children's curiosity is released. The thrust to learn seems to be latent in every

child, at least within a very wide range of normality. But however good the opportunities, some children may not be able to take advantage of them. Failure may have taken away from them their urge to learn.

137. A teacher cannot and should not give the deep, personal love that each child needs from his parents. There are ways he can help:—

(a) He can relieve children of responsibility without dominating them in a way which prevents them from developing independence. Deprived children may have been forced into premature responsibility. They are often given the care of younger children and are free to roam, to go to bed or to stay up, to eat when and where they can. This produces what is often a spurious maturity. Confidence can be encouraged by tasks which are fully within their capacity. A measure of irresponsibility has to be allowed for: it will pretty certainly come later, and in a less acceptable form, if not permitted at the proper time.

(b) A teacher can do much by listening and trying to understand the context of the questions the children ask. It will be much easier if he knows the child's family and the neighbourhood surrounding his home.

(c) Children in deprived neighbourhoods are often backward. There is a risk that an inexperienced teacher will think there is not time for anything but the three Rs if the child is not to be handicapped throughout his life. This is quite wrong. These children need time for play and imaginative and expressive work and may suffer later if they do not get it at school.

(d) Teachers need to use books which make sense to the children they teach. They will often have to search hard for material which is suitable for downtown children.

(e) Record keeping is especially necessary for teachers in schools in deprived neighbourhoods. There is so much coming and going by families that a child's progress may depend very much on the amount and quality of information that can be sent with him from school to school.

Hope for the Future

138. In our cities there are whole districts which have been scarcely touched by the advances made in more fortunate places. Yet such conditions have been overcome and striking progress has been achieved where sufficiently determined and comprehensive attack has been made on the problem. In the most deprived areas, one of H.M. Inspectors reported, "Some heads approach magnificence, but they cannot do everything . . . The demands on them as welfare agents are never ending". Many children with parents in the least skilled jobs do outstandingly well in school. The educational aspirations of parents and the support and encouragement given to children in some of the poorest neighbourhoods are impressive. Over half of the unskilled workers in our National Survey (Appendix 3, Table 26) want their children to be given homework to do after school hours; over half want their children to stay at school beyond the minimum leaving age. (Table 27). One third of them hoped their children would go to a grammar school or one with similar opportunities (Table 28). The educational aspirations of unskilled workers for their children have risen year by year. It has been stressed[1] to us that the range of ability in all social classes is so wide that there is a great reservoir of unrealised potential in families dependent on the least skilled and lowest paid work. A larger

part of the housing programme than ever before is to be devoted to rebuilding and renewing obsolete and decaying neighbourhoods. The opportunity must be seized to rebuild the schools as well as the houses, and to see that both schools and houses serve families from every social class. It will be possible to make some progress in reducing the size of classes in primary schools in these areas as well as elsewhere. Colleges of education which have taken a special interest in deprived areas report that their students respond in an encouraging fashion to the challenge of working in these neighbourhoods. Most important of all, there is a growing awareness in the nation at large, greatly stimulated, we believe, by our predecessors' Reports, of the complex social handicaps afflicting such areas and the need for a more radical assault on their problems. These are the strengths on which we can build. How can they be brought to bear?

139. We propose a nation-wide scheme for helping those schools and neighbourhoods in which children are most severely handicapped. This policy will have an influence over the whole educational system, and it colours all the subsequent recommendations in our Report. It must not be put into practice simply by robbing more fortunate areas of all the opportunities for progress to which they have been looking forward; it can only succeed if a larger share of the nation's resources is devoted to education. So far-reaching a set of proposals must be firmly rooted in educational grounds, yet the arguments for them inevitably extend beyond this field into many other branches of the nation's affairs. Before explaining these proposals we give a brief outline of the reasoning which led us to make them.

Educational Assumptions and Policies

140. Our study of these problems compelled us to consider the process of economic and social development and the contribution made to it by the schools. Industrial development in many respects is the motor of social progress. We recognise that there are limits to the resources that can be mobilised for education and the primary schools. But it does not necessarily follow, as many have assumed, that the fruits of economic growth, together with the present pattern of public services, will in time give every child increasing opportunities of contributing to the nation's progress. It does not follow that education, because its development depends in the long run on the growth of the economy, must therefore follow in its wake, rather than contribute to the promotion of growth. Nor does it follow that a "fair" or "efficient" distribution of educational resources is one that provides a reasonably equal supply of teachers, classrooms, and other essentials to each school child in each area. Nor does it follow that the government's responsibility for promoting progress within the limits permitted by these resources must be confined to encouraging development in the most capable areas, spreading word of their progress to others, and pressing on the rearguard of the laggard or less fortunate whenever opportunity permits. Though many of these assumptions are already being questioned or abandoned, our own proposals are unlikely to convince those who still accept them, and we must, therefore, challenge each in turn.

141. During the second world war there was a considerable improvement in the living conditions which bear most directly upon children in deprived

groups and areas. In spite of this there has not been any appreciable narrowing of the gap between the least well off and the rest of the population. This is most obvious among children, particularly those in large families. "It is ... clear that, on average, the larger families in all classes, and also those containing adolescents and children, constitute the most vulnerable groups nutritionally."[2,3]. Signs of rickets have recently been reported again from the slums of Glasgow; mortality among children during the first year of life has fallen sharply since 1950, but the difference between social classes remains great[4]. Much the same goes for stillbirth rates which, in different social classes "despite a dramatic wartime fall, were as far apart in 1950 as in 1939". Meanwhile "class differentials in perinatal mortality are as resistant to change as those of infant mortality. The results of the (Perinatal Mortality) Survey suggest, indeed, that the gap may be increasing rather than narrowing"[5]. The Milner Holland Committee's study of housing conditions in London covered a period in which this country probably achieved a faster rate of economic growth than it has ever experienced before, and an area in which conditions are generally better and improving faster than elsewhere. But it showed that progress has been most rapid in those parts of the town where conditions were already best. In less fortunate neighbourhoods there has been less improvement and in some respects an appreciable deterioration. Families with low incomes and several young children were among those who suffered most[6].

142. If the fruits of growth are left to accumulate within the framework of present policies and provisions, there is no assurance that the living conditions which handicap educationally deprived children will automatically improve—still less that the gap between these conditions and those of more fortunate children will be narrowed.

143. The contribution made by education to economic development poses complicated questions, upon which systematic research has only recently begun, and we cannot present firm conclusions about it. Comparisons with other countries—all of them more recently industrialised than Britain but all now at a similar stage of economic development—suggest that we have not done enough to provide the educational background necessary to support an economy which needs fewer and fewer unskilled workers and increasing numbers of skilled and adaptable people. One example can be drawn from a pioneer piece of research in comparative educational achievements. This compares mathematical skills at several stages of secondary education[7]. It shows that in the early stages England was distinguished from other countries not by the average standard attained (which was closely similar to the average for the other countries compared) but by the scatter of its results. English children achieved more than their share of the best results, and more of the worst results. Our educational system, originally moulded by the impress of Victorian economic and social requirements, may not yet have been fully adapted to present needs. In the deprived areas with which this chapter is concerned too many children leave school as soon as they are allowed to with no desire to carry their education further and without the knowledge to fit them for a job more intellectually demanding than their father's or their grandfather's. Yet they face a future in which they must expect during their working life to have to change their job, to learn new skills, to adapt themselves to new economic conditions and to form new human relationships.

They will suffer, and so will the economy; both needlessly. It should not be assumed that even the ablest children can surmount every handicap. They may suffer as much as any from adverse conditions.

144. If the schools are to play their part in resolving and forestalling these problems much of the action required must be taken at the secondary and higher stages of the system. But this action cannot be fully effective if it does not touch the primary schools. Recent research has shown how early in the lives of children the selective processes begin to operate[8]. There are primary schools from which scarcely any children ever take a secondary school course which leads them to 'O' level in G.C.E. Children of good potential ability enter them, but the doors to educational opportunity have already closed against them when their schooling has scarcely begun. Reforming zeal and expenditure directed to later stages of education will be wasted unless early handicaps can be reduced.

145. The schools unaided cannot provide all the opportunities their pupils deserve, or create the labour force this country needs. Industry, and the authorities responsible for housing, planning, employment and other services must also play their part. But, from the earliest stages of education, the schools enlarge or restrict the contribution their pupils can make to the life of the nation. Money spent on education is an investment which helps to determine the scope for future economic and social development.

146. Our argument thus far can be briefly summarised. As things are at the moment there is no reason why the educational handicaps of the most deprived children should disappear. Although standards will rise, inequalities will persist and the potential of many children will never be realised. The range of achievement amongst English children is wide, and the standards attained by the most and the least successful begin to diverge very early. Steps should be taken to improve the educational chances and the attainments of the least well placed, and to bring them up to the levels that prevail generally. This will call for a new distribution of educational resources.

The Distribution of Resources

147. The principle that certain local authorities (but not districts within local authorities) should receive special help from the rest of the community is already recognised. At the national level the government takes needs into account when distributing grants to local authorities for educational and other purposes. The basic grant consists of so much per head of population plus so much for each child under 15 years of age. The supplementary grants allow for:

the number of children under five,
the number of people over 65,
school children in excess of a prescribed proportion,
density,
sparsity,
declining population, and
Metropolitan Areas.

There is also a formula that increases the grant paid to authorities with lower rateable values and reduces it for wealthier ones. The same principle of district priorities applies to educational building programmes. The needs of districts with a growing population come first; the next buildings to be sanctioned must be for the purpose of making good the deficiencies of existing schools. This principle can also be seen at work in the distribution of teachers. Local education authorities with an exceptionally high proportion of immigrant children may apply for an addition to their quota of teachers.

148. Redistribution of resources within local authority areas has been less marked. "Equality" has an appealing ring, "discrimination" has not. It is simpler and easier, for example, to defend staff-pupil ratios that are roughly the same in each school than to explain why they should be better in some and to decide which are to be the favoured. Even so, more and more local authorities do discriminate. They look with a more generous eye on schools whose "social need" is greatest, as reckoned by the free dinner list, by the proportion of children who do not speak English at home, or (which may be an even better guide) by the opinion of experienced teachers and administrators. These schools may be allowed an extra teacher or more non-teaching help, or a slightly bigger ration of "consumable stocks".

149. These are no more than a tentative beginning. The formulae for allocating grants are designed to equalise the financial resources of poorer and wealthier authorities. But equality is not enough. The formulae do not distinguish between the districts within authorities' areas in which children and schools are most severely handicapped. These districts need more spending on them, and government and local authorities between them must provide the funds. Permission is required before the money can be spent on what is most needed—additional teachers and better buildings. The authority's quota must be raised before extra teachers can be engaged, and additions to the building programme must be sanctioned by the Department of Education. Even if this happens the battle is not over. Some authorities whose need for teachers is great find it impossible to recruit for deprived schools the teachers to whom they are entitled. The vicious circle continues.

150. A study of the educational expenditure of 83 county boroughs has been made for us by Mr. B. P. Davies[9] (See Appendix 14). He compared the way money was spent with the evidence about the needs of each borough. He found no link between the amount spent on primary schools and their pupils and the social character of the area they served. In general, deprived areas were neither more nor less likely than others to get a bigger share of the total expenditure. A large proportion of expenditure was devoted to the salaries of teachers, whose distribution is subject to quota rules, and to the provision of those essential services which give little scope for variation. Other services, on which an education authority has great scope for independent decision, often tended to have more spent on them in those boroughs where the needs appeared to be less urgent. There are signs of this in the expenditure on nursery schools, and (less clearly) on child guidance. The same applied to school meals where parental preferences exert an influence. More striking, perhaps, was the persistence of these patterns. The boroughs in which expenditure was generally low were much the same in 1960–61 as they were in 1950–51.

Educational Priority Areas

151. The many teachers who do so well in face of adversity cannot manage without cost to themselves. They carry the burdens of parents, probation officers and welfare officers on top of their classroom duties. It is time the nation came to their aid. The principle, already accepted, that special need calls for special help, should be given a new cutting edge. We ask for "positive discrimination" in favour of such schools and the children in them, going well beyond an attempt to equalise resources. Schools in deprived areas should be given priority in many respects. The first step must be to raise the schools with low standards to the national average; the second, quite deliberately to make them better. The justification is that the homes and neighbourhoods from which many of their children come provide little support and stimulus for learning. The schools must supply a compensating environment. The attempts so far made within the educational system to do this have not been sufficiently generous or sustained, because the handicaps imposed by the environment have not been explicitly and sufficiently allowed for. They should be.

152. The proposition that good schools should make up for a poor environment is far from new. It derives from the notion that there should be equality of opportunity for all, but recognises that children in some districts will only get the same opportunity as those who live elsewhere if they have unequally generous treatment. It was accepted before the first world war that some children could not be effectively taught until they had been properly fed. Hence free meals were provided. Today their need is for enriched intellectual nourishment. Planned and positive discrimination in favour of deprived areas could bring about an advance in the education of children in the 1970s as great as the advance in their nutrition to which school meals and milk contributed so much.

153. Every authority where deprivation is found should be asked to adopt "positive discrimination" within its own area, and to report from time to time on the progress made. Some authorities contain schools or even one school of this kind where deprivation is so serious that they need special help. Most of these schools and areas are already well known to teachers, administrators, local Inspectors and H.M. Inspectors. Local knowledge will not be sufficient to justify decisions which are bound on occasion to be controversial. Objective criteria for the selection of "educational priority schools and areas" will be needed to identify those schools which need special help and to determine how much assistance should be given by the government. Our National Survey showed the prime importance of parental attitudes, and it might be thought that a measure of these attitudes could be devised. But the data for the selection of priority schools and areas must be readily available, without additional surveys, and in any event the validity of answers given by parents with the education of their children at stake might fairly be questioned. The criteria required must identify those places where educational handicaps are reinforced by social handicaps. Some of the main criteria which could be used in an assessment of deprivation are given below. They are not placed in order of importance, nor is any formula suggested by which they should be combined. They may require further study. The criteria are:

(a) *Occupation.* The National Census can report on occupations within quite small areas, and, for particular schools, the data can be supplemented without too much difficulty. The analyses would show the proportions of unskilled and semi-skilled manual workers.

(b) *Size of Families*. The larger the family, the more likely are the children to be in poverty. Wages are no larger for a married man with young children than they are for a single man with none. Family size is still associated with social class, and men with four or more children tend to be amongst the lowest wage earners. Family size also correlates with the results of intelligence tests—the larger the family, the lower the scores of the children. The children are liable to suffer from a double handicap, both genetic and environmental—the latter because, it is suggested, they have less encouragement and stimulus from parents who have more children amongst whom to divide their attention. Those earning the lowest wages often make up their incomes by working longer hours. Often, too, their wives have less time and energy to devote to their children. Family size likewise correlates with nutrition, with physical growth and with overcrowding, and is therefore an apt indicator (when allowance is made for the age structure of the local population, and particularly the number of mothers of child bearing age) of the poor home conditions for which schools should compensate. The National Census, supplemented by the schools censuses made by the education authorities, would provide the information required.

(c) *Supplements in Cash or Kind from the State* are of various kinds. Where the parents are needy, children are allowed school meals free. The proportions so benefiting vary greatly from school to school, and afford a reasonably good guide to relative need. The procedures laid down are designed to give free meals according to scales similar to those used by the Ministry of Social Security. Another criterion of the same type is the number of families depending on National Assistance, or its future equivalent, in a particular locality. The weakness of these criteria taken by themselves is that some people do not know their rights or are unwilling to seek them.

(d) *Overcrowding and Sharing of Houses* should certainly be included amongst the criteria. It will identify families in cramped accommodation in central and run-down areas of our cities. It is a less sure guide than some others because it may miss the educational needs of some housing estates and other areas which can also be severe.

(e) *Poor Attendance and Truancy* are a pointer to home conditions, and to what Burt long ago singled out as a determinant of school progress, the "efficiency of the mother". Truancy is also related to delinquency. The National Survey showed that four per cent of the children in the sample were absent, on their teachers' assessment, for unsatisfactory reasons. (Appendix 5, paragraph 27).

(f) *Proportions of Retarded, Disturbed or Handicapped Pupils* in ordinary schools. These vary from authority to authority according to the special schools available and the policies governing their use. But, everywhere, the proportions tend to be highest in deprived districts. It is accepted that special schools need additional staff, and the same advantages should be extended to normal schools with many pupils of a similar kind.

(g) *Incomplete Families* where one or other of the parents is dead, or not living at home for whatever reason, are often unable to provide a satisfactory upbringing for their children without special help.

(h) *Children Unable to Speak English* need much extra attention if they are to find their feet in England. This is already recognised in arranging teachers' quotas, but should also be used as a general criterion.

154. All authorities would be asked to consider which of their schools should qualify, to rank them according to criteria such as those we have listed, and to submit supporting data. Advice would also be available from H.M. Inspectors of Schools. In this way the Department of Education and Science would have full information both about the social and the educational needs of the schools and areas. Many of the criteria would be closely correlated. With experience the data required could be simplified so as to ease administration; but meanwhile, a wide variety of criteria should be employed. The schools near the bottom of the resulting rankings would be entitled to priority. We envisage a formal procedure enabling the Secretary of State for Education and Science to designate particular schools or groups of schools as priority schools or areas. Those so designated would qualify for the favourable treatment described later in this chapter. Local education authorities would submit regular reports on these schools to the Secretary of State for the purpose of determining what progress was being made, how long their designation should continue, which aspects of the programme were proving most effective, and what further steps should be taken.

Special Groups

155. However good the information secured, and however extensive the experience gained in using it, the administration of this policy would always call for wise judgement and careful interpretation. An infallible formula cannot be devised. Severe deprivation can be found among particular groups which are unlikely to be singled out by such criteria. Canal boat families are an example. Another are the gypsies whose plight is described in Appendix 12. They are probably the most severely deprived children in the country. Most of them do not even go to school, and the potential abilities of those who do are stunted. They tend to be excluded by their way of life and their lack of education from entering normal occupations and confined to others that compel continual travelling. Thus, unless action is taken to arrest the cycle, their children will in turn suffer educational deprivations which will become increasingly severe in their effects as general standards of education rise. The age distribution of this group bears a telling resemblance to that of England in 1841 and so does their education or lack of it. The numbers of gypsy children are small—those of compulsory school age probably amounting in total to less than four thousand. But they are increasing, and in the next 20 years their numbers are likely to double. In their own interests and in the nation's, they merit help of the kind we recommend. Yet the criteria listed in paragraph 153 would not select them. They move too frequently to be accurately recorded in census data, they are too seldom in school to appear in figures (of free school meals, for instance) derived from the school population, and the districts in which they are found, particularly the rural areas

surrounding the South Eastern and West Midland conurbations, are unlikely to contain many educational priority areas.

156. Another group of children which would not be identified by the suggested criteria are from Army and Air Force families in areas with large service populations. There is evidence of serious backwardness among them and of high turnover of pupils and teachers.

157. The case of the gypsies illustrates another aspect of the policies required in educational priority areas. Improved education alone cannot solve the problems of these children. Simultaneous action is needed by the authorities responsible for employment, industrial training, housing and planning. There will be similar, though less extreme, needs for co-ordinated action on behalf of other groups deserving priority. The experience of those engaged in the "war on poverty" in the United States gives warning of the disappointments which sometimes follow from attempts to improve the education of the poorest which are not coupled to an effective attack on unemployment. Where there are plans for new centres of economic growth in the less prosperous regions, extra resources for education should be temporarily concentrated in areas where the whole pace of development is likely to be increased. In such places, joint operations of this kind could before long go far to eliminate educational deprivation.

More Teachers

158. Once educational priority areas have been selected, the next step must be to give them the help they need. Each authority would be asked not only to say which schools had been selected, and why, but also what it proposed by way of remedy. The most important thing is to bring more experienced and successful teachers into these areas and to support them by a generous number of teachers' aides (see Chapter 24). Until there are more teachers all round, the possibility for increasing their numbers in these schools will, of course, be limited. But a beginning could be made, and the right framework created for the future. To start with, quotas should be raised for authorities with educational priority areas. But the schools in greatest need often cannot recruit their full complement at present, and to increase it, if that were all, would do nothing but cause irritation. Additional incentives are needed. We therefore recommend that there should be extra allowances for teachers and head teachers serving in schools in difficult areas. In many ways their work is already more arduous than their colleagues'. They will in future be expected to assume yet further responsibilities, not only in making contact with parents but also in arranging activities for their children outside the normal limits of the school day, and in collaborating with other local social services. Teachers in such schools deserve extra recognition and reward, and to give it to them would be one way of achieving something even more important, greater fairness between one child and another. The government has already reached the same conclusion in its search for means of recruiting doctors to the less popular areas; financial incentives are being offered to those who are willing fo work in them. Salary incentives, of course, present difficulties for the professions concerned, but we believe that the teachers, who understand better than most the urgency of the need, will be prepared to accept the remedies their medical colleagues are already adopting.

159. The Dame Jean Roberts Committee on Measures to Secure a More Equitable Distribution of Teachers in Scotland studied these problems independently and we were unaware that they had reached similar conclusions until our own Report was nearly completed. They call in their Report[10] for the designation of individual schools in which the scarcity of teachers is particularly severe, and for the payment of an additional £100 a year to all teachers serving in these schools. Our scheme differs from the Scottish plan in one important respect. The criteria we recommend are all social, not educational, so that priority schools and areas will not lose their privileged status, whether they have enough teachers or not, until the social conditions improve. As we understand the Scottish proposals, designation as a school of temporary shortage is to be subject to annual review and the additions to salaries will be paid only during the time when the school is so designated.

160. There is an important distinction between "mobile" teachers, often young and sometimes still unmarried, and the "immobile", who are more often married. Many authorities have succeeded in attracting back to work women teachers who had resigned after marriage, and the more who return the better. But the schools to which they go are often those near their own homes, and therefore in middle-class neighbourhoods not in the queue for priority. Each woman who returns could release an additional mobile teacher for priority areas, but that will not be achieved unless more carefully drawn distinctions can be made between the mobile and immobile, and the quotas to be applied to each. The principle underlying these arrangements should be that authorities must employ every immobile teacher in their areas before drawing on mobile teachers who may be available for the priority areas. The administrative difficulties of such an arrangement are considerable, but while teachers remain so scarce every effort should be made to overcome them.

161. There are two obvious problems about this scheme which should be mentioned. The first is the risk that, while the black areas may become white, the neighbouring grey areas may be turned black by an exodus of teachers attracted by salary incentives. But the fact that the priority areas will seldom, if ever, cover a whole authority will be a safeguard. They will usually consist of much smaller districts, some containing one or two schools only, within the territory of an authority and the authority can exercise considerable control over the recruitment and deployment of its teachers and ensure that a balance is maintained between the claims of all its schools, good and bad. The second concerns our proposals for different rules for the employment of mobile and immobile teachers. The Department of Education and Science does not know where the immobile live, especially if they left teaching some years ago. This information might be collected by local education authorities. This should form the basis of information for the Department, who should modify its quota arrangements to take into account the varying resources of immobile teachers in each area.

162. Priority areas are not the kind of place where teachers normally live. Yet those whose homes are near their pupils' can often do a better job than those who travel great distances. They belong to the same community; they can understand their background better. What is more, the creation of vast one-class districts from which all professional people are excluded is bad in itself. Sustained efforts ought to made to diversify the social composition

of the priority areas. Many professional workers feel the need to start buying a house early in their careers because mortgage terms may be more favourable, and because once they own a house it is easier for them to secure another one if they move elsewhere. Their needs should be recognised by the housing and planning authorities. There should be a mixture of houses for renting, for owner-occupation, and for co-ownership, and cost-rent schemes run by housing associations. As our enquiries showed, many authorities can, and some do, provide housing for teachers and others whose claims derive not from the urgency of their housing needs but from the contribution they make to the community which provides the houses. The housing needs of families in badly overcrowded places are likely to be more urgent than those of teachers; but their children will not get the education they deserve if teachers are systematically excluded from the locality. The Dame Jean Roberts Committee urges, and we agree, that local education authorities "should be allowed greater freedom than at present to purchase, and if necessary to adapt, houses to let to teachers willing to serve at shortage points. Expenditure incurred on the purchase and adaptation of such houses should not be regarded as a charge on an authority's capital investment allocation for school building" (p. 25). We agree with this. It does not follow that any help with housing would entitle teachers to subsidies designed for tenants with lower incomes. The Dame Jean Roberts Committee recommended also that there should be travel allowances for teachers working in difficult areas at a distance from their homes. We recommend that local authorities consider this.

Colleges of Education

163. Teachers in training also have a part to play. In our visit to the United States we were much struck by the value of linking teacher-training establishments with schools in deprived areas. In some cities young teachers are attracted to such places and helped to settle down there by the appointment of special consultants who regularly visit new teachers in schools where the conditions are difficult, support them in their work, and are available on call to give advice. On a smaller scale, the benefits of such links can already be seen in England. We urge that colleges should be asked to establish wherever possible a continuing link with schools in priority areas. Students should be sent to them for a part of their teaching practice. We also hope that in many of these areas a generously equipped teachers' centre can be set up for the in-service training of teachers already working there, partly staffed by the affiliated college of education and partly by local inspectors, H.M. Inspectors and experienced local teachers and heads. The improved staffing ratio we recommend should make an in-service training programme possible. Longer courses to equip teachers for work in the priority areas could be run from such centres and in colleges of education, and be recognised for purposes of Burnham allowances. Over the years this work would help to build up a body of knowledge about the best ways of teaching children in socially deprived neighbourhoods. Co-operation for research purposes with university departments and with colleges of education would also enable the successes, and failures, of the whole venture to be properly assessed.

Buildings

164. The shortage of buildings is going to be as acute as the shortage of teachers. New building is committed for several years ahead to keep pace with

the birth-rate and the rise in the school-leaving age. There will not be much to spare for the priority areas in the immediate future. Our criteria should be given great weight when determining which of the schools with old and out-of-date buildings is to be replaced first. It would also help if the element in the total building programme reserved for minor works were increased specially for the benefit of these areas. Schools in the greatest plight could be given preference, for the improvement of lavatories and wash places, and for modifications to classrooms. They also should be frequently redecorated. There is urgent need for decent staff rooms to replace those ones thought good enough sixty years ago, if indeed there were any at all. In making estimates of the costs involved we have assumed that an average of £5,000 should be spent on each of these schools. Some will need more; others will need very little. What goes into the building is likewise important. The need for extra "consumable stocks" has already been mentioned. Additional books and audio-visual equipment of various kinds, including television sets and tape-recorders, would be particularly valuable in these schools.

Nursery Education

165. We argue in Chapter 9 that part-time attendance at a nursery school is desirable for most children. It is even more so for children in socially deprived neighbourhoods. They need above all the verbal stimulus, the opportunities for constructive play, a more richly differentiated environment and the access to medical care that good nursery schools can provide. It will be many years before they are generally available. The building of new nursery schools and extensions to existing schools should start in priority areas and spread outwards. As a minimum we suggest that all children aged four to five who live in the areas should have the opportunity of part-time attendance and that perhaps 50 per cent should have full-time places (although their need for a gradual introduction is the same as that of all other children).

Other Priorities

166. The development of social work carried out in conjunction with the schools is discussed in Chapter 7. This too should be concentrated first in the priority areas.

167. It might be thought that our proposal for community schools, made in the previous chapter, would be hardest to implement in these districts. But in many of them the demand for centres for activities outside the home of various kinds is keen, as the existence of university settlements and similar bodies shows. It will take special skill to seize these opportunities and use them for educational purposes. But the gains that could be made in mutual understanding between teachers and parents through the work of a well run community school in a priority area make the scheme well worth trying.

First Steps

168. Local education authorities which have a number of priority schools will not be able to embark on a policy of positive discrimination until they know what help they can get from the central government. The nation's supply of the principal resources required—teachers and school buildings—is known and committed, several years in advance, often to other parts of the

educational system. We must, therefore, think in terms of an immediate programme, on which a start can be made without waiting for additional resources or major changes in existing plans, and after that a longer term programme to follow.

169. The principles on which we have based the immediate programme are as follows:

(i) A start should be made as quickly as possible by giving priority to the schools which by our criteria contain the ten per cent of most deprived children. Starting at two per cent in the first year this percentage should be reached within five years. The additional budget for these areas should not engross the entire increase in educational resources available for the whole country, year by year. There must be a margin permitting some improvement in the schools serving the rest of the population.

(ii) The programme should begin as quickly as possible at varying dates for different elements in the system (teachers' aides, for example, may be available sooner than an over-all increase in the school building programme).

170. During a period to start in 1968 and to reach its peak in 1972 the following steps should be taken in educational priority areas (or in individual priority schools):

(i) The staffing ratio should be improved so that no class need exceed 30.

(ii) Additions to salary of £120 (as are given to teachers of handicapped children or those with other special responsibilities) should be available at the rate of one for every teacher in the priority areas. But it would be open to local education authorities to award these increases according to any plan approved by the Department of Education and Science as being likely to improve education in the designated schools. The additional resources should be used flexibly; for example, an allowance might be allocated to a remedial teacher specialising in helping these schools, or allowances might be withheld and become payable only after a brief qualifying period. They would not, of course, be paid to staff working mainly in other schools. These arrangements will require an amendment of the Burnham Report.

(iii) Teachers' aides should be provided to help teachers, on the lines described in Chapter 24, but at the more generous ratio of one aide for every two classes in infant and junior schools.

(iv) Those educational priority schools with poor buildings should be allocated, within the first five years, a minor building project. The average costs between all priority schools might be £5,000 though some will need little or no new building.

(v) The full provision for nursery education should be introduced for children aged four and five as proposed in Chapter 9 of this Report. A higher proportion than in the rest of the country will attend full-time (up to 50 per cent).

(vi) Research should be set on foot to determine which of these measures has the most positive effect as a basis for planning the longer term programme.

(vii) We estimate, in Chapter 31, that by 1972/73 the educational priority areas will add £11 million to the total current costs of the maintained primary schools. It is clear therefore that the total of Exchequer grants to local authorities will have to be increased to take account of this. It is not for us to plan the mechanism for the distribution of these grants. A new specific grant for authorities containing priority areas may be required, on the lines of the proposed grant to authorities with large numbers of Commonwealth immigrants; or the formula for the distribution of the new rate support grant might be modified.

A Continuing Policy

171. The longer term programme will call for additional resources, over and above those at present allocated to education. Our proposals are not intended to be a once-for-all expedient. The lead in the ratio of teachers to pupils which the priority areas should have attained by 1972 must be maintained. It is suggested they should be restricted to an arbitrary figure of ten per cent of the population initially, in order to provide a serious test of the effectiveness of different elements of priority within the resources that can be found without depriving the rest of the country of scope for improvement. It will be much longer before reliable conclusions can be reached about the outcome, but already by 1972 it should be easier to decide how far and in what way to extend the programme. The need may well be shown to go beyond ten per cent of children. The Council's last report estimated that just under a fifth of modern school pupils were in "problem areas", very similar to what we describe as educational priority areas[11].

172. The arguments for this policy are general, and apply to whole districts that have been educationally handicapped for years. They are not confined to primary schools and apply to secondary schools as well. But a start should, in our view, be made in primary schools. They have long had less than their share of new building and their classes have always been larger. Since they draw their pupils from smaller catchment areas they feel the full impact of social conditions in their immediate neighbourhood, whereas rather more secondary schools can draw from a mixture of neighbourhoods, with the more fortunate offsetting the less.

Conclusion

173. Positive discrimination accords with experience and thinking in many other countries, and in other spheres of social policy. It calls both for some redistribution of the resources devoted to education and, just as much, for an increase in their total volume. It must not be interpreted simply as a gloss upon the recommendations which follow in later chapters. This would not only be a misunderstanding of the scheme; it would destroy all hope of its success. For it would be unreasonable and self-defeating—economically, professionally and politically—to try to do justice by the most deprived children by using only resources that can be diverted from more fortunate areas. We have argued that the gap between the educational opportunities of the most and least fortunate children should be closed, for economic and social reasons alike. It cannot be done, unless extra effort, extra skill and extra resources are devoted to the task.

Recommendations

174. (i) As a matter of national policy, "positive discrimination" should favour schools in neighbourhoods where children are most severely handicapped by home conditions. The programme should be phased to make schools in the most deprived areas as good as the best in the country. For this, it may be necessary that their greater claim on resources should be maintained.

(ii) A start should be made as soon as possible by giving priority to the most severely deprived pupils, starting with two per cent of the pupils and building up to ten per cent over five years. The purpose of the short term programme would be partly to discover which measures best compensate for educational deprivation. In the longer term, the programme may be expanded to cover a larger proportion of the population.

(iii) Every local education authority having schools in which children's educational handicaps are reinforced by social deprivation should be asked to adopt the measures suggested below and to report from time to time on the progress made. Local authorities should be encouraged to select schools within their areas for special attention even though they are not eligible for extra help from national resources.

(iv) A wide variety of criteria should be employed initially. Experience will show which of these criteria are most useful.

(v) Authorities should be asked to say which of their schools should receive extra help from national resources. The Department of Education should formally designate those schools and areas in most need as educational priority areas. Priority areas and the progress made in them should be reappraised regularly by local education authorities and the Department of Education and Science.

(vi) Authorities and the Department of Education and Science should ensure that the needs of other educationally deprived groups, such as gypsies, which will not be picked out by the general criteria laid down, are not overlooked.

Steps to be Taken: 1968 to 1972

175. (i) Measures should be taken to improve the ratio of teachers to children in educational priority areas to a point at which no class in these areas exceeds 30. Additions to salary amounting in total to £120 for every teacher in the priority areas should be paid. It should be open to authorities to award increases according to any plan approved by the Department of Education and Science as being likely to improve education in these areas.

(ii) Teachers' aides should be provided in the priority schools at a ratio of one to every two infant and junior classes.

(iii) In building programmes, priority should be given to these areas for the replacement or improvement of schools with old or out of date premises. The element of the total school building programme reserved for minor works should be increased specifically for their benefit. Approximately £5,000 should be allocated for minor works in each school.

(iv) Extra books and equipment should be given for schools in priority areas.

(v) The expansion of nursery education should begin in the priority areas.

176. (i) The Department of Education and Science should modify its quota arrangements so that they take into account the varying resources of immobile teachers available in each area. Authorities with large numbers of qualified married women willing to teach but unable to work in other areas should gradually be persuaded to employ all of them before drawing on mobile teachers who might be available for priority areas.

(ii) Colleges of education should, wherever possible, establish a continuing link with priority schools. Students should do part of their teaching practice in these schools.

(iii) Teachers' centres should be set up for in-service training. They might run longer courses with the co-operation of local colleges of education. Such courses might be recognised for salary purposes.

(iv) The development of social work in conjunction with schools should begin in priority areas and be more heavily concentrated there subsequently.

(v) Community schools should be tried out first in priority areas.

177. (i) Sustained efforts should be made to diversify the social composition of the districts where priority schools are so that teachers and others who make an essential contribution to the life and public services of the neighbourhood are not excluded from them. Co-ordinated action will be necessary on the part of authorities responsible for employment, industrial training, housing and town planning if educational deprivation is to be rapidly reduced.

(ii) Research should be started to discover which of the developments in educational priority areas have the most constructive effects, so as to assist in planning the longer term programme to follow.

(iii) Exchequer grants to local authorities with educational priority areas should be increased and the necessary changes in the grant making system made.

REFERENCES

[1] Professor S. Wiseman. Oral evidence to Council.
[2] National Food Survey, 1963.
[3] Lambert, R., Nutrition in Britain 1950–1960, Codicote Press, 1964.
[4] Arneil, G. C. and Crosbie, J. C., 'Infantile Rickets Returns to Glasgow', Lancet (1963), ii, 423. Quoted in Arie, T., 'Class and Disease', New Society, 27th January, 1966.
[5] Illsley, R., and Kincaid, J. C., 'Social Correlation of Perinatal Mortality', p. 271 in Butler, N. R. and Bonham, D. G., Perinatal Mortality, Livingstone, 1963.
[6] Milner Holland Report. Report of the Committee on Housing in Greater London, Cmnd 2605, 1965.
[7] 'A Comparative Study of Outcomes of Mathematical Instruction in Twelve Countries'. Ed. T. Husén. Almqvist and Hicksell, Stockholm. (Forthcoming). Attainment: The Implications for Primary Education.

[8] For example, J. W. B. Douglas, Home and School. MacGibbon and Kee 1964. The same data forms the basis of arguments in Robbins Report, Vol. II.

[9] Davies, B., Relative Inequality and Interrelationships Between Standards of Provision of Primary, Secondary and Other Forms of Education and Socio-Economic Factors Affecting Education Performance. (To be published).

[10] Report of the Dame Jean Roberts Committee on Measures to Secure a More Equitable Distribution of Teachers in Scotland, H.M.S.O. 1966.

[11] 'Half Our Future', 1963, paragraph 31.

CHAPTER 6

Children of Immigrants

178. So far we have said nothing, except in passing, about immigrant children. Some of their needs are very similar to those of children in educational priority areas; others are not. They have often been abruptly uprooted, sometimes from a rural village community, and introduced, maybe after a bewildering air flight, into crowded substandard housing in an industrial borough. This happens to European immigrants from Cyprus, Italy or Eire, as well as to the Commonwealth immigrants from the West Indies, parts of Africa, India or Pakistan. When the immigrant is Hindu or Muslim, and has special religious or dietary customs, difficulties for both child and teacher increase greatly. The worst problem of all is that of language. Teachers cannot communicate with parents; parents are unable to ask questions to which they need to know the answers. It is sometimes impossible to find out even a child's age or medical history. Opportunities for misunderstanding multiply.

179. Most experienced primary school teachers do not think that colour prejudice causes much difficulty. Children readily accept each other and set store by other qualities in their classmates than the colour of their skin. Some echoes of adult values and prejudices inevitably invade the classroom but they seldom survive for long among children. It is among the neighbours at home and when he begins to enquire about jobs that the coloured child faces the realities of the society into which his parents have brought him.

180. The concentration of immigrant families in the crumbling areas of industrial cities and boroughs has greatly complicated the tasks of their teachers. We wish to pay tribute to the devoted work that is being done in many schools.

Numbers

181. The number of immigrant children in schools has risen sharply during the last decade. Immigrant parents often have larger families than the rest of the population. Many immigrants work hard and save to bring their families to the United Kingdom. The voucher system, as operated since the White Paper of 1965, limits entry of immigrant workers for settlement to 8,500 a year, but children up to the age of 16 can join their parents so that some three or four children may enter for each father who enters on voucher. In addition to children born abroad, a recent estimate[1] is that 200,000 children of Commonwealth citizens have been born in this country since immigration began on a large scale.

182. Accurate figures of immigrants in schools have hitherto been hard to obtain. Returns in 1966 from local education authorities to the Department of Education and Science show the following totals for four of the main groups of Commonwealth immigrants:

Table 2 Numbers of Children from Certain Commonwealth Countries in English Schools, 1966: (Primary and Secondary Schools)*

West Indians	Indians	Pakistanis	Cypriots
57,000	24,000	7,800	13,200

Some 25 boroughs (including 11 in the Inner London Education Authority) have an immigrant population in school of more than five per cent, the highest single figure being 21 per cent. Because immigrants are concentrated in particular parts of these boroughs, the children attend few schools. In some schools, more than half the pupils are from immigrant families.

Educational Problems

183. These families, though handicapped by unfamiliarity with the English way of living, by their language and too often by poverty and cramped living conditions, are often drawn from the more enterprising citizens of their own country. Though the range of ability and temperament is wide, many children are intelligent and eager to learn. Indeed, this eagerness sometimes proves an embarrassment when it is for the disciplined book learning and formal instruction of their own culture and when the language barrier prevents the school explaining fully to parents the different way we go about education in England.

184. Although some immigrant children are at first upset by the English climate, they are usually well nourished and well clothed[2]. When their health is poor this is usually due to complaints which were common among working class people before the last war[3]. Some special problems face local education authorities and others in areas with high concentrations of immigrants. Many immigrant children are at a disadvantage because of the poor educational background from which they have come. It is difficult to discriminate between the child who lacks intelligence and the child who is suffering from "culture shock" or simply from inability to communicate. As a result, few immigrant children find places in selective schools. In one borough with nearly six per cent of immigrants in its school population, not a single child was selected for a grammar school in 1966. Children with high mathematical or technical ability are at a disadvantage because of their poor command of written English.

185. Teachers have generally not been trained during their courses at colleges of education to teach immigrant children. They, therefore, lack knowledge of the cultural traditions and family structure that lie behind the children's concepts and behaviour. Experienced teachers of immigrant children testify that they have found it of great help to know about family tradition and habits of worship, and about food, clothing and customs, which differ from ours. Unfortunately it is not easy to find authoritative books on these subjects suitable for teachers in training, and there has been a lack of in-service training courses.

*These are children in schools in which there are ten or more immigrant children. An "immigrant child" is defined as a child born abroad of immigrant parents or born in this country of parents who immigrated after 1955.

186. A start has been made by the Association of Teachers of Pupils from Overseas, the British Caribbean Society and others, who are helping teachers to acquire background knowledge. The National Committee for Commonwealth Immigrants has begun the publication of a series of background booklets for teachers. The next step must be the inclusion in initial training courses for some teachers, and in some refresher courses, of discussion of the background of immigrant children. Local education authorities, where there are large numbers of immigrants, could hold induction courses for new teachers in these areas.

The Curriculum

187. The curriculum of the primary school with a substantial intake of immigrant children should take account of their previous environment, and prepare them for life in a different one. Their culture can enrich the school's geographical and historical studies and, if used imaginatively, can improve other children's appreciation of the newcomers besides enabling immigrant children to value their own culture and language. This is easier to achieve with older than with younger children. It is particularly important to introduce the younger children to their new environment. Visits to shops and factories, to the local fire station, to the library, the museum, and the country can provide a useful background to their school work. Meanwhile, books used in schools should be re-examined. Some display out of date attitudes towards foreigners, coloured people, and even coloured dolls. Some are linguistically unsuitable, and some assume a social background incomprehensible to the newcomer[5].

188. Contacts with the home are especially important and, because of language difficulties, far from easy to establish. In one school[6], for example, 80 per cent of immigrant parents interviewed as compared with 20 per cent of the rest, did not know the name of their children's class teacher. The appointment of suitably trained immigrant teachers who would combine part-time teaching with welfare functions could be helpful. They could interpret the school's aims to immigrant parents and the parents' wishes and anxieties to the schools.

189. The education of the parents must not be neglected. Many of them are anxious to learn English, and to educate themselves in other ways. There is a possible role here for married women teachers willing to give up part of their time to teaching immigrant family groups in the afternoon or evening. They would require courses in teaching English as a foreign language.

190. It is absolutely essential to overcome the language barrier. This is less serious for a child entering the infant school. He rapidly acquires, both in the classroom and outside, a good command of the relatively limited number of words, phrases and sentences in common use among the other children. He can then learn to read with the rest, by normal methods.

191. Immigrant children who arrive later in their school life have much greater problems. They need to learn a new language after the patterns and often the written forms of their own language have been thoroughly mastered. This calls for special techniques and materials and poses problems to which little research has been directed. It is necessary to distinguish between the

non-English speaking Cypriot or Asian child and the West Indian who speaks a vernacular form of English, influenced to some extent by "creole" English. It is a dialect form which, if not supplemented by a form nearer to "received pronunciation", may place the speaker at a disadvantage in seeking employment and in ordinary social contacts. Techniques suitable for the child who goes home in the evening to a family speaking Urdu, or Greek, will not be suitable for the child whose parents speak a dialect of English which may be close to "received pronunciation" or distant from it, depending on the island, or the social class, from which they come.

192. So far there has been very little opportunity for teachers to learn how to teach English to foreigners. The University of London Institute of Education has provided a few places; more are needed. No colleges of education have yet run courses, but we are told that seven plan to start this year. Some local education authorities are providing in-service training. The University of Leeds Institute of Education, sponsored by the Schools Council, is preparing and testing materials for teaching English to children of immigrant families from Asia and Southern Europe.

193. When the concentration of non-English speaking children in a particular school reaches a level which seems to interfere with the opportunity for other children to learn, or with the teacher's ability to do justice to the immigrant children, there may be a demand for dispersal of the immigrants. The Secretary of State for Education and Science, in Circular 7/65[7], advised local authorities to avoid heavy concentrations of immigrants in particular schools. As the Circular points out, experienced teachers believe that a group containing up to one fifth of immigrant children can fit in a school with reasonable ease, but if the proportion goes beyond a third serious strains arise, and it may become difficult to prevent the proportion rising further. The Department's views are shared by many teachers and were reached only after the most serious study of the implications.

194. Yet some local education authorities after equally careful thought and a great deal of experience have preferred not to implement the Circular. One teacher of long experience in a notoriously deprived district has written: "We have to accept that there are going to be schools in many of our cities with an intake largely coloured. . . .Dispersal at the primary stage, except on a limited geographical basis, is administratively difficult and psychologically unsound". This authority has preferred to trust to extra staffing and enrichment of the curriculum in smaller classes. Other authorities are trying a variety of solutions[8] using partial dispersal, centres to which children go until they have some command of English, or a mixture of both. Whenever immigrant children are dispersed it must be done with great care and sensitivity. Children should be given special consideration on account of their language and other difficulties and not on account of their colour.

195. The Department of Education and Science have increased quotas of teachers for areas with substantial numbers of immigrants. Some authorities have been unable to fill these quotas, however, for the same reasons that they have been unable to staff the schools in their deprived areas. Our proposals for the priority areas (Chapter 5) may help to meet these staffing problems and our proposals for the training and recuitment of teachers' aides (Chapter

26) have a special relevance. The central government are already helping in other ways: the Local Government Bill now before Parliament provides for a new specific grant to those local authorities with concentrations of Commonwealth immigrants.

196. We have had evidence that volunteers in the year between sixth form and university have helped by being available to work with small groups of children, under the supervision of a trained teacher. We were interested to learn that one authority plans to keep open some of its schools during the summer holidays for the continuous teaching of English to immigrant children so that they do not forget what they have learnt. There should be further experiment on these lines.

197. Remedial courses in spoken English are also needed for those immigrant teachers, especially from Asia, who, though in theory qualified to teach, find it impossible to obtain posts because their speech is inadequate. Holding university degrees and similar qualifications, they often cannot understand why they are not appointed as teachers. It is not easy to detect one's own speech peculiarities. Four remedial English courses are planned by the Department of Education and Science for 1966/67. All are heavily oversubscribed. There is a pressing need for an expansion of such courses which could also provide an introduction to English primary school methods and prepare some teachers for social work.

198. The purpose of the various measures we have discussed should be to eliminate, not perpetuate, the need for them. The time required to make the newcomers fully at home in the school and community will be an index of their success. The steps taken ought to be constantly reviewed as immigrant groups are absorbed into the native population. Special measures inevitably identify children as "different" and their duration should be as brief as possible.

Recommendations

199. (i) Colleges, institutes of education and local education authorities should expand opportunities through initial and in-service courses for some teachers to train in teaching English to immigrants and to increase their knowledge of the background from which children come.

(ii) Work already started on the development of suitable materials and methods for teaching English to immigrants should continue and be expanded.

(iii) Dispersal may be necessary but language and other difficulties should be the criteria employed.

(iv) There should be an expansion of remedial courses in spoken English for immigrant teachers.

(v) Schools with special language problems and others of the kind referred to in this chapter should be generously staffed: further experiments might be made in the use of student volunteers.

D

REFERENCES

[1] Memorandum from the National Committee for Commonwealth Immigrants and the Survey of Race Relations (September 1965).

[2] London Head Teachers' Association: Memorandum on Immigrant Children in London Schools, 1965.

[3] Yudkin, Simon, 'The Health and Welfare of the Immigrant Child'.

[4] Peppard, Miss N., Oral Evidence to the Council.

[5] See ([1]).

[6] Young, M., and McGeeney, P., 'Learning Begins at Home', Routledge, forthcoming in 1967.

[7] Department of Education and Science: Circular 7/65, June 1965.

[8] Hawkes, N., 'Immigrant Pupils in British Schools', Institute of Race Relations, Pall Mall, London, 1966.

CHAPTER 7

The Health and Social Services and the School Child

200. The scale and character of the work done for families by the social services vary widely. Virtually all families with school children use the services of doctors, dentists and the schools; the great majority attend welfare clinics and are called upon by health visitors. Fewer have contact with educational welfare officers or have to rely at some time on the National Assistance Board. Even fewer seek the help of Children's Departments and Child Guidance Clinics[1]. Social work and psychological services are of great importance to the small minorities with whom they deal but also have considerable general influence.

201. *This chapter deals with these social services and with the links between these services and the schools. A large part of this field is now being studied by a Committee (appointed jointly, on December 20th, 1965, by the Home Secretary, the Secretary of State for Education and Science, the Minister of Housing and Local Government and the Minister of Health) "to review the organisation and responsibilities of the local authority personal social services in England and Wales, and to consider what changes are desirable to secure an effective family service". This Committee is making a more extensive study of the personal social services than we have attempted but we hope our own analysis, conducted from the standpoint of those concerned with the primary schools, will prove helpful to it. Much of what we have to say here concerns only the minority of children in need of special help.

The Health of the School Child

202. The improvement in the health of young children during the last thirty-five years has been tremendous. They are on the average taller. Routine medical examinations in 1965 showed that the general physical condition of more than ninety nine per cent of those examined was satisfactory. Their teeth are beginning to be better cared for; and the incidence of skin diseases has been greatly reduced. The number of children treated for scabies, ring-worm or impetigo fell from some 115,000 in 1947 to about 12,000 in 1963. Despite an increase in the school population of nearly two million the number

*The main sources of our evidence are listed at the end of this chapter. But we must here acknowledge our debts to a series of government committees—particularly to the Young-husband[2], Ingleby[3] and Kilbrandon[4] Committees—to various professional, inter-professional and administrative bodies[5,6,7,8] which presented evidence to us, to the Home Office, and to the County Borough of Preston—whose staff prepared evidence[9] for us and invited us to attend discussions with head teachers and social workers. We are especially indebted, however, to research workers from three universities who agreed at short notice to make special studies in three local areas, and to the chief education officers, teachers and social service staff whose help made the research possible. A summary of the three studies appears as Appendix 8 of our Report. We also had access to an earlier study, dealing with similar questions in a fourth area, made by Mrs. Margot Jeffreys and since published under the title 'An Anatomy of Social Welfare Services'. The health services are dealt with at greater length in Appendix 2.

of deaths of school children between the ages of 5 and 14 fell from 11,813 in 1931 to 2,437 in 1963 (see Table 3). The reduction in the number of deaths from diphtheria, tuberculosis and poliomyelitis has been especially marked— 1,744 children died from tuberculosis and 1,344 from diptheria in 1931; the corresponding figures for 1963 were ten and nil. Measles is now the only serious infectious disease which attacks young children on a large scale. In 1963, for instance, 200,705 school children caught the infection of whom 29 died. Otherwise, the infections from which school children suffer are now chiefly respiratory or gastro-intestinal and the great majority of the other ailments which come to light in routine medical inspections in schools are developmental.

The School Health and Dental Service and the Health Visitors

203. Close attention is generally given to mothers and their babies during the weeks immediately before and after childbirth. Until children enter school or nursery, the initiative for further contacts with the health services is taken either by parents or by health visitors who select for special attention those few families who need it. All children are medically examined when they enter school, and further examinations generally take place at the end of both primary and secondary education. Most mothers attend their child's medical examinations. Children are also examined and treated by the school dental service.

Table 3—Main Causes and Numbers of Deaths in Children Under 15 (with percentages of total deaths in brackets) 1931 and 1963

	1931		1963	
Causes of Death	Age 1–4	Age 5–14	Age 1–4	Age 5–14
All causes	18,038	11,813	2,780	2,437
Tuberculosis (all forms)	1,600 (9%)	1,744 (15%)	22 (1%)	10 (0·4%)
Other infectious diseases	5,524 (30%)	2,708 (23%)	175 (6%)	82 (3·3%)
Respiratory diseases	6,704 (37%)	1,680 (14%)	676 (24%)	242 (10%)
Malignant disease (including leukaemia)	Not recorded		307 (11%)	449 (14%)
Congenital defects	207 (1%)	86 (0·7%)	249 (9%)	233 (9%)
Accidental (including traffic accidents)	1,135 (6%)	1,442 (12%)	626 (22%)	736 (34%)
Cardio-vascular diseases	103	1,138	17	33
Rheumatic fever	42	401	6	15
Digestive disease	649	111	94	16
Diabetes	11	99	8	21
Age specific death rate per 1,000 Total Population	7·53	1·80	0·86	0·38
School Population in millions	—	5·57	—	7·09

204. In 1963 there were over 7,400 school nurses (equivalent to 2,667 full-timers) of whom nearly 6,000 held health visitors' certificates[10]. Health visitors are state registered nurses with obstetrical experience who take an additional year of study leading to the Certificate of the Council for the Training of Health Visitors. Their training emphasises the social environment of the individual, his mental and physical development at all ages, and the wide range of advice the health visitor can offer[11]. Many health visitors are not school nurses, but the majority of school nurses are health visitors. This combination of functions helps them to fulfil the intentions of a Ministry of Health Circular which urged that the "sphere of work of the health visitor should be broadly based and should extend to the whole family. They will be in touch with most families where there are children". In many areas they provide a unified service for people of all ages, although most of their work is with children under five. Some local health authorities are introducing schemes whereby health visitors are attached to general practice. The health visitors carry out their usual duties but with the families on the general practitioner's list instead of those in a limited geographical area.

205. In 1963 there were 2,521 doctors employed in the school health service (a full-time equivalent of 982) of whom 623 (103 full-time equivalent) were also general practitioners or married women employed part-time. Of the 1,900 employed by local authorities, 1,700 work both in the school health and in the public health services[12]. The schools can seek the advice of medical officers and nurses about behaviour problems as well as more strictly medical problems, and children may then be referred to other social services.

206. The improvement in the health of school children is not wholly attributable to the better care provided by the health services, important though that is. Much is due to general advances in medicine, to a more rigorous practice of immunization and to the improvements in diet and hygiene which have resulted from a general rise in the standard of living. Nevertheless, the continued existence of malnutrition, and the fact that more than 300,000 children are still given free meals, show that much poverty still persists. It seems from our surveys that the schools themselves consider the School Health Service to be highly successful. Its job is widely understood and accepted. Its staff is highly trained, even though some, like the school doctors, have no special preparation for work with school children. Its responsibility, much more advisory then therapeutic, is to ensure that children function normally and live and grow in harmony with their environment. It is primarily a preventive service, and it does not compete with the general practitioners or hospital services. In its early years the service was preoccupied with arranging treatment that could be found nowhere else. Since the war, however, general improvements in the health of school children and the development of the National Health Service have enabled the School Health Service to give more of its attention to normal and handicapped children and less to the treatment of the diseases of childhood. Yet it must evolve more effective means for identifying early and helping the handicapped and those subject to special risks.

207. The School Health Service is now establishing closer links with other branches of the health services. There is an almost complete integration between the local public health and school health service in all but two local authorities. The combination of the functions of school nurses and health

visitors, the attachment of health visitors to general practice, and the employment of general practitioners as part-time school medical officers, are all developments which are being encouraged. Although slow progress is being made in forging links between the School Health Service and the hospital paediatrics services, much remains to be done in this direction. Links with non-medical services are likewise a cause of concern. The members of a group practice who serve part-time in the School Medical Service and have a health visitor and, as in a few experimental cases, a social worker attached to them, are in a good position to know which families are likely to need help for their children, and to keep in touch with the teachers and social workers who may be dealing with them. But such arrangements are exceedingly rare.

Medical Examinations

208. To enable school doctors to give the best service they can, the system of routine medical inspections must be further modified. Thirty years ago doctors began to question whether a superficial inspection of large numbers of normal healthy children made the best use of their skill. After the issue of the 1953 School Health Service and Handicapped Pupils Regulations more thorough examinations of selected children in some areas has taken the place of medical inspections of children of 10 to 12. By 1964 more than a third of the education authorities had adopted systems of this kind. A variety of selection methods have been used, including questionnaires completed by parents and teachers, special requests by teachers and health visitors for examination of children known to be causing concern at home or in school, and scrutiny of attendance registers. Where these methods have been introduced carefully and with conviction, parents, teachers and doctors have welcomed them. Often they have meant that school doctors visit schools more frequently and communication between teachers and doctors has improved. The implications are wide, for they illustrate how one service can be improved by closer collaboration and a freer interchange of information with other services, and how scarce professional staff may be more efficiently used.

209. Further points call for attention. Information collected by health visitors, clinics and the School Health Service could be used to warn other medical and social workers of families in danger arising from social circumstances. The information should be treated as confidential and be given only to those who are likely to deal directly with a family. Facts disclosed by parents ought not to be passed on to other social departments without parental consent except in special circumstances and then only after discussion with a parent. These families could be helped, and in time. Records should contain perinatal information, evidence from medical development tests of potential disorders, and information furnished by other social services. This information should go forward with the child, forming the basis of later developmental and selective medical examinations, and prove useful if social work or other help is called for. All children should, if possible, be examined before they start school: legislation may be needed for this. The first examination should be concentrated on the assessment of development as well as of other medical conditions, and it should take place a few months before entry to school so that decisions about part-time or delayed entry can be taken in

appropriate cases. Later examinations can then be limited to children shown to need them by "screening" procedures.

210. Too many children still arrive at school in need of treatment. There are areas in which this is true of 14 per cent of the children. Of this number, between 20 and 50 per cent have not been treated[13]. It is upon these children and those whose family and social circumstances give cause for concern that attention should be concentrated. If our proposals for nursery education are accepted, the school health service will have access to many more children between the ages of three and five. Our concern, however, is not simply to provide more medical inspections but to make better use of the resources available, and to ensure that more selective information is secured and more effectively used by all those who can help children and their families. Meanwhile it must be remembered that serious gaps remain to be filled in the more specialised branches of the health services. More dentists have been recruited in recent years and some school dental services are now fully manned, but others, in the North, Midland and Eastern regions, are still seriously under-staffed[14].

Child Guidance, School Psychological, and Speech Therapy Services

211. The child guidance clinics and the school psychological service, which are at present the subject of enquiry by a departmental committee, are of fairly recent origin. Their growth has been hampered by an acute shortage of staff. They are more fully developed in the south and south-east than in the north. The Underwood Committee, reporting in 1955, recommended a growth in child guidance services which would by 1965 have called for a full-time equivalent of 140 psychiatrists, 280 educational psychologists and 420 psychiatric social workers. These were regarded as realistic interim objectives. By 1965 the child guidance services of local education authorities were still manned by a full-time equivalent of only 101 psychiatrists, 151 educational psychologists (the full-time equivalent of a further 172 were working in the school psychological service) and 140 psychiatric social workers —less than half the total recommended strength overall—and only a third of the required psychiatric social workers.

212. The school psychological service has a variety of functions. The educational psychologist may be asked to advise on the way in which children should be allocated at the age of 11 to the various types of secondary school. It is common for teachers to seek his advice if they are concerned about the academic progress of an individual child, and he may help them in remedial work with slow learning children in ordinary schools. He is frequently called upon to identify and assess those children who may need special educational treatment. He can also give parents and teachers a fuller understanding of the needs of children and an appreciation of the range of behaviour that may properly be regarded as normal, so that they can distinguish between minor difficulties which are incidental to growth and those for which outside help may be needed. He can often help the teacher to deal with the puzzling behaviour of emotionally disturbed children. In many areas the educational psychologist is also a member of the child guidance team. Joint appointment to those two services forms a valuable link between the schools and the child guidance clinic.

213. It is rare, however, for child guidance clinics to be able to spend time on the problems of very backward children. The reason lies in their long waiting lists. There is a disturbing amount of maladjustment and unsettled behaviour among the very backward, who may not be given sufficient support and positive guidance, even when placed in special schools. Fortunately many primary schools are able to help children who are slightly maladjusted. They need not, therefore, be removed from their normal environment.

214. Speech therapists provide another relatively small, but vital, service that cannot be adequately developed owing to staff shortages. Some studies have suggested that there should be one therapist for every 10,000–12,000 children in the population. This would give a city the size of Birmingham an establishment of 18; but the approved establishment in that city is now 13 and owing to staff shortages and high turnover the number actually in post early in 1966 fell to two. The speech therapists' professional association carried out a survey during the previous year from which they concluded that about 37 per cent of the established posts were unfilled.

Recommendations

215. We now sum up our main recommendations about the school health services and their connections with other branches of the social services.

(i) All children should be examined before entry to school for the purpose of assessing their developmental and medical needs.

(ii) Selective but more intensive medical examinations should become the normal practice in later school life.

(iii) Particular attention should be paid to the development of "observation registers" based on perinatal information, developmental tests and other procedures for identifying children showing tendencies to disorders. Social information should appear in these registers. Social workers collaborating with the school health services should be informed in confidence of needs and problems which concern them, subject to parental consent.

(iv) Co-operation between family doctors, school and public health services and hospitals should be closer.

(v) More staff is needed in almost all branches of the school health service.

(vi) Closer collaboration between social workers and medical and nursing staff is necessary; but the doctors and nurses will themselves need an increasing knowledge of social work. We welcome the introduction of a greater social work element in the training of health visitors and school nurses, and hope that it will extend to the training of doctors who become school medical officers.

The Education Welfare Officers

216. The number of education welfare officers, and their distribution between different authorities are not known with certainty, but in 1964 there were about 2,000 in England, distributed unevenly amongst 129 local education authorities. A survey of 55 County Boroughs made in that year by the National Association of Chief Education Welfare Officers showed that the average number of pupils to each officer was about 3,000, but it ranged from

2,000 pupils in one authority to over 6,000 in another[15]. In 16 counties the average number of pupils to each officer was larger, about 4,000, and the range wider from just over 2,000 an officer to 7,500. The service is staffed almost entirely by men. Many of them are in their forties or fifties, and they have a lower rate of turnover than most groups of social workers.

217. The role of the education welfare officers is described in the evidence presented by their own Association as follows:

". . . Securing regular attendance of all children of school age. Acting as the liaison officer between home, school and local authority and agencies for the welfare of children . . . giving advice to parents of delinquent children . . . referring children to Child Guidance Clinics . . . interchange of information and co-operation with all other social workers and attendance at case conferences . . . supervision of families where there is child neglect and arranging for the provision of school meals and clothing to necessitous cases . . . investigation of wrongful employment . . . acting on behalf of the local authority with regard to children brought before the courts concerning education problems. . . ."

218. The greater part of their time is spent on school attendance work and routine enquiries, although in one of the local authorities studied the officers thought that absence or truancy was the main problem in slightly less than half their cases. The rest of their work with primary school children is mainly concerned with free meals and clothing, keeping track of changes in the child population of their areas and following up children with verminous conditions. While most authorities employ an all-purpose body of education welfare officers, some still divide this work between attendance officers and a smaller group of welfare officers concerned with special types of case.

219. Most of the education welfare officers' work is concentrated on children of compulsory school age, and particularly on those in secondary schools where most attendance problems are found. In some areas they deal with children below school age, assisting with welfare work, or even with the identification of children requiring medical examination. But the responsibility of the local authorities for children under the age of five rests mainly with the health visitors.

220. A new Certificate in Education Welfare has recently been established to be awarded after examination by the Local Government Examinations Board. Those who possess this certificate will be accepted for salary purposes as falling within the administrative, professional and technical divisions of local government service instead of the miscellaneous category. In 1964[16] the great majority of education welfare officers held no formal qualifications, though 30 of the membership of 1,200 held a university certificate, diploma or degree in the social sciences, and over 300 had begun studying for the Certificate in Education Welfare, an impressive response to the introduction of the new certificate. The fact that this is largely a correspondence course inevitably limits its value for so personal a service as welfare work; but there can be no doubt of the demand for training.

The Child Care and Probation Services

221. The children's departments of the local authorities were set up in 1948, to care for children deprived of a normal home life. But in the course of time they have been drawn increasingly into helping families whose children are

living at home. This development has been encouraged by recent legislation —particularly the Children and Young Persons Act of 1963. The Ingleby Report[17], calling for more effective "prevention of suffering of children through neglect in their own homes", the recent White Paper on "The Child, the Family and the Young Offender"[18], which proposes for discussion the establishment of Family Councils in which social workers of the children's service and other persons would play a central part, and the enquiry now being carried out by the Seebohm Committee may all foreshadow further developments that may eventually lead to the creation of a more comprehensive social work service. Its relation to the schools will be important. The children's departments and their responsibilities are now in a state of rapid but uneven development. In some more than half the children currently being helped are living in their own homes and are not technically "in care" of the authority. The great majority of the children in their care may be living in foster homes or in small family group homes, attending the local schools. Some juvenile courts are making less use of approved schools and commit children instead to the care of the children's authority which is entitled to arrange any appropriate form of supervised care. But in other places the work of these departments still does not extend far beyond caring for deprived children for whom no other arrangement can be made.

222. The probation service has always devoted much of its efforts to the welfare of children appearing before the courts, and to families who seek its help without coming through the courts. But probation officers are more often concerned with secondary school children, amongst whom delinquency and school attendance problems are more common, than with younger children. Their new obligations for after-care of discharged prisoners may further increase the proportion of their work with adults, but their concern for the family situation of those whom they help will always bring them into contact with children of primary school age.

223. The demands on the child care and probation services have been continuously growing in recent years and, although many more training courses, including in-service training courses, have been introduced with support from the Home Office, many of their staff do not have a recognised professional training. Nearly a third of the 2,150 child care officers and two-thirds of the 2,319 probation officers in post in 1965 had completed professional courses of various kinds. Over a fifth of the probation officers have gained a professional qualification after taking a university course in the social sciences. Others, about 28 per cent of child care officers and four per cent of probation officers, have university qualifications in the social sciences which provide some preparation for their work without amounting to a professional qualification.

Voluntary Services

224. Voluntary organisations dealing with primary school children provide services of many kinds and much of this work is exceedingly valuable, as is shown by the studies described in Appendix 8. In some cases these organisations have been employed by the local authorities on an agency basis.

Social Work and Related Services

225. There is no agreed or simple definition of the human needs to be met by the social work services. Schools in two of our local studies (see Appendix

8) produced "welfare sub samples" of seven per cent and three per cent of all children. In the third study, two areas of one large city (both mainly working class in composition, though one was in a suburban district and the other an old and cramped central area) produced "welfare samples" respectively of eight per cent and 21 per cent of all children. These wide divergences are not wholly explained by variations in types of area or by differences in the definition of "welfare cases". They result partly from variations in the demands made upon the services, in the connections formed between different services and in the generosity of provision.

226. We believe the demands made upon the services will increase during the next decade. They will certainly change. There will be more children. More children needing the help of social workers now remain in the ordinary schools, living in their own homes or in foster homes. More and more families move house, as fathers go to new jobs, and as towns are expanding and partly as at last the slums are being pulled down. Some move because they want to; some are forced to go. Most will benefit, but sometimes there will be serious problems for families who will lack the support of relatives and old friends in times of difficulty. There are many immigrant families fresh to this country. Many of them have special problems. Meanwhile, public understanding of the social services and public sensitivity to the needs they meet are likely to increase, bringing more insistent demands for service.

227. The most striking shortages in the services we have examined are probably to be found in the child guidance service. In one of our local studies it was found that the work of the child guidance clinic was hamstrung for lack of a consultant psychiatrist. The service, which had only been established a few years earlier, was concentrating mainly on the primary schools[19]. In another of the areas studied, the psychiatric time available was thought by one of the consultant psychiatrists to be one third of that required for the number of children sent to the clinic. Things are now slightly better, but the less serious cases still have to wait up to ten months for an appointment[20]. Because the clinic's work was concentrated on a few difficult cases the expert knowledge of its staff was not generally available to other social workers in the district. We also think that clinics sometimes concentrate their efforts on the families from whom most co-operation can be expected since co-operation is essential for successful treatment. They are not necessarily those whose need is greatest, and it may be that the children of unskilled workers, for instance, get less help than they should. In B. P. Davies's study of county boroughs (Appendix 14) the ratio of Child Guidance staff to pupils tended to be slightly lower in authorities where families were large and houses more crowded.

Organisation and Deployment of Services

228. We were unable to make a detailed study of the deployment of trained manpower within the social services, but it is clear that not all is well. Since they are likely to be short of staff for many years to come, the few trained workers must be efficiently used. This is difficult to secure as long as the social services dealing with the family remain separate and independent of one another. Trained workers cannot be deployed or re-deployed to meet

changing needs. Staff difficulties are made worse by the inadequacy of office facilities and clerical assistance—a point made in the Younghusband Report[21] and by the education welfare officers in their evidence to us[22]. The efficiency of some services is hampered by a lack of agreement about their functions. There are signs that the education welfare officers suffer in this way. Census work must be kept up to date by the education department, but it is not a task for which a social work training is required. The welfare officers, for example, now have to do a great deal of routine work, of which some is unnecessary and some should be regarded as purely clerical. School attendance work is bound to take time, although more of it might be done from school or education office by correspondence and, eventually, by telephone. The investigation of children's absences from school is an important matter; but most primary school children who are not at school are in fact ill. In one area the welfare officers found that this was the explanation in three quarters of the cases they investigated. Many of these visits were clearly a waste of time. Welfare officers should be enabled to concentrate on the real problem cases and have time to give them the benefit of general case work. If some of the welfare officers are to carry increasing responsibilities for social work, and we think they should after training, a distinction must be made between their welfare duties and the administrative work which ought to be done by others.

229. We have been told of the skill of psychiatric social workers, the combination of disciplines brought together in the clinics where they work, and the devotion and enthusiasm of these teams. But while the child guidance clinic was a natural base for these workers between the wars, when this branch of the profession was new and not widely understood, the current demand for their services may not justify their concentration in these clinics. Concentration need not mean isolation but it sometimes does. Increasingly psychiatric social workers are able to carry their influence outside the clinics to other social workers, to health visitors and to teachers. And, of course, many are now employed altogether outside the clinics and outside the educational service too. It may well be that some should work more in direct connection with the schools rather than in child guidance clinics.

Co-ordination

230. Many problems affecting families with young children, though infinitely varied in detail, are fundamentally similar and call for similar qualities among those helping the families. Where, when and from whom the help comes often depends on the relative strengths of local services, their relations with one another and with the public, and on pure chance. For example, a disturbed and difficult child may be referred to the Child Guidance Clinic, especially if his parents can travel there regularly, and keep and effectively use the clinic's appointments. Alternatively his poor attendance at school may bring in the education welfare officer as the principal worker involved. But if the child appears in court, the probation officer may become responsible or the child may be placed under the supervision of a child care officer. Later he may be committed to an approved school or to the care of the children's department. But the right solution might have been to diagnose maladjustment or subnormality, to provide special educational treatment and so to avoid the sequence of failures. It is possible, too, that none of these services would have

been involved if a teacher had noticed that the child had special problems and gone out of his way to help at a sufficiently early stage.

231. Co-ordination is not simply an administrative or procedural problem. It demands a reappraisal of family needs and of the skills required to help those in difficulty. It requires a greater measure of training common to all the services. We should above all be suspicious of any tendency to set up yet further services which will complicate the issue, create more joints in the communication system through which leakages can occur and generally dissipate energy and effort.

232. While the education welfare officers say in their evidence to us that they work closely with other agencies, they also complain[23] that others neglect them, and that teachers and education officers sometimes fail to understand their role. Health visitors[24] give evidence of the need for improved connections between the social services affecting the primary schools, and one of our own studies[25] strongly implies that health visitors themselves are sometimes unwilling to make contact with social workers. The Younghusband Report, whilst concluding that a "multiplicity of visitors" was not a serious problem, recognised that social service staff often fail to understand each other's functions. The Ingleby Report[26] made much the same point.

233. Co-ordination can take place at two levels. Meetings of heads of departments or their senior staff can deal with the general development of services and policies. Meetings of field workers can deal with the needs of individual families, avoid overlapping or conflicting activities, clarify their joint aims and exchange information. Their meetings should be regarded as "case conferences" rather than "co-ordinating committees". Most authorities have both kinds of procedure. In the three authorities we studied there were committees which were concerned with individual problems and difficult cases rather than with the general co-ordination of departmental policies. Such conferences can only deal with a small minority of cases. If too much reliance is placed on them, poor team work affecting a much larger number of cases may be concealed or perpetuated. Often one person should have primary responsibility for each child or family needing help, and it should be his duty to see that other agencies and workers are called in when required. A major reappraisal of personal services dealing with families made in one of the areas we studied has shown that the present structure of the social services cannot be radically changed without legislation. The education committee, the health committee, the children's committee, the probation service and other bodies cannot shed or share their legal responsibilities. Thus although co-ordination can and should be improved, it cannot provide a complete solution to the problems we have discussed.

Training and Recruitment

234. The social services will be short of staff for a long time to come, but they could do more to help themselves. The new Council for Training in Social Work, the colleges working with it, and the National Institute for Social Work Training have already gained valuable experience in organising new forms of training. The Central Training Council in Child Care sponsors a wide variety of training courses aimed at encouraging every type of recruitment into the children's service. They, and the health and welfare departments

of the local authorities, have found that the provision of courses and the requirement of qualifications do not deter recruits but encourage them. The education welfare officers are a natural source of recruits for some forms of social work training and, once trained, they are unlikely to leave social work. Other sources of recruitment might also be found if the social services generally were as energetic as some education authorities have been. Late entrants to the profession must be encouraged. Married women, both trained and in need of training, are available and should be offered suitable working hours.

The Schools and the Social Services

235. Relations between the schools and the social services should be improved. First, there is the problem of the teachers' own knowledge—their capacity to identify social problems and to be aware of the services available to help children. Secondly, there are problems of communication between the schools and other services—the ability and willingness to keep each other adequately informed. Thirdly, there is the broader problem of the schools' contacts with their pupils' homes—a question of the teachers' understanding of what goes on at home which we have discussed in Chapter 4.

236. Nearly half the teachers in two of the three areas studied said either that they could not remember receiving any systematic instruction about the social services during their training or that they would have liked more. Head teachers in the third area said it was difficult to pick up this kind of knowledge on the job. It was when they became heads that many of them realised how much they had to learn about the social services. Social workers probably get equally little instruction about the part played by the school in the life and development of children.

237. "Welfare cases" are generally handled by the head teacher. Class teachers have little contact with social workers and depend on the head for information about pupils who are being helped by outside agencies. But the head teacher himself is not always kept informed. Of 39 children in one of our samples[27] who were being helped by child care officers, only ten were discussed with teachers by the officers concerned. Sometimes there is no need for such discussion, but where social workers have assumed a large part of the responsibility normally borne by parents we would expect them to see the child's teachers from time to time.

238. Although a teacher may be the first person outside the child's home and immediate neighbourhood to know of difficulties he is experiencing, we do not bleieve this occurs very often when the difficulties are severe. We found in our own studies that other agencies were already in touch with the majority of children for whom the schools sought outside help—particularly where children's problems were serious. But teachers can often help others who are working with their pupils, and can learn a great deal about the children and their needs in return. There is, of course, a limit to the time and energy teachers can devote to these contacts but especially, although not only, in the deprived areas they should be helped to learn more about the home background of their pupils and to make closer contacts with parents. The fact that teachers and social workers have a different outlook on the problems of the children they are both helping can itself be an advantage. What the schools.

need is a readily available social worker whom they know and trust, and who can act quickly. Through day to day contact, the most can be made of teachers' understanding of children. Teachers can become more perceptive and knowledgeable, and the right action is more likely to be taken promptly by all concerned. Social workers collaborating closely with the schools will not restrict the teachers' responsibilities but enable them more effectively to do their own work which includes some welfare work of a less general kind.

239. There has, to date, been no official report covering all the services we have discussed. But the Younghusband[28], Ingleby[29] and Kilbrandon[30] Committees—although starting from different, and restricted, terms of reference—reached similar general conclusions about the need for an integration of the social services. What are the implications of this for the schools? Many American school districts employ school social workers with a general training in social work and a minimum of specialisation. They work in a group of schools and are responsible to the principal, and ultimately to the Superintendent of Schools, but they can call on the help of specialist social workers in other fields. Most of our evidence[31,32] however, has led in a different direction, making a strong case for a broader integration of the personal social services.

240. We think the following arguments carry great weight: (a) workers in a variety of services are increasingly finding they are concerned with similar families having similar needs; (b) the atomisation of social services leads to contradictory policies and to situations in which "everybody's business becomes nobody's business"; (c) continuity of care is difficult under present arrangements; (d) a more unified structure would provide better opportunities for appraising needs and planning how to meet them; (e) it would also accord with the present tendency of social work to treat people as members of families and local groups rather than to deal with specific individuals or separate needs isolated from their social context; (f) it would make it possible to create viable teams to operate in areas of special need. Although such teams should cover carefully selected areas they could be physically located in many different places, for instance in clinics, in the local offices of welfare and children's departments, or medical group practices. Since all children spend several hours a day in school for most of the year, and since it is relatively easy for parents to visit schools, there is much to be said for choosing the schools as a base for social work units responsible for helping families facing many kinds of difficulties. For social work units that were also concerned with old people, single people or the mentally disordered, other bases would be necessary.

241. Other models are suggested by schemes operating in Glasgow and in London. The Glasgow scheme, which is based on secondary schools and makes some provision for associated primary schools, is similar in many respects to the American schemes mentioned in paragraph 239. The principal strengths of the scheme are that the school has access to a readily available, known person who is treated as a colleague by teachers and who can act quickly. The Glasgow social workers all have some training. But these workers are based in secondary schools; and, although they have some responsibilities for the primary schools in their areas, they do not have time to give them the same attention. Primary schools are too small and too numerous to place a social worker in each of them, even if such a scheme

were restricted to educational priority areas. The special characteristic of the London scheme[33], based on the Care Committees, is the use made of some 2,500 volunteers who are guided by 80 full-time paid organisers. But it is not easy to recruit sufficient voluntary workers in all parts of the country, particularly in the areas in which they are most needed. Moreover, scarce trained staff may become so burdened with the supervision of voluntary workers, for whom few training opportunities exist, that their skills are not most efficiently used in helping children and families. In many parts of Hertfordshire, we understand, a large part of the welfare work that elsewhere falls within the sphere of the education welfare service is carried out by the children's department, operating as the agent of the education committee. The arrangement arose from historical circumstances peculiar to this authority but it appears to work well. We have borne all these possibilities in mind when formulating our own proposals.

Conclusions

242. Our conclusions are deliberately tentative, stressing needs and opportunities rather than formulating detailed schemes. More specific proposals are to be expected from the Seebohm Committee.

243. The schools' interest in social work arises from their need to identify and help families with difficulties that lead to poor performance and behaviour of their children in school. Construed narrowly, these responsibilities mean that an education authority must prevent unnecessary absence from school and deal with problems that obviously prevent attendance, for example, inadequate clothing. Construed more positively, they call for social work amounting to general family case work, supported by specialist services equipped to deal with the more serious physical, environmental and psychological problems. Teachers are responsible for establishing a good understanding between the school and parents. There will, however, be difficult cases beyond the competence, time or training of the head or class teacher. These should be the responsibility of trained social workers, collaborating closely with the schools, readily available to teachers, and capable of securing help quickly from more specialised social services. The school social worker can also encourage the more reluctant parents to visit their children's schools and talk with teachers. The help and advice he offers to families in difficulties can provide a practical demonstration of the school's concern, not only for children but for the welfare of the whole family. Within the school, he can help teachers understand some of the difficulties their pupils contend with at home, alert them to problems they would not otherwise be aware of, and thus put teachers in a position to do their own job more effectively.

244. The principal need is for an organisation, which need not be an additional organisation but could be a grouping of existing organisations, and which will enable these functions to be fulfilled. The "school social worker", or a social worker collaborating closely with the school, needs to be clear about his powers to act on truancy, about the additional forms of guidance, supervision and help he may be asked to provide, and about his right and need to call upon other services when required. He must be known to teachers in the schools he serves and be accepted by them as a colleague. The size of his case load should be strictly controlled. These conclusions will remain

valid whether or not present services are unified within one local social work department.

245. If some or all of this work is to be carried out by the present education welfare officers, they would have to shed duties which could be carried out more effectively by staff without responsibilities for social work, who would remain based on the local education office rather than the schools. Routine investigations of attendance could often be carried out more selectively and with less waste of time; they should probably be associated with social work (since serious attendance problems often prove very complex) although different grades of worker including that of welfare assistants may be required for different types of case. It is not satisfactory that the service mainly responsible for welfare work in connection with the schools should be largely untrained.

246. The work and aspirations of the education welfare officers are developing in a way that encourages us to believe that some of them are capable of filling the places left open by the shortage of trained social workers. Selected education welfare officers might be given an intensive one year course, provided this were regarded as a temporary arrangement and not as a precedent for the establishment of a general level of training inferior to that now being offered to social workers elsewhere. In time a two year training similar to that required for the Certificate in Social Work or the Letter of Recognition awarded by the Central Training Council in Child Care would be needed.

247. The experience of existing councils for training in social work and child care will provide guidance about the type of course required. We hope that room might be found for this training within the courses the councils are now developing. There are, we believe, many potential social workers, with adequate academic qualifications, who would enter these courses, given appropriate career opportunities and salary structure. More resources, too, will have to be made available for training if there is to be any expansion. The principal shortage is of field work supervisors.

248. Anxious though we are that there should be rapid improvement in the services directly concerned with the schools, it is obvious that plans for reorganisation and training must be related to the whole social work field, and we hope that a comprehensive plan of action will be prepared without delay. A clear and generally applicable plan for social work in schools has not yet been devised. In carefully selected and different areas, where such help is most urgently needed, experimental teams should therefore be established which would include workers from many of the relevant fields together with social workers largely responsible for school social work. The school social workers should also have ready access, through their fellow team members when appropriate, to the help of the school medical and psychological services and other more specialised staff. In some places the school workers may have to spend so much of their time in the schools that they become, in effect, members of the schools' staff. While school social workers should always operate with the consent of the head teacher, and be immediately responsible to him for their work within and on behalf of the school, their administrative responsibility should normally be to a team leader in a service with broader functions through whom a large range of specialist resources would be available to them. Experiments on these lines should be started as

soon as possible and linked with research designed to test their value. A start should be made in the areas of greatest need, particularly some of those selected to become educational priority areas of the kind described in Chapter 5.

249. We note that in Glasgow the staff of school welfare officers (working alongside a larger number of attendance officers) have all taken a two year university course in the social sciences, or the two year C.S.W. course. The city has now seconded on full salary their first worker for professional training at university level. The English education welfare service should enable some of its staff to have this kind of professional training. But it is clear that different grades of work will remain to be done for the schools. Much of it will be routine work. Social workers attached to schools should therefore be assisted by "welfare assistants" with less training, as again is done in Glasgow. We recommend that consideration be given to the creation of a grade of welfare assistant in this field.

250. It may be possible that volunteers or part-time workers could play a useful part in social work teams after a short period of training and work under the supervision of professionally qualified staff.

251. Whether teams are established or not, we believe that greater care is needed in deciding on the number of social workers required in an area. This is plain from the varying burdens carried by social workers in the three areas we have studied in detail.

252. Finally, we return to the teachers. Too many do not know enough about the social work being undertaken on behalf of their pupils. Medical and social workers should inform the schools of action being taken in respect of their pupils whenever this would help teachers in their work with children. Parental permission must be sought for this step and it will normally be forthcoming. Teachers, we are sure, will welcome information that may explain a pupil's behaviour and performance in school, and they will treat it as confidential. It is essential that teachers should accept social workers as colleagues with whom there can be informal and frequent communication, but this will not happen of itself. It needs planning.

253. A teacher who has to consult with a social worker about a pupil is likely to learn quickly something of the organisation with which he is dealing. But this kind of localised knowledge is not enough. The initial training of teachers ought to take more account of the social factors that affect school performance, and of the functions and working of the social services. Short conferences and other forms of in-service training are clearly called for, especially for head teachers and deputies. Similarly, social workers need to be better informed about the educational system. We recommend that there should be experimental schemes for the joint training of social workers and teachers, (such as started in Scotland in 1966), and that social work courses should contain adequate instruction about the role of the school in the community and in the development of children, and about welfare work in and around the schools.

254. Social workers will never be concerned with more than a small minority of school children. It must always be remembered, therefore, that the main responsibility for developing good relations with parents rests with teachers.

Summary

255. This chapter reaches conclusions which are necessarily tentative. We have summarised the main points on the health of the school child in paragraph 215. The rest of our conclusions are as follows:

Social Welfare Work in the Schools: Structure

(i) There is a need for adequately trained social workers who would collaborate closely with schools, would be readily available to teachers, capable of assuming responsibility for cases beyond the competence, time or training of the head or class teacher, and capable of securing help quickly from more specialised social services. The principal need is for a grouping of existing organisations within a comprehensive plan of action which will enable these functions to be fulfilled.

(ii) In those areas where help is most urgently needed, teams should be established to include experienced workers from the relevant fields including social workers largely responsible for school social work. In schools with special difficulties, social workers may spend so much of their time in the schools as, virtually, to be members of the school staff. Experimental teams should be set up as soon as possible, particularly in some of the educational priority areas, and linked with research designed to test their value.

(iii) Local circumstances and experiment should decide whether school social workers could be best based on the education office, or on the schools, or should belong to a more varied social work team, including social workers doing different jobs. Social workers should, however, always work in the schools with the consent of the head teacher and be immediately responsible to him for their work on behalf of the school. Their administrative responsibility should normally be to a team leader located in a service having broader social work functions where a large range of specialist resources would be available to them.

(iv) A new grade of welfare assistant working with social workers might take over much of the routine work carried out by education welfare officers. Some of the work at present carried out by E.W.Os. could more appropriately be undertaken by clerical workers.

(v) Medical and social workers should inform the schools of action being taken in respect of their pupils whenever this information would help teachers in their work with children. Such information should be treated as confidential, and its use should be subject to the consent of parents.

Training

(vi) Education welfare officers could be trained to carry out wider social work functions. The present shortage of social workers might be partly met by selecting some education welfare officers for intensive one year courses. A two year training similar to that required for the Certificate in Social Work or the Letter of Recognition of the Central Training Council in Child Care should be established for selected education welfare officers. These Councils might include such training within the courses they are now developing.

(vii) The training of teachers, including in-service training, should take more account of the social factors that affect school performance and of the structure and functions of the social services. Such training is particularly necessary for head teachers and deputies.

(viii) There should be experimental schemes for the joint training of social workers and teachers. Social work courses should contain adequate instruction about the role of the school in the community and in the development of children, and about welfare work in and around the schools.

REFERENCES

[1] Political and Economic Planning. Family Needs and the Social Services. Allen and Unwin, 1961.

[2] The Report of the Working Party on Social Workers in the Local Authority Health and Welfare Services. (The Younghusband Report, 1959).

[3] The Report of the Committee on Children and Young Persons (The Ingleby Report, 1960).

[4] The Report of the Kilbrandon Committee on Children and Young Persons, 1964. Command 2306.

[5] Evidence to the Council from the National Association of Chief Education Welfare Officers.

[6] Evidence to the Council from the Education Welfare Officers National Association.

[7] Evidence to the Council from the Council for Training in Social Work.

[8] Evidence to the Council from the Standing Conference of Organisations of Social Workers.

[9] Preston Education Committee. Family Welfare and the School. Evidence to Council.

[10] Health of the School Child. 1962 and 1963. Report of the Chief Medical Officer of the Department of Education and Science Page 5.

[11] Council for the Training of Health Visitors: Syllabus Examination for Health Visitors in the United Kingdom, 1965.

[12] See (10) above. Page 129.

[13] See (10) above. Chapter III. Page 23.

[14] See (10) above. Chapter XIV. Page 103.

[15] See (6) above.

[16] See (6) above.

[17] See (3) above.

[18] The Child, The Family and the Young Offender. Command 2742. August, 1965.

[19,20] These facts are taken from our three local studies which are summarised in Appendix 8.

[21] See (2) above. Paragraphs 403 to 406.

[22] See (6) above.

[23] See (6) above.

[24] Evidence to the Council from the Council for the Training of Health Visitors. Paragraph 8(f).

[25] See (19) above.

[26] See (3) above.

[27] See (19) above.

[28] See (2) above.

[29] See (3) above.

[30] See (4) above.

[31] See (7) above.

[32] See (8) above.

[33] Evidence to the Council from the London County Council.

Form of Report Involving Parents

REPORT FOR SCHOOL YEAR ENDING JULY 1966

CHILD *Anthony Brown*   CLASS *4Y*

SUBJECT		EFFORT	ATTAINMENT	GENERAL REMARKS
MATHEMATICS	MECHANICAL	C	C	*Has made especially good progress in English and interest studies as a result of his wide reading. Often displays real artistic talent in his interest studies. His mathematics do not quite match with his other achievements. I feel sure he will do well in his secondary school.*
	PRACTICAL	B	B	
ENGLISH	READING	A	A	
	WRITTEN	B	A	
INTEREST STUDIES		B	B	

SOCIAL ATTITUDE

Tony is self confident and has a good number of friends. He is a good organizer of games and handicraft projects.

A EXCELLENT   B VERY GOOD   C AVERAGE   D BELOW AVERAGE   E POOR

CLASS TEACHER............   HEADMASTER...............

Please cut off and return to school

REMARKS—from PARENTS

(Please add any comment, information or concern which may be helpful)

We are very pleased that Anthony has improved in his work since we came to the open day at Easter. He still seems worried about his Arithmetic and we would be glad to know how we can help him. I have tried but he says, he does not do it like that.
Thank you for your help.

A Letter which might be sent by an Infants' Head Teacher to Parents at the end of the First Term

Dear Mr and Mrs..........

We thought you would like to know how Tony has developed during his first term at school.

He made a confident start as he had been well prepared by you and his sister. I know you were disappointed that he was reluctant to come to school on some mornings later in the term, when his first enthusiasm had waned. This is not unusual, however, and may have been caused by his not being quite well at the time, some upset with one of his friends or by a very natural desire to stay at home sometimes! We think he would profit by a further period of attending in the mornings only as he does get tired in the afternoons. Perhaps you could call to see us about this.

He loves stories and books especially about animals. Perhaps you or his father could spare time to read to him. I think you will find him beginning to pick out words to recognise. He can already read the names of most of the children in his class. He can count correctly up to five and is beginning to want to paint and write.

He is more independent in putting on his clothes etc. though he still needs a good deal of help in this.

He is a sensitive boy who is often thoughtful for other people.

Yours sincerely,

A Letter which might be sent by the Head Teacher of a Junior School to Parents at the end of the First Term

Dear Mr and Mrs..........

We thought you might like to know how Diane is getting on in her first term in the junior school.

She began very timidly. She is small for her age and perhaps feared the larger children but she is now a happy member of the group. She is greatly respected by the other children because she is so agile and fearless in physical activity and this has helped her to gain confidence.

Her reading is satisfactory, though slow. Could you spare time to take her to the Children's Library in . . . . . St.? She would be quite able to choose suitable books for herself and would improve her reading speed by reading a greater number of fairly easy books.

She is coming rather slowly to an understanding of number. We feel it is important that she should not be hurried in this, because that would add to her confusion. It would be helpful if you could entrust her with small sums of money for shopping and help her to count the change.

She does not like to take part in acting but is most ingenious in preparing costumes for other children. Her painting is really lovely. We hope you will find time to look in some morning next term to see it and to see the children at work.

Yours sincerely,

The Structure of Primary Education
Part Four

CHAPTER 8

Primary Education in the 1960s:
Its Organisation and Effectiveness

256. Part IV of our Report is concerned with the general structure of primary education: we discuss later the internal organisation of primary schools. This chapter compares the present provision with the arrangements in force when the Hadow Reports were new. It also compares our predecessors' verdict on the schools they knew with our estimate of the quality of schools today. The chapter concludes with descriptions of primary schools which may give the reader a more detailed picture of what we mean by good practices.

The Legal Position

257. The law of education, as embodied in the 1944 Education Act and subsequent legislation, does not fully describe its structure. It fixes the lower and upper limits of primary education; but it says nothing about the age of transfer from infant to junior education, and it does not stipulate whether boys and girls should be educated together or separately. The main statutory provisions about primary education are:

(a) "The statutory system of public education shall be organised in three progressive stages to be known as primary education, secondary education and further education." (Education Act 1944, Section 7.)

(b) Primary education is defined as full time education for children below ten years six months and children above that age but below 12 years whom it is expedient to educate with them (1944 Act, Section 8(1)(a) as amended by Section 3 of the Education (Miscellaneous Provisions) Act 1948). The 1964 Education Act allows proposals to be submitted to the Secretary of State for the establishment of schools with age limits below 10 years 6 months and above 12 years. The Act applies, however, only to new schools and was not intended to make a major change of structure.

(c) Education must be provided for all children from the term after that in which they reach their fifth birthday (1944 Act, Section 35 and Education (Miscellaneous Provisions) Act, 1948, Section 4(2)).

(d) Local education authorities under Section 8(2)(b) of the 1944 Act, must "have regard to the need for securing that provision is made for pupils who have not attained the age of five years by the provision of nursery schools or, . . . by the provision of nursery classes in other schools, where the authority consider the provision of such schools to be inexpedient."

Reorganisation of Primary and Secondary Education

258. The substantial "three decker" schools which stood, and often still stand, in London and some other towns high above terraced rows of working class housing were designed to fit the educational system as Hadow found it. Its divisions can still be seen commemorated in the clearly carved inscriptions over the doors of many schools—Infants, Girls, Boys. The infant department

was on the ground floor. At the age of seven boys and girls were promoted to one of the other storeys which normally housed separate boys' and girls' departments where pupils stayed until they left school at the age of 14. In effect the first Hadow report in 1926 proposed a re-arrangement of the two upper storeys. It suggested that there should be a change of department at 11 as well as at seven years of age. The typical three decker could be re-arranged quite easily to meet these suggestions. The three storeys could house infant, junior and senior departments instead of infant, girls' and boys' departments. Country schools and the older schools in towns were not built to this pattern and often had no separate infant department. The progress of Hadow re-organisation can be seen in the following diagrams[1]:

Diagram 3

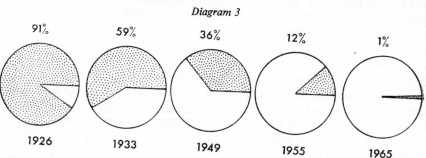

The shaded area represents the proportion of pupils aged 13 in unreorganised or "all-age" schools, i.e. schools with an age range from five or seven to the end of compulsory education. By 1955 all-age schools had virtually disappeared from the towns; in the last ten years they have nearly gone from the countryside. Hadow reorganisation is usually thought of as preparing the way for "secondary education for all". It was just as valuable because it made possible genuine primary education for boys and girls from the age of 7 to 11.

Changes Within Primary Education

259. The infant department had usually been a mixed school; but for older pupils the normal pattern of English education until comparatively recently was to teach boys and girls in different schools wherever possible. In 1925 half the children aged nine were being educated in single sex schools; today the proportion is three per cent. The following diagrams show how rapid has been the changing pattern since 1926:

Diagram 4

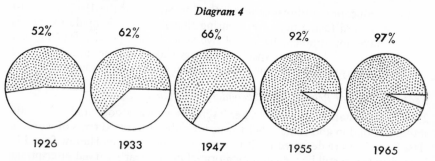

The shaded area represents the proportion of nine year olds in co-educational schools.

260. In 1952 two fifths of all schools with children of primary age had less than 100 pupils. By 1965 the proportion was less than a third. But it is more important to consider the declining number of these small schools than the proportion they bear to the total. This is illustrated in the graph in Diagram 5 (page 107) which shows the position in 1947, the first year for which statistics in this form are available, in 1950 and then at five yearly intervals. The graph shows three possible definitions of a small school. According to each, the number of small schools has declined. It is the smallest schools which are least defensible both financially and, except in special circumstances, on educational grounds.

261. The English infant school, and it is a distinctively English institution, has a long history because it has been accepted for a century now that children up to six or seven need quite different treatment from older boys and girls. Wherever numbers made it economically possible, the policy had long been to provide separate infant schools. "Hadow reorganisation" in towns did not make sweeping changes in this respect because it was for the most part only the older schools in which the "all age" structure had included infants. In fact there has been a reduction in the last 40 years in the proportion of six year olds who are being educated in separate infant schools. In 1925 it was 70 per cent; in 1965 it had dropped to 56 per cent. Ten years earlier it had been 60 per cent.

262. "In the country districts", the 1933 report suggested, "the typical unit will eventually be a primary school which contains all the children up to the age of 11. The infant class or division will form an integral part of such a school[2]." It is not because separate infant schools are educationally less valuable than combined junior and infant schools that their numbers have declined. Country schools and voluntary primary schools are usually combined schools. What has been happening recently is that in many new housing estates the distribution and density of population have fitted better with a combined school than with separate infant and junior schools.

263. The corollary to the secondary school under "Hadow reorganisation" was the establishment of separate junior schools. The Education Act of 1918 enforced compulsory education up to the age of 14 and, by making it a duty of local education authorities to provide courses of advanced instruction for older and more intelligent children, encouraged some of the more enlightened authorities to revise their arrangements for children below the age of 12. From 1919[3] several authorities began to create junior schools and departments. It was not, however, until the Hadow reports of 1926 and 1931 that much progress was made. Then it came with startling rapidity. Over a brief period of three years, from 1927 to 1930, the number of pupils in separate junior departments rose from 150,000 to 400,000, or an increase from over seven per cent to 16 per cent of the total child population aged between eight and 12[4]. By 1965, half of the children between the age of seven and 11 were in separate junior schools. There were one and a quarter million of them.

Nursery Schools and Classes

264. From 1907 it became the policy of the Board of Education to encourage the exclusion from school of children under five, who were often attending in surprisingly large numbers, unless special arrangements could be made for

them. One effect was to stimulate the foundation of nursery schools by private effort. Rachel and Margaret McMillan were outstanding among the pioneers. Nursery schools first became eligible for grant in 1919 but growth has been slow, although the last war gave them a temporary boost. Nevertheless, many schools continued to admit children to infant classes before the age of compulsory attendance. In other schools, nursery classes were formed, often including children of the same age as those in admission classes elsewhere. The proportion of children attending any form of school before the age of five has remained roughly stable since 1930. Table 4 illustrates this. The Department of Education statistics do not show separately the numbers of children attending nursery classes. We therefore made our own enquiries of local education authorities. Table 5 shows the distribution of children under the statutory age between nursery schools and nursery and admission classes of primary schools.

Some Other Features

265. Other features besides structure have changed. Perhaps the most common experience of the last 30 years has been the great variations in numbers that the primary schools have had to take at short notice. (See Diagram 6). We refer to these changes and their effects on class sizes in Chapter 23.

266. There are nearly 21,000 English maintained primary schools which between them contain about 4,000,000 pupils who are taught by nearly 133,000 full time teachers and by part-time teachers equivalent to nearly another 6,900 (see Table 6). The cost of nursery and primary education in 1964/65 in England was £300 million excluding the cost of training teachers, and of meals and milk. In terms of manpower and of the children accommodated in the schools, the primary schools form the largest sector of the whole educational system. Table 6 contains the main figures which describe primary education.

Assessments of Primary Education

267. So far this chapter has been confined to the organisation of education on which definite statements can be made and comparisons drawn. Although this is more difficult when judgements of quality are concerned, we think that the attempt should be made. First, however, we should remind ourselves of a comment made by the Hadow Committee on aspects of the later stages of primary education:—

"It can, however, hardly be denied that there are places in our educational system where the curriculum is distorted and the teaching warped from its proper character by the supposed needs of meeting the requirements of a later educational stage. . . . The schools whose first intention was to teach children how to read have thus been compelled to broaden their aims until it might be said that they have now to teach children how to live. This profound change in purpose has been accepted with a certain unconscious reluctance, and a consequent slowness of adaptation. The schools, feeling that what they can do best is the old familiar business of imparting knowledge, have reached a high level of technique in that part of their functions, but have not clearly grasped its proper relation to the whole. In short, while there is plenty of teaching which is good in the abstract, there is too little which helps children directly to strengthen and enlarge their instinctive hold on the conditions of life . . ."[5].

268. We visited as many schools as possible, received much written and oral evidence and had many informal conversations. But we could not possibly claim that we had in this way obtained anything like a complete picture of the state of primary education throughout the country. We felt the need for an assessment covering all the primary schools. Since H.M. Inspectors were in the best position to undertake a comprehensive survey we asked them to do so.

269. All the 20,664 primary schools in England were included in the survey, apart from 676 which were either too new to be assessed or for some other reason could not be classified. The whole body of H.M. Inspectors responsible for the inspection of primary schools took part. It is probable that misjudgments which must have occurred in particular cases cancelled each other out. The survey was planned to ensure that the various categories into which the schools were placed were exhaustive and did not overlap, to eliminate as far as possible the idiosyncrasies of personal judgement and to make certain that the identity of individual schools could not be discovered.

270. In the first category were placed schools described as "In most respects a school of outstanding quality". These are schools which are outstanding in their work, personal relationships and awareness of current thinking on children's educational needs. They are the pacemakers and leaders of educational advance. This category contained 109 schools in which there were about 29,000 children, representing one per cent of the total primary school population. The second category, "A good school with some outstanding features", indicated schools of high quality, far above the average, but lacking the special touch of overall rare distinction needed to qualify for the first category. There were 1,538 of these schools educating nine per cent of the total number of primary school children. That ten per cent of the schools should fall into these two categories of excellence is highly satisfactory. 4,155 schools (23 per cent of the children) were in the third category: "A good school in most respects without any special distinction". These are schools marked by friendly relationships between staff and children, few or no problems of discipline, a balanced curriculum, good achievement and an unmistakable recognition of children's growth and needs as they are known. One third of the children in primary schools go to schools which are quite clearly good.

271. Category 9 was "A bad school where children suffer from laziness, indifference, gross incompetence or unkindness on the part of the staff". Into this category fell 28 schools with 4,333 children, or 0·1 per cent of the whole. We were at pains to discover not so much how such schools had come to be since in any large group of human beings or institutions there must always be a few complete failures, but what was done about them when they were identified. Each of the 28 schools was followed up by the local authorities and by H.M. Inspectors, and action taken. There may always be bad appointments of head teachers; and deterioration in health or character may explain schools such as these. We doubt whether any school in this category would be suffered to stay there long.

272. The number of schools in Category 8—"A school markedly out of touch with current practice and knowledge and with few compensating features"—is a little more disturbing. 1,309 schools with five per cent of the children were placed in this category. This is a small proportion, but large enough to cause concern. But the situation is not static, nor is it simply tolerated. The local authorities and H.M. Inspectorate do all they can to assist such schools to improve, but their weakness makes them less susceptible to constructive suggestion than better schools. We would like to see systematic efforts to provide special in-service training for teachers in these schools and to see they take advantage of it.

273. Category 6 is "A decent school without enough merit to go in Category 3 and yet too solid for Category 8". This is the largest single category. It contains 6,058 schools and 28 per cent of the children. These are "run of the mill" schools. The fact that these schools, with Categories 8 and 9, considered above, contain only a third of the children gives some ground for satisfaction. Obviously all the schools in these groups are capable of improvement and ought to be improved, but the figures mean that the general distribution is quite markedly "skewed" towards good quality. This is a cheering aspect of the assessment. It is re-inforced when the remaining three categories are included. These three were deliberately framed as "odd-men out". Category 4 is "A school without many good features, but showing signs of life with seeds of growth in it". This category contained 3,385 schools and 16 per cent of the children. It is really an offshoot of Category 6. The schools in it might well recently have been there, but all of them are on their way to Category 3. Some may not get there; some may go further; a few perhaps will drop back; but all are at present moving in the right direction and can reasonably be regarded as promising.

274. Category 5 is "A school with too many weaknesses to go in Category 2 or 3, but distinguished by specially good personal relationships." This was devised for schools in very poor areas, often with large numbers of immigrant children, which cannot hope to match the achievements of the higher categories but which yet do splendid social work. Into this category the Inspectors put 1,384 schools with six per cent of the children. It is one to which any school so circumstanced might be proud to belong.

275. The remaining Category 7 ("Curate's egg school, with good and bad features") contained 2,022 schools (nine per cent of the children). It is likely to be an unstable one. The schools in it might drop into 8, move almost imperceptibly into 6 or 4, or rise to 3 or even further. The disparity is sometimes between the upper and lower part of the school in, for example, a full range primary school where infants may be taught more individually than the juniors, or where the work of the older children may be more interesting than that of the younger children.

276. There was no evidence in the survey that good or bad schools were characteristic of north or south, town or country. The various categories were far from being evenly spread over the areas of different authorities, but they were almost exactly balanced as between counties and county boroughs and the north of England and the south. We consider that it would be worth while to undertake similar surveys at intervals of ten years. They must always be based on subjective judgments and, in the absence of a fixed datum line,

comparisons would have a limited value, but they would tell the Secretary of State and the people of the country something that they ought to know and be the means of revealing trends which would otherwise be only surmises.

Description of Schools

277. Finally, we should like to accompany an imaginary visitor to three schools, run successfully on modern lines, which might fall into any of the first three categories. The pictures given are not imaginary, but the schools are composite.

278. The first is an infant school occupying a 70 year old building, three storeys high, near the station in a large city. The visitor, if he is a man, will attract a great deal of attention from the children, some of whom will try to "make a corner in him". He may even receive a proposal of marriage from one of the girls. This has nothing to do with his personal charms, but it is a sure sign of a background of inadequate or absentee fathers. A number of children are coloured and some of the white children are poorly dressed. All, however, are clean. The children seem to be using every bit of the building (the top floor is sealed off) and its surroundings. They spread into the hall, the corridors and the playground. The nursery class has its own quarters and the children are playing with sand, water, paint, clay, dolls, rocking horses and big push toys under the supervision of their teacher. This is how they learn. There is serenity in the room, belying the belief that happy children are always noisy. The children make rather a mess of themselves and their room, but this, with a little help, they clear up themselves. A dispute between two little boys about who is to play with what is resolved by the teacher and a first lesson in taking turns is learned. Learning is going on all the time, but there is not much direct teaching.

279. Going out into the playground, the visitor finds a group of children, with their teacher, clustered round a large square box full of earth. The excitement is all about an earthworm, which none of the children had ever seen before. Their classroom door opens on to the playground and inside are the rest of the class, seated at tables disposed informally about the room, some reading books that they have themselves chosen from the copious shelves along the side of the room and some measuring the quantities of water that different vessels will hold. Soon the teacher and worm watchers return except for two children who have gone to the library to find a book on worms and the class begins to tidy up in preparation for lunch. The visitor's attention is attracted by the paintings on the wall and, as he looks at them, he is soon joined by a number of children who volunteer information about them. In a moment the preparations for lunch are interrupted as the children press forward with things they have painted, or written, or constructed to show them to the visitor. The teacher allows this for a minute or two and then tells the children that they must really now get ready for lunch "and perhaps Mr. X. will come back afterwards and see what you have to show him." This is immediately accepted and a promise made. On the way out two of the children invite the visitor to join them at lunch and he finds that there is no difficulty about this. The head teacher and staff invariably lunch with the children and an extra adult is easily accommodated.

280. Later in the day, the visitor finds a small group of six and seven year olds who are writing about the music they have enjoyed with the headmistress.

He picks up a home-made book entitled "My book of sounds" and reads the following, written on plain unlined paper:—

"The mandolin is made with lovely soft smooth wood and it has a pattern like tortoise shell on it. It has pearl on it and it is called mother of pearl. It has eight strings and they are all together in twos and all the pairs make a different noise. The ones with the thickest strings make the lowest notes and the ones that have the thinnest strings make the highest notes. When I put the mandolin in my lap and I pulled the thickest string it kept on for a long time and I pulled the thinnest wire and it did not last so long and I stroked them all and they didn't go away for a long time."

281. Quite a number of these children write with equal fluency and expressiveness, and with concentration. The sound of music from the hall attracts the visitor and there he finds a class who are making up and performing a dance drama in which the forces of good are overcoming the forces of evil to the accompaniment of drums and tambourines.

282. As he leaves the school and turns from the playground into the grubby and unlovely street on which it abuts, the visitor passes a class who, seated on boxes in a quiet, sunny corner, are listening to their teacher telling them the story of Rumpelstiltskin.

283. The next school is a junior mixed school on the outskirts of the city in an area that was not long since one of fields and copses and which has been developed since 1950. The school building is light and spacious with ample grass and hard paved areas around it and one of the old copses along its borders. The children are well cared for and turned out and a high proportion of them go on to grammar schools. The visitor finds his way into a fourth year B class (the school is unstreamed in the first three years) and finds a teacher who is a radio enthusiast. The children, under his guidance, have made a lot of apparatus and have set up a transmitting station. They have been in touch with another school 80 miles away and sometimes talk to their teacher's friends who are driving about in their cars in various parts of England. While the visitor was present, part of the class disappeared into another classroom and there broadcast through a home-made microphone a number of poems chosen by themselves and all dealing with winter. "In a drear-nighted December", "When icicles hang by the wall" and "This is the weather the shepherd shuns" were clearly and sensitively spoken and closely listened to. In another classroom the children had been asked to make models at home which showed how things could be moved without being touched. They had brought to school some extremely ingenious constructions, using springs, pulleys, electro-magnets, elastic and levers and they came out before the class to demonstrate and explain them. When the visitor left they were preparing to describe their ideas in their notebooks. A random sample of these books showed that accuracy and careful presentation were as characteristic of the less able children as of the obvious grammar school candidates.

284. During break some of the children went into the hall and listened to the headmaster's wife playing the C major prelude. In another room the chess club was meeting and the visitor saw a Ruy Lopez and a King's Pawn opening and the school champion lose his Queen. In yet another room the natural history club was meeting to discuss its programme for the coming year, while outside the school football team was having a short practice. The library was

filled with children. The visitor was interested to notice that there was no contrast between this rich and varied out of school life and the life in school hours which offered just as much choice and stimulus. The library, for instance, was in constant use throughout the day, and at many different points in the school were to be found examples of good glass, pottery, turnery and silver, all of a standard higher than would be found in most of the children's homes. With all the children the visitor found conversation easy. They had much to tell him and many questions to ask him and they seemed to have every encouragement and no obstacles to learning.

285. The third school, a three teacher junior mixed and infant school, is in the country. It was built in 1878 by the squire and since 1951 it has been a Church of England voluntary controlled school. The church is a few yards away. The original building, with its high roof and window sills and its tiny infants' room, has been made over by the L.E.A., the infants' room being now a cloakroom and there is a big new infants' room at the back. This has encroached on the now very small playground, but there is a meadow just across the lane where the children play when it is dry enough. The village has grown and there are many commuters of varying social background who travel to the big country town nine miles away.

286. When the visitor arrived all the children in the first class were either on top of the church tower or standing in the churchyard and staring intently upwards. The headmaster appeared in the porch and explained what was happening. The children were making a study of the trees in the private park which lay 100 yards beyond the church. The tower party had taken up with them the seeds of various trees and were releasing these on the leeward side, and were measuring the wind speed with a home-made anemometer. The party down below had to watch each seed and measure the distance from the tower to the point where the seed landed. The children explained that ten of each kind were being released and that they would take the average distance and then compare the range of each species and calculate the actual distance travelled. When they had finished they went back to school to record their results, some in graph form, in the large folders which already contained many observations, photographs and sketches of the trees they were studying. The visitor was interested to notice a display of materials from which children were going to learn about their village, and social life generally, at the time the school was opened. They included photostats of pages in the parish registers, the school log book and a diary kept by the founder, as well as a collection of books and illustrations lent by the county library.

287. The second class of sevens to nines were rather numerous for their small room, but had spread out into the corridor and were engaged in a variety of occupations. One group was gathered round their teacher for some extra reading practice, another was at work on an extraordinary structure of wood and metal which they said was a sputnik, a third was collecting a number of objects and testing them to find out which could be picked up by a magnet and two boys were at work on an immense painting (six feet by four feet) of St. Michael defeating Satan. They seemed to be working harmoniously according to an unfolding rather than a pre-conceived plan. Conversation about the work that the children were doing went on all the time.

288. In the large new infants' room, too, many different things were going on. Some children were reading quietly to themselves; some were using a recipe

E

to make some buns, and were doubling the quantities since they wanted to make twice the number; a few older children were using commercial structural apparatus to consolidate their knowledge of number relationships; some of the youngest children needed their teacher's help in adding words and phrases to the pictures they had painted. The teacher moved among individuals and groups doing these and other things, and strove to make sure that all were learning.

289. These descriptions illustrate a point perhaps not often enough stressed, that what goes on in primary schools cannot greatly differ from one school to another, since there is only a limited range of material within the capacity of primary school children. It is the approach, the motivation, the emphasis and the outcome that are different. In these schools, children's own interests direct their attention to many fields of knowledge and the teacher is alert to provide material, books or experience for the development of their ideas.

Recommendation

290. Surveys similar to that carried out by H.M. Inspectorate to assess the quality of primary education for the Council should be undertaken at ten year intervals.

REFERENCES

[1] These and other statistics in this chapter are taken from the appropriate Annual Reports of the Board, the Ministry of Education and the Department of Education and Science, or from the 'Statistics of Education'.

[2] Report of the Consultative Committee on Infant and Nursery Schools, 1933, paragraph 66.

[3] Report of the Consultative Committee on the Primary School, 1931, paragraph 22.

[4] See (3), paragraph 20.

[5] See (3), paragraph 74.

Diagram 5

Small Schools in England: Primary (Including All Age)

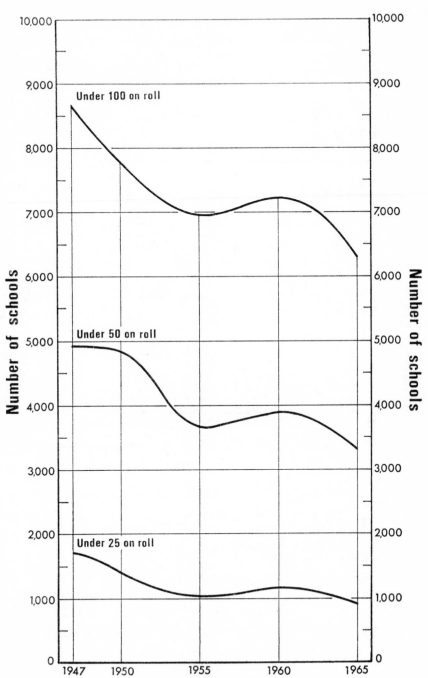

Table 4

Provision In England For Children Under Five: 1932 Compared To 1965.

Year	(1) Total No. of children in age groups 0–4	(2) Total number of nursery schools under the supervision of the Department of Education and Science, (a) maintained (b) direct grant (c) recognised Independent (d) other Independent	(3) Pupils in nursery schools in (2) (a) maintained (b) direct grant (c) recognised Independent (d) other Independent (Full-time equivalents)	(4) Pupils under 5 in (a) maintained primary or public elementary schools (b) recognised Independent schools (c) other Independent schools	(5) Number of Institutions under the supervision of the Ministry of Health (a) day nurseries (b) voluntary and other private day nurseries	(6) Number of children in (5) (a) day nurseries (b) voluntary and other private day nurseries	(7) Number of children under 5 in Institutions under the surveillance of the Home Office	(8) Total No. of children under 5 in schools and nurseries. (Full-time equivalents)	(9) (8) as % of (1)
March 1932	2,787,000*	(a) 30 (b) — (c) 25 (d) not available	(a) (b) }4,520 (c) (d) not available	(a) 135,791 (b) not (c) available	(a) 19 (b) 83	(a) }3,726 (b)	Not Applicable	144,000	5·2
January 1965	4,100,000	(a) 420 (b) 16 (c) 9 (d) 194	(a) 21,849 (b) 672 (c) 286 (d) 5,102	(a) 174,939** (b) 948 (c) 2,787	(a) 448 (b) 2,164	(a) 21,396 (b) 53,048	10,000 (appox.)	283,000	6·9

*Report of the 1931 Census—General Tables. Table 17.
**Includes 110,527 'rising 5s', that is, pupils reaching the age of 5 during the spring term 1965.

Notes: The figures shown for 1932 and 1965 are not strictly comparable because:—
(a) The totals of children and percentages have been crudely adjusted to apply to England only. The figures for 1932 in Column 6 and for 1965 in Column 7 apply to both England and Wales and exact figures for each are not available.
(b) No information is available about the number of children under 5 in Independent schools and nurseries in 1932.

Sources: The statistics for 1932 are taken from Annual Reports of the Board of Education and the 1931 and 1933 Hadow Reports.

Table 3

Pre-School Provision in England: Information from Department of Education and Science, Ministry of Health and Home Office

(Total number of children aged 2–4 in January 1965: 2,100,000.)

(I) Establishments inspected by the Department of Education (January 1965).

Type of establishment	No. of establishments	Children aged 2	Children aged 3	Children aged 4	Total 2–4	Pupils per teacher	Other information
1. Nursery schools	420	1,668*	9,439*	10,553*	21,660*	25·0	1,021 Class 1 nursery assistants employed. 174 Class 2 nursery assistants employed.
2. Infant schools		109	4,798	95,030	99,937	29·1**	In nursery classes: January 1964 1,194 Class 1 nursery assistants employed, 306 Class 2 nursery assistants employed. (No later figures available).
Junior schools with infants		59	2,522	71,732	74,313	27·6**	
Junior schools without infants		3	2	76	78	29·5**	
All age schools			27	581	611	25·9**	
All primary schools		171	7,349	167,419	174,939***	29·9**	
3. Direct grant nursery schools	16	51	322	299	672	21·0	
4. Recognised independent nursery schools	9	39	131	106	276	11·5	
5. Other independent nursery schools	194	84	806	1,907	2,797	8·6	
6. Recognised independent schools other than nurseries							
primary		5	212	2,280	2,497	12·8**	
all age		15	110	1,565	1,690	13·9**	
7. Other independent schools other than nurseries							
primary		107	1,409	6,612	8,128	14·4**	
all age		61	442	2,135	2,638	13·9**	
Total	639	2,201	20,220	192,876	215,297		

*2 part-time pupils are shown as 1 full-time pupil. Approx. 18,000 children in nursery schools attend full-time.

**Pupil: teacher ratios for 2–4 year olds are not available. The ratios shown relate to all pupils and teachers.

***This figure includes 32,008 children in 1,017 nursery classes at January 1964 of whom 7,313 were aged 3 and 17,340 aged 4. Since then a further 38 nursery classes have been established under Addendum 2 to Circular 8/60. The numbers attending them are not known.

Table 5—continued

II. Establishments for which the Ministry of Health is the Responsible Central Department (December, 1965): England.

Type of establishment or provision	No. of establishments	Number of children or places	Numbers and types of staff in day nurseries run by local health authorities
1. Local Health Authority nurseries	448	approved places: 21,396; av. daily attendance: 16,470	Matrons: 440 (239 S.R.N., R.S.C.N. or R.F.N. 201 N.N.E.B.) Deputy Matrons: 411 (83 S.R.N., R.S.C.N. or R.F.N., 328 N.N.E.B. Wardens: 305 (Mostly N.N.E.B.) Nursery nurses: 1,510 (Mostly N.N.E.B.) Nursery Assistants and nursery students 2,181
2. Private nurseries run by factories.	56	2,098	
3. Other private nurseries	2,108	50,950	
4. Child minders retained by Local Health Authorities	865	1,482	
5. Registered Daily Minders	3,347	Not available	

II Children under the Surveillance of the Home Office (March, 1965) (England and Wales)****

Type of establishment or provision	No. of children aged 2–5
1. Local authority homes; boarding out	9,138*****
2. Homes provided by voluntary child care organisations	1,785
3. Boarding out by voluntary organisations	521
Total Approx.	10,000*****

****Separate figures for Wales are not available.

*****Some children in the care of local authorities are in homes provided by voluntary organisations, and are included in the total at IV.

Diagram 6

Numbers of Children in Maintained Primary Schools Aged 5 to 11 in 1947–1965: England

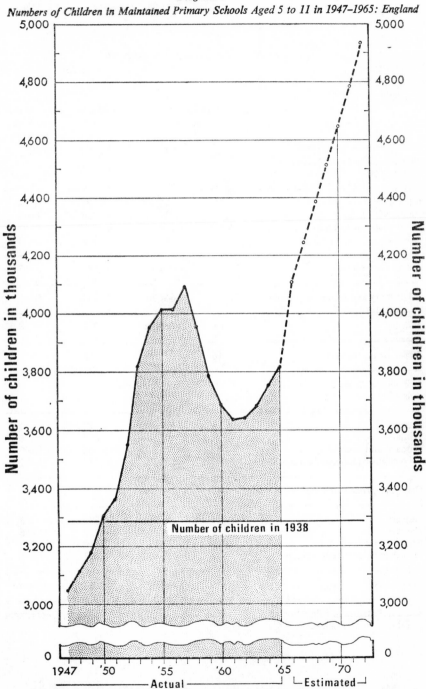

The projected primary school populations between 1965 and 1972 are based on figures for England and Wales, adjusted for England only.

Source: Statistics of Education Part 2: 1964

Table 6

English Primary Education: January 1965

	Schools or Departments	Pupils	Full-time Teachers	Part-time Teachers — Full-time Equivalent
Maintained by Local Education Authorities				
Infants	4,948	945,405	30,627	1,803
Junior with Infants	11,212	1,729,633	59,590	3,040
Junior without Infants	4,431	1,284,487	41,544	1,994
All—age	198	44,409	1,619	98
All primary schools	20,789	4,003,934	133,480	6,997
All primary and secondary schools	26,261	6,644,307	206,444	15,540
Nursery	420	21,849	831	14
Direct Grant Nursery	16	672	32	
Independent Schools recognised as efficient				
Nursery	9	286	22	2
Primary	743	86,304	6,099	756
Primary and Secondary	445	138,380	8,804	1,190
All recognised independent schools	1,481	296,551	20,757	2,502
Other independent schools				
Nursery	194	5,102	323	2
Primary	1,128	74,549	4,299	866
Primary and Secondary	446	52,049	3,060	745
All other independent schools	1,972	148,042	8,892	1,871
All schools	33,115	7,468,091	259,563	23,488

Source: Statistics of Education, 1965, Part One, Table 9 and Statistics Branch, Department of Education and Science.

Table 7

Children Aged 5-11 in Different Types of School: England

(a) 31st March, 1932

	Infants	Junior			All Age*			Total Primary and All Age
		Boys	Girls	Mixed	Boys	Girls	Mixed	
No. of Departments % of Total	5,780 22	2,133 8	2,241 9	10,699 42	497 2	556 2	3,647 14	25,553
No. of Children % of Total	977,628 30	285,486 9	276,571 8	848,057 26	143,180 5	124,692 4	658,444 20	3,314,058

(b) January, 1965

	Infants	Junior without Infants			Junior with Infants			All Age			Total Primary and All Age
		Boys	Girls	Mixed	Boys	Girls	Mixed	Boys	Girls	Mixed	
No. of Departments % of Total	4,948 24	247 1	198 1	3,986 19	4 0·1	69 0·3	11,139 54	23 0·1	26 0·1	149 1	20,789
No. of Children % of Total	945,405 24		1,284,487 32			1,729,633 43			44,409 1		4,003,934

*The statistics of the time ("Education in 1932", Table 6, page 100 and Table 12, page 110), show:—
(a) infant departments included many children outside the normal infant age range; some were between 3 and 5 or between 7 and 9, or of other ages;
(b) junior schools contained some children of infant age;
(c) most all age schools took children from 7 but that many contained children from 5.

Sources: Statistics of Education, 1965, Part One, Table 9, and Statistics Branch, Department of Education and Science.

Table 8

Maintained Primary Schools: England

Number of Schools or Departments According to Numbers

of Pupils on the Register: January 1965

	Up to 25	26 to 50	51 to 100	101 to 200	201 to 300	301 to 400	401 to 600	601 to 800	801 to 1,000
Infants	52	127	502	2,021	1,786	399	60	1	—
Junior with Infants	835	2,237	2,324	2,213	1,904	1,080	567	47	5
Junior without Infants	2	27	138	853	1,459	1,199	713	39	1
All-age	8	5	15	66	59	25	20	—	—
Total	897	2,396	2,979	5,153	5,208	2,703	1,360	87	6

Source: Statistics of Education, 1965. Part One, Table 16.

Table 9

Maintained Primary Schools or Departments by Denomination
January 1965: England

Type or Denomination	No. of Schools	As % of All Primary Schools	No. of Pupils	As % of All Primary Schools
County	12,320	59·3	2,821,362	70·5
All Voluntary				
Aided	4,554		767,343	
Controlled	3,912		414,657	
Special Agreement	3		572	
Total	8,469	40·7	1,182,572	29·5
Church of England				
Aided	2,777		335,077	
Controlled	3,780		398,601	
Special Agreement	2		266	
Total	6,559	31·5	733,944	18·3
Roman Catholic				
Aided	1,730		425,318	
Controlled	3		380	
Special Agreement	1		306	
Total	1,734	8·3	426,004	10·6
Methodist				
Aided	13		982	
Controlled	65		7,720	
Special Agreement	—		—	
Total	78	0·4	8,702	0·2
Jewish				
Aided	11		2,826	
Controlled	—		—	
Special Agreement	—		—	
Total	11	0·1	2,826	0·1
Others				
Aided	23		3,140	
Controlled	64		7,956	
Special Agreement	—		—	
Total	87	0·4	11,096	0·3

Source: Statistics of Education, 1965, Part One, Table 26 and Statistics Branch, Department of Education and Science.

CHAPTER 9*

Providing for Children before Compulsory Education

291. The under fives are the only age group for whom no extra educational provision of any kind has been made since 1944. Since then successive governments have raised the minimum school leaving age and decided to raise it again in 1971. They have abolished all-age schools, expanded further education, increased the number of university places and done much for the youth service. Nursery education on a large scale remains an unfulfilled promise. Whether a mother has even a bare chance of securing a nursery place for her child depends on the accident of where she lives. The distribution of nursery schools and classes bears no relation to present day needs or wishes. But to start to meet the demand must cost much money, involve considerable building and employ many teachers. When all three are so scarce, can we honestly recommend expansion; or must we, however reluctantly, agree with the inaction of successive governments? We have thought it our duty to examine rigorously the educational case for and against nursery education as well as to consider the economic implications of expansion.

I. THE PRESENT POSITION

292. We have briefly described in Chapter 8 the earlier history of provision for the under fives. Immediately after the war some day nurseries were transferred to the education service. But there has been no expansion, first because of the pressure on the building industry, and later because of the shortage of teachers. Recently a slight increase has been allowed, but only to enable qualified married women teachers to return to work in maintained schools. Both the restriction and this partial relaxation have been introduced to try to preserve existing standards of staffing in the compulsory stages of education at a time when they are threatened by the great increase in the child population and by persistent wastage in the teaching profession.

293. In 1965, about seven† per cent of all children under five in England were receiving some form of education in a school or nursery class. The proportion has hardly changed since the 1930s (see Table 4) although the quality of provision has almost certainly improved. A much smaller number of children attend local authority and private day nurseries for which the Ministry of Health is the responsible Department, and residential nurseries under the control of the Home Office. The types of institutions and numbers of children of two to five years in them in January 1965 are given in Table 5. In addition, about 20,000 children are under the care of local authority or registered child minders and certainly many more are supervised by unregistered minders who, according to a recent survey, are increasing in number[1].

*See Notes of Reservation on this Chapter.
†Children attending part-time are counted as full time equivalents. Most under fives in school attend full-time as do many in nurseries.

116

294. One in six of the children in the National Survey* (Appendix 3, Section 3, paragraph 2) had attended nursery school or nursery class. The highest proportions came from professional and unskilled workers' homes—25 per cent and 20 per cent respectively. Since, according to the N.U.T. Survey[2], three-quarters of all maintained nursery places are in working class areas, it seems clear that many professional parents are making use of private nurseries. According to the National Survey (Appendix 3, Table 38) there were marked regional variations in the distribution of nursery places. Thirty-four per cent of children in the Metropolitan area had attended nurseries as against eight and nine per cent in East Anglia and West and East Ridings respectively. Provision of day nurseries is equally patchy—of the 11,000 local authority day nursery places in England and Wales in 1964 surveyed in one enquiry, 2,800[3] were in Lancashire as were 15 of the 57 factory nurseries. Of a total of 1,585 private nurseries in England and Wales in one survey, 82 were in Orpington. "Nursery schools, as opposed to classes[4], are surprisingly concentrated in a broad crescent stretching from Greater London through the northern and western Home Counties to Oxford and Birmingham, thence to the Potteries and the textile towns of East Lancashire, across the Pennines to the Bradford area and northwards to County Durham. The highest number of nursery schools in a single authority's area is to be found in Birmingham; London comes next. Outside this 'nursery-school crescent' there are only a few minor concentrations, notably in Bristol, Nottingham, Liverpool and Hull." Three-quarters of nursery places are in classes in infant schools. Surprising variations exist between towns of similar sizes in similar regions.

295. Most, but not all, maintained nursery places are given to children who suffer some kind of social handicap. Some children are admitted because they lack companionship, others because their homes are too crowded or poor in other ways. They may come from flats lacking space, or because housing conditions are poor. Some are admitted on medical grounds or to help mothers nearing the end of their tether. Some mothers are working, although our enquiries show this is not the reason for most admissions. Often there is more than one reason. Teachers' children get priority because this is a condition for the expansion of nursery education under Addendum No. 2 to Circular 8/60. Since a nursery should not be simply a refuge for children in trouble, some children without handicaps get places with the unavoidable result that other children in need have to go without. The fault lies, however, with the restrictions on expansion rather than the selection of children.

The Case for Nursery Education

296. There is a wide measure of agreement among informed observers that nursery provision on a substantial scale is desirable, not only on educational grounds but also for social, health and welfare considerations. The case, we believe, is a strong one.

297. Only two individual witnesses questioned whether expansion was desirable and that mainly because they thought teachers and buildings were more urgently needed elsewhere. Of the principal local authority and teacher associations all were agreed that it would be desirable, although some local authority associations were doubtful whether expansion would be feasible in the present shortage of teachers. Of the 1,852 primary school teachers who

*No distinction is made in the Survey between independent and maintained nurseries.

answered our Questionnaire (Appendix 1, Table B.2) nearly 73 per cent said that nursery education should be available to all children whose parents wanted it, over 22 per cent said that it should be available only for those in special need and 2·7 per cent said it should not be provided. In the National Survey enquiry into parental attitudes (Appendix 3, Tables 41 and 42) a third of the parents would have preferred their children to have started full-time schooling (including nursery school or class) before the age at which they had in fact started schooling. The 1964 N.U.T. Survey of Nursery Education[5] showed that, where nursery education is available, the waiting lists are often double the size of the school, though some children may be placed on more than one waiting list. In 1966 in one urban area there were 1,818 children attending nursery schools and classes and 5,410 on the waiting list. In two thirds of nursery schools, the waiting period between application and admission is at least a year and may be considerably more.

298. The Nursery Schools Association told us they wanted more nursery places because most children can benefit from the physical care, the enriched opportunities for play both indoors and out, the companionship of other children and the presence of understanding adults which nursery education provides. Children need opportunities to get to know people outside their own family circle and to form some relationships which are less close and emotionally charged. The earlier maturity of children increases their need for companionship and stimulus before the age of attendance at school.

299. Many young children, of course, have a stable home background, companionship with their parents and their brothers and sisters, and sufficient space indoors and out. But there are aspects of modern life in cities which disturb us. The child who lives with his parents in a tall block of flats is likely to be house bound as the child in a bungalow or small house is not. The "extended family" with cousins and aunts and grandparents close at hand provides, where it still exists, a natural bridge between the intimacy of life at home and life with strangers in the wider world of school. But there are fewer extended families because more men change jobs and move to new districts. Mothers have less relief from their young children, lose the social contacts they have been used to, and may become less good mothers in consequence. And, of course, increasing numbers of married women are at work. The consequence of this is the new occupation of registered or unregistered child minders. Many professional families, too, rely on "au pair" girls or other help to look after their young children during part of the day. Child minders and au pair girls are rarely trained to look after the young child. Their growing number points to the need for the transitional world of the nursery school or class with its trained staff to do for today's children what modern family life often cannot do.

300. Long before a child is five he is already using words and is often familiar with books, toys and music. The issue is not whether he should be "educated" before he reaches school age because that is happening anyway. What has to be decided is whether his education is to take place in increasing association with other children and under the supervision of skilled people, as well as of parents, in the right conditions and with the right equipment.

301. Finally, there is evidence[6] on the special needs of children from deprived or inadequate home backgrounds. Some homes have positive disadvantages:

children from families in overcrowded or shared houses, or from broken homes, or even children of obsessive mothers may have few opportunities for normal and healthy development. Early help is also needed for handicapped children and for those with physically handicapped parents.

302. Our witnesses were those who had worked with and observed the needs of young children. They quoted research on the extent to which nursery education can compensate for social deprivation and special handicaps. Hindley[7] shows that even amongst children below compulsory school age, the growth of measured intelligence is associated with socio-economic features. There is strong support among witnesses for the view of Bernstein and Deutsch[8,9] that poverty of language is a major cause of poor achievement and that attempts to offset poverty of language are best made as early as possible. These researchers argue that thought is dependent on language and that some working class children have insufficient encouragement, example and stimulus in the situations of their daily life to build up a language which is rich and wide ranging in vocabulary, is a tool for categorisation and generalisation, and which, being complex in structure, develops concepts of time, space and contingency. The argument thus leads to the conclusion that since development in communication begins in the earliest years, one way in which the consequences of social deprivation can be overcome is to provide richer experience as soon as children are ready for nursery education. Other research consists mainly of studies of the improvement in mental defectives and in children from orphanages after nursery school experience, as well as of some work on children from more normal backgrounds. Hunt[10] outlines these investigations and, while recognising their importance, indicates the difficulties in evaluating them and the inconclusive argument that has focused on them. Examples of some of the difficulties are to be found in a recent paper by J. W. B. Douglas and J. M. Ross outlining the later effects of nursery school attendance[11]. The educational performance of children from the nursery schools was higher at eight than that of other children, but this advantage was lost by 11, and at 15 they did slightly less well than their contemporaries. In no year, however, were the differences statistically significant. Maladjustment among children who had attended nurseries was higher than amongst other children but, as is pointed out in the paper, children may have been admitted to nursery schools because of problems of behaviour, and "the conclusion to be drawn depends . . . on the original selection of the children . . . (It) may well be that a group who were highly vulnerable at entry have been given substantial help." The National Child Development Study (Appendix 10) may at a later stage produce further evidence on this issue.

303. The research evidence so far available is both too sparse and too heavily weighted by studies of special groups of children to be decisively in favour of nursery education for all. We rely, therefore, on the overwhelming evidence of experienced educators.

304. Each of the countries we visited provides education for children before the age of compulsory entry to school on a more generous scale than we do. Evidence from foreign countries must, however, be used cautiously to support or reject arguments for nursery education, first, because the age of compulsory entry is one or two years later than ours and, secondly, because the purposes and methods of education of children between three and seven are often different from ours. Yet the fact remains that many of these countries

believe that educational stimulus for young children is of great importance, particularly for the deprived. In the U.S.A. at the present time federal and other authorities, and private foundations, are providing large sums of money for programmes of nursery education, to counter the effects of extreme deprivation.

Mothers at Work: The Economic Argument

305. A further argument in favour of nurseries touches on equally complex and controversial subjects. The British economy and society are likely to change greatly in the next decades with results for child care which cannot be ignored. Mothers are demanding more and better quality services in schools, and more medical and social services generally. Many more married women now go to work and more will. The proportion of married women in employment in Great Britain, when corrected for changes in age composition, doubled between 1931 and 1951. The National Institute of Economic and Social Research has made projections of married women's employment to 1975 which show a further substantial rise since 1960 and predict that it will continue[12]. Many of these working wives, of course, have not got children below school age; but many have and it seems that their number will grow. Different studies [13, 14, 15, 16] show that the numbers of women who work range between 12 per cent and 35 per cent of those with a child under five, while as many as 13 per cent have had a full-time job at some time since they have had children. Further information may be available from later reports of the National Child Development Study (1958 Cohort). In our own small supplementary sample of 249 children entering school in the summer of 1965, 21 per cent of mothers were working (Appendix 6, paragraph 31). The general pressure to raise living standards causes mothers to go to work to raise money and employers to search for additional labour of which the most obvious source is married women. Although economic reasons are the most important in sending married women back to work, it is also true that many anyhow prefer to work, often with their husband's approval, because running a home now offers insufficient employment for them. Such research as we have been able to examine does not prove that children with mothers at work are necessarily worse off. Prolonged and early separation from mothers is known to be disadvantageous, but a short absence during the day does not harm the child who is ready for it. There was no evidence from the National Survey that mothers who were working had less time than others for their children in the evening. Many middle class parents pay someone to look after their children and send them, if possible, to nursery schools—as is evident from the data quoted in paragraph 294. In quoting this research we are not saying that it is better or unharmful for mothers with children under five to work. Our conclusions are that many mothers will work, and that their children will, as a result, need places in nurseries. And since, in the absence of positive steps to stop it, the numbers of mothers working will increase, it is possible to offset the contribution made by married women workers against the costs of providing nurseries. We assess these indirect benefits in Annex B to Chapter 31.

Arguments against Nursery Education

306. The first argument advanced against nursery education is that the place for the young child is with his mother in the home—a view expressed in the

1933 Report[17]—and that, in many homes, children have the experiences that the nursery school or class provides. Where this happens, nursery education is an unnecessary elaboration of these experiences and cannot give as generous a measure of adult support as the good home.

307. Some of those who have studied in detail the mother-child relationship in the early years [18, 19, 20, 21] hold that harm may come to some children through removal from their mother's care and companionship at too early an age before they realise that separation is only temporary. They stress the need for the greatest care in the gradual process of separating the child from his mother. They argue that a child's sense of security depends on the presence of a familiar figure. In the first three years of life only those whom a child sees regularly can give him a sense of security, particularly when he is in an unfamiliar situation or confronted by strange adults or children or by unaccustomed events. If anxiety is aroused it tends to be cumulative and, so far from promoting healthy independence, such experiences might make the child either too clinging or too detached and unable to form relationships. Evidence of this kind points to the danger of allowing children to attend nursery school or class at too early an age or for too long a period each day.

308. Another argument against an expansion of nursery education is based on the shortage of teachers. This might indeed suggest that there should be a contraction in order to divert teachers to pupils of compulsory school age. Inevitably, more nursery education will cost money and make heavy demands on manpower and will compete with the needs of other sectors of the economy and social services which, like the hospitals, require large numbers of girls with similar educational qualifications (see Chapter 31).

II. OUR RECOMMENDATIONS: FUTURE PATTERNS OF NURSERY EDUCATION

309. The arguments in paragraphs 306 to 308 have an important bearing on the conditions in which nursery education should be provided, but do not disprove the case for it. We conclude that there should be a large expansion of nursery education subject to the following points:

(a) It should be part-time rather than whole time because young children should not be separated for long from their mothers. Attendance need not be for a whole half-day session and in the earlier stages only one, two or three days a week will often be desirable. In the words of Susan Isaacs "the nursery school is not a substitute for a good home: its prime function . . . is to supplement the normal services which the home renders to its children and to make a link between the natural and indispensable fostering of the child in the home and social life of the world at large . . ."[22]

(b) A minority of children will, however, need full-time nursery education for a variety of reasons.

(c) The expansion of nursery education, which these recommendations involve, ought not to be at the expense of existing standards in the primary schools.

310. The major obstacle to expansion has been the shortage of teachers. The scheme we now outline seems to us to offer a way round this and other difficulties.

311. Our recommendations are, in summary, that expanded nursery education should be available for children from three to five in "nursery groups"

of 20 places.* Two or three groups might make one unit—to be called a "nursery centre"; or they might be combined with day nurseries or clinics in "children's centres". We believe that groups should always be under the ultimate supervision of a qualified teacher, but that the main day to day work should be undertaken by two year trained nursery assistants, of whom there should be a minimum of one to every ten children.

312. Where a group is supervised by a member of a primary school staff, the group will be formally part of that school. Groups not attached to a school but sharing the supervision of a qualified teacher might form a single nursery group even though they might be in two or three separate buildings.

Nursery Groups and Day Nurseries: A Unified Service

313. We have not so far distinguished between a nursery school or class, which is part of the education service, and a day nursery, which comes under the Ministry of Health. Day nurseries have made, and are making, a contribution towards the intellectual and emotional, as well as the physical, well being of children from the age of six months until they enter school. Their purpose is now mainly to relieve family problems. Reasons for admission include the difficulties of widowed or unmarried mothers, poverty severe enough to oblige the mother to work and unsatisfactory physical conditions at home. The day nurseries are concerned primarily with physical health, and are designed for children whose mothers are unable to care for them. They make their greatest contribution at the lower end of the age range. At present they take babies from six months or even from shortly after birth until entry to school. At the upper end, nursery education, properly so called, should be of increasing importance. An educational emphasis does not mean a lessening of concern for the physical health of the child. But help for older children calls for supervision by those whose training has given them broad educational perspectives and skills. In some areas day nurseries and nursery schools have good co-operative arrangements through the help of a joint committee which shares the expert knowledge of officials from both the health and education departments. This we welcome.

314. Although there is no obvious break in children's development in the years below school age we think that, since lines must be drawn somewhere, the day nursery is the proper place for those children who have to be away from their homes before the age of three. An institution with a more directly educational aim is right for children of three and over and for this reason it should be provided by the local education authority under the Education Acts instead of being administered by the health authorities. This argument is strengthened if our proposals for changes in the dates of entry to compulsory schooling for some children are accepted (see Chapter 10). Children in long term care might also attend the nursery groups, provided that the special strains to which the children are subject are taken into account before they are assumed to be ready for nursery education.

315. If the nursery provision for children aged three and over is to be in nursery groups administered under the Education Acts, the character of the day nurseries will change. Furthermore, day nurseries provide care through-

*When there is more than one nursery group, children and the assistants responsible for them will work co-operatively.

out normal adult working hours and in the holiday periods for children with difficult home circumstances. Only a few nursery schools care for children beyond normal nursery hours. These problems can be overcome if the larger nursery centres, and particularly those that form part of the children's centres containing day nurseries as well, make arrangements for children who must stay all day. At present the number of children involved is small: the average daily attendance at day nurseries of children under five was 16,470 in 1965— although the majority attend beyond normal school hours.

The Age Range of Nursery Education

316. The evidence suggests that most children are too young at two to tolerate separation from their mothers (see paragraphs 306 and 307 above). Some will be ready at three, but for others four will be a better age to join a nursery group. It will be for parents to decide and most parents will exercise this right sensibly. Nursery education should be available to children at any time after the beginning of the school year after they reach the age of three.

Part-Time Nursery Education

317. Since it is harmful to remove a child too suddenly or for too long from his mother, part-time attendance should be the normal pattern of nursery education. Children should be introduced gradually even to part-time education. It is the practice in many nurseries for the mother to stay with her child when he first enters and this should be encouraged. Teachers and parents should take account of the differing needs of young children in deciding at what age and, to begin with, for what periods each week and for how long each session, they should attend a nursery group. The minority of children who will attend full-time will have an even greater need for gradual introduction.

The Encouragement of Attendance

318. Evidence from such bodies as the Save the Children Fund and the Family Service Units shows that while many parents of children from impoverished home backgrounds respond to the advice of health visitors and others, a minority are unwilling or unable to make the effort even to take their children to a clinic, let alone a nursery. There is no easy solution. Compulsory attendance at a nursery group would be unworkable, even for those with special needs, for enforcement would place an intolerable burden on both the local authorities and on nursery staffs, and would create a relationship with the parents contrary to the whole concept of nursery education. A more widespread provision of nursery groups will help in reducing the distance mothers have to travel. In exceptional cases local education authorities or voluntary bodies might arrange for children to be brought to the nursery groups or taken home again.

319. We hope that these parents will appreciate the nursery groups and that as the health, social work and education services become better co-ordinated there will be more and better contact between them. In any event local education authorities can make full use of the advice of health visitors and others from whose records information about children in need can be gained. As nursery education becomes more generally available health visitors may

find it easier to persuade families to make more use of it. How far the nursery places are used by children in special need should be carefully studied by local authorities and by the Department of Education and Science so that further methods of persuasion can be brought into play if this proves necessary. More positively, the problem must be tackled by the development of parental education, including that of parents of children of pre-school age, which we suggest in Chapter 4.

Nursery Education and Parents

320. Nursery education creates contacts between parents, the educational service and the related health and welfare services, and can thereby improve the quality of the whole educational process. As the Hadow Report of 1933 pointed out, nursery education brings parents and teachers together in a setting where good attitudes towards community problems can flourish and where advice on all aspects of child rearing can be easily sought. At that time as many as 40 per cent entered school at five in need of medical attention. Even now, while three-quarters of mothers attend child welfare clinics during the first year of their child's life, only a quarter persist between one and five. Nursery education should throughout be an affair of co-operation between the nursery and home and it will only succeed to the full if it carries the parents into partnership. Support does not mean mild consent; it means the kind of active concern which can only come out of joint activity and out of close knowledge by the parents of what the schools are doing and why. The nursery group needs to be an outpost of adult education if it is to attain its goal for young children.

321. In Chapter 4 ways of enabling parents to participate in the life of the school have been described. Their active help can more easily be used in nursery groups. Some mothers may train as nursery assistants and work in the nurseries. Others may be content to help in less skilled ways. In some instances in this country, mothers are already being drawn into the life of the nursery. The head of one nursery school in which parents are encouraged to help wrote: "It increases their sense of belonging and gives their children tremendous joy." The child sees teacher and mother working together and accepting the same standards of behaviour. We saw this being done in one area of California with outstanding success. In some kindergartens visited it was a condition of children's admission that mothers should help and be present at discussions. We should not wish to go as far as this, as it might exclude some children who should be admitted.

322. Parental involvement with the nursery is bound to be close if only because at this stage mothers must bring their children to it. If parents become used to talking to teachers, more may continue to be interested in the work of the schools as their children get older. Contact with parents will be an important duty of the qualified teacher who is in control of the nursery group.

The Future of Voluntary Nursery Groups

323. Many voluntary nursery groups have done valuable work with little financial or other encouragement, and their contribution deserves to be widely recognised. They draw upon parental enthusiasm and effort of a kind that we

hope parents will put into the maintained nursery groups. There are about 600 groups established by the Pre-School Playgroups Association which are run on a part-time basis in such accommodation as is available, staffed mostly by mothers who are not qualified teachers and with active participation from other parents. Although guidance and help are available from the Association's headquarters the groups mainly exist where parents have the initiative and ability to set them up and to run them. Costs are met by daily charges for attendance. The Department of Education and Science have recently made a small grant towards the Association's headquarter expenses. Groups run by the Save the Children Fund also provide part-time places and are in the charge of nursery assistants, supervised by qualified teachers. In meeting requests for groups to be established, the Save the Children Fund gives priority to areas of social need. Costs are met largely from the funds of the Society, although in some areas grants have been made by local authorities. We understand that the Pre-School Playgroups Association wish to continue and extend their activities and the Save the Children Fund wish to continue to provide groups in especially difficult situations where experimental methods are needed, at least until maintained groups are generally available.

324. Nursery groups should be provided, in the long run, by local education authorities. Until enough maintained places are available, however, local education authorities should be given power and should be encouraged to give financial and other assistance to non profit making associations which, in their opinion, fill a need they cannot meet. This should include some arrangement for the training of their staff to be approved by the endorsing body which we suggest should be responsible for the training of nursery assistants.

325. At present, the premises of voluntary groups are inspected by the local health authorities. Where they continue to exist, with or without help from public funds, and the majority of children attending are between three and five years, we recommend that inspection of them by local education authorities and Her Majesty's Inspectors of Schools should be similar to that of the maintained nurseries.

Siting of Nurseries

326. Ideally, all services, including nursery, for the care of young children should be grouped together and placed near the children's homes and the primary schools. However, the nursery groups will have to be placed at first where they will fit most easily, and that will often be in existing primary schools. Elsewhere, they might be on the same site as children's clinics. It is intended to build 500,000 new houses a year and in the re-building of an area it should be possible to build nurseries near a health centre, a group practice of doctors or other community facilities. Since industry would benefit from an expansion of nursery education because labour will be easier to recruit (see Annex B to Chapter 31) factories might provide premises for a group which can then be maintained by the local education authority. In new housing development, particularly in blocks of high flats which increasingly are being built in the cities, space should be left for nursery education. The planning of accommodation for nursery groups should become as much a commonplace in the development of new areas as that of other community facilities, although we hope that their siting will be undertaken with more sensitivity to users' needs than is common at present. Nursery groups will

need to be in addition to the play centres and "one o'clock clubs" which cater all the year round for children and their mothers and which are part of the amenities of a district. The needs of young children for spaces where they can play safely with other children and yet be near enough to be in constant contact with an adult have been too often forgotten in post-war urban development. The planners have accepted, in recent years, that a family must have a space for a car, but few have considered the needs of pre-school children.

III. THE EXPANSION OF NURSERY EDUCATION: THE PLACES NEEDED, THEIR STAFFING AND ACCOMMODATION

327. We turn now to the problems of supply, staff, buildings and money that arise from our proposals that nursery education should be expanded. The ideal pattern that all nursery teachers would like to see established, if there were no shortages of teachers and buildings, would be one in which groups of 20 children would be assigned to the care of one trained teacher and one assistant with N.N.E.B. or other recognised training. But it will not be possible for some decades to find the 30–40,000 teachers for nursery education that this pattern would demand and we therefore propose a somewhat different pattern that will allow nursery education to develop, even if under conditions which are not ideal.

The Number of Places Needed

328. Eventually there should be nursery places for all children whose parents wish them to attend from the beginning of the school year after the age of three.* Since attendance will be voluntary it is not easy to estimate the number of places that will be needed. We have based our estimates of demand on the following assumptions:—

(a) nursery education will be available either for a morning or an afternoon session for five days a week except that over the country as a whole provision will be made for 15 per cent of children to attend both a morning and an afternoon session (see paragraphs 329 and 330 below). We should, however, expect some of the younger children to attend fewer than five sessions a week and less than a full session and that some will enter nursery groups at different times throughout the year;

(b) the average annual age group in England will be 880,000 children in the mid 1970s and over 900,000 by 1980†;

(c) not more than half the three year old children will attend nursery groups, either full or part-time, because many parents will consider their children too young to attend until they have reached the age of four;

(d) a maximum of 90 per cent of four year old children may attend nurseries. Some parents will be unwilling to allow them to attend nursery groups,

---

*In this Chapter we refer to 'three year olds' and 'four year olds'. In fact, their ages will range at the beginning of the school year from 3·0 to 3·11 and 4·0 to 4·11 respectively. Some three years olds will therefore reach four early in the school year.

†These figures are based on current population projections. If, however, the most recent trends in births continue, some downward movement is likely.

others will continue to make private arrangements and others, particularly in the country, will find the nearest nursery group inaccessible.

Full-Time Attendance for a Minority

329. We assume that 15 per cent of children between three plus and five plus will attend full-time. The figure of 15 per cent is built up on the following assumptions:—

(a) as we have said in paragraph 305, many mothers of children under five years work and many of them work full-time. The numbers are likely to increase if more married women continue to return to employment. The various studies[23] show different figures but the general picture that emerges is that at least five per cent of mothers with children between three and five work full-time;

(b) as many as ten per cent of mothers have been identified as unable to care effectively for their children[24]. Most of their children ought to receive full-time nursery education;

(c) an unidentified number of children ought to attend full-time because home circumstances are poor. The children of very large families, those from overcrowded homes, homes with only one parent or with sick mothers will have claims on full-time places;

(d) for the reasons given at (a) to (c) above, it seems that at least 15 per cent of children should have full-time nursery education. This is only a rough estimate. For one thing, we do not know the number of children of working mothers who are and can be well looked after by grandparents, relatives and neighbours. Nor can we estimate the extent to which parental apathy will prevent attendance by some of those who need it most. In Chapter 5 we have suggested that children in areas of social difficulty should get nursery places more quickly, and that half of them might attend full-time.

330. The extent to which mothers of young children should be encouraged by the provision of full-time nursery places to go out to work raises a question of principle. Some mothers must work because they need the money. The government, for reasons of economic policy, wish to see more women working. But, to work full-time, a mother must expect that her child will attend nursery for extended hours and during school holidays. Our evidence is, however, that it is generally undesirable, except to prevent a greater evil, to separate mother and child for a whole day in the nursery. We do not believe that full-time nursery places should be provided even for children who might tolerate separation without harm, except for exceptionally good reasons. We have no reason to suppose that working mothers, as a group, care any less about the well-being of their children than do mothers who do not work. Indeed, it is interesting that, in our supplementary sample (Appendix 6, paragraph 31) of children just starting school, 42 per cent of the working mothers would prefer their children to start part-time as opposed to 35 per cent of non-working mothers. But some mothers who are not obliged to work may work full-time, regardless of their children's welfare. It is no business of the educational service to encourage these mothers to do so. It is true, unfortunately, that the refusal of full-time nursery places for their children may prompt some of them to make unsuitable arrangements for their

children's care during working hours. All the same, we consider that mothers who cannot satisfy the authorities that they have exceptionally good reasons for working should have low priority for full-time nursery for their children.

Places Needed

331. We cannot forecast what proportion of the threes and fours will eventually attend the nursery groups. We think most of the places will be filled by children attending morning or afternoon sessions but that a minority will attend full-time. But it may be, at least in the early years of the scheme, that a smaller proportion of the three and four year olds will attend than we have assumed. The National Survey shows that more than two thirds of parents would have liked their children to have started full-time school before the age of five. Our figures are intended to be estimates of the maximum number of places which would be required. On this assumption, 746,000 full-time places might be required by 1975 and 776,000 by 1979, as is shown in Table 10.

*Table 10. Nursery Education: Number of Full-time
Equivalent Places Needed*

| | Full-time equivalent places needed | |
	1975	1979
Porportion of children in each age group		
'3s—4s' full-time attendance (15%)	132,900	137,400
'3s—4s' part-time attendance (35%)	155,050	160,300
'4s—5s' full-time attendance (15%)	130,800	136,650
'4s—5s' part-time attendance (75%)	327,000	341,625
	745,750	775,975

Staffing the Nurseries

332. How should the nurseries be staffed and how many teachers and other trained staff will be needed for them? Will it be possible to find as many as are needed?

333. We suggest that the day to day running of the nurseries should be in the hands of trained nursery assistants but that every 60 full-time places should be supervised by a qualified teacher. In practice, this will mean that qualified teachers working on the premises all the while will be in charge of the largest nursery centres consisting of three nursery groups of 20 children each. Nursery places will, however, also probably be provided in single groups of 20 children, or less, and we envisage one qualified teacher supervising three such groups, dividing her time between them as she sees fit. Elsewhere, in a small school with small classes, a nursery group might conveniently be supervised by the head or assistant teacher of the school to which it is attached. These supervisory arrangements must be tailored to fit local circumstances but two main principles should be observed:—

(a) all groups should be under the ultimate authority of a qualified teacher;

(b) each group should be staffed so that at least one experienced nursery assistant is present in each group. When a teacher is not permanently on the premises one of the assistants should take responsibility for the children's safety. As we suggest in Chapter 26, the most experienced assistants should be able to qualify on merit for a responsibility allowance.

Teachers

334. The nursery groups need not create demands for more teachers. For the most part, they will use in different ways teachers who are already responsible for children of nursery age. In January 1965 there were nearly 7,000 infant and junior mixed and infant schools in which more than half of the classes had less than 30 pupils. Most were in the rural areas, though some, including quite large ones, were in the cities. These schools are, however, generally small and a nursery group providing places for children in the area would be correspondingly small. If accommodation is available, a school with predominantly small classes could provide supervision of a nursery group without needing an additional teacher. It might be possible, for example, for a two teacher school of 50 children to provide supervision for a nursery group of six or seven children so long as a trained nursery assistant was provided. In many schools where the classes average 30 or less the head teacher is herself in charge of a class. This need not present insuperable problems as long as the other teacher or teachers are qualified. But if other problems such as those presented by a large number of recently arrived immigrant children are also evident, the further responsibility of a nursery group may have to be avoided. If accommodation is available possibly as many as 70,000* nursery places could be supervised without additional teachers but with additional nursery assistants. Only a careful survey by local authorities will establish the exact numbers.

335. The second way in which qualified teachers might be found for the supervision of the nursery groups would be by a diversion of some of those who would otherwise be teaching infant classes. We make the case in Chapter 10 for a single date of entry in each year which will delay entry to school for some children and thus reduce the load on the total teaching force. But nursery places will be needed for children who would otherwise have places for part of the year. How many teachers this change will make it possible to employ in the nurseries cannot be estimated with any precision but at the most it might be eight thousand. In addition there were nearly 200,000 children below the statutory age in school or in nursery school in January 1965. This figure will almost certainly diminish as the pressure on places increases during the rest of the 1960s and it is equally uncertain whether places will be restored in the 1970s. We therefore assume, taking all of these sources of teachers into account, that there may be as many as ten thousand teachers to supervise the nursery groups when the single date of entry is introduced, probably in the late 1970s (see Chapters 10 and 31). This number may be sufficient to supervise the majority, though not all, of the nursery places needed.

*This figure is based on the number of nursery age children in the catchment areas of infant and junior mixed and infant schools in which more than half the classes have less than 30 pupils.

Nursery Assistants

336. Whilst the number of full-time equivalent places in nursery groups might be 746,000 in 1975 and 776,000 by 1979 (see Table 10) some groups will contain fewer than ten children so that a somewhat larger number of assistants than one for every ten children will be needed throughout the country. Taking this into account, we estimate that the total number of nursery assistants needed will be 82,000 by 1975 and 85,000 by 1979.

337. In Chapter 26 we describe a combined scheme for the recruitment and training of nursery assistants and teachers' aides. In Chapter 31 we discuss whether, given other demands for manpower, the women needed for both schemes can be recruited. On the assumption that about three quarters of those trained will enter the schools as teachers' aides and a quarter enter the nursery groups as nursery assistants until the schools have enough aides, there might be enough trained assistants to staff the whole of our scheme for nursery education by the early 1980s. Table 37 shows the numbers entering training and service and the number of places for which they can be responsible, if training begins in 1968 and a build-up takes place systematically from then on. We consider this further in Chapter 31 where we also argue that the recruitment of teachers' aides should be regarded as being of higher priority than that of nursery assistants.

338. From paragraphs 334 to 337, it will be seen that a substantial expansion of nursery education will become possible mainly through the employment of infant teachers, supported by nursery assistants. Yet we are conscious of the difficulties. Some areas may not be able to find teachers to fill their quotas even now and may have no teachers for nursery education. They would have some when the single date of entry is introduced. We hope, however that in the educational priority areas (see Chapter 5) special efforts will be made to attract teachers. If not, provision will be patchy and some of the areas whose claims are greatest will not get nursery education. The expansion we propose is to be envisaged against the improved rates of teacher recruitment in the 1970s foreshadowed by the Secretary of State in his speech of 12th April 1966*. We have also assumed that the numbers of women who can be attracted to training as nursery assistants will increase substantially. We believe, but cannot be sure, that the estimated numbers can be recruited. If not, the rate of expansion must be slower than we suggest. The success of the scheme will depend above all on the efforts made by local education authorities. We take up in Chapter 31 the ways in which the recruitment of assistants, diversion of teachers, and availability of buildings must be synchronized.

Buildings

339. Much building will be necessary if all the nursery places needed are to be provided but even now there are some empty places. Since 1954 building

---

*In his speech to the National Union of Teachers in April 1966 the Secretary of State said that, by Easter 1971, the teacher shortage in England should be no more than 8,000 and that although the raising of the school leaving age would inevitably cause a temporary set-back in staffing standards a speedy recovery would be ensured through the heavy reinforcement which the schools would be receiving from the greatly expanded colleges of education. The next five years to 1976 should see recovery of all the lost ground and the elimination of oversize classes. Pressure would then still be necessary to ensure a better distribution of teachers between different parts of the system and to help the primary schools reduce the size of their classes.

programmes have had to meet the large demand for new school places as people moved from north to south and from city centre to outlying suburb. New schools provided on new housing estates have sometimes meant empty places in others. Where there are enough empty places of this kind, and where the lack of amenities common to old school buildings can be put right, there is the possibility of nursery groups without new buildings. We cannot, however, calculate the number or distribution of unused places which exist. Secondly, the number of children under statutory age in primary schools, including nursery classes but excluding nursery schools, totalled 175,000 in January 1965. If our short term proposals for entry to school (see Chapter 10) are adopted, more children will delay entry full-time until they are over five. The places which they will occupy during the two terms when they will attend part-time will be, to all intents and purposes, nursery places. Thirdly, if our proposal for one annual intake is accepted, the equivalent of one third of the five year old age group will be taken out of the primary schools—a further 214,000 children on present numbers, or 290,000 on the average school population expected in the 1970s.

340. Only careful surveys by local education authorities and the Department can show how many of the 776,000 places can be provided without new building. We make here an informed guess at the space that can be found through changes in admission policies, and the use of places at present under-used, so as to complete our estimates of cost. If all under fives ceased to attend school full-time, on 1965 figures, nearly 175,000 places would be released, but we do not know how many under fives will be in school in the late 1970s. We arbitrarily assume that the number might be reduced to 100,000 because of the evidence already quoted that local education authorities are increasingly excluding under fives. Secondly, 290,000 places might be released by the introduction of the single date of entry. Thirdly, the number of places under used, including those in very small schools and small classes, might be a further 100,000. There might therefore be a theoretical maximum of nearly half a million places. But nursery groups will not contain more than 20 children whereas the spaces they will occupy have held as many as 40 children. The theoretical maximum should thus be reduced to 250,000 and we assume that other difficulties might reduce this figure even further. The number of places might therefore range between 175,000 and 250,000. We estimate costs for the additional places to be built in Chapter 31.

Conclusion

341. The timing and priorities that we consider right for nursery education are discussed more fully in Chapter 31. We emphasise, however, that unless a start, no matter how modest, is made soon, there will not be a sufficient build up of staff for the large scale expansion to approach completion in the late 1970s. There are areas where a start can be made right away. We have already suggested in Chapter 5 that a large scale expansion should take place between 1968 and 1972 in the educational priority areas. But there will be neighbourhoods outside these areas where general social conditions, such as high flats or lack of recreational space, make nursery education essential.

342. In this chapter we have discussed the ways in which a large educational reform might be put into effect. Our proposals may meet with objections. Teachers may fear that nursery groups will have too little supervision by

trained teachers but at least the young children in them will be in small groups; the adult pupil ratio will be at least one to ten and these adults will be trained. What we suggest will be far better than the sub-standard arrangements which have often been made in the past for children under five. Those responsible for the planning and staffing of primary education will know of many alternative uses for the staff and the money which will be needed—perhaps £80 million gross when the full plan is complete. Yet we believe that what we propose will at last make possible an expansion of nursery education which will be generally welcomed.

Recommendations

343.   (i) There should be a large expansion of nursery education and a start should be made as soon as possible.

(ii) Nursery education should be available to children at any time after the beginning of the school year after which they reach the age of three until they reach the age of compulsory schooling.

(iii) Nursery education should be available either for a morning or afternoon session for five days a week except that over the country as a whole provision should be made for 15 per cent of children to attend both a morning and afternoon session.

(iv) The take up of nursery places by children in special need should be carefully watched by local education authorities and by the Department of Education and Science so that further methods of persuasion can be used to bring in all children who are in need of nursery education.

(v) Low priority should be given to full-time nursery education for children whose mothers cannot satisfy the authorities that they have exceptionally good reasons for working.

(vi) Children should be introduced gradually to nursery education.

(vii) Nursery education should be provided in nursery groups of up to 20 places. More than one and up to three groups might be formed as one unit to be called a nursery centre or to be combined with day nurseries or clinics in children's centres.

(viii) The education of children over three in day nurseries should be the responsibility of the education rather than health departments.

(ix) All nursery groups should be under the ultimate supervision of a qualified teacher in the ratio of one qualified teacher to 60 places. The main day to day work of the groups should be undertaken by two year trained nursery assistants in the ratio of a minimum of one to every ten children. There should be at least one experienced nursery assistant in each group and where no teacher is always on the premises, one assistant able to cope with accidents and safety risks. Experienced assistants should be able to qualify on merit for a responsibility allowance.

(x) Nursery groups which are under the supervision of a teacher or head teacher of an adjoining primary school should be part of that school. Groups not attached to a school should form a single nursery centre with the other groups which are supervised by the same qualified teacher

(xi) Until enough maintained places are available, local education authorities should be given power and be encouraged to give financial or other assistanee to nursery groups run by non-profit making associations which in their opinion fill a need which they cannot meet. Voluntary groups, with or without help from public funds, should be subject to inspection by local education authorities and H.M. Inspectorate similar to that of the maintained nurseries.

(xii) Ideally, all services, including nursery, for the care of young children should be grouped together and placed near the children's homes and the primary schools. The planning of new areas and the rebuilding of old should take account of nursery education.

(xiii) Local authorities should undertake local surveys at an appropriate time to assess the net cost of extra accommodation needed to establish nursery provision in their area and to see how many qualified teachers will be available following changes in the age of entry to the first school.

References

[1] 'Under 5': Howe, E. Conservative Political Centre, June, 1966, page 19.
[2] 'The State of Nursery Education'. N.U.T. 1964.
[3] Labour Women's National Survey into Care of Children. National Labour Women's Advisory Committee. 1966. Page 11.
[4] English Primary Education: A Sociological Description. Vol. I. W. A. L. Blyth 1965. Page 31, quoting information made available by the Nursery Schools Association.
[5] N.U.T. 1964 Survey. Page 13. (See 2).
[6] Evidence submitted to the Central Advisory Council by the N.U.T., the Nursery Schools Association, the L.C.C. and many other associations and individuals.
[7] Hindley, C. E. 'Social Class Influences on the Development of Ability in the First Five Years'. Child Education. Ed. Skard, A. G. and Husen, T. Copenhagen, Munksgaard. 1962.
[8] Bernstein, B. 'Social Structure, Language and Learning'. June 1961. Educational Research, Vol. III, No. 3, and other publications including unpublished work, 1966, on children of primary school age, received as this Report was going to press.
[9] Martin Deutsch. 'The Influence of Early Social Environment on School Adaptation'. 1963.
[10] J. McV. Hunt. 'Intelligence and Experience'. New York, Ronald Press Co. 1961.
[11] J. W. B. Douglas and J. M. Ross. 'Subsequent Progress of Nursery School Children'. Educational Research Vol. VII 1964. pp. 83–94.
[12] W. Beckermann et al. 'The British Economy in 1975.' National Institute of Economic and Social Research, Cambridge University Press, 1965.
[13] V. Klein. 'Working Wives'. Institute of Personnel Management. Occasional Papers, No. 15. 1960. Pages 9–10 and 'Employing Married Women'. Institute of Personnel Manage-Management. Occasional Papers No. 17. 1961, pages 5 and 9.
[14] B. Thompson and A. Finlayson. Married Women Who Work in Early Motherhood. Brit. Journal of Sociology, June, 1963.
[15] S. Yudkin and A. Holme. 'Working Mothers and Their Children'. Michael Joseph. 1963.
[16] J. W. B. Douglas and J. M. Blomfield. 'Children Under Five'. 1958, page 118.
[17] Report of the Consultative Committee on Infant and Nursery Schools, 1933. Section 81, page 113.

[18] Evidence submitted by Dr. J. Bowlby to the Council.

[19] Evidence submitted by the Tavistock Institute to the Council.

[20] Dr. Terence Moore. 'Children of Full Time and Part Time Mothers'. International Journal of Social Psychology. 1964.

[21] Evidence submitted by the British Psychological Society to the Council.

[22] Isaacs, Susan. 'Educational Value of the Nursery School. Nursery Schools Association. 1938, Pamphlet No. 54.

[23] R. K. Kelsall and S. Mitchell. 'Married Women and Employment in England and Wales'. Population Studies. Vol. 13. 1959–1960. The Labour Women's Survey (see 3) contains an excellent summary of both American and British Studies.

[24] See ([16]) above. Page 45.

CHAPTER 10

The Ages and Stages of Primary Education

When Should Primary Education Begin?

344. The last chapter was concerned with the upbringing of children before they reach school age. The arguments led to the conclusion that they should have the opportunity of belonging to a nursery group. This will be the more possible because we are suggesting changes in the ages at which they are admitted to primary schools. We now examine the case for these alterations in its own right.

345. The choice of five as the age at which children must begin school was made almost by chance in 1870, but the Consultative Committee reported in 1933 that it was working well in practice, and thought there was no good reason for modifying the law. But, with the exception of Israel and a few states whose educational systems derive from ours, the United Kingdom is alone in the world in fixing so early an age. In most countries it is six; in some seven. This sharp contrast makes it right for us to consider carefully the grounds for admitting children to school when they are so much younger.

346. Children are born every day of the year. In England they are admitted to infant schools at intervals of four months (most countries have one yearly intake), and promoted to junior schools or classes only at intervals of twelve months. They must go to school at the beginning of the term after their fifth birthday; they are promoted to the junior school (or junior classes) in the September following their seventh birthday.

Table 11. Compulsory Education in Infant Schools Under Present Arrangements

	Year 1			Year 2			Year 3		Junior School
Month of Birth	Age of Child in Autumn Term	Age of Child in Spring Term	Age of Child in Summer Term	Age of Child in Autumn Term	Age of Child in Spring Term	Age of Child in Summer Term	Age of Child in Autumn Term	Age of Child in Spring Term	Age of Child in Summer Term	Length of Infant Schooling on Promotion
Sept–Dec.	—	5	5	5 to 6	6	6	6 to 7	7	7	8 terms
Jan–April	—	—	5	5	5 to 6	6	6	6 to 7	7	7 terms
May–Aug.	—	—	—	5	5	5 to 6	6	6	6 to 7	6 terms

Table 11 shows that:

(a) there is a considerable difference in age and in the length of time children have been at school when they are promoted to the junior school. Either annual admissions, or termly promotions, would remove one or other of these differences; it is the combination of the two which imposes a double difference.

(b) the number of pupils in the infant school varies greatly from term to term: a school which has about 240 children in the summer term may have less than 200 before Christmas.

Disadvantages of Termly Entry

347. There is evidence both from our witnesses and research[1,2,3,4] that children born in the summer, who are younger and have a shorter time at school than others before they are promoted, tend to be placed in the "C" stream of those junior schools which are organised in this way. The N.F.E.R. study of streaming (Appendix 11, Section 1(2), paragraph 4) found that "the A streams had the highest average age and the lowest ability streams the youngest". The difference persists. One county borough[5] has found that a high proportion of the pupils born between September and December gained grammar school places compared with those born between May and August. The latter often have to transfer to junior school before they have finished learning to read. Their new teachers, not always realising their relatively late start, may believe them to be slow learners, expect less of them and often in consequence get less from them. The "age allowances" made in selection procedures cannot offset their psychological handicap.

348. In many schools there is either a spare classroom in the first term of the year, or the rooms are over filled in the summer. Few authorities staff the infant schools on summer numbers and fewer still will do so as staffing problems increase. For this reason it is common to find that children are promoted each term. This practice has been encouraged by authorities who have often provided two form-entry schools with one especially well equipped room for the admission class. Its teacher's task is unrewarding. She helps children to adjust to school and gets to know their parents; but, before she can use this knowledge, the children are transferred to another teacher. She feels the lack of a group of "old hands" among the children to show newcomers how things are done.

349. The shuffle up of children from admission classes often affects the whole school. Children and teachers may have to get used to a new class each term. The effect on young children may be serious. The teacher is to them something like a parent. Nobody would like to change parents once a term; children in infant schools should not have to change teachers at this rate. A minority of schools avoid this problem by the form of organisation known as vertical grouping (see Chapter 20). But this would not be acceptable in all schools.

350. It seems, therefore, that termly entry results in unsatisfactory organisation in the infant school and has serious disadvantages for the summer born children. This view was endorsed by many of our witnesses and by the sample of teachers whom we invited to comment on the age of entry (Appendix 1, Table B.1.) We recommend, therefore, that all children should begin compulsory schooling in the same period of the year and that this should be in the autumn term. Even though the children born in the summer would be younger than the rest, they would have the same number of terms as other children in the infant school.

351. So far we have assumed that all children first go to school when they are legally required to. This is far from true. It is common practice for children to be admitted in the term before that in which their fifth birthday falls. In some areas, where there is a long tradition of women's work, children are admitted to school at the beginning of the year in which they turn five. Interviews with parents of children who started school in the summer term

of 1964 (a small sample forming part of the National Survey) showed that two-thirds of their children had entered school under five years (see Appendix 6, Table 2). The National Child Development Study (Appendix 10, Table 15) gave a lower figure—49·1 per cent. Statistics provided by the Department show that the majority of children who are "rising five" in January enter school that term. Undoubtedly more autumn born than summer born children enter school before five. If summer born children are admitted before their fifth birthday they often enter classes which are overcrowded and schools which are less well staffed than earlier in the year. We are told that a third of all local authorities are now having to exclude "rising fives" through the year. In a few areas there has recently not been room for even all of the statutory age. The age at which a child may go to school is affected by the conditions of the area in which he lives. Subject to these limitations, however, the age at which he does go to school depends on his parents' choice between one term and the next or even, perhaps, between three possible terms. In this way some children get nine terms and some only six in the infant school.

Chronological Versus Developmental Age

352. Chronological age, which can be a misleading a guide to a young child's development, decides when he can and when he must go to school. Some of the teachers who gave evidence would have liked to substitute "developmental age" but, for the reasons given in Chapter 2, it would not be easy to assess this accurately even with tests of the same complexity, expense and unpopularity as those which have been used in transfer to secondary education. It would seem wise, therefore, to continue to relate entry to school to chronological age. The law should, however, allow a good deal of variation in practice.

Easing Entry to School

353. Many parents probably have a fair idea of when their children are ready for school. The possibilities open to them should be widened and they should be given advice when it is needed. Today most children move in one step between the age of 4 years 9 months and 5 years 3 months from full-time home to full-time school. In the last chapter we recommended that children might move gradually, according to their individual needs, from occasional attendance to half-time attendance between the ages of three and five. We think also that part-time attendance should remain possible after a child reaches the chronological age, which is fixed by statute, for him to start school. Decisions ought to rest with the parents in consultation with head teachers. Children who now enter school under five—and many who are older—would be as well, and often better, served by part-time attendance at small nursery groups because the ratio of adults to children can be more generous and education informal. The nursery type of education would have to be available in the infant schools for those children who still needed it. Equally there would have to be sufficient stimulus in the nursery groups for the older and more advanced children.

354. We have received a considerable amount of evidence that part-time education would enable a child to settle more easily at school. The Nursery Schools Organiser in one county wrote "I am convinced that if more flexible

F

part or full-time entry was permitted during a child's first year at school, that he or she would be ready to accept compulsory full-time at six". A county Inspector said "The present arrangement of full-time education at five is too abrupt a transition from home for many children". A headmaster wrote "Many children who begin their school life at five find the full school day too long and show signs of fatigue. Some show marked signs of strain". Other witnesses felt that most children settled easily into a full day. Twenty three per cent of mothers interviewed for the National Survey (Appendix 3, Table 44) would have liked their children to have started part-time. This proportion rose to 36 per cent in the supplementary sample (Appendix 6, paragraph 6) of children just settling into school. Yet all the new starters began full-time.

355. The N.C.D.S. Report indicates (Appendix 10, Table 80) that seven per cent of the boys and five per cent of the girls were reported still to be unsettled after the first three months in school. Our proposals for nursery education should ease the introduction to school. Admissions to the infant school should be staggered over half a term by arrangement between parents and head teachers. In this way each new child and his mother could be sure of an individual welcome. In the last resort there will, however, be some children who are not ready for full-time* education when the law expects them to be. If they are in a nursery group we suggest that they should stay there a little longer. If they have not been to one, we think that they should begin with attendance for half a day at the infant school. Care would have to be taken to see that while they were part-time, they got a balanced education without undue emphasis on learning to read, write and count. They need the play and creative expression which infant schools generally provide. This transition period within the statutory age for full-time education ought normally to last not longer than a term but this should be extended, if parents wish, until the child reaches the age of six. The child must come first.

356. We have been told that it is mostly professional parents who would like their children to start part-time and that to delay the full-time entry to school of children of parents in unskilled occupations would penalise their development. Yet the transition from home to school is a great change for all children and may be even greater for the child from a poor home. Care should, therefore, be taken to explain to parents why it is better for children to adjust gradually to school. We hope that, even in those areas where there has been a long tradition of entry to school before the statutory age, the part-time entry to a nursery type of education we have suggested as a short term measure (paras. 399 to 405) will be adopted.

Age of Entry

357. The argument so far leads clearly to two decisions. It is better to have one intake a year to infant schools or classes than three. It is desirable to be able to delay full-time education for those few who are not ready for it at the appointed time, and to lead up to it by part-time attendance. But what should be the age for entry? As we have seen, the other countries of the world, with few exceptions, favour a later age than ours. Some of our witnesses agreed with them. A few favoured the age of seven. The rest were divided between five and six. Clearly no decision will be absolutely right for everybody. To

*We use the terms 'full-time' and 'part-time' education to mean two sessions and one session a day respectively.

raise the age to six and define it as "the September following the sixth birth-day" would mean that the median age on admission would be six years six months and a good many children would be nearly seven. This would cer-tainly reduce the number of children who would need continued part-time education, but for the same reason it would be frustrating for the many who would be ready for school well before. It seems to us, too, that there is a sound educational argument for admitting five year olds to school. It was with this age group that informal ways of learning, and teaching geared to individual needs, were first extensively developed in this country. There is a marked contrast between education given to six and seven year olds in England and in most countries with a later age of entry. In this country, learning through play and creative work continues throughout most infant schools; elsewhere this approach seemed to us on our visits often to be lack-ing. We think that it is probably sacrificed to the formal work which a later date of entry may easily seem to demand. We should not want this to happen in England.

358. We, therefore, recommend that the statutory time by which children must go to school should be defined as the September term following their fifth birthday. This measure would require legislation. Attendance at a nursery group should be permitted for the first term of compulsory educa-tion. A child should, if his parents wish, be allowed to attend school for a half day only until he reaches the age of six. Some children would be nearly six before they went to school; some no older than at present. The median age would be five years six months. This modest raising of the age of entry for some children by a few months would, we think, have several beneficial effects:

(a) It would simplify the organisation of the infants schools which could then be staffed and equipped for a full three year course.

(b) Children would no longer need to be promoted each term.

(c) The unfairness which springs from varying lengths of education in the infant school would disappear.

(d) The saving of teachers and classrooms would, as we saw in the last chap-ter, help to make possible a preparatory period of part-time nursery education for all who want it.

(e) This would ease the transition from full-time home to full-time school, as would the slightly later start of school life for two-thirds of the five year olds. Those children who still need an introductory period of part-time school after reaching the statutory age would, we think, largely come from those who were barely five on admission.

359. As we have said this change should not be made unless nursery educa-tion is available for all who wish it for at least one year before school starts. The older children within an age group should, when possible, be admitted earlier. Over two-thirds of parents want their children to start school before the age of five. Their wishes are entitled to respect. To raise for some children the age of entry to school and not to provide some alternative education for the year before the new age of entry would be inexpedient as well as educa-tionally unsound. We think that alternative education should, however, usually be part-time in a nursery group.

The Length of the Infant School Course

360. If our recommendation of one entry date a year stood alone all children instead of roughly a third would be limited to a two year course in the infant school. Yet we have received convincing evidence that the present course is too short and that children transfer to the junior school before they are ready for it.

361. Many infant schools are outstanding for the quality of the relationships between teachers and children. They excel in the opportunities they provide for play and the talk that accompanies it, the stress they put on individual learning and the skill with which teachers select from the various methods of teaching reading those that suit themselves and the individual children. Infant school teachers also have good opportunities for building up a knowledge of both children and parents. The children are usually open and trusting and parents have been shown by the National Survey to be more interested in their children's work at this stage than at any subsequent period (Appendix 3, Section 2, paragraph 34).

362. Two years is too short to profit fully from these qualities of the good infant school. In this period many children cannot establish social confidence and their slowly maturing personal relationships may suffer a severe setback, when they transfer to a new and unfamiliar junior school. This setback is especially characteristic of children in socially deprived areas who often enter infant schools lacking both social experience and the ability to express themselves in speech. Similarly, there is overwhelming evidence that many children have not achieved a mastery of reading by the time they leave the infant school. A reading survey conducted by the N.F.E.R. in Kent; showed that though standards were rather higher than in the country as a whole, 45 per cent of the children in the first year junior classes still needed the kind of teaching which is to be found in infant schools. Yet most of their teachers had received no training in infant methods and a substantial minority had no knowledge of how to teach the beginnings of reading. The survey also demonstrated that the prospects of success in reading for children who are poor readers when they transfer to the junior school are very gloomy indeed. The N.C.D.S. survey tells the same story (Appendix 10, Section 6(a)). Many seven year old children continue to need systematic teaching in reading. At this age girls are superior to boys as judged by objective tests and by the primers they have reached. Early transfer to the junior school may be one reason why more boys than girls are to be found in remedial classes.

363. We conclude, therefore, that children should have three years in the infant schools and that they should not transfer until the age of eight. A three year course will allow teachers and children to work steadily without anxiety. It will give infant school teachers the satisfaction of seeing more results to their labours and of knowing that children have reached, before eaving them, a stage at which they can tolerate a change of school.

364. We believe, therefore, that all children (instead of only some as at present) should have at least three years in the infant school. But would a four year course be preferable? Two main arguments have persuaded us to the contrary. If the infant school course were to last four years, some children would be nearly ten before transfer. It would then be difficult both to cater adequately for the most advanced children and at the same time to preserve

the best of infant education. Secondly, as we argue later, 12 seems to us a better age of transfer to a secondary school than 13, and we believe that four years is the right length for junior education. Thus, there is a cumulative case for a three year infant school, deriving from what is best educationally for children between five and eight or nine, and from what are the desirable lengths of the junior and secondary courses. We recommend that transfer to junior schools should take place in the September following a child's eighth birthday.

Should the Age of Transfer to Secondary Education be Raised?

365. "11+" seems now as firmly fixed in Englishmen's minds as 1066. One of the matters referred to us, the age of transfer to secondary education, forces us to ask whether it should soon become as much a matter of past history. It is no longer to be the dreaded landmark marking off the grammar school child from the modern school child. Should it also ceas? to mark the transition from small primary to large secondary school?

366. The choice of the age of 11 was the result, it seems, partly of the desire to give "scholarship winners" from the old elementary schools the benefit of the established five year course in the county secondary schools and old grammar schools and partly of the desire to provide secondary education for all in a system where most boys and girls left school as soon as they became 14. A later age than 11 would have meant for most pupils a secondary school course of "one and a bit years" instead of "two and a bit". The second alternative just made sense: the first was plain nonsense. The choice between them was easy. Practical considerations decided the matter; theory, in so far as it came in at all, was used in support.

367. The present dividing line is governed by Section 8(I) of the Education Act of 1944 as amended by Section 3 of the 1948 Act. In 1944 Parliament laid down that there were to be "sufficient primary schools for junior pupils under ten and a half years of age and for those over that age whom it was expedient to educate with such pupils". There were also to be sufficient secondary schools for senior pupils over 12 and for those junior pupils over ten and a half whom it was expedient to educate with them. Pupils, therefore, were to move from primary to secondary schools between the age of ten and a half and 12, that is, at about the age of 11.

368. The 1964 Act enabled proposals to be made to the Secretary of State for the establishment of schools which straddled the dividing line laid down by the 1944 Act between primary and secondary education. The intention was to allow experimental patterns to be tried out, rather than to modify the general age structure. It was expected that the outcome would be the establishment of a small number of middle schools for children of 8 to 12 and 9 to 13. Since then, Circular 13/66, announcing the Government's plans for raising the school leaving age, allows local education authorities to change the age of transfer to 12 or 13 if justified "by reference to some clear practical advantages in the context of reorganisation on comprehensive lines, or the raising of the school leaving age, or both."

369. The bewildering variety of schemes which are being canvassed, and to a less extent, applied made it all the more necessary for us, in view of our terms of reference, to study from first principles what the best age of transfer to

secondary education should be. We took, as starting points, the information on children's development described in Chapter 2, the written and oral evidence received from associations, individual witnesses and members of H.M. Inspectorate, and the arguments put forward for the Leicestershire plan and by some local authorities for 9 to 13 schools. We held discussions with head and assistant teachers from different types of secondary school and with teachers from primary schools. Some of us have visited areas in which experiments are being made in teaching children aged 11 to 13 in separate, self contained schools. Our recommendations take into account the extension to 16 of the period of compulsory attendance at school.

370. The present age of transfer, as opposed to the mechanism of selection, has been little challenged until recently. This is a reason for caution. Moreover, there are good arguments against a change. From the point of view of the primary schools there is an objection to interfering with junior schools at a time when they are rapidly becoming leaders in educational advance. This, it may be said, is no time to disturb by organisational changes a revolution in ways of teaching and learning that is wholly to the pupils' good. From the secondary point of view there are two strong aruguments for the present age. It gives the secondary school time to get to know its pupils well before decisions are made on choice of courses at about the age of 14. It allows eleven and twelve year olds the stimulus of teaching by, or at least of teaching supervised by, the specialists who are in charge of secondary school departments. This is especially valuable in subjects such as mathemetics and science in which skilled teachers are scarce. There is also the point that transfer at 11 allows a small majority of pupils time to adjust to their new school before meeting the strains of puberty. But, as Chapter 2 shows, the variations in the age at which puberty occurs are so wide that it is impossible to fix a transfer age which would be generally satisfactory from this point of view.

371. Some of the arguments for a change of age arise from a belief that the junior school course now ends at too early an age. The experience of teachers and other educationalists suggests that for many children the changes of curriculum and method associated with a break at 11 cut across a phase in learning and in attitudes to it. An unselfconscious period in art, dramatic movement and writing, for example, may last till 12 or 13. Many children, too at the top of the primary school develop confidence in devising experiments and using books in specific situations (often unrelated to "subjects"). Their progress may be slowed down by premature emphasis on class instruction, adult systematisation and precision in secondary schools. These arguments are supported by the findings of Piaget and his English followers on the late emergence of powers of abstract thought. Equally, the junior school curriculum is wider than it was. A foreign language, science (as opposed to nature study) and mathematics (as opposed to arithmetic) used to be confined to secondary schools. They are now taught in junior schools. Today there is a basis for a "middle school" curriculum.

372. Other arguments from the secondary school side turn on the disadvantages to the 11 and 12 year olds and to the schools as a whole which now arise from transfer at 11. Eleven, it is argued, is too early for the educational decisions which follow from a change of school. Our evidence from witnesses goes to show that transfer between streams in comprehensive schools is

uncommon just as transfers between modern and grammar schools are. The strictly educational, as opposed to social, argument against a selective system starting at 11 does not lose its force because the selection is between streams instead of between schools. This rigidity inside comprehensive schools may be unnecessary and may be temporary; but it has to be taken into account.

373. The second line of argument turns on the fact that so many more boys and girls than formerly stay at school to 16 and 18. The demands made by the growing numbers of these senior pupils in secondary schools are such that highly qualified teachers have little time and energy to devote to younger pupils. Specialist organisation is necessary for the older pupils. It is often extended to the younger pupils for whom it is not. It is difficult to cater in one institution for the needs of 11 year olds and pupils of 15 to 18: either the presence of children will prevent the development of the near adult atmosphere that older pupils need; or, if priority is given to creating an adult community, the younger pupils may feel lost, or even by contrast be treated as younger than they are.

374. There are also the middle years of the secondary school course to consider. To the newcomer the secondary school may be as delightful, once his initial shyness has passed off, as his junior school has been. For the seniors at the top there often are the necessity for hard work and, for some, the enjoyment of intellectual effort. There is established position, responsibility, seniority in fact, to enjoy. But in between there may be drab years of boredom when the fulfilment which school denies may be sought elsewhere and show itself in restlessness. Whatever the age span, the middle years are dangerous. It should not all be blamed on adolescence. Seven years to 18 for the able, five years to 16 for most pupils is a long time. These are longer periods than than those spent in any other part of the educational system. There is something to be said for shortening the total span of secondary education, and this can only be done by starting it rather later.

375. Another argument for a higher age of transfer turns on the increasing size of secondary schools. The voluntary lengthening of school life and the raising of the minimum school leaving age will make schools bigger unless countervailing action is taken. So will the increase in the number of comprehensive schools for 11 to 18 year olds. The Newsom report recorded the conviction of heads of schools in deprived areas that their pupils needed small schools. Quite apart from this special case it seems clear that 11 and 12 year olds may easily feel lost in too large a school. A later age of transfer than 11 would to some extent offset this trend and protect the younger children, who are the ones most likely to suffer from size. There is no reason why a junior or middle school need be large. A two tier secondary system starting at 11 is an alternative method of reducing the size of comprehensive schools. But, with a five year secondary course, one or other stage must be limited for many pupils to two years—"all legs and no body" as one witness put it.

376. Some of those with whom we have had discussions see no difficulty in common provision for pupils from 11 to 18. Others find it necessary to take avoiding action where they can. Thus, library provision is often separately made for juniors. Where this is not done, they are often inadequately catered for. Out of school activities are usually biased towards the interests of the older pupils, and frequently they are insufficient for the younger. The evidence

of the Incorporated Association of Head Masters refers to the need for separate buildings for the youngest pupils in schools with large sixth forms. The headmaster of a large selective boys' school has told us that he had found it necessary to make special arrangements for the community life of the younger pupils. Some comprehensive schools are organised in lower, middle and upper schools, an arrangement which gives the younger pupils a community of their own but does not isolate them, and which breaks up large numbers and extensive buildings into units of manageable size.

377. Granted that 11 and 12 year olds fit less well than they did into secondary schools unless special provision is made, is there reason to believe that they would fit better or with less difficulty into a school with children of eight, nine and ten? The main difficulty in answering this question lies in the different development of boys and girls. Girls are ahead of boys from birth and reach adolescence some two years before them. One possibility would be to provide single sex schools at this stage of divergent development and interests. This arrangement would run counter to the general trend towards co-education and few have suggested it. All boys and most girls would be at home in a middle school*, but there might be difficulties for a 13 year old girl who had reached adolescence early. If the transfer age is fixed at 13, earlier transfer would probably be needed for a minority of girls who were exceptionally mature.

378. The different rate of development towards sexual maturity among boys and girls is only one of the physiological and psychological factors which have to be considered. The differences between individuals are at least as important as the difference between the sexes. The important thing is to remember how extremely wide the range of variation is. This means that wherever the age of transfer is fixed, there will be some children who would have been better left in the primary school, and some for whom the reverse would be true. There is, therefore, need to treat the years immediately before and after transfer as a transitional period. What happens at present, and the arguments we have been considering, both make us believe that most of this period is best spent in a primary school. We conclude that the case for a higher age of transfer is made out. But should it be 12 or 13?

12 or 13?

379. The answer to this demands a fairly close look at the working of the present schools. Both ages would protect the pupils somewhat longer from the downward reaching examination pressures which the G.C.E. ,and perhaps even C.S.E., may create. Pupils transferred at 12 would have four years before taking a first external examination in their secondary school. Even transfer at 13 would allow pupils an introductory year and two years for an examination course. So far there is no decisive advantage either way. But we have only been considering pupils who propose to take a full secondary course and probably sit for an examination at the end. Many will not, and will leave as soon as they may. For these, if they were born between September and February, the earliest date of leaving after 1970 will be the Easter after their sixteenth birthday. If the age of transfer is 13, their secondary course would have lasted only two years and two terms which we and most of our witnesses think too short. Transfer at 12 would be better for them.

*For an explanation of the term 'middle school' see para 406.

380. For many subjects of the curriculum 12 and 13 would be equally satisfactory transfer ages. This holds good for all the English subjects, for home economics and probably for art. There is, perhaps, a slight, but certainly not a decisive, advantage in the lower age where foreign languages are concerned. Latin and a second modern language are usually introduced in the second year of the secondary course, but there would be no harm in leaving them for a further year. Science, handicraft and physical education present rather more difficulties with the higher age. Some extra accommodation and equipment would be needed in middle schools for all three subjects if the age of transfer is raised at all; if it is raised to 13 more would be needed than if it is fixed at 12. Staffing for science and mathematics in middle schools would be more difficult to provide, because more specialist teaching would be needed, with the age of transfer at 13 than at 12. Accommodation in a two form entry junior school would probably be adequate for an eight to 12 school provided that one or two general practical rooms were added; and that there was easily accessible space for books and a place to read them. On these curriculum matters the balance of advantage seems to us to lie with a transfer at the age of 12.

381. It is also necessary to consider whether transfer at 12 or 13 is more likely to produce the kind of middle school we wish to see. Eleven year old pupils often transfer from a school based entirely on class teaching to a secondary school which, because of the needs of the older pupils, is organised for specialist teaching. A school with semi-specialist accommodation shared between cognate subjects, and teachers skilled in certain areas of the curriculum rather than in single subjects, could provide a bridge from class teaching to specialisation, and from investigation of general problems to subject disciplines. The influence of semi-specialist teachers primarily concerned with the older pupils might be reflected in more demanding work being given to nine and ten year-olds, while the primary tradition of individual and group work might advantageously be retained for a longer period than at present, and might delay streaming.

382. Effective staffing of middle schools would call for recruitment of teachers both from present junior schools and from those experienced with the younger age groups in secondary schools. At the same time some teachers mainly concerned with the younger juniors would need to transfer to first or infant schools. Many junior teachers would need to deepen and extend their knowledge; former secondary teachers would have to absorb the best of primary school attitudes and practice, and also to increase their personal resources since they would no longer have available to them the knowledge and advice of specialist heads of department. An imaginative programme of in-service training would be called for, but in-service training is just as necessary for satisfactory education within the present structure. Junior-secondary courses in the training colleges offer a basis on which suitable initial training courses could be developed. The principal need would be for courses which offer a group of related subjects for study in relative depth, for instance in the creative arts, in English and English subjects, or in a combination of mathematics, geography and science. Middle schools might well attract more men than junior schools have done, which would probably give them a more stable staff. They might also attract graduates, interested in the possibility of working experimentally.

383. If the middle school is to be a new and progressive force it must develop further the curriculum, methods and attitudes which exist at present in junior schools. It must move forward into what is now regarded as secondary school work, but it must not move so far away that it loses the best of primary education as we know it now. The extended programme will require teachers with a good grasp of subject matter, but we do not want the middle school to be dominated by secondary school influences. Clearly these aims could be achieved with transfer set either at 12 or 13.

384. The danger of the extension of the middle school course for one year only would be that the change might not provide sufficient challenge to the schools to think afresh about what they provide for the older pupils. The danger of a two year extension would be that the middle school might forget that it was still a primary school. There is a risk either way; on the whole we think that transfer at 12 is more likely to give us the middle school we want to see.*

385. The arguments in favour of 12 and 13 as the age of transfer are fairly evenly balanced, and there is, we repeat, no one age which is right for every child. But on nearly every count it seems to us that the balance of advantage is just with 12 year old transfer, that is to say transfer in the September following a child's twelfth birthday which gives a median age of 12 years 6 months on admission to a secondary school.

386. Our recommendations for the structure of primary education, therefore, are:—

(a) there should be part-time nursery experience for those whose parents wish it;

(b) a three year course in the first (at present the infant) school with one annual intake in September at a median age of five years six months;

(c) the first school should be followed by a four year course in a middle (at present the junior) school with a median age range from eight years six months to 12 years 6 months.

387. We emphasise that the merits of this structure depend on the inter-locking of its parts. The arguments in its favour must not be used to support one part without the other two. In particular we wish to stress that our proposal for one intake a year to the first school is inseparable from our recommendation of part-time nursery education for all whose parents wish it.

Provision for Exceptional Cases

388. Up to this point we have been concerned with the structure of nursery and primary education. One of the major difficulties has been the fact which we have had tiresomely to reiterate, that there is no universally right age for

---

*The Scottish Council for Research in Education sponsored a detailed enquiry into the age of transfer from primary to secondary school, the results of which were published in 1966[6]. The age of transfer in Scotland has been 12. They concluded, as we have done, that "The answer to the question 'What is the appropriate age of transfer' must be that there is no one 'correct' age ... The transition from primary to secondary education should extend over the whole period from age ten to age 13. These years should be regarded as a transitional period, during which there is a gradual change in curriculum and style of teaching. Prescribing age limits within this period for a change of school is justifiable for administrative reasons, not on psychological grounds". (p.89).

any step, so various are human beings. They are so various that it is in our view right that special provisions should be made for exceptional individual circumstances. It is wrong to take refuge in the old saying that hard cases make bad law when it is clear that the strict application of regulations would defeat the educational purpose for which they are framed. It is therefore necessary to consider the kind of circumstances which merit individual consideration.

389. The wide variation in the maturation of children has been described in Chapter 2. A class of five year olds may not only have an age range of a year in chronological age but may also cover a span of two or three years in developmental age. As the child grows older, this span widens. A girl becomes an adolescent; the boy in the next seat remains a child. Teachers have to adopt an individual approach to each child in order to help a class of children at widely different stages of development even when the chronological range is narrow. Even so, there are a minority of children who, in all aspects of development, are so ahead of their contemporaries that they ought to work with older children.

390. Some authorities and schools rightly allow flexibility of transfer between the infant and junior stages for the minority of children who fall outside the normal range of maturation. There is, however, under the present law no provision for postponing the beginning of compulsory education where this would be desirable, and no provision even for attendance to be part-time at first for those children who would be the better for it. When the single date of entry is adopted there will be an even stronger case for flexibility. A mature child, who may be amongst the oldest in his nursery group, may well be ready before the others to go to school. He should be allowed the opportunity. Similarly, it may well be right for an immature child to remain an extra term in the nursery group.

391. We enquired how many children at present move from primary to secondary schools when they are either 10 or 12 instead of 11. The number is insignificant. Our National Survey showed only 44 under age and 10 over age transfers out of a total of some 20,000 children. Early transfers usually take place at the initiative of parent or teacher and depend on head teacher estimates, objective tests and in some instances on the opinion of the educational psychologist. Late transfers almost invariably follow a period of illness. The small amount of flexibility revealed by the National Sample cannot reflect accurately the wide variations in maturity which exist between individual children. We believe that there should be a greater number of early and late transfers, at each stage of education, based on consultations between teachers and parents. A margin of six months on either side of the official transfer age would probably cover the needs of all but a few children. Late transfers should be fewer than early. Only in exceptional circumstances is it right for a child to be kept back in a primary school after his friends leave. Occasionally it may be right to arrange a transfer in the course of a school year instead of waiting for the next autumn.

392. Our conclusions on the degree of discretion that should be allowed to parents and schools as to the ages of entry and of transfer are:—

(a) at least one year of part-time nursery education should be made available before compulsory education for those children whose parents wish it;

(b) children should be allowed to enter the first school at any date in the first half-term of the school year, subject to agreement between the parents and the head teacher;

(c) they should also be permitted to attend for a half day for the first term and, exceptionally, up to the age of six, at the request of parents in consultation with the head teacher;

(d) attendance at a nursery group by agreement between parents and school should be treated for the purposes of the Education Acts as full-time education for the first term to which the law of compulsory attendance applies;

(e) transfers to middle schools within a range of six months on either side of the normal age should be permitted by agreement between school and home. Great care should be taken to avoid isolating a backward or advanced child from his friends of the same age;

(f) the arrangements for transfer to middle schools should also apply at the next stage to secondary schools. There is a greater risk here that children who are intellectually advanced will be considered as necessarily ready for early transfer. Overall development should be taken into account when decisions are made;

(g) more flexibility than at present is needed, but its use should be exceptional if the primary and secondary schools increasingly cater for each child individually.

The Need for a National Policy
Why a Uniform Age of Transfer is Necessary

393. Government policy is directed towards creating a mobile labour force. Education must be awake to its implications, one of which is a single nation-wide age of transfer. We agree that this will take time to achieve, but the interim period should be as short as can be contrived. The inconveniences it will cause should not be tolerated for long. Two illustrations may be given. A child in moving home might find himself moving backwards educationally from full-time education in an infant school in an unreorganised area to part-time education in the reorganised system of his new home. Another older child in similar circumstances might have to transfer out of secondary education to a middle school in the primary system.

394. How frequently do families move home and children change schools? Most removals, of course, are local and do not result in a change of school; but our National Survey (Appendix 3, Section 3, paragraph 7) showed that nearly a quarter of the children at the top of the junior schools had changed schools because their families had moved to a different district. Eighteen per cent of the seven year olds in the N.C.D.S. Survey (Appendix 10, Table 73) had attended more than one school. Ministry of Labour statistics showed an increase in gross regional migration for employed persons from 505,000 in 1952, to 610,000 in 1964[7]. Many of these half million workers must have children of school age.

Making the Changes

395. We, therefore, recommend that the Department should announce as soon as possible a national policy on the structure of nursery and primary

education and that it should fix a date by which new ages of entry and transfer should become binding. We naturally hope that these decisions may follow our recommendations summarised in paragraph 392.

396. We believe that they reflect the balance of educational advantage, and that they are also the most practicable to carry out. We cannot be quite sure of this because, although we tried to make an estimate of the building costs of different ages of transfer, we were unable to extend it to secondary school building or to find out the extent to which individual existing buildings could be put to new uses. We do not therefore take this factor into account in deciding to recommend transfer at 12 instead of 13. It will be necessary for the Department and local education authorities to make a careful survey of all school buildings before they decide when changes in ages of transfer can be made nationally. We hope this will be put in hand at once.

397. Meanwhile, it is clear that authorities will have to make the best use they can of the buildings they have. In the rest of this chapter we are concerned with suggestions for this interim period for which the Department sanction local variants on the national plan. This interim period is bound to last until a great deal of building can be sanctioned for re-organisation. Some authorities may, and probably will, in the interval be forced to adopt a two tier system of secondary education with the lower tier devoted to children aged between 11 and 13. This should be recognised only as a purely temporary expedient. A two year school is not educationally sound, particularly at this stage of children's development. In the first year they will be settling down; in the second they will be getting ready to leave. There will be no time to become the school community which children of this age particularly value. Where such a school has to be introduced, the accent, especially in the first year, should be on the continuation and development of the ways of learning found in the best junior schools, carried out by teachers some with the deeper subject knowledge expected in secondary schools.

398. Small primary schools will probably be the hardest to fit into the new national pattern. Most of them are combined junior and infant schools; many of them are voluntary schools. In urban areas, some small schools might be amalgamated, and some sites would allow for additional building. But most of them are in the country and there are rural counties where two class schools are still usual. We consider the problems of rural schools in Chapter 14.

An Emergency Plan for Infant Schools

399. We have attached importance to the simultaneous introduction of nursery provision for all who want it and a single intake each year into the infant schools. Except in the educational priority areas we are afraid that these changes cannot come for ten or a dozen years until the late 1970s. Meanwhile, school conditions for young children grow worse. Even in 1963, 26 per cent of our special sample of infant starters (Appendix 6) entered classes over 40. In an increasing number of areas the rising fives are being excluded. The first batch to be excluded are the summer born children, because the summer term is when the infant school is most crowded.

400. A long day—there is no provision for part-time education—in a large class is no way to start school. Some measures must be designed to enable

children to start school part-time in small classes. We think that the worst effects of the present situation can be mitigated by the following arrangements:

(a) Children should begin full-time attendance at school twice a year, those reaching the age of five between February 1st and August 31st in the following September, at a median age of five years three months, and those reaching this age between September 1st and January 31st in the following April, at a median age of five years five months.

(b) Children should be obliged to attend school as now from the beginning of the term following their fifth birthday but those children not entitled by their date of birth to full-time education should attend one session only each day.

(c) Part-time education should be available at a morning or afternoon session, for two terms before full-time entry.

(d) For staffing and other purposes, part-time pupils would count as if they were full-time so that they could be taught in classes of half the normal size.

(e) As in our long-term proposals a child should be allowed to attend part-time, at the request of his parents, until he reaches the age of six. A change in the Schools Regulations would be necessary.

401. The way the plan would work is illustrated in Table 12. It should be compared with Table 11 which shows the present age of compulsory education.

Table 12 *Interim Plan for Entry to First Schools*

Month of Birth	Year 1			Year 2			Year 3			Junior School
	Term			Term			Term			Max. terms of school experience on promotion
	Autumn	Spring	Summer	Autumn	Spring	Summer	Autumn	Spring	Summer	
Sept–Jan	Age 4·7 — 5·0 *	Age 4/5 *	Age 5·3 — 5·8 **	Age 5+ **	Age 5/6 **	Age 6+ **	Age 6+ **	Age 6/7 **	Age 7+ **	9 (8 f.t. equiv.)
Feb–Aug.	—	Age 4·4 — 4·11 *	Age 4/5 *	Age 5·0 — 5·7 **	Age 5+ **	Age 5/6 **	Age 6+ **	Age 6+ **	Age 6/7 **	8 (7 f.t. equiv.)

* Optional half-time attendance in half classes.
** Compulsory full-time attendance in whole classes.

402. It will be seen that:

(a) no child whose parents take up the two term part-time option will get less than the equivalent of his present entitlement to full-time education, and some will get more;

(b) no child will get less full-time education than summer born children now get in areas which exclude "rising fives";

(c) no more teachers will be needed than at present;

(d) the eldest children in each half yearly intake will start full-time education a term later than they do at present;

(e) the average age of the second intake will be slightly lower than the first at the time of entry.

403. The scheme would also have the following advantages which, we think, entitle it to be regarded not only as an emergency salvage measure but as a foretaste of our permanent plan:

(a) it would introduce children to school part-time;

(b) it would reduce pressure on teachers of, and children in, admission classes;

(c) part-time schooling for the first two terms would make it easier to employ part-time teachers. Teachers' aides or nursery assistants could be introduced as they become available and thus a beginning made in establishing an adult/child ratio similar to that in nurseries. The scheme would help by providing a little additional space in schools;

(d) in the autumn term the teacher of the youngest children might be either:

(i) be a probationer who would thus start with a small class and could help with a small group of other children in the afternoon;

(ii) an experienced teacher who would then be free to help probationers or students in the afternoon;

(e) the first year would be a combination of nursery and infant work and would provide favourable conditions for children starting school;

(f) children starting school would not be faced with the added strain of attending school meals. By the time a child stayed he would be used to school.

404. Care should be taken to introduce children to school by preparatory visits and contacts in the way discussed in Chapter 12. This applies both to those who are going to start part-time and to those who will begin full-time.

405. We have stressed earlier the advantages of a three year course in the infant school. This scheme moves towards it. Yet we hope that, in the period before the general structure of primary and secondary education is changed, authorities will extend the infant course to a full three years from five to eight whenever buildings make this arrangement possible. This length of infant course should certainly be possible in authorities which are establishing middle schools as part of their plan for introducing comprehensive education.

Conclusion: A Change of Name

406. A new structure for primary education seems to us to make a change of names desirable. The parents of eight year olds will not want them called infants; 12 year olds, whose older brothers have been in the secondary school at that age, will object to being juniors. There will inevitably be a sense of being "kept down". We suggest "first school" for the five to eight age group and "middle school" for the eight to 12. Where a school serves all children from five to 12 we suggest that it should be called a "combined school". A nursery forming part of a first school might be called a "nursery group".

Long-Term Recommendations

407 (i) As soon as there is nursery provision for all children whose parents wish it, for a year before starting school, the normal time by which a child should go to school should be defined as the September term

following the fifth birthday. This would require legislation. Schools should be allowed to space admissions over the first half term of the year.

(ii) There should be a three year course in the first (at present the infant) school.

(iii) This should be followed by a four year course in the middle (at present the junior) school.

(iv) There should be flexibility in entry to school and in transfer between the stages of education to allow for the circumstances of individual pupils.

(v) Children should be allowed for the first term after the normal time of entry to attend a nursery group, if the parents wish, and may attend school for half a day only for the term or until their sixth birthday, if this is later than the end of the term, at the request of parents.

(vi) The Department should announce as soon as possible a national policy on the structure of nursery and primary education and on the ages of transfer from stage to stage and should fix a date by which these should become binding.

Interim Recommendations

(vii) Until this date children should begin whole-day attendance at school twice a year, those reaching the age of five between February 1st and August 31st in the following September, and those reaching five between September 1st and January 31st in the following April. This would also require legislation which should permit staggered admissions over half a term.

(viii) Part-time attendance should be available at a morning or afternoon session for up to two terms before full-time entry. Exceptionally, a child should be allowed to attend part-time at the request of his parents until he reaches the age of six.

(ix) The same flexibility in arrangements for starting school should be allowed in exceptional cases as is proposed for the long term in paragraphs (iv) and (v) above.

REFERENCES

[1] Williams, P., 'Date of Birth, Backwardness and Educational Organisation', Brit. Journ. Ed. Psychol., Nov. 1964.

[2] Jinks, P. C., 'An Investigation into the Effect of Date of Birth on Subsequent School Performance', Educational Research, Vol. VI, No. 3, page 220.

[3] Nightingale, T. W., 'The May to August Births', Journal of the Durham Institute of Education, Nov. 1962.

[4] Armstrong, H. G., 'Special Educational Treatment in the Ordinary Schools', Brit. Journ. Ed. Psychol., June 1965, Vol. XXXV, Part 2.

[5] Morris, J. M., 'Reading in the Primary School', 1959, Newnes.

[6] Nisbet, J. D. and Entwistle, N. J., 'The Age of Transfer to Secondary Education', Univ. of London Press Ltd., 1966.

[7] Ministry of Labour Gazette, July 1965. Table 2, page 300 and information provided by the Ministry of Labour.

CHAPTER 11

Selection for Secondary Education

408. When the Council began their work, the future of selective secondary education was still uncertain. Strong trends against it had been apparent for some time. In 1964, an N.F.E.R. analysis[1] of local authority practices in the allocation of pupils to secondary schools showed that all but 29 per cent of local authorities had established—or intended to establish—one or more comprehensive schools. Many authorities were showing less interest in allocation procedures because they intended to change the educational system which made them necessary. Comprehensive education is now the declared policy of the Government. In July 1965 local authorities were invited to submit plans for reorganising their secondary schools on a non-selective basis.

409. But the less enterprising primary schools are what they now are partly, at least, because of the influence of the selective system and it is not yet clear how soon and how completely authorities will abandon selection. For these reasons this chapter assesses briefly the various methods of selection and their impact and discusses the use of objective tests.

410. Before, however, we turn to the future, we think it right to recall the intentions of those who introduced methods of selection. Their aim was fundamentally egalitarian. It was to open the doors of the grammar schools to children of high ability irrespective of their social background. For the first 20 years after Hadow the problem was often to persuade working class parents to take up the "free places" their children had won. For the last 20 years, however, the 11 plus has shut off from grammar schools many who wanted to go there and whose subsequent careers have shown that they would have profited from the opportunity.

Impact of Selection Procedures

411. A number of our witnesses thought that both the fact of selection and the way it is carried out made parents and children anxious, and that secondary modern schools had to contend with a sense of failure in their pupils. Definite evidence is difficult to obtain. The results of an enquiry made by the British Psychological Society into strain in children aged about 11 were inconclusive[2]. Though some children are certainly worried this seems often to be the result of their parents' or teacher's anxieties rather than their own. The number of complaints from parents to the Department about errors in selection has declined recently. The growing opportunities offered by G.C.E. courses in secondary modern schools probably explain why parents are complaining less often about selection.

412. It is said that selection procedures lead to a narrowing of the primary school curriculum, an excessive emphasis on the acquisition of measurable skills and rigid streaming. Yet an assessment by H.M. Inspectors of the ill effects of selection in schools in the National Survey suggested that these effects were lessening, perhaps because teachers' estimates were tending to replace externally imposed attainment tests. Inquiries were also made into the

quality of primary school work in areas where comprehensive schools have been set up or where testing has been replaced by teachers' estimates. Not surprisingly, some teachers continue their established routines when the reason for them has disappeared. The books of English exercises and of mechanical computation remain in many schools. But when there is encouragement from local advisers and when refresher courses coincide with the disappearance of formal selection arrangements, the work of the junior schools is liberated.

Selection Procedures

413. In the past 50 years persistent efforts have been made to refine methods of selection. As a result the World Survey of Education in 1962[3] commented that "Great Britain has made the greatest advance . . . in developing reliable and valued methods of testing and examining scholastic aptitude and ability. Few countries . . . have yet adopted such reliable methods of standardising or normalising the marks in assessments used for selection purposes." Any substantial further improvement in accuracy is unlikely. When the best available methods are used, the number of children likely to be misplaced varies between ten per cent and 20 per cent of the total number of children transferred, depending on whether accuracy is defined in relation to achievement at 13 or 16. This estimate of error does not take account of the fact that selection procedures may create the future they predict. The reputation, good or bad, which a pupil earns by his performance at 11 tends to influence what his teachers and parents expect from him in the future and what he feels he can do. Boys and girls tend to live up to, or down to, their reputations.

414. The methods of selection most commonly used consist of:—

   (i) a battery of standardised verbal ability and attainment tests;

   (ii) teachers' estimates scaled by verbal reasoning tests;

   (iii) teachers' estimates scaled by a study of borderland cases and feed back of information from the secondary school.

415. The N.F.E.R., in their enquiry in Twickenham in 1956[4], found the greatest accuracy was achieved when account was taken both of attainment tests and of the head teacher's order of merit scaled by the results of an intelligence test. Nevertheless, the order of merit was the best single predictor. Only a slight reduction in accuracy was caused by leaving attainment tests out of the calculation. This loss of accuracy must be weighed against the effects of externally imposed attainment tests on the curriculum of the primary school. Some teachers undoubtedly prepare for attainment tests and give this preparation undue weight in the curriculum. Some authorities try to reduce the backwash on the curriculum of standardised attainment tests by including English composition in the tests, or by new English tests which allow a greater freedom of response than did earlier types. Arithmetic tests have been constructed in which speed and computation are reduced in importance and items included which attempt to measure understanding. Although these tests are improvements they will not allow enough freedom to primary teachers if they are externally imposed. We conclude that where selection procedures continue to be used, a slight loss of accuracy is better than the risk of a harmful backwash on the curriculum, and that externally imposed attainment tests should be abandoned.

416. Another selection method uses teachers' estimates calibrated by a verbal reasoning test. An intelligence test is taken in all schools and the result decides the number of grammar school places allocated to each primary school, which are then filled in the head teacher's rank order. The use of an intelligence test, even if only as a calibrator, is likely to cause undue attention to be given to practice which can improve performance. The more effective the coaching, the more it nullifies the purpose of giving the tests. Where intelligence tests continue to be used as calibrators, great care should be taken in presenting the scheme to parents and teachers so that they understand its purpose and do not try to increase school quotas by coaching at home or at school.

417. An alternative method of calibration rests upon two observations. In the first place, although different primary schools get different proportions of grammar school places, the proportion awarded to the same school in different years does not vary much. Secondly, a comparison of secondary school form orders shows that some primary schools produce "improvers", who do better than those with the same marks from neighbouring schools. Other schools produce "deteriorators", who do worse. The Thorne system, so called from the neighbourhood where it was first tried, was designed to take account of these two observations. An initial quota of selective places is given to each primary school and is generally based on the results of the previous three years. The accuracy of this figure for the current year is checked by a careful investigation of all borderland pupils undertaken by a panel of head teachers. A further check is provided by the feed back of information from the secondary schools to the primary schools. The purpose of this system is to avoid distortion of the primary school curriculum by dispensing with an externally imposed test. It achieves this object without loss of accuracy. It is acceptable to teachers and parents and has led to co-operation between primary and secondary schools. We are impressed by its advantages and hope that authorities which continue to use selection procedures will study its merits.

418. Selection at 11 is coming to an end, a trend we welcome in view of the difficulty of making right decisions and the effect of selection on the curriculum in primary schools. This does not, however, get rid of the need for an assessment of primary school pupils before they leave. The comprehensive school has decisions to make about the work suitable for individual pupils, and for this it needs guidance from the primary schools which children have been attending. The alternative of setting tests to children as soon as they arrive in their new school is deplorable. As one head teacher said "I found I was testing what children had forgotten in the holidays". There should therefore be some assessment of a child before he leaves his primary school. Should this be based on achievements in a single year or throughout the primary course? Because decisions based exclusively on tests taken on a single occasion have been thought unjust, some authorities, and some teachers in their estimates, have been led to rely on children's performance from the age of seven onwards. The effect may be to turn an 11 plus into a seven plus, an age at which some children may know more just because they have been longer at school. The earlier the origin of the information about children, the more likely it is to be obsolete at 11. Teachers should not make premature judgements about children's achievement, and so help to create the response

in children which they expect. A further point is particularly relevant to teachers' estimates. If parental occupation is taken into account in assessment procedures, their predictive accuracy is improved. This might be taken to suggest a debit or penalty for poor parental backing because children from poor homes tend to do less well. The ability of a child as known to its teachers should not in our opinion be written down because his parents may in the future fail to encourage him. In Chapter 4 we have discussed ways in which this risk can be reduced and parents brought to a deeper participation in their children's education. Here we are concerned only with the assessment of children from varying social backgrounds.

419. Teachers, who, whatever their origins, tend to have middle class values, have a difficult task in assessing correctly the children of unskilled workers, partly because they speak a different language and have different conventions, and partly because a smaller proportion of these children can count on informed parental backing. There is a risk that their potential may be under-estimated because their actual achievement is not seen in relation to their starting point. No test with predictive value can be "culture free", but a non verbal intelligence test is a sensible check to use on impressions gained from attainments in class work or verbal tests.

420. Teachers who have to interpret test results need to bear in mind that a child's achievement is always in a given setting, in a particular school and with an individual teacher or teachers, so that an attainment test may predict imperfectly what will follow changes of situation and possible changes of motivation. Those who use tests should realise that there is a greater possibility of error in the test assessment of an individual than of a group, that tests are valuable only if they are standardised on a sufficiently representative sample and that the intelligence which is measured varies according to the test used (see Chapter 2). They should also realise that intelligence and attainment tests may be biased in favour of girls or of boys and that they must be suited to the age of children for whom they are being used. As the 11+ tests disappear, the internal use of tests may increase and it becomes even more important that teachers should be well-informed about them.

421. It is usual to welcome the over-achiever, the child whose achievement runs beyond his apparent ability. That there should also be under-achievers is statistically inevitable. When they are recognised teachers should consider whether changes of attitude and fresh stimulus from the school are called for. Information about under-achievement should always be passed on from class to class and school to school.

422. Teachers who want to compare their pupils with those from other schools, as will become more necessary with the disappearance of selection examinations, can use, in their own school, group intelligence and attainment tests or ask for a feed back of information from secondary schools, as in the Thorne Scheme. They may also wish, on occasion, to use tests for individual pupils about whose work they are worried. At this time of rapid change in the curriculum, the means of assessment of progress are almost bound to lag behind. We hope that attention can now be diverted from the design of tests for the purpose of selection to the development of tests suited to the changing primary curriculum, and helpful to teachers who need to diagnose children's difficulties in learning. Teachers themselves might devise tests, of an objective type, based on the concepts which they wish their pupils to form in such

subjects as mathematics. Tests which would help teachers to recognise inventiveness and originality would also be valuable. Although tests are useful, there is some danger of spending too much time on testing, at the expense of teaching.

Recommendations

423. (i) Authorities who for an interim period continue to need selection procedures should cease to rely on an externally imposed battery of intelligence and attainment tests.

(ii) Further work is needed on tests for use by teachers in the context of the changing curriculum.

REFERENCES

[1]Local Authority Practices in the Allocation of Pupils to Secondary Schools, N.F.E.R , 1964.
[2]'Secondary School Selection'. British Psychological Society, 1957.
[3]World Survey of Education, 1962, U.N.E.S.C.O.
[4]Secondary School Selection N.F.E.R., 1956.

CHAPTER 12

Continuity and Consistency between the Stages of Education

Home to School

424. This chapter is mainly about what ought to happen when a child passes from one school to another, but it must start with a different kind of transition—from home to school. The relation between these two halves of a child's life is so obviously of fundamental importance that it will recur at intervals throughout this chapter just as it does throughout the whole Report. In Chapter 10 we suggest that admissions to the first school ought to be staggered over half a term so that each child and each child's mother can be separately welcomed and made to feel at home. It ought not to be just a matter of bringing a child to school, but of placing him in a co-operative undertaking in which teacher and mother both have parts to play. Over half the schools in the National Survey made no special arrangements. Nearly half said they were not free to do so. Our recommendation then is not just a pious approval of an all but universal practice. Neither is it a shot in the dark. In the autumn of 1963 a third of the schools in the National Survey did not expect their new children all to start school on the first day of term—12 schools spent three days in welcoming the newcomers, four spent over a week and nine a fortnight or more. Another six said five year olds were free to join any day in the term they became five, and four that children entered in the week of their fifth birthday. This was a very thorough form of staggering. When only one yearly intake is in force there will be even greater need to stagger admissions, and they will have to be spread over a longer time.

425. But welcoming a child is more than a matter of reserving proper time to attend to him. It is the quality of the welcome and the imaginative insight given to it which counts. H.M. Inspectors told us what they thought of the way in which this was done in the infant and junior mixed and infant schools in the National Survey. Over a third showed themselves resourceful and enterprising in what they did. A sixth were poor. The kind of things that impressed the inspectors, and they seem right to us, were invitations to mothers and children to spend some time in the children's first class before admission, encouragement to mothers to stay with children who are anxious during the first few days at school, welcoming letters to parents with suggestions on how to help their children to make a successful start, and meetings for discussion between the school staff and the parents of five year olds. Satisfactory contacts with homes are one of the strengths of the village school. "In this small, friendly favoured village where the headmaster and his colleagues know every family well," one report ran, "there are simply no problems or difficulties. Each individual parent has a chat with the headmaster at some time; young children sometimes come to a school function; but nothing specifically planned is called for." Given a good staff, this happens naturally in a village; even given a good staff, it has to be industriously contrived if it is to happen in the anonymous society of a city.

158

Separate or Combined Schools

426. The next problem of continuity arises now at the age of seven, and will occur at eight if our recommendations are accepted. Ought there to be separate first and middle schools, or are combined schools better? One of the strengths of English education has been its sense of community, which is hardly possible if the age range is very wide and the numbers too large for children to know one another. It is proper that schools for the youngest children should emphasise individual play and learning, and that schools for somewhat older children should make the most of their tendency to go about in groups. Research evidence on the relative merits of combined and separate junior and infant schools is inconclusive[1], but experienced observers say that outstanding work by seven year olds is more frequent in separate infant schools. Teachers in separate junior and infant schools have been able to concentrate on educating children who are at different stages of developments. All schools tend to over value their oldest pupils, by whom the success of the school is usually judged. This tells against a school with an age span so wide that there is almost bound to be a conflict between the interests of the oldest and youngest children. We have suggested that the age of transfer to secondary education should be raised to 12. We doubt whether a single school can provide entirely satisfactorily for children from five (or three if there are nursery groups) to 12. If the school is intimate enough for the youngest children, it is unlikely to justify a staff varied enough in their abilities and interests to meet the needs of the older children. We conclude that the most suitable organisation of primary schools is in separate first and middle schools, though a combined organisation may be necessary in rural areas and for some voluntary schools.

Avoiding Strain at Time of Transfer

427. Children, like adults, enjoy and are stimulated by novelty and change. The first day at school, the transfer to the "big school", are landmarks in the process of growing up. Even when children are apprehensive, they look forward to change, the man teacher, the "terribly hard work" of the junior school, the new subjects in the secondary school. They exaggerate and boast about the difference from the "kids" place where everything was easy. So strong is the myth that "going up" must mean going to something better that some children, who are hopelessly bewildered by secondary school work, persist in saying that all is well. But if change is to stimulate and not to dishearten, it must be carefully prepared and not too sudden. The new school must know enough of the old school's ways to carry on where it left off, and neither to repeat what is already known nor to jump unthinkingly ahead.

428. The disadvantage of separate schools is that they lack the natural contacts between infant and junior teachers in the staff room of a combined school. Contacts between separate schools have to be cultivated instead of being spontaneous, and indeed unavoidable. The evidence is that they are not cultivated enough, though H.M. Inspectors' enquiries in connection with the National Survey show that there is a real improvement. The gulf between junior and secondary teachers is even wider, though there is some evidence that as selection procedure with its standardised information about pupils declines, more secondary school head teachers are coming to primary schools for information.

429. Primary and secondary school teachers not only need to know each other, but to know each other's work. This is something that can greatly be helped if they are trained together in the same colleges. Colleges of education have been developing groups deliberately designed to overlap two stages of education, infant-junior, and junior-secondary groups catering for teachers of children of 5 to 9 and 9 to 13. Great as is the need for colleges of education to train more primary teachers, an increase would be bought too dearly if it meant that almost all secondary teachers were trained in universities, and the separation already evident in the present system made even more acute.

430. In spite of their training, teachers in the admission classes of infant schools may try to press on with reading, the teachers of the lower juniors to bring all eight year olds up to the same level and the teachers in the lower forms of secondary schools to begin to think of preparing children at 11 for the long road to external examination. It is after a few years' service that there is need for radical in-service training. It is then that nursery and infant class teachers can most profit from discussion of play for children, that infant and junior teachers need to share their views on the work that is possible between six and eight (and we hope later, between seven and nine); and that junior and lower secondary school teachers can discover that both have found that "how" rather than "why" is what interests their pupils. Groups of primary and secondary teachers who belong to the same subject associations or are taking part in the same Nuffield projects can learn much from one another. The primary teachers need the subject knowledge of the specialists; the secondary teachers can profit from hearing of the astonishing standards some children reach in some primary schools.

Contacts Between Teachers in Successive Stages of Education

431. Neither initial nor in-service training is a substitute for personal contact between the primary school teacher who taught a boy in the summer term and the secondary school teacher who will look after him in the autumn term. These contacts are often difficult to arrange. Though many schools share common sites, many are isolated from the schools that contribute to them and those to which their children go. There are more than mechanical difficulties to face. Schools are shy of one another. The secondary or junior head may fear that his junior or infant colleagues may suspect interference: the feeling that to teach younger children is somehow inferior often makes the infant teacher diffident about approaching the junior head, the junior head uneasy about inviting the secondary head to his school. These are human weaknesses. Authorities and professional organisations should help teachers to overcome them. It is important for the children that they should. Given the will, many forms of working together are possible, as we have seen from our enquiries. The children who are due to go up are sometimes visited not only by the head of their new school but also, which is more immediately important to them, by their future class teacher. There are schools where joint meetings of the two staffs are held to discuss work and policy. Occasionally a teacher moves up with her class from the infant school and remains their class teacher in the junior school. The same policy is rare, but not unknown, in the transition from junior school to secondary. But many contacts are of the formal kind that consist in visiting other schools for speech days and other ceremonial occasions that give little opportunity for conversation about individual pupils.

There are schools which work side by side in almost total ignorance of one another. We have heard of a teacher who had been taking the youngest class in the junior school for a number of years but who did not know, even by sight, the deputy head of the infant school who was normally responsible for the oldest class. Such instances may be exceptional; but where schools live in enclosed worlds the local education authority might close the schools in the area for one day and arrange a conference for the teachers to establish some footing on which the schools can work together in equal partnership.

432. In some districts parent-teacher associations serving a group of schools have strengthened the bonds between school and home and between schools. In other districts an overlap in the membership of governing and managing bodies has proved useful. There are large secondary schools where contact with contributory primary schools is one of the most important responsibilities of the head of the lower school. One selective school holds an annual conference with its contributory primary school head teachers. The secondary form masters enquire about their new pupils and the primary heads see and discuss the reports on their former pupils. The primary school staff are told about proposed changes in the secondary school curriculum and are invited to comment.

Interchange of Knowledge of Pupils

433. Most of the information which a secondary school needs about individual pupils ought to be put into writing. After the war a type of record card was popular which asked for so much information, most of it assessed on a five point scale, that many teachers found it took far too much time to complete. They also questioned the reliability of assessments of personality characteristics, recognising that children may behave differently with different teachers. Some information asked for was, they felt, too confidential to be committed to a record card. There was often a feeling that children should be given a fresh start and not saddled with a bad name.

434. As a result many authorities shortened and simplified their record cards. Differences in the use made of information are as great as those in the amount and kind sent on. In some schools, records remain in the head teacher's room and are never seen by class teachers unless a special problem arises. But the person who needs nine tenths of the information to do his job is the class teacher.

435. It is time that new thought was given to both sides of the exchange. We think the authorities might well call area conferences of teachers to discuss the information that is passed on and the use that is made of it, and draw up proposals for the future. Our own suggestion is that there should be a folder for each child containing:

   (i) medical records—at present not always seen by head teachers and rarely seen by class teachers;

   (ii) facts about illness, absence from school, and composition of the family;

   (iii) results of intelligence tests with a note on the test used and interpretation;

   (iv) results of attainment tests and, where necessary, of diagnostic tests;

(v) examples of the child's work and the names of some of the books he has read;

(vi) full notes of personal handicaps or special gifts;

(vii) possibly a pen picture of the child.

436. The material in the folder could provide a basis for the regular review with parents of children's progress, and notes on these discussions might be added. For the majority of children and schools, entries under (i) and (ii) will be brief and those under (iii) and (iv) will not begin till the upper junior school. The time gained by this brevity might be spent on detailed comment in special cases. Some authorities may prefer to use a record card to collect information under (ii), (iii) and (iv). If they do, teachers should be encouraged to make comments only where they have something to say. Full value will not be gained from the folders unless they are available to class teachers in junior schools and to form teachers or personal tutors in secondary schools*.

437. Written records are only of limited value unless the writers know one another, and feel free to ask supplementary questions with confidence that they will be answered. A teacher who has finished a folder and sent it on to the next school does not lose interest in the child he has taught. It is not idle curiosity, and the desire to know how former pupils are getting on in their new schools ought to be satisfied. If the new school takes the trouble to let the old school know, it is likely to get even more useful information about future intakes partly because the teacher who is completing a folder will know that the information is being used, and partly because he will gradually find out what is specially worth reporting.

Introducing Pupils to New Schools

438. When schools are near one another, children are often invited to plays and other functions. Visits are also often arranged in the term before transfer. Towards the end of the summer term in one school, each third year junior is encouraged to befriend one of the infants, to take him on a tour of the junior school building and to help him find his way around in the first few days after he moves up. In another school, junior teachers take their future classes from the infant school to see where they will work next term. They talk to them about the excitements that await them as juniors, and tell them which door to come in on the first day, where to hang their coats and other details about which children often worry.

439. Some secondary schools invite new entrants to spend half a day in the school in the term before entry. Another proved device is for new pupils to come a day before the rest so that they can explore the building, meet the staff, and get their books and time-tables in relative peace. By the second day they can begin to work in earnest. A prompt start helps morale. There is some evidence that transition to secondary schools is particularly difficult for pupils from small primary schools. To overcome this in one rural area, top juniors from small primary schools work half a day a week in the local secondary school. The effect has been to familiarise them with the school to

---

*In France, the "dossier scolaire" includes much the same information. It is used at the end of the primary school course and again at the end of the "cycle d'observation" for making decisions on the course best suited to a pupil in the secondary school.

which they will transfer, to enrich the curriculum of ten year olds in small country schools, and to build a bridge between primary and secondary education. Where schools are far apart, these introductory devices are more difficult to arrange but also far more important then for those schools which are close together. For the children from a remote country school, going to a new school is an adventure into a strange land. All children should make at least one visit to their new school in the term before they transfer.

Support from Parents

440. Children need an extra measure of support from their parents when they change schools, and not only when they go to their first school. Some junior heads, in the term before children enter, invite parents to a meeting to see the school, hear about its activities and meet the staff. Sometimes this meeting is associated with an open day for the younger classes, an arrangement which works well enough, provided that time is left for the teachers to meet the parents both of the newcomers and of those who are already there.

441. It would be helpful if all authorities adopted the practice already followed by some and sent parents a leaflet explaining the choice of available secondary schools and the courses provided within them. The leaflet might also, as is very rarely done, prepare parents for the differences between primary and secondary education. But a personal contact is always more valuable. In some primary schools a meeting is held in the summer term for parents of fourth year pupils, which is attended by the heads of the secondary schools to which pupils will be transferring. Many secondary schools send parents details of school routine and arrange meetings and personal interviews for them with the head master and masters or mistresses of junior forms. In some schools further meetings are organised early in the school year at which parents' problems can be raised. There is no one ideal pattern for these arrangements but all secondary schools need to meet the parents of new entrants. Fathers are as easily interested as mothers and feel they have something of their own to contribute.

Consistency in Work and Organisation

442. Some years ago, H.M. Inspectors, looking at the work being done by children before and after transition to the junior school, felt that three to six months after transfer there was a narrowing of opportunities, a tendency towards regimentation and a substitution of group or even class teaching for individual work. Many children tackled less difficult work and wrote less in their own words than they had done some months before. The libraries in the youngest junior classes were often inferior in quality and range to those the children had left behind in the top infant classes, and children spent more time on "readers" and less on library books. Individual interests in music and art and craft had petered out. Some boys whose ability and attendance were average or poor had fallen back in almost every respect when seen four months after transfer. They made little perceptible headway by the end of the year.

443. It is possible that conditions have improved in the last two or three years as an increasing number of junior schools have adopted a more liberal approach to the curriculum. But the National Survey shows (Appendix 5)

that nearly a third of the first year junior classes were taught by beginners Where the first year was streamed, there was a tendency, confirmed by the N.F.E.R. streaming survey, (Appendix 11, Section II, Table XI), to put the weakest teacher with the least able children, perhaps because this was the smallest class. The contrast between the education provided in the infant school and the junior school is often accentuated because it is frequently the deputy head who teaches the older infants. Some of the difficulties we have described will be reduced if children are transferred, as we recommend at eight. It will still be necessary to ensure that there is no sharp break between "infant" and "junior" methods, and to see, whenever possible, that weak teachers are not made responsible for children who are adjusting to a new school. One study of a small sample of children suggests that refusals to attend school reach a peak at the age of eight[2].

444. There is even more danger of setbacks and standstill at the transition from primary to secondary schools. They are particularly demoralising to 11 year olds who expect transfer to a secondary school to bring the challenge of new work. Sometimes a secondary school draws from so many primary schools that it is extremely difficult for it to know much about all of them. But real knowledge of the work at the top of a few primary schools enables secondary schools teachers to know what they ought to expect, to set their sights high for able children and lower for others. In this way all the newcomers benefit, whether or not their form master knows the school from which a child comes.

445. In the primary school the class teacher knows all about each child's work and can, if he likes, provide plentiful opportunities for pupils to work on their own, in groups or as a whole class. A secondary school run on specialist lines is not in the same position. Nobody knows, except by hearsay, about a child's work in all subjects. For this reason many secondary schools have less specialist teaching in the first year or two years and try to see that the form master or mistress teaches the form for at least one period a day. Other devices such as "tutor sets" are introduced to try to offset the difficulties caused by specialist teaching. It is outside our province to consider the methods of working in secondary schools but we wish to record our belief that 12 and even 13 year olds need to be taught by teachers whom they really know and who really know them, however this is secured. We have received evidence that this does not happen enough at present.

Content of Curriculum

446. Not unexpectedly, it is the new subject with new equipment which beginners in the secondary school most often enjoy. Disappointment is more usually expressed with work in the fields of study already familiar from the primary school, in which many secondary teachers involuntarily or deliberately repeat work that has already been attempted. The secondary schools are in a difficult position in that, despite tradition and other influences, there may be big differences of content and method even from one primary school to another in the same area. Increased opportunities for individual work in secondary schools could reduce the overlap in children's work before and after transfer. Some revision is due to the mistaken hope that repetition in, for example, computation will lead to perfect accuracy. Similarly, there is a

tendency for schools to go back to the Stone Age in history and to return to the British Isles in geography. These are deliberate, if mistaken, overlaps which will only be abandoned as teachers realise that they lead to boredom. Accidental overlaps such as the use of the same text books in history and geography at the top of the primary school and the bottom of the secondary school could readily be avoided by discussion between primary and secondary teachers and a study of pupils' records. It is particularly unfortunate when the same literature is read in successive years, when there are so many books of quality suitable for children. English secondary schools have an international reputation for their school libraries, but in some schools too little provision is made for the younger children who may have a poorer choice of books than they had in their primary schools. Collaboration often occurs when new subjects or new perspectives in subjects become common in primary schools. The introduction of a foreign language in primary schools has led to discussion of the development of language teaching in both primary and secondary stages. Similar collaboration has come from recent changes in mathematics and science teaching. But unless joint discussions continue, the new primary school subjects will add to the opportunities for stale repetition.

447. No magic changes six, seven and eight year olds from infants to juniors as they move from one school to the next. They are the same children. Children of 10, 11 and 12 are not transformed by entering the secondary school. Changes bring setbacks as well as stimulus. The solution lies in close professional contacts, not only between head teachers but also between all who teach children on either side of the frontiers, which should not be barriers, that divide school from school.

Recommendations

448. (i) Mothers and children should spend some time in the school and class before admission, and mothers stay with children when necessary during the first few days at school. Meetings between staff and parents should be arranged.

 (ii) The most suitable organisation of primary education is in separate first and middle schools, though combined schools may be necessary in rural areas and for some voluntary schools.

 (iii) The initial and in-service training of teachers should overlap more than one stage of education.

 (iv) There should be a variety of contacts between teachers in successive stages of education.

 (v) Local education authorities should close schools for one day to arrange conferences for teachers, when there is evidence of lack of contact between those in successive stages.

 (vi) Authorities should call area conferences of teachers to consider the information passed on within the primary stage and from primary to secondary schools and the use made of it.

 (vii) There should be a detailed folder on each child which could provide a basis for a regular review with children's parents of their progress. The folders should accompany the child into the middle and secondary schools and should be available to the child's class or form teacher. Information about former pupils should be sent back from secondary to primary schools.

(viii) All children should make at least one visit to their new school in the term before they transfer.

(ix) Authorities should send parents a leaflet explaining the choice of secondary schools available and the courses provided within them.

(x) All secondary schools should make arrangements to meet the parents of new entrants.

(xi) There should be no sharp break between infant or first and junior or middle school methods. In allocating staff, heads should try to avoid giving responsibility to a weak member of staff for children adjusting to a new school.

(xii) Discussions should be held between primary and secondary teachers to avoid overlap in such matters as text books and to discuss pupils' records.

REFERENCES

[1] D. A. Pidgeon. School Type Difference in Ability and Attainment. Educational Research, June, 1959.

[2] T. Moore. Difficulties of the Ordinary Child in Adjusting to Primary School. Journal of Child Psychiatry and Psychology, 1966.

CHAPTER 13

The Size of Primary Schools

449. The size of primary schools is determined in large measure by the distribution of population and by other circumstances in the community or area which they serve. Most small schools are in the country or in urban areas where the population is falling. Rural schools and their sizes are treated in the following chapter. Many small schools both in town and country are voluntary schools and their size must depend on the number of children for whom a denominational school can be shown to be needed. Substantial changes in the size of existing schools are not likely in the near future since most schools must continue to use their present buildings. Yet many new primary schools will have to be built and it may be possible to reorganise existing schools. It is, therefore, of value to discuss the most satisfactory size of school. Though our evidence was necessarily based on schools as they now are, we have made suggestions for the sizes of schools in the various age ranges which we recommend.

The Existing Situation

450. Table 8 shows the different size of primary schools in England in January 1965. It will be seen from it that:

(a) most infant schools have between 100 and 300 children on the roll;

(b) just under half of the junior with infant schools have fewer than 100 children on roll;

(c) nearly one third of all primary schools, including all age schools of which only a few remain, have 100 or fewer children on roll. They contain, however, only about 12 per cent of the primary school population;

(d) junior schools, which are concentrated in urban areas, tend to be larger than junior mixed and infant schools.

Suitable Sizes of Schools for Primary Children

451. Most witnesses who expressed an opinion favoured schools small enough for children to move freely about the buildings without anxiety, and to get to know the adults and many of the children. It is difficult to be sure whether the youngest children are aware of the total size of the school community, particularly if their part of the building is separated from that used by the older children. Witnesses held that primary schools should be of a size in which the head and other teachers can know children as individuals. A study of the incidence of delinquency in primary schools in a large urban area[1] suggests that there is rather less delinquency in smaller schools, when allowance is made for the neighbourhood. Heads of the special group of "schools in the slums" studied in the Newsom report thought this to be so.

452. Witnesses believe—and we concur with their view—that schools should be small enough for heads to know parents personally and to involve them in the work and life of the school. Whether parents visit a school frequently

will depend partly on its distance from their homes. Distance also matters to children, who should not be expected cross busy roads, particularly if it is difficult to provide traffic wardens at all dangerous crossings.

453. Witnesses also agree that schools should, when possible, be large enough to justify a staff with varied gifts, and to permit a flexible organisation which does not force classes with a wide age range on teachers who are not convinced of their value. At the same time, schools should be small enough for a head to be able to give effective leadership to their staff and, in particular, to inexperienced teachers, and for the staff to work together as a team without too formal an organisation.

454. The evidence of research about the attainments of children in schools of varying size is inconclusive. Studies of reading in Kent[2] showed that reading attainments were higher in larger schools. The Manchester Primary School Study (see Appendix 9) found a similar correlation between size of school and attainment. The authors of both these studies are aware that the larger schools are found in those areas where parents tend to belong to higher socio-economic groups than are characteristic of communities where the schools are small. The National Survey shows that, when other factors are held constant, no clear relationship emerges between size of school and attainment in reading.

455. The advice of almost all our witnesses is that, with the present age range and class size, two form entry junior or infant schools and one form entry junior mixed and infant schools are the most satisfactory. This amounts to about 240 children in an infant school, about 320 in a school for juniors only and 280 for a combined junior mixed and infant school. Advice from the Department to local authorities in recent years has been on this basis and has usually been followed in the building of urban schools. We have analysed by size a list of schools of especial distinction compiled by H.M. Inspectors. The proportion of schools on this list, which are of the sizes commended by our evidence, exceeds markedly the national proportion of schools of these sizes. The excess of good schools occurred in each type of primary school— junior mixed and infant, junior, and infant schools. It is also interesting that the proportion of schools in the National Survey which were rated average and above average was rather higher in schools of 200–350 pupils than in larger or smaller schools (Appendix 5, paragraph 8 and Table 5).

456. Almost alone among our witnesses the L.C.C. (now the I.L.E.A.)[·] while in favour of variety in size and organization of school, recommended experiments in schools of up to 500 children aged five to 11, and saw no overriding argument against infant schools of 360 and junior schools of 480, if other circumstances, such as the area of the sites, made this possible. They believed that there were advantages in the varying gifts of a large staff and in the wider range of equipment available in a big school. Larger schools can absorb a higher proportion of men teachers and can reduce the demand for women in positions of responsibility. This is an important point since there are few applications from women for headships or posts of responsibility. The L.C.C. also thought that the promotion prospects created by large schools might attract more men into primary schools. In common with most of our witnesses, they preferred for urban areas a school which admits at least one form each year and makes possible classes which contain one year

group only. Finally, they suggested that, in schools which are bigger than one form entry, the annual entry was less likely to vary so much that there would have to be children from more than one age group in a class.

Economic Arguments

457. In making a decision on the most satisfactory size of schools, local education authorities have to take into account the cost of building and maintenance, of transport and of staffing, both in manpower and in money. These economic factors are relevant to this and the following chapter.

458. The cost limits for building new schools allow more for each pupil in small than in large schools. It is assumed that classes with wide age ranges need to be smaller than classes with a narrow age range, and this assumption is made explicit in the Building Regulations, which provide for two teaching spaces (or classrooms) to be built for 26–50 children, three for 51–80 children, four for 81–130 children and five for 131–160 children. It is therefore more economical to build larger schools. As Table 13 shows, the rate of savings diminishes in schools which have more than 280 pupils. Smaller savings are not negligible, however, at a time when many schools need to be replaced or improved, and when education must compete with other equally important services for its share of money and labour for building.

Table 13 Cost Limits for Different Size of Primary Schools ! June 1966

Pupils Numbers	Cost per pupil £
50 pupils on roll	285
100 pupils on roll	266
180 pupils on roll	221
280 pupils on roll	193
320 pupils on roll	190
360 pupils on roll	185·5
400 pupils on roll	180·5
480 pupils on roll	174

459. We examined the relationship between the major running costs of a sample of 81 primary schools and their size and age. Building maintenance costs were shown to be related to the age of the school, but not to its size. Cleaning and caretaking costs per pupil showed some tendance to rise with increases in the size of school, and fuel and lighting some tendency to fall, but none of these costs was related to the age of the building. The failure to find a significant relationship between running costs and size may be due to the nature of the sample. Different methods of heating and different kinds of fuel were used in different schools. Maintenance costs are affected by the type of building construction, the extent to which schools are used outside normal hours and the care taken of the buildings. A further study by the Department of Education and Science of schools in county areas of England and Wales shows a somewhat erratic connection between running costs (other than in staffing) and size. Areas where the average size of school is 70 pupils or fewer had very high costs which decreased as sizes reached 120–130 pupils but then increased again. But these areas were not matched for size or other aspects of buildings or of their use. It may be that as the stock of new building increases, such costs as heating and caretaking will become more uniform among schools of equal size. Further analysis is called for with a carefully matched sample of schools.

Staffing Costs in Manpower and Money

460. Small schools have better ratios of staff to pupils than large schools. The figures in Table 14 show that the pupil-teacher ratio rises sharply in schools up to 200 but that, though there is some further increase in larger schools, it is proportionately much smaller. We agree with our witnesses that, except in those classes of young children which are vertically grouped by deliberate policy, classes combining two or more year groups should be smaller than classes which provide for only one year group. Because of the shortage of teachers, the need for more generous staffing in smaller schools is a strong argument for organising, whenever possible, schools of at least one form-entry in urban areas. The economy in staffing in very large schools is less genuine and will disappear, if as we recommend, schools are staffed on the basis of a pupil-teacher ratio as well as on size of class. Competent head teachers should be able to carry heavy responsibilities in the guidance of staff and pupils. But, if more than one teacher is absent, as must often happen in a very large school, classes have to be combined. Heads cannot see as much of the work of the staff in a large school as in a school of medium size, unless the heads themselves give up teaching. If they delegate some of their responsibility for advice to deputy heads and others, these teachers ought to be relieved of some periods with their own classes. In either case, teachers who are not in charge of classes become necessary.

Table 14 Distribution of Pupil/Teacher Ratios by Size of School:
January 1965 (England)

				Number of Schools or Departments with the following number of pupils on roll						
	Up to 25	26– 50	51– 100	100– 200	201– 300	301– 400	401– 600	601– 800	801– 1,000	All Schools
Number of Schools/ Departments	897	2,396	2,979	5,153	5,208	2,703	1,360	87	6	20,789
Actual Pupil/ Teacher Ratio	14·0	19·0	24·9	29·0	30·7	31·9	32·7	33·0	34·5	30·0

Source: Statistics of Education, 1965, Part One, Table 16 and Statistics Branch, Department of Education and Science.

Transport Costs

461. We have not obtained figures for the cost of transporting children to schools outside the area or village in which they live. The costs themselves may be less important than the time and energy consumed in long journeys.

Foreign Practice

462. Many of the schools visited by members in the U.S.A., the U.S.S.R. Denmark and Sweden were larger than those normally found in this country. In Sweden there is centralised planning by the Royal Swedish Board of Education which relates the size and situation of individual schools to popula-

tion and housing trends[3] and often allows the first school (seven to ten years) to be part of quite large combined schools containing older children as well. In the U.S.A., some elementary schools (generally catering for children between 6 and 12 years of age) have more than 1,000 pupils on roll, and a high proportion of the child population is in these big schools. These schools, mainly to be seen in large cities, may mislead the visitor into thinking that most American elementary schools are large. In fact many American elementary schools are as small as our own. Schools in other countries are often larger than ours because there are few separate infant and junior schools and primary schools cover therefore a wider age range than here. Parents and children benefit from a longer association with the same school. The disadvantages of large size may be less because there may be less emphasis on the school as a community, and more on the importance of classroom instruction. In a large school the head teacher is an administrator rather than a principal teacher, and in the U.S.A. is often referred to as such. Foreign practice as to the size of primary schools has therefore little relevance for us because of varying concepts of the school and the different ways in which schools are organised.

Conclusions

463. In Chapter 10 we recommend that there should be schools for children from five to eight and from 8 to 12 years and in Chapter 14 we suggest an option of between eight and nine in rural areas. When new schools are provided or existing schools reorganised to fit this changed structure, we believe that a two form entry will usually be most satisfactory for a first school (that is about 240 children) and a two to three form entry (300–450 children) for a middle school.

464. The figures which we have quoted relate to schools with classes for 40 children, except that it is assumed that children aged 11–12 will be in classes of 30. When class sizes are reduced it may be sensible to work to the same total numbers but to provide more classes since the pupil-teacher ratio will be better. Three form entry first schools (with classes of 30 pupils making a roll of about 270 children) could transfer children to three form entry middle schools. Alternatively two first schools, each of two form entry, could be linked with one four form entry middle school (with about 480 children). Other arrangements of a similar kind could be made. A middle school of this size should be able to employ teachers particularly competent in the main aspects of the curriculum. The larger the middle school, the easier it will be to provide simple facilities for practical work in science, and in art and craft and sufficient space for physical education.

465. It is more difficult to recommend the most suitable size for a combined first and middle school. If our recommendations on the age of transfer are accepted, combined schools will have less to recommend them than they have now. Either the school community will be too large for the younger children or, if it is small enough for them, the staff will be few and may not give enough stimulus to the older children.

466. In general there seems to be little serious conflict between the size of schools desirable on educational, economic and other grounds, except perhaps for the three and four class schools which are often inevitable in the

country. Larger schools than are educationally desirable might be a little more economical to run, but the evidence is far from clear. The question of size of school is of sufficient interest to merit further study from both educational and economic points of view. The economic data should be closely analysed on well matched samples of schools.

Recommendations

467 (i) The most satisfactory size for new or reorganised first schools will normally be two form entry (240 children) and for middle schools two to three form entry (300 to 450 children). When class sizes are reduced, the same number of children can be retained on roll but schools should be organised on the basis of three form entry first and middle schools, or two form entry first schools and four form entry middle schools.

(ii) With the exception of small schools in rural areas and voluntary schools, combined first and middle schools are undesirable.

(iii) Further study should be made of the educational characteristics of schools of different sizes, and the economic data should be analysed on well matched samples of schools.

REFERENCES

[1]Information supplied by Liverpool Local Education Authority and analysed by Mr. G F. Peaker.

[2]Morris, J. M. 'Reading in the Primary School', 1959, Newnes.

[3]Discussion with officials of Royal Swedish Board of Education and 'Can Population and Housing Censuses Be Used in the Localisation of Schools?' B. Jacobson. Statistisk Tidskrift 1964:5 p.317 to 326.

Table 15

Number of Small Schools in England: 1962-65

Schools	1962		1963		1964		1965	
	Up to 25	26 to 50	Up to 25	26 to 50	Up to 25	26 to 50	Up to 25	26 to 50
Infants	67	173	65	170	55	142	52	127
Junior with Infants	1,052	2,428	989	2,375	901	2,341	835	2,237
Junior without Infants	4	32	6	32	3	32	2	27
All Age	17	46	18	27	10	18	8	5
Total Primary	1,140	2,679	1,078	2,604	969	2,533	897	2,396

Sources: Statistics of Education, 1962. Part One. Table 11.
Statistics of Education, 1963. Part One. Table 9.
Statistics of Education, 1964. Part One. Table 12.
Statistics of Education, 1965. Part One. Table 16.

CHAPTER 14

Education in Rural Areas*

468. In 1962, the last year in which Ministry of Education statistics distinguished between urban and rural schools, just under two out of every five primary schools in England and Wales were rural. If the child population was proportionate to the total population as shown by the 1961 census, about one in five pupils attended a country school. According to the N.U.T. Survey of schools (1962) about 17 per cent of rural schools had one or two classes. Most of the remainder contain three or four classes. Two class and three class schools constitute the two main groups. Most village schools provide for children from 5 to 11.

School Closures

469. Affectionate accounts of village schools figure prominently in autobiographies and in descriptions of schools published in the last 20 years. Nevertheless, many are closed every year, partly as a result of shifts of population, partly by the deliberate policy of local education authorities.

470. During the period 1962 to 1965 the number of primary schools with up to 25 pupils on roll declined by 243 and the number of schools with 26 to 50 pupils was reduced by 283 (see Table 15). Closure of one teacher schools was proportionately greatest; these schools, increased in number by the removal of pupils over 11 to secondary schools, are particularly difficult to run. If the teacher is ill, there may be no alternative to sending the children home, and no one to see that it is done. Many of the smallest schools are in the worst buildings; the N.U.T. Survey showed that the smaller the school, the more likely it was to have been built in the nineteenth century. Frequently, no applications may be received for headships of isolated one teacher schools. Teachers who are not outstandingly gifted find it difficult to educate more than two age groups of junior children together unless the class is very small or extra help is given. That small schools are expensive to build and to staff has been shown in the previous chapter. The evidence we have received both from teachers in small schools and most of the educational associations is that a three class school for the age range 5 to 11 is the minimum effective unit.

Changing Social Conditions

471. For those living in the country, even more than for the rest of the community, change has been rapid in the last 30 years. Television has introduced new interests. London or the nearest sea side resort is often better known, and more readily imagined, than the county town. Mechanisation is reducing the number of farm workers, never more than a proportion of villagers, needed to work the land and it is demanding more technical ability of those who

*The Central Advisory Council For Education (Wales) have, we understand, made a detailed study of problems of rural education. It contains much that is relevant to the size of rural schools and to rural education in England. Its relevance is, however, limited by the difference in rural communities between Wales and most parts of England.

remain. Though wages have gone up and much overtime can be earned seasonally, earnings lag behind those in the towns. Many villages are almost emptied of their working population during the day: public and private buses and cars take men and women to factories in the nearest towns. The drift of the young from the countryside continues.

472. Yet there are large differences from one part of the country to another and from one village to another. Many villages are near enough to urban counties to be preferred by commuters to suburban dormitories. Whole areas of the home counties come into this category. Parents expect and press for as good an education for their children in the village as they would have had in the town. Some of the most active P.T.As. are in commuter villages. In the true country, some villages grow larger because of housing development, the introduction of small industry, adequate shopping facilities and reasonable public transport. In others, transport is poor, no council houses are built and the young must move away to work and later to set up their own households. In some villages, only a minority of the inhabitants were born there. In others the old cohesion remains, and a proposal to close a village school may raise a storm of protest from parents and from others who have no immediate concern with the school. To close a primary school may in fact diminish a village in more senses than one and provide a further reason why young married couples will want to leave it. Yet there are great variations between villages and between regions. Some schools, especially in the North, were never integral to a village but were placed centrally for hamlets and outlying farms.

Rural Schools: The Premises

473. The pioneering work of the National Society in providing schools for the villages in the nineteenth century has left a heavy legacy of problems. Though many of these schools become "controlled" after the 1944 Act and the buildings could therefore be improved with local education authority help, progress has been held up by the priority given to secondary school reorganisation and to the provision of schools for new housing estates. In any case until reorganisation was completed and the older children transferred, improvement would have often taken up too much space. Now that this has been done improvements must rely on minor building programmes which, though increased, do not make sufficient impact. Yet there have been some remarkable achievements. The co-operation of local education authorities and the Ministry (and, later, Department) of Education Development Group has resulted in the planning and building of village schools, designed for the conditions of rural education and so able to serve as models for new schools and for adaptations.

474. Yet, many country schools, like the older primary schools in the towns, lag behind what is tolerable, let alone what is desirable. Some schools are without facilities for physical education, either indoors or outdoors. Even though more space has been provided by the transfer of secondary pupils the infants' room is often so poky that it will not take new furniture. There is rarely any place where teachers can withdraw from the children or talk to a parent. Storage is inadequate. Many schools still lack piped hot water and the chemical closet and the earth closet still survive. In some schools conditions are worse than at home, and training in hygiene difficult to achieve.

Staffing

475. On the whole, the uniform Burnham scale and staffing quotas have been favourable to rural schools. Yet while some counties can pick and choose others have difficulty in recruiting the teachers they want. It has already been suggested that difficulty in obtaining teachers has been one reason for the closure of one teacher schools. We have been told that the average age of the village teacher is rather higher than that of all teachers and many will retire shortly. Difficulty in appointing teachers to country schools may therefore increase. Much depends on the attractiveness of the area, on its accessibility, on the size of the village, on the provision of modernised school houses and on what is known of an authority's reputation for helping country schools. Although some authorities are deliberately increasing the number of men teachers in rural schools, others do not employ many men. Enterprising teachers, who want to try fresh ideas, often prefer headships in a country school, with responsibility for a class, to a deputy headship or a graded post in a larger school and this is bringing new strength to some small schools. Some of these teachers live in the villages and identify themselves with it; yet as more teachers own cars, more probably live away from their work.

476. It is even more difficult to find suitable assistant teachers for small schools than heads. Unqualified supplementary teachers who have helped to staff rural schools in the past are retiring. Except in the commuter villages there are relatively few married women teachers available. Teachers are easier to recruit for villages near to towns but then they usually live in the town and the identification of the school with the village, one of the advantages often claimed for the village school is weakened. We have heard of some authorities, which employ men assistants in two teacher schools, a policy which is apparently working well, even though much of their work must be with infants. Traditionally the head, whether man or women, takes the older children who can more easily be left when the head is called away. Many counties have to draft teachers to remote schools, in much the same way that county boroughs often staff schools in socially deprived areas. Probationers often do not stay after the end of the year, partly because of their dislike of isolation, partly because suitable lodgings are hard to find. We have heard of schools in which there is a yearly change of assistant teachers.

477. Acknowledgement must be made of the devoted work of many village school teachers. Often working alone in their schools and with few opportunities for discussion with their colleagues, sometimes heavily handicapped by their buildings, responsible for children of a wider age range than most junior school teachers think practicable, they have created schools characterised by warmth, mutual forbearance and an almost family affection. Many teachers showed great adaptability in responding to the needs of a 5 to 11 school as distinct from the all-through school to which they had been accustomed. Recent recruits to country schools have continued this tradition and, as we have seen for ourselves, have set an example for national progress in primary education, both in the flexible organisation of their schools and the excellence of their work.

Children and the Schools

478. Enquiries into the measured attainment of children in rural and urban schools have tended to show lower mean attainment for country children than

for urban children. It has often been suggested that this is because the enterprising in all classes make for the towns. Yet a summary of the evidence in 1959 suggested that, when socio-economic class is taken into account, the differences between town and country children disappear[1]. In villages accessible to towns where the occupational distribution of the parents is changing, the children's attainment may also be expected to change. Some country people speak less and speak more more slowly than people in town. It may be that country children have been handicapped by silence at home and that test vocabularies have been biased in favour of urban children. Certainly there is evidence that speed tests give advantage to children from town schools. Some authorities, concerned about the small proportion of village children who obtain grammar school places, have reserved some places for children from country schools. It has been found that these children have justified their places[2]. Similarly an enquiry in Cambridgeshire showed that pupils from rural areas who obtained places in selective schools fulfilled their promise more consistently than those from the towns[3].

479. There are both advantages and disadvantages in the circumstances of the country school. The National Survey showed that beginners settle easily in a village school to which all their acquaintances go and whose teachers, parents, and children they almost always know. The small numbers in the school and the wide age range in classes encourage a spirit of co-operation and children quickly assimilate the established traditions of learning and behaviour. Yet the older children and particularly the abler ones may lack the stimulus of their peers. The wide age range within a class is to some teachers an incentive to individual work; to others a burden. At worst, the five year olds may begin book learning before they are ready, so that they do not disturb the others, and the older children make their way with little guidance through English "work books" and arithmetic text books. A handful of really backward children may make no progress at all. At best, the small school provides for much hard thinking arising from genuine problems and discussion, and for personal writing and art and craft of as high a quality as we have seen in any schools in England. The knowledge of children that a good village school teacher can build up is invaluable. Yet one weak teacher can destroy a child's educational opportunities and a clash of personality between a teacher and a child may be disastrous. A good head can quickly influence a small school, particularly if, as is becoming more common, a rigid class organisation is broken down and teachers pool their ideas and gifts. The immediate environment of many country schools is rich with interest and children can make visits for themselves out of school hours. Yet they may often need help from an enlightened and sensitive adult to awaken their interest in what to them is common place. It is in fact the country schools which have set the pace for the development of environmental studies.

Size and Age Range of Rural Schools

480. Despite the achievements of one and two teacher schools, their difficulties and their cost, particularly in teachers, lead us to recommend that schools with an age range of 5 to 11 should usually have at least three classes, each covering two age groups. But local circumstances will make exceptions inevitable.

481. If the age range of primary education is extended to 12, it will be difficult to provide a sufficiently challenging curriculum for the older pupils who may become, as one witness suggested, "unwilling veterans" unless an additional teacher is appointed or substantial help is given by peripatetic teachers. If some rural schools in the area become larger, other village schools will have to be closed.

482. We are concerned about the number of five year old children who travel by bus to schools outside their villages. These children are often less ready for school at five than town children. Their mothers are unable to go with them to school or to make informal contact with their teachers, and from the first children must spend two sessions at school unless special arrangements are made for their transport. For the sake of these young children, and because we should like middle schools to be geared to the needs of pupils between 8 and 12, we should prefer a two tier system of primary education in the country as in the town. First schools serving one or two country villages might contain two or more classes of children from five to eight or nine and a nursery group; if there were only enough children for one class, the class might be regarded as an annex to a larger school and the teacher might be given the support of an aide or nursery assistant. Middle schools might be centrally placed in large villages or small country towns.

483. We have been unable to investigate whether a two tier rural reorganisation is practicable. We understand that enquiries made by three local education authorities for the Welsh Central Advisory Council for Education showed that it would be easier to organise 5 to 12 schools partly because this structure would make use of existing three class schools; a two tier plan would perpetuate or increase expensive one class schools, or annexes, as we have suggested. Yet we have received evidence from rural authorities, admittedly not based on detailed enquiry, which favours two tier schools. Much must depend on the distribution of population, the siting of villages and the amount of remodelling of rural schools which has taken place. Planning must take into account whether villages are decaying, static or growing and the possible effect of school closures on them. Where authorities find that 5 to 12 schools are the only possible pattern, the older children must not be denied the broader curriculum they would have had at the top of a middle school. Earlier transfer for exceptionally mature children at 11 or, in a two tier system, at seven or eight will be particularly important when the number of classes in rural schools is small. If schemes involve travelling for five year olds, their transition to school should be eased by the provision of part-time education even if it adds to the cost of transport. Parents must be involved in the schools and whenever possible part-time nursery groups set up in the villages. Country children who often do not have other children of their own age to play with and whose language may be stunted because of infrequent opportunities for talk with adults particularly need nursery experience but rarely get it. To some extent, these disadvantages are compensated for by the freedom and interest of their environment. We have suggested that in some instances parents' obligation to have their children educated might be satisfied by children's attendance at a nursery group. This arrangement might be particularly helpful for children who are not ready for a whole day at school away from the village.

Help for Rural Schools

484. We are impressed by the work of a local authority that has pioneered the adaptation and rebuilding of country schools. It is building a new primary school, a welfare clinic and a branch library associated with a further education centre on the site. It is considering attaching village rooms with their own cloakroom facilities and access to new primary schools as a means of associating community and school, the more necessary perhaps now that this authority is finding that it cannot retain a school in each village. Most interesting of all are the close relationships which are being developed by groups of small schools. Although heads retain responsibility for their own schools, the local education authority consults the needs of the whole group when it appoints new teachers. In one group members of staff interchange schools so that they can learn of experiments taking place, initiate new methods, and give help in matters in which they are knowledgeable both to their colleagues and to groups of children. A liaison assistant has been appointed to look after the secretarial work for the group and for individual schools. She is also responsible for a group collection of film strips, tapes, expensive books and display materials. Children visit each other's schools for team games, music making and country dancing. A minibus is available. It is intended that the managers of the schools shall have some group meetings. This organisation has developed from informal friendly relationships which have existed between the schools for many years and have been fostered by the advisory teachers whose contribution to the work of rural schools is an outstanding feature of this authority.

485. The developments in this authority point to the general needs of country schools. Among the most important are support for teachers, more contacts for country children with their contemporaries and improved buildings. Rural schools need to open up rooms to provide more space and movement and to encourage the staff, which will almost certainly include a head in charge of a class, to work as a group. New methods are also needed to preserve and improve further the co-operation between school and community which has been a strength of many village schools.

486. The number of village teachers who have been brought up in the country is dwindling partly because more people live in towns, partly because assistant teachers from town schools find promotion as heads of country schools. Care must therefore be taken to see that teachers who may work in the country know what it has to offer, what it is like to live there and have a sympathetic understanding of the rural society they serve. Some town schools are over used for teaching practice by colleges of education. Some village schools are still under used. Admittedly lodgings in villages are often difficult to obtain but students might lodge in a market town and travel by bus to a group of villages, as some already do.

487. In-service training and easy contacts between country school teachers are at least as important as initial training. Valuable help can be given by advisers and by advisory teachers. In some areas, at least, an advisory teacher comes into the schools not by right but by the staff's goodwill, and teaches as a teacher with teachers. He can fill a vacancy for a brief spell in an emergency. He can spend several days in succession in a school to support a probationary teacher who is having difficulties (as we suggest in Chapter 25); he can advise an established teacher who is modifying his methods or bring

new quality to an aspect of the curriculum on which the adviser is expert and the school lacks resources.

488. The staffs of country schools need, and respond to, arrangements to bring them into regular association with one another. The grouping of primary schools which has already been described is an effective way of bringing this about and leads naturally to links with the secondary schools to which children transfer. Some authorities find that almost all teachers attend area courses or conferences. Country teachers also need to meet teachers from a wider range of schools. One authority which has given much attention to in-service training has developed a "junior workshop" or group of junior teachers within the county. It holds general meetings on topics of common interest and subdivides into study groups for teachers in small schools and those who are particularly concerned with certain aspects of the curriculum. One of the liveliest of these groups is concerned with environmental studies. It is hoped to establish a centre for environmental studies for primary school children which would give children a short experience of residential education and could be used to train teachers in the use of the environment in the education of primary children.

489. If heads who are in charge of classes are to give sufficient guidance to their staff and to make contact with parents, they need, as suggested in Chapter 24, part-time teaching help and ancillary assistance. Peripatetic teachers can be helpful in new subjects, such as French, and established subjects such as music. With assistance from educational psychologists they can help in the education of the most backward children. Teachers in country schools who have to provide for children in more than one age group, and children from remote rural areas can make particularly good use of such aids as radio, television, tape recorders, film strips and programmed learning. The county libraries have already done much to enrich the education of country children; museum and picture loan services might be provided more generally than at present.

490. To help the teachers is to help the children. There are advantages in the country school of the flexible forms of organisation which are described in more detail in Chapter 20. We commend regular visits by children to nearby primary schools and occasional visits or interchanges with town schools. It has been brought to our attention by several witnesses that country children, particularly those from scattered communities, may lack companionship and find little to do after school hours. There is a place for the community school in the country no less than in the town. In one school, 81 children out of 98 eligible attended clubs which the school provided for an hour each evening. The transition from a small country primary school to a centrally situated secondary school can be a considerable strain for the children. We refer in Chapter 12 to a scheme by which primary school children in their last year attend once a week the secondary school to which they will transfer. This arrangement could enrich the curriculum for children in a 5 to 12 school and would fit well with the suggested grouping of primary schools.

491. Changes in village life make it necessary to organise what has hitherto been a largely informal association of the village school master with the parents of his pupils. Certainly when a village school has to be shut and a school serves more than one village, it would be helpful for the head to visit regularly each village in order to meet parents. As many villages become less

cohesive, more formal procedures including P.T.As. may become necessary even in a school which serves only one village. The closer the relations between the village and the school, the easier it will become to solve the school's many problems: to find lodgings for an assistant teacher; to build the swimming pool without which village children would have no opportunity to learn to swim; to provide supervision for out of school activities and, occasionally, to find sources to satisfy a child with a special interest about which no one on the school staff is knowledgeable. Parental encouragement, based on parental knowledge of what the school is trying to do, is as important for country as for town children.

Recommendations

492. (i) Schools with an age range of 5 to 11 should usually have at least three classes, each covering two age groups.

(ii) If the age range is extended to 12, further teaching help may be needed to provide adequately for the older children.

(iii) A two tier system of primary education is preferable in the country as in the towns. Great flexibility will be needed in the age of transfer to meet local circumstances and to fit the needs of individual children.

(iv) One or two class first schools or annexes should be provided for younger children, who would otherwise have a long journey to school.

(v) Teachers' aides should be employed in small rural schools.

(vi) Teachers in rural schools need help from advisers and advisory teachers, and opportunities for regular association with other teachers and schools.

REFERENCES

[1]Barr, F. 'Urban and Rural Differences:—Ability and Attainment'. Educational Research, Vol. 1, 1959, page 59.
[2]Evidence collected by West Riding and other local education authorities.
[3]Cross, G. R. and Revell, C. J. 'Note on Grammar School Selection in a Rural Area'. Bulletin 7, N.F.E.R. March 1957.

Part Five

The Children in the Schools: Curriculum and Internal Organisation

Part Three

Four Failures in the Schools: Curriculum and Internal Organization

CHAPTER 15

The Aims of Primary Education

493. All schools reflect the views of society, or of some section of society, about the way children should be brought up, whether or not these views are consciously held or defined. The old English elementary school derived, in part at least, from the National Society for the Education of the Poorer Classes in the principles of the Established Church founded in 1811, the aim of which was to provide for what were then thought to be the educational needs of the working class. The effects of the hierarchical view of society which this title implied persisted long after the view itself became unacceptable and out of date. American schools have had, as an avowed purpose, the Americanisation of children from diverse cultures, races and climates. Russian education is strictly geared to particular political and social beliefs. Our society is in a state of transition and there is controversy about the relative rights of society and the individual. What agreement can be reached in the midst of this uncertainty about the objectives of English education, and in particular of English primary schools, in the last third of the twentieth century?

494. One obvious purpose is to fit children for the society into which they will grow up. To do this successfully it is necessary to predict what that society will be like. It will certainly be one marked by rapid and far reaching economic and social change. It is likely to be richer than now, with even more choice of goods, with tastes dominated by majorities and with more leisure for all; more people will be called upon to change their occupation.

495. About such a society we can be both hopeful and fearful. We can hope it will care for all its members, for the old as well as the young, for the handicapped as well as the gifted, for the deviant as well as the conformer, and that it will create an environment which is stimulating, honest and tolerant. We can fear that it will be much engrossed with the pursuit of material wealth, too hostile to minorities, too dominated by mass opinion and too uncertain of its values.

496. For such a society, children, and the adults they will become, will need above all to be adaptable and capable of adjusting to their changing environment. They will need as always to be able to live with their fellows, appreciating and respecting their differences, understanding and sympathising with their feelings. They will need the power of discrimination and, when necessary, to be able to withstand mass pressures. They will need to be well-balanced, with neither emotions nor intellect giving ground to each other. They will need throughout their adult life to be capable of being taught, and of learning, the new skills called for by the changing economic scene. They will need to understand that in a democratic society each individual has obligations to the community, as well as rights within it.

497. When we asked our witnesses for their views on the aims of primary education we found a wide general measure of agreement, though many of the replies seemed to have as much relevance to other phases of education

as to primary. The heads of both junior and infant schools laid emphasis upon the all round development of the individual and upon the acquisition of the basic skills necessary in contemporary society. Many added a third aim, that of the religious and moral development of the child and some a fourth, that of children's physical development and acquisition of motor skills. Phrases such as "whole personality", "happy atmosphere", "full and satisfying life", "full development of powers", "satisfaction of curiosity", "confidence", "perseverence" and "alertness" occurred again and again. This list shows that general statements of aims, even by those engaged in teaching, tend to be little more than expressions of benevolent aspiration which may provide a rough guide to the general climate of a school, but which may have a rather tenuous relationship to the educational practices that actually go on there. It was interesting that some of the head teachers who were considered by H.M. Inspectors to be most successful in practice were least able to formulate their aims clearly and convincingly.

498. Even the second aim, that of acquiring the basic skills, proved less tangible than would appear at first sight or than public opinion would consider it. Most witnesses were thinking in terms of the three Rs, but there are other skills besides those of reading, writing and arithmetic which are necessary for those who are to live happily and usefully both as children and as adults. Communication by the spoken word is at least as important as writing and for the majority perhaps more important. In Chapters 16 and 17 we consider the curriculum in detail and try to show how the aims of the school, the needs of the children and the means at the disposal of the teachers fit together and react upon each other. Here we are concerned with aims in general.

499. A special difficulty is raised by the third aim mentioned by our witnesses, that of the religious and moral development of the child. We discuss Religious Education in Chapter 17 and the standards of behaviour of the child are referred to in other parts of the Report.

500. An aim, which was hardly mentioned by head teachers and yet one which, if challenged, they would almost certainly have admitted, is the cooperation of school and home and, with it, that of making good to children, as far as possible, the deficiencies of their backgrounds. That this aim found so little expression is significant. The implications of the relationships between school and home have still to be worked out; some teachers are anxious about the extent to which the school is taking the responsibility for the child's welfare and thus undermining the responsibility, as some would put it, of parents. The stronger partnership that there should be between teacher and parents has been discussed in Chapter 4.

501. It is difficult to reach agreement on the aims of primary education if anything but the broadest terms are used but formulations of that kind are little more than platitudes. We invited the help of a number of distinguished educationists and professors of educational philosophy, and enjoyed a lengthy and interesting discussion with them. They all confirmed the view that general statements of aims were of limited value, and that a pragmatic approach to the purposes of education was more likely to be fruitful. We now turn to the implications of this conclusion.

502. An individual as distinct from a general statement of aims may be more worth making. It clears the writer's mind and compels him to examine what

he is doing and why. This is a useful professional exercise for all teachers. Head teachers have for long written statements of this kind to help their staffs. They are useful insofar as they promote real thought and are not confined to a mere set of directions. They should encourage class teachers to look critically at their day to day work, relating it to guiding principles and not simply to short term objectives. One of our witnesses gives such a list: "physical health, intellectual development, emotional and moral health, aesthetic awareness, a valid perspective, practical skills, social skills, personal fulfilment", and so on, with each main heading divided into appropriate subheadings. But he goes on to say: "such an itemised statement of purposes has doubtful value, except as an academic exercise or as a check list". Check lists, however, have their uses and the items on the lists should be double checked against current practices. What practices in my school develop these qualities? Which of these qualities are developed by this particular practice? Rather commonplace little exercises such as these encourage the staff of the school to keep thinking about what they are doing. Because statements of aims of this kind are written for a small and intimate circle there is less risk of disagreement about the underlying assumptions than with documents intended for a wider public.

503. Another approach might be to draw up a list of danger signs, which would indicate that something has gone wrong in a school: fragmented knowledge, no changes in past decade, creative work very limited, much time spent on teaching, few questions from children, too many exercises, too many rules, frequent punishments, and concentration on tests. Such a list, of course, involves value judgements at the outset, but it is an invitation to thought and argument and not simply to compliance. Then it could be asked what aims are implicit in, for example, play activity, painting, free writing, "movement", games, the new mathematics, learning by heart, grammar and so on. To subject all educational practices to this kind of questioning might be healthy. Habit is an immensely strong influence in schools and it is one that should be weakened though it is never likely to be removed. These words are particularly addressed to practising teachers and especially to head teachers, rather than to educational theorists, who seldom fear innovation, but whose ideas may founder because of their ignorance of what schools (and sometimes teachers) are really like.

504. If these methods were applied to all primary schools it would be apparent that the trend of their practices and outlook corresponds to a recognisable philosophy of education, and to a view of society, which may be summarised as follows.

505. A school is not merely a teaching shop, it must transmit values and attitudes. It is a community in which children learn to live first and foremost as children and not as future adults. In family life children learn to live with people of all ages. The school sets out deliberately to devise the right environment for children, to allow them to be themselves and to develop in the way and at the pace appropriate to them. It tries to equalise opportunities and to compensate for handicaps. It lays special stress on individual discovery, on first hand experience and on opportunities for creative work. It insists that knowledge does not fall into neatly separate compartments and that work and play are not opposite but complementary. A child brought up in such an

atmosphere at all stages of his education has some hope of becoming a balanced and mature adult and of being able to live in, to contribute to, and to look critically at the society of which he forms a part. Not all primary schools correspond to this picture, but it does represent a general and quickening trend.

506. Some people, while conceding that children are happier under the modern regime and perhaps more versatile, question whether they are being fitted to grapple with the world which they will enter when they leave school. This view is worth examining because it is quite widely held, but we think it rests on a misconception. It isolates the long term objective, that of living in and serving society, and regards education as being at all stages recognisably and specifically a preparation for this. It fails to understand that the best preparation for being a happy and useful man or woman is to live fully as a child. Finally, it assumes, quite wrongly, that the older virtues, as they are usually called, of neatness, accuracy, care and perseverance, and the sheer knowledge which is an essential of being educated, will decline. These are genuine virtues and an education which does not foster them is faulty.

507. Society is right to expect that importance will be attached to these virtues in all schools. Children need them and need knowledge, if they are to gain satisfaction from their education. What we repudiate is the view that they were automatically fostered by the old kind of elementary education. Patently they were not, for enormous numbers of the products of that education do not possess them. Still more we repudiate the fear that the modern primary approach leads to their neglect. On the contrary it can, and, when properly understood, does lay a much firmer foundation for their development and it is more in the interests of the children. But those interests are complex. Children need to be themselves, to live with other children and with grown ups, to learn from their environment, to enjoy the present, to get ready for the future, to create and to love, to learn to face adversity, to behave responsibly, in a word, to be human beings. Decisions about the influences and situations that ought to be contrived to these ends must be left to individual schools, teachers and parents. What must be ensured is that the decisions taken in schools spring from the best available knowledge and are not simply dictated by habit or convention.

CHAPTER 16

Children Learning in School

Towards Freedom of Curriculum

508. The ending, in 1898, of the system of payment by results, under which a proportion of teachers' salaries was dependent upon the results of an annual examination of pupils held by H.M. Inspectors, led to an increasing freedom for teachers to exercise their own judgment in matters of syllabus. In 1905 the Board of Education first issued a Handbook of Suggestions for the Consideration of Teachers, a title that itself indicated a change in outlook. The Elementary Code laid down some very broad requirements, but a large measure of choice was left to the individual school. In the preface to the 1918 edition of the Handbook occurs the following significant passage: "Neither the present volume nor any developments or amendments of it are designed to impose any regulations supplementary to those contained in the Code. The only uniformity of practice that the Board of Education desire to see in the teaching of public elementary schools is that each teacher shall think for himself, and work out for himself such methods of teaching as may use his powers to the best advantage and be best suited to the particular needs and conditions of the school. Uniformity in detail of practice (except in the mere routine of school management) is not desirable, even if it were attainable. But freedom implies a corresponding responsibility in its use." This passage was reprinted in the preface to the 1937 edition of the Handbook. In 1944 the Code, which had become increasingly permissive, finally disappeared, and in the 1944 Education Act the only statutory requirement that remained was that children should be educated according to "their age, ability and aptitude".

509. During the 46 years that elapsed between the abolition of payment by results and the abolition of the Code, the use made by teachers of their growing freedom varied considerably. The force of tradition and of the inherent conservatism of all teaching professions made for a slow rate of change. The requirements of selection examinations for grammar schools also exercised a strong influence towards uniformity. In the earlier part of the period, too, H.M. Inspectors, who for the previous thirty years had been examiners, were probably restraining influences on innovation, though as time went on they tended increasingly to be agents of experiment and change. A minority of teachers, particularly in the infant schools, responded eagerly to freedom. The infant schools themselves were influenced by ideas on nursery education partly because training for nursery work was often given in colleges which specialised in infant education.

510. A considerable body of liberal thinking on the education of children was available to teachers. Rousseau, Pestalozzi, Froebel, Whitehead, Dewey, Montessori and Rachel Macmillan, to mention only a few, had all written on lines that encouraged change and innovation. Yet it may be doubted whether the direct influence of these or of any other writers was great. It was rare to find teachers who had given much time to the study of educational

theory, even in their training college days. Perhaps the strongest influence was that of Froebel, mediated through the Froebel training colleges which bore his name.

511. In some infant schools, a "blocked" time table began to take the place of a day fragmented into 15 or 20 minute periods, which was as long as little children could tolerate when most of the instruction was oral. It became quite common to give two periods each day to physical activity and, in the more enlightened schools, the distinction between physical education and play was blurred. In some schools, the "occupations", which owed their place in the curriculum to Froebel but were usually very different from what he had intended, were superseded by dramatic play and large scale construction. There was an increased tendency to allocate blocks of time to the three Rs and within these periods to provide, as is described in this and the next chapter, for group and individual work.

512. For children between the ages of 8 and 11, experiments were mainly in method, class organisation and use of materials. The curriculum, in the narrow sense of the subjects studied, remained almost unchanged. It included Scripture, English, arithmetic, history, geography, art, craft, music, nature study and physical training. It was rare, in the period 1898 to 1944, to find a primary school in which any of these subjects was omitted and any other included. But there was, especially after the publication of the Consultative Committee's 1931 Report, much variety of content and approach. English was beginning to involve a freer use of composition, and drama was making an appearance. The first signs of a change in the conception of mathematical learning were there for those who searched. The boundaries of history and geography were sometimes blurred and something called environmental studies—or social studies—which embraced them both, was beginning to be talked of. Art was already moving rapidly away from the dreary pencil drawing that had been universal. Craft was still limited and formal. A beginning was being made in the use of musical instruments. Nature study increasingly took place outside the classroom and physical education advanced greatly when the old conception of drill was swept away by the publication in 1933 of the Board of Education's new syllabus. Here and there schools were making a much more radical approach to education than this would indicate. The freedom was genuine, even if it was seized a little gingerly

513. During the war, when there was a growing consciousness of social problems, much thought was given to the hitherto largely neglected report of 1931 and to the writings of educationalists such as Susan Isaacs. Despite overcrowding and large classes, many post war primary schools did much to enlarge children's experience and involve them more actively in the learning process—the main themes of the 1931 Report. This was a period when a great many descriptive books, of considerable practical help to teachers, were being written about both infant and junior schools, and, for the first time, a sizeable number of junior schools, backed by H.M. Inspectors and local inspectors, began to work on lines similar to those already common in infant schools. For a brief time "activity" and child-centred education became dangerously fashionable and misunderstandings on the part of the camp followers endangered the progress made by the pioneers. The misunderstandings were never as widespread in the schools as might have been supposed by reading the press, and certainly did not outweigh the gains which were

especially notable in the English subjects. Then as now, the schools which continued on traditional lines to emphasise instruction exceeded the number of those which erred by excess of innovation. In any case, correctives came in an emphasis on quality in the learning experiences provided for children, and on the positive function of the teacher.

514. Among the many influences which have eased the task of the teachers wishing to experiment have been the new school buildings, in which a third of primary school children are housed, more generous equipment allowances, and increased in-service training.

515. Recently, there have been changes in the curriculum which must be attributed to influences sufficiently distinct from those just mentioned to require separate treatment. A second language, in almost every case French, has been introduced in a substantial number of primary schools. The teaching of mathematics is undergoing a radical change and a wider field of science is replacing nature study. The cause of these changes will be discussed in detail in Chapter 17. All that need be said here is that these changes seem to be taking place unusually rapidly, often because of the in-service training which has been encouraged and sometimes planned by the Department in concert with other bodies.

516. Looked at from any point of view, the changes that have taken place between 1898 and the fifties and sixties have been striking, but they have been largely unco-ordinated, except perhaps by in-service training. It was argued that the establishment of some central organisation could accelerate the process of change, and co-ordinate and evaluate whatever changes were taking place. Such thoughts as these led to the setting up in 1964 of the Schools Council for the Curriculum and Examinations.

517. The organisation and operation of the Council have been fully described in its own publications. The Council is a consortium of bodies concerned with education, the teachers' organisations, the local education authorities, the universities and colleges of education, the Department being one member among others. One of its main functions is to enlist teachers' help in curricular development. The Council's activities in the short time they have been established have been principally concerned with secondary education, save for their interest in the Nuffield primary school projects in French, science and mathematics. The Council have a great number of subject sub-committees as well as steering committees concerned with the different stages of education, including one for primary education.

Research on Children's Learning

518. Towards the end of the nineteenth century, research began to supplement general observation of children's methods of learning, though even now it would be difficult to find many teachers who could relate what they are doing in the classroom to any particular piece of research. Here, as in other fields, the pace has recently quickened. Many teachers, for example, are following research on various methods of teaching children to read. More fundamentally, an encouraging number of teachers are beginning to concern themselves with theories of learning. By their practical work in the classroom, teachers have perhaps as much to contribute to psychology as the psychologists to educational practice.

519. Research into the ways in which children learn has produced, broadly, two interpretations of the learning process. One, which is still dominant in the United States, and is associated with the names of Thorndike, Hull, Pavlov and Skinner among others, is essentially behaviourist. It is concerned with simple and complex operant conditioning, the place of reinforcement in learning, habit formation and the measurement of various kinds of stimulus-response behaviour. Much of the more recent work derives from animal studies and its main relevance is to motor learning, though some work has been done on the learning of information, concepts and skills by children and adults. It does not offer very much direct help to teachers since, for the most part, the motives and sequence of children's learning are too complicated for analysis in terms of simple models. A recent review of programmed learning[1] suggests that even simple segments of learning do not always conform closely to models of learning theory such as Skinner's. It is in a whole situation with a history behind it that a child or adult learns. Success in using a machine may be due as much to relaxation from anxiety or to a feeling of self-importance as to the small steps used in linear programming on the Skinner system. Most teachers of young children have seen the value of a gradual build-up of vocabulary in the teaching of reading. But they have also had evidence of the rapid strides that children can make when a particular book holds such interest for them that they are determined to read it quickly.

520. Some of the experiments of the behaviourists confirm that prolonged periods of routine practice in, for example, computation or handwriting reduce rather than improve accuracy. This is a lesson which is particularly relevant to schools working on traditional lines.

521. A second school of research, which is dominant in Great Britain and apparently gaining ground in the United States, is associated with the names of Baldwin, Isaacs, Luria, Bruner, and in particular Jean Piaget. This school is interested in discovering the ground plan of the growth of intellectual powers and the order in which they are acquired. One of its most important conclusions is that the great majority of primary school children can only learn efficiently from concrete situations, as lived or described. From these situations, children acquire concepts in every area of the curriculum. According to Piaget, all learning calls for organisation of material or of behaviour on the part of the learner, and the learner has to adapt himself and is altered in the process. Learning takes place through a continuous process of interaction between the learner and his environment, which results in the building up of consistent and stable patterns of behaviour, physical and mental. Each new experience reorganises, however slightly, the structure of the mind and contributes to the child's world picture.

522. Piaget's thought, which influenced the 1931 Report and our own, is not easy to understand. It is almost impossible to express in other than technical terms. Although he is not primarily an educationalist, his work has important implications for teachers. His observations of the sequence in the development of children's concepts are being tested on samples of children in many countries and these tests are tending to confirm his main findings. Much more investigation is needed on the extent to which the school environment and the guidance and teaching provided by teachers can accelerate children's progress. The effect of social expectations on the way children learn also calls for study. Nevertheless Piaget's explanations appear to most educationalists in this

country to fit the observed facts of children's learning more satisfactorily than any other. It is in accord with previous research by genetic psychologists and with what is generally regarded as the most effective primary school practice, as it has been worked out empirically. The main implications of that practice are described in the following paragraphs and, where relevant, reference is made to the support given them by the Piagetian school of thought.

Aspects of Children's Learning

523. Play is the central activity in all nursery schools and in many infant schools. This sometimes leads to accusations that children are wasting their time in school: they should be "working". But this distinction between work and play is false, possibly throughout life, certainly in the primary school. Its essence lies in past notions of what is done in school hours (work) and what is done out of school (play). We know now that play—in the sense of "messing about" either with material objects or with other children, and of creating fantasies—is vital to children's learning and therefore vital in school. Adults who criticise teachers for allowing children to play are unaware that play is the principal means of learning in early childhood. It is the way through which children reconcile their inner lives with external reality. In play, children gradually develop concepts of causal relationships, the power to discriminate, to make judgements, to analyse and synthesise, to imagine and to formulate. Children become absorbed in their play and the satisfaction of bringing it to a satisfactory conclusion fixes habits of concentration which can be transferred to other learning.

524. From infancy, children investigate the material world. Their interest is not wholly scientific but arises from a desire to control or use the things about them. Pleasure in "being a cause" seems to permeate children's earliest contact with materials. To destroy and construct involves learning the properties of things and in this way children can build up concepts of weight, height, size, volume and texture.

525. Primitive materials such as sand, water, clay and wood attract young children and evoke concentration and inventiveness. Children are also stimulated by natural or manufactured materials of many shapes, colours and textures. Their imagination seizes on particular facets of objects and leads them to invent as well as to create. All kinds of causal connections are discovered, illustrated and used. Children also use objects as symbols for things, feelings and experiences, for which they may lack words. A small girl may use a piece of material in slightly different ways to make herself into a bride, a queen or a nurse. When teachers enter into the play activity of children, they can help by watching the connections and relationships which children are making and by introducing, almost incidentally, the words for the concepts and feelings that are being expressed. Some symbolism is unconscious and may be the means by which children come to terms with actions or thoughts which are not acceptable to adults or are too frightening for the children themselves. In play are the roots of drama, expressive movement and art. In this way too children learn to understand other people. The earliest play of this kind probably emerges from play with materials. A child playing with a toy aeroplane can be seen to take the role of both the aeroplane and the pilot apparently simultaneously. All the important people of his world figure in this play: he imitates, he becomes, he symbolises. He works off aggression

or compensates himself for lack of love by "being" one or other of the people who impinge on his life. By acting as he conceives they do, he tries to understand them. Since children tend to have inflexible roles thrust on them by adults, they need opportunities to explore different roles and to make a freer choice of their own. Early exploration of the actions, motives and feelings of themselves and of others is likely to be an important factor in the ability to form right relationships, which in its turn seems to be a crucial element in mental health. The difficulties of blind and deaf children whose play is restricted show how much play enriches the lives of ordinary children. Adults can help children in this form of play, and in their social development, by references to the thoughts, feelings and needs of other people. Through stories told to them, children enter into different ways of behaving and of looking at the world, and play new parts.

526. Just as adults relive experience in thought or words, so children play over and over the important happenings of their lives. The repetition is usually selective. Children who re-enact a painful scene repeatedly are not doing it to preserve the pain but to make it bearable and understandable. They incorporate those parts of the difficult situation which are endurable and add others as their courage and confidence grows. This is one of the ways in which they bring under control the feelings of frustration which must be experienced by those who are dependent on the will and love of adults. This kind of play can preserve self esteem by reducing unpleasant experiences to size, and reinforce confidence by dwelling on success.

527. Much of children's play is "cultural" play as opposed to the "natural" play of animals which mainly practices physical and survival skills. It often needs adult participation so that cultural facts and their significance can be communicated to children. The introduction into the classroom of objects for hospital play provides opportunities for coming to terms with one of the most common fears. Similarly the arrival of a new baby in the family, the death of someone important to the child, the invention of space rockets or new weapons may all call for the provision of materials for dramatic play which will help children to give expression to their feelings as a preliminary to understanding and controlling them. Sensitivity and observation are called for rather than intervention from the teacher. The knowledge of children gained from "active" observation is invaluable to teachers. It gives common ground for conversation and exchange of ideas which it is among the most important duties of teachers to initiate and foster.

528. A child's play at any given moment contains many elements. The layers of meaning may include a highly conscious organisation of the environment, exploration of physical and social relationships and an expression of the deepest levels of fantasy. Wide ranging and satisfying play is a means of learning, a powerful stimulus to learning, and a way to free learning from distortion by the emotions. Several writers have recently emphasised the importance of a period of play and exploration in new learning as, for example, in mathematics and science.[2,3] Adults as well as children approach new learning in this way.

529. The child is the agent in his own learning. This was the message of the often quoted comment from the 1931 Report: "The curriculum is to be thought of in terms of activity and experience rather than of knowledge to be acquired

and facts to be stored". Read in isolation, the passage has sometimes been taken to imply that children could not learn from imaginative experience and that activity and experience did not lead to the acquisition of knowledge. The context makes it plain that the actual implication is almost the opposite of this. It is that activity and experience, both physical and mental, are often the best means of gaining knowledge and acquiring facts. This is more generally recognised today but still needs to be said. We certainly would not wish to undervalue knowledge and facts, but facts are best retained when they are used and understood, when right attitudes to learning are created, when children learn to learn. Instruction in many primary schools continues to bewilder children because it outruns their experience. Even in infant schools, where innovation has gone furthest, time is sometimes wasted in teaching written "sums" before children are able to understand what they are doing. The N.C.D.S. Survey (Appendix 10) shows that 17 per cent of children start doing sums in infant schools before the age of five and a half.

530. The intense interest shown by young children in the world about them, their powers of concentration on whatever is occupying their attention, or serving their immediate purposes, are apparent to both teachers and parents. Skills of reading and writing or the techniques used in art and craft can best be taught when the need for them is evident to children. A child who has no immediate incentive for learning to read is unlikely to succeed because of warnings about the disadvantages of illiteracy in adult life. There is, there-fore, good reason for allowing young children to choose within a carefully prepared environment in which choices and interest are supported by their teachers, who will have in mind the potentialities for further learning. Piaget's observations support the belief that children have a natural urge to explore and discover, that they find pleasure in satisfying it and that it is therefore self-perpetuating. When children are learning new patterns of behaviour or new concepts, they tend both to practise them spontaneously and to seek out relevant experience, as can be seen from the way they acquire skills in move-ment. It takes much longer than teachers have previously realised for children to master through experience new concepts or new levels of complex concepts. When understanding has been achieved, consolidation should follow. At this stage children profit from various types of practice devised by their teachers, and from direct instruction.

531. Children will of course vary in the degree of interest that they show and their urge to learn will be strengthened or weakened, as we have suggested in Chapter 3, by the attitudes of parents, teachers and others with whom they identify themselves. Apathy may result when parents show no interest, clamp down on children's curiosity and enterprise, tell them constantly not to touch and do not answer their questions. Children can also learn to be passive from a teacher who allows them little scope in managing their own affairs and in learning. A teacher who relies only on instruction, who forestalls children's questions or who answers them too quickly, instead of asking the further questions which will set children on the way to their own solution, will disin-cline children to learn[4]. A new teacher with time and patience can usually help children who have learnt from their teachers to be too dependent. Those who have been deprived at home need more than that. Their self-confidence can only be restored by affection, stability and order. They must have special

attention from adults who can discover, by observing their responses, what experiences awaken interest, and can seize on them to reinforce the desire to learn.

532. External incentives such as marks and stars, and other rewards and punishments, influence children's learning mainly by evoking or representing parents' or teachers' approval. Although children vary temperamentally in their response to rewards and punishments, positive incentives are generally more effective than punishment, and neither is as damaging as neglect. But the children who most need the incentive of good marks are least likely to gain them, even when, as in many primary schools, they are given for effort rather than for achievement. In any case, one of the main educational tasks of the primary school is to build on and strengthen children's intrinsic interest in learning and lead them to learn for themselves rather than from fear of disapproval or desire for praise.

533. Learning is a continuous process from birth. The teacher's task is to provide an environment and opportunities which are sufficiently challenging for children and yet not so difficult as to be outside their reach. There has to be the right mixture of the familiar and the novel, the right match to the stage of learning the child has reached. If the material is too familiar or the learning skills too easy, children will become inattentive and bored. If too great maturity is demanded of them, they fall back on half remembered formulae and become concerned only to give the reply the teacher wants. Children can think and form concepts, so long as they work at their own level, and are not made to feel that they are failures.

534. Teachers must rely both on their general knowledge of child development and on detailed observation of individual children for matching their demands to children's stages of development. This concept of "readiness" was first applied to reading. It has sometimes been thought of in too negative a way. Children can, as we indicate in Chapter 17, be led to want to read, provided that they are sufficiently mature. Learning can be undertaken too late as well as too early. Piaget's work can help teachers in diagnosing children's readiness in mathematics, and gives some pointers as to how it can be encouraged.

535. At every stage of learning children need rich and varied materials and situations, though the pace at which they should be introduced may vary according to the children. If children are limited in materials, they tend to solve problems in isolation and fail to see their relevance to other similar situations. This stands out particularly clearly in young children's learning of mathematics. Similarly, children need to accumulate much experience of human behaviour before they can develop moral concepts. If teachers or parents are inconsistent in their attitudes or contradict by their behaviour what they preach, it becomes difficult for children to develop stable and mature concepts. Verbal explanation, in advance of understanding based on experience, may be an obstacle to learning, and children's knowledge of the right words may conceal from teachers their lack of understanding. Yet it is inevitable that children will pick up words which outstrip their understanding. Discussion with other children and with adults is one of the principal ways in which children check their concepts against those of others and build up an objective view of reality. There is every justification for the conversation

which is a characteristic feature of the contemporary primary school. One of the most important responsibilities of teachers is to help children to see order and pattern in experience, and to extend their ideas by analogies and by the provision of suitable vocabulary. Rigid division of the curriculum into subjects tends to interrupt children's trains of thought and of interest and to hinder them from realising the common elements in problem solving. These are among the many reasons why some work, at least, should cut across subject divisions at all stages in the primary school.

Some Practical Implications
The Time Table

536. These beliefs about how children learn have practical implications for the time table and the curriculum. One idea now widespread is embodied in the expression "free day" and another, associated with it, is the "integrated curriculum". The strongest influence making for the free day has been the conviction of some teachers and other educationalists that it is through play that young children learn. Nursery schools began by devoting half an hour to free play. This is still done by many kindergartens which we visited abroad. Now the whole day is spent on various forms of play, though groups of children may break away to enjoy stories or music with an adult. Infant schools usually give at least an hour a day to play, though it may be called by many different names. If teachers encourage overlap between what is done in periods of self chosen activity and in the times allocated, for example, to reading and to writing, a good learning situation will probably result. Children who are not yet ready to read can go on playing and building up vocabulary while other children are reading. Play can lead naturally to reading and writing associated with it. Children do not flit from activity to activity in their anxiety to make use of materials not available at other times of the day. Some infant schools are now confident enough in the value of self chosen activity to give the whole day to it, except for times which are used for stories, poetry, movement, and music—and even these may be voluntary, particularly for the younger children. The tendency is spreading in junior schools. Children may plan when to do work assigned to them and also have time in which to follow personal or group interests of their own choice. In a few infant and junior schools the day is still divided into a succession of short periods. In the great majority, we are glad to say, there are longer periods and these can be adjusted at the teacher's discretion.

537. These changes represent a revolution from the type of time table implied by the forms completed by schools for local education authorities until quite recently. Heads were expected to show exactly what each class was doing during every minute of the week and to provide a summary showing the total number of minutes to be spent on each subject. In extreme cases, the curriculum was divided into spelling, dictation, grammar, exercises, composition, recitation, reading, handwriting, tables and mental arithmetic. It is obvious that this arrangement was not suited to what was known of the nature of children, of the classification of subject matter, or of the art of teaching. Children's interest varies in length according to personality, age and circumstances, and it is folly either to interrupt it when it is intense, or to flog it when it has declined. The teacher can best judge when to make a change and the

moment of change may not be the same for each child in the class. In many schools, as we have said, children plan much of their work. Yet the teacher must constantly ensure a balance within the day or week both for the class and for individuals. He must see that time is profitably spent and give guidance on its use. In the last resort, the teacher's relationship with his pupils, his openness to their suggestions and their trust in him are far more important than the nominal degree of freedom in the time table.

Flexibility in the Curriculum

538. The extent to which subject matter ought to be classified and the headings under which the classification is made will vary with the age of the children, with the demands made by the structure of the subject matter which is being studied, and with the circumstances of the school. Any practice which predetermines the pattern and imposes it upon all is to be condemned. Some teachers find it helpful in maintaining a balance in individual and class work to think in terms of broad areas of the curriculum such as language, science and mathematics, environmental study and the expressive arts. No pattern can be perfect since many subjects fall into one category or another according to the aspect which is being studied. For young children, the broadest of divisions is suitable. For children from 9 to 12, more subject divisions can be expected, though experience in secondary schools has shown that teaching of rigidly defined subjects, often by specialist teachers, is far from suitable for the oldest children who will be in the middle schools. This is one of our reasons for suggesting a change in the age of transfer to secondary education.

539. There is little place for the type of scheme which sets down exactly what ground should be covered and what skill should be acquired by each class in the school. Yet to put nothing in its place may be to leave some teachers prisoners of tradition and to make difficulties for newcomers to a staff who are left to pick up, little by little, the ethos of a school. The best solution seems to be to provide brief schemes for the school as a whole: outlines of aims in various areas of the curriculum, the sequence of development which can be expected in children and the methods through which work can be soundly based and progress accelerated. It is also useful to have a record of experiences, topics, books, poems and music which have been found to succeed with children of different ages, and for attention to be drawn to notable experimental work. In good schools, schemes are often subject to a process of accretion which may make them so long that few teachers have time to read them. It is better for them to be sifted and revised, for matter to be dropped as well as added. Individual members of staff, with such help as the head and others can give, will need to plan in more detail the work of their particular classes. Often it will develop in an unexpected direction. A brief report on the topics, literature and so forth which have absorbed children during the course of the year will be necessary for teachers who take them later in their school career.

540. The idea of flexibility has found expression in a number of practices, all of them designed to make good use of the interest and curiosity of children, to minimise the notion of subject matter being rigidly compartmental, and to allow the teacher to adopt a consultative, guiding, stimulating role rather than a purely didactic one. The oldest of these methods is the "project". Some topic, such as "transport" is chosen, ideally by the children, but frequently

by the teacher. The topic cuts across the boundaries of subjects and is treated as its nature requires without reference to subjects as such. At its best the method leads to the use of books of reference, to individual work and to active participation in learning. Unfortunately it is no guarantee of this and the appearance of text books of projects, which achieved at one time considerable popularity, is proof of how completely a good idea can be misunderstood.

541. A variation on the project, originally associated with the infant school but often better suited to older children, is "the centre of interest". It begins with a topic which is of such inherent interest and variety as to make it possible and reasonable to make much of the work of the class revolve round it for a period of a week, a month or a term or even longer. Experience has shown that it is artificial to try to link most of the work of a class to one centre of interest. It has become more common to have several interests—topic is now the usual word—going at once. Much of the work may be individual, falling under broad subject headings. One topic for the time being can involve both group and class interest, and may splinter off into all kinds of individual work.

542. When a class of seven year olds notice the birds that come to the bird table outside the classroom window, they may decide, after discussion with their teacher, to make their own aviary. They will set to with a will, and paint the birds in flight, make models of them in clay or papier maché, write stories and poems about them and look up reference books to find out more about their habits. Children are not assimilating inert ideas but are wholly involved in thinking, feeling and doing. The slow and the bright share a common experience and each takes from it what he can at his own level. There is no attempt to put reading and writing into separate compartments; both serve a wider purpose, and artificial barriers do not fragment the learning experience. A top junior class became interested in the problem of measuring the area of an awkwardly shaped field at the back of the school. The problem stimulated much learning about surveying and triangles. From surveying, interest passed to navigation; for the more difficult aspects of the work, co-operation between members of staff as well as pupils was needed. For one boy, the work on navigation took the form of a story of encounters of pirate ships and men-of-war, and involved a great deal of calculation, history, geography and English. Integration is not only a question of allowing time for interests which do not fit under subject headings; it is as much a matter of seeing the different dimensions of subject work and of using the forms of observation and communication which are most suitable to a given sequence of learning.

Use of the Environment

543. Another effective way of integrating the curriculum is to relate it through the use of the environment to the boundless curiosity which children have about the world about them. When teachers talk about "first-hand experience" what they often have in mind is the exploration of the physical environment of the school, though the expression of course includes other kinds of experiences as well. Whereas once the teacher brought autumn leaves into the classroom and talked about the seasons and their characteristics, now he will take the children out to see for themselves. Rural schools can be

overwhelmed by the variety of material on their doorsteps. Crops and pastures, wild flowers and weeds, farm animals, wild creatures of every kind, roads and footpaths, verges, hedges, ditches, streams, woods, the weather, the season, the stars, all provide starting points for curiosity, discussion, observation, recording and enquiry, at every level from that of the five year old to that of the 12 year old and beyond. Much of this material is also available to the newer urban schools though their sites are often laid out too formally to be suitable for children's play or for interesting studies. The most difficult problem of all is not so much that of the older urban school, despite its often restricted site, as that of the school on the large housing estate. But the weather and the stars are available to all; so are the occupations of fathers which offer a way of enlisting co-operation and interest in their children's education as well as an approach to local industry.

544. Teachers in town schools can make use of railways and other transport systems, and the local shops and factories, all of which can provide suitable material. Building sites are almost ubiquitous and can provide an approach to geography, mathematics and science. We have heard of children doing "traffic counts", discovering from shop keepers the source of their goods and even, in one case, exploring unofficially the sewage system of their area. Museums, geared to children's interests, may also be within reach and are becoming ready to let children handle as well as look, and to lend to schools some of the surplus stock which is otherwise often stored away in basements. It may be well to look a little at this approach as it can work out in a favourable environment. A group of H.M.Is. working in a division in which some particularly good work is to be found, write as follows:—

"The newer methods start with the direct impact of the environment on the child and the child's individual response to it. The results are unpredictable, but extremely worth while. The teacher has to be prepared to follow up the personal interests of the children who, either singly, or in groups, follow divergent paths of discovery. Books of reference, maps, enquiries of local officials, museums, archives, elderly residents in the area are all called upon to give the information needed to complete the picture that the child is seeking to construct. When this enthusiasm is unleashed in a class, the time table may even be dispensed with, as the resulting occupations may easily cover mathematics, geology, astronomy, history, navigation, religious instruction, literature, art and craft. The teacher needs perception to appreciate the value that can be gained from this method of working, and he needs also energy to keep up with the children's demands."

545. Another possibility is to take children out of their own environment into a contrasting one, either for the day or for a longer period. This of course applies as much to rural children visiting towns as to urban children visiting the countryside. Such visits, carefully prepared for and not just sight-seeing, are generally used as the culmination of an interest or interests. They would often serve better as starting points. For day visits, when the school situation makes it possible, those places are best which are near enough for children to visit and to revisit, individually, in groups or as a class when new questions arise. There is then a strong incentive for them to look closely at the objects which have made a further visit necessary.

546. In one northern city a school, well situated in a park on the outskirts of the city, is being used for a fortnight at a time by children from the central

slum areas. The school has a small resident staff and is well equipped. Since the visiting children's own teachers accompany them, they can be taught in small groups of 15. During the summer months the school day is extended into the evening so that the children, who are conveyed by buses, can gain the maximum from their experiences.

547. Authorities can help schools, as some indeed do, by providing hutted camps and other residential centres which do much for children socially as well as educationally. Useful experiments have also been tried in linking country and urban schools and arranging for exchange visits. Expeditions too far afield are to be avoided, as they are generally speaking pure sight-seeing tours. We have considerable doubts about overseas expeditions for primary school children.

548. A third possibility, which is open to all schools, is to make the school environment itself as rich as possible, Nearly all children are interested in living forms, whether they be animal or plants. Some acquaintance with them is an essential part of being educated. To care for living creatures offers an emotional outlet to some children and demands discipline from all. However rich the locality, emphasis must always be put on the school itself, which is an environment contrived for children's learning.

Discovery

549. A word which has fairly recently come into use in educational circles is "discovery". It includes many of the ideas so far discussed and is a useful shorthand description. It has the disadvantage of comprehensiveness that it can be loosely interpreted and misunderstood. We have more to say about the value of discovery in the section on science. The sense of personal discovery influences the intensity of a child's experience, the vividness of his memory and the probability of effective transfer of learning. At the same time it is true that trivial ideas and inefficient methods may be "discovered". Furthermore, time does not allow children to find their way by discovery to all that they have to learn. In this matter, as in all education, the teacher is responsible for encouraging children in enquiries which lead to discovery and for asking leading questions.

550. Free and sometimes indiscriminate use of words such as discovery has led some critics to the view that English primary education needs to be more firmly based on closely argued educational theory. Nevertheless great advances appear to have been made without such theory, and research has still a long way to go before it can make a marked contribution. At many points even so fruitful an approach as that of Piaget needs further verification. What is immediately needed is that teachers should bring to bear on their day to day problems astringent intellectual scrutiny. Yet all good teachers must work intuitively and be sensitive to the emotive and imaginative needs of their children. Teaching is an art and, as long as that with all its implications is firmly grasped, it will not be harmed by intellectual stiffening.

Evaluation of Children's Progress

551. We have considered whether we can lay down standards that should be achieved by the end of the primary school but concluded that it is not possible to describe a standard of attainment that should be reached by all or most children. Any set standard would seriously limit the bright child and be impossibly high for the dull. What could be achieved in one school might be

impossible in another. We have suggested in Chapter 11 that, with the ending of selection examinations, teachers—and parents—will need some yardstick of the progress of their children in relation to what is achieved elsewhere. Without it teachers may be tempted to go on teaching and testing in much the same way as they did before. We therefore envisage that some use will continue to be made of objective tests within schools. Such tests can be helpful—and their norms can serve as a basis of comparison—as long as they are used with insight and discrimination, and teachers do not assume that only what is measurable is valuable (see Chapter 11). Primary schools should hear regularly from the secondary schools to which they contribute how their pupils compare over a period with children from other schools. One of the principal functions of H.M. Inspectors is to help teachers to know what to expect from children in the circumstances of their neighbourhood and to advise teachers on standards in aspects of the curriculum where objective measurement is not practicable.

552. We have already suggested that surveys of the quality of primary schools should be made by H.M. Inspectorate at regular intervals. We also think that there should be recurring national surveys of attainment similar to that undertaken in reading by the Department of Education, and those carried out by the N.F.E.R. in reading and mathematics.

553. In this chapter, and in Part V as a whole, we describe how children learn and make broad suggestions for the curriculum and organisation of primary schools. Our views derive from evidence given to us and our own observations of good practice in the schools. At some points research supports strongly our emphasis on active learning. But many problems remain unresolved and we have, therefore, recommended further enquiry into child development and the results of new methods. We endorse the trend towards individual and active learning and "learning by acquaintance", and should like many more schools to be more deeply influenced by it. Yet we certainly do not deny the value of "learning by description" or the need for practice of skills and consolidation of knowledge. This part of our Report should be read in conjunction with Part IV where we discuss the teacher's responsibility for ensuring that what children learn is worth learning. At the extremes of the ability range, as we have said in other chapters, there will always be children who need special help. Not enough is known about how far, apart from variations in ability, children differ, according to temperament in the way they learn. Even as children differ so do teachers. They must select those of our suggestions which their knowledge and skill enable them to put int practice in the cicumstances of their schools.

Recommendations

554. (i) There should be recurring national surveys of attainment similar to those undertaken in reading by the Department of Education, and those carried out by the N.F.E.R. in reading and mathematics.

(ii) Primary schools should hear from secondary schools how their children compare over a period with children from other schools.

REFERENCES
[1] Williams, J. D., 'Programmed Instruction Not Yet Proven?' National Foundation for Educational Research, Article in New Society, 20th January, 1966.
[2] Skinner, B. F., Harvard Educational Review, 1954.
[3] Dienes, Z. P., 'Building Up Mathematics', Hutchinson Educational Press, 1960.
[4] Holt, J., 'Why Children Fail', Pitman, 1964.

CHAPTER 17

Aspects of the Curriculum

555. Throughout our discussion of the curriculum, and particularly in this and the previous chapter, we stress that children's learning does not fit into subject categories. The younger the children, the more undifferentiated their curriculum will be. As children come towards the top of the junior school, and we anticipate they will be there till 12, the conventional subjects become more relevant; some children can then profit from a direct approach to the structure of a subject. Even so, subjects merge and overlap and it is easy for this to happen when one teacher is in charge of the class for most of the time. Schools and individual teachers group subjects in various ways, as well as allowing for work which cuts right across them.

556. Yet an expanding curriculum makes great demands on the class teacher. For this reason we recommend in Chapter 20 that teachers expert in the main fields of learning should give advice to their colleagues throughout the school. The work of the oldest children could be shared by a few teachers who, between them, can cover the curriculum.

557. In considering the curriculum, we have discussed with expert witnesses the experiences and ideas within the traditional subjects which are suitable for primary school children, and give examples of work at most stages of the school.

*A. RELIGIOUS EDUCATION†

558. The Council is divided in its views on religious education because of the personal beliefs of its members. The fundamental difference between the theist and the non-theist is not one we can try to resolve. A minority of members believe that religious education should not figure in the curriculum at all. They have stated their reasons in a note of reservation at the end of this Report and dissociate themselves from the views we express. Other members believe that religious education and the Act of Worship should influence the entire curriculum and set the tone of living and learning for the whole school community. The views of the remaining members of the Council range between these two extremes. We have decided to discuss in this section what reforms are possible and desirable within the framework of the 1944 Act. In doing so, we have borne in mind that a survey in 1965[1] showed that 80 per cent of those interviewed thought that the present arrangements for giving religious education in schools and for daily worship should continue. This interest in religion is supported by other surveys[2,3].

559. The Act, in effect, improved the financial position of voluntary schools of which there are two main categories, aided and controlled. In aided schools, all religious education may be denominational; in controlled schools there is

*We prefer to call it religious education (R.E.) although the Education Act 1944 refers to religious instruction.

†See Notes of Reservation which follow the main Report.

provision for not more than two periods of denominational instruction each week for children whose parents desire it. Most voluntary schools are Church of England; there is a substantial minority of Roman Catholic schools and a smaller number of Jewish, Methodist and undenominational Christian schools (see Table 9).

560. In both county and voluntary schools, the Act gave statutory force to the provisions of corporate worship (the "Act of Worship") and of religious education, but it did not introduce either school prayers or scripture lessons, which were all but universal in schools before the Act came into force. It laid upon local education authorities the duty of providing or adopting a syllabus for R.E., which would be agreeable to the local education authorities, the churches other than Roman Catholic churches, and the teachers, but which would not be distinctive of any particular denomination. The Agreed Syllabuses were not an invention of the Act, but Parliament made general and obligatory what was already common practice. The use of the Agreed Syllabus is obligatory in county schools and controlled schools (apart from periods provided for denominational instruction) and it is quite common in voluntary aided schools.

561. The Act laid down that the Act of Worship should begin the school day: R.E. which previously had to be given at the beginning or end of a session could now be given at any time, the way being thus opened to specialist teaching. The rights of teachers who did not wish to give R.E. or to attend the Act of Worship were safeguarded. The rights of parents were also safeguarded so that at their request their children might be excused from R.E. and the Act of Worship, or be withdrawn for denominational instruction or for Agreed Syllabus instruction within some limits.

562. At the moment R.E. is the only subject which the law requires to be taught and the only subject from which both the individual child and teacher may be excused. Its unique status causes difficulties. We stress elsewhere in this and the previous chapter the importance of the integration of the curriculum, particularly for the younger children. Can an integrated curriculum include religious education when individual parents may not wish their children to receive it and certain teachers may not feel competent or wish to give it? What is, and should be, the position of the child or teacher who wishes to withdraw, or the non-Christian head teacher? What form should the Act of Worship take? Are most Agreed Syllabuses in accordance with what is known about children's ways of learning? Is the very notion of an Agreed Syllabus compatible with the flexibility of the modern primary school? We try to answer some of these questions in the paragraphs that follow.

Teachers' Attitudes

563. The willingness of teachers to give religious education is a matter of some delicacy and, so far as we are aware, no direct approach has ever been made to the teaching profession to ascertain the facts. In 1964, however, a survey was undertaken by H.M. Inspectors. All those who happened to be carrying out full inspections in county schools during the Christmas Term of 1963 and the Easter Term of 1964 were asked to estimate, with the help of the head teachers, the proportion of teachers in these schools who would be likely to volunteer to give religious education if volunteers were called for. The lowest estimate of teachers willing to give instruction in any one primary

school was 70 per cent. Of teachers actually heard giving religious education during these inspections, H.M.I.s concluded that eight per cent of the women, and 16 per cent of the men, were reluctant or not much interested. It should be noted that, in all but eight of the 163 primary schools included in this survey, religious education was given by all the class teachers in their own classes. In the light of this evidence it seems probable that, if religious education were to be given only by teachers who volunteered to give it, there would be no difficulty in staffing it overall, though there might, of course, be some difficulty in individual schools.

564. The fact that schools seldom have to arrange for classes to receive religious education from other than their class teachers suggests that, although teachers are aware of their right to refuse to give religious education, not all those who wish to exercise this right on conscientious grounds actually do so. This may be because of the inconvenience which would be caused within the school, or because it is believed that a profession of agnosticism is a handicap to promotion. It seems to us that these reasons must operate, though with what frequency or force we are unable to say.

565. The morning assembly may create a greater difficulty for the agnostic aspiring to a headship than religious education itself. It is comparatively easy for a head teacher to arrange that other teachers of his staff should be responsible for religious education but, if he opts out of taking the morning assembly, his withdrawal is bound to be a subject of remark, and, since assembly is a social, as well as a religious, occasion, such a head is likely to be at a real disadvantage.

566. There is some evidence that head teachers and assistants are not sufficiently aware of their freedom in relation to the Agreed Syllabuses. In many instances, the Syllabus itself is very brief and the detailed commentary which may accompany it can be followed or not as teachers wish. In other Syllabuses, it is clearly stated that teachers may select topics and draft their own schemes to suit the children they teach. It may well be that the very existence of an Agreed Syllabus discourages teachers from thinking out schemes for themselves.

Difficulties of the Present Position

567. It does not imply any criticism of the excellent and imaginative work done in religious education in many schools to recognise that there are serious shortcomings in the present arrangements. The chief difficulties seem to be the following:

(a) Many devout Christians want for their children more convincedly Christian teaching than in present circumstances they sometimes get.

(b) For the non-Christian parent there is a difficult choice: either he must acquiesce in his child being taught beliefs which he holds to be untrue and harmful, or he must take the initiative and ask for his child to be excused from religious education, thus setting him apart from the rest of the school. He may not be prepared to do this because he does not wish to make his child appear different.

(c) For the teacher who does not accept the Christian faith, the present arrangements may encourage dishonesty or cynicism, and some sincere teachers are known not to have applied for headships because they would not pretend to a faith they did not hold.

The School Community

568. The school should be a community within which children should learn to live a good life. They learn from their relationship with their teachers and with each other and from observing the way the adults in the school behave with one another and with children. By example at first hand children can learn to love and to care for others, to be generous, kind and courageous. Good experiences in personal relationships in early life will make a most important contribution to an understanding of spiritual and moral values when children are older. Teachers should have clearly thought out and positive views on what constitutes good moral and social behaviour. In the later stages of the junior school, children should be encouraged to discuss the basis of conduct. Junior children can feel true compassion. Children need a vivid experience of service to others. It is not enough to give money for refugees and famine areas. We have heard of a school whose "adoption" of an Indian boy included personal friendship expressed in gifts and the exchange of letters. Another school invites the local old peoples' club for an afternoon of entertainment and hospitality. Such activities enlarge children's imagination and deepen their sympathy. Through th m they learn that charity is about people.

569. Each school is composed of individuals, teachers and children, from various religious backgrounds. We believe that to provide for them and to carry out the spirit of the 1944 Act all parents should be told, when children are admitted to school, of their rights of excusal both from the Act of Worship and from religious education. They should be told how both these forms of religious education are conducted in the school and what provision, if any, is made for the children who are withdrawn from them.

The Act of Worship

570. We believe that the Act of Worship has great value as a unifying force for the school and that in it children should find, in brief moments, a religious expression of their life in school. They should be able to understand and to take part in what is happening. Yet there should be more freedom in the interpretation of the law. It is not always suitable, particularly in a junior mixed and infant school, for an assembly to include the whole school. There are occasions when it is appropriate for different age groups to have separate assemblies. Many schools have found advantages in placing the assembly at other times than the beginning of the day. In a school of mixed religious or non-religious backgrounds, it is essential that the assembly should be conducted in such a way that as large a part of the school community as possible, both teachers and children, can take part in it without offence being given to anyone's conscientious scruples. We are sure that, at this stage of education, common standards and values are of extreme importance, and we cannot overemphasise the need for the security which a sense of these will give, especially to children in infant and lower junior classes.

571. The Act of Worship should illuminate personal relationships and introduce children to aesthetic and spiritual experience. It can derive material from other than Christian sources. There is no reason why heads should always conduct the Act of Worship; other members of staff may plan and lead the assembly. Arrangements such as we have described, both as to the

content and the leadership of the assembly, already work—and work well—in many schools. We hope that heads of schools and administrators will be sensitive to the needs of minority groups, both for worship and for religious education. The need is especially evident when numbers of immigrant children of other than Christian religions are educated in schools which were hitherto largely Christian. It has long been common for special provision to be made in some schools for Jewish children. We have heard of a school with a large Mohammedan intake where pupils have been encouraged to bring their prayer mats to school, and go into a room provided for prayer, rather than go out of school and travel some distance for religious observances in the town.

Religious Education

572. Our theological witnesses stressed that religious education should be given by those with a knowledge of young children. The vast majority of teachers have been brought up as Christians, and accept the Christian code of morality though they are often insufficiently informed and mature about Christian beliefs and their application in the twentieth century. We believe that religious education should, when it is possible, be given by the class teacher. In practice most religious education in primary schools emphasises the cultural heritage of Christianity and the effect it has had on generations of men and women. There may be some schools in which parents' views are so divided that special periods in the time table should be allocated for it. Whether it is given by the class teacher or assigned to a separate period, in either of these conditions, it should meet the wishes of those parents who have specifically accepted that their child should have this instruction. It should recognise that young children need a simple and positive introduction to religion. They should be taught to know and love God and to practise in the school community the virtues appropriate to their age and environment. Children whose parents do not wish them to have any R.E. will have to be catered for separately, but they should otherwise conform to the general life of the school. It is essential that the teacher who is prepared to give religious education should be honest and sincere in his teaching, and should not pretend to beliefs he does not hold. For the non-believing teacher or one of different religion this may mean stressing the ethics and the history of Christianity rather than its theology. Children should not be unnecessarily involved in religious controversy. They should not be confused by being taught to doubt before faith is established. Inevitably at some stage of the child's growth the truth of religious teaching will be questioned and a free judgement made as to its truth or falsehood. These judgments will only exceptionally be made by children of primary school age. If children ask, as they will, whether stories are true they should be given an honest answer by each teacher according to his lights. Neither the believing nor the non-believing teacher should try to conceal from his pupils the fact that others take a different view. All teachers giving religious education should have some knowledge of Biblical criticism. There is reason to suppose that too much emphasis is still being put on the Old Testament rather than on the New Testament.

The Agreed Syllabus

573. There is an urgent need for a reconsideration and re-appraisal of what aspects of religious faith can be appropriately presented to children, at what

time and in what way. That there is anxiety about the Agreed Syllabus is apparent from the evidence we have received. One witness wrote "In almost every case the syllabus was based on factual knowledge which it was felt a child ought to have. . . . Educational thought today is questioning whether the basis ought not rather to be the development of religious concepts, and the meeting of the religious needs of children at each point of their lives". Investigation on these lines into the spiritual development of the young child is already being carried out[4]. We welcome research which is trying to determine what religious subject matter and concepts are relevant to children's interests, their experience of life and their intellectual powers. We recognise that children may appreciate poetically what they cannot grasp intellectually. It is to be hoped that the recasting of Agreed Syllabuses will take account of all these points. It seems that children who are introduced very early to the more difficult Christian stories and beliefs are likely, especially when they come from a non-Christian home, to form concepts which are shallow and limited, and attitudes which are legalistic. If they remain Christian, they may not grow beyond childish ideas and attitudes; alternatively they may reject religious ideas as their critical faculties develop, and, at the same time, the morality which they associate with them. There will certainly be some stories about the life and teaching of Jesus which children can be told at an early age. They may be led to find in him the expression of that which, in ways appropriate to their development, they have learnt to be good and true. A more systematic study of the life and teaching of Jesus should be delayed until the later years of the junior school, when children can be encouraged to think critically. At this stage children can begin to understand that the Bible is neither a work of science nor of history, and that its value is in the account it gives of man's relationship with God.

574. The selection of Bible stories to be told to children of various ages and of the hymns and prayers which they use require much thought. While young children enjoy and appreciate some Bible stories, they lose their force by too frequent repetition, and some stories are certainly better postponed until the junior or secondary stage. Prayers and hymns should be related to the child's interests and maturity, but care should be taken to avoid the use of banal language and music.

575. During the last years of the junior school more specific religious education should be given, and, from such areas of the curriculum as history, literature, poetry, geography and music, discussion may arise which bears on religion and brings in judgements on values. Among the historical characters about whom the older children should hear, care should be taken to include sympathetically those who represent a non-Christian tradition, Saladin for example, as well as St. Bernard. Children's moral judgements and personal aspirations will also be stimulated by hearing about great figures of both the present and past, who like themselves combine strengths and weakness, and who achieve much for others, despite their weaknesses. At this stage, as at any other, teachers should be sensitive to the feelings of children of parents who are non-Christian, agnostic or humanist as well as to those of Christian parentage.

576. The future of religious education in the primary school depends on the training of teachers. Although many bring skill and devotion to this part of their work, many more are aware that they are inadequately equipped to teach

it. A more thorough training of all who are likely and willing to give religious education is certainly necessary, difficult as it may be to reconcile with all the other demands of the training course. Religious education is often given too little time in the secondary school and students are likely to come to college with inadequate knowledge and immature concepts. They should be able to relate the background and facts of the Christian revelation to situations which are within children's experience, and so give their teaching vitality and greater relevance to the problems of life. When the 1944 Act made religious education compulsory too little thought was given to the training of teachers. It seems reasonable to expect that some voluntary colleges should be a major source of teachers able to act as advisers to their colleagues in primary schools, who are willing to give religious education but aware of their limitations. If practising teachers are to be brought up to date in the knowledge required to give religious education satisfactorily, and if they are to become familiar with modern methods of teaching the subject, systematic provision of in-service training should be made. Another important way of raising the standard of religious education should be the appointment of advisers in this subject by local authorities. At present advisers have been appointed by only four authorities.

Recommendations

577. (i) Parents should be told when their children are admitted to school of their rights of excusal from the Act of Worship and from religious education.

(ii) There should be more freedom in the interpretation of the law on the Act of Worship and it should not necessarily be conducted by the head teacher.

(iii) Further enquiry should be made into the aspects of religious faith which can be presented to young children.

(iv) Further in-service training should be provided to familiarise teachers with modern thinking on religious education.

REFERENCES

[1]Survey by Research Department, Odhams Press (1962) of young people aged 16 to 25 years.
[2]Survey by Institute of Christian Education (1964) of parents of sixth-formers.
[3]Survey by National Opinion Polls Ltd. (1965) for 'New Society' in five regions of England, Scotland and Wales.
[4]Goldman, R. J., 'Readiness for Religion: A Basis for Developmental Religious Education', Routledge, 1965.

B. ENGLISH

578. Despite the obvious importance of English both as a means of communication and as literature, it has not had a brilliant place in the history of education, at least until modern times. In the public schools English was long subordinated to the classics. The first schools for the poor concentrated on teaching children to read the Bible. Later they aimed at equipping them, in

the short period available before they went to work, with those minimum skills in reading, writing and cyphering which would fit them for a humble and useful station in life. The past is still with us in the trend in some schools to emphasise the techniques of reading and writing at the expense of speech and in the survival of a theory of grammar that derives from the inflected language of Latin. It is significant too that, central as English has now become in the curriculum and time table of most primary schools, revolution came later than in art, partly no doubt because English became one of the two subjects by which fitness for secondary education was assessed.

579. But revolution has certainly come. It began when infant schools recognised how much and how spontaneously children learn of the world and of language in the four or five years before they come to school, more than they will ever learn again in the same span of time. Experience and language interact all the time; words come to life in the setting of sensory experience and vivid imaginative experience. It is equally true that experience becomes richer when talked over and recreated. Its meaning can be clarified and refined, feelings about it are brought more into harmony and it becomes the basis for further learning. The achievement of many infant schools has been to build on and to extend children's experiences, to provide opportunities for talk about them and to create a warmth of relationships which encourages children to talk and to listen.

Speech

580. Much has changed in the schools since children sang

"What is infant education?

Universal information

While the children round are walking

None should ever be found talking"

In successive phases, schools tried to make formal provision for speech by the object lesson, the conversation lesson and the "news" period; now there are many schools where the day is spent in long periods of work and play accompanied by talk between teacher and children as individuals, in groups and occasionally with the whole class drawn in. But how difficult it is for teachers of large classes to spend long enough with individuals, even those who have had scant opportunities for the interplay of conversation at home. Teachers can certainly reassure children, but there is rarely time enough to wait for their hesitant words or to put the questions which will help children to classify, and so to forge the instruments of thought.

581. For this reason among others, there seems to be no justification for the sudden decrease in the ratio of adults to pupils as children pass from nursery to infant schools. Similarly there is reason for grave concern about those children who get to the top of the infant school, and even more, the lower reaches of the junior school, before they have become fluent in speech. If teachers are over-anxious to establish literacy at this stage, they may concentrate too narrowly on graded readers and spend too little time on stories. They may clamp down on children's interests and on the conversation and planning arising from them, even though they provide an incentive for reading and writing. Towards the top of the junior school, the situation

usually rights itself, at least for the abler children. Group interests and individual hobbies provide incentives and opportunities for children to talk at some length, though perhaps because of the stress on high standards in written work, as well as on account of differences between English and American society, it is rare to find quite the same degree of confidence in speech that some of our members noted on their visits to schools in the U.S.A. Yet there is no doubt about the improvement in children's fluency, articulation and confidence in speech in the last 20 years. Its effects are already apparent in the speech of young teachers now entering the schools. Since example in speech is all important, we can expect a further improvement in the speech of children, especially since the influence of radio and television, and of easier relationships in society, are working in the same direction.

582. It goes without saying that children should be encouraged to speak audibly, though that is certainly not the same as being asked to "speak up" which often in practice leads to children speaking raucously and straining their voices. As they grow older and their self assurance increases, occasions should be devised for them to talk, according to their capacity, to a group, to the class and at assembly, when audibility, and practice to ensure it, become a necessity. But we are less confident about the elements of speech indicated by such terms as "correctness" and "accent". Usage is always changing and teachers must not burden their pupils with the observance of out-worn conventions. Correctness should be sacrificed rather than fluency, vigour or clarity of meaning. When relationships are sound, children can usually accept and benefit from correction by their teachers of gross grammatical errors and of the use of phrases like "kind of" which impede clear communication. It is more difficult to decide whether accent is to be tolerated, welcomed, or modified. All sorts of personal and social as well as pedagogical questions are bound up in this problem, and whenever the matter is discussed in the press, wide differences of opinion and strong feelings are revealed. We hope that Project English, a research programme of which we have a little more to say later, will throw light on this and offer guidance to teachers.

Teaching Children to Read

583. Traditionally one of the first tasks of the infant school was to teach children to read. It is still, quite rightly, a major preoccupation, since reading is a key to much of the learning that will come later and to the possibility of independent study. In many infant schools, reading and writing are treated as extensions of spoken language. Those children who have not had the opportunity at home to grasp the part that they play are introduced to them by the everyday events and environment of the classroom. Messages to go home, letters to sick children, labels to ensure that materials and tools are returned to their proper place; all call for reading and writing. Many children first glimpse the pleasures of reading from listening to stories read to them at school; as teachers' aides are introduced (see Chapter 24), it should be possible for even more children to have the opportunity that others have at home of looking at pictures and text as a picture book is read to them individually or in small groups. Books made by teachers and children about the doings of the class or of individuals in it figure prominently among the books which children enjoy. They help children to see meaning in reading and to appreciate the purpose of written records. Children who show interest in reading but

who are not ready to make steady progress on a graduated series often profit from using home-made books and picture books. They can get much interest from them, without mastering the whole vocabulary, and they will be protected from feeling that they are failures because they have not passed quickly to a second book in a series.

584. As to the systematic teaching that follows this introduction to reading and writing, the most successful infant teachers have refused to follow the wind of fashion and to commit themselves to any one method. They choose methods and books to fit the age, interest and ability of individual pupils. Children are helped to read by memorising the look of words and phrases, often with the help of pictures, by guessing from a context which is likely to bring them success, and by phonics, beginning with initial sounds. They are encouraged to try all the methods available to them and not to depend on only one method. Instead of relying on one reading scheme, many teachers use a range of schemes with different characteristics, selecting carefully for each child: some schemes emphasise sight reading, others phonics; some consist of short books, with a very slow build up of vocabulary, and suit children who need quick success; other schemes help children who are able to advance rapidly and to discard primers. Reading schemes should never determine the practices adopted for all children. A few children are able, with a little help, to teach themselves to read from books of rhymes and stories learnt by heart. Rather more can pass direct from home-made books to simple story books. Many children will not need to go right through a series of books: others will require a great deal of supplementary material.

Standards of Reading

585. Successive investigations into reading ability undertaken by the Department of Education from 1948 to 1964 (see Appendix 7*), make it clear that, despite the dismal reports that appear from time to time in the press, the standard of reading in the country as a whole has been going up steadily since the war. Children of eleven have advanced by an average of 17 months since the first report was made, and backwardness now has a different connotation from that which it had in 1948. For this improvement the schools can take much of the credit, but it does not dispose of all the questions asked about reading. The most important which remain are: what can be done to help the minority of children for whom learning to read is a slow business and for a few, never achieved? What use is made of the skill once it is acquired?

586. On the first question we must repeat our conviction of the set-back which children often suffer from a change of school at seven. At this age many children are at a turning point in their mastery of reading. A week, a month, a term more and their future progress may be assured. Except for those children whose experiences in the infant school have resulted in disheartenment, nothing could be worse than a change of school at this time, after a long holiday during which their half-won understanding may have faded away. Even those children who appear to have failed completely might have fared better in the infant school had their teachers known that the introduction

*A fuller account of this study is to be found in 'Progress in Reading' (1966), H.M.S.O.

to systematic reading could be left a little later, and that there would still be time for unhustled progress. English children are taught to read earlier than in most other parts of the world. Evidence from research[1] has confirmed that transfer at seven can have disastrous results on children's achievement in reading. It has shown that nearly half of the children in a representative sample of schools continued to need after transfer the skilled teaching associated with the infant school. But, as we have pointed out in Chapter 10, they do not get it.

587. We are concerned about the quality and content of many primers and particularly of those used by children who come late to reading from an unbookish background. Too often, the difficult problem of combining interest with a controlled vocabulary is not solved. The middle class world represented by the text and illustrations is often alien to the children, the characters shadowy, the content babyish, the text pedestrian and lacking in rhythm and there is rarely either the action or the humour which can carry children through to the end of the books. We agree with the recommendation made to us by the National Association for the Teaching of English, that research should be instituted into the types of primer and library book which are most effective with children from different backgrounds and of varying levels of ability.

588. A hundred and fifty years ago, Coleridge, anxious about his own child's progress in reading, complained about "our lying alphabet". How great an obstacle is it to children who have difficulty in learning to read? The Initial Teaching Alphabet has attracted great public attention and has been the subject of heated argument. Should the claims made for the use of this alphabet be substantiated, it would mean that all but a small minority of those children who find reading difficult would find it so no longer. Since at present a substantial minority find difficulty, the claims merit careful scrutiny.

589. The Initial Teaching Alphabet is the subject of research[2] which is being carried out by the University of London. It is not yet complete but interim results have been reported. The Alphabet is in use in something like five per cent of the infants' schools in England and possibly in as many as ten per cent of the elementary schools in the U.S.A. An investigation of all the available evidence is currently being undertaken by the Schools Council and its results may be published before our Report is out. It would therefore be inopportune to make an assessment here. All that needs to be said now is that I.T.A. is not a method of teaching reading. It is an alphabet which is more efficient than Caxton's alphabet (adapted from the Latin). It is intended only to get children over the difficult first stage of learning to read and they usually transfer from it to a fairly simple primer in traditional orthography. It can be used with various methods and, like other instruments, it can be used well or badly. We welcome the investigations being made into the evidence of its use and success with beginners, and with children who have failed in learning to read the conventional alphabet. We also welcome research into the effects of improved methods of teaching reading in traditional orthography. It is important to stress that even if methods are found which make possible an early beginning in reading, it does not follow that children's time is best spent on reading. The earlier children read and the more time spent on it, the more important it becomes to see that books are worth reading and that their substance does not outrun children's experience and maturity.

590. Some of our witnesses have suggested the existence of specific developmental dyslexia (sometimes called word blindness), a failure in reading which is thought to be due to neurological causes. There are so many possible reasons for poor reading, such as late maturation, ill-timed or poor teaching, sensory and speech defects, strephosymbolia (misperceptions of letters or numbers which usually correct themselves in time) and the emotional disturbances which may both cause, and result from, retardation in reading, that it is difficult to be sure whether specific dyslexia exists as an independent factor. An acute difficulty in reading appears to be confined to a very small number of children, perhaps five or fewer in a thousand. Research into it is now being carried out in Leeds, with the financial support of the Department of Education and Science. In the meantime, we are advised that if children have not learned to read by the age of nine they should be referred to an educational psychologist. If they are also clumsy runners, and unable to draw a diamond shape, a neurological examination is advisable[2]. If possible the educational psychologist should come to the school and discuss the individual children with the teachers.

A Range of Books

591. As the skill of reading is established, it must be used and here a really remarkable change has taken place since the war. The provision of books, which was usually meagre in quantity and in quality in the elementary schools, is now much improved. The average number of school and class library books in schools in the National Survey was 1,800 (Appendix 5, Table 10). Junior school libraries of 4,000 to 5,000 books are quite common, although we show in Chapter 28 that many authorities are still insufficiently generous in book allowances. The establishment of a representative collection of children's books by the Department (commonly known as the "Tann" collection), and its exhibition at teachers' courses and conferences all over the country, the provision of similar collections by many local authorities and by some colleges of education, the work of children's librarians, the collaboration of the publishers, some children's book shops and the displays arrang d by the National Book League have all played their part in bringing the rapidly increasing range of children's books to the attention of teachers. The exhortations of Lord Eccles when Minister of Education, the readiness with which some authorities have responded to them by increasing their grants for books and the initiative which many head teachers have shown in building up school library funds in a multitude of ways have all added to the number of books in the schools. There is now a wide range of children's books, notably enriched by translations of the better books written abroad. Inevitably, there is dross as well as gold and a difficult problem of choice confronts the teachers when some 3,000 new children's books are published each year. Many schools have no book shop within reach and, save when an exhibition is arranged in their area, must send for examples of books, relying on the publications of the School Library Association and the reviews in the more reputable journals, some of which take special account of children's books. One of the functions of teachers' centres (referred to in Chapter 25) would be to house a collection of children's books which could be regularly kept up to date and could provide starting points for discussion by teachers of how children have responded to books. This discussion is important since adults

may provide too many of the books which they enjoy themselves and which only appeal to exceptional children. There is still an insufficient supply of good light literature for the less able children.

592. Among the most welcome changes which have accompanied the growing informality of the primary school has been the move away from categories of books, each confined to a special time and purpose. In many schools there are now no longer class readers, supplementary readers, group readers, text books and library books: though library books were often the most exacting and rewarding of all, they were frequently relegated to odd moments when other tasks were finished. There are simply books—to be used as and when they are needed. Though there may still be occasions when class sets of books are useful, pe hap; as a basis for discussion between teacher and children on the ways in which information can be sought, collated and summarised, much of the money that used to be spent on dull and over-generalised geography and nature study books is now available for the pu chase of "books of information". Many are admirable but some certainly suffer from the same weaknesses as the text books they are tending to replace; over-generalisation, inaccuracy and poor illustrations.

593. Inevitably there are inequalities in the use as well as in the choice of books. There should certainly be a time for browsing among books; there is also a time for purposeful reading and consulting books to find the specific information needed, for instance, when a group project is begun, or to develop an individual interest. The starting point for an interest is often the teacher's knowledge and enthusiasm; this can carry children far beyond their usual intellectual range, the laggards and apathetic with the rest. Yet imposed interests are a contradiction in terms and are likely to result in worthless transcription from books, a danger of which teachers need to be aware. Whether interests originate with the children or are stimulated by the school, the teacher must not abdicate in favour of books but give continuing guidance and support. At the same time it is true that reading will often awake new interests as well as nourishing existing ones. Some children have a voracious appetite for facts and will read even reference books and encyclopedias from cover to cover. But it is the teacher's responsibility to see that such books are a support rather than a substitute for first hand evidence, whenever the latter is available. An adult reference book is often more serviceable to children, particularly for example for identification of flowers and birds, than the children's books in which the illustrations are usually, to quote a six year old's explanation, "too beautiful" to be useful.

594. It may be children's appetite for fact in a world in which knowledge is increasing at an astounding rate that explains the dominating place of informative books in many school collections. Whatever the reason, fiction is often represented by a random collection of books lent by the public library, their uniform bindings sometimes comparing unfavourably with the books bought by the school. Yet most libraries will do their best to provide specific books if teachers ask for them and will leave books in schools as long as teachers need them. Many libraries set an example to schools by their choice and display of books. Certainly fiction ought to form part of the permanent collection of books in every school, since some children will come back to the same books again and again; and it is often the books which demand re-reading which are most worth reading. Probably, teachers are not sufficiently informed about

the excellence of many contemporary children's stories or their availability in cheap editions. Since literary quality cannot be detected quickly, teachers tend to rely on the "safe" classics and on the books they read in their own childhood. Often they are poorly produced and are in rehashed versions from which the quality has been drained away. Many of the outstanding children's classics, particularly the Victorian ones, continue to appeal, especially to the abler children. But the books of yesterday, perhaps because they derive from a period when children were artificially insulated from adult life, are often more remote from children than the timeless traditional stories and those of the classical and medieval world.

595. We are convinced of the value of stories for children, stories told to them, stories read to them and the stories they read for themselves. It is through story as well as through drama and other forms of creative work that children grope for the meaning of the experiences that have already overtaken them, savour again their pleasures and reconcile themselves to their own inconsistencies and those of others. As they "try on" first one story book character, then another, imagination and sympathy, the power to enter into another personality and situation, which is a characteristic of childhood and a fundamental condition for good social relationships, is preserved and nurtured. It is also through literature that children feel forward to the experiences, the hopes and fears that await them in adult life. It is almost certainly in childhood that children are most susceptible, both to living example and to the examples they find in books. As children listen to stories, as they take down the books from the library shelves, they may, as Graham Greene suggests in "The Lost Childhood", be choosing their future and the values that will dominate it.

596. We have written in some detail about the value of story because there are still too few books of literary quality in primary schools and too little time is given to reading them. Even in good schools, it is sometimes thought sufficient to allow a weekly library period, when books for reading at home may be changed, but there is little opportunity for guidance or stimulus. There has certainly been no glorious past here. Reading the same classic "round the class" for a term or more, or working comprehension exercises on passages of literary quality—a practice which still lingers—can be looked back on without nostalgia.

Poetry

597. It is doubtful whether poetry has ever been well treated in the majority of schools. Matthew Arnold recommended Mrs. Heman's poems to the schools, admittedly with some reservations. Another inspector included "There are fairies at the bottom of our garden" in the immensely popular English text books which he wrote before he joined the inspectorate. Until fairly recently, it was common to find class sets of poetry books including far too many of the traditional anthology "pieces", and too much tinkling verse about fairies and elves written specially for children. A period was usually set aside for poetry each week: at best children made individual anthologies and memorised some of the poems they chose to copy out: at worst the whole class copied a poem a week from the blackboard and poetry became little more than a writing lesson. Occasionally, choral verse speaking brought some vitality to the poetry period but the poems chosen were not

always well suited to the technique. Now the class sets of poetry books are disappearing fast though individual copies of them are not infrequently the sole representatives of poetry in class and school libraries. The number of really good anthologies for children—many of them compiled by poets and well produced—has increased rapidly in the last few years. Most of them are expensive and relatively few have found their way into the schools. Selections from the works of individual poets are particularly uncommon. Similarly, poetry is poorly represented in teachers' reference libraries and is often confined to collections intended only for school use. Some good teachers lack conviction about the value of poetry and are more confident about giving children opportunities to write poems than about nourishing them with great poetry. Few children learn poems because, once the nursery rhyme stage is past, few teachers speak poems to them. Children may lose much when they are not set an example of getting poetry by heart.

598. To leave an account of literature and poetry here would be to present too pessimistic a picture. There is some evidence that the tide is beginning to turn. In a growing number of schools, the head or one of the assistants makes himself an authority on children's books and gives advice to the rest of the staff. It is not uncommon to find some interchange of classes so that children can enjoy poetry with an enthusiast. The proportion of young teachers who are sensitive to quality in literature, and knowledgeable about children's books, seems to be increasing. This may well be one of the gains of the three year course and the deeper study of English and of education which it makes possible. Supported by teachers, children can reach out to stories and poetry that they could not manage unaided. But a teacher can only share with children what he understands and likes. He can only choose wisely what to share when he has both a well developed critical sense and an understanding of children. In poetry, above all, children can be carried by the pleasure of sound over difficulties in language, but the mood must have some relevance to their experience. In schools where the place of literature is becoming stronger, teachers will give much time to reading aloud when they are introducing a book to their class. They cast their net wide in what they read, often making use of short passages from their own personal reading. They take chances with contemporary literature, especially poetry, recognising that children may be more in tune with the spirit of the time—to which poetry often gives heightened expression—than their teachers are themselves. Poetry written for adults, or written at least by those who are poets in their own right, is usually to be preferred to children's verse. In some schools teachers vary their own interpretation of poetry by the use of recorded verse. Occasionally a group of children put on tape a programme of poems on a particular theme. They have an incentive for the best reading they can manage, or for getting their poems by heart so that they can speak them better. The ordering of the programme can lead to much thought about the poems themselves. Teachers, too, encourage children to think about poems more by the sequence and contrast of what is read than by direct comment, and are content to leave the outcome largely to children's questions.

599. When teachers read much aloud, sometimes giving children only a taste of the pleasure that awaits them and referring them to the sources, the quality of children's own reading is influenced for the better. Time and peace for solitary reading must also be found, not always easy in a school which is

humming with activity. If it is not possible to allow all types of books, other than expensive reference books, to go home, it means that a school has too few books. Some children will be literary cormorants, swallowing all that comes within their reach; it is for teachers to see that some of it at least is of a kind to give "an obscure sense of possible sublimities", to be worth reading and re-reading.

Drama

600. Some of our witnesses regarded drama as an integral part of English. Yet drama embraces movement, gesture and mime, and these primitive features of drama should be emphasised with young children, especially since plays written for them are usually of indifferent quality and do little to extend or clarify their experience. In practice, drama bridges English and movement. This is apparent from the dramatic play of children in the infant school. They rely mainly on movement yet, even at the stage when play is largely individual and a group may contain three heroes and only one unwilling villain, words will force a way in as part of the movement. We have been much impressed by the dramatic work which has developed in junior schools in some parts of the country. Children re-enact and reshape experiences of everyday life and those derived from literary, Biblical and historical sources. Unscripted speech plays a part but, if it is emphasised too much, it may cramp movement and kill action. As children become more accustomed to this way of working, improvisations can be discussed, revised and rehearsed until they grow into coherent plays from which children begin to understand something of the problems and strengths of dramatic form. When the amount of dialogue increases, some children may want to polish their plays by putting words on paper. If pupils remain in the middle schools till 12, some will probably be ready to interpret the plays of others, beginning perhaps with the mummers' plays or mystery plays whose conventions are near to the children's own. A few exceptional teachers have communicated an enthusiasm for Shakespeare to children of junior school age and have even produced scenes with them, but it is doubtful whether this should become general. It is significant that the liveliest drama in the first year of the secondary school is of the unscripted kind that we have described earlier. Certainly, though some primary school children enjoy having an audience of other children or their parents, formal presentation of plays on a stage is usually out of place.

Children's Writing

601. Perhaps the most dramatic of all the revolutions in English teaching is in the amount and quality of children's writing. The code of 1862 required no writing other than transcription or dictation until Standard VI, or about the age of 12 to 13. In the thirties, independent writing in the infant school and lower junior school rarely extended beyond a sentence or two and the answering of questions, and for the older children it was usually a weekly or fortnightly composition on prescribed topics only too frequently repeated year by year. Now it is quite common for writing to begin side by side with the learning of reading, for children to dictate to their teachers and gradually to copy and then to expand and write for themselves accounts of their experiences at home and at school. Often these accounts also serve as their first reading books. As with speech, new routines have developed which, if followed too exclusively, or with all children, can also be deadening: the

picture always accompanied by a caption, the class news book or individual diary filled in whether or not there is anything to be said, and the "story". What is most remarkable now in many infant schools is the variety of writing: writing arising out of dramatic play, writing associated with and explaining the models that are made, writing which reflects the sharpening of the senses, "the peppery smell of the lupins", "the primroses clustered so closely that the stalks can't be seen", the writing that derives from the special occasion, the tortoise brought in for the day—"I could hug him and snug him and our teacher wanted to tell us the story of the hare and the tortoise but we had all heard it before". Much of the writing derives from the experiences of individual children, much from the excitement of a shared visit, "the most day that fascinated me", a visit to a zoo which led after a longish spell of time to a description of a snake "slithering slowly through the long grasses. Up, up, up the tree he coiled and rested his head on his tall slim body". Less frequently the spirit and language of a story are caught, "one day however the prince was lucky for he found to his joy on the topmost branch of an oak the Golden Bird and he said in a joyful voice 'Great Golden Bird, come down and let me pluck a feather from your breast so I may marry the princess'. The Golden Bird shivered. . . "

602. Some teachers at the bottom of the junior school become so anxious about children's insecure hold on reading that they make too frontal an attack on it. Equally, they become concerned about inaccuracies in children's writing and about the long-winded rigmarole which sometimes follows children's discovery that they can write. They worry about the consequences of the belief, occasionally encouraged by an over-enthusiastic infant teacher, that there is virtue in sheer volume, irrespective of what is said. But here again the remedy does not lie in narrowing children's activities or confining them to a starvation course of six simple sentences on "Myself" or on "My School". When inaccuracy impedes communication, that is the moment, without worrying about inessentials, to help children to see how their meaning can be more clearly and economically conveyed. It may also be prudent to concentrate for a time on writing about the shared experiences of teacher and children—first hand or vicarious—which will be clarified to some extent, and therefore controlled by previous discussion.

603. In a growing number of junior schools, there is free, fluent and copious writing on a great variety of subject matter, similar to—but extending beyond—that found in infant schools. Sometimes it is called "creative writing", a rather grand name for it. Its essence is that much of it is personal and that the writers are communicating something that has really engaged their minds and their imaginations. To this kind of writing, here as in the infant school, we give an unqualified welcome. It is nearly always natural and real and sometimes has qualities which make it most moving to read. Several collections of children's writing[4] have been printed and for this reason we give only brief examples here.

604. It is becoming less usual for personal writing to take the form of an invented "story". Save for exceptional children who have a story telling gift, and should be given the opportunity to use it, this type of writing tends to be second rate and derivative from poorish material. The great story can change children's ways of looking at the world and at themselves; but poorer story

writers often have more influence, in the short run, on children's style because their conventions are mechanical and easily borrowed. In the long term, the quality of children's reading will certainly influence their writing.

605. The best writing of young children springs from the most deeply felt experience. They will write most easily and imaginatively about their homes, their hobbies and interests, about things seen and done in science, mathematics, geography and on school visits. When relationships are good, the slower children often achieve most when they have talked over with their teacher the day to day experiences of school and family life. In a few sentences, a child from a fourth stream can portray her mother: "she is not tall or short and quite ordinary looking. She is patient and good natured and helps us in all we do. She always gives in to my sisters and to me. She says sometimes, she wishes she was dead". Children need extension of experience, both at first hand and through reading and listening, if they are to write well. They are often stimulated by hearing good poetry read aloud, partly by its whole flavour, partly perhaps because they are encouraged to convey their meaning in relatively few words. It was after hearing, and reading for herself, some extracts from T. S. Eliot that a girl of modest ability described how she had felt at home on the previous evening;

> "The smell of fish and chips
> Cooking in the kitchen.
> The baby crying for its feed
> And our old Dad reading the newspaper.
> Slippers lying around the house,
> And big sister telling us off.
> Mother has got a headache
> And so have I.
> The doors are slamming to and fro.
> Seven o'clock.
> Time for television."

More remarkably, the poetry a boy had heard extended his vision as he looked at scaled models of the planets, strung across his classroom. Most of them were clustered against the sun, drawn on the wall, but Pluto was placed away in the corner of the room,

> "Pluto the lonely traveller
> Far out in the unconquered universe,
> Like a hermit
> In the mysterious desert of space.
> Mercury the baby of the family,
> The Sun the mother,
> Watching over her nine sons.
> Pluto the shy and lonely one,
> Earth the educated son."

606. The ablest children can benefit particularly from the disciplined writing which ought to accompany first hand observation in geography or science. Exact observation and exact language should go hand in hand and children can be helped to see that the validity of a simple experiment may depend on exact recording. But there are other aspects of the curriculum, notably

history, which cannot be based to the same extent on experience at first hand. Whether a topic makes an impact will often depend on whether children are given, by oral lesson or through books, authentic detail on which their imagination can play. Detail, and therefore focus on selected topics, are vital in stimulating knowledge and language in every aspect of the curriculum at the top of the junior school. This is one reason for moving towards some subject divisions with the ablest children at this stage.

607. It is not easy to determine whether this flowering of children's writing has been accompanied by a decline in formal excellence—neatness, good handwriting, accuracy and arrangement. Some of our witnesses think that it has, but few collections exist which would make possible any comparison between the writing of the thirties and that of the present day. The far greater variety of subject matter now used and the decline of the "fair copy", though it still has a place for the special occasion, make the matter even harder to decide. We very much doubt whether there has been any deterioration in the appearance of children's work, but we think that there is room for improvement. Schools which make a feature of good handwriting, often in the Italic mode and sometimes in other styles, lose nothing in the freedom and imaginative quality of children's writing and can gain in other ways.

608. Some comment must be made on the efforts of schools to improve the accuracy and arrangement of ideas in children's writing. There are some schools in which, as an insurance policy for the eleven plus examination, teachers continue to prescribe and prepare with the children compositions on traditional subjects in the later years of the junior course. It is perhaps almost inevitable that the writing of older children will become rather bookish and pretentious. They may copy the hackneyed phrases which adults often use as as a substitute for thought and which even nowadays children are encouraged to adopt by being set worthless exercises of the "cool as . . ." type. There is certainly no point in forcing children into stock phrases and insincerity by setting them to write on the conventional subject: the walk in spring, the autobiography of the penny, the loaf of bread, or the tree, which may culminate in "I am happy as a table, but I was happiest as a tree". Children may well want to write in autobiographical form but how much more exciting and indeed more possible to imagine themselves with Columbus as he first glimpsed land, with Elizabeth as she reviewed the troops at Tilbury, or in Jerusalem on the first Good Friday.

609. Preparation of written work has more place in connection with the factual summaries which secondary schools will expect children to be able to write if their transfer from the primary school is deferred by a year. The child's view of what is important ought still to hold the field. Discussion is needed with individuals and groups about the kind of questions they will want to answer on an "interest" or "topic" and the ways in which material can best be ordered. In all types of writing, children will need tactful help in conveying their meaning and in the craftsmanship of writing. Ideally, it is best given orally to individuals, but the size of classes may make some written comment necessary and it may help to fix a point in a child's mind. Care should always be taken not to discourage children, particularly the younger and the less able, by too much criticism. What should children be told about their work? They ought to know if they have succeeded in sharing their meaning and, however tactfully, what impact the meaning made. Teachers should, that is to

say, be at least as much concerned with the content as with the manner of what is said. They should be quick to notice an absurd combination of natural phenomena on a spring morning or bombs facilely disposed of by opening a plane window (though this kind of nonsense is usually the product of an imposed subject). Often the probing question is the best comment. Some "correction", if so inadequate a word must be used, should be directed towards inaccuracies, not so much the careless slips that everyone makes throughout life, as the repeated errors in sentence construction, in punctuation and in spelling which get in the way of communication. Similarly such techniques as paragraphing can be taught when it can be made clear to children that the technique will serve their purpose in writing. With the abler children, there is room for some concern about form and style so long as it does not make children self-conscious.

610. Any follow-up of written work should be tailored to individual and group needs. The N.F.E.R. survey has shown that there is relatively little group teaching in English, except in reading. Some schools provide assignment cards to correct specific weaknesses, and references to a single exercise or two in an English course book that can serve a similar purpose. Programmed texts are likely to be developed which can be similarly used to help individuals to correct errors in those particular matters in which they have difficulty. There is no sense in classes working systematically through books of exercises. Much money is wasted on these books which would be better spent in building up school libraries. Much time also is wasted by children on English course books. They learn to write by writing and not by exercises in filling in missing words.

611. The growth of the study of linguistics, with its interest in describing and analysing how language works, the differences between written and spoken language and the influence of language on children's thought and mental development, will no doubt come to be reflected in teachers' courses and in classroom techniques. Already the linguist has done a good deal to clarify the vexed question of the role of grammar in teaching English, by his distinction between "prescriptive" and "descriptive" grammar. Speech is how people speak, not how some authority thinks they ought to speak. The test of good speech is whether any particular use of language is effective in the context in which it is used, not whether it conforms to certain "rules".

612. The Schools Council's "Project English" will study among other questions the lessons that linguistics has to offer to teachers, and its findings will be awaited with interest. In the meantime we offer the following propositions for the consideration of teachers:—

(a) Children are interested in words, their shape, sound, meaning and origin and this interest should be exploited in all kinds of incidental ways. Formal study of grammar will have little place in the primary school, since active and imaginative experience and use of the language should precede attempts to analyse grammatically how language behaves.

(b) The time for grammatical analysis will come but it should follow a firmly laid foundation of experience of the spoken and written language. When "rules" or generalisations are discussed these should be "induced" from the child's own knowledge of the usage of the language. The theory of grammar that is studied should describe the child's language and not be a theory based on Latin, many of whose categories, inflexions, case systems, tenses and so on do not exist in English.

(c) While there is no question of the teaching of linguistics in the primary school, some work in linguistics at colleges of education or in refresher courses will help teachers to a sound view of how language works.

613. There has been since the war such progress in the teaching of English that it might have been thought, that, with Project English on the way, we might have treated it more briefly. But English permeates the whole curriculum as it permeates the whole of life. We cannot afford to slacken in advancing the power of language which is the "instrument of society" and a principal means to personal maturity.

REFERENCES

[1]Morris, J. M., 'How Far Can Reading Backwardness be Attributed to School Conditions?', an address presented to the International Reading Association, May 1964.

[2]Downing, J. A., 'Initial Teaching Alphabet', Cassell & Co., 1966.

[3]Evidence submitted by Medical Officers of the Department of Education and Science.

[4]For example :—

'The Excitement of Writing', West Riding Education Committee. Advisory Centre for Education, Cambridge 1966.

'Children as Writers', Annual Anthology of entries to the *Daily Mirror* Children's Literary Competition, started 1960.

'Free Writing', Pym, D., Bristol University Institute of Education, London University Press, 1956.

'Young Writers, Young Readers', ed. Ford, B., Hutchinson, 1960.

C   MODERN LANGUAGES

614. For many years there have been sporadic, individual and quite uncoordinated attempts to teach a modern language, nearly always French, in primary schools. The age at which boys in independent preparatory schools began Latin and French had already shown that there was no fundamental difficulty in teaching a second language to at least some children of primary age. Whether it was possible to teach a second language to all or most children was unknown, and the scattered experiments (if they deserved the word) just mentioned threw no light on the problem. They were generally confined to the most able children in the fourth year and were undertaken because of the appearance on the staff of someone who was "good at" or "keen on" French. Often the subject was not begun until after the selection examination had taken place and was thus limited to the period March–July. All too frequently the weekly time-allowance was too short and badly distributed and if, as often seemed to happen, the key teacher left, French dropped out of the curriculum without trace. The plain fact was that the majority of primary school teachers were not qualified to teach a modern language. Furthermore, the secondary schools to which the children concerned went, showed, often with some justification, a bland indifference to their claims to have "done some French already". The whole proceedings were an example of the least admirable side of the English traditional of independence, and, as recently as 1959, the Department's handbook of suggestions for teachers, Primary Education, gave little encouragement to the introduction of a second language.

615. In the last few years a complete change has occurred. It is possible that the general cl mate was already more favourable in 1959 than the writers of Primary Education supposed. More English people, including many teachers, had been travelling abroad and there was a feeling that links with the rest of Europe ought to be strengthened. The cultural advantages of knowing a second language, as distinct from the strictly linguistic ones, had always been understood, but it was now increasingly felt that they ought to be available to a much larger section of the population. In 1962 the Nuffield Foundation offered the sum of £100,000 for the production of materials for experiment in teaching French in primary schools. The Department of Education and Science undertook responsibility for organising the necessary teacher training and a joint steering committee, on which the Department, the Foundation and the local education authorities were represented, was set up.

616. The experiment is still in progress and this is not the place to describe it in detail, still less to assess its results. The preliminary period, during which the 13 experimental areas and the 53 associated areas were chosen, the teachers trained, a process that included a three months' course in France, and the early stages of the teaching material prepared, came to an end in September 1964, when the second stage, that of beginning to teach French to the eight year olds, was introduced. At the time of writing (Summer 1966), these children are nearing the end of the second year of French, and a second cohort of eight year olds are finishing their first.

617. There are a number of points which seem to be worth making at this comparatively early stage:—

(i) The careful and systematic planning of the experiment was in contrast to the haphazard methods of the past, involving, as it did, a reasonable assurance of sound foundations and continuity and a firm agreement with the receiving secondary schools.

(ii) The Nuffield teaching material, despite its close connection with the experiment, is not an essential part of it. There is no compulsion to use it and in fact about 20 per cent of the pilot areas are using other material, some of it devised in France, some in the U.S.A. and some in this country. The schools which are using the Nuffield material have been given every opportunity for shaping it and improving it. The continuing and constructive collaboration between all concerned—Foundation, Department and teachers—is one of the most heartening and significant features of the experiment.

(iii) We appreciate the reasons which led to the experiment being almost entirely confined to French at primary level. The number of primary teachers who know any other language well enough to teach it is minimal and French is the "safest" language from the point of view of transfer to a secondary school. Nevertheless we must regret that the experiment is perpetuating the dominance of one language, even though it is the language of our nearest neighbours and one with a rich literature. We hope that if the present experiment is successful, the possibilities of including another language will be explored.

(iv) The introduction of a modern language into primary schools raises acutely the question of specialisation. It will be easier when many more primary teachers are qualified to teach French, but that time is still a long way off. In the meantime there is bound to be some anxiety lest the methods used in teaching French vary sharply from those used for the rest of the curriculum. The developing tradition in primary education since 1945 has been away from class teaching and from formal lessons, but the early stages of learning a modern language inevitably involve some class teaching and many teachers fear that much hard-won ground will have to be given up. The approach adopted in the Nuffield material, and in any of the other three sets of material in use in the pilot areas, need not occasion anxiety; but there are other courses on sale and in use which are completely out of harmony with good primary practice. Some are intended for older children, and others introduce the reading and writing of French at too early a stage. Any school embarking on French ought to scrutinise critically the course that it proposes to use. We hope that work in French will flow over into other areas of the curriculum and that care will be taken to brief specialists and peripatetic teachers about the general principles of young children's learning.

(v) It is unfortunate that many schools and areas which are outside the experiment have chosen to add French to the curriculum without ensuring reasonable conditions for success. There is obviously not the smallest reason why a free-lance school or area should not do just as well as an "experimental" one. The fact remains, however, that far too many schools have introduced French without having a teacher who possesses even minimum qualifications, without consideration of what constitutes a satisfactory scheme and time-table and without any consultation with receiving secondary schools. This can only be deplored. No good purpose can possibly be served by it. Without a teacher who is well qualified linguistically and in methods suitable for primary schools, it is better to have nothing to do with French. The presence of a native French speaker, while it guarantees the former, often fails to provide the latter.

618. The experiment has aroused keen interest in many primary schools but we retain certain reservations about it. The later stages of learning a language are more difficult than the earlier ones. It is when the later stages are reached that the learning problems of less able pupils can be assessed and the difficulties of staffing so great an expansion of language teaching can be appreciated. For this and other reasons we hope that the experimental nature of the project will be recognised and that no attempt will be made to press further the teaching of a second language in primary schools until the results of the experiment can be fully assessed.

619. We discuss the problem of teaching English to children of foreign origin in Chapter 6.

D. HISTORY

620. History for children is a subject on which it is not easy to reach agreement. The heroine of "Northanger Abbey" "pitied the hard fate of historians filling great volumes and labouring only for the torment of little boys and girls". Charlotte Yonge was so spellbound by the six volumes of ancient history which she was given before her sixth birthday that she was despondent a year later when her mother refused to christen her brother Alexander Xenophon. In adult life she was to add to the histories for boys and girls, and

some of these books are still in print. Since then many new problems have arisen in the teaching of history to children. Personalities have tended to recede from the stage and when they hold their commanding position, their motives are difficult to disentangle. Economic influences and institutions have come to the fore. History, it is said again and again, is an adult subject. How then can it be studied by children without it being so simplified that it is falsified? There is the further problem that it is not until the later years of the primary school, if then, that some children develop a sense of time. Yet we received oral evidence of an infant school where several of the older children became absorbed in historical subject matter of the most varied kind, and we visited an infant school where one exceptional child had memorised the dates of the kings and queens of England—"all except the muddling Anglo-Saxons". There is, it seems, a need for further enquiry into the impact of history on children, in terms of the interest, attitudes, knowledge and concepts which it develops. In particular, more studies are needed of children's understanding of time.

621. These uncertainties may go some way towards explaining the widely differing situation of history in the schools. We have received evidence that there has been a great improvement in history teaching since the publication of the 1931 report. This must almost certainly be true. The 1931 report took it for granted that history teaching would be based on a textbook. Now, the most common criticism of work in history is that it derives from textbooks and that chapter headings form the syllabus. Despite the doubts about history in school, it has been seized on by the writers of children's books and the publishers as subject matter popular with children. Informative books on history and historical novels are often found in considerable numbers in school and class libraries, and they rarely stand idle on the shelves.

622. In most junior schools history continues to appear as a separate subject in the time-table, certainly in the last two years and often before. It usually suffers the disadvantage of being confined to two periods a week and even this meagre time allowance is occasionally sacrificed to coaching for the eleven plus in the first half of the fourth year. But the dreary notes copied from the blackboard have largely disappeared and children are at least given the opportunity to make their own summaries in which emphasis may quite rightly be very different from that of adult historians of all shades of thought. History frequently provides a successful starting point for spontaneous drama, for narrative of the "I was there" kind and for lively art and craft. This spilling over of history into other aspects of the curriculum is probably the most general advance of recent years.

623. Work of quality of which we have heard usually occurs in schools which break away from the conventional time-table divisions, either by giving a concentrated spell of time first to one aspect of the curriculum, then to another, or by working on topics such as exploration which link history and geography or by studies of the environment. Some schools are fortunate enough to have an enthusiast for history on the staff who may show his colleagues how for a time a class can be steeped in the past. Children may study it in such detail that probing questions are asked, connections are seen and discoveries are made as authentically from written sources as from environmental study or scientific investigation. This kind of work does not usually develop until children are 10 or 11 and is equally suitable for children

in the lower forms of secondary schools. A topic may be formally introduced by the teacher because the subject matter is interesting, important and balances other work done by the children, or it may begin with a child's question arising from a local antiquity or from a historical novel. Once interest is stirred, materials are collected from the school library, and the public library and elsewhere; stories for background, children's reference books, adult books, printed source material, illustrations, film strip, photostats of documents from the local record office or elsewhere. Collections of contemporary documents and illustrations are now on the market and some are suitable for use by children between 10 and 12. If the local museum has a school loan service, it may be possible to supplement displays of pictures and books with real objects from the period. Class discussion clarifies the aspects of the period which individuals or small groups of children can investigate. It may be advantageous to let choice take its natural course and for several children to study the same topic. Provided that the books used are not full of generalities, even primary school children may begin to glimpse that history is in part created by the historian. It is essential for teachers to help individuals and groups to clear their minds about what they want to find out, though children will often find themselves led by the material itself in unexpected directions, and to guide them with exact references to source and adult books so that they do not waste time.

624. Visits to houses and churches of the period and to museums are best made early in the school year or in a study of a topic, so that, if children have further problems, they can make return visits. They are often most evocative when children are prepared, not by lists of things to look out for, but by first-hand source material which will fire the imagination. Only one brief quotation can be given from a wealth of exciting narrative which followed a visit to an Elizabethan manor house, full of priest's holes. The children had heard extracts from the Autobiography of John Gerard and could feel in some degree what it was like to be cooped up in a tiny cavity, with nothing but an earthenware bottle of water and the jar of quince jelly that the mistress of the house had in her hands when the alarm was sounded. "As the day wore on", a ten year old wrote, "the searchers came to the library and began scratching, tapping and measuring. Every minute they drew nearer to my hiding place. I recognised their leader's voice. He was Benedict. "I know that Father Domine is here" he said, "he must be here somewhere". When he said this I pressed myself against the wall and trembled. I wanted to cry out but I repeated again and again a fervent prayer. I quivered as a child might when about to be smacked by an angry parent. Suddenly my heart seemed to stop beating. A soldier stopped outside by the beam which I had lifted to get into my hiding place. I bit my lip, "No, no", I almost cried aloud . . ."

625. At the end of six weeks or a term, when children have been led on by direct teaching, by reading and by visits, and have discussed with each other their findings, they will have escaped temporarily from their own world, have been confronted with a different world, with the fact of change in the past and its implications for change in the future. By the top of the junior school, a few children may begin to have an imaginative intuition of period, of how things hang together and men are the creatures as well as the creators of their time. They may be helped to taste, for example, the flavour of Elizabethan exuberance: the extravagant clothes of the gentry, "sooner is a great ship rigged

than a gentlewoman made ready"; the increasing comfort at home, the heavily carved and bulbous table legs akin to the slashed and exaggerated breeches; a passion running all through society for whatever "is dear bought and far fetched". Though they will not talk about cause and effect, they may sense a connection with the boom in overseas trade in the middle of the reign and the private fortunes that were being made right through to its close.

626. Study in depth of the kind we have described frequently originates from children's curiosity about their environment, from the modest survivals—the fire society mark, the milestone, the Victorian letter box, the toll house—as well as those on a grander scale. Often history will be only a small part of a study which cuts across subject divisions. How big a part history should play depends on the children and the particular environment. Even in so rich a historical environment as Bath, it was enough for one class of slow learning children to spend a day or two on history, on a vivid reconstruction of Roman life, a visit to the bath, and the modelling and painting that followed. That this much was worth while was apparent from a boy, ascertained as educationally subnormal, who looking at a culvert commented "think what things must have flowed down that drain". The same boy turned away from a model hypocaust saying that he would rather look at the real thing.

627. An example of an environmental study with a historical bias comes from a Shropshire school. Children visiting Ludlow for another purpose began to speculate about the castle; who built it, how old was it, who lived and died there, why were there so many castles in Shropshire. At this stage, class teaching on the Norman Conquest, relying heavily on the Bayeux Tapestry, became a necessity and children were soon taking sides—Norman or Saxon, and no half measures. Having begun to see the need for castles in conquered territory, held by a handful of men, the children visited early Norman castles near the school. Running up a 100 ft. motte, they imagined what it felt like to be Saxons or Welsh trying to storm the wooden keep, defended by Normans using arrows, stones and burning pitch. Stories of attacks and sieges stimulated ballad writing. A large-scale model of a motte and bailey castle was built, using clay for the mound and to line the moat, and wood for the keep and stakes. Extracts were read from stories like Puck of Pook's Hill, Hereward the Wake and the Gauntlet. Interest turned to weapons and particularly to archery, and led to work of a mathematical kind on the speed and distance of flight and some on the trajectory of the arrows. Before the topic came to an end, children had visited Ludlow and Stokesay and seen that a more comfortable life could be lived there than in the early purely military castles. They became enthusiasts for heraldry and devised their own coats of arms. They searched their surnames and vocabulary for traces of Norman-French influence.

628. A limiting factor on the use of school environments is their very varying nature. Suburbs and housing estates in particular may be historically poverty-stricken. Yet even in the newest estate it may be possible to build up from children's memories and those of their parents and grandparents, from old photographs and newspapers and bric-a-brac, a record of some of the vast changes that have taken place in the last 50 years. Within this limited period children can get an idea of sequence and change: from long skirts and woollen stockings and cotton prints to rayon and nylon (though the process has now ceased to be regular), from candle and oil or gas lamp to electric lighting.

from the first probing with the cat's whisker and the broadcasts from 2LO to the valve set and then TV, and so on. This, like exploration, is one of the aspects of modern history that primary school children can appreciate and it can be given reality for them by being founded on first-hand evidence and focused on the changes in their own town or village.

629. Other springboards into the past have been found in children's names, their games, their phrases, their conventions and their hobbies. Their interest in steam engines (which grows as the steam engines themselves become fewer) and in the history of some of the everyday things mentioned in the previous paragraph has supported history based on so-called "lines of development" which has the advantage of being backed by good reference books for children. One of the weaknesses is that, like some work on the environment, it may over-emphasise gradual evolution whereas children are often more interested in the contrast of past and present. Too often, work centred on railways, ships, buildings and costumes leaves out the people who made and used them.

630. Children are interested in history because they are interested in stories. We have already suggested in the section on English that children may be starved of stories, even in good junior schools. Many of the stories through which children approach history in the earlier part of the primary school and which should balance environmental and other studies at a later stage are not to be distinguished from literature. Odysseus, Beowulf, the Norse stories, Roland, some of Chaucer's Tales, Arthur, Robin Hood: children should not be denied these stories. As they grow older and understand that the stories are legends, they may begin to realise, if Beowulf is linked with the Sutton Hoo remains, that the story illuminates a shadowy period of history when Christianity was beginning to triumph but monsters and dragons had not lost their sway. In Robin Hood they can see the memory of an England where great tracts were given over to forest and to hunting. The forest law was so harsh that even the dogs had to be crippled. Even more clearly, children can appreciate that the Arthurian stories have something to tell about medieval knights, if little about Arthur. In the story of Edward I and his son swearing on the swans that they would be revenged on the sacrilegious Robert Bruce, and the young Edward pledging himself never to sleep in the same bed till Scotland was reached, some mature children may begin to see that if history makes legend, legend also makes history.

631. It is heroes and villains, fairy tale extremes, that young children look for in legend. But even before they leave the infant school, some children press to know whether a story is really true. Stories which have actually happened have an added force for them. This is surely the moment for heroic stories, despite the many difficulties they present, for giving children "the habitual vision of greatness" which Whitehead believed to be essential to moral development. Leonidas, Boniface, Alfred, Francis, explorers from the fifteenth to the twentieth century: these are among the characters who can be exciting company for children.

632. Whether in a story or in some other form of historical work, it is detail, not the generalisation of the textbooks, that carries conviction and stimulates enquiry. Detail for the imagination to play on is a parallel to the concrete situations from which young children may form their mathematical concepts.

Children ask exactly what their heroes looked like. Sometimes there is no authentic information but when it exists they should be given it—Edward I's great stature and drooping eyelid, the wart on Cromwell's nose and his linen "plain but not clean". It is not enough to learn that Elizabethan ships were small and that music was popular in Elizabethan England. Children benefit from knowing the exact dimensions of the ships that ventured into unknown seas, that explorers like Drake and Davis found room for a small orchestra on board ships so tiny that adequate supplies could not be carried, and that Elizabethan barbers provided citherns rather than magazines for their waiting clients.

633. History may be studied in its own right or as a dimension of the many topics in which children are interested. In either case, its quality will depend on the sources available for children and teachers alike. In this, as in most other aspects of the curriculum, a consultant is needed on the staff, who will see that good historical material is available for pupils and teachers, (including the many cheap editions of sources that are now in print). He ought to make himself knowledgeable on the historical resources of the neighbourhood and to discuss with his colleagues which of children's historical interests are most worth underlining and reinforcing.

634. Though there is doubt about the belief that young children memorise more readily than adolescents, children profit from having some landmarks in chronology. Certainly if they remain in the middle school till 12 plus, they should be helped to see by time charts and other means the broad sequence of the events and aspects of history they learn about, and to acquire in effect a short "alphabet" of history.

E. GEOGRAPHY

635. A key problem in the teaching of geography is to balance the knowledge which can be learned by children through their own senses with knowledge about distant places, which can only be learned through reports of various kinds made by other people and which demands imagination and interpretation on the part of the children. It has long been recognised that the first sort is a necessary prelude to any real appreciation of the second. For this reason many teachers have regarded local geography as the foundation upon which may be built sensitive and accurate imagining about strange lands and customs. Such teachers are prepared to accept the difficulties of organisation, the hazards of being confronted with questions which they cannot answer, and the demands upon professional skill to select from among a miscellany of experiences, all of which are the consequences of out-door work. One of the notable changes in geography teaching in the primary school over the last 20 or 30 years has been the steady increase in out-door work. Some schools not only conduct local studies but arrange visits to a contrasting area, often using exchange visits with another school or a brief period of residence in one of the field study centres which a growing number of local education authorities are establishing. Other schools have made little or no serious attempt to assess the potentialities of their neighbourhoods for geographical study. There has thus been an uneven growth of learning out of doors, and, concurrently with it, an uneven reassessment of the qualities that children's geographical books should possess.

636. Forty years ago primary schools were largely dependent on series of text books written in simple language specifically for young children. Some text book writers sought to use the dependence of Britain upon imported food and raw materials as a link between the children and other lands: there grew up a fashion for the geography of products which often told of "workers" and gave descriptions of meaningless industrial processes, rather than people and the lives they lived. Other writers sought an orderly framework of world geography; Herbertson's "natural regions" (elements of an advanced geographical concept) were often used as the basis of world study and the children were told of the great climatic and vegetation belts as broad types of environment within which it was erroneously claimed that human activity conformed to set patterns. Terms like tundra, selvas and deciduous forest became the stock in trade of junior geography, and lessons dealt with "the lumbermen of the cold forests", "the pygmies of the hot wet forests", and "the nomads of hot deserts". These generalised cardboard characters belonged to no specific place. Subsequent writers have realised the importance for young children of the specific before the general, and there has been a steady increase in books which deal descriptively with a single family or small village, with a real farm or plantation, or with a few workers in an actual mine or factory. These sample studies carry much of the authenticity of local geography and permit genuine comparisons with the home region. There are now many hundreds of books for children, often illustrated with photographs or attractive line drawings, which tell of life as it is actually lived in many parts of the earth. These books stimulate some of the most searching questions from children and the most assiduous reference to maps and globes. There are also text books which fall between these two extremes and stimulate sample studies by manufacturing characters and names and situations which are claimed to be typical of certain areas. They rarely achieve authenticity.

637. A third element which has assumed increasing importance in the last 20 years in many schools is the use of mechanical aids; film strips, ciné film, sound radio and television have made available new and vivid sources of information which call for discriminating use by the teacher.

638. Visits to schools today show an enormous variation in the extent to which teachers are prepared to exploit their localities as teaching laboratories, and to use new kinds of geography books and other teaching aids. The head of the procession has advanced far beyond the tail.

639. The work done by many teachers in primary schools suggests that there are three broad stages through which children pass in their geographical education in the primary school:

(i) The first stage, which is appropriate to younger, and some older, infants is concerned with indiscriminate examining and observing of objects, events and phenomena, and learning the vocabulary needed to communicate about them. Weather, people and their actions, growing plants, inanimate objects, scenes in the road or street are all matters of curiosity and comment. A walk out of doors was recorded by infants on a large wall frieze in which houses, the church, trees, clouds, a lorry driver, a dog and the children themselves were prominently depicted: three dimensional models were made and some words, phrases and sentences written to accompany the pictorial record.

(ii) In the second stage the continued enlargement of vocabulary (which indeed persists into adulthood) is accompanied by more discriminating and selective examination. Single objects or phenomena are isolated and analysed; changes in the weather, farming activities or the traffic flow are discussed, the different layers of soil are compared by feel, colour and texture; leaves of one tree may be set against those of another. Questions of a quite penetrating character may be asked and explanations given by parents or others may be remembered and repeated. At this stage observation can be acute and children find themselves striving for modes of expression which they have not yet mastered. The following piece of writing by a seven year old boy after seeing a picture in a geographical magazine illustrates this stage:

> "Once a lovely liner was noseing down a Norwegian fjord. High steep rocky mountains towered the sides of it, and the captain of the liner was gazing out all around him. It was quiet lovely and lonely. A fjord is an arm of water, like a channel with mountains at the side. All fjords are in Norway, and some are used for harbours. The captain was on his bridge eating egg sandwiches and drinking lemonade. The captain's ship was called the 'Golden Glory'. The funnels were red with gold stars. The ship had three funnels, a Union Jack at the front and back. It had two anchors one for the front and one for the back. The ship weighed a 150 tons. It had 21 portholes at each side. The Golden Glory was 2,000 yards long. It had a mast at each end with a flag on. The ship was two miles up the fjord."

(iii) In the third stage the analysis and comparison of phenomena take on precision as mathematical skills, language and simple argument come to be employed. A sequence of events in human activity is recorded; temperatures are measured, clouds are classified and the directions of their movements described by points of the compass, traffic is counted and classified. Tables, graphs and written descriptions are commonly used as well as models and pictures. As children pass into this stage many of them are able to elucidate relationships and offer explanations. One group of juniors who kept a graphical record of atmospheric pressure and rainfall discovered that a large fall in pressure was accompanied by rainfall. On the single occasion when the correlation failed they wrote to the Meteorological Office to discover why.

640. Most junior schools allocate specific weekly periods to geography though the time-table is not necessarily followed slavishly. In others the name may not appear on the time-table but the subject matter with which geographers are concerned—embracing the landscape, both natural and man-made, weather and climate and many aspects of the activities of people—is included in the curriculum in one form or another.

641. There are many first hand experiences through which primary school children can become acquainted with objects and events of geographical significance, can gain a vocabulary associated with them, and can lay the foundation of that essentially geographical skill, map reading. But the situation of the school invariably limits the teacher's choice among these experiences. In some districts a stream may be both accessible and safe and

the observed speed of flow, the depth of water, its muddiness or clarity can become topics for observation, measurement, and, at a later stage, explanation. Terms such as source, current, bed, sediment, confluence and estuary are used and questions may need to be answered about the relationships between weather and flow. Work of this kind may enable a child to understand more clearly what the Aswan dam can mean in a country like Egypt. In another area the river may be regarded as a source of water supply, as a barrier to movement that has necessitated bridges or ferries with their dominating influence over road and rail patterns, or as a means of transport linking the interior of the country with the sea. Some schools, particularly those in northern and western Britain, may find a source of interest in rocks in their many forms. Children may become acquainted with their textures, colours and weights, observe the strata in which they occur, and in some favoured areas the fossils they contain. They may observe how rocks are used for building stone and road metal or, in the case of chalk and limestone, sent to the cement factory. Other schools have access to the coast where cliffs, beaches, sand dunes and the flotsam lines of high tide are matters of interest. Animals, machinery, crops and farming routine are part of the rural setting available to some schools. Schools in urban areas can study shops, transport, housing estates and industry. There are very few schools indeed that cannot make useful studies of building materials, that cannot observe and record weather changes, and that cannot dig a small hole in a garden or adjacent field to find out what soil is like and how it changes with depth. Elements such as these are being employed by teachers to help children to gain vivid impressions by seeing, hearing, touching, smelling and examining the world around them. Measuring and calculating come at a later stage and often accompany a change from pictorial recording to graphs, maps and written accounts. Older juniors may relate one phenomenon to another such as rainfall to stream flow, slope to cultivation, land use to elevation or industrial sites to railway or canal.

642. There are various means by which local studies carried out by children themselves may lead outwards to the study of areas that cannot be visited. Sometimes a local feature possesses a direct link with a distant place; for example, a stream may send children to maps to discover its source, the hill where it rises, other streams which share its basin, the towns on its banks and the port at its mouth; a railway, road, canal or ship may carry children in imagination from the northern industrial district to the farmlands of Lincolnshire or the Fens, from the uplands and valleys of Wales to the industrial Midlands, from London to the holiday resorts of Cornwall or the lonely Scottish highlands, from Hull to Oslo or Copenhagen. A more profitable device, especially for older children, is to stress the thematic aspects of local study. Thus a farm which is well known to the children becomes the heart of a series of farm studies; dairying in Cheshire may be compared with sheep farming in Wales, stock fattening in Northumberland, fruit growing in Kent, wheat farming in Saskatchewan, rice cultivation in Java or subsistence agriculture in Nigeria. Weather studies and graphical records may be used for comparison with exotic climates and some awareness conveyed of the great contrasts that occur in temperature and rainfall and their seasonal fluctuation from one place to another. Older children may thus enquire into some of the reasons that differentiate their home area from other areas. Younger juniors marvel at the way in which the homely matters of food, clothing and houses in

J

strange regions stand in contrast to those which they know, and seek for simple explanations of some differences. In such excursions the children are called upon to exercise their powers of imagination and this is where modern aids can bring powerful support to the teacher and child.

643. The ciné film, transparencies and clear pictures are a valuable complement to first-hand experience and extend indirect experience; but time must be given for studying and discussing them or much of the impact may be lost. Broadcast programmes which provide local background colour in the form of typical sounds and conversations have a similar value, but they, too, need preparation and time for discussion if their value for the children is to be fully reaped.

644. To a large extent the teacher learns to control or to be prepared for the directions in which children's questions lead outwards to the world from local study, film and broadcast lessons. But there are other influences at work outside the classroom which inform children and stimulate questions. The cinema, the press, and most of all television have made available to everyone a general visual knowledge of the world such as was impossible for adults, let alone children, before their invention. Simply left to himself, the television viewer sees more of the world and its peoples than the most travelled man of a century ago. Such knowledge may be superficial but it bears the ring of authenticity. This makes the task of the school at once easier and more difficult; easier because the sources of knowledge are much greater than school geography alone, and more difficult because the wealth of impressions possessed by children will be incomplete, confused and often coloured by the selection and purposes of the programme observed. The producer of a programme on the animal life of Borneo is under no obligation to explain to his viewers that the clothing, weapons and houses of the people seen as background to the main theme may represent skilful adaptations to natural environment, available materials, social organisation and the present state of technological skills which prevail. Detailed descriptions of a variety of environments and modes of life are needed before children can realise the wise balance of adaptation that has been achieved by a great many communities. In this respect some textbooks are open to serious criticism because they convey an over-simplified and often grossly distorted version of the lives of children and grown up people in other lands. The textbook flat conical hat of the south Chinese peasant is not "funny" to Chinese; it is sensible headgear made cheaply from available materials and well suited to a climate in which heavy rain and hot sun may alternate. Recent developments in northern Canada and Greenland have enriched the way of life of the Eskimo communities in a manner quite foreign to many standard textbook accounts.

645. Even the best books will need constant revision. There is an increasing supply of well written and well illustrated reference books, and the sources of reliable, unbiased information of the sample study type as well as of good films are constantly being enriched.

646. Some form of national and world geography ought to be studied by older juniors and the emphasis ought to be primarily on the relationship between a way of life and the total environment rather than on natural features in themselves or economic products. If such studies are accompanied by the

regular use of globes and maps, the sophisticated conventions which they employ are gradually absorbed by the children and help to bring order to the many diffuse environments and cultures to which they have been introduced. But the important thing ultimately is that people should understand people, and in the primary school a significant contribution may be made to this end.

F. MATHEMATICS

647. Until comparatively recently a typical "scheme of work" in a primary school could have been summarised somewhat as follows: "Composition and decomposition of 10. The four rules. The four rules in money. Tables. Vulgar fractions. Simple decimals. Simple problems." Emphasis was laid upon knowledge of tables, computation and quick and accurate "mental arithmetic". About twenty years ago the first signs of change appeared, but it is perhaps only in the last five or six that the new ideas have spread so as to affect at least a majority of primary schools, and to justify the name of revolution in a substantial minority.

648. Rapid revolutions are not common in English education and, before describing the change and saying what we think about it, it is worth indicating briefly how it has been brought about. Changes of this nature and magnitude probably occur only when there exists a fairly widespread dissatisfaction with the current state of affairs and a predisposition to look in new directions. The dissatisfaction had certainly been there for many years and it was not confined to this country. It was associated with the growing need of society for mathematics at an advanced level. Those who supported the accepted ways argued that a sound mechanical foundation was essential before anything more adventurous could be attempted and that children must learn to walk before they tried to run. There was, however, a growing conviction that the accepted approach laid too exclusive an emphasis on mechanical operations, was too little concerned with the practical uses of mathematics, and that the traditional syllabuses included much useless lumber.

649. For 30 years or more attempts had been made both by teachers and by the writers of textbooks to make arithmetic more practical and more interesting, but it was not until a mathematical, rather than a purely arithmetical, approach began to be made, that the whole subject began to take on a new look. The various kinds of number apparatus for the use of infant schools, none of which was perhaps essential to the change that has taken place, have helped teachers to think in a fresh way about number and broken down some of the misgivings that many women teachers undoubtedly had about mathematics as distinct from "infant number". Even more important was the work of many infant teachers, and their advisers, who realised that learning in school and out of school went on all the time and who directed children's attention to the mathematical aspects of their environment and of their play. Many of these teachers came to realise the contribution of experience to the formation of concepts and the limited value of processes learnt by rote. Books, too, had their influence—Piaget's researches, books about the history and nature of mathematics and the Mathematical Association's "The Teaching of Mathematics in the Primary School", which was a tremendous encouragement to change.

650. There is little doubt that the next most important move came from the Department of Education and Science. Individual members of H.M. Inspectorate had, since the mid-forties, been encouraging a more mathematical approach and the Mathematical Panel of Inspectors, which had formerly been mainly concerned with secondary mathematics, had for some time taken a greatly increased interest in primary schools. In 1959 one of its members was seconded almost full-time to the task of organising courses and conferences for teachers. As a result, about 15 per cent of all primary teachers in England have by now attended courses and conferences organised by H.M.Is., with much valuable co-operation from local advisers, and lecturers in colleges and departments of education. The aim was to introduce teachers to new ideas, to encourage them to set up local groups for further study and exchange of experiences, and to remove the insecurity and inadequacy of which many were all too conscious. These groups were an essential part of the development that took place. Some mathematical specialists from secondary schools took part in all courses. According to the National Survey 26 per cent of teachers attended courses in mathematics between 1961 and 1964 (Appendix 5, Tables 30 & 31).

651. The most encouraging result has been the great interest known to be aroused amongst teachers attending, including those who had always thought mathematics beyond them. The collaboration of mathematicians from many different institutions has led to an enrichment of mathematical knowledge and to a clearer understanding of each other's needs and problems. The experience gleaned in the years from 1959 to 1964 has been embodied in the Schools Council Curriculum Bulletin No. 1 "Mathematics in Primary Schools" ([1]), a work of much interest and, we think, of great usefulness. It contains many fascinating accounts of children's work and activities and can be recommended to any reader who wishes to know in detail what modern teaching of mathematics in the primary schools is like. It has greatly influenced the current Nuffield project in primary mathematics. A deliberate change in the curriculum has been brought about not by the issue of programmes by states or universities as is often done in the U.S.A., but by pioneer work by teachers, clarified and focused by advisory services to teachers, and diffused on a national scale by in-service training in which self help has played a major and essential part. This may prove to be the beginning of a new era associated with the establishment of the Schools Council.

652. The Nuffield project, which is being sponsored by the Schools Council and which has been financed by the Nuffield Foundation, involves the issue of material for the use of teachers. At every stage primary teachers have been involved in its production and at every stage it is being "tried out" in primary schools. It will thus have undergone a more rigorous testing than any ordinary mathematical textbook, which is normally the work of a single writer. But the material is not a textbook, nor is it a course. It is best described as a "do-it-yourself" series of handbooks. Furthermore, when it is published and made available for general use, it will carry no authority other than what its own inherent qualities command and will compete on equal terms with other books and courses.

653. It would not be timely to describe in detail the present state of mathematical teaching or to pass judgement on it. We offer a brief general account of new ideas on mathematical teaching, followed by some comments derived

from what we have seen on our visits to schools and heard from our witnesses.

654. In Curriculum Bulletin No. 1 (Chapter 3, page 9) the following summary is given of the principles underlying this new approach:

(1) Children learn mathematical concepts more slowly than we realised. They learn by their own activities.

(2) Although children think and reason in different ways they all pass through certain stages depending on their chronological and mental ages and their experience.

(3) We can accelerate their learning by providing suitable experiences, particularly if we introduce the appropriate language simultaneously.

(4) Practice is necessary to fix a concept once it has been understood, therefore practice should follow, and not precede, discovery.

Some of the practical consequences of adopting these principles are:

(a) Instead of being presented with ready made problems in a textbook the children find their own problems or are given them in a "raw form" with the idea of their learning a mathematical concept. The old ready-made problems were often concerned with irrelevant situations such as filling baths, and calculating how many men would take how many hours to dig so many yards of ditch, if it took another lot of men a different number of hours to dig a different length of ditch. These were simply mechanical sums in disguise. They involved no constructive thinking, only the choice and application of a process. Now many infant schools arrange equipment so that children can themselves discover relationships between numbers in the counting sequence. The genuine problem may arise very early as when infants notice the varying length of shadows at different times of the day and ask the reason. They are encouraged to begin to look for an answer even if the description of the problem, the measuring of the shadow, is as far as they are interested or able to go. Later on a dripping tap in the cloakroom, not an imaginary one in the textbook, might provide a "real" problem. How much water is being wasted in 24 hours, in a week, in a year? Later still the problems may be quite complicated. Some ten year old children had collected a number of bird and animals skulls and became interested in comparing the capacities of the brain cavities. They had to think out an efficient method of measuring them, and then construct some cubic receptacle for measuring the dry sand that they had poured into the cavities. The cubic inch that they had used for the cat's and the rabbit's skulls proved to be too large for the bird's and the interesting discovery that a cubic quarter inch was not the same as the quarter of a cubic inch was not likely ever again to be forgotten.

(b) The communication of results in mathematical symbols and graphs develops alongside the practical experiences. Children do not first of all learn fractions, then graphs, then equations, then indices as was done in former days. They learn the appropriate symbols and techniques as they need them and often show a capacity for mathematical thinking and for processes formerly regarded as "advanced" much earlier than was ever dreamed of under the old methods. The correct vocabulary is often quite naturally introduced at an early stage.

(c) "Pure mathematics" appear to have a fascination for many children, and such things as number series, sets, magic squares and the geometry of shapes now appear in the primary school curriculum. Some schools are experimenting with teaching mathematics through the language of sets. This approach has been taken up more strongly in the United States. There is hardly enough evidence as yet to judge the success of these experiments.

(d) Although the new approach has brought much new experience and material into primary schools and has made for a much greater flexibility in matters of presentation and sequence, it has not removed the necessity for a very carefully thought out scheme of work in junior schools, for careful individual records of progress, for practice in computation and for accuracy.

655. Our first comment upon these generalisations would be that this sort of approach demands a considerably greater knowledge of mathematics or rather degree of mathematical understanding in the teachers than the traditional one. If the children have to think harder, so do the teachers. Some have difficulty in identifying the mathematical aspects of topic work. Many teachers, especially women, faced the change with a poor equipment of mathematical training, and it is a measure of their willingness to learn and ability to profit by their learning, that so much has been achieved in so short a time. The changes in the study of mathematics in colleges of education ought to produce a generation of teachers with a much better initial equipment than formerly.

656. There is ample evidence that many of the claims made for the new approach are well founded. Moreover, the number of non-mathematicians floundering in a welter of half grasped rules and inaccurate figures is noticeably less.

657. The extent to which the primary schools have adopted the new approach is difficult to measure precisely. The general impression of H.M. Inspectorate is that at least a majority of schools have been influenced by the developments of the last five years and that a substantial minority, something between ten per cent and 20 per cent, have completely rethought and reorganised their mathematical syllabus and teaching methods. One of the most encouraging features of these developments is the evident enjoyment that many teachers themselves display on encountering mathematics in its "new" form.

658. Will the modern methods lead to a decline in computation and accuracy? A modern approach can be mishandled like any other, and a lazy or unsympathetic or muddle-headed teacher could fail in this approach, no less than in the traditional one. Occasionally children may be given too little guidance but there is nothing new in this. When taught by older methods, children were sometimes either kept together as a group or left to "work on" in their book without enough teaching, stimulus or discussion. Accuracy, indeed, is likely to improve, since in this kind of work there is a built-in incentive to accuracy. The children are much more personally involved and are often called upon to exercise their own judgement on the degree of accuracy, either in measurement or in computation, that each particular operation requires, whereas in the old arithmetic books inches appeared in the same sums as miles. It has been feared by some that computation would

be given too little place. The more fascinating the mathematics, the less the enthusiasm that might be felt for "sums", but here again there is an automatic safeguard. Computation can be seen to have a clear purpose, that of "fixing" a necessary process and increasing the speed of its performance. The introduction of the decimal system should reduce the time necessary for arithmetical computation.

659. If, as we think, it is desirable that this development should continue, the process which brought it about may indicate the means of furthering this. We believe that the local groups of teachers which sprang up in the wake of one H.M.I. and those who worked with her, provide a useful model. If the stimulus is provided by industry, local education authority organisers, university lecturers, researchers and H.M.Is., the initiative and responsibility for development must lie mainly with primary school teachers themselves. They must form working groups which exist not primarily to listen to lectures but for the discussion of experience and ideas and for practical work. The centres for teachers which are being established in some areas will fail in their object if they encourage either a passive attendance or attendance with the object of learning how to teach a programme. They must have as their main objective the encouragement of initiative and of imaginative and constructive thinking.

660. It is obvious that, in a large number of smaller primary schools, mathematics must be taught by those who are in no sense mathematical specialists, while even in the largest schools a full-fledged mathematician cannot, even if it were desirable, do all the mathematics teaching. We think that the teachers' groups that have been described will be the most useful means of ensuring that the mathematicians and the non-mathematicians work in a team and that the latter learn from the former. The specially devised machinery of the Nuffield project must be succeeded by established machinery. The future will depend upon the extent to which we can produce teachers with the necessary knowledge and understanding to use and improve upon the material made available to them, and to keep themselves up to date. This is the responsibility of the colleges of education, supported by whatever permanent arrangements are made, locally and nationally, for in-service training.

661. The "Southampton School Mathematics Project" in which a number of maintained and independent schools have co-operated, was the first of several experiments at the secondary level. Nevertheless children who have learned to think mathematically in the primary school are too often faced with little more than mechanical computation, repetitive sums and revision when they arrive in their new schools. The moral is that arrangements made for the in-service training and the re-education of primary school teachers should be increasingly available to the teachers of the younger pupils in secondary schools, and that the latter should be actively encouraged to take advantage of them. The raising of the age of transfer will make this an urgent necessity.

662. It happens that our enquiry has coincided with a period of change in the teaching of mathematics and we have been privileged spectators of it. While it must be evident from our remarks that we are full of enthusiasm for what we have seen and of hope for the future, we must emphasise that the last thing we wish to see is a hardening of the new approach into an accepted

syllabus supported by textbooks, work books and commercially produced apparatus and consecrated by familiarity. The rate of change must obviously slow down, but the initiative must remain firmly in the practising teachers' hands.

REFERENCE

¹'Mathematics in Primary Schools', Schools Council Curriculum Bulletin No. 1 H.M.S.O., 1965.

G. SCIENCE

663. Traditionally, the only science taught in primary schools was nature study which varied from a close study of living things at first hand to avid note making and illustrations of animals, birds, plants and insects seldom actually seen and often scarcely recognisable. B.B.C. talks and the admirably produced pamphlets which accompanied them often aroused interest but resulted too rarely in first-hand observation. Unless the individual teacher had a real knowledge of natural history, the subject tended to be one of the less satisfactory in the primary school.

664. We must emphasise that there is hardly any material more suitable for study by young children than living forms. The observation, identification and recording of fauna and flora found in the neighbourhood of the school, the elementary study of ecological features, simple studies in human biology, the breeding and care in good conditions of insects, small mammals and fish, are all educational and appropriate. Some authorities are setting up animal "banks" from which animals, much greater in variety than those formerly seen in the classroom, can be supplied. The presence of animals encourages a great deal of writing and practical work. Interest in living things tends to be particularly long-lived.

665. Quite naturally, the children's enquiries can lead to some understanding and respect for the fundamental life processes of breathing, feeding and movement, of sensitivity and reproduction. Discussion of the significance of these could be sufficiently wide-ranging to include some reference to human organs and their functions; but it must be handled with delicacy and should avoid eliciting too morbid an interest in self. Curiosity so aroused can lead to simple experiments which test the efficiency of digestive juices like saliva, of the design and arrangement of muscle, sinew and bone, and of the heart and circulation. Some enquiry into the workings of sense organs and their efficiency and limitations is another fascinating topic and should lead to studies of reaction-times and even to some interest in the functioning of the brain and nervous system. Although we include later in the report a separate section on sex education it may best arise in the context of a general study of life processes, and teachers would perhaps be wise to channel and encourage enquiries to this end. It would certainly seem natural and desirable to foster in older children a sense of wonder at the power of organisms, including man,

to adjust to environment, to escape enemies, to grow from tiny origins and complete a life-cycle, covering remarkably varied spans of time, and to produce young like themselves. Indeed, with this in mind many schools consider it important to supplement classroom studies with visits to farms and the growing of suitable plants.

666. But there is no reason to confine scientific studies to biology even in environments particularly favourable to that kind of work. There are some teachers who are more at home in the field of physical science, which is certainly a source of absorbing interest to most children. Young children have enjoyed playing with models, magnets, siphons, low voltage electricity, lenses and so on for as long as anyone can remember. For some years, interest tables in many infant schools have been stocked with magnets, pulleys, levers and magnifying glasses and have proved stimulating when supplemented by oral or written suggestions from the teacher. Teachers have drawn children's attention to physical phenomena through water play without trying to explain too much. But, for no clear reason, little place was found for these matters at the junior stage and for most children their first serious introduction to physical science was in the secondary school.

667. In 1957 a meeting of teachers was called by the Department of Education and Science and conducted by H.M. Inspectors. It was followed by national and local courses, the publication by the Department of a pamphlet "Science in the Primary school" and, in 1963, by a Nuffield project, planned on similar lines to the mathematics project and in close co-operation with it. The material produced by the Nuffield team became available on a limited scale in the autumn of 1965 and is still in an experimental stage. By late 1966 a teachers' guide, a volume of case histories of science in the primary school, and a series of teachers' books on a variety of general topics will be available for purchase by the many local education authorities who wished to take part in the first phase of the Nuffield project but who could not then be accepted. This second phase, of testing materials, used on a large scale, over a period of six years or so, will be evaluated by a study commissioned by the Schools Council. The project is planned to cover not only the primary years as at present defined but also the years up to 13.

668. A twofold change is therefore occurring—first the introduction of a much greater variety of subject matter into primary schools and secondly a new approach. The physical environment of a school, as of an individual child, contains an immense variety of objects and phenomena. Besides the natural world of living forms and of sun, moon, stars, wind, rain, snow, frost, fog, heat and cold, night and day, there is the man-made world in all its technical complexity. The conventional ways of categorising these phenomena as biology, branches of physics such as optics, electricity and magnetism, chemistry, engineering and so on are neither natural nor, except very crudely, understandable classifications to young children of primary school age. If, for the terms used above, rabbits, railway engines, telescopes, T.V. sets and aeroplanes are substituted, these are at once seen to be things about which children show a spontaneous curiosity and ask endless questions. The subject matter of primary school science thus almost settles itself. It is those objects and phenomena in the physical world which attract and interest. The choice,

within that vast range, must depend partly on the immediate environment, urban or rural, plain or mountain, coastal or inland, partly on the special resources and interests of the teacher who may be a keen birdwatcher, a radio amateur, an enthusiast for railways or for twenty other different things, and will do best if he shares his special interest with his pupils. Clearly, the topic must be suitable for study by children of primary school age. Mains voltage electricity would be fascinating, but might also be fatal, and electronics would involve concepts too difficult for all but the most able children to grasp.

669. The treatment of the subject matter may be summarised in the phrase "learning by discovery". In a number of ways it resembles the best modern university practice. Initial curiosity, often stimulated by the environment the teacher provides, leads to questions and to a consideration of what questions it is sensible to ask and how to find the answers. This involves a great exercise of judgement on the part of the teacher. He will miss the whole point if he tells the children the answers or indicates too readily and completely how the answers may be found, but he must not let them flounder too long or too helplessly, and can often come to the rescue by asking another question. But, though constant dialogue between teacher and children is an essential feature of the approach we are describing, it would be wrong to picture it all as taking place in a classroom or even a laboratory. Essential elements are enquiry, exploration and first-hand experience which may mean expeditions, perhaps no further than to the playground, but sometimes to a railway station, a factory, a wood or a pond. The making of models and the construction and repetition of experiments will also play an important part. Young children may want to repeat experiments over and over again and the comparison of results will often lead to further enquiry. If, as children become older, they jump to generalisations too readily from the results of a single experiment, the teacher should see that they repeat their experiments. By this means children's understanding of precision, reliability and the nature of evidence can be increased. Some enquiries will certainly lead children to books, and information picked up from books or from television will also provide starting points for enquiry. But if primary school science is confined to knowledge taken from books, the whole purpose of the study of this area of the curriculum will be lost.

670. Although we welcome the extension of primary school science to include the physical sciences, we would regret any tendency to underestimate the importance of the opportunities of natural history. Our first example of first-hand study of the environment is therefore drawn from the latter, and is an extract from a much longer account by the headmistress of a little country school.

"In the spring of last year a mother carried a jar of frog spawn to school for her five year old son following his interest in a discussion we had after a ramble down the lane to find any material indicating that spring had arrived. He had asked his mother to take him for a walk after school and they had seen the frog spawn in a dirty pond so father was sent with the jar to get some for school.

The spawn was put into the tank and next day pond water and plants arrived from many sources. Daily observations were made, always somebody was popping over to see if the "black things" were frogs yet. We found shy children giving their views as to whether they were bigger than yesterday, and what movement could be seen. The older children began to note down and sketch the changes, but the Easter holidays broke into this piece of observation, and the interest was flagging when one of my managers visited the school and invited us to fish for tadpoles in her lily ponds.

Next day nylon stockings, wire and sticks, for fishing net making, arrived. The following day a shuttle service with cars conveyed all the infants and then any juniors who were without bicycles to Hailey House.

My helper took charge of the infants to fish in the lily ponds while we fished in the disused swimming pool. Although it poured with rain their spirits were not dampened, and very reluctantly after an hour, the party left with tadpoles and jars of creatures and mud from the swimming pool. Days were spent in naming newts, beetles, water boatmen, making charts with pictures cut from old books or magazines from home and information added which had been sought for in library books. Feeding habits were watched at odd times and inhabitants were counted as it was realised that some were being eaten. Some of our original tadpoles were put in their tank too, so that the water in the tadpole tank could be lowered and stones put above the water line so that they could now be amphibious, and as the change to frogs seemed too slow I suggested they should have natural surroundings but not too far away for us to watch. After discussion it was decided that plastic would hold water and having some big plastic bags the boys dug a hole and made a very satisfactory pond which lasted until the summer holidays. This gave them the chance of seeing the final development into frogs and the comparison of indoor and outdoor growth. Discussions arose naturally on stagnant water, fresh water, drinking water and flowing water which took us down into the village to note the currents, depth, etc., and to fish. Plants in the water and at the edge were named. The use of bridges and fords was another topic, the flooding and the debris left behind, and the flowing of the streams into the River Thames and its journey to the sea.

After this a girl brought a jar of water from the football field to show me that it was not fit to drink although it was always used for the players' tea. Then the boys wanted to find out if the rain water running down the bank contained any debris, so more jars of water were left to settle and the children were again experimenting a bit farther."

This account, besides giving a vivid picture of an activity, illustrates at several points the ways in which this kind of approach serves and enlivens the three Rs.

671. Our second example is an account of some group work by second year juniors on heat. It illustrates the interplay of the children's discovery and the teacher's guidance. We print it at the end of this section, as it was written.

672. Once again we emphasise the importance of language in this kind of approach. We have been told of a class of rather backward children who, after a term of being taught science in this way, showed a startling improvement in both spoken and written English. What they had said and written had a meaning and purpose for them which they had scarcely known previously. For the first time, perhaps, school was offering them first-hand

experience which demanded exact recording. For some less able children it may be appropriate for this free-ranging enquiry to continue beyond the primary school; it may still be for them the best way of learning. For others, perhaps the older and abler ones, a pattern of experience may emerge from their work that engages their attention and impels them to confine their enquiries within a chosen framework. For them a narrower field and deeper, cognate enquiries may become more satisfying. This development could fit them well for the more mature and systematic work that is more evident at the secondary stage.

673. The development that has been described has not been greeted with unanimous enthusiasm in all quarters. Some teachers of science in secondary schools have feared that children would come to them possessing all kinds of fragmentary, unclassified information, some of it inaccurate or at least "unscientific", all of it incomplete. Although it is too early to make a general assessment of the new approach, this particular objection to it can be fairly summarily disposed of. Knowledge is always incomplete, and it is only gradually that children can build up a coherent understanding of any aspect of it. The kinds of classification that are useful and necessary at an advanced stage may be meaningless at the age of 11. If children leave their primary schools with their natural curiosity not only unimpaired but sharpened, with experience of first-hand discovery in several different fields, with some idea of what questions to ask and how to find the answers, they will be well equipped to proceed with a scientific education. We believe that many secondary school teachers of science welcome this already and we hope that soon all of them will do so.

674. Whatever the outcome of the current projects, we are confident that the teacher's groups described in the section on mathematics will have an important part to play. The close connections between science and mathematics point to it, and the groups might well in practice be identical. Much of the material needed for science and mathematics is the same. Most science equipment is simple, and can be obtained from local shops or made in school. Some is expensive and requires careful "housing". Further, science is constantly extending its boundaries and though the frontiers of pure science are remote from the primary school, the practical application of new discoveries are not. Children now ask questions about space flight and transistors, neither of which existed a generation ago. We hope that, as in mathematics, teachers' centres will encourage initiative in teachers and will certainly not be used to draw up school syllabuses, though examples of the materials which can be handled by children at various ages, and of the ways in which investigation has developed in individual instances, can be useful. They should provide opportunities for teachers to extend their own scientific knowledge by practical work, and by study courses and lectures given by experts. The new methods demand more knowledge in teachers. There ought also to be opportunities for them to make apparatus to use in school and to discuss with their colleagues the innovations they are trying out, and opportunities for them to see each other's work in the classroom. There already exist the field study centres at Flatford, Malham Tarn and elsewhere, which have done much for the further education of teachers in biology and, more particularly, ecology, and a similar need undoubtedly exists in the non-biological sciences.

The precise relationship which ought to exist between teachers' centres, institutes of education and colleges of technology will probably vary from area to area but we have little doubt that some kind of partnership is needed. In the long term, the development of this work is bound also to depend heavily on the success of colleges of education in educating teachers who have broad scientific interests.

675. We have indicated the close connections which exist between science and mathematics and science and English, but the kind of science that we have been describing has even wider connections than these. A visit to a stream with the avowed object of collecting specimens may lead to non-scientific consequences—to a poem, or a painting, or to drawings which may be at once accurately observed and artistically pleasing. A visit to a church, with history and religion in mind, in one instance that came to our notice, resulted in a decision by the children to find out how the church was built, what were the engineering problems involved and, surprisingly, how much it weighed! The project involved much careful planning and hard work in mathematics and science, and a great deal of speaking, reading and writing. In a modern primary school this kind of thing is increasingly apt to happen. We applaud it because it reflects not only the nature of young children and their methods of learning but interconnections of subjects which have been more or less arbitrarily classified.

Is Polystyrene Warm?

We were puzzled in our group because the polystyrene feels warm to your hand. I'm sure I felt warmth when I held the palm of my hand about half-an-inch away from a cube surface.

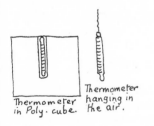

Thermometer in Poly. cube. Thermometer hanging in the air.

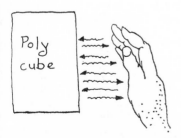

Poly cube

We thought at first the warmth must come from inside the polystyrene so we drilled a deep hole in one cube, and placed a centigrade thermometer inside the hole and hung another thermometer outside near it. But they both said 21½C. so there couldn't be warmth coming out of the material. For a long time we were puzzled and couldn't solve the mystery . . . where was the warmth coming from? Then Penny tumbled on the truth (we think!). The warmth coming from your hand hits the face of the cube and bounces back to your hand. So the material doesn't contain heat, doesn't soak up or absorb the heat—it throws it back. Our teacher says the name for *such a material is an insulator*. He then put our long iron poker in the fire and we felt the heat coming up to the handle. *Iron* must take up heat, not reflect it, so we learned that it *is a conductor*.

Finding More About Polystyrene as an Insulator

Now we decided to find out if any heat at all will pass through polystyrene. So we set up sheets of polystyrene in front of the stove, where it is very warm.

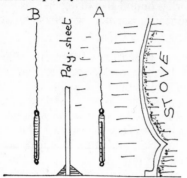

Next we hung a thermometer on each side of the sheet of polystyrene. After 5 minutes A read 31½°C, B read 22½°C. Suddenly I realised it wasn't a good experiment because A thermometer was nearer to the stove than B, and so we couldn't tell how much heat the polystyrene really stopped.

How We Improved The Experiment

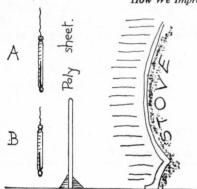

We hung both thermometers on the side of the polystyrene away from the stove, but only one shielded by the material and the second one much higher and with nothing to protect it from the heat of the stove.

We did this experiment with ½″, ¾″ and 1″ sheets of the material and these were the results.

	Room Temp.	A	B
1″ Sheet	21½°	27°	22½°
¾″ Sheet	21½°	27°	22½°
½″ Sheet	21½°	27°	22½°

I expect the air round the stove would be warmer than anywhere else in the room, so that will account for the one degree higher readings on thermometer B. But apart from that it looks to us as though polystyrene is a very good insulator, not soaking up any heat nor letting heat pass through it.

Out of curiosity, we got our teacher to open the stove damper to make more heat come from the stove, and we put the three sheets of polystyrene through the same tests against more heat.

The B thermometer stayed at 22½°C though A rose and rose. We were amazed to find that the thinnest sheet of polystyrene kept the heat in just as well as the thickest sheet.

Results	A	B
Poly ½″	18¾°	22½°
Poly ¾″	30½°	22½°
Poly 1″	34½°	22½°

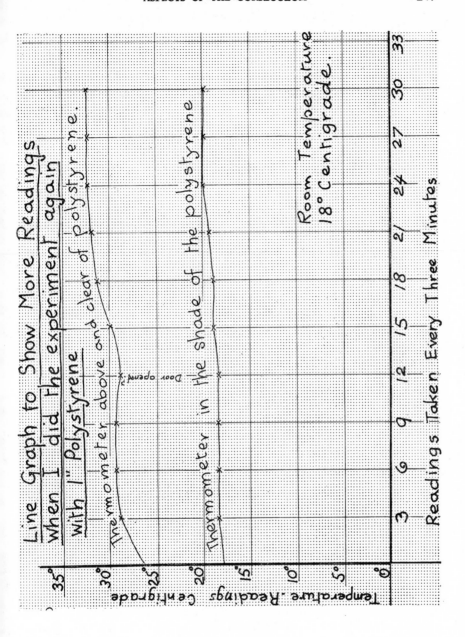

Line Graph to Show More Readings when I did the experiment again with 1" Polystyrene

Thermometer above and clear of polystyrene.

Thermometer in the shade of the polystyrene

Door opened.

Room Temperature 18°Centigrade.

Temperature Readings. Centigrade

Readings Taken Every Three Minutes

H. ART AND CRAFT

676. Art is both a form of communication and a means of expression of feelings which ought to permeate the whole curriculum and the whole life of the school. A society which neglects or despises it is dangerously sick. It affects, or should affect, all aspects of our life from the design of the commonplace articles of everyday life to the highest forms of individual expression.

677. The beginning of the revolt against formalism occurred in the realm of pictorial art. In the late 1920s the influence of Marion Richardson began to be felt and by 1939 a considerable number of schools had broken away from the old tradition and were trying something new. The old tradition consisted of the careful copying of objects—flowers, twigs, fruit, geometrical forms and sometimes pictures—usually in black and white and usually with a hard lead pencil. If colour was introduced, it was to fill in outlines, and crayons were much commoner than paint. If paint was used, it was cheap water colour. There was little in this tradition to commend. It encouraged neither vision nor invention. The close observation and careful recording that might have been its merits were disappointingly absent from the work of the majority of children, for whom the demands made were quite inappropriate. The essence of the new approach was to let children use large sheets of paper and big brushes, requiring larger movements of hand and arm, more suitable to their age than the fine, delicate movement required by the old tradition. Powder colour in plenty and free brush work were introduced from the earliest moment and the children were allowed to paint "what they liked". Little attempt was made to teach them perspective or techniques, but certainly Marion Richardson and those close to her did much to arouse children's powers of observation.

678. The immediate result of the inter-war approach was the production of vast quantities of childlike pictures, boldly executed, usually aglow with colour, often showing freshness and originality of vision and sometimes a remarkable power of organising two-dimensional space. This stage of almost complete freedom from teaching of techniques was necessary. It was probably the only means of breaking away from the arid formalism of the tradition, but it was only a stage, and good primary school art has developed considerably beyond it in recent years.

679. There are many more teachers now than there ever were with an appreciation of painting and other arts and an understanding of their value for children. They still do little teaching of techniques, but do much more than those of 30 years ago to stimulate children's vision, to develop the "seeing eye", to multiply the possible sources of inspiration and to enrich the school environment. They supply the better art books and magazines and make use of everyday objects of good design from this country and others, as well as of the resources of the past. The subject matter, the treatment and the media of children's painting show a much greater variety than those of the thirties. The primary schools have, indeed, participated to the full in the more general flourishing of art in the whole community. Some primary schools encourage close observation of the detail and subtleties of colour and texture to be found in bark, stones, shells, plants and seaweed. Many delightful coloured and black and white drawings are acutely observed and lovingly executed. Much that was banished in the thirties, and rightly banished because it was feebly conceived and inadequately provided for, has now returned to its rightful place, infused with life and assisted by the use of better tools and media.

680. We think, at its best, primary school art is very good indeed. But there is no cause for complacency. Many schools still show too little sign of having moved far from the outlook of the thirties and although this is better than the tradition that preceded it, it is too limited in scope to be acceptable. There is

often too little progression, and the work of the ten year olds is less developed than would be expected from what is done by the sixes, sevens and eights. This is partly attributable to a failure on the part of teachers to realise their pupils' possibilities, and partly to teachers' lack of confidence in their power to help. As long ago as 1933 some children in Wiltshire painted large murals in the school and expressed a desire to brighten up in a similar way the local station waiting room, a suggestion in which the railway company took no interest! We are convinced that the artistic capabilities of children are much greater than many primary teachers realise. This underestimate will become more serious if some children remain in the middle school till nearly 13. Too many teachers still believe that after that "first fine careless rapture" children's imaginative powers diminish and wither. Others teachers have proved the reverse. What has to be recognised is that, as children grow, their vision and also their interests and viewpoint change. For example, although not all twelve year olds "see" perspective in the adult sense, many become deeply absorbed in what the adult world calls "drawing". The form and construction of things, both natural and man-made, are of consuming interest to some boys and girls of this age. If the school can feed and satisfy this interest, all should be well. Of course twelve year olds will paint differently from nine year olds; but, if they have a full life, their work will certainly not be empty or derivative: it will be as exploratory and as satisfying to themselves as it ever was. Moreover, the impact of commercial art and the influence of the camera, particularly through television, must be recognised. The school has to manage these forces tactfully. In both there is something stimulating and good as well as bad, and the discerning teacher will know how to guide his children's emerging powers of criticism. A more fundamental obstacle to full develop-ment is the lukewarm attitude not only of the public but also of many teachers and many schools, especially grammar schools, to the importance of art in education. If the word "frill" is not now often used of it, the attitude that it implies is still widespread. We shall return to this point later, and will only say here that we are ourselves satisfied that the practice of art by children is a fundamental and indispensable part of their education.

681. Craft in the elementary school was traditionally separated from art. For the boys it meant woodwork, cardboard models and geometrical drawing and for the girls needlework and knitting. Certain other crafts, notably basket-making, book-binding, weaving, block-printing and occasionally pottery became common in the senior elementary schools in the thirties, but the primary schools were not much affected. Latterly a much greater variety of crafts, including wood-carving, clay-modelling, dyeing and block-cutting, have come into the primary schools and the distinction between what is done by boys and girls has partly disappeared. Except possibly for the oldest children, it is quite artificial and unhelpful: boys enjoy stitchery and girls can benefit from work in wood and metal.

682. The basis for much of the best work done in the primary school has been the willingness of many infant teachers to make materials and tools of good quality available to young children. There has been a welcome trend away from didactic to natural materials and to those whose use is rooted in our tradition. Clay has replaced plasticine, the well-kept "piece box" has taken the place of the hessian mats and school knitting cottons, and wood

and waste materials have been substituted for paper as a medium for three dimensional models. Children need to experiment with a wide range of materials, natural and man-made.

683. The connection of art and craft with the rest of the curriculum is of paramount importance. The development of sensitivity and the growth of techniques come partly as the result of play and experiment with materials. But, just as in mathematics, techniques are learnt most easily when they are needed for the purposes children have in mind.

684. At its best, the craft of English primary schools is outstanding. We have seen work of extraordinary beauty and technical perfection which we could hardly have believed had been produced by young children had we not watched them doing it; but here, equally, there is much still to be done. There is far too much mechanical and repetitive work, especially in needlework, far too much dull and tasteless craft, far too widespread an acceptance of poor standards, far too little integration of the craft into the curriculum as a whole. If children stay in the middle school for an extra year, more account must be taken of their growing concern to know how things work and how to do a job "properly", almost to pursue a technique for its own sake. There must be a more workmanlike and ambitious outlook for the older children. Some girls will certainly wish to make simple outfits for themselves. They should be given opportunity to discriminate between the fabrics which are suitable for their purpose and for their degree of skill, and should be helped by frequent discussion. Guidance should be given in the ways of holding and manipulating tools and materials, and the sewing machine should have a place. Many of the crafts associated with textiles, block printing, tie dyeing, embroidery and weaving appeal to boys and girls alike. An over-academic emphasis in the work of the abler streams in the grammar schools and the neglect of craft in their education has left its mark on the great majority of teachers in primary schools. Some of the colleges of education have done splendid work in the correction of this lopsided education, as also have some of the advisers to local authorities. Exhibitions of children's work have also provided much stimulus, but a considerable upheaval in the educational world and the world in general will be needed before art and craft take their proper place in the education of the young.

685. For most of their history the English people have shown at least as much genius as any other for the creation of a physical environment suitable for human living, The eighteenth century town, the village, the country house, the parkland, the cottage garden, the farm with all its appurtenances—the ages which produced them could be criticised for their inequality, their poverty, their squalor and their harshness, but not for their taste and crafts-manship. The industrial revolution saw a decline in many things aesthetic, a decline which became steeper as the nineteenth century advanced, though we are beginning to perceive achievement even in the worst period. The results of this decline are about us, above all in our large towns, and the schools of the period are characteristic. Until recently people had become accustomed to the idea that schools were ugly and dark places surrounded by dreary stretches of asphalt without and painted dark brown within, though some teachers worked wonders by the environment they created inside the school. Opinions will differ about contemporary school buildings, but it is generally

agreed that they represent an advance in lightness, spaciousness and convenience, and anyhow in aesthetic good intentions. But much of the rest of the environment, rural as well as urban, in which children grow up is all too evidently the product of a crude indifference to aesthetic values and of an insensitiveness to many of the deepest human needs. We should like to see the schools becoming, much more than most of them now are, places in which the children are surrounded by many examples, old and new, of taste and discrimination—furniture, clocks, fabrics, ceramics, pictures and books. It should be the object of every school to do all in its power to add to the beauty of its equipment and environment, in exactly the same way as a householder with a sensitive eye for beauty will make such constant additions, improvements and adaptations as his means allow to the house and garden in which he lives. In recent years the public have become familiar with the interiors of many great houses which were once closed to all but a privileged few, and which are now worth seeing because their former owners had taste, thought their own surroundings important and took trouble with them. We should like to see schools set out on the same course, so that in time every school in England is worth visiting, not only for what goes on in it, but for the surroundings it gives to its children and the example it sets of civilised living, Much of the beauty in the school environment should be created by the children themselves and by the care taken in the display of their work. There are schools which already do much and which are showing others the way. Though opportunities and circumstances are very unequal, every school could do something and in the aggregate the schools could become a strong, perhaps a decisive, influence on public taste.

I. MUSIC

686. Music had a place in the elementary schools from their earliest days, though until the second third of the 20th century it was almost exclusively vocal. Where a member of the staff was musically educated, the singing of hymns and songs was often admirably done, but in a great number of schools, where no such teacher was to be found, standards were low. Out-of-tune and sometimes broken pianofortes and wheezy harmoniums were beyond the skill of even the most gifted to use well; but far too often, even if the instrument was satisfactory, the playing was wretched and the choice of music deplorable. Some large schools made a feature of massed choral singing and, at its best, this provided a good, if limited, musical experience and education for the children. The appointment of music organisers by a number of local education authorities helped to raise standards, but progress was, and still is, very slow, mainly because of the neglect of systematic musical instruction in the grammar schools and colleges of education and the consequent musical illiteracy of the great majority of teachers.

687. In the early thirties the percussion band and the bamboo pipe made a welcome innovation in infant and junior schools, but here again progress was often disappointing and for the same reasons. There was a dearth of competent teachers and, too often, the instruments provided and the music

performed were of poor quality. Percussion bands and music were often introduced to children who were too young for them. When good progress was made in the primary schools, there was rarely any follow-up in the secondary school. This lack of continuity between primary and secondary school work is still a weakness. Non-competitive festivals became popular at this period, and did much to bring schools together for musical help and for the sympathetic guidance of experienced conductors. Competitive festivals, while helping to raise standards of repertory and performance, sometimes tended to narrow musical training.

688. Although the position today is rather better than before the war and exhibits several promising signs, it cannot be described as satisfactory. The recorder has made considerable headway in the primary school; the pitch percussion instruments, including those associated with the name of Carl Orff, as yet a much slighter one. The teaching of stringed and wind instruments by peripatetic teachers is increasing slowly, and primary school orchestras are by no means rare and sometimes very good. These influences have increased the scope of musical education. The School Broadcasting Council too have made a great contribution in providing music of quality for the schools at a time when many teachers have lacked the knowledge and skill to help their pupils. The close liaison of the School Broadcasting Council with the teachers has added to the value of its work. The greater accessibility of recorded music of all kinds since the invention of the microgroove record has given teachers one of their most valuable resources. Finally, the growth of professional orchestras, the organisation of children's concerts and the establishment of children's and young people's orchestras have increased the opportunities for listening and the incentives for music making.

689. The present unsatisfactory position will have to be tackled systematically and resolutely. Perhaps the first requirement for this is already in being. Music of all kinds is now almost universally "available". The population in general are much more aware of its possibilities than they were 30 years ago. It is accepted as a source of pleasure for all, especially in recent years when the popularity of the guitar has brought with it mass interest in music amongst the young. The climate is more favourable to musical education than ever before.

690. It is to the musical education of the teacher that attention must first be given. By this we do not mean the education of the music specialist. Provision for the latter exists and has recently been expanded. Large numbers of young musicians are being trained in the colleges of music and their musical competence may be assumed, though they may lack training in how to teach young children. Comparatively few primary schools, however, can, for some time to come, expect to have a music specialist as a full-time member of the staff and it is even doubtful whether a specialist responsible for most of the teaching is desirable. It is the musical education of the non-specialist which, in our view, is the key to the problem. This education takes place mainly in the secondary schools and in the colleges of education, and until both these institutions regard a music course as part of their obligation to all their students and particularly to intending teachers, progress will continue to be slow. But in the meantime much can be achieved by the use of peripatetic teachers and private teachers and by the development of short and extended

courses for teachers in service. Music centres such as are being established could provide in-service training for teachers and also opportunities for gifted children.

691. Next, we think that all authorities should look to the musical equipment in their schools, which is often still inadequate in quantity and quality. Pianofortes are probably better in quality and better kept than they were, but there are not always enough of them, while other instruments are often woefully scarce and, when found, frequently of poor materials and workmanship. The Committee set up by the British Standards Institution is publishing a useful series of booklets on the qualities to be sought for in musical instruments of all kinds. There is some tendency for the hymn chart, so common before the war, to reappear. It is a poor substitute for hymn books with music. A thorough review of the musical equipment of most primary schools is overdue and should result in a drastic "turn-out" and generous restocking.

692. As for what goes on in the classroom, we put forward the following points for the consideration of all who teach music:

(a) In many schools mass instruction is given in music, and in music alone, to whole classes or even combined classes: little is attempted in groups or by individual methods, and teacher direction persists in this field even in schools where it has almost disappeared in language, mathematics and art. Massed hymn practice and massed festival songs sometimes dominate the scene in both infant and junior schools, and the musical merits of teachers tend to be judged on the basis of their capacity to direct, and accompany on the piano, such choral activities.

(b) The principle of individual progression is seldom consistently and successfully carried into the musical sphere. In schools where progress in language is carefully checked, the achievements expected in music of older pupils as compared with younger ones are often ill-defined and vary enormously from school to school. This is a frequent ground of criticism from specialists who take over the children in the first year of the secondary school; there is, however, another side to the question—the secondary specialist often does not know how to link up with what has been taught.

(c) The importance of musical literacy is not fully understood. Without it, independent effort, progression and discovery are impossible, and unfamiliarity with musical notation breeds the kind of suspicion that verbal illiteracy usually brings in its train. Some teachers believe that learning to read music increases difficulties and diminishes enjoyment, whereas the contrary is true. Literacy must however, be closely related to active music-making; it must be functional, not theoretical.

(d) The planning of music as a creative subject lags behind work in language and the visual arts and crafts. There are two aspects of musical creativity— the making of original patterns in sound (extemporisation, composition) and the re-creation of patterns already devised by a composer (performance, interpretation). The latter is easier to control and direct, is usually more in line with the teacher's own musical training, and as a rule gives more pleasing results to outsiders than the former. Nevertheless, a balanced musical education should allow scope for both:—

(i) Exploration of sounds in their raw state is a useful first stage in independent creation, a first stage which many infant schools have reached, but the need for control, selection, discipline and technique soon arises if the work is not to become static and repetitive. It is easier to start improvisation than to continue it into the junior and secondary stages. Not enough is yet known about how to develop children's creative powers in music. Here, research is needed.

(ii) A valuable teaching situation is often produced when teacher and children work upon the basis of material already "processed"—for example a simple folk tune and add their own ideas to it, perhaps through the use of percussion instruments, instead of by taking over a ready made arrangement.

(iii) "Musical appreciation" has lately fallen a little into disrepute, partly because what used to be done under that name was often ineffective and partly because, rightly in our opinion, the best way of learning to appreciate music to is to make it. But there is a place for listening to good music whether played by the teacher or a visitor or heard by means of recorded sound. Young children's listening powers are usually exhausted fairly quickly and the choice of music, the occasion for listening and the duration of the performance all call for great judgement on the part of the teacher. There can be a link here with other branches of the curriculum. A medieval hymn, such as "A great and mighty wonder" that the children sing at Christmas, the dances and madrigals of the 17th century, the water music of Handel, the Hebridean Overture, can all be illuminated by, and can themselves illuminate, non-musical material.

693. It has been suggested to us that the most musically gifted children cannot be properly provided for in the ordinary schools and that special schools of music should be set up for them, a question to which we return in Chapter 22. The U.S.S.R. and Hungary have done this and, in this country, a school has been recently established to give to especially talented pupils of both primary and secondary age a musical and general education. It is self-evident that the musical education of children thus segregated will benefit and we are far from opposing experiments of this kind in the private or indeed in the public sector; but they will always be exceptional and care has to be taken that the general education and development of children are looked after when they are in separate schools. However that may be, we are clear that it is the musical education of the generality of children that most needs critical examination and reform and it is to that need that our attention has been chiefly directed.

694. If the upper age limit of the primary school is extended to 12 some fresh problems will result, but there will also be new opportunities. As far as boys are concerned, many of their voices will be at their best, and singing of high quality, which should include singing in parts, will be possible at the primary stage. With earlier maturing, however, some boys and not a few girls of this age will be passing through a phase of uncertainty, and it may be advisable to reduce the amount of singing expected from some children, to limit the register range of what they sing and to provide other means of practical music making.

695. Those who have begun the study of instruments may by this time have developed considerable facility and will need expert guidance and opportunities for playing together. Where the existence of outstanding talent is suspected, the schools should feel a responsibility for fostering it, and consult with the local education authority's advisory staff or anybody else who is qualified to help on such cases. The proliferation of musical activities at this period greatly increases the need for planned accommodation for group and individual tuition and for the storage of instruments.

696. The primary school bears the main burden of responsibility for sending out pupils who have had a wide range of musical experience, are familiar with the idioms of sound in pitch, time and timbre, and able to help themselves in creating and re-creating music by interpreting and using the visual symbols of conventional notation. The schools have an excellent starting point in children's enjoyment of music and rhythm, but much work remains to be done.

J. PHYSICAL EDUCATION

697. The "1933 Syllabus of Physical Training for Schools" forms a useful starting point for this section of the Report. It was in preparation at the time of the 1931 report, and the two publications must have had a common source of reference in the newer ideas and developments to be seen in various parts of the country during the previous ten years. The term "physical training" was still in general use for one aspect of physical education, and the 18 "lessons" and 42 "tables" of exercises in the Syllabus were so planned as to form a common scheme for infants and juniors, and even for older pupils, in schools all over the country during the "physical exercise lesson". Teachers were trained in and expected to adhere closely to the nine tables of exercises drawn up for each year in the primary school. The first half of each lesson consisted of localised exercises for different parts of the body, arranged and applied in an anatomical sequence; formal commands and formal class arrangements were recommended and many of the exercises had remedial or corrective objectives. There were, however, signs of a break with formality in the introductory activities in the form of games and in the greater emphasis given in the second part of the lesson to individual and group practices and to games.

698. For some years after 1933, the main effort in the initial and in-service training of teachers throughout the country was directed towards putting the Syllabus into practice, although, almost from the time of its publication, progressive teachers and schools were experimenting and extending their work beyond what it defined. The re-training of teachers was achieved by the widespread appointment of local education authority organisers and advisers in physical education. The importance of gym-shoes and suitable clothing, which were often a charge on parents, had to be pressed, and in the poorer areas, some opposition was encountered on the grounds of modesty as well as on those of economy. But by 1939 much progress had been made.

699. During the war and in the early years after the war, several influences combined to produce simultaneous developments in different parts of the

country. The interplay between new concepts of primary education and a reappraisal of the purpose and nature of physical education brought about innovations corresponding to those to be found in other aspects of the curriculum. When improvements in material conditions and in the supply of equipment were made after the war, further progress was made and the momentum still continues.

700. The introduction of large climbing apparatus into infant and junior schools had begun before 1939. Scrambling nets, which formed part of the training of army commandos, were adapted for use in schools. When supply became easier after 1945 there was a rapid increase in the use of all kinds of apparatus, including climbing frames, ladders, bars and ropes. Children were encouraged to explore the possibilities of such apparatus rather than required to practise specific activities, an approach which had for some time been typical of nursery and infant schools, and which spread upwards into the junior schools and beyond. The increased provision of playing fields and, more recently, of learner swimming pools has been a further help to a fuller and more varied programme.

701. Another major development was the abandonment of formal class teaching. This arose partly from a general change in the relationships between adults and children and consequently between teachers and pupils, and partly from a recognition that marks for standing still and team marks for the straightest line limited the activity that physical education was intended to provide. Formal commands, formal class arrangements and the performance of exercises in unison gave way to informal, conversational teaching and to an acknowledgement that individual children needed to work at their own rate and at their own level of ability and, therefore, to have scope for individual practice. The level of performance came to be regarded as more important than ability to respond to a command or to conform to a class rhythm; localised exercises ("head, arm, leg, trunk" is a sequence that will be recalled by older readers) gave way to movements of the whole body with an emphasis on activity, agility and skill.

702. A third development, the most significant so far, has been the adoption of general principles of movement training and their application to different aspects of the physical education programme. Various systems of gymnastics and eurhythmics have attempted a generalised training in movement, but their concern has been predominantly with the strucure and anatomical parts of the body rather than with the process of moving based on a comprehensive analysis of movement. More recent developments derive to a large extent from the teaching and writing of Rudolf Laban, and from a growing acceptance of the analysis and principles of movement enunciated by him. Laban's early work was related to the theatre and to dance, but he was interested in all aspects of human movement, and when he settled in England in 1936, he established connections with industry and education as well as with the stage. His early influence in schools, mainly in secondary schools for girls, was through the medium of Modern Educational Dance, but his principles have been increasingly adopted for their value in all aspects and stages of physical education.

703. In the primary school, a harmony was recognised between the general approach to movement and current educational ideas and ideals. With new

emphasis on the building up of a child's resources in movement and their extension into many different situations, and with scope for individual exploration, choice and practice, physical education made a more significant contribution to educational development.

704. An associated development has been the increasing recognition of the place of expressive movement in primary education. Children have a great capacity to respond to music, stories and ideas, and there is a close link through movement, whether as dance or drama, with other areas of learning and experience—with speech, language, literature and art as well as with music. In the U.S.A., modern dance has led to a highly developed theatre art form but it has had little or no influence in the elementary schools whereas, in certain parts of England, there has been a flowering in the primary schools which, at its best, reaches a high standard. Anyone who has visited schools or seen films of the work cannot fail to be impressed by its quality and by the pupils' total absorption and involvement in it.

705. All these developments were already in evidence in 1952, when the 1933 Syllabus was replaced by the Department's "Moving and Growing" (Part I of "Physical Education in the Primary School"; Part II of this publication "Planning the Programme" became available in 1953 and deals more specifically with the organisation and planning of lessons). This publication, with its wealth of illustrations, relates these various developments to the needs of the children. It has been influential in shaping the philosophy of physical education in the primary school in the last 12 years and it prepared the way for a further recognition of the value of expressive movement. It refers to "the movement period" instead of the "physical exercise lesson" of earlier publications. In many schools and other educational institutions the mainstay of the physical education programme has come to be referred to as "movement". There is some misunderstanding about the use of this term, and several special meanings have come to be associated with it. It should be used broadly and comprehensively, and it may be concerned with agility, on the ground or on apparatus, with ball or athletic skill, or with expressive movement of dramatic or dance-like quality. In such work, exercises or techniques are unlikely to be taught; the aim is rather to develop each child's resources as fully as possible through exploratory stages and actions which will not be the same for any two children. When these ends are pursued successfully, the children are able to bring much more to any situation than that which is specifically asked of them; the results transcend the limits of what can be prescribed or "produced", and lead to a greater realisation of the high potential of young children.

706. We welcome what is being done and lay particular stress on the need for a balanced programme. Children need activities of an acrobatic and athletic type as well as ball games, swimming, dance and drama, and to neglect any of these is to impoverish the programme. Work with the lower age groups is likely to be of an experimental and exploratory nature. Children will invent different sequences of movement and will enjoy discovering their bodily powers and capabilities. This stage cannot be hurried,and time is needed to enjoy it to the full; variety also is needed. In the upper age groups, and especially with an extension into the thirteenth year, lessons and teaching will need to be more systematically planned and directed as the children's capacity for sustained and co-ordinated performance increases. With young

children, the work will be very general and it will not always be easy to separate different modes of movement and experience. By the time they are ready to leave the primary school, however, the work and the teaching will be more closely related to specific ends: gymnastics, games, dance, drama and swimming will be the normal elements of a weekly or seasonal programme.

707. Between the ages of 11 and 13 girls and boys are at their most agile and responsive, and a blend of vitality, inventiveness and control can lead to high accomplishments. They need space and apparatus to challenge and extend their powers. Lessons must be planned with skill and understanding, and response guided by knowledgeable and perceptive comment. In spite of differences in physique and aptitude, no child's effort should be inhibited by fear of failure or ineptitude. Later attitudes and achievement will derive to a large extent from the bodily resources built up at this stage.

708. Early play and free practice with balls, bats and sticks, which will begin in the infant school, will lead to simple games in association with partners and against opponents. Girls and boys at the top of the primary school will be acquainted with the rudiments of the main national games—netball, hockey and tennis for the girls, football and cricket for the boys. For their future progress as well as for their current enjoyment, girls as well as boys need a firm foundation for their games in the primary school. But the range of ability is wide, and care is needed to relate the teaching and coaching to the ability and "readiness" of the performers. Some 12 year olds enjoy and respond successfully to the complexities of a full team game, others need a much simpler organisation. We hope that the approach to games training will emphasise the essential nature of the game and the true spirit of play. The establishment of sound attitudes is important from the start.

709. Swimming and athletics also appeal to juniors—in fact, many infants may have learnt to swim and in any case enjoy movement in water. In recent years, the building of indoor shallow water swimming pools has enabled many young children to be introduced to swimming. The older juniors respond enthusiastically to taxing demands and strenuous routines, and their full potential is seldom realised. We hope that under wise guidance the maximum number of juniors will develop and enjoy their powers to the full, but we believe the first priority is rightly placed on teaching the highest possible number of young children to gain confidence in water and to swim; we have been impressed by recent efforts in this direction. Running, leaping and throwing are a natural part of a child's activity, and are often stimulated by a desire to run faster, jump higher and throw further or more accurately than others. A well equipped primary school offers ample scope in the open air for these activities from which athletic events will later take shape, and we welcome their inclusion in the programme. But whilst juniors will practise and compete with zest in running, jumping and throwing contests, a more specific introduction to athletics is more appropriate to the secondary stage of education.

710. The marked post-war development of outdoor pursuits in education has not passed over the primary school. As more older pupils in secondary schools embark on mobile camping, sailing, canoeing and mountain activities, many junior schools and local education authorities are recognising that nine is a good age to introduce campcraft and country activities in general. The

competence and pleasure with which some schools organise their own camps lead us to hope that many more children will be able to enjoy similar opportunities.

711. We have stressed the need for a balanced programme, and have considered some of the activities included in it. We would also stress the importance of good quality in performance. Exploratory and experimental stages are essential—so also are skill and mastery. How something is done matters as much as what is done. At a time when in some fields notability is rather easily won, this is especially important. Children have the capacity for high level performance, an eagerness to learn, an urge to explore, a hunger for skill and a thirst for adventure. At the top of the primary school, they readily identify themselves with stars of the games field, of the athletics track and of the stage. Some will show a flair for technical accomplishment. All will apply themselves with intense and unselfconscious effort unless their interest is dulled.

712. There are some obvious dangers, and some not so obvious, in the situation. The achievement of some children may lead to their being introduced to techniques before they are ready for them and to their being submitted to an adult conception of sport and personal performance. Techniques are necessary, and the technical ability of some top juniors is impressive, but if patterned movements are introduced too soon, they may quench the ability to play creatively. Competition clearly has a place, but it can be overdone and we think it sometimes is, in the form of inter-school leagues and championships.

713. What is desirable in modern primary physical education will only be nurtured, and what is dangerous avoided, if the arrangements made for training teachers are satisfactory. We have been told that in the upper forms of some secondary schools, little time or attention is given to physical education; in others the pupils are allowed little freedom to choose the type of activity they wish to pursue. The result may be that physical education is too infrequently chosen as a subject by students in colleges of education. In some colleges the curriculum course in physical education is optional. We do not wish to see specialist teaching of physical education in primary schools, though an advisory teacher with a specialist qualification would be invaluable in a large school. There is however some danger of a dearth of young teachers whose training has fitted them to teach physical education. We hope that all primary teachers will take an adequate curriculum course in this subject, which they will be expected to teach regularly.

K. SEX EDUCATION

714. We have felt some reluctance about including a section on sex education in our Report. It rarely appears on the time-table of a primary school. In many schools it receives little mention, while in others it is treated, if at all, in biology or in general talks between the class teacher and his class. But it is a matter to which we have given consideration and on which we have something to say. As it is one on which teachers may feel a need for guidance, it seems simplest to treat it separately here.

715. We have no doubt that children's questions about sex ought to be answered plainly and truthfully whenever they are asked. Some questions will be repeated over the years and on each occasion the answer must satisfy. What is a proper and full answer for a six year old will not do for him four years later. The answe s given must provide an acceptable and usable vocabulary for the child. This raises a difficulty. The "popular" vocabulary, the four-letter words, is the one that the children will use clandestinely or openly among themselves. It is less "taboo" than it used to be, but most people would probably still consider it unacceptable for use in schools. Its associations are still too powerful. The circumlocution ("the little nest inside mummy") is often confusing, tends to be purely personal and has a sentimental, shamefaced sound. The scientific terms are really the only ones available.

716. We are unanimous that, if they are able to do it, the proper people to answer children's questions are parents. Young children often find the facts of sexual intercourse incredible. They associate their sexual organs with excretion and that they are also instruments not only of reproduction but of love is difficult for them to believe. When the information is given in the context of a happy home by loving parents it may be more acceptable than if given by someone else, however well intentioned. The fact, however, is that not all homes are happy and some parents still find it embarrassing to discuss the physical details of sex with their children. Who, in such cases, ought to answer the questions and in what circumstances?

717. If the parents make their own arrangements there is no problem. If they approach the head teacher of their child's school, he must fit their request into the general pattern. The simplest plan seems to be for the school, though not necessarily all the teachers in it, to undertake to answer questions, though making sure that the parents agree with what is being done. Any tendency to specialise, or to import a specialist, destroys the spontaneity of question and answer. The questions may arise at any time—in the scripture lesson as well as in biology. Ideally, questions should be answered then and there, though some are best answered individually. Not all teachers will feel equally comfortable in tackling questions and this is something to which the colleges of education must give some thought. Every school must make the arrangements that seem best to it and should have a definite policy, which, in consultation with parents, covers all the children. It is not good enough to leave matters vague and open, hoping for the best.

718. Some primary school heads feel that a regular course of instruction ought to be given to fourth year pupils and, when the extra year is added on, this number may increase. We have been impressed by the care and sincerity with which this work is done and we should be the last to condemn it. On the whole, however, we feel that a more informal method is to be preferred and that the essential questions will all either crop up or be easily stimulated without any systematic course being initiated. Now that an increasing number of girls are beginning to menstruate while in the primary schools, it is important that the facts should be explained early to them and that proper arrangements should be made for them in schools. There are a number of excellent books on human biology which are suitable for juniors and some of these should find a place in the school or class libraries.

719. So far we have been thinking mainly of the more or less strictly biological aspects of sex, of those which are essentially present in the mating of animals as much as in that of human beings. But human sex involves relationships, and relationships involve ethics; although this side of the matter seldom directly affects primary school children, at least to any depth, it will be there, implicitly or explicitly, in many of their questions. Direct questions must be answered as honestly as possible, with due regard for parental opinion, but a great deal will depend on the general human relationships that exist in the school. We return to this in Chapter 19. The foundation for good sexual ethics can be laid in a school in which the children learn to respect and appreciate each other as personalities, to treat everyone with consideration and never to make use of human beings or treat them callously or contemptuously and where they find in adults the same attitude towards each other and towards themselves.

720. From time to time teachers in primary schools will come across manifestations of what is often called "an unhealthy interest in sex". It may take such forms as the passing round of indecent pictures, the sending of obscene notes, graffiti in the lavatories or elsewhere, various Peeping Tom practices and sometimes what, in adults, is known in law as "indecent exposure". All this is clandestine. It is probably a good deal more frequent than some teachers believe, and, when it is discovered, is often an occasion for moral indigation and severe punishment. We feel quite sure that such manifestation should not be taken too seriously. In the sort of atmosphere described above they are a good deal less likely to occur than in a repressive one. They represent much more a response to adult attitudes than any undesirable sexual precocity. If dealt with rather as breaches of good manners, and even then without too much solemnity, rather than as grave moral delinquencies, we think that their true weight will have been accorded to them, and the tension that produced them largely dispersed.

721. A society in which the mass media are preoccupied with the physical aspects of sex and seem unable to put them into perspective must not be surprised if its children are affected. It would be unfair to look to the schools to cure this sickness, but they can make a beginning.

CHAPTER 18

Aids to Learning and to Teaching

722. The oldest and most universal aids to learning are the picture and the book. To these aids frequent reference has been made throughout the chapter on the curriculum. Two points should perhaps be emphasised. Books and illustrations must be accessible at least as much for individual as for class use. The implication is that, especially for the younger children, collections of books and illustrations should be housed mainly in the rooms or adjacent to the rooms where children are normally working. There must be a central collection as well, since some books, illustrations and maps are too expensive to be duplicated. Children should have access to books which are finely produced and illustrated and to some adult works of reference. These central collections must also be accessible and not shut away in a room so often occupied by a class that individual children can only use them once or twice a week. The school's collection of illustrations, tapes, filmstrips, photostats, discs and programmed texts needs to be indexed so that teachers and children can find out what material there is of interest to them. Much of this work can be done by a teacher's aide under the supervision of the head teacher or of an advisory teacher.

723. Some primary school teachers think that such aids to learning as broadcasting, television, ciné film, filmstrip and discs are the negation of modern primary methods which stress individual learning. This helps to explain the relatively small use that has been made of them in some of the best primary schools. But it is a mistaken view. They should be used to bring into the classroom personalities and voices, scenes and places, that could never appear there by any other means. They enrich enormously the resources available to teachers and children. Intelligently selected and used, they provide excellent background material, historical, geographical, biological and aesthetic. Teachers have from the start been enabled by their membership of B.B.C. and Independent Television Authority committees, and by requests for criticism, to play a big part in planning sound and television programmes.

724. There is a further reason for introducing more aids into school. Television is now, as films and sound broadcasting have long been, a part of ordinary life to which children are accustomed. It has even been described as "a rival system of education". Children must be taught to use it profitably and to associate it with learning as well as with entertainment. This point of view has to be balanced with another: for the youngest children, in particular, who spend more time in front of the television screen than any other age group, there is a particular need for the school to provide direct experiences when all the senses come into play. In this way precision, associations and meaning can be added to what is seen and heard on television.

725. Many teachers in the past, with some reason, preferred ciné film, filmstrip and discs, to broadcasting. The former can be seen or heard in advance, can be chosen by the teacher to suit his own purposes, can be used at the most suitable moment in the day and can be stopped or repeated by the teacher or

262

by the children themselves. Strips can be cut up and transformed into individual slides, a highly desirable method of dealing with them, since many filmstrips are too long and too repetitive. Many teachers, indeed, make their own slides. Flexibility of this kind has not in the past been shared by radio or television broadcasts save in so far as teachers could predict from the excellent supporting publications what was likely to be coming, and could switch off the set if what in fact came was unsuitable. The tape recorder, and the permission given to schools to record and use sound broadcasts for a period of twelve months, have made it possible to use them in much the same way as discs and film and to reconcile their use with a flexible time table. Video tape may in the long run do the same for television broadcasts.

726. Another important development, perhaps potentially the most important of all those so far noted, is that it is no longer necessary for these aids to involve class teaching. Hand viewers and slide projectors are increasingly used by individuals and by groups. Ear-phones enable children to listen to speech recorded by themselves or teachers, or to the spoken word accompanying a written text. The more flexible school buildings become, the more they are provided with small group rooms, the easier it is for children to use aids without disturbing others.

727. Though some radio series are intended to be followed in sequence, others have been designed as an a la carte menu from which teachers choose individual programmes to suit the rest of the work that is being done with their classes. If unstreamed classes and provision for group viewing and listening become more general, more programmes might profitably be designed as entities to be followed by such particular groups as very able or very slow children.

*Programmed Learning**

728. We have left till last the consideration of the most recent and controversial of teaching aids, the making of teaching programmes and their presentation in books or by machines. It has roused strong feelings in the teaching profession because more than any other aid it has seemed to some that it might take over part of the teacher's job. Since most programmes for primary

---

*A programme presents the learner with all the material he needs to master a particular task. At the present time most programmes are written on one of two systems. In linear programmes material is presented in a carefully prepared logical sequence and in such a way that progression from one small step (or 'frame') to the next is almost certain. The size of the steps and their sequence are determined empirically by trying out the programme on a representative sample of the pupils for whom the programme is intended and what proves difficult is altered until a successful approach is achieved. A basic principle of linear programming is that success should be virtually inevitable at every step and that the student should be told of his success at each point. The pupil's interest is held by the way the material is presented, the easy small steps and by the fact that he is told immediately he takes any action whether or not he has done right: the next piece of information is not presented until the one before has been mastered. In branching programmes, each step of the programme contains more material, is planned on the assumption that some mistakes will be made, and that the pupil will profit by discovering why he has gone wrong. This method is more closely related to that of existing teaching practice in that the writer of the programme sets out to anticipate the pupils' difficulties. At each frame the pupil is given a choice of responses: the correct answer leads him forward; an incorrect one takes him through a branch sequence designed to correct the error he has made.

school children have been concerned with the acquisition of factual knowledge, programmed learning has seemed counter to current trends of basing children's learning on interest and discovery.

729. Yet programmed learning could relieve the teachers of some routine tasks and free them to exercise their influence more constructively. The motive for learning may arise from the children, or may be stimulated by discussion between teacher and children. The teacher can help children to become aware of problems, and to recognise the need for specific knowledge. At that point a programme might provide knowledge, techniques and practice in them, its great advantage being that both the programmed text and the programmed machine can be used individually. Once children have assimilated knowledge, the possible uses to which it may be put become again a matter for discussion. Few programmes have been devised for or tested with primary school children and their use is not yet sufficiently widespread either here or in the U.S.A. for firm judgments to be made.

730. In one area teaching machines have been successfully used for teaching a few backward juniors and secondary pupils to read. It seemed from this experiment that children who, because of past failure, are too unsure of themselves to form a relationship with a teacher, can learn from a machine, gain in this way in confidence and so are helped to return to normal relationships. It is claimed that the machine and the programme have special advantages for this kind of child; the child learns in private and does not have to share his learning device; he has no fear of punishment, the small steps of the programme make success likely and yet the child can withdraw from the learning situation without seeming aggressive. We have also heard that some children become bored with programmed learning.

731. We are glad to know that the Department are supporting research projects which are designed to discover the best methods of programming school learning and of using programmes in schools of all kinds. The Department have also encouraged institutes of education to provide short courses to train teachers to write programmes. Until more programmes have been produced, research results cannot be convincing. Furthermore it is stimulating for teachers to make programmes since they are forced to think hard about what they are teaching and why and to test its success. Scrutiny of the difficulties encountered by pupils in using programmes can give teachers new insight into the processes of teaching and learning.

732. One final word should be added on these aids for teachers. It is often a matter for mild amusement at educational conferences that nothing is more certain than that, at a session in audio-visual aids, the aids will in some way fail: the films break, the record player is so sensitive that it exaggerates extraneous noise, and, at the very least, the plug is of the wrong size. There is here certainly a moral for the schools. Children are used to high standards in commercial film projection and in television. Not only must the standard of educational films, broadcasts and television be high but the machines themselves must be in good order. Local authorities might well employ technicians to service the mechanical aids which we hope will be found in most primary schools. It is, however, doubtful whether authorities should provide all this equipment automatically for schools. The automatic supply of equipment

Plate 2.   Children at Work   1937

and 1966

Plate 3.

Plate 4. Listening to a Story

Plate 5. Experimenting with Clay

Plate 6.   Care in Building

Plate 7.   An Incentive to Read

Plate 8.

Plate 9.

Looking Forward to Adult Life

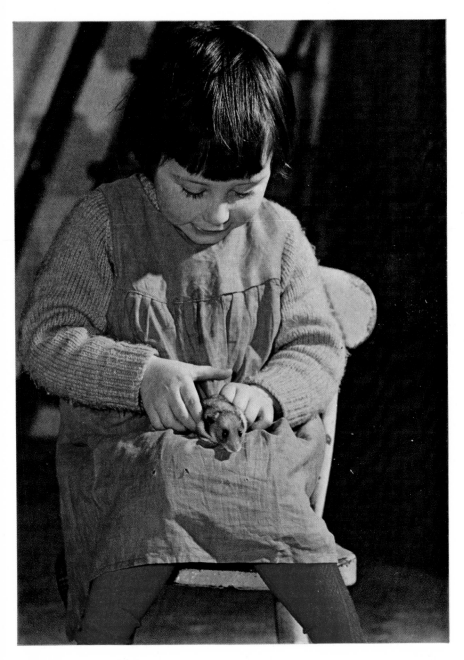

Plate 10. Living Things

Plate 11.   A R___ and of the Devil

Plate 12.   Reading

and
Writing

Plate 13.

Plate 14.   Concentration

Plate 15.   Work or Play?

Plate 16.   Freedom to Move

Plate 17.   Dramatic Encounter

Plate 18. A School in its Environment

Plate 19.

Plate 20.   The Environment the same School Creates

Plate 21. School in a Congested Suburb

Plate 22. A Suburban Infant School without Traffic Dangers

Plate 23.   Primary Schools in the Centr

A. A primary and a secondary
   school—opened 1876.

B. Infant schools—opened
   1877 and 1893.

C. Primary schools—opened 1883.

D. Nursery schools.

E. Voluntary school—opened 1837.

Schools lacking open space and play
facilities— subject to traffic and access
hazards and nearly all below present
minimum site area standards.

Plate 24.   Primary School and Clinic adjacent to a Secondary School

Plate 25.   Junior Children are most Agile

Plate 26.   Expression in Movement

Plate 27.   Finding out the Properties of Things

Plate 28.   —and Numbers

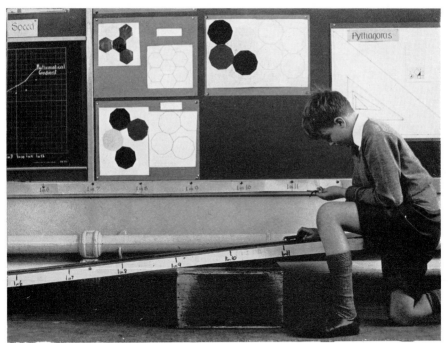

Plate 29.

Mathematical
Problems arise
from Real Life

Plate 30.

Plate 32.   Comparing Temperatures in a Puddle

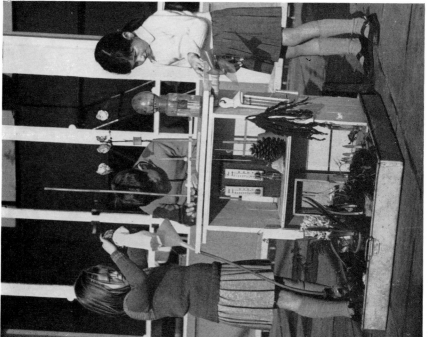

Plate 31.   Weather Station

Plate 33.

Plate 34.

Using Mechanical Aids in Small Groups

Plate 35.

Plate 36.

Learning about Colour and Design.

Plate 37.   Imagination and Accuracy in Reconstructing the Past: Top Juniors

Plate 38.   Lifting Weights with Pulleys

Plate 39.

Plate 40.   Differences between Art and Crafts for Boys and Girls
are disappearing

Plate 41.

Plate 42.

Following individual Interest

Plate 43.   Inventiveness with Materials

Plate 44.   Individual and Group Work

Plate 45.

Plate 46.

The Beginning of Life-long Interests

does not ensure good use. But the allowance made to primary schools should be sufficient for them to buy and use such of this equipment as they are prepared to use to the full.

733. This is an age of increasing mechanisation. Inevitably, more and cheaper mechanical aids will find their way into the primary schools. Teachers must, therefore, consider how they can use them best to enrich the ways in which children can learn.

K

CHAPTER 19*

The Child in the School Community

734. Many changes have taken place in the past 30 years or so in the relationship between children and adults. The causes of these changes include the increased employment of mothers outside their homes, the greater earning power of young people generally, the virtual disappearance of juvenile employment and the greater appreciation of children and their needs that has spread through the population. As a result, the children of today are more independent and less ready to accept parental authority than their parents were. The resulting relationship has some obvious good features, actual as well as potential. It allows a much freer interchange of opinions and a greater friendliness between parent and child than was usually possible under the old authoritarian relationship. At the same time it raises problems which have not yet been solved and which may give rise to anxiety and unhappiness. If authority simply decays the results can be negative. A new and positive relationship between parent and child, and indeed between old and young, still needs to be worked out. Some families have gone a long way towards it. Others are bewildered.

735. There are other changes, too, which have had an unmistakeable effect in the schools. The first of these is the increased diversity of occupations available to school leavers and the decreasing extent to which particular occupations are tied to social class. Every school has to prepare its children for a wider range than 30 years ago. Even young children demand, and are given, if not always willingly, a much broader choice of outlook and conduct as well as of subsequent occupation. A school which tried to impose the kind of discipline that was common before the war would soon find itself in difficulties. The effects of these changes are naturally more acute in the secondary schools, yet it is the primary schools which have moved most quickly in the new directions that they demand.

Relationships in Primary Schools

736. The general public is hardly aware of what a primary school run on modern lines is like and of the extent as well as the profundity of the changes that have taken place since the war. A middle aged visitor, educated in an ordinary elementary school at the time of the 1931 Report, who visited a good primary school in 1966, would find much to surprise him. If he arrived at the official opening hour he would find that many of the children had been there long before him, not penned in the playground, but inside the school, caring for the livestock, getting on with interesting occupations, reading or writing, painting, carving or weaving or playing musical instruments. Probably some of the teachers would also be early, but whether they were there or not, would not affect what the children were doing. The visitor might be surprised to notice that when the bell rang, if there was a bell, no very obvious change took place. As the morning went on he would see various pieces of more organised

*See Note of Reservation at the end of the main Report.

activity, backward readers being taken as a group, an assembly of the whole school for prayers and hymns, an orchestra, some movement, some group instruction in mathematics, some exploration outside and so on. During all this time he would hear few commands and few raised voices. Children would be asked to do things more often than told. They would move freely about the school, fetching what they needed, books or material, without formality or interference. Teachers would be among the children, taking part in their activities, helping and advising and discussing much more frequently than standing before a class teaching. Mid-morning break and even midday break for lunch would show little change and at the end of the day there would be no sudden rush from school, leaving an empty building, but a much more leisurely and individual departure, so that important tasks could be finished and interesting questions answered. In this kind of school it is common for some of the older children to spend two or three weeks away with their teacher in another environment. In this way many children have their first experiences away from the family in a secure setting, and also an opportunity for getting to know their teachers better.

737. These schools are not exceptional. What here concerns us about them are the implications for relationships and discipline and these are many. They raise the following questions. What kind of assumptions about children are involved in running a school on these lines? By what process does a school run on authoritarian lines change into the kind of school just described? In what circumstances is it impossible or too difficult to run such a school and, in such a case, what is to be done about it?

738. The relationships of the school described are certainly not the product of mere permissiveness. For all the appearance of free-and-easiness, for all the absence of the traditional forms of discipline, there is behind it all, not only a deep understanding of children, but careful planning. The two basic assumptions are that children respond in kind to courteous and considerate treatment by adults, and that they will work with concentration and diligence at tasks which are suited to their abilities. Neither assumption is true for all children, or for any child all the time, but both are true enough to make them a workable basis for many primary schools. With them must go a great deal of perceptive thought and action. The balance between free choice and directed choice, the safeguarding of intellectual discipline, the few rules that are to be insisted upon, the richness, suitability and variety of what is provided, the means of ensuring and recording progress, the treatment of misfits —all these and many other problems need careful and skilful leadership. When the head or his or her staff can bring it off, it is a way of running a school which we think is ideally suited to the needs and nature of children and to their development as human beings. We believe that the atmosphere in a school run on these lines is healthier than one in which discipline is authoritarian, and can foster self-discipline, a sense of responsibility for others in the community, and honesty in action and in thought. There is, for example, no reason to cheat or to crib. If each child is valued for himself, there is less reason to lie, whether from fear, idleness or the desire for self-aggrandisement.

739. It is clear that to change a school run on traditional lines to one run on free lines requires faith and courage. The fact that a substantial number of schools have made the change is evidence that these qualities have not been wanting. They are certainly the first requirements in a reforming head, but

they are not the only ones. It is not a question of saying "freedom is in, discipline is out", an attitude which could lead to instant disaster. The change involves the total life of the school, and the staff, or a substantial proportion of it, must at least be ready for change and must understand something of the philosophy underlying it. A small country school which had been run on traditional lines was able to make the change quickly because the staff of two retired simultaneously, and were replaced by a man and his wife who knew what they wanted to do and were able to set about it without delay. The children responded and, in less than a year, the school closely resembled that described at the beginning of this chapter. On one occasion the head-master was obliged to be absent for two days and was unable to obtain a substitute. The children in his class were then left to their own devices, with only such supervision as the infants' teacher in another room was able to give them. "There was no trouble" said the headmaster, "and they had done two good days' work when I got back". A ten year old boy at this school observed to a visiting H.M.I.: "The trouble with this place is that we haven't enough time to do all we want. We are trying to get Mr. . . . . to start a night school for us, so we can get on with our work in the evening". There will be many readers including teachers, who will find this story almost incredible, remem-bering, as they will, the instantaneous, disorderly relaxation which used to characterise a class when the teacher went out of the room. The change is a major one which is beginning to revolutionise the primary schools of England, but it needs teachers of great personal qualities, strong character and a deep understanding of children, and it also needs first rate organisation. If, for example, children are allowed choice in what they do the choice must be genuine and the alternatives interesting and worth doing. Boredom is a deadly enemy. Time wasting occupations and exercises "to keep the children quiet while the teacher is busy, or marking the Registers" are fatal to good discipline and to good learning and there is no place for them, or need for them, in the kind of school we are discussing. Furthermore, although in such a school rewards and punishments in the ordinary sense may seem to have little or no place, there is in fact a substitute in the form of approval and dis-approval. The more sympathetic a teacher is, the more successfully he or she establishes with the children a relationship of affection and respect, the more clearly will approval be a reward, and withdrawal in some sense a punish-ment. Such a system is preferable to arbitrary authoritarianism, but if it involves the abrogation of one kind of power, it bestows another and must be used with understanding and scrupulousness. Children like to know where they stand and what to expect. They must depend upon adults for their moral standards and for guidance on what behaviour is tolerable in society; an adult who withholds such guidance is in fact making a decision which involves as heavy a claim for his own judgement as is made by the martinet. There may be occasions, as the children grow older, when such guidance ought to be withheld so that children can think out problems for themselves, but this only underlines the fact that the teacher has a crucial role to play at every point in the "free" school.

740. We must now consider why it is that this happy state of affairs is not commoner and whether there are schools, or areas, or circumstances in which it would be foolish or impossible to try to introduce it. Many older teachers brought up on authoritarian precepts may feel hostile or contemptuous when

they are told of "free discipline" and, even if sympathetic to the idea, may feel afraid of trying it. The thought of the possible chaos is too daunting. Some may genuinely doubt whether, even if it comes off, it is good for the children. They fear that the school would be too unlike the world outside where people have to struggle, learn to take orders and face uncongenial and uninteresting tasks. We sympathise with these fears and anxieties, but the last one at least is quite unfounded. We believe that the modern, relaxed, friendly approach is a much better preparation for life in contemporary society than the old authoritarian one.

741. Not all reforming heads are in the fortunate position of the one described earlier. They may have staffs who cannot "take it" and may feel that it would be unwise as well as unjust to the staff to force the pace. They will have to move slowly and wait patiently for favourable signs and developments. In addition, there are certainly schools and even whole areas where the difficulties involved in freedom are very grave. If a large proportion of the children come from insecure or unloving homes, they will be disturbed and, although they may need freedom more desperately than children from good homes, the transition may be too perilous to face. It is just the "difficult" schools which find it hardest to recruit and keep good staffs and no one with any knowledge of such schools will wish to weaken the influence of teachers, or make their task any harder. In a single class there may be children who are regularly and perhaps brutally thrashed at home, children who are taught implicitly or explicitly that all authority is an enemy and children who have never known any consistent discipline or control, let alone warm affection and interest.

742. Quite apart from these specially difficult cases, there are children, usually boys, in all areas and in most schools who need to feel the pressure of authority in order to come to terms with it. The high spirited, mischievous child is traditionally regarded with affectionate tolerance. "Boys will be boys", "You're only young once", "I was just the same when I was his age", people say, and generally win an approving nod. A boy who never gets up to mischief, it is suggested, is not a proper boy and a good spanking will keep him within bounds. The mental picture often seems to have an archaic rural background and to evoke the suggestion of a little mild apple stealing. Stealing from a supermarket seems to put the matter in a different light. Everybody loves Huck Finn, but he can be a thorn in the side of young and inexperienced teachers. Yet boys need an element of adventure and out of school activities can often satisfy this need legitimately.

Punishment

743. We have made it clear that the kind of school that we should like to see is one in which the delights as well as the rigours and demands of learning are built into the whole life of the place, so that there is little or no need for the stimulus of marks and class places and rewards, or for the sanctions of punishment in the cruder sense. Such schools, as we have said, are not visions of the future. There are many of them. Nevertheless, many teachers will feel that punishment is sometimes necessary and that the right to give it when it is judged to be necessary ought not to be withheld. Few indeed will now consider it in any way positively "good for children" to be punished, and few will regard punishment as a cure either for deep seated evils, such as persistent

cruelty, or for laziness, inattention and poor work. Punishment will be defended simply as a means to order. A single unruly member cannot be allowed to upset the whole of a class. The boy who "tries it on" just to see how much the teacher will take, must discover quite soon that he will not take much. The child who persistently ignores rules of safety, for example, when crossing the road, must be sharply reminded of them. This we accept and we think that the decision whether to punish or not must be left to the individual teacher acting within the policy of the school. It is unwise to try to lay down precise rules which would confine individual professional judgement, but the excessive use of punishment of any kind should be regarded as an acknowledgement of someone's failure.

744. What kind of punishment should be given is more open to doubt. We have little hesitation in saying that punishment ought not to humiliate a child, though it sometimes ought to humble him. But children differ. Something that will bitterly humiliate one child may be accepted with cheerful indifference by another. Sarcasm is a weapon that should never be employed. A punishment must be understood by the child and be seen to be just and to this extent accepted by him; the most difficult children may be, at least temporarily, beyond this kind of understanding and be afflicted with a sense of injustice in spite of every attempt to remove it. The conclusion seems to be that in the matter of how to punish as well as in that of whether to punish, the judgement of the teacher must be respected, although, in the most difficult cases, expert advice on problems of behaviour should be sought from school doctors and child guidance clinics. We do not feel justified in leaving the argument there. Corporal punishment appears to us to be in a special category and to need special consideration.

745. We have considered the opinions of the teaching profession and of H.M. Inspectors and have studied the regulations of local education authorities. We have also considered the views of psychologists, a sample of parental opinion and practice in other countries.

746. From the evidence available to us the following conclusions can be drawn:

(a) The overwhelming majority (between 80 per cent and 90 per cent) of the teaching profession are against the abolition of corporal punishment, though few support it except as a final sanction[1,2,3,4].

(b) Public opinion appears to be in favour of its retention and a considerable majority of parents agree to its occasional use.

(c) Only one local education authority forbids its use, but there is great diversity in regulations, some of which have not been revised for 20 to 30 years. To some extent local authority regulations reflect public opinion and the lack of any pressure for change; the infrequent revision of regulations may also be explained by a decline in corporal punishment[5].

(d) While there are few primary schools in which corporal punishment is never used, there are a large number in which it is used only rarely, and its use is on the decrease. Infants and girls seldom receive it[6].

(e) The associations of psychologists consulted by the Council agree that the advantages of corporal punishment are outweighed by its disadvantages[7,8].

47. The present legal position is that a teacher, who stands in loco parentis to a school child, is held to be justified in using a reasonable amount of force by way of correction. Magistrates can and do convict when they judge that an unreasonable amount of force has been used. Although it would be technically possible to make it a legal offence for a teacher to inflict any degree of corporal punishment on a child in school, this would present difficulties in practice. It would in particular make a teacher vulnerable to malicious prosecution. Moreover, it could be asked whether the same sanction should not apply to parents as well as teachers. In Denmark it has been possible to abolish corporal punishment in both school and home, because public opinion was strongly behind the measure.

48. It has been almost universally outlawed in other western countries[9]. It can be associated with psychological perversion affecting both beater and beaten and it is ineffective in precisely those cases in which its use is most hotly defended. We think the time has come to drop it. After full consideration, we recommend that the infliction of physical pain as a recognised method of punishment in primary schools should be forbidden.

49. The most convenient method of carrying out our recommendations in the case of maintained schools seems to be an amendment of the Schools Regulations to provide that the infliction of physical pain as a method of punishment should not be allowed. No comparable sanction is available for independent schools generally and to prohibit corporal punishment in them would involve an amendment of the law. We believe that the law should be amended so as to give power to the Secretary of State to deny registration to any independent school in which the infliction of physical pain is a recognised form of punishment. In the meantime we recommend that no independent school in which this practice obtains should be granted recognition as efficient and we urge the professional associations of the independent schools to do everything in their power to ensure that it is discontinued in non-recognised schools. We hope that the schools themselves will take steps to abandon the practice entirely.

50. Our recommendations are likely to meet with some opposition. We may be accused of encouraging softness and of indulging the evil doer. The majority of teachers sincerely believe that corporal punishment may be necessary as a constraint. Indeed, a lack of corporal punishment in school will often contrast sharply with what happens in the child's home. We believe, however, that the primary schools, as in so much else, should lead public opinion, rather than follow it. Often corporal punishment is the result of school conditions trying the patience of both teachers and pupils. Smaller classes and the presence of teachers' aides (see Chapter 24) in all schools, particularly in the educational priority areas, may help those schools whose conditions are such that corporal punishment seems difficult to avoid. Teachers need to give time and individual attention to children who get into trouble; persuasion is a time-consuming business and cannot easily take place if a class is too large. On theoretical grounds alone, we believe that the kind of relationship which ought to exist between teacher and child cannot be built up in an atmosphere in which the infliction of physical pain is regarded as a normal sanction. The psychological evidence which we sought also supports this view. Our Report makes it clear at many points that we believe in discipline. But it can only come from a

relationship between teacher and child in which there is mutual respect and affection. There is nothing soft or flabby about this relationship. It is impaired by disorder, untidiness, boredom and slackness and only flourishes in an atmosphere of order and purposefulness. To achieve the right balance between encouragement and restraint, between permissiveness and direction between reward and admonition, between withdrawal and intervention, is the teacher's art. It is with this art that much of this Report is concerned and the art is not simply an amalgam or sum total of skills, knowledge, methods and aids, but rather a combination of these with judgment, discrimination sensitivity, sympathy, perception and imagination, all of which are involved in the exercise of discipline and the education of children.

Recommendations

751.   (i) Decisions on punishment should generally be left to the professional judgment of the individual teacher acting within the policy of the school.

    (ii) The infliction of physical pain as a method of punishment in primary schools should be forbidden. Schools Regulations, which apply only to maintained schools, should be amended accordingly

    (iii) The Secretary of State should be given power to deny registration to any independent school in which the infliction of physical pain is a recognised method of punishment. Until such time as a change in the law can be made, no independent school in which this practice obtains should be recognised as efficient, and the professional associations of the independent schools should endeavour to ensure its discontinuance in non-recognised schools.

REFERENCES

[1]National Foundation for Educational Research: A Survey of Rewards and Punishments 1952.
[2]The Council's Questionnaire to 2,500 teachers (Appendix 1, Volume 2).
[3]The National Union of Teachers. Memorandum submitted at Council's request.
[4]The National Association of Schoolmasters. Memorandum submitted at Council's request.
[5]Survey based on Council's enquiries to local education authorities' on regulations or corporal punishment in primary schools.
[6]See[5].
[7]The British Psychological Society. Memorandum submitted at Council's request.
[8]The National Association of Mental Health. Memorandum submitted at Council's request.
[9]The Council also sent enquiries and received information on practice abroad from the following countries:
      Belgium.
      Denmark.
      Federal Republic of Germany.
      Holland.
      Norway.

CHAPTER 20

How Primary Schools are Organized

I. DEVELOPMENTS IN THE CLASS TEACHER SYSTEM

752. Most primary school work is done in classes. The children who form a class spend most of the day with their class teacher. This is what teachers are used to, and what overwhelmingly they think right. More than two thirds of those in our sample of primary school teachers (Appendix 1, Table D.22) thought that the class teacher should be mainly responsible for his class, while a further quarter accepted the system but thought that the class teacher could reasonably share more of his present responsibilities with other teachers. The bulk of the evidence received also supported the class teacher system.

753. But a class need not necessarily be taught as a whole. There has always been much class instruction and we believe that there is still too much. Yet to some extent, the early age at which English children were admitted to school has always put limits on it, as can be seen from reports from the early twentieth century of three year olds falling asleep on the floor from the gallery benches where 80 at a time were assembled for needle-threading drill or for object lessons. There was also a far more liberal tradition deriving from Robert Owen and reinforced by the ideas of Froebel and Montessori. By the time of the 1933 report, the majority of infant schools divided their classes into groups for teaching reading. Some teachers found they could arrange their work in such a way that children learnt individually at their own pace. The 1931 report on the junior school was more cautious in advocating group and individual learning except for younger juniors. Throughout the thirties, the number of groups within a class of 40 or 50 tended to be limited to three or four, whether or not this number corresponded to the range of achievement in the class. In junior schools "group reading", with each group supervised by a child teacher (whose fate was usually to read below his own ability), and the teacher circulating round the groups was and is a popular device for increasing the number of occasions on which each child read aloud. It was an improvement on reading in chorus or reading aloud round the class but is shown by recent research to be far from effective. Class instruction in arithmetic was often followed by practice in two or three groups which were given sums of varying difficulty. Other schools allowed individual children to work through the sums in their text book at their own pace.

Individual Group and Class Learning

754. In the last 20 years schools have provided far more individual work, as they have increasingly realised how much children of the same age differ in their powers of perception and imagery, in their interests, and in their span of concentration. The more obvious this becomes, the less satisfactory class instruction seems. When children first come to school they learn most effectively if they choose what to do from amongst a range of materials carefully selected by their teachers. Similarly, throughout the primary school, children should have time to follow their own interests and hobbies, to read for pure

273

enjoyment and to record their personal findings and experiences, in words, in pictures and in movement. But from the start, there must be teaching as well as learning; children are not "free" to develop interest or skills of which they have no knowledge. They must have guidance from their teachers. The younger the children, the more solitary their pursuits are apt to be and the more short-lived the groups they form. The demand for help in the exercise of techniques and skills, whether, for example, in reading or in so different a skill as sewing usually arises "on the job". Teaching must often be individual, though other children will look on, and often learn in the looking. The varying interests of older children and their differing ability and knowledge means that they too ought often to be taught as individuals both for reading and mathematics. Sharing out the teacher's time is a major problem. Only seven or eight minutes a day would be available for each child, if all teaching were individual.

755. Teachers, therefore, have to economise by teaching together a small group of children who are roughly at the same stage. Ideally, they might be better taught individually, but they gain more from a longer period of their teacher's attention, even though it is shared with others, than they would from a few minutes of individual help. This is particularly true of children who have reached the same stage in reading and computation. A group of this kind should be formed for a particular purpose, and should disappear when the purpose is achieved. But it is rare to find a class all of whom will fit tidily into groups. If children are learning according to their capacity, some are almost bound to be racing ahead and some will barely have reached the starting point.

756. Choral singing, games and physical education for the older children are obvious examples of things usually taught to a whole class. Experiences like listening to a story, a poem, or music may be heightened by being shared with a class, but it is often best to leave children to make their private and individual response. There are no infallible rules. Recapitulation, explanation, or question and answer may standardise and devalue the more deeply felt experiences, yet on occasion the right comment, briefly made, may illuminate them. A vivid reconstruction of the past or an account of life in another part of the world can also be presented to a whole class. Sometimes a topic for group or individual work is introduced to the whole class which is again brought together for discussion and instruction as the work develops. Some modern language teaching is also usefully given to all together. Class teaching for these various purposes is sensible and helps to make the class a unity. On the other hand, the practice of setting a whole class laboriously to copy notes from a blackboard, and other similar mass drills are best avoided.

757. Children of junior school age tend naturally to go about in small groups. Groups of three to 15 pupils are good for many kinds of school work. In this way children learn to get along together, to help one another and realise their own strengths and weaknesses, as well as those of others. They make their meaning clearer to themselves by having to explain it to others, and gain from opportunities to teach as well as to learn. Some children are so timid and inarticulate that they need to hear their companions put to teachers the questions they themselves are unable to frame. Apathetic children may be infected by the enthusiasm of a group, or decide to sit back as idle passengers, a danger which the teacher needs to watch. Able children benefit from being

caught up in the thrust and counter thrust of conversation in a small group of children similar to themselves. They would also profit from reading with a teacher a book which is too difficult for the rest of the class. But this is an opportunity they rarely get.

758. Group work has often demonstrated the capacity of primary school children to plan and follow up mathematical and scientific enquiries. They are less shy of risking a hypothesis in a group than before the whole class, and sometimes the extravagant guess turns out to be right. More children, too, get the chance of discussing, and so understanding more clearly, what their problem is. Expeditions gain in value when the class is broken up into smaller groups. More children can help to plan the visit and each group can be given a different target. But each individual child needs some time during the expedition to follow up his own interests.

759. A class or group "interest" depends for its value on the children being absorbed in it and the teacher giving it skilful guidance. There should be opportunity for each child's individuality to show itself. The production of a class magazine illustrates this. It calls for class discussion of the general outline, for the formation of groups to plan sub sections, and freedom for children to make their individual contribution.

760. Some types of group work are too ambitious. Local historical or geographical surveys, for example, may demand from each child an artificial narrowing of the field of study, and a measure of collaboration which few adults can achieve. Success depends on the teacher's skill in knowing when to drop a topic, when to intervene, to sustain or reinforce the interest of an individual, a group, or occasionally, the whole class. Then the pieces of the jig saw can be fitted together—or seen not to fit. Usually children's records of their work should be individual. Occasionally the outcome may be a group or class record and will give children an incentive to reach a particularly high standard of presentation. The final product may be a useful addition to the school collection of books.

Team Teaching

761. In making a case for children to have experience of individual, group and class work are we merely justifying what exists? Are the class and the class teacher necessary? Supporters of "team teaching", a method developed in the U.S.A., raise this question. The broad principle of team teaching is that, instead of each teacher working mainly on his own, teams are organised within a school so that the experienced and able carry responsibility, the newly trained receive guidance, and students and teaching aides are integrated into the work of the school. Use is made of the special skills and knowledge of individual teachers. A team of teachers may be responsible for the work of a number of children ranging from 60 to 200. For teaching purposes, the children are arranged in groups which vary in size and composition according to what is being taught. Some groups may contain only a handful; others one or two hundred. In some schemes, the class as a teaching unit disappears. Any number larger than 15 is considered a big group, so that a class of 30 is thought little better than an assembly of 100 or more children. The pupils, however, usually have a "home room" and a "home teacher" who registers their attendance and is generally responsible for their welfare.

762. Many English primary schools have for long tried, and liked, several of the practices which, taken together and raised to a principle, are described in America as "team teaching". But they have done so without abandoning the framework of the class and its class teacher, our principle of stability. It is common, for instance, for junior school teachers to exchange classes. In this way special strengths are made use of, special weaknesses avoided. The musical and the tone deaf will change places; a teacher with scientific interest will take more than one class: a young teacher will relieve an elderly one for physical education. New subjects for primary schools such as French are leading to more interchange of classes.

763. Classes in the junior schools are sometimes re-arranged for mathematics and reading because a child's achievement often varies considerably from one to the other. Sometimes the classes in one or two year groups—or even the whole school—are redivided into sets based on the children's attainment. The size of sets can be varied according to the amount of help their members need. If a part-time teacher is available, or if the head teacher takes a set, there can be more sets than classes and smaller teaching groups all round. But in spite of these advantages, this practice seems to be less favoured than it was (see Appendix 11, Section 6b, paragraph 1), probably because it has been applied too rigidly and emphasised subject divisions on the time-table before they were desirable or necessary.

764. For part of the week, the senior classes in the junior school are sometimes reorganised into clubs for music, drama or art so that children get an opportunity to make further progress than they can achieve within their own classes. Several classes may be linked together in arts and crafts, and children may go term by term to pottery, painting or needlecraft, each taken by a teacher with a particular bent for it. These arrangements are especially helpful for children who develop special interests at an early age.

766. The informal arrangements possible in small schools have probably done more to make teaching flexible between classes as well as inside a class than the organised time-tabled arrangements discussed in the last two paragraphs. The recognition that nursery children gain from living in a family group of mixed ages made it artificial to divide the school into separate rooms and classes for different ages. Because the entire school is rarely more than 60, it is common for children to have the freedom of the whole building and be in touch with all the staff including the nursery assistants and students. But each member of the staff has a small group of children who are her special charge. They naturally turn to her. An infant school classroom is too small and too confined for all the things the children need to do. They overflow into the open air where there are no walls to shut off one class from another; they stray into corridors which are not marked out into pens like sheep folds. The classroom is the children's home, their teacher's base; but outside it any teacher may be drawn into any child's concern. The school becomes a unity.

766. A similar situation is becoming more usual also in the junior school. Room for individual work is found in corridors and foyer. Here may be the central collection of books which are more accessible and more fully used than in a library room, in which each class may have only one or two time-tabled periods. In an increasing number of schools, classroom doors are,

metaphorically at least, open. Teachers know what is going on all over the school. Children are encourged to visit classes other than their own, to use equipment kept there, or to consult a teacher who has the particular knowledge that they need. In overcrowded town schools where an additional teacher is provided but where there is no room in which to form an extra class, two teachers sometimes work side by side and find that in this way they can learn from each other and do more for children individually.

767. Another kind of flexibility, arising from a different situation, has been developed in many two teacher country schools. The strict class teacher system would mean that children would be taught for three or four years by one teacher who would be unlikely to possess all the necessary gifts. Instead both teachers and the ancillary helper, if there is one, take some responsibility for all the children. Space is shared as seems best from time to time. On occasion one teacher supervises the majority of the children in order that the remainder can be given special help.

768. Until recently primary schools were designed merely as a collection of classrooms and a hall. Thirty years ago they were furnished in such a way as to make class instruction easy, group and individual work difficult. We have seen how they are now used. This in turn has stimulated the building of experimental schools in which classrooms are linked, some facilities shared and quiet individual working spaces provided. Experiment in buildings has reinforced experiments in teaching. If this is team teaching, we welcome it.

The Class Teacher

769. How far should schools break down class organisation? Even young children can work happily with more than one adult. In fact, some change of teacher during the week is stimulating to most children. It also makes easier the transition from one class teacher to another after the summer holidays, or when there has to be a change in the course of the year. A particular child and a particular teacher may find it difficult to get on with one another. An occasional change gives relief from the situation, a sense of perspective and a second opinion to help decide whether a change of class is necessary. Yet it is not surprising that when children are asked what class they are in, they usually give their teacher's name in reply. The youngest children in particular need a steady relationship with one teacher who should know them well. It is hard enough to know 40 children; it is virtually impossible to know 160. If there were no class teachers, nobody in a school would have the depth and clarity of knowledge of individual children on which their education depends. The most economical way to get to know children is to supervise their learning, to talk to them, to teach them, to be with them for enough of the day to see their changing moods and responses.

770. Children may sometimes see too much of each other as well as of their teachers; a few need a fresh start with new class mates. Yet the dismay that children usually show at a change of class in the middle of the year suggests that they benefit from a stable community whose values they can assimilate and where they know what to expect. A class is large enough to have groups which can form and reform for different purposes. A skilful teacher is able to some extent to influence the roles that individuals play within the groups and to provide some measure of success for most children. Meantime the class

takes on a personality, with its own history, its own jokes, its own favourite words, all in some sense a protection from the mass of the school.

771. It is, in fact, class teachers working for much of the day in their classrooms who have succeeded in establishing individual and group learning as the usual way of education in infant schools, and who are on the way to achieving a similar pattern of learning in junior schools. Teachers are able to make time to help individuals when they have most of the day at their disposal. For the same reason it is possible to take account of children's varying spans of attention, and children are able more often to bring their work to a conclusion instead of being interrupted for a change of teacher or group when interest and thinking are at a climax. The more children move from teacher to teacher, the more time and thought are bound to be absorbed in organisation, and the more anxious teachers may become about whether they are covering enough ground in the curriculum.

Conclusions

772. We conclude that the class, with its own teacher, should remain the basic unit of school organisation, particularly for the younger children. The great bulk of teaching of children up to eight or nine should normally remain with the class teacher. Yet even at this age there are benefits in the children knowing and having access to other teachers. The classroom doors should no longer be shut, as still happens in some schools, with the teachers, both experienced and inexperienced, isolated in their rooms. There may be circumstances when the best course will be for a class to be shared by two part-time teachers, or for two classes to be shared by a full-time teacher and two part-time teachers. But teachers sharing a class must work together and be consistent in their attitudes. There is a good deal to be gained if teachers, especially those who have classes of the same age, or a year younger or older, can arrange to plan some of their work together and to share equipment. Teachers' aides would fit well and easily into this kind of association. Interconnecting classrooms and some shared working spaces can encourage teachers to make adjustments, to vary the size of groups for different purposes and to form some groups from more than one class.

773. The older children might benefit from a more systematically planned contact with two or three teachers, each expert in one of the main aspects of the curriculum and able to teach related subjects. As the range of the primary school curriculum widens, it becomes increasingly difficult to equip students in a three year course to teach all subjects to older pupils. It will be even more desirable, if our recommendation for the extension of the middle school by one year is adopted, to provide the oldest pupils with teams of teachers who, between them, have some mastery of the English subjects, of a modern language, of mathematics and science, and of the arts. We recommend that experiments should be tried out in associating two or three classes—up to about 100 children—in the care of two or three teachers. Some of these experiments might treat the age group as a social unit, subdivided for various teaching purposes, to test whether children gain or lose from the larger unit. The effects on the teachers ought also to be watched. There is some danger that the staff would become stratified and that teachers would be confined to a narrow age range within the school.

774. There will be occasions when the work of both younger and older children should be enriched by occasional or regular teaching from a specialist in a subject such as music. But it needs to be recognised that the result of this may be that some teachers who exchange classes with specialists are left to "fill in" subjects which become isolated from the rest of the curriculum without the compensation of gifted teaching.

775. The case for giving children some individual teaching and allowing them to work in small groups is strong. We have therefore tried to discover activities in which it is profitable for a large number of children to be put in the care of one teacher so that the other teachers may have time to work with smaller groups. It has not been easy. When children watch television or listen to radio, all the teachers who are concerned with follow up work need to be there. We have received oral evidence which suggests that attention diminishes when a group is larger than the ordinary class. It is also significant that music, which is the subject for which primary school classes are most frequently combined, is one of the least developed. Perhaps the most promising line is for the large group to be engaged on individual work in which many children can get on by themselves without the help of a teacher.

776. Teachers who allow a substantial amount of individual work may have reason to fear that they do not have the knowledge they need of each child's progress and difficulties. But apparent attention to a class lesson may be no more than mask of inattention. Teachers who rely on rigid grouping may have the security of feeling that they know where the children have got to, but the price which is paid for this may be that some have not got far enough, or do not really understand what they are doing. Careful records are essential, but the task of keeping them increases with the amount of individual work. We recognise therefore that the blend of individual, group and class work in any one class must be the one that the particular teacher can manage.

777. Similar conditions apply to the more flexible grouping of classes and teachers that we hope to see. Room must be left for the teacher who is an individualist and works best on his own. The children too will differ in the changes of relationship which they can tolerate. For over sheltered and timid children a gradual introduction to an enlarging circle of adults and other children is best. Even more, those children whose home life lacks structure and consistency will need a simple class organisation from which they can move out to the wider community of the school. The organisation of each school ought to fit the individual circumstances of the children and the qualities of the staff.

II. THE SIZE OF CLASS

778. In 1931 the Consultative Committee deplored the "stereotyped instruction and mass discipline and lack of help for the individual" that resulted from a class of 50 and recommended that no class should be larger than 40, a recommendation which was not adopted in Ministry of Education Regulations till 1944. As the abnormally large age groups of children born immediately after the war entered the primary schools the size of classes increased but from 1954 there was a gradual fall in average size of class and in pupil-teacher ratio. For the past two years the position has been roughly

stable, in spite of rising numbers. This has been achieved by employing more unqualified teachers and, to a less extent, by closing some very small schools, which are extravagant to staff. Diagram 7 shows the proportion of classes of various sizes at intervals since the war. Table 16 shows the number of children and the percentage of all pupils in classes of varying sizes:

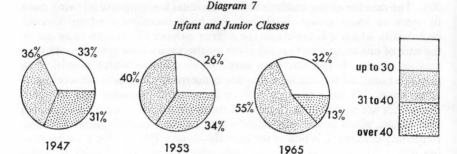

Diagram 7

Infant and Junior Classes

1947   1953   1965

up to 30

31 to 40

over 40

Table 16 Size of Primary Class, England: January, 1965

(1) Size of Class	(2) Number of Pupils (Thousands)	(3) Pupils in (2) as percentage of all pupils
1—15	40	1
16—20	117	3
21—25	256	6
26—30	528	14
31—35	980	24
36—40	1,402	35
41—50	676	17
51 and over	5	0·1

Source: Statistics of Education, 1965, Part One, Table 20.

779. In 1965, 17 per cent of primary school pupils were in classes over 40, the average size of class was 30·7 and the pupil teacher ratio, taking into account the full-time equivalent of part-time teachers, was 28·5 (see Table 18). It is clear from the tables that the average size of class and the pupil-teacher ratio are derived from a wide range of sizes and ratios. The smaller classes are in the smaller schools. The National Advisory Council on the Training and Supply of Teachers suggested in 1965 that infant school classes would increase in size in the next few years and that the improvement, which might have been expected in the primary schools after 1970, is likely to be checked by the transfer of primary teachers to secondary schools after the school leaving age is raised.

780. Almost all our witnesses believe in the value of smaller classes. They see the supply and quality of teachers as the two crucial factors in primary education. The L.C.C. evidence urged that an improvement in the pupil-teacher ratio should be a major objective of policy. Most witnesses, asked to suggest what size of class should be the objective for the next 20 year period, chose 30. Some said that 30 was the maximum number of children of the same

age that an average teacher could teach effectively without strain. But, if, for example, a class contained children from 8 to 11, they thought the number ought to fall to around 25. Some witnesses added that a class of fewer than 15 to 20 did not provide sufficient stimulus for teacher or children besides making obvious difficulties for physical education, music and drama. Rather smaller classes were suggested for infants than for juniors and the admission class should, it was thought, be the smallest of all. Support for these views can be found in Swedish practice where the statutory class size for the first three years of schooling—from seven to ten years—is smaller than in the later years. There is a striking measure of agreement between the witnesses who gave individual evidence and the sample of teachers who responded to our questionnaire on primary education. Some 61 per cent of head and assistant teachers believe that 30 is the maximum reasonable size of class. Of the remainder, the majority favour classes of 25 or smaller (Appendix 1, Table D.18). Parents certainly believe in small classes. That is one of the main reasons for sending children to independent schools, where the average number of pupils to teachers is less than half that in maintained schools.

781. Despite all this agreement, some research surveys have shown no significant relationship between class size and attainment in reading or other aspects of the curriculum in which results can easily be measured. Other surveys[1,2] (see also Appendix 9) have even shown a positive relationship between attainment in these skills and large classes. What is the reason for this discrepancy?

782. The most up to date and thorough analysis of the relation between attainment in reading and school and home conditions is provided by the National Survey (1966) (Appendix 4). Its results derive from an analysis in which the association of size of class with reading comprehension is isolated, and many other variables, such as the size of the school, home circumstances and attitudes, the effects of streaming are held constant. In those surveys which produced a positive association this was done for far fewer—or no— variables. The National Survey itself has provided no evidence that when other things are equal large classes are associated with good results in the reading comprehension test. This squares with common sense. But why has not research confirmed the equally common sense judgement that small classes positively make it easier to learn to read? A possible explanation is that, as we know, small classes tend to be found in small schools; and that small schools tend to be either in the country, or in those older areas of towns where bad social conditions may have a cumulative effect on children. In both instances, classes may contain children of several different ages.

783. There is further evidence from the National Survey bearing on this problem. If, instead of comparing school with school, each school is studied individually, we find that the pupils with the better reading scores tend to be in the larger classes. But general experience, confirmed by the N.F.E.R. Survey of Junior School Organisation, (Appendix 11, Part 11, Section 5:6) shows that backward pupils are often, as a matter of policy, put into small classes. There is also a tendency for young and inexperienced teachers to be put in charge of them, partly no doubt because their classes are small.

784. The importance of size of class may vary according to an individual teacher's objectives and methods[3]. If the teacher treats the class as a unit, its size is relatively unimportant. If the aim is to teach individuals and small

groups, there is a limit to the number of pupils for whom one teacher can be responsible. Large classes may encourage concentration on a narrow curriculum. As a consequence, pupils' scores may improve in the measurable but limited range of work with which research has mainly been concerned. The advantages of small classes may lie in the possibilities they offer for developing individual work.

785. We agree with the observation of the Scottish Research Council[4] that "the results of an investigation based on accepted organisation . . . are biased from the beginning . . . that an investigation of this topic (class size) would require a specific design, in which the accepted principles for organising classes would be altered for the purpose of the experiment". Experiments should be made to test the effects of small classes and generous staffing ratios.

Conclusions

786. Although positive evidence from research in favour of small classes is lacking, this does not outweigh professional advice, public opinion and the example of other countries. The present statutory maximum size of a primary school class in this country is larger than in most European countries and in most American states, where primary classes are also sometimes smaller by regulation than secondary classes. The parents of children in maintained schools, interviewed for the National Survey (Appendix 3, Section 3, paragraph 56) had two principal complaints and anxieties about primary schools. The buildings were old and the classes were too large.

787. Some of our witnesses would not go so far as to maintain that a teacher necessarily did better with his class when it was less than 40 or worse when numbers rose above it. Much depends on the skill of the individual teacher. There are even some who find big classes a challenge to their determination and professional competence. Some infant teachers immediately after the war developed individual work with classes of 50 and triumphed over every disadvantage.

788. But achievement in the face of such difficulties cannot be expected of all teachers, and should be asked of none for long. The fact that the improvement in primary schools is so widespread and general reflects in part at least the reduction in size of classes. Further progress depends on the development of individual and group learning. Teachers must be able to prescribe and provide for each child what he needs. We do not believe that any but exceptional teachers can know, in this sense, more than about 30 children and their parents. We, therefore, recommend that the maximum size of primary class should be reduced and that within the primary schools classes for the youngest pupils should be the smallest. We discuss staffing prospects, proposals for their betterment, and the effect on size of class in Chapters 23 and 24.

III. THE COMPOSITION OF A CLASS

789. During the last war two of the set questions which army recruits were asked were: "What standard were you in when you left school? Was that the top standard?" From 1862 onward the classes in English elementary schools were described as standards. The "standard" was the level which an average child, taught by an average teacher, was expected to have reached at

the end of a year's work. The normal rate of progress was one standard a year from the age of six. There was a strong incentive to move children into Standard I as soon after six as possible because under the system of "payment by results" this was to the school's financial advantage. But there was no financial point in accelerated promotion through the standards because there was no extra grant for children who had got beyond Standard VI. Some schools but not all, had a Standard VII—hence the interviewers, second question. The idea of "standards" regulating promotion survived the end of "payment by results" in 1898, and was indeed given a new twist by the introduction of the junior scholarship system. This secured "free places" in what we now call grammar schools for the ablest children in the elementary schools. A child was held to have a better chance with competitive examination at the age of ten or 11 if he could get quickly to the top of the elementary school. Naturally he was encouraged to do so. Accelerated promotion for some was counter balanced by delayed promotion for others who repeated the same work year after year. Some left from Standard II or III. Practice had not made perfect.

790. The decision to have separate schools for children over 11 meant, where it was carried out, the rejection of classes with a very wide age range. The building of senior elementary schools left empty places in the old all-age school. These places were not, of course, left empty but filled with other children aged between seven and 11. Their greater number meant that there had to be more classes for them. The development of mental tests by educational psychologists had made clear, and apparently measurable, the differences between children, differences which were thought to be roughly constant but whose effect on attainment increased with age.

791. The Consultative Committee in 1931, therefore, recommended that, where classes were rather large, grading in ability within an age group (now called streaming) should be introduced into junior schools. It had reservations about jumping to conclusions about children's ability as soon as they had left the infant school, and stressed the importance of easy transfer between streams. These reservations tended to be forgotten. Grading by ability, in one form or another, became almost universal in all but the smallest schools. Some shift of opinion and of practice has now become apparent, partly in response to the idea that, since the world contains people of all grades of ability, children should learn to mix with them at school. This has become more practicable as group and individual work within classes has been developed.

Infant Schools and Classes

792. Infant schools are exceptionally difficult to organise because of their termly intake but annual output. The number of children is bound to rise throughout the year; whether the size of the staff expands and contracts in the same way depends upon the authority's policy. Few authorities staff for the year on September numbers; the majority base the number of teachers on the January roll, providing an extra teacher in the summer if the pupil teacher ratio becomes very unfavourable and a teacher can be found. Quite often an additional class of the youngest children is formed for the summer term only. Occasionally the classes for the youngest children in September are deliberately kept small enough to take in their newcomers in January and after Easter so that the other classes may be left undisturbed. More commonly,

all the classes are arranged to be roughly equal in size at the beginning of the year, and there are sufficient termly promotions to balance the termly admissions. This principle may be applied to all classes, or the top classes may be left undisturbed.

793. Some schools arrange all their classes strictly by age. Often, however, the children who are making progress in reading are promoted first and in a two form entry infant school the classes in the final year may be clearly differentiated by attainment. It is rare to find this acknowledged in the way the classes are named. An accurate picture of grading in the infant school could only be obtained from a survey as detailed as that made by the N.F.E.R. on the junior school (see Appendix 11). Such information as is available to us (Appendix 10)[5, 6] suggests that in a quarter to a fifth of infant classes, children of six are graded by attainment. In some schools grading begins even earlier.

794. As long ago as 1933, in a few areas, many infant schools which could have organised on an age basis were experimenting with "vertical classification". Each class contained children aged from five to seven or eight. The advantage was said to be that at the infant stage, as in the nursery, children learnt from one another and learnt more successfully when there was an age range wider than a year. It was also argued that children gained from a longe association with one teacher. This type of grouping remains a minority practice. It is prevalent in two or three areas which are among those which have the most lively infant school work in the country. It is now being tried in the lower classes of a few junior schools. We return to a discussion of this organisation in paragraphs 799–804.

Junior Schools and Classes

795. About four fifths of the junior schools and three fifths of the junior mixed and infant schools in the National Survey took into account attainments as well as age in deciding in which class to place their pupils (Appendix 5, paragraph 9). The much larger N.F.E.R. survey of junior schools puts the proportion at 56 per cent for certain with another 14 per cent of probables (Appendix 11, Table 1). In big schools, it is easy to be sure. There are, for instance, eight classes in a two form entry school—two for each year—and these are normally divided into an "A" stream and a "B" stream. In smaller schools with anything between two and six or seven junior classes it is less easy to be sure how children are divided between the classes. The most common practice in schools with between five and seven classes is to consider the eight and nine year olds together and divide them between classes according to their attainments and to do the same for the 10 and 11 year olds. A good many schools of this size, and more of the smaller ones, still work on something like the old standard system, though with fewer over age and under age pupils in a class than in the days before Hadow and, of course, a smaller age span because the 12 and 13 year olds are in another school.

796. When a junior school pays attention to attainments or ability in placing a child how does it assess them? Most head teachers rely in the first instance on the infant school. Often the record card will make specific recommendations about the most suitable "stream". Rather less than half the junior schools in the N.F.E.R. survey use a standardised intelligence test. Some other methods, in decreasing order of popularity, are the head's own judgement, the result

of internal school examinations, a child's position within the age group, and standardised attainment tests. In the later years of the junior school, increasing reliance is placed on school examinations, teachers' judgements and standardised attainment tests. Most schools would claim that they group children both on attainment and on ability. In fact, the intelligence test itself measures a kind of attainment (Chapter 2), though it is less influenced by subject knowledge than are the skills usually measured by attainment tests.

797. Some 21 per cent of the children in schools included in the N.F.E.R. survey were placed in classes which were intended to include the whole range of ability in the school (Appendix 11, Table 2, Part 1). The most usual arrangement in a large school is to separate the older and younger children within a year group. Some schools do their best to ensure classes exactly parallel in ability by relying on children's records, test results and so forth. Others allocate children to classes at random, or according to where they live, or alphabetically, by their surnames.

The Criteria Discussed

Age

798. A flexible age of transfer between schools based on developmental age was considered in Chapter 10 and rejected. The same arguments apply to movement from class to class as to movement from school to school. If work within a class is adjusted to individual capacity, there seems little case for moving children out of their age group. If the class is taught as a unit, "skipping" classes may mean gaps in the course, and retention for a second year can result in wearisome and disheartening repetition of the same work. Investigation in Belgium and in other European countries where promotion from grade to grade depends on achieving a specified standard have shown that failure tends to be cumulative and that pupils who repeat a grade on one occasion, far from catching up with their contemporaries, are more likely to have to do so again a second or a third time[7]. They do less well than those pupils who are promoted despite their poor attainment. These results, and similar ones from research in the U.S.A., confirm the experience of English schools when a similar system was in force. We recommend that promotion should normally be by age. Some children are so exceptionally advanced or retarded that they are better placed with an older or younger group. Decisions for acceleration or retention should take into account children's all-round development, physical and emotional, just as much as intellectual. The presumption should be that children are better with their friends in their own age group, unless there is clear evidence to the contrary.

"Vertical Classification"

799. Is it desirable deliberately to extend the age range of each class to two or three years, in order to extend the range of attainment that teachers might expect from their pupils and so make it easier for them to provide for children who are exceptionally able or retarded? Some schools in the United States are ungraded, but the evidence they provide is hardly relevant to our situation.

800. Experience of vertical grouping exists in some English infant schools where one of the reasons for its adoption has been termly admissions. Even if all children are admitted, as we have recommended, at the beginning of the school year, some of the difficulties it is designed to avoid will remain. Even

though children first enter school in small groups, week by week, or month by month, teachers of the first year classes will be hard pressed to give enough time to beginners who may up to now have had their mother's full-time attention. If the class covers a two or three year age span, a small group of newcomers can be absorbed into a settled routine in a community which may well include a brother or sister, or a neighbour's child. The new entrants learn by imitating the older children and talking to them. During the first few months the teacher can concentrate on giving personal attention and re-assurance to the younger children when it is needed. Later in the year, extra time can be found for the older children who demand daily or twice daily help with reading. Among the newcomers may be a few children who have begun to read at home or will quickly read if they are given help. These children will be attracted to the simple reading books provided primarily for the older children. Certainly no less important, those older children who are not yet ready to read can play and talk with the younger children without any feeling of failure. The teacher becomes increasingly sensitive to her pupils' needs as she gets to know them and their parents over two or three years.

801. But there are also disadvantages. For children to spend the whole of their infant school life with one or at most two teachers may be to distribute the strengths and weaknesses of the staff unfairly. It may also limit children's contacts with adults to too narrow a circle and some children may be too sheltered or lack stimulus. In practice, however, schools which deliberately widen the age range of classes are usually closely knit communities. Teachers work with children from classes other than their own, and children seek help outside their own class.

802. There may be some danger that the younger children will be over-shadowed by the older ones, may imitate them too closely, and have in-sufficient experience of the kind of play that is an investigation rather than a use of materials. Great skill is called for from the teachers, both in supporting the young children and in seeing that the older ones are given enough stimulus. They may need to be taken separately for story telling and music. Yet many of the traditional children's stories have the quality of myth, and can be enjoyed at many different levels: and even when a story may seem too difficult for the younger children, they often pick up much from it, as do children in a family who listen eagerly to stories intended for older brothers and sisters. Interests, like stories, may be enjoyed at many different levels. For most infants prehistoric animals are hardly to be distinguished from dragons and from fantasy, and therein lies their attraction. Some of the older children are ready to learn about them quite seriously, measuring their bones in the local museum and memorising their extraordinarily difficult names. The need to make suitable provision for the older and abler children ought to be very much in the mind of teachers of a "vertically grouped" class.

803. The older children become, the more widely the range of their achieve-ment fans out. Many schools find a year's range in attainments so un-manageable that they group children by attainment at seven. It is of some interest that many of the heads of junior schools of five to seven classes in the N.F.E.R. streaming survey complained of the difficulties of a wide age range in a large class. Many of these schools have more than one age group within a class of more than 35 pupils. They share, that is to say, the conditions of a school which voluntarily widens the age range in its classes.

804. We have been impressed by the liveliness and good quality of the work in infant schools where classes extend over two or three age groups. We think that this organisation has advantages at the infant school stage though they may become rather less marked if our recommendations for a single term of entry and part time introduction to schooling are adopted. In the meantime, it is for each head teacher, in consultation with her staff, to balance the gain and loss of classes containing more than one age group. No evidence is available to show whether a double age group is advantageous in the junior school.

Classes Including Less Than a Year Group

805. Some schools extend the age range in their classes. Others, particularly infant schools and some large junior schools which do not grade children by attainment, adopt a precisely opposite policy and narrow the age range in each class to a six months period. The effect in the last year of the infant school may be to concentrate in one class too many children who are needing help in reading. It may also persuade a teacher that she has a class who are all at much the same level, and blind her to the exceptions. There is some evidence that, when senior and junior unstreamed classes are formed within a year group, the younger children do less well by the end of their junior school course, even when allowance is made for their age. The explanation may be that the younger children at first appear less able, both because of their age and because they have had a shorter time at school, than the older children. Teachers may then ask less of them so that their achievement is further depressed in comparison with that of the older class. More research on this topic is needed, particularly since this kind of grouping is becoming relatively common. There may be occasions when it is useful to collect the younger children together for a limited period so that they can be given additional help. Teachers, however, need to be aware that a younger class may easily be considered a less able class.

Classification by Attainment or Ability (Streaming)

806. Streaming is, as we have seen, by far the most common way of organising junior schools, but there is reason to think that practice is changing. Only four per cent of junior schools had rejected streaming according to a 1962 survey[8]. The next year the N.F.E.R. found in their enquiry into junior schools that six per cent did without it. Their report also showed that recent changes in organisation in the schools surveyed had lessened the amount of streaming and that other schools were intending to introduce mixed ability groups.

807. Teachers' views may be moving faster than practice has done. In the 1962 Survey, 85 per cent of primary teachers favoured streaming, six per cent had mixed views and nine per cent were hostile. Of the replies of teachers to our own enquiry (Appendix 1, Tables D.19, 20) only 34 per cent approved of streaming for all or most junior children, 25 per cent approved of streaming for older pupils and 30 per cent were hostile. It should be added that our enquiry, unlike the earlier one, included teachers in schools which were too small to stream and teachers in infant schools. It may also be significant since heads plan school organisation that many more heads than assistants are critical or undecided about streaming.

808. To judge by the parents in the National Survey (Appendix 3, Section 3, paragraph 40 and Table 56) professional opinion is swinging more rapidly against streaming than is public opinion generally. In 1964, two thirds of the parents preferred their children to be taught in classes streamed by ability. There was no difference according to social class. A clear majority favoured streaming even among those parents who thought that their children were being taught in classes of mixed ability. There may be some connection with the preference expressed for grammar school education.

809. Before the 1939 war, streaming was seen as a device for opening the grammar schools to talented working class pupils. The grammar school in its turn was expected to make available to its pupils a choice of occupation and of a way of life. Selection for secondary education has been challenged on three main educational grounds: the accuracy of the selective process, the contrast in the provision made for children of differing ability and the effect of segregating them on their achievement. It has also been criticised as being socially divisive both because it gives middle class children a better chance than manual workers' children to secure grammar school places, and because it gives better career openings to grammar school than to modern school pupils. The same arguments are also used against selection for primary school classes, or streaming. We must now consider them.

810. In coming to our conclusions we have taken into account our impressions of schools which we have visited, the evidence we have received and the results of research. Streaming is almost unknown on the continent of Europe, and repetition of the year's work, which is a form of streaming, is declining. While we have tried to take account of all the research findings which have been brought to our notice, we owe a special debt to the investigation into streaming in the primary school which was undertaken by the N.F.E.R. and financed by the Department of Education and Science. But, as will be clear from the summary printed as Appendix 11, this research is far from complete. A survey of junior school organisation in 1963, a study of matched streamed and unstreamed schools and a cross-sectional inquiry into the achievements and characteristics of pupils in all four junior years in 1964, is to be succeeded by a longitudinal study of the seven and eight year olds as they pass through the junior schools, and by intensive work on a small number of schools.

811. Streaming involves selecting. In schools which are streamed throughout, children are selected at seven. We know of no satisfactory method of assigning seven year old children, still less those who are even younger, to classes graded by attainment or ability. When head teachers rely on their own judgement and those of the infant school heads, they may underestimate the difference which the home makes to the speed of learning to read. But this is one of the main yardsticks by which teachers compare children. Differences in attainments may be more due to differences in age than heads recognise—after all some seven year olds have had half as much education again as others. Objective tests have the advantage that these tests make allowance for age but few group tests are satisfactory at seven and few primary school teachers can find time to give individual tests. There is, too, a danger that if objective tests are known to be used a seven plus test with its pressures and tensions may be substituted for an 11 plus examination. It is known that of the predictions made at 11, by the best methods available, between ten per cent and 20 per cent turn out to be mistaken within the next three to five years. The earlier

that tests are given, the less relevant they are bound to be to an education which will continue to 15 or later. The younger the children, the larger the number who will be clustered together in the middle ranges of ability and attainment. The less useful, therefore, the tests will be as a means of discrimination.

812. If many children are bound to be wrongly placed at seven, the amount of transfer between classes is important. Professor Vernon has estimated that it would be reasonable to expect ten per cent of pupils to be transferred each year. It is clear that the actual proportion of transfer is smaller. One sample of two streamed schools showed an annual rate of transfer of 2·3 per cent between eight and 11[9]. In a small sample of three streamed schools there was a transfer rate of six per cent[10]. The conclusion drawn by the N.F.E.R. from their survey was that there was a relatively small amount of transfer in 1961–62.

813. The reasons for a small amount of transfer are not clear. Teachers, when asked to estimate a figure, almost always over-estimate it. It may be that assessments as children progress through a school are no more reliable than those first made and give no firm grounds for reversal of judgements. Once in a class, children probably take on its characteristics, including its average level of attainment, and this may result in part from their adapting themselves to the rate of progress or work which the teacher expects. Some teachers are understandably reluctant to upset children who have settled down with their friends in a class and who may suffer some set-back if they are promoted and still more if they are "put down" to make room for another child.

814. Some of the effects of early selection are evident both from the N.F.E.R. enquiry and from other research. The system of streaming favours girls who are, age for age, more mature than boys and more disposed to play "the good pupil role" and therefore to gain the approval of their teachers. Research is certainly not needed to substantiate the evidence of any observant visitor to schools that lower streams and remedial classes contain more than their share of boys. The lower the stream, the younger the average age, and the higher the proportion of children who will have had only six terms in the infant school. Conversely, the higher the stream, the older the average age and the higher the proportion of children who will have spent nine terms in infant classes. Of the children in remedial classes in schools studied by the N.F.E.R., (Appendix 11, Part II, Table 10), 39 per cent had been at the infant school for the minimum period of six terms and only 12 per cent for the maximum course of nine terms.

815. There is also much evidence that streaming serves as a means of social selection[11]. It is not simply that middle class pupils congregate in upper streams and the children of semi-skilled and unskilled workers in lower streams. That might be expected from the association of intelligence with social class and occupation. Evidence is also available that more middle class children are to be found in upper streams and fewer in lower streams than would be expected from their results in objective tests[12]. Similarly a higher proportion of children, known from earlier records to have received poor maternal care in early childhood, were in lower streams than their test scores warranted. How much of this placing was due to characteristics in the

children which might have made them unsuccessful in an upper stream, how much to teachers' assumptions that clean and well kept children are abler, it is impossible to say.

816. Selection will inevitably be inaccurate. If the conditions for upper and lower streams were equally good and if all children stood equally high in the respect and affection of the staff, it would not perhaps matter very much whether children were wrongly placed. One of the principal advantages claimed by teachers for streaming is that it makes possible smaller classes and individual help for the slower children. That significantly smaller classes are in fact organised for these children is demonstrated quite clearly from the N.F.E.R. survey. But it is also true that a bigger class is thought to demand a stronger teacher, and the smaller classes, where almost every child may have difficulty in learning and many also have emotional problems, may therefore fall to the less experienced teachers. Their lack of experience may make it exceptionally difficult for them to set their sights—or rather the children's sights—high enough. The multiplicity of the problems with which some teachers have to deal, their low assessment of the children's capacity and the slow rate of progress at which they aim may explain why, at the end of the year, few children stand out as needing transfer. There are of course many schools where teachers alternate between upper and lower streams and where much thought is given to the selection of teachers for classes of slow learning pupils. Nevertheless experience, borne out by research (N.F.E.R., Appendix 11, Part II, Section 5, paragraph 5), suggests that in the main the older and more experienced teachers and particularly the deputy heads and holders of graded posts are assigned to the upper streams. Teachers may be streamed, no less than pupils. The more established the teacher the more probable it is that he will get one of the better classrooms and a generous supply of books and equipment. The N.F.E.R. survey showed that a higher proportion of the lowest streams were in classrooms which faced north (Appendix 11, Section 5:6). A low stream may be housed in a canteen or annexe because the children will have more space or be able to make a noise without disturbing the rest of the school, but the gain may be offset by the children's isolation from the rest of the school.

817. Finally what is the effect of streaming on children's achievement and attitudes? In 1959 a summary of research on streaming[13] concluded that it was not possible, on the evidence available, either to establish a case against streaming or to prove that it was a more effective form of organisation. Since that date further evidence[14, 15, 16] (Appendix 9 and 11) has been published, but it has not materially altered the conclusion. There has been some indication that the standards of attainment of the weaker children may rise when schools are deliberately unstreamed[17]. But the Manchester Survey 1964 (Appendix 9) shows that attainment in objective tests tends to be better in streamed schools and that this association does not disappear when allowance is made for the size of school, which is usually related to the type of neighbourhood and therefore to good attainment. It also gives no support to the view that streaming has an adverse effect on children of low ability. The National Survey, in which many more variables are held constant, shows no association, positive or negative, between streamed schools and reading attainment, except for a small positive association in the case of top infant girls. The results of the N.F.E.R. cross-sectional study of attainment in matched streamed and unstreamed schools

are particularly interesting (Appendix 11, Section 4, para 2). Reasonably enough, the tests chosen are similar to those generally used in junior schools. Both at seven and at ten children in streamed schools did somewhat better than those in unstreamed schools. But in no case save in mechanical arithmetic, which is known to give poor prediction of later success in mathematics, was the average difference more than two or three questions right on a test of 30 or 40 items. The advantage for children in streamed schools was most marked when tests assessed the more formal work such as computation and least marked in reading. By ten the lead of children in streamed schools had been reduced in all tests and there was no significant difference in reading, a result identical with that found in the National Survey. There is other evidence which suggests that children who are taught by informal methods make a slower beginning and catch up towards the end of the primary school [18, 19].

Conclusions

818. There is some evidence which suggests that achievement in the limited field of measurable attainment is higher in streamed schools. It is not so marked as to be decisive, and our view—which is supported by the results of the N.F.E.R. enquiry—is that forms of organisation are less critical than the underlying differences in teachers' attitudes and practice which are sometimes associated with them.

819. Nevertheless organisation can reflect and reinforce attitudes. Schools which treat children individually will accept unstreaming throughout the whole school. When such an organisation is established with conviction and put into effect with skill, it produces a happy school and an atmosphere conducive to learning. Not all teachers are yet ready or able to go so far. Even so, it has now been generally accepted that it is impossible to assess accurately the potential of children of primary school age. The younger the children, the greater the inaccuracy is bound to be. We welcome unstreaming in the infant or first school and hope that it will continue to spread through the age groups of the junior or middle schools.

820. Whatever the decision about the organisation of classes for the older children there will be certain problems to be faced. If streaming is retained, children should be classified in a way which is related to the distribution of abilities in the particular school. For example, in some three form entry schools the usual large "A" class is bound to contain a wide spread of ability. It would become only a little wider, and some of the dangers of streaming would be removed, if two parallel classes were formed, together with one really small remedial class. In another school where there was too little stimulus for able children, it might be right to form for at least part of the day or week, a group where these children could work together.

821. It is essential to ensure that the staff realise that any classification is bound to be faulty, that there certainly will be big differences between individuals in each class and that those differences can be expected to increase as children grow older. Differences in attainment as well as in interest demand individual and group learning in the streamed class as well as in the class which is avowedly of mixed ability. When all the children in a class appear to work at the same pace and the same level, they are probably conforming to what their teacher expects of them.

822. The division into classes made, every possible means should be adopted of blurring the distinction between streams. In this connection the suggestions made earlier in this chapter for informal co-operation between classes are relevant. If for some purposes classes work together and are regrouped, some of the disadvantages of streaming will be reduced. It is difficult to know to what extent teachers remain with the same stream or the same age group but we are clear that it happens too often. If almost all classes are bound to include a range of ability it is important that teachers in streamed schools should turn their attention now mainly to one section of the range, now to another, so that they will be aware of what children can achieve. There may be some teachers who temperamentally or in other ways are not suited to the slower children. Usually it is stimulating to teachers to take their turn with each of the streams. In that way, attitudes and expectations are less likely to harden and the strengths and weaknesses of the staff will be fairly distributed. Survivals from the past linger too long in English education. For the fourth year "A" class to cease to be the preserve of one or two teachers in each large junior school might be one way of speeding the disappearance of exercises which serve little purpose save to prepare for an examination which is itself now disappearing.

823. Streaming can be wounding to children. Great care ought to be taken not to suggest that trust and responsibility, or prowess in games, or the ability to look after library books are the preserves of certain classes. No more certain way could be found of alienating children from school or of creating irresponsibility.

824. The problem in the unstreamed class will be to translate into practice the principle of individual learning. If class teaching plays a large part, the abler children will be held back and the slower will lose heart. Clear cut streaming within a class can be more damaging to children than streaming within a school. Even from the infant school there still come too many stories of children streamed by the tables they sit at, of "top tables" and "backward reader" tables, and newcomers to school mystified by what they conceive to be the art of "reading backwards". There must be groups, of course, based sometimes on interest and sometimes on achievement, but they should change in accordance with the children's needs. One difficulty in the unstreamed class will certainly be to provide for the very able and for the slow learners. The slower children can gain from the enthusiasm and interests of the able children but only if the teacher sees that the slow children are absorbed into the class community and into small groups, and given praise, attention and instruction enough to encourage them to fresh effort. For the able children much more can be done by making accessible, in the classroom and the school as a whole, a liberal range of books and other equipment, though they ought sometimes to be fired and challenged by working with like minded children from another class. Checks will be needed that children are working to their capacity. Careful individual records are essential. Schemes for the whole school will need to be in every classroom and classes, as well as individuals, ought to have records which show, for example, the literature that has been read to them and the interests which have provided a point of departure for the class as a whole or for substantial groups within it.

825. It is possible to exaggerate the contrast in the problems and difficulties which confront teachers in streamed and unstreamed classes. In both there

will be big and growing differences in children's ability and attainment but they will follow no tidy pattern because interest and motive can make havoc of prediction. In both there will be children who are far more alike in their common human needs than they are differentiated by their background and abilities.

IV. THE LENGTH OF THE SCHOOL DAY AND TERM

826. Schools Regulations require that "on every day on which a school meets there shall be provided for the pupils:

(a) ....

(b) in a school or class mainly for pupils under eight years of age, at least three hours of secular instruction, and

(c) in a school or class mainly for pupils of eight years of age and over, at least four hours of secular instruction,

divided into two sessions, one of which shall be in the morning and the other in the afternoon unless exceptional circumstances make this undesirable." In practice most primary schools work for longer hours than the regulations require.

827. We found on our visits abroad that the school day was shorter than in England, although children may go to school on Saturday, and homework is usually set. There is more variation abroad than in England in the length of school day for children of various ages. For example, in Denmark, children work for only three hours in the first year and the length of day increases steadily up to the fifth year. The shortness of the day and the early hour at which it begins in some countries makes possible more flexible use of staff and buildings than are usual in England. The longer day here may, however, have allowed an informal pattern of education to develop more easily.

828. Relatively few of our witnesses have commented on the school day except to suggest that a full day's attendance should not be required of the younger children. We have recommended that part-time attendance should be usual for nursery, optional for beginners at school and available in exceptional circumstances until the child is six. It might, however, be preferable for somewhat older children to be in school for a slightly shorter period than now so that they can be in smaller classes for part of the time. Local education authorities might permit schools, in consultation with parents, to shorten the dinner hour so that children get home earlier, or to experiment, where classes are large and cannot be reduced in any other way, with staggered hours for slightly younger children. For example, some children might come to school at 9 a.m. and remain till 3 p.m., others might come at 10 a.m. and remain till 4 p.m. This arrangement would result in sessions the length of which would be within the limits imposed by Schools Regulations.

829. According to Regulations all schools must meet for 400 sessions (half days) in the year. Almost all schools take their main holidays at Christmas,

Easter and August (with varying amounts added in July and September). An increasing number of schools have a week at Whitsun and in some areas a full week's holiday is taken in October and February.

830. It is commonly held by teachers and parents, and our witnesses agreed, that the summer holiday is too long for the younger children. Many children get bored and there is some evidence that delinquency increases. Our witnesses suggested that four evenly spaced terms with shorter intervening holidays would be of greater benefit to the children. They also expressed the view that holidays should be arranged by the local education authority in consultation with the schools and that primary school holidays should be co-ordinated with those of secondary schools. There is a general move towards the staggering of holidays and the change of date of the August Bank Holiday is an example of it. Although traditions fade slowly, it is likely that holidays will in future be more evenly spread through the summer months.

831. The spring and winter terms impose some strain upon teachers and children both of whom tire towards the end of term. These are times of the year when children and members of the staff are most liable to illness. Young children do not work well in school during the long days of June. They might be better served if they were on holiday at this time and at school during August. Yet in some schools, a good deal of time may be spent at the beginning of each term before the work gets into top gear and a similar period is given to winding up work at the end of each term. An increase in the number of breaks might therefore lead to a reduction in the amount of effective learning.

832. We welcome experiments by authorities with a four term year and other variations in the time in which the schools are on holiday. The holidays of primary and secondary schools within each area should be co-ordinated.

Recommendations

833. (i) We recommend a combination of individual group and class work and welcome the trend towards individual learning.

(ii) The class should remain the basic unit of school organisation, particularly for the younger children; even so, children should have access to more than one teacher, and teachers should work in close association.

(iii) Experiments should be tried in associating two or three classes of the older children—up to about 100 children in the care of three teachers. Some experiments might treat the large group as a social unit.

(iv) The maximum size of primary school classes should be reduced. Experiments to test the effects of small classes and generous staffing should be established.

(v) We welcome unstreaming in the infant school and hope that it will continue to spread through the age groups of the junior school.

(vi) Flexibility in the length of the school day and the spacing of the school year should be encouraged.

REFERENCES

[1]Morris, J. M., 'How Far can Reading Backwardness be Attributed to School Conditions?', an Address presented to the International Reading Association, May 1964.

[2]Kemp, L. C. D., 'Environmental and Other Characteristics determining Attainment in Primary School', British Journal of Educational Psychology, Vol. XXV, Ps. 67–77, 1965.

[3]Markland, S., 'Scholastic Attainments as Related to Size, Homogenity of Classes', Ed. Research, Vol. 6, No. 1, November, 1963.

[4]Scottish Scholastic Survey of 1953, Scottish Research Council, 1963, p.168.

[5]Jackson, B., 'Streaming: An Education System in Miniature', Routledge and Kegan Paul, 1964.

[6]'Streaming in the Primary Schools', Statement prepared for the Council by the Metropolitan Division of H.M. Inspectorate.

[7]Wall, W. D., Schonell, F.J. and Orson, W. C., 'Failure in School', U.N.E.S.C.O., 1962.

[8]See [5] above.

[9]Douglas, J. W. B., 'Home and School', MacGibbon and Kee, 1964.

[10]Daniels, J. C., 'The Effects of Streaming in the Primary School', B. J. Ed. Psychol., Feb. 1961.

[11]See [5] above.

[12]See [9] above.

[13]Yates, A. and Pidgeon, D., 'The Effects of Streaming', Ed. Research, Vol. 2, No. 1, November, 1959.

[14]See [5] above.

[15]See [10] above.

[16]See [12] above.

[17]See [10] above.

[18]Gardner, D. E. M., 'Experiment and Tradition in Primary Schools', Methuen, 1966.

[19]Mc.V. Hunt, J., 'Intelligence and Experience', New York, Ronald Press Company, 1961.

CHAPTER 21

Handicapped Children in Ordinary Schools

834. However nearly we approach in future the ideals we have suggested, however small classes can eventually become, however well the learning of children within these classes can be guided individually, there will always be a minority of children in need of special help. A child may be handicapped mentally, physically, emotionally, or, as we have shown earlier, by his environment. The extent and seriousness of handicaps are likely to change in different medical and social conditions, but they are unlikely to be altogether eradicated. Indeed, although the incidence of some handicaps has declined the advances in many fields of medical knowledge have resulted in the survival of thousands of children who in rougher or more ignorant times would have died in infancy. The schools and particularly the special schools have therefore to face more severe and complex handicaps. At the same time society has created new stresses and strains. Modern society accepts responsibility for the welfare of its handicapped members to a greater extent than did earlier generations and much has been done during the last 50 years to enable children suffering from all kinds of handicap to take their place in society as they grow up. This is specially true since the 1944 Act, but much remains to be done.

835. We have not been able to study the education of children in special schools which is, in any case, the particular concern of the Secretary of State's Advisory Committee on Handicapped Children. Our terms of reference, however, make it appropriate for us to comment on the way in which handicapped children, some of whom will eventually be in ordinary primary schools, are identified and on how their needs are met. The problems of backward children, most of whom are in ordinary schools, are of particular concern to us.

836. Under Section 34 of the Education Act of 1944 it is the duty of each local education authority to ascertain which children in their area require special educational treatment. To fulfil this obligation they may require parents to submit their children from the age of two "for examination by a medical officer of the authority for advice as to whether the child is suffering from any disability of mind or body and as to the nature and extent of such disability". When a disability is severe it is almost always recognised in early infancy and the parents themselves usually take the initiative in informing and seeking the help of the local authority. Children with handicaps such as blindness, deafness, severe behaviour disturbance and the more severe forms of physical handicaps are usually sent to special schools, where specialised equipment, small classes, and, usually, specially trained teachers are available to meet their particular needs. Other handicaps however are neither so serious nor so easily identifiable. A decision on the kind of schools most suitable for a particular child is not always easy to reach. There are borderline cases about which opinions differ.

837. The policy of the Department of Education and Science is that each individual child should be placed wherever he has the best opportunities of developing his resources to the fullest extent. For most children this will be their ordinary primary school. Circular 276 (1954) gives clear expression to this view: "No handicapped child should be sent to a special school who can be satisfactorily educated in an ordinary school". Nearly all our witnesses supported this policy and we are in agreement with it. A handicapped child who will spend his life in the society of normal people and often in competition with them must learn to accept his disabilities and his differences though he needs the assurance that he is not alone in them and that help is available. The unnecessary segregation of the handicapped is neither good for them nor for those with whom they must associate. They should be in the ordinary school whenever possible.

838. Early and accurate identification of handicapped children is essential however slight or severe their disability. Rapid mental and physical development in the first four or five years of life makes their early environment of particular significance. Some children with physical handicaps will not develop residual skills unless they have been encouraged to use them in early childhood. For those children who are gravely handicapped in their intellectual development, whether by reason of hereditary endowment, their environment, or both, a wide range of experiences and opportunities is necessary, so that they may be enabled to realise their full potential. It might in this way be possible to help them attain a higher level of functioning than they do at present.

839. Full use should be made of the wide range of local authority, general practitioner and hospital services which may be available for the diagnosis and assessment of handicapped children from the time of their birth. Some authorities have established diagnostic classes and units for children from two or three upwards. In several cases children have been able to go from them into ordinary schools. These classes can provide opportunity for contact with parents under easier and more natural conditions than those in clinics and hospitals. The child benefits from being with other children and seeing other adults. But it is essential that the teachers have the full support of medical and educational specialists. Speedy identification and assessment must depend on the efficiency of the local authority whether in maintaining a risk register, in using the records of maternity and child welfare clinics or establishing diagnostic units or classes. When a child is ready to start school some handicaps indicate clearly the type of school needed. Others only begin to show or to carry obvious disadvantages after a child has started school. Partial sight and limited mental ability are examples of these. Teachers need to be alert to detect children and bring forward for expert examination without delay any child who fails to make satisfactory progress or seems to have sensori-motor, social or emotional difficulties. In this connection we are disturbed to learn that there are still a few authorities which do not test vision or hearing on entry to school.

840. As shown in Table 17 there are for purposes of administration ten categories of handicapped children. These are defined in Regulations made under Section 33(1) of the Education Act 1944*. However useful they may

*The current Regulations are the Handicapped Pupils and Special Schools Regulations 1959 as amended by the Regulations of 1962.

be administratively they are inevitably somewhat artificial and children do not necessarily fit neatly into them. An acute and prolonged difficulty in learning to read, which does not appear in the list at all, may spring from a variety of causes. A large and growing number of children are found to have more than one disability. A deaf child may be mentally retarded; maladjustment is often a consequence of a physical or mental handicap; physical handicap can include a wider range of disabilities. Some of our witnesses have expressed concern over the lack of adequate provision for children with two-fold or multiple disabilities.

841. In addition to these handicapped children there are the severely subnormal children who are designated "unsuitable for education in schools" and who are the responsibility of the local health and hospital authorities and of the Ministry of Health. Some witnesses have made the point that there can be no firm and accurate division between children who are suitable for "education" and those who are not. From our knowledge of the difficulties of interpreting the response to intelligence tests and of distinguishing how much the environment contributes to children's effectiveness, we would agree with them.* These witnesses stress the need for the educational service to be linked with the health service responsible for junior training centres for the mentally subnormal. They have drawn our attention to interesting experiments in dealing with borderline children, which are the shared responsibility in some areas between the health and education services.

842. The assessment of a handicapped child is not simple and cannot be made with finality. It is a continuing process and because of the complexity of the task both the process itself and the treatment of the total situation demand teamwork, in which teachers, doctors, psychologists and parents must co-operate. Assessment of handicap is needed not only for educational purposes, but also to ensure medical and social support.

Parents

843. Teamwork is necessary between all concerned and, in this connection, we must stress the vital role of the parent. Legally, parents must be informed of their right of appeal to the Secretary of State against any decision about their child's education. There is an elaborate appeal procedure. But essentially this is a problem of human relations. Whether parents have discovered their child's handicap for themselves or not, they will be, at least, worried about it and they may feel acute distress, bewilderment, resentment or even shame. They will almost certainly need help, first in accepting that their child is not like other children and then in understanding his needs, and in adopting a balance between excessive protectiveness on the one hand and indifference or even rejection on the other. All our evidence emphasises the need to advise and support the parents and to associate them as closely as

---

*The British Psychological Society in "Children in Hospitals for the Subnormal" (1966), a study of 403 children aged 1–15, found that 24 per cent had I.Q.s over 50, 14 per cent over 70, and 4 per cent over 100. (155 children were testable). They recommended: "The educational work of both Junior Training Centres and schools in hospitals for the subnormal should become the full responsibility of the Department of Education and Science. Pending the assumption of such responsibility, more flexible arrangements should be made whereby educational advisers, psychologists and inspectors of schools can advise staff of hospital schools and Junior Training Centres".

possible with the education of their child. This is not primarily a matter for an official letter but for sensitive and sympathetic advice given personally by a familiar figure, doctor, health visitor, social worker or teacher whom they have learned to trust. The head teacher should regard it as a special part of his duties to advise parents and to bring about close contact between them and their child's teacher, and any medical or social staff who are involved. If it is necessary for a child to go to a special school, or still more to a training centre, parents need to be helped to accept and understand the decision, and they should always be consulted well before it is made. This is not only a question of courtesy and humanity; it has practical importance. The readier the parents are to help and co-operate, the more likely is the child's education to be successful.

844. There is need for an advisory or counselling service for the parents of handicapped children, which should be available when the handicap of the child is first identified, often before the child has started school. The service should of course report back to those who have referred parents or notified cases to it[1]. It should co-ordinate those matters which are the concern of welfare, health, education and youth employment departments and it would be the responsibility of health visitors, doctors, teachers and hospital almoners to refer parents and to notify cases to it. Such a service would ensure continuity of help for parents and would enable them to make the best use of the services which are available. It would also give them support and encouragement and help them to feel less isolated.

Table 17

Numbers of Handicapped Pupils Receiving and Awaiting Special Education (in Special Schools, Classes, Units, in Hospitals and at Home) and Prevalence per 10,000 of the School Population in England and Wales, 1961 and 1966

Categories	1961		1966	
	No. of Children	Prevalence per 10,000 of School Population	No. of Children	Prevalence per 10,000 of School Population
Blind	1,474	1·9	1,337	1·7
Partially Sighted	2,182	2·8	2,326	3·0
Deaf	3,594	4·7	3,281	4·2
Partially Hearing	2,013	2·6	3,296	4·2
Physically Handicapped	10,757	14·0	11,616	14·8
Delicate	12,724	16·6	10,418	13·3
Maladjusted	6,033	7·9	8,548	10·9
Educationally Sub-Normal	47,247	61·7	55,514	70·9
Epileptic	903	1·2	877	1·1
With Speech Defect	151	0·2	224	0·3
TOTAL	87,078	113·7	97,437	124·4

Source: Statistics Branch, Department of Education and Science.

The Handicapped Child in the Ordinary School

845. We turn now to the provision made for the handicapped child in the ordinary school. No device or organisation will be much good unless the teachers concerned understand the nature and implications of the handicaps they meet. This is partly a matter of initial and in-service training to which we shall return later but it is also one of the "climate" of the school and one in which the other children have a concern. If handicapped children, either as individuals or as a group, are looked upon as a nuisance, or with pity, they will not flourish. If follows that a school such as we have described in Chapter 19 is not only right for the normal but right for the handicapped, for their fundamental educational needs are similar though there may be differences in the way they are satisfied. The school must provide for and cherish all its members. Some handicaps evoke more sympathy than others. Blindness, for instance, excites almost universal sympathy, deafness much less, while maladjustment is often exasperating, and certain kinds of physical deformity are felt by many to be repellent. Not every teacher is able to overcome the emotional and psychological reactions which some handicapped children arouse. If children such as these are to be placed in a normal class it is essential that the co-operation of the teachers is secured, after the nature of a child's disability has been made clear. It must not be forgotten that even one or two severely handicapped children add greatly to the responsibilities of a busy teacher in a large class. In such instances some ancillary help may be essential. If relationships in a school are good and if other children have had the nature of the handicapped child's difficulty explained to them they will rarely be cruel or hostile, but they may express their concern by being too sympathetic and too eager to help so that the handicapped child becomes spoiled and excessively dependent.

846. Many children whose handicap is not severe are taught in ordinary classes. In some instances more severely handicapped children have been successfully placed in them too. For instance a number of limbless children including some from the thalidomide group are satisfactorily placed in ordinary classes. We have been told of one congenitally limbless child who, provided with powered limbs, has gone successfully through the junior school. It is significant that since the birth of this child his mother has been well supported by the consultant paediatrician and that all concerned have shown excellent co-operation. We have also been told of six children from a special nursery school who were transferred not to another special school but to the ordinary infant school. They included a child with spina bifida and a girl with cerebral palsy. The local authority made special sanitary arrangements for these children, and provided ancillary help. They also ensured that specialist advice was available to teachers. In such circumstances some children can be fitted satisfactorily into primary schools, though their continuing development needs to be carefully watched.

847. It may well be that similar arrangements will be made more frequently in the future, but there will always be other children needing more specialised education either in a special school or in a special class in an ordinary school. The aim when such a class is set up is to concentrate on the learning disability in the special class and to allow the child to take as much part in the ordinary life of the school as possible. There are a small but growing number of special

classes in many areas for the partially hearing. There are also a very few for the partially sighted. The need here is, of course, for specialised equipment and for teachers trained in its use. The expense of the installation and the prevalence of the handicap mean that special classes must serve a wider area than the school's normal catchment area.

848. Fewer authorities provide special classes for maladjusted children, although referrals to child guidance clinics reach a peak at about nine. Difficulties often increase at adolescence. But demanding, aggressive, unco-operative or withdrawn behaviour may appear before this and teachers need to have sufficient knowledge of the emotional and social developments of children to notice it and to refer children when necessary. Check lists of children's difficulties, imperfect as they are, can be valuable in helping a teacher to describe a child's difficulty. In schools where there is absence of stress and generous attention to individual and group needs, disturbed children often remain and improve in their ordinary classes. One organisation in their evidence to us[2] estimated that 15 per cent of children in primary schools may at some time need special help and understanding from their teachers. But disturbed or aggressive children can be upsetting and disruptive and some authorities have established classes for them on two or three mornings or afternoons a week with considerable success. Similar arrangements have been made for children discharged from mental hospitals and psychiatric units in hospitals. This has helped them to settle down in ordinary schools.

Slow Learners

849. By far the largest number of handicapped children who need special education are those described as educationally sub-normal. This term causes unnecessary distress to parents and we suggest that the term "slow learners" is adopted instead. Both descriptions include children who are genetically poorly endowed as well as those of average ability who are seriously retarded in their attainments. Although it is doubtful whether it is yet sufficient, a great variety of provision exists for this large category of children. Some are educated in special E.S.N. schools, others are in ordinary schools either in special classes with special staffing ratios and specially qualified staff; others remain in the ordinary classes. In 1966, 45,000 such children were in special schools and at least another 10,000 in ordinary schools awaiting admission to special schools.

850. There is serious delay in identification of these children. In 1964 although one in four pupils in special schools for the physically handicapped was under eight, the corresponding figure for the E.S.N. schools was one in 18. The needs of the slow learner, as we shall henceforward refer to him, are not so obvious as those of the physically handicapped and no doubt some of the discrepancy in age of assessment is attributable to this. But there are good reasons why all slow learning children should be identified early. Until an authority is fully aware of the numbers of these children, it is not in a position to plan adequately for them, nor is there any incentive to do so. Only after a full investigation is it possible to assess the needs of children in difficulties; the investigation should reveal ways in which the teacher and

the parents can be helped to meet the needs of the child, whether he remains in the ordinary school, or until he can be admitted to a special school. Some teachers are hostile to the idea of early referral for assessment, and do not ask for children to be examined. This may be because they have found in the past that no action follows referral, because there are no vacancies at special schools or because, with some reason, they doubt the reliability of tests for young children. As it becomes clear that the special education selected for children depends on all their circumstances and not simply on an I.Q. or attainment score, and that assessment is regularly reviewed, teachers should become more ready to refer children early. To enrich their educational background is likely to be the surest way to compensate for earlier disadvantages.

851. Five per cent of the children in the N.C.D.S. sample (Appendix 10, Section 5(a)), were receiving some form of special education and heads estimated that a further eight per cent were in need of special help, 13 per cent in all. The Department have estimated that approximately one child in every ten aged over seven is sufficiently retarded to need special education, though this number is significantly greater in some areas. The vast majority of these pupils will rightly remain in their ordinary primary schools. Whatever the precise figure may be, and it is one that is bound to depend to some extent on personal judgement, it is clear that the ordinary school must make special provision for a substantial number of children, unevenly distributed in different areas.

852. Slow learning children in the ordinary schools are best served by the approach which characterises the most progressive primary schools of today. Somewhat different provision may be required by those children who will always develop slowly and those who, with help, should be able to make relatively rapid strides. Remedial or "opportunity" classes are sometimes provided for slow learners and in other instances children join a remedial group only for a part of the school day. If they are good these classes or groups provide an effective education which enables the child to remain in the ordinary school. But to be educated in an unsatisfactory remedial class can be the worst arrangement of all for a slow learner. The danger of a remedial class or group becoming a place from which none escape and which perpetuates a sense of failure and hopelessness ought to be recognised. The aim should be to limit the stay of a retarded child in such a class and to regard it as a ladder back to the normal level. Even the child who will never catch up may profit from the stimulus of a change of teacher and companions and ought not to remain in the same "slow learning" class for more than two years, if it can be avoided. Opportunities should be made for children in slow learning classes to mix with other children in the school.

853. Slow learning children, many of whom are emotionally disturbed, may profit even more than other children from movement, drama, music, craft and painting. Though they should have opportunities for choice, these may need to be restricted to some extent and the pupils patiently and consistently guided by teachers. They need many opportunities for talk about people, places and things. Though slow children may need a more gradual and explicit introduction to the world about them than other children, their interest is unlikely to be held by materials designed for much younger children. They often spend hours at home before the television screen and some of the

elevision programmes they watch may provide good starting points for
iscussion as also will some of the school television broadcasts. It is prob-
ble that programmed learning and other mechanical aids could help these
hildren to overcome some of their specific learning difficulties.

he Teachers

54. It is implicit in all that we have said that the handicapped child in the
rdinary school needs an understanding and gifted teacher; children with
ertain disabilities need to be taught by specially trained teachers. Our main
oncern is with the ordinary teacher who in the ordinary school has to deal
vith handicapped children, most of them the slow learners who may be in
  special class, or in a C stream, or in ordinary classes. Many teachers have
leveloped a particular interest in handicapped children and become success-
ul practitioners without having had any special training, but we think that
nore preparation is needed. Every primary school teacher will have to help
low learners sooner or later and should have sufficient knowledge to be able
o recognise children who need special help and to provide it for the majority
»f them. If the problem is beyond his resources he should know clearly to
vhom to turn. There should be opportunities for teachers to discuss individual
hildren with school doctors or educational psychologists.

?55. Our evidence suggests that some colleges and departments of education
ncourage teachers to acquire a good deal of knowledge of the differing rates
»f children's intellectual, social and emotional growth, usually as part of the
ourse in child development. This might be extended possibly by the provision
of an optional course during the final year, so as to give young teachers more
ielp in dealing with the difficulties of slow learning and other handicapped
hildren in ordinary schools.

?56. A number of one year courses are available to serving teachers who
vish to teach handicapped children, and serving teachers should be encouraged
o attend them. Even so, only a minority will be affected. We are, therefore,
glad to learn of the increasing number of courses lasting one term, and of
short in-service courses dealing with the needs of handicapped children;
head teachers as well as teachers of handicapped children should be en-
ouraged to attend them.

?57. Many local authorities make use of part-time peripatetic teachers to
give help to individual or to groups of children who have difficulty in learning.
Peripatetic teachers are particularly useful when they act as a bridge between
the school psychological service and practising teachers. Some part-time
teachers, however, are not experienced or knowledgeable in the methods
needed to teach slow learning children. While the individual attention they
are able to give almost always produces some beneficial results they could
achieve more if they were given initial help and retraining. To these teachers
the school psychological service can provide valuable advice and support.
In some cases it has proved more successful for part-time teachers to take
the normal children, releasing the class teacher to help the handicapped.

858. It must be emphasised once again that any arrangement that is made for
the education of the handicapped child must be subject to constant review.
Whether a child is sent to a special school or to a special class of whatever
kind in an ordinary school the decision must not be regarded as final[3]. There

must be no vested interest in preserving an arrangement which is no longer necessary and teachers, parents and psychologists and doctors must all co-operate in ensuring this.

859. Though we have viewed the problem of the handicapped child only from the periphery and have concerned ourselves primarily with the problem of the handicapped child in the ordinary school, it is apparent that children with similar degrees of disability are provided for differently. In one area a child may be in a diagnostic unit attached to an ordinary primary school whereas a child with the same disability in another area may be excluded from school as unsuitable. Some special schools have children who in another authority's area might be in a special class in the ordinary school. Some special schools and training centres are sited close together and are even under the same direction. We recommend a study of the needs of the handicapped child, including the slow learner, and of the provision made for him, with an assessment of the methods and organisation in use, and the extension of carefully supervised experiments and trials of new systems. Account should be taken of the changing pattern of handicaps, the new optimism about the educability of children once thought "ineducable", the increasing ability of some schools to provide for children with very different handicaps and the increased number of special schools able to experiment in various ways.

Recommendations

860. (i) Early and accurate identification of handicapped children from birth onwards is essential. Teachers need to be alert to children showing difficulty and to arrange for them to have expert examination without delay.

(ii) Assessment of handicap should be a continuing process in which teachers, doctors, psychologists and parents must co-operate as a team.

(iii) A counselling service is needed for the parents of handicapped children.

(iv) A detailed enquiry should be made into the needs of handicapped children including slow learners and the provision made for them.

(v) The term "slow learner" should be substituted for "educationally sub-normal".

(vi) Teachers in training should be equipped to help handicapped children as far as they can.

REFERENCES

[1]Department of Education and Science: Circular 9/66, dated 31st March, 1966.
[2]Association for Special Education: Evidence to the Council.
[3]Ministry of Education: Circular 11/61 dated 3rd July, 1961.

CHAPTER 22

The Education of Gifted Children

861. We have not undertaken, or commissioned, any special study of the education of gifted children. This has been done by others[1] but we have formed some impressions, in the course of our general enquiries, which it may be useful to describe briefly at this stage in our Report.

862. While it is universally admitted that exceptionally gifted people do exist, both the identification of them as children and the treatment that such children need are a matter of some disagreement. There is first of all what may be described as an egalitarian suspicion of the whole concept of giftedness. This is no less strong for being a confused mixture of, among other things, dislike of privilege, doubts about intelligence tests and defensiveness about comprehensive schools. At the outset giftedness meets with an irrational obstacle. Even when this is overcome, there remains a real problem of identification. Giftedness is not a clearly defined category. It is characteristic of a small minority and the size of that minority is a matter of choice. It can be five per cent, one per cent or 0·1 per cent according to the degree of giftedness that is being postulated, but any definition in terms of I.Q. or, indeed, of any other attempts at measurement, is certain to be too inaccurate to be worth much. Giftedness varies in incidence in particular schools. In one independent preparatory school of which we have been told, as many as six per cent of the children are said to have an I.Q. of over 140, yet only 0·5 per cent of the whole population have, so far as measurement at that level is reliable, an I.Q. above that figure. In schools where the contributory population is less gifted, a child with an I.Q. of 125 (five per cent of the population) might be exceptional. Finally, there are forms of giftedness which are imperfectly revealed by intelligence tests; the tests devised to reveal creativity so far do not possess much validity.

863. In any ordinary group gifted children are bound to have particular needs. Their quality of thinking shows itself in the power to organise material and to perceive early the need for many different words to express shades of meaning, and the power to make analogies and use images. They seem to have the capacity of adapting methods and even of lowering sights in the pursuit of some idea. Self-criticism, beginning usually with criticism of others' work, often develops early, and it is often a problem to deal with the gifted child's dissatisfaction with his own capacity to carry out his ideas. The ability to see and to make a joke is an important if small indication of high ability. These children are often better adjusted and more cheerful than normal ones. Their distribution in the population makes it unlikely that chance will result in their meeting others of their kind. The attitudes of their contemporaries vary with the school and neighbourhood, but they may be unsympathetic. If their parents and teachers are not understanding, they may well find the world discouraging. Their interests may be branded as unhealthy or precocious, and their questions, which may seem tiresome and difficult to answer, resented and discouraged. These children may therefore

305

become frustrated and impatient. One must not restrict the search for the highly gifted to children who are doing well in school, to the "good" children; one must look at the "difficult" ones as well.

864. Some difficulties can arise from failure to recognise gifted children early enough. It is too often assumed that gifted children will be able to do the same things as the others but better. It is probably true that they could, but they often do not. They tend to be less conforming: their handwriting is often behind their mental development. They may suffer from boredom and set up a habit of day dreaming and escaping.

865. Even when the gifted child is recognised for what he is he may experience difficulties which will need very sympathetic handling by his teacher. He will often work and play with children older than himself, and be unable to match the physical skill or prowess of his companions, something which is highly prized by juniors. He may not feel at home with his contemporaries and yet he may not be accepted by those who are older.

866. The general conclusion to be drawn is sufficiently obvious. The needs of the highly gifted, however we define them, must be met. Their first and most important need is for perceptive parents. Though the genetic factors cannot be precisely determined they are unquestionably weighty. It is more likely than not that the parents of the exceptionally gifted will themselves be highly intelligent or will have highly intelligent immediate forbears. But this is far from being a certainty and, in any case, the parents may have had environments unfavourable to the development of their intelligence. We think that advice and help should be available to all parents who, for whatever reason find their children hard to understand or to handle and, what is perhaps more difficult, that they should be persuaded to make use of it. The proposals that we make elsewhere for the establishment of nursery groups ought to help in the early identification of the gifted. The child welfare service also has a part to play. But it is when the children arrive in the infant school and move forward year by year towards conceptual thinking that the gifted begin to stand out and their needs therefore become clamant.

867. A possible solution of the problem is to concentrate them in certain schools. The question as to whether special schools for the gifted are as necessary as those for the handicapped has frequently been asked and demands consideration. In our own country some of the independent school have been, in effect, something like this. In a stratified society such as our this is perhaps not surprising, but in the United States, in spite of its long tradition of equality and of a common programme, classes for the gifted have for some time now been making their appearance. There are undoubtedly particular artistic gifts which either show themselves or need to be developed at an early age. Music and ballet, for example, are difficult to provide at high enough level except in a school staffed and equipped for the purpose It must of course provide a balanced education as well.

868. Most of our members believe that schools for the gifted should be limited to those providing training in such arts as music and ballet. In the first place, it is not desirable that the gifted should think of themselves, more than is necessary, as a class apart, still less that they should have no experience of living and getting on with more ordinary children. Secondly, the majority of us believe that the English system of primary education at its best

is better adapted than any other we have seen to provide for the needs of the gifted individual, without segregating him. We are aware that the best is more often sought than attained, and that gifted children are often at present bored in the upper reaches of the junior school. As we have said in Chapter 10 there will be some exceptional children who, because of their all-round development, intellectual, emotional and physical, should transfer from one stage of education to another earlier than their contemporaries. These children need to be with older children who are close to them in intellectual level. Most of us are confident that it is possible to provide satisfactorily for the majority of gifted children in the kind of primary school described throughout the Report. In a school where children are not confined to their own classroom, teacher and equipment, exceptional children should be able to spend part of the day with others of like ability and have access to the school collection of books and materials.

869. To teach a brilliant child, to receive from him a thought that could not have come from the teacher himself, ought to be a source of delight, yet it may not be easy for all teachers to admit to themselves that a pupil is more intelligent than they are. A teacher who finds himself with such a child must offer his sympathy, encouragement and delight in good work and never take refuge in the dangerous half truth which many people are fond of uttering that "the clever child will look after himself". He needs just as much support from his teacher, though of a different kind, as the dull and backward. He needs to be helped to cultivate his gifts and to place them at the service of the community. He needs subject matter beyond the normal range. He needs a richer curriculum, not simply a quicker journey through the ordinary one. He needs to go deeper and wider and he must have and use the resources that this implies—a really good library, the p rogrammes of B.B.C. and I.T.V. and whatever contacts can be contrived with individuals outside the school who share his interests or can further them—the local museum curator, for instance, or any practitioner, architect, ornithologist, physicist, painter— who is willing to help him. The schools have a responsibility towards these children which must be taken seriously. We cannot afford to waste their talents.

870. In one area the problem is tackled by sending 60 highly intelligent children to a college of education where, on one day a week, they are given special lessons with an emphasis on concentrated work to which they are said to react with positive pleasure. In some areas, too, the needs of specially gifted young artists and musicians, are met by out of school activities at art centres, at colleges of music, in children's orchestras and at schools of ballet and drama. Some of these special attempts are conducted on a voluntary basis and without tests for admission. They have, nevertheless, attracted the gifted and provided opportunities for developing specific talents.

871. A growing amount of attention, especially in the United States, is now being paid to the education of the gifted child and there is now little likelihood of his problem being overlooked in good primary schools. Indeed, there is some danger that the results of research undertaken in other countries may be too readily applied to the condition of our own. We think there is much still to be discovered, and we welcome all attempts to improve the life and prospects of the gifted in the primary schools of this country. Long term studies should be mounted to elucidate further their needs and achievements.

Recommendation

872. Long term studies should be made on the needs and achievements of gifted children.

REFERENCE

[1]Terman, Lewis M., Oden, Melita H., and others, 'The Gifted Child Grows Up. Twenty-five Years Follow-up of a Superior Group', Stanford University Press, 1947, is perhaps the most famous of many studies in this field.

Part Six

The Adults in the Schools

Introduction: The Role of the Teacher

873. In every section of our Report we have been forced back to the teacher's role and its importance. A superficial conclusion from the National Survey might be that schools and teachers are less crucial to children's education than was formerly thought. Our inference is that teachers must enlarge their endeavours, and enlist parents' interest to a greater extent in their children's education. When children are materially, intellectually or emotionally deprived, teachers must strive to serve as substitutes for parents, to make children feel that they matter, however little they are able to respond, and however unattractive they may appear to be. Much is asked of teachers in these circumstances: to be patient when children develop slowly or regress, to provide experience rather than short cuts to it, to care tenderly for individual children and yet retain sufficient detachment to assess what they are achieving and how they are developing.

874. Our study of children's development has emphasised the importance of maturation to learning. The corollary is not to make the teacher's role passive but to underline the importance of diagnosing children's needs and potentialities. Teachers face the difficult task of assessing individual differences, appraising effort in relation to them and avoiding the twin pitfalls of demanding too much or expecting too little. Teachers must support apathetic children until they gain a momentum of their own. They must challenge and inspire children who are too readily satisfied and, on occasion, force independence on those children who wait to be prompted. They must sometimes recognise a child as being more gifted than they are themselves and be perceptive enough to provide through books or by invoking the help of another teacher the stimulus which they cannot themselves furnish.

875. Similarly, as we have surveyed the way children learn, the demands made on teachers have appeared frighteningly high. The primary school curriculum must touch on the scientific and mathematical knowledge on which the modern world depends and in which children are particularly interested. The teacher who used to give set lessons could manage on a little knowledge and use it over and over again. Far more knowledge, both about subject matter and about how children learn, is called for in teachers who have continually to exercise judgement, to "think on their feet", to keep in mind long term and short term objectives. They have to select an environment which will encourage curiosity, to focus attention on enquiries which will lead to useful discovery, to collaborate with children, to lead from behind. That instruction is going on throughout periods of free play has been well demonstrated by a recent enquiry into the role of the teacher in the infant and nursery school[1].

876. To a unique extent English teachers have the responsibility and the spur of freedom. They adapt schemes of work to the children for whom they are responsible and in an increasing number of schools they plan how the day will be spent. It has long been characteristic of the English educational system that the teacher has been expected to carry the burden of teaching by example as well as by precept. He is expected to be a good man and to influence children more by what he is than by what he knows or by his

311

methods. "First he wrought and afterwards he taught" is particularly relevant to the teacher of young children and extends to every facet of education. Teachers cannot escape the knowledge that children will catch values and attitudes far more from what teachers do than what they say. Unless they are courteous, they cannot expect courtesy from children: when teachers are eager to learn and turn readily to observation and to books, their pupils are likely to do the same. There is little hope that children will come to an appreciation of order and beauty either in nature or what is man-made, unless these qualities are enjoyed by their teachers and exemplified in the schools.

877. So broad and ill defined a role is almost bound to be at one and the same time satisfying and yet over demanding. The teacher's work can never be seen to be completed. Its outcome is usually undramatic, and success can never be finally or tidily assessed. The more sensitive and conscientious teachers are, the more they will realise that some failures are inevitable and the greater the danger that they will become so absorbed in their work with children that they will deny themselves an adult life of their own and thus dry up the sources of the help they give to children. The deference and respect that children show to good teachers may to some extent isolate them from other adults, especially since, with justification, every parent claims to know something of the upbringing of children and many fail to see the subtleties of the teacher's task.

878. There can be no doubt of the importance or the exacting nature of the teacher's task. On the teachers, on their skills and on their good will, far more than on organisation or on buildings, the future of education depends. Yet we write at a time when, despite all the efforts of the colleges of education, the primary schools are 20,000 teachers short of the number needed on present staffing standards.

CHAPTER 23

The Staffing of Schools

879. It is not our intention to write yet another report on how to get enough teachers, but our proposals for making better use of the teachers we have must be seen against the national situation. The first factor is necessarily the number of children to be taught. In pre-war years England had grown accustomed to the dwindling numbers entering her schools each year. In 1938 there were half a million children aged five years. After the war the position changed. In 1952 there were three quarters of a million and in the following year 829,000. In 1955 there were over a million more children in primary schools than there had been in 1946. This was the post-war "bulge", the result of marriages and child bearing postponed during the war. It was assumed that it would be a temporary emergency, and the fall in the number of births after 1948 seemed to confirm this. For a time there was a slight easing in the primary schools, and mounting pressure in secondary schools as the children born immediately after the war reached the age of 11 and an increasing number of older boys and girls decided to stay at school after 15. Then the birth rate rose again. Ten years ago, before the "bulge" was quite clear of the primary schools, the pressure on them began to return. It has grown steadily worse, and now affects both primary and secondary schools. These two forces, the biological facts of bigger age groups, which educational policy can only accept, and the social pressure for longer school life, which it would be wrong to oppose, have created a record demand for teachers.

880. Many more teachers are needed. Until recently new recruits for the profession have had to come from the small age groups of the pre-war and war years. In spite of this, spectacular progress has been made. In 1947 there were some 115,000 teachers taking primary classes; by 1958, the number was 138,000. There have been two great changes since the inter war period—far more careers were open to women so that more competition had to be faced; women teachers no longer had to resign on marriage so that, immediately at least, the supply of teachers was increased. Today over half the women teachers in maintained schools are married women. But the removal of the ban on marriage carried with it a middle distance threat of heavy wastage as wives became mothers and only a long term promise of a return to teaching once child bearing and child rearing was past. The exodus has been catastrophic; the return slow

Men and Women Teachers

881. Wastage is a particularly serious problem for primary schools because so many primary teachers are women. In primary schools as a whole women outnumber men by three to one; in the secondary schools, men outnumber women by four to three. In infant schools in 1965 there were only 97 brave men out of a total of 33,000 teachers. One in four teachers in junior mixed and infant schools and about two in five teachers in junior schools are men. The tradition that women are better suited than men to work with younger

children also affects the allocation of classes within schools. The National Survey shows that 90 per cent of teachers of first year juniors were women as compared with 55 per cent of the teachers of fourth year juniors. The N.U.T. Survey of the Primary Schools[2] showed that in 40 per cent of primary schools there were no men teachers at all. A further point should be made: in those areas where the proportion of women teachers is particularly high and where married women teachers tend not to live, the turnover of staff in primary schools is bound to be very considerable. Schools in these districts are staffed by a succession of young women who marry and leave after a few years service[3].

882. The proportion of men and women teachers in posts of responsibility is different. In 1965 there were approximately as many men as women primary school head teachers. Almost all infant school heads are women; men outnumber women heads in other primary schools. In schools included in the National Survey more than half the men teachers, but less than a quarter of the women teachers were heads, deputies or graded post holders.

Full-Time and Part-Time Teachers

883. It follows from the preponderance of women teachers in the primary schools that these schools have in the long run more to gain than the secondary schools from the return of married women teachers, and, what is part of the same situation, more need to employ part-time teachers. In the twelve months up to February 1966, the numbers of qualified married women teachers returning to teach full-time was about 3,400, approximately the same number as in the previous 12 months. There was, however, a net increase of nearly 5,000 part-time teachers in the same period. Local education authorities have long been readier to employ these teachers in secondary schools, because they fitted into the structure of specialist teaching, particularly in shortage subjects. In 1962 two thirds of the primary schools still had none, and almost another 30 per cent had only one or two part-time teachers. The average primary school employed only 0·9 of a part-time teacher for one day a week[4]. By February 1966, 17,373 teachers were employed part-time in primary schools (the full-time equivalent of 8,189 teachers), compared with 18,330 in secondary schools (the full-time equivalent of 9,032). Ninety four education authorities (out of a total of 162) had reached the target of five per cent set by the Departmental Circular (6/65) issued in May 1965 while in one in ten education authorities ten per cent of the teachers were employed part-time. The pattern is still too uneven; 14 education authorities still employ less than three per cent. Some variation may be explained by the absence of married women teachers in many areas: elsewhere it is due to the policy of the education authority. The employment of married women teachers, both full-time and part-time can bring strength to the schools. They are to be welcomed, and they will form part of the permanent pattern. We have suggested in Chapter 5 that all authorities should be encouraged to identify and employ "immobile" married women teachers and that, if necessary, the Department should refine the quota system to make their employment universal.

Unqualified Teachers

884. Though regulations have laid down that only qualified teachers should be employed on a permanent regular basis, there has never been a time when

all primary school teachers have been qualified. The employment of unqualified teachers is to be deplored, and should be discontinued as soon as possible. Nevertheless it has helped to prevent a growth in the number of oversize classes and the pupil-teacher ratio. Unqualified occasional teachers may be employed on a daily basis to meet a particular emergency. Many authorities are in a permanent state of emergency and thankful to recruit anyone who can keep a class occupied. Those eligible for admission to a college of education may become temporary teachers and it has been common practice for students waiting to go to college to become temporary teachers. In areas which are well staffed they are supernumerary. They can then be given opportunities to observe work at various stages in the school and can gradually take some responsibility. In other districts boys and girls straight from the sixth form are put in charge of a class.

885. The N.U.T. Survey of 1962[5] found that only six per cent of teachers in primary schools were unqualified. There seems little doubt that this figure has now risen substantially. An analysis of teacher supply[6] showed an increase in primary schools from 1964 to 1965 of 665 temporary teachers and 284 occasional teachers. The proportion of unqualified teachers in infant schools is substantially greater than in junior and junior mixed and infant schools. In 1965, in the Christmas term when staffing is usually at its best, the percentage of unqualified teachers had risen to 35 in two authorities and was well above 20 in three other areas.

Ratio of Teachers to Pupils

886. The staffing of a school can be expressed in two ways—by class size or by number of pupils per teacher. Both are shown in Tables 18 and 19. These figures are a measure of the efficiency of national policy and of the severity of the teacher's task. They are encouraging in view of the difficulties, daunting when one remembers how the educational service has had to struggle in order to stand still, or make relatively slight gains.

887. To those teachers who have to face oversized classes the situation must seem intolerable. It is also depressing when a rehousing programme reduces numbers, so that a hard pressed authority has to take away staff, and the equipment allowance falls. The effect of shortages of staff, coupled with the growth of the secondary schools and their staff, have reinforced a suspicion that the dice are unfairly loaded against the primary schools. The attempt to divert teachers from the primary schools to the secondary schools in the 1950s as the "children of the bulge" grew older was not matched by equal endeavour to get them back again when the next wave hit the primary schools. Training colleges were asked to concentrate mainly on preparing students for primary schools, but this change could only take effect after a delay of three years as the length of the course was raised at the same time. Primary school teachers had to pay heavily for this reform. Special campaigns by the Department and local authorities are being aimed at bringing back married women teachers, recruiting graduates after short courses and employing more part-time teachers. The emphasis is on the needs of the primary schools particularly those for infants.

Distribution of Teachers

888. We need to know not only how many teachers there are, but where they are in order to appreciate the situation in the schools. A crude, but reasonably reliable, way to show this is to divide England into counties and county boroughs. A few of the counties are almost exclusively rural; most are made up of a mixture of villages, small and middle size towns and the commuter belts which surround the great cities. There are rather more than twice as many children in the counties as in the county boroughs. Tables 20, 21 and 22 set out the position.*

*The Isles of Scilly, for obvious reasons, had a more generous staffing ratio. They are excluded from Tables 20, 21, 22.

Table 18 Primary School Staffing, 1947–1965: England

Year (January)	(1) No. of pupils on roll (thousands)	(2) No. of teachers (including f.t. equiv of p.t. and unqualified teachers) (thousands)	(3) Pupil-teacher ratio	(4) Proportion of pupils in oversize classes (over 40) (percentage)
1947	3,500	116	30·2	not available
1953	4,146	130	31·9	37·8
1956	4,294	139	30·9	not available
1958	4,214	138	30·5	not available
1959	4,025	135	29·8	not available
1960	3,925	134	29·4	21·4
1961	3,866	133	29·0	20·0
1962	3,865	134	28·8	19·2
1963	3,881	134	29·0	19·8
1964	3,938	136	29·0	18·4
1965	4,004	140	28·6	17·0

Source: Statistics Branch, Department of Education and Science.

Table 19 Number of Classes of Different Sizes in Primary Schools, 1947–65: England

Size of class	No. and % of classes						No. and % of Pupils 1965	
	1947		1953		1965			
	No.	%	No.	%	No.	%	No.	%
Under 20	10,681	11	7,707	7	9,584	8	156,866	4
21—30	20,645	21	21,865	19	29,653	24	783,746	20
31—40	35,897	36	45,806	40	66,419	55	2,382,290	59
Over 40	31,421	31	39,825	34	15,791	13	681,032	17
TOTAL	98,644		115,203		121,447		4,003,934	

Source: Ministry of Education, Annual Report, 1947. Table 10.
Ministry of Education, Annual Report, 1953. Table 10.
'Statistics of Education', 1965. Part One. Tables 20 and 21, and Statistics Branch, Department of Education and Science.

Table 20 Numbers of Primary Pupils Per Full-Time Teacher, January, 1965: England

Pupil-Teacher Ratios	No. of Counties	No. of County Boroughs
21·1—25	2	—
25·1—30	40	16
30·1—35	7	65
35·1—40	—	1

Table 21 Numbers of Primary Pupils Per Full-Time Teacher (*Total Full Time and Full-Time Equivalent of Part-Time*), January, 1965: England

Pupil-Teacher Ratios	No. of Counties	No. of County Boroughs
20·1—25	4	—
25·1—30	43	57
30·1—35	2	25
35·1—40	—	—

Table 22 Average Sizes of Class, January, 1965: England

No. of Pupils	Counties	County Boroughs
20·1—25	1	—
25·1—30	16	—
30·1—35	30	57
35·1—40	2	25

*Source: Statistics Branch, Department of Education and Science. They make it clear that big classes and a widespread resort to part-time teachers are much more characteristic of the county boroughs. The full range of pupil-teacher ratios is from 23·2:1 in the best staffed county to 32·3:1 in the worst county borough (Table 21). This means that a primary school of 250 children might have ten teachers on the first ratio but only seven on the second. But, of course, an authority's staffing ratio as set out here is the average for all its pupils. This average conceals wide variations from school to school just as the national figures conceal the variations between authorities and it does not show the distribution of unqualified teachers.

889. The variations in staffing ratio would have been much greater still if there were not a quota system. The system works by holding steady, rather than depressing, the standards of the best-off authorities. Although it can give no guarantee that deprived authorities will be able to fill their quotas it gives them a better chance to do so by preventing the more popular areas exploiting their natural advantages. Since 1956 the gap in quota standards between the worst and the best placed authorities has at least halved and an increasing majority are now close to the mean.

Ancillary Helpers

890. The continuous shortage of teachers and the increasing range of their duties have made the Department and the local education authorities anxious to use their services more efficiently. No longer are teachers expected to do everything that needs doing in school except clean it. School dinners have brought with them not only cooks but, in the end, "dinner helpers". Head

teachers have some secretarial help. Other assistants are being appointed to relieve class teachers of some of the burden involved in looking after very young children. This process has gone a long way; but not, in our judgement, far enough. The ancillary services that exist are not yet provided everywhere, and they are not comprehensive enough.

891. In 1962 the N.U.T.[7] reported that 87 per cent of primary schools had school meals helpers, and 68 per cent secretaries, but only 22 per cent had the help of welfare assistants to relieve teachers in caring for some of the needs of young children. A report of the Association of Education Committees[8] showed that in 1965 all but seven counties and seven county boroughs provide school secretarial assistance for primary schools and that all but three local authorities employ meal supervisors. It also recorded a very considerable increase in the number of welfare assistants, though it has to be remembered that the figures in the Table below refer to authorities, not schools as in the N.U.T. Survey, and say nothing about the scale of provision.

*Table 23 Ancillary Help Employed in Primary Schools, 1965. (England and Wales)**

Type of School	No. of Authorities Providing Welfare Assistants to Work:		Total
	In Classrooms	Only Outside Classrooms	
Nursery	115 (a)	5	120
Infants	58 (b)	50	108
Junior	17 (c)	13	30

*This report was based on returns by 156 authorities in England and Wales: not all returns were complete.

Notes: (a) including 14 who describe duties as 'quasi educational',
         (b) including 8 'quasi educational',
         (c) including 3 'quasi educational'.

Source: 'Employment of Ancillary Helpers', Section VI, Paragraph 1. Report of Association of Education Committees, 1966.

892. One hundred authorities employ trained nursery assistants in nursery schools, 21 authorities employ these assistants in infant schools and one authority made use of nursery assistants in junior schools. In two authorities trained nursery assistants are employed but they are not allowed to work inside the classroom. Information received recently from H.M. Inspectorate suggests that the number of authorities employing nursery assistants in primary schools is increasing rapidly.

893. There is little logical pattern to be seen in the employment of unqualified teachers and of ancillary helpers other than secretaries and meals' assistants. It is clear that some authorities prefer to allow class size to grow beyond the statutory maximum, while others keep class sizes down by appointing unqualified teachers. There appears to be little connection between the size of the classes, the number of unqualified teachers and the readiness of the authorities to make use of ancillary helpers for quasi-educational functions. Certainly some authorities where classes are very large do not employ ancillary helpers who can work with teachers within the classroom.

It seems then that some authorities are hesitating to employ helpers of this kind because of their cost, because they are uncertain how to use them or because they share the anxiety of some teachers about "dilution" or fear the consequences of forcing their employment on a reluctant profession.

The Future

894. There are brighter prospects ahead, though teachers might say "I've heard that one before". Certainly as far as we can tell there will be more teachers. The problem is how they will be divided between the primary and the secondary schools. The Government is committed to implementing the long promised reform of raising the minimum school leaving age in 1970/71. This is estimated to increase secondary schools rolls by 350,000 pupils who will need teachers. The National Advisory Council on the Training and Supply of Teachers in their Ninth Report[9] anticipated that there would be a transfer of 10,000 teachers from primary to secondary. We understand that they were not advocating this step, but indicating only what seemed likely to happen if matters were left to take their own course. It seems to us that this would be a foolish way of staffing the increase from the point of view of the secondary schools. The older pupils whom this reform will retain in the secondary schools need, as the Council's last report indicated, work of a different kind from that which they are now getting, and this "requires that many of the teachers themselves should have experience of the industrial situation . . . men and women recruited to teaching after experience of other kinds of work may have a special part to play"[10]. This means new blood, not a blood transfusion. To transfer teachers for the raising of the school leaving age would be disastrous for the primary schools. It must not be allowed to happen.

895. It is sometimes maintained that there is a "gravitational pull" towards the teaching of older children, and there is some recent evidence which appears to show this. The colleges of education are the main providers of primary school teachers, but more than the expected number of the students who took junior-secondary course have gone to work in secondary schools. It is reasonable to ask why this has happened. Some of the reasons may be deep seated and beyond administrative action to repair. There may be some, however, which are remediable. How do the career prospects of men and women going into primary and secondary schools compare? How does a student who has had teaching practice in both kinds of school weigh the large classes and absence of free periods which confront the primary school teacher against the often more serious disciplinary problems in secondary schools? How far, in fact, would the consequences of the reforms we suggest, more favourable staffing ratios and a fuller provision of ancillary helpers, correct what seems to be a "gravitational pull"? These questions deserve careful and immediate study.

896. The greatest shortage in the primary schools is of infant teachers. The cause is clear, but the remedy elusive. They have the most severe wastage rate because most of them are young women who tend to marry early and leave the profession. The National Survey (Appendix 5, paragraph 11) showed that only 34 per cent of the teachers who had been in the infant schools between September 1961 and June 1964 were in post at the beginning of the period. The core of stable teachers was smaller and newcomers stayed

less long. The seemingly hopeless prospect of retaining infant teachers may be one reason why there are local education authorities which show less persistence in seeking them out when there are equal shortages in other parts of the educational system. If so, it is not a good reason.

Table 24 Primary School Staffing: England

Year (January)	(1) No. of pupils on roll (thousands)	(2) No. of qualified teachers (incl. f.t. equiv. of p.t. teachers) (thousands)	(3) Pupil: qualified teacher ratio	(4) Deficiency or surplus of qualified teachers for reducing classes to 40 (i) and 30 (ii) if all objectives stated in Report are met** Thousands	(5) Deficiency or surplus of teachers for reducing classes to 40 (i) and 30 (ii) if objectives for E.P.As. met but no expansion of nursery education elsewhere Thousands***
1966	4103·6	135·8	30·0	—20·2 (i)	—20·2 (i)
1967	4239·6	140·7	29·9	—20·5 (i)	—20·5 (i)
1968	4382·4	147·3	29·5	—21·0 (i)	—21·0 (i)
1969	4515·7	154·8	28·9	—20·4 (i)	—20·4 (i)
1970	4646·3	162·4	28·4	—19·5 (i)	—19·5 (i)
1971	4781·9	170·4*	27·9	—18·3 (i)	—18·3 (i)
1972	4932·1	177·9	27·5	—18·3 (i)	—18·3 (i)
1973	5005·3	185·1	26·8	—13·9 (i)	—13·9 (i)
1974	5084·6	192·5	26·2	— 9·5 (i)	— 9·5 (i)
1975	5175·1	199·9	25·7	— 5·6 (i)	— 5·6 (i)
1976	5248·0	207·3	25·1	— 0·9 (i)	— 0·9 (i)
1977	5313·2	213·4	24·7	+ 2·7 (i) ⎫ —56·3 (ii) ⎭	+ 2·7 (i) ⎫ —57·7 (ii) ⎭
1978	5372·9	219·0	24·3	—53·7 (ii)	—55·1 (ii)
1979	5428·5	226·9	23·7	—48·7 (ii)	—50·1 (ii)

*Assumes no transfer of teachers from primary to secondary schools for raising of the school leaving age.

**Includes extra teachers for E.P.As. (see Chapter 5). Assumes no diversion for expansion of nurseries (except for E.P.As.) (see Chapter 9) but that single date of entry to school introduced in 1977.

***Assumes no expansion of nursery provision other than in E.P.As. and no single date of entry.

897. The situation calls for measures which have to be taken from the centre. We make three recommendations:

(i) those who are concerned with appointing teachers should do their utmost to persuade all those who have been trained for primary work not to transfer to secondary schools;

(ii) a larger number of training courses for teachers of children from three to nine should be provided, and students who would otherwise train for work with older children persuaded into them; colleges of education should emphasise work with young children more heavily in infant-junior and junior-secondary courses. In-service training for married women returners should stress work with young children;

(iii) if necessary, a selective quota system should be considered to give teeth to this persuasion.

On the assumptions that no transfer of primary teachers to secondary schools takes place, and that the primary schools receive the full number of teachers which the colleges of education are planning to train for primary work, the earliest date by which all classes over 40 could be abolished would be 1976*. Beyond then classes can be further reduced. The pupil-teacher ratio in primary schools would have to be reduced from 30:1 today to 25:1 in 1976. The steps by which this would be brought about are shown in Table 24.

Primary and Secondary School Staffing

898. Finally, continuing study should be undertaken of the right proportion of teachers to pupils of different ages, given modern equipment and the employment of ancillary staff. The Consultative Committee of 1931 rejected the view that primary school classes should be larger than those for children over 11. In 1944 the regulation maximum size of class was reduced from 50 to 40 for primary schools. But, at the same time, classes in all types of secondary schools were limited to 30, a size which had previously applied only to grammar schools. Primary school children continued to be at a disadvantage. Two of the Joint Four Associations have told us that they seen no reason why children below 11 should be in larger classes than children up to the age of 13. Witnesses from all types of secondary schools said that primary classes should range in size from 25 to 30. Differences between pupil-teacher ratios for primary school age children and secondary pupils up to the age of 15 are similar to those between average class sizes (28·4 for primary schools and 20·8 for secondary school pupils up to 15). But to isolate the secondary school ratio for pupils up to 15 does not give the whole picture. These pupils get some advantage from the far more favourable ratios for pupils of 15 to 18. In consequence, most secondary school teachers have non-teaching periods, whatever the age of the classes they teach. Unlike secondary teachers, primary teachers spend the whole day with their class.

899. The primary schools have a strong case for smaller classes. The younger the children, the less they can benefit from large group instruction or use mechanical devices. They need help from a teacher, and for much of the time they need individual help. Although, as a Council, we have no knowledge of secondary schools, it seems obvious that, as their size increases and the number of pupils following advanced courses (whether at 16 or later) grows, economies in staffing become possible. Nevertheless, secondary schools have big problems to face in the next decade. Reorganisation into comprehensive schools will increase the number of schools whose pupils are scattered among several buildings; the majority of schools will be learning how to meet, in one school, the needs of pupils of all levels of ability; they also have to work out suitable courses up to the age of 16 for all boys and girls, including those where special problems were highlighted by our immediate predecessors on the Central Advisory Council. The available teachers have to be shared between the primary and secondary schools. In these circumstances

---

*As Table 24 shows, if preference were not given to educational priority areas (see Chapter 5) oversized classes would be abolished by 1974.

we do not think it practicable to suggest the exact number to which primary school classes should be reduced during the next decade and even beyond. We believe, nevertheless, that, as a general rule the maximum size of primary classes should be the same as that in the first two or three years of the secondary school. This principle should be taken into account as teachers are placed in post in preparation for the raising of the school leaving age. It will mean that the size of secondary school classes will have to increase slightly, though temporarily, in order to prevent primary school children being at a continuing disadvantage. Adjustments should be made to the Regulations for maximum class sizes to allow for the flexibility that we suggest.

900. The Secretary of State has declared his sympathy with an ultimate objective for a class size of "say 30/30" for primary and secondary schools. We have studied the ways in which teachers and ancillary helpers are and should be used in the primary school and have come to the conclusion that a class teacher cannot satisfactorily work with more than 30 to 35 children. We suggest that such studies should continue to be made in the future: studies are also needed of secondary school staffing.

901. It is clear that "education" is becoming easily the biggest employer of the most educated citizens. The National Advisory Council for the Supply and Training of Teachers estimated that half the products of the higher education would be absorbed in the educational system[11]. When we add our own demands in the Report to the number of teachers required to meet the lengthening of secondary school life and the expansion of the universities, we cannot make the sum any less. It is then imperative that the manpower employed in the teaching profession should be used as economically and productively as possible. The only way to ensure this is by detailed and patient study.

Recommendations

902. The situation calls for measures which have to be taken from the centre. We make five recommendations:

(i) those who are concerned with appointing teachers should do their utmost to persuade all those who have been trained for primary work not to transfer to secondary schools;

(ii) a larger number of training courses for teachers of children from three to nine should be provided, and students who would otherwise train for work with older children persuaded into them; colleges of education should emphasise work with young children more heavily in infant-junior and junior-secondary courses. In-service training for married women returners should stress work with young children;

(iii) if this persuasion is not sufficiently effective, it may be necessary to rely on a selective quota system;

(vi) continuing study should be undertaken of the right proportion of teachers to pupils of different ages;

(v) as a general rule, the maximum size of primary classes should be the same as that in the first two or three years of the secondary school; this principle should be taken into account as teachers are recruited for the raising of the school leaving age.

REFERENCES

[1]Gardner, D. E. M. and Cass, J. M. 'The Role of the Teacher in the Infant School'. Pergamon. 1965.

[2]'The State of Our Schools'. A Report of the findings of the National Survey of Schools. 1962. N.U.T. Part I, paragraph 9.

[3]Taylor, G. 'Analysis of Teacher Supply'. Education, 17th December, 1965. (Refers to both primary and secondary schools in England and Wales).

[4]See[2] above. Part I, paragraphs 10 and 11.

[5]See[2] above. Part I, paragraph 12.

[6]See[3] above.

[7]See[2] above. Part I, Table 10.

[8]'Employment of Ancillary Helpers', Report prepared by the Association of Education Committees to the Joint Working Party of Representatives of Local Education Authorities and of Education Committees, with the Inner London Education Authority, and of the Teachers' Association, 1966. Sections I and IV.

[9]'The Demand for and Supply of Teachers 1963–1986'. Ninth Report of the National Advisory Council on the Training and Supply of Teachers. H.M.S.O., 1965, paragraph 197.

[10]'Half Our Future', H.M.S.O., 1963, paragraphs 295–6.

[11]See[9] above, paragraph 20.

CHAPTER 24

The Deployment of Staff

The Proportion of Men and Women Teachers in Primary Schools

903. The last chapter discussed the sources of supply of teachers and how schools are staffed. We now consider how they can be deployed to the best effect in the primary schools. More men are now teaching young children in England than was formerly the case*, and the number of men head teachers in primary schools is rising. The interest shown by men in the teaching of young children is also demonstrated by their attendance at courses on child development and work in infant schools. There are both educational and practical grounds for urging that as far as possible there should be men teachers in all primary schools. Some young children, particularly boys, may respond better to teaching from a man than from a woman, and most schools and communities benefit from the contributions of both men and women teachers. It is also clear that a staff on which there are men teachers is likely to be more stable than a staff made up exclusively of women.

904. The effect of the planned increase in the number of men students in colleges of education would be to increase to 52 per cent the proportion of men teachers in junior schools by 1980. At present, colleges find it difficult to reach the present targets. We believe that this proportion of men teachers could be effectively employed in primary schools, assuming present age ranges. But we see no reason why men should not teach in first schools, particularly if our recommendation is accepted and children remain there until eight. Present failures in continuity might become more serious if schools for children up to eight were staffed entirely by women, and if in middle schools more than half the staff were men. In any case it is sensible for as many primary teachers as possible to have first-hand experience of the education of the youngest children. Many slow children in junior schools need the methods commonly used in infant schools. We hope that the plans to increase the number of men admitted to training for primary education will be successful and will not lead to a lowering of entry standards. We also suggest that men should be encouraged to teach in first schools.

905. It has often been the practice for the head and deputy head teacher to be of opposite sex, particularly in the case of junior with infant schools. This is desirable, but may no longer be practicable as a general rule because of the small number of women who will accept promotion. This makes it even more necessary that men should have direct experience of work with young children. At the least, in-service training for work with infants should be provided for men appointed to combined schools. Yet we hope that authorities will employ enough women heads and deputies for the characteristic contribution of women to primary education to be maintained. The National Survey shows that it is in danger of being lost (Appendix 5, Table 18).

*The proportion of men assistants at the primary stage in England is higher than in countries abroad we visited.

324

The Criteria for Staffing Schools

906. We have had some difficulty in discovering precisely how the present body of primary school teachers is deployed, partly because of the different ways in which staffing establishments are fixed for individual schools. Some authorities make their first object the elimination of oversize classes. Others staff their school according to a pupil-teacher ratio, which may or may not include the head teacher. The Department of Education and Science speaks with two voices; its statutory regulations refer to class sizes, but its quota system is based on pupil teacher-ratios.

907. We agree with the National Advisory Council for the Supply and Training of Teachers[1] that the number of oversized classes in a school does not adequately describe its staffing, and that the number of oversized classes in the country as a whole is an equally misleading indication of the national situation. A class of 15 boys and girls of varying ages may be as exacting to teach as 35 children of the same age. The reason one class is oversize may be the head teacher's decision to make another small because he has a group of very backward children or a weak teacher. In other schools, classes may be large because there are too few rooms or because some small rooms can only accommodate 20 to 24 children. If the trouble is caused by lack of sufficient rooms, an additional teacher is sometimes provided who can help the class teachers by taking small groups whether in the classroom or perhaps the staff room, or relieve his colleagues by making occasional free periods available. A few head teachers prefer to keep one teacher free of responsibility for a class even when they have accommodation enough to reduce the size of classes. The relief which a head teacher himself can give to class teachers depends on the size of the school and the number of classes which have to share his help. For all these reasons class size is an inadequate index, though an important matter.

908. It is doubtful if the pupil-teacher ratio is by itself a satisfactory clue to the staffing of schools. Authorities differ about the size of school in which they expect the head teacher to take charge of a class, and some head teachers who are without this responsibility nevertheless teach for a substantial part of the week. The most useful way of using a staffing ratio for comparative purposes seems to be to classify schools by size and within each classification to include the head teacher in the ratio. It is, of course, essential, if valid comparisons are to be made, that all authorities should follow the same convention which they do not do at present. The present situation is like recording temperatures sometimes in Centigrade and sometimes in Fahrenheit without making it clear which is being used. It is important that the inclusion of the head teacher in a pupil-teacher ratio is not used to conceal a deterioration in ratios and is not thought by teachers to be a device for this purpose.

909. To parents and teachers it is class size that matters. Even though there is less class teaching, the class will continue to be important as the group of children for whose welfare a teacher is responsible. A minimum average pupil teacher staffing ratio and the elimination of oversized classes should become a two fold objective for local education authorities and the subject of Department of Education and Science Regulations. Returns from local education authorities and the Department's statistics should continue to record both these aspects of staffing.

910. The quota already makes some allowance for authorities who have large numbers of immigrant children, and, as we have suggested in Chapter 5, it might make similar provision where there are an unusually large number of children with a poor social background. Only the local education authority knows enough about individual schools to fix appropriate staffing establishments. In doing this the following factors might constitute a claim for generous treatment:—

(a) a large number of retarded children, immigrants, or children from poor home backgrounds;

(b) exceptional inexperience or weakness among several members of the staff;

(c) experimental work requiring temporary additions to the staff;

(d) unusual difficulties in accommodation;

(e) very large or very small schools.

911. The size of schools is the most important single cause of differences in pupil-teacher ratios from authority to authority and from school to school. That is why all authorities would do well to relate their staffing ratios to the size of schools, and permit individual modifications. Very large schools as well as small schools need special consideration in staffing. In the former, the head teacher has too many classes under him to be able to give much time to anyone; in the latter, he himself has full-time duties as a class teacher. There are a number of ways in which small schools can be more economically staffed than they often are at present without sacrificing their efficiency. We suggest that where it is essential to keep them open for social or geographical reasons:

(a) part-time teachers might in some instances replace full-time teachers;

(b) a single full-time teacher with an ancillary helper might replace two teachers in very small schools where the reason for the second teacher has been to ensure that children are not left without adult supervision in an emergency;

(c) a group of small rural schools might be given the support of advisory teachers;

(d) children up to the age of eight or nine might be taught in their own village in detached classes of nearby primary schools.

Some of the arrangements we suggest are already common practice.

The Recruitment and Use of Part-Time Teachers

912. It is good that the Burnham Committee have decided to recommend the adoption of uniform arrangements for assessing part-time teachers' pay. We are also glad to know that a Working Party set up by the Secretary of State have formulated proposals for the admission of part-time teachers to a superannuation scheme. Enquiry is also continuing into the best ways of enabling married women teachers who are out of service to keep in touch with their profession and to return at the earliest possible moment. A national register of such teachers, if practicable, would be of great value in forecasting the supply of teachers and in planning their distribution. Local registers, with arrangements for interchange of information, would probably be a more effective way of keeping these teachers in touch with teaching and with the

local education authorities to whom they will eventually return. It would be helpful if all authorities would follow the example of those who have already compiled local registers of this kind. "Return to Teaching Clubs" have been organised in one authority in five education centres. Talks are given by practising teachers and school visits arranged. These are attended by married women out of service, so that they can keep in touch with the schools.

913. The Department of Education have published information about ways which have proved successful in recruiting part-time teachers and helping them to pick up the threads after a period of absence from the profession (see Chapter 25). We are in sympathy with these suggestions and add only the following points:—

(a) authorities ought to see that part-time teachers are reasonably distributed among their schools. There are still a few schools in residential areas with a low turnover of staff where the appointment of part-time teachers would bring more variety of experience and background. Schools in other more difficult areas would benefit from the experienced full-time teachers who would be released;

(b) two or more teachers need to be employed for rather longer in total than one full-time teacher if they are to share a class efficiently. A class taught by one teacher in the morning and another in the afternoon suffers if there is no opportunity for discussion between the two teachers. This arrangement is also unsatisfactory when formal work in English and arithmetic in the morning is divorced from creative work in the afternoon. At least one authority permits joint responsibility for a class only when the two teachers spend some time together in school. A highly successful arrangement of which we have heard is a class shared by two teachers, one of whom teaches for four days, the other three days each week; for part of the week both teachers are present, and some help can be given in other classes;

(c) part-time teachers who can work in the same classroom as another member of the staff are likely to learn the school's ways easily and naturally. One useful method of employing two part-time members of staff as class teachers is to make one full-time and two part-time teachers jointly responsible for two classes. At the least, teachers who give one session a day should be encouraged to remain in school during the lunch hour. This would allow them to consult the head and other teachers in addition to their partner in the class.

914. Apart from class teaching, part-time teachers are principally used for:—

(a) "specialist" subjects such as music, physical education and French—sometimes the teacher may be in full-time service with the authority;

(b) remedial work in basic subjects;

(c) relieving head teachers and deputy heads from some teaching;

(d) relieving class teachers by withdrawing groups or sharing the work within the classroom;

(e) providing sets, smaller than the normal class, for certain subjects of the curriculum;

(f) supporting young teachers who have large classes.

915. Part-time help for such subjects as music, physical education and French is particularly useful to small schools. We have referred earlier to the value of part-time teachers in rural schools. Most part-time teachers employed in remedial work need guidance from a remedial centre or an educational psychologist. It is often best for the full-time class teacher to take the slower children, whose work should arise naturally from their life in the classroom, while the part-time teacher concerns herself with the others. Our evidence suggests that head teachers are often reluctant to assign classes or groups of able children to part-time teachers. Yet these may be the very children who find it easy to adjust to more than one teacher and may in fact be stimulated by change.

916. The success of part-time help for a teaching head is often to be explained by the head's readiness to brief the part-time teacher. In large schools, part-time help for deputy heads would enable them to assist the head teacher in looking after young teachers, probationers and students.

917. Ideally, we should like to see all classes of younger children in charge of a full-time teacher with additional part-time or ancillary help. Yet in the present staffing situation, the choice may be between two qualified part-time teachers or one unqualified teacher. Co-operation between the part-time teachers is vital; five year olds are particularly likely to be confused by conflicting standards or methods.

Various Kinds of Ancillary Help and Helpers

918. We have given most serious thought to the amount and kind of help that can be given in schools by those who are not qualified teachers. The teachers' associations are unanimous in asking for increased help from secretaries and school meals supervisors, and from welfare assistants as long as they do not work in the classroom. The N.U.T. Report of 1962[2] suggested that most heads were satisfied with the moderate amount of help that they had got. Yet this report included, in a special study of the replies to some general questions, the comment that "innumerable teachers mentioned what a boon it would be to have helpers, auxiliaries, welfare assistants and the like". This is much the impression that we have from witnesses and from our visits to schools up and down the country. In answer to our questionnaire to 3,000 teachers, 49 per cent of heads and 37 per cent of assistant teachers thought there was a place for non-qualified assistant helpers inside the classroom. (Appendix 1, Table E.31). We are naturally aware that some teachers are anxious, as are the teachers' associations, in case the profession should be diluted by allowing ancillaries* to operate within the classroom. We sympathise with those who fear that the informal relationships and teaching, which make many infant schools the good places they are, might come to be regarded as the sphere of the ancillary, and the teacher be confined to straight instruction. Junior schools too need to be preserved from such division

919. Nobody, however, feels this objection to secretaries, meals assistant or welfare assistants. They have been universally welcomed, but more profitable use might be made of them. In some smaller schools the duties of meals

---

*Ancillaries and ancillary staff are terms used henceforward for all paid workers who are not qualified teachers, and who assist in the school in any capacity.

assistant, secretary and welfare assistant (or any two of these) might be combined and the assistant play an even fuller part in the life of the school. This arrangement is already working in some areas, but in others, although teachers have asked for it, nothing has happened because of difficulties over the varying rates of pay. If some at least of the meals assistants have duties which employ them in the school at other times, attitudes and discipline at dinner are more likely to conform with what is expected during the rest of the day.

920. Much of a school secretary's job is confidential, though a good deal is necessarily routine clerical work. Given more time, she could help the staff by ordering books and equipment, looking after stock, and cataloguing library books. Welfare assistants already do many useful services for teachers; they give invaluable help with hygiene and first aid, look after sick children in school, and escort them home or to clinics. Rather less commonly they make and mend apparatus and repair books. There is no reason why they should not prepare the materials for art and craft, look after plants and animals, help with displays and exhibitions, and record school broadcasts on tape so that they are available when needed. It is perhaps unrealistic to hope that these "all rounders" could, except in exceptional cases, care for mechanical and musical equipment. But as the use of this equipment develops, authorities might appoint a technician to service the mechanical aids in a group of schools.

921. Most of this help is given outside the classroom, but there are many reasons why ancillaries should work in any part of the school where their help is needed. A large number of children are being taught by unqualified teachers, who have no training and who only get guidance in the little time the head teacher has to spare. In our visits, we were occasionally told of the excellent work of unqualified teachers; but we often heard how fortunate a school was in its "outstanding" welfare assistant and how many sided were her gifts. We believe more ancillaries of this quality can be recruited if it is known that they will work in close association with teachers and be trained for the job. We discuss their training in Chapter 26. As the whole school building becomes more and more a workshop for the children, the distinction between help inside and outside the classroom loses meaning. There are almost insoluble difficulties in defining what is and what is not teaching and what can and what cannot be done by ancillary staff. The only reliable guide is experience. Our suggestions for using ancillaries are in fact a record of help that teachers have found valuable. The effectiveness and status of teachers will eventually be improved by their having assistants who can be used as they judge best. The safeguard against ancillary assistants taking on responsibilities which ought to belong to teachers is the fact that these assistants are appointed for the specific purpose of helping teachers, that their duties lie within the discretion of head teachers and are carried out under the supervision of head or class teachers. Ancillary help should be used not simply to maintain, but to raise educational standards. For this reason, and to allay the anxiety of teachers, any scheme for the employment of ancillaries should be accompanied by an assurance that objectives in pupil-teacher ratios will not be adversely affected. For the same reason, we recommend that all local education authorities, including those which are well staffed, should be encouraged to experiment with different ways of using ancillary help. Colleges

M

of education should train prospective teachers to make good use of these helpers, and so should in-service training programmes.

*Teachers' Aides**

922. There is an increasing amount of experience on which to base our views of what can be done inside the classroom. Recently the scope of the National Nursery Examinations Board syllabus has been extended to prepare students for work with children up to seven instead of five. Infant schools may, therefore, now be used to train N.N.E.B. students. Some authorities have for a long time employed unqualified helpers in such subjects as needlework though these helpers have often been classed as "occasional" teachers. The type of help that is, or might be, given by teachers' aides, who ought to have equal status with nursery assistants and have a comparable training, falls into three kinds:

(a) Help that amounts to an extra pair of hands for the teacher. Young children working as individuals or in small groups need encouragement and help in their play, their reading and other activities. They want stories read to them and several groups and many children want help at the same time. The teacher can only tend one at a time. Other children, individually or in groups, use visual aids, tape recorders and simple learning machines; they learn on their own, but not without help. Teachers' aides can accompany teachers and children on out of school expeditions and help inside and outside the classroom in the preparation and maintenance of materials and equipment;

(b) help, often part-time, from those with special skills. This could be available for needlework, art and craft, handicraft, gardening, games and swimming, drama, music (including acting as pianist), library work and knowledge of children's books. These aides would give the help the class teacher asks for—it might be within school hours or in club sessions after school. In some areas help of this kind is already used;

(c) supervising children after school hours while they are waiting for their parents (such an arrangement might require special provision for insurance).

923. Teachers' aides can make a contribution to junior as well as infant schools and their employment in both will reduce the risk of their being thought "good enough" only for the younger children. In practice, general purpose aides would be most useful with children up to eight or nine (or rather older in areas with special problems), and aides with special skills, who can also give some general help, would be valuable with older primary children. It is assumed that some aides would be full-time and some part-time.

924. It has not been easy to suggest how many aides should be employed. If the figure is high, the quality of applicants may fall, and recruitment of nursery assistants may be adversely affected. The National Association of School Masters recommended that one general assistant should be assigned to an infant school of up to 200, and two assistants to an infant school over 200 (and for a junior school one for numbers up to 400, and two assistants for a school above that size). Our concept of an aide is broader than that of a "general assistant". We think that, as a first step, aides should be employed

*Teachers' aides is the term used for trained ancillaries who give substantial help to teachers inside and outside the classroom.

on a scale which will provide the equivalent of one full-time aide for 60–80 infants (two classes), and one aide for 120 to 160 juniors (four classes). For the educational priority areas we have suggested a rather more generous scale. These proposals will mean the training and recruitment of over 50,000 aides by 1973/4.

925. The nature of ancillary assistance for schools is bound to vary according to local circumstances. In small schools in rural areas, all purpose assistants are likely to be most helpful. In large schools, separate secretarial help will probably be essential and, for an interim period at least, welfare assistants may be needed in addition to teachers' aides. But as more of the latter become available they will take over the duties at present covered by welfare assistants. It would be desirable that a salary structure should provide for equality of status between nursery assistants and trained aides, though special allowances would be less necessary for aides than for nursery assistants. The status and salary of aides and nursery assistants would be superior to that of welfare and meals assistants. A national agreement between the authority and teachers' organisations on the functions of teachers' aides is desirable, but we hope that a good deal of discretion will be left to the head teachers.

926. To avoid keeping children out of school, authorities with insufficient qualified staff employ unqualified temporary and occasional teachers to take charge of a class. Constructive suggestions in this field, more than in any other, are apt to be blocked by the understandable anxiety of the teaching profession to avoid dilution. We cannot, however, avoid the responsibility of advising what should be done. On no account should children be in charge of untrained helpers without supervision by a qualified teacher. It is preferable that, when circumstances make some arrangement of this kind necessary, children should be looked after by a trained aide and their class linked with a qualified teacher. Responsibility allowances should be paid to teachers whose duties are increased in this way. Where accommodation permits, the total number of children under the supervision of a teacher and a teacher's aide should be smaller than Schools Regulations provide for two classes taught by qualified teachers. Where the two classes have to be big two teachers' aides should be assigned to one teacher.

927. Parents sometimes accompany school expeditions or make equipment for use in school. We do not wish to limit the sources from which help can come, or the conditions under which it is given, so long as it is at the invitation of, and under the strict control of, the head teacher. Too many primary schools assume that schools naturally contain only teachers and pupils. There are mutual advantages in opening the schools to the community. Mothers can help in school libraries and in other ways as is common in the U.S.A.; in New York it is organised by the School Volunteer Service. Parents and others can assist in clubs as was happening in schools which some of us visited in the U.S.S.R. There are schools in England where the village policeman trains the boys' football team, a local choirmaster helps with the school concert, and local studies are pursued with help of those who know the area well. We should like to see this kind of help enlisted on a larger scale. There is no reason why help should be limited to out of school activities. The head teachers of a few London infant schools which have many children from problem families have enlisted Care Committee workers to look after small groups of children with behaviour difficulties for a day each week. This extra

attention has had a valuable effect on the children. Head teachers (or secretaries of P.T.As.) might keep a record of help which parents are willing to
give and local education authorities might make it their business to interest
the local community and to keep a central register of offers of help, much as
has been done in connection with the Youth Service. This help would take
little of the time of any one individual, and would usually be voluntary. It
might be a useful source for the recruitment of paid ancillary workers.

928. Help of this voluntary kind will be hardest to come by in the areas
which are most short of teachers. They will have to rely more heavily on paid
help for which systematic arrangements should be made.

The Head Teacher and His Staff

929. The independence of the head teacher within his school is great. The
intervention of local authority or managers in the curriculum and organisation is no more than nominal. It is for the head teacher in co-operation with
the staff to crystallise the school's aims and to see that schemes and organisation serve them. The head teacher must know the staff, both the teachers and
others, be aware of their gifts and weaknesses and assign their duties in such
a way that children are well taught. It is also the head teacher's responsibility
to ensure that the staff are provided with essential equipment and are kept in
touch with new ideas.

930. It is rare to find a primary school so large that the head teacher cannot
know every child, which is particularly valuable at this time of rapid turnover
of assistant teachers. The best way to get to know children is to teach them,
and be with them inside and outside the classroom. In this way a good head
teacher can stimulate the children, inspire the staff, weld the school into a
unity and set its values. If there are areas of a curriculum which other teachers
cannot effectively cover the head teacher will have to equip himself as far as
possible to deal with them.

931. During the last war, and in the immediate post-war period, the administrative duties of head teachers increased and they had no secretarial help.
They had as a result to teach less. We are glad to learn, from an enquiry[3]
made for us into the role of primary school teachers, that the heads in the
small sample were spending much of their time in visiting classrooms and
teaching small and larger groups. There is no better way of commending their
leadership to the staff than by demonstrating their skill in the classroom. The
fact that the head continues to teach raises the whole status of teaching.

932. The head teacher must also keep in touch with parents and know where
to get help if children's problems or their home circumstances call for specialist advice. It is also primarily the head teacher's responsibility to be in
personal contact with the schools from which his pupils come and to which
they go.

933. Whether all this really happens depends a good deal on the extent to
which the whole staff share in the making of school policy and are given the
right blend of freedom and guidance. Some research suggests that young
teachers, who should be a sensitive measure of how well collaboration is
working, benefit greatly from informal discussion with their colleagues and
with head teachers but little from staff meetings. There is an important place
both for informal consultation and for more formal discussion among the
staff as a whole. A staff meeting may sometimes have little value because it is

given too limited a function. It is more important to discuss educational topics than arrangements for a party or a sports day. Matters of routine can properly be cleared by circular notes to the staff; changes of policy and policies which have been unchanged for many years are worth detailed examination. Staff meetings should, we think be held regularly. There should usually be a central topic for discussion of which advance notice has been given, and topics ought to be suggested and introduced by assistants as well as by the head.

934. In the past head teachers were responsible for all schemes of work. Now that the primary school curriculum is being widened, it is increasingly difficult for them to be up to date with all the developments and sensible that they should invite the help of assistant teachers in preparing schemes, in giving advice to their colleagues and in the selection of books, materials and equipment. Since students in colleges of education now study at least one subject in some depth there should be no lack of response from teachers, though at present it is improbable that any school will have sufficient choice to build up a staff which is nicely balanced in specialist knowledge. It is important that head teachers should be consulted by the authority on staff appointments so that, whenever possible, marked deficiencies in a staff can be made good.

935. It will, we think, strengthen primary schools if heads go further than is commonly done in delegating duties. The deputy head usually stands in for the head teacher in his absence and may relieve him of such jobs as interviewing parents or taking the morning assembly, though these responsibilities should not be confined exclusively to head teachers and their deputies. Occasionally a deputy head teacher has no class of his own though we doubt the wisdom of this. It is also often suitable, particularly in large schools, for the deputy head teacher to give guidance to probationers and to students. Out of school activities which involve parents and children are often well left to deputy head teachers. A large school may have need for two deputy head teachers.

936. The Burnham structure provides for graded posts in the primary school. The intention is that they should be awarded for specific duties. In practice the duties for which they are assigned are sometimes trivial. It is usual, and it should continue to be usual, for a graded post or a deputy headship to be given to a member of staff who takes charge of the infants in a junior mixed and infants school. The same principle might be adopted for other age groups in the school. A member of staff might act as consultant for the teachers and ancillaries working with one or two age groups. Whether or not a graded post is available, heads will often want to arrange for an experienced and an inexperienced teacher to take parallel classes and work together. But there are no invariable rules. Occasionally, when a staff has become set in its ways, it may be helpful for two young teachers to be associated with an age group so that, with the head teacher's help, they may reinforce one another in experiment.

937. In the assignment of classes, in the award of graded posts and in the nomination of consultant teachers, head teachers will also want to take into account their teachers' knowledge of subjects. The main role of a consultant teacher should be advisory, but he might sometimes take over a class for part

of the week. This may be desirable in order to raise the quality of work, or indeed to ensure that a subject such as music or physical education is covered in some classes. It is also important that consultant teachers or teams of teachers do not remain permanently with the same age group. Two successive years may consolidate understanding of the problems involved. But there are too many schools in which teachers settle down with a particular age group or even with a stream within an age group, for the bulk of their career.

938. There are at present striking differences between authorities on the size of school in which head teachers are expected to take charge of a class. In some areas the head must teach full time when there are as many as 200 children in the school; in others, he may be freed of a class in a school of 100 or fewer. We are clear that, except in one class schools, all heads need part-time assistance so that they can get to know both children and parents and advise the staff including, probationers. It is equally essential that head teachers of larger schools should not have to spend so much time on adminis-trative duties and on general supervision that they are unable to teach. One authority has told us that they think head teachers should spend three quarters of their time in teaching. Relief for head teachers could be given by additional secretarial assistance. The returns required by authorities and by the Department should be kept under continuous review to see whether they can be reduced in number or simplified. Part-time teaching help ought to be provided in large schools to enable deputy head teachers and consultant teachers to share with the head teacher the responsibility of guiding the staff. Unless these teachers are freed for some part of the week from their work with their own class they will be unable to exercise satisfactorily the respon-sibilities assigned to them. It is particularly important that the teachers in charge of the infants in a junior mixed and infants school should be able to spend time in all the infant classes.

939. There must, according to the Burnham scale, be a deputy head teacher in a junior mixed and infants school of more than 100 pupils, and in a separate junior or infant school of more than 200. Local education authorities have discretion to create posts in smaller schools. Difficulties occur in primary schools of 200 and less when the head teacher is absent and there is no deputy to take his place. We hope that authorities will use more generally the powers they have to appoint deputy heads in small schools. There may be one or more posts for heads of departments in the larger primary schools. New arrangements allow some increase in the number of graded posts in primary schools which previously may have been insufficient. A school with 300–500 pupils may have two Scale I posts; with 500–700 pupils it may have four such posts; the available points may be used to provide fewer but more valuable posts.

940. It has been put to us that the hierarchy of deputy headships, headships of departments and graded posts in large primary schools makes for frequent changes of staff. A sub-committee of the Burnham Committee is now examining the points system; we hope it will take account of the overriding need of primary schools for a more stable staff. Clearly, an assistant teacher in a small school who seeks promotion must change his school. There is less need for movement when graded posts are to be filled in a larger school, though promotion should be a reward for merit and not for seniority. It seems also that the policy of some authorities in appointing head teachers is

out of date. It is not unknown for candidates to be denied promotion because they have not had experience in a sufficient number of schools. We believe that attention should now be directed more to the variety of experience and responsibility that teachers have exercised within schools, the short courses they have followed and the visits to other schools which they have made, and less to the number of schools in which they have taught.

Advice and Inspection

941. We have described the support the individual teacher can get within the school from being a member of a team guided but not dominated by the head teacher. But help from within the school is not enough, especially at this time of a rapidly changing curriculum, methods and organisation. The freedom of the class teacher to prescribe for his pupils, and of the head teacher to prescribe for his school must be informed by a knowledge of the successes and failures of others. Both will benefit from outside advice from somebody who knows the inside of their school.

942. How is the knowledge and advice to be supplied? Is there too much of it or too little? Though on at least one occasion we heard the familiar description of the teaching profession as the most inspected of all professions, the general impression given by our evidence is that teachers are still too isolated and that they are under rather than over advised.

943. Two bodies exist to inspect and advise the schools, H.M. Inspectorate and local inspectors. Both originated in the 19th century in the need to supervise the expenditure of public money. Since that time the education and training of primary school teachers have been greatly improved and the teaching profession has established its own traditions. But we doubt if the time has yet come to throw over entirely the principle of inspection and simply substitute advice. Assessment of a school is a necessary preamble to giving relevant advice, and a safeguard against the preaching of an educational gospel, regardless of the different circumstances of different schools. Very occasionally children and the public still need to be protected. There are rare occasions when a report, whether by H.M. Inspectors or local authority inspectors, ought to draw attention to the fact that a school is positively harmful to children. Local inspectors must also assess schools since they often advise managers on promotion. Without this knowledge, selection would have to depend mainly on the impression at an interview, a notoriously hazardous method. Yet we welcome the growing stress on the role of adviser rather than of inspector, and note with pleasure the friendly relationships which are usual between H.M. Inspectorate and the teaching profession. The more informal the schools become in their organisation and relationships, the more informal ought to be the routines of inspection.

944. The roles of the national and local inspectorates are complementary. H.M. Inspectorate is a relatively mobile body which can watch the development of education in maintained and independent schools throughout the country. Advances in education or practice are often surprisingly local and often owe much to local inspectors and advisers. They can be made widely known by H.M. Inspectors.

945. Local inspectors through courses, visits and placing of staff can help to build up a group of outstanding schools which may serve as a spearhead of

advance within their own authority and often in the country as a whole. These schools should not become show schools. Often a monthly teachers' meeting, held in different schools in succession, is the best way of propagating educational ideas without seeming to single out individual schools.

946. There is a danger that at this time of shortage of teachers too much of the time of the local inspectorate may be devoted to the placing of teachers. We have been much impressed by the work of advisory teachers* who have a small group of schools, and who concentrate on help for teachers. What distinguishes them from other inspectors and advisers is that much of their time is spent in teaching in the classroom, often side by side with the class teacher.

947. The National Association of Inspectors and of Educational Organisers has been unable to tell us with any exactitude how many local authority advisory officers there are or what subjects or stages of education they cover. Authorities are obliged to employ a youth officer and a school meals officer. The Association thinks that not more than 50 out of all local education authorities appoint a range of advisers or inspectors which is significantly larger than this minimum. On the whole it is the counties which are best provided. These authorities certainly have many small schools in which there may be a lack of stimulus for teachers. Nevertheless the County Boroughs where there are the biggest problems of social deprivation are worse staffed. Even in authorities where there are a number of posts, the majority tend to be assigned to physical education, music, housecraft and handicraft, subjects which were added to the minimum curriculum in the 19th century and were thus thought to require special supervision. Traditions yield slowly. Some of these subjects are usually taught today by specialists who should require little help from advisers. We see three main needs for development in the advisory services. There should be additional inspectors or, even better, advisory teachers in primary and particularly in infant education. Only in this way can the large number of young teachers receive sufficient help. Advisory posts should be established for such developing subjects as mathematics, science and drama, for English, in which class teachers have too long been left to their own devices, and in religious instruction in which the need for change is generally acknowledged and where few primary teachers have thought out their position clearly. Experiments might be tried in appointing advisers who combine knowledge in two or three subjects with interest in primary education. Finally small authorities which cannot individually maintain an adequate range of advisers might combine for the organisation of courses and to provide other advisory services. We have heard of only a handful of instances in which an arrangement of this kind is made, though without it it is difficult to see how otherwise probationary teachers can be given a minimum of care or all teachers the help they need. We are aware that these suggestions rest on incomplete evidence. We believe that a comprehensive survey should be made of advisory services and of the work which they do.

*We distinguish between "consultant teachers" whose function is to advise members of the school staff on which they serve, and "advisory teachers" on the authority's general staff who serve a group of schools.

Recommendations

948. (i) More men are needed in first schools. Prospective men head teachers or deputies of first or combined schools should have had direct experience or in-service training in infant as well as junior work. A sufficient number of women heads and deputies should continue to be appointed.

(ii) Neither class size nor the pupil-teacher ratio gives a sufficient picture of the state of a school. Both should be used in reporting conditions and defining objectives. Separate returns should be made for schools of different sizes. Head teachers should be included in the ratio.

(iii) More generous staffing should be given to schools satisfying certain requirements which we specify.

(iv) Satisfactory conditions of service of part-timers need to be negotiated. Local registers of immobile teachers should be compiled.

(v) Part-time teachers should serve in well staffed as well as understaffed schools to release full-time teachers for more difficult areas.

(vi) More profitable use should be made of meals assistants, secretaries and welfare assistants, and in smaller schools their duties might be combined.

(vii) Trained teachers' aides in the ratio of one full-time aide to 60–80 children (two infant classes) and one aide to 120–160 children (four junior classes) (except in educational priority areas) should be employed in primary schools under the supervision of qualified teachers to provide them with help within the classroom. The conditions of service of aides should be regulated by local education authorities but discretion in the matter of their duties should be left to head teachers. A national scheme for the employment of aides should be accompanied by an assurance that objectives in teacher pupil ratios will not be adversely affected. Authorities which are well staffed should be encouraged to experiment with different ways of using ancillary help.

(viii) Nursery assistants and teachers' aides should be on a higher salary scale than welfare and meals' assistants.

(ix) In exceptional circumstances qualified teachers and teachers' aides should be associated for the supervision of larger groups of children than those laid down by Regulations and the additional responsibility of the teachers should be recognised by the payment of an allowance.

(x) Schools should enlist the voluntary help of parents and other members of the community both in school and for out of school activities, provided such help is at the invitation and under the strict control of the head teacher.

(xi) Head teachers ought to teach. Those in charge of a class should be given part-time teaching and secretarial help.

(xii) In bigger schools part-time teaching help should be provided for deputy heads and holders of graded posts so that they may assist the head with guidance of probationers and students, interviews with teachers and in other ways.

(xiii) The planning of schemes of work should increasingly be undertaken by assistant teachers.

(xiv) The present review of the points system should pay attention to the need for reducing the turnover in school staffs.

(xv) Authorities should consult head teachers about the filling of staff vacancies to ensure proper balances in the staff as far as possible.

(xvi) Authorities should use more the powers they have to appoint deputy heads in schools with less than 200 on roll.

(xvii) Schools need inspection as well as advice.

(xviii) There is need for a greater number of local authority advisers, with special knowledge of primary education. Some authorities may need to combine for this.

(xix) There should be a general review of advisory services.

(xx) Advisory posts should be established for such developing subjects as mathematics, science and drama, and in English and religious education. Experiments should be tried in appointing advisers who combine knowledge in two or three subjects with interest in primary education.

REFERENCES

[1]'The Demand for and the Supply of Teachers 1963–64'. Ninth Report of the National Advisory Council for the Training and Supply of Teachers, paragraph 29, H.M.S.O., 1965.
[2]'The State of our Schools', N.U.T. 1962, Part I, paragraphs 17 and 23.
[3]'Roles and Responsibility of Head Teacher and Teaching Staff in Primary Schools'. Report of a Pilot Survey by Miss I. E. Caspari, Department for Children and Parents, Tavistock Clinic, London.

CHAPTER 25

The Training of Primary School Teachers

949. The rapid turnover of teachers, however disastrous it may be in other ways, does at least provide the opportunity for new ideas in education to make themselves rapidly felt in the schools. Because of this, the colleges of education and university departments have at this moment a more influential position than they would have in more settled times. This is the time when there should be a full study of the whole subject of the training of teachers. Undertaken now, it could help to influence the ways in which expansion takes place instead of being an inquest on what has been done. The training of teachers was examined by the Robbins Committee only as part of a much wider survey. An analysis of the effectiveness of different patterns of teacher training should form a major part of such an enquiry. The most that we could do was to study the training of teachers from the angle of primary education and to consider the part the schools can play in training.

950. Teacher training institutions have been working under great strain in the past decade. The three year course was introduced generally in 1960. The years immediately before 1960 were devoted to the intensive planning of the extended course, to the preparation of members of staff and the recruitment of the many additional lecturers who were needed. Yet in the very year in which the first students entered the three year courses, the Ministry of Education, faced with an impending shortage of primary school teachers, asked the colleges to increase substantially the proportion of those who were preparing to teach in primary schools. Since 1960 the colleges have been engaged on an expansion programme which has more than doubled the number of places. It was under 30,000 in 1958/59; it was over 70,000 in 1965/66. This year it will be 80,000.

951. The colleges and departments of education are preparing teachers for several different roles. Many women students need a sound basic training which will enable them to make a useful contribution to the schools for a few years until they start their own families. Their training should equip them with constructive and adaptable attitudes towards children and teaching. When they later return to teaching, full-time or part-time, a refresher course will enable them quickly to pick up the threads. Many men and women students will make education their life work. Among them will be the innovators, the future heads of schools, the teachers in colleges and departments of education, the advisers and administrators. Both the admission procedures and the courses arranged in the colleges must be flexible and imaginative enough to be suited to students who will play these differing parts in the educational structure of the future.

The Present Position: A Factual Summary

952. There are about 67,000 students taking courses in general colleges of education in England and Wales. In spite of the grave shortage of primary

* See Suggestion on the Supply and Training of Teachers at the end of the main Report.

and particularly infant teachers only one third, nearly all of them women, are preparing to work with very young children by taking nursery-infant, infant or infant-junior courses. About 19,000 students are taking junior-secondary courses; about half are men.

953. Not only are there twice as many students as there were seven years ago, but they are better qualified. In 1965/66 about 66 per cent had one or more Advanced level passes in the General Certificate of Education compared with 62 per cent in 1961/62. The great majority have qualifications well above the five Ordinary level passes, which is the statutory minimum (see Table 25).

954. The standard length of course is three years but some 3·5 per cent of all students in colleges of education are in shortened courses. These students are normally over 25. Mature students as a whole are an important group which provided 14 per cent of all first students in 1964 and 1965. Many of them go to special day colleges, or to "outposts" of other colleges. These outposts have been set up in areas which are likely to provide a continuing flow of recruits who are unable to live far from their homes.

955. The training of graduates is either concurrent, in which academic and professional courses take place alongside each other, or consecutive, in which professional preparation follows degree work. Concurrent training has been provided in two undergraduate university courses and in a small number of colleges of education. The amount of concurrent training will increase rapidly in the next few years as the four year course for the B.Ed. degree becomes established. Most universities are planning to hold their first examination for the B.Ed. degree in 1969.

956. Six university departments of education in England and two in Wales offer one year post-graduate training for primary education. Less than four per cent of post-graduate students in university departments of education were following one of these courses. There are also some post-graduate students in colleges of education, but, although the proportion taking primary or primary-secondary courses was much higher (29 per cent), the total number was negligible. In 1965/66 there were only some 300 graduates training for primary school work.

957. The colleges and departments of education are grouped in 20 institutes or schools of education, which act as area training organisations. All but one of them are university bodies. While they vary in structure, they all co-ordinate the facilities in their areas for training teachers and oversee the content of the training courses. They are also responsible for the examination of students and recommend successful students to the Secretary of State for qualified teacher status, subject to a satisfactory probationary period.

The Structure of Training

958. Most colleges of education prepare students for one career only, that of teaching. This arrangement has the advantage that academic and professional studies are carried on side by side, a point to which we return later in paragraph 972, and that vocational interest can give a sense of purpose to all the work. But there are disadvantages. A choice of career is forced on students at 18 or earlier, before some know their own minds, and future teachers are segregated from those preparing for other types of work. It is not easy to

balance the advantages and disadvantages; and at present it could only have academic interest. The grave problem of the supply of teachers would prevent any considerable modification of the present system.

959. A concurrent course of training for teachers need not be the only course provided in a college of education. There are already one year "consecutive" courses for graduates and certain specialists. Some colleges of education include an optional course in youth work in their teacher training courses. A college in the Midlands trains students for teaching, youth service, work in community centres and for other careers. One Scottish college provides a two year course for social workers as well as training for teachers.

960. We hope there may be some institutions in which social service students and students preparing for teaching can share much of their first year work, especially as this should encourage closer collaboration in the field. Certainly all students preparing to teach need to know much more about social work and family needs, just as most social workers would benefit from a deeper insight into the work of schools. We also welcome experiments now about to be put into effect for training teachers in selected technical colleges, especially because they will increase the opportunities of prospective teachers to train side by side with students in other disciplines who are preparing for other professions. At the outset lecturers dealing with main subjects in such colleges might well feel the disadvantage of slight knowledge and experience of the primary school and it must be hoped that they will look for help from their colleagues in the Education Department, who are likely to be specially recruited for this work. All such courses for the training of teachers should be affiliated to the institutes of education.

Admission of Students

961. Although the general level of academic qualifications of students is satisfactory, there are aspects which cause disquiet. Too many students have concentrated in the sixth form on English, history and geography. Too few are qualified to take college main courses in mathematics, science or music. All primary school teachers need to be numerate in the Crowther sense as well as literate. A minimum standard of numeracy involves the capacity to secure a pass at Ordinary level in mathematics in the G.C.E. A quarter of the men and two fifths of the women entering college have not reached this level and the proportion is deteriorating. The future teacher needs as well to have some understanding of scientific method and a recent acquaintance with the practice of one of the arts. The secondary schools with their specialist tradition in teaching are not, we think, sufficiently aware of the need of the primary schools, and we would include the proposed middle schools, for teachers whose value lies to a marked degree in their versatility. The main courses in secondary schools and the use of sixth form minority time need scrutiny with this problem, among others, in mind.

962. Assessment of candidates' suitability is made by individual colleges which use many different selection procedures. Their criteria include examination success, school reports, intelligence and other tests, evidence of experience with children and the impressions created on interview. Many colleges now share the responsibility for selection widely amongst members

of staff; a few invite primary school head teachers to take part, a useful practice though it may make too heavy demands on a head teacher's time.

Balance of Men and Women Students

963. There is little to choose (as shown by Table 25) between the qualifications of men and women students recently admitted to the colleges. At first sight, therefore, it seems possible to increase the proportion of men without risk to the quality of intake. But scrutinies of unplaced candidates undertaken by the Central Register and Clearing House tend to confirm the view held by the colleges that the average quality of men applicants is lower than that of women. There is a particularly marked shortage of able men wishing to enter primary courses. More could be done to bring the work of the colleges to the attention of sixth formers, particularly those in boys' schools. Visits might be arranged for members of sixth forms to colleges and also to primary schools, as is already done in some parts of the country. College-based courses might be held for sixth formers during the Easter vacation.

Mature Students

964. Mature students are an important group of future teachers. They are valuable in the colleges because of the additional experience they bring to their corporate life; they are valuable in school not only because of their training and experience, but also because they are more likely than young women to stay in teaching. Those we met were thoughtful people, working hard and likely to become good teachers. It is worth while planning facilities for training in such a way as to make it possible to enlist more. The day colleges and "outposts" have been successful largely because they are ready to adapt their hours to students' family obligations. The courses in technical colleges will make teacher training available to more day students. We should like to see experiments in part-time courses for mature students and understand that some will begin in 1967.

Graduates

965. Graduates have been regarded with some suspicion by other primary school teachers, since some graduates entering primary schools are poor teachers. Some are untrained, and try to base their methods on those of grammar schools. Yet the primary schools need graduates for two specific reasons. Our evidence has shown a critical shortage in colleges of education of lecturers for "education" departments with qualifications in psychology, sociology and philosophy. The right people to fill these posts need good d grees in these subjects and teaching experience in primary schools. The second reason is that the introduction of new subjects in junior schools and, still more, the prospective demands at the top of middle schools, if our recommendations are accepted, will make it important for more primary school teachers to have specialist knowledge. Graduates who enter primary teaching will find that it offers intellectually challenging work. Primary schools will need all the benefits which trained minds, interested in writing and research, will be able to bring.

966. The B.Ed. degree ought to be a major, perhaps the major, source of supply of graduates for primary schools. How far it will in fact take into account the special requirements of primary education depends on decisions

being made by the universities. They will determine whether the B.Ed. will give us the teachers we need. Clearly it is most important that the universities should equip students of good ability for this work. We take up this question in paragraphs 977 and 978.

967. If the university departments of education expand to the extent that is likely in the next few years, more of them will be able to provide suitable training for work in primary schools. We should like to see all of them offer this training provided that they have sufficient staff of the right experience and a large enough group of students intending to teach in primary schools. But the colleges of education have special advantages for training post-graduate students to teach in primary schools since so much of their experience is with primary work. We hope that the total number of post-graduate students in colleges of education, and also the proportion who are preparing for teaching in primary schools will increase substantially.

968. Increased recruitment of graduate students to courses of primary training will depend, to some extent, on better contacts with secondary schools. A campaign is needed to make the opportunities for graduate teachers in primary schools known in secondary schools and universities. The teachers' associations might play their part. Colleges of education might tell secondary schools how their former pupils are doing, and keep in touch with those of their applicants who withdraw to take up university places but who may remain interested in primary teaching. A fresh approach could be made to university appointments boards. The Department of Education and Science should give more publicity to courses of primary training for graduates and to the career prospects for those who take them.

969. Under present regulations, professional training is not a compulsory requirement for the award of qualified teacher status to graduates. We must make it quite clear that we share the views of the whole of the educational service that graduates should be required to receive training before they teach, above all if they are going to work in primary schools.

The Courses in Colleges of Education and University Departments of Education

970. We have not been in a position to assess the courses in colleges and departments of education; but we have given some thought to the strengths and weaknesses of the teachers they produce, and how far they meet the needs of the schools.

971. We have also taken into account the evidence we have received, both formally and informally. We have heard many favourable comments on the work of the colleges and departments of education but also a considerable amount of criticism open or implied. Half the head teachers to whom our questionnaire was sent (Appendix 1, Table E.24) thought that students were adequately prepared in colleges of education; over a third disagreed. Nearly three fifths of the assistant teachers were satisfied; nearly a third were not. There was stronger criticism of the training in university departments of education. The views expressed in evidence or in answer to the questionnaire could not, of course, have been based on long experience of the effects of the three year course because it only started in 1960, and the first teachers trained in it did not reach the schools until late in 1963. Some teachers may not have

realised the strain under which colleges have been working. But there are criticisms which ought to be taken seriously. These are complaints about:

(i) the quality of college courses: some of the abler students are dissatisfied with the standards of some courses;

(ii) the balance between theory and practice in the professional training: too little practical help, for instance, on such matters as class organisation and the teaching of reading; too little time in the schools; and inadequate preparation for work with slow or socially deprived children.

(iii) the qualifications and experience of some members of college staffs: too few lecturers with up to date knowledge and experience of primary work; and the colleges, in general, too remote from the problems of the schools.

Our main conclusion from these criticisms is that colleges and schools need to be brought into closer contact and to understand one another better. This point is amplified later; other points are taken up in the following survey of college courses and in our comments on them.

Main Courses

972. The content of the course varies both between institutes and between individual colleges, but there is much common ground. All students undertake an advanced study of one or two subjects (main courses). Some teachers question whether this is necessary for students training to be primary school teachers. We accept the general view that study in some depth forms an essential part of the education of any teacher. The practising teacher will be learning to be a teacher all his life but he may have less opportunity, once he leaves college, for the systematic study of a subject for its own sake. Students need resources of knowledge and judgement upon which they can draw both as teachers and individuals, and these will not necessarily be related to the day to day work in the primary schools. We are advised that there is a wide variation in the standards attained by students in their main courses. The best already reach the level of an ordinary degree, but at the other end of the scale are students who pass at a level little beyond the advanced level in the General Certificate of Education examination.

Education Course and Teaching Practice

973. The education course contains some common sections and others designed to prepare students for teaching a particular age range. Students training for primary teaching usually spend a substantial part of their time in studies of child development, a practice we commend and should like to see extended to all students in junior-secondary courses. We also share the view that educational theory and practice should support one another throughout the course. For this reason, the sooner students get into school—though not at first to teach—the better. We have been told that the work in the theory of education shows a wide variation in quality. It may range from courses of a rather discursive and descriptive nature to others which make a much more rigorous intellectual demand and involve reading, discussion and written essays of a high standard. Part of the difficulty lies in the dual nature of education courses. The lecturer most competent in the schools may not be suited to teaching the more theoretical aspects of children's development, or the psychology, sociology and philosophy of education. We welcome the

trend towards the appointment of specialists in these fields, and hope it will go further. As far as possible these specialists ought to have had direct experience of primary schools, and a post-graduate course relevant to primary education.

Curriculum Courses

974. Curriculum courses, intended to inform students both about the subject matter that children will learn in school and the way in which they will learn it, are essential. It is difficult to know how best to prepare students who may have to take responsibility for the full range of work in a single class. An attempt to cover everything can lead to fragmented and superficial work; the selection of a restricted number of subjects for intensive study can leave gaps which many students find awkward. The student needs help at his own level and detailed guidance in working with children. If too little attention is given to the former, teaching may be impoverished by, for example, a lack of a sensitivity to the arts, or too little knowledge. If too little attention is given to the way children learn, a junior school teacher may be quite unable to teach children to read. Students' time can be saved if their curriculum courses are chosen and designed with a view to individual needs. Some colleges try to ensure that students, either through their main courses or a curriculum course, study an example from each main aspect of the children's curriculum, language, mathematics, learning by discovery and experiment, and creative work in the arts. In other colleges, curriculum courses begin with an integrated study of the neighbourhood, a way of learning highly relevant to children, or a study of a primary school in its setting. It is particularly important that students who are taking junior-secondary courses and from whom many of the teachers needed for primary schools must come have a sufficient range of curriculum courses to feel competent to teach in primary schools.

Staffing of Colleges of Education

975. The old anxiety lest colleges should become inbred has been allayed by the rapid expansion bringing in many newcomers direct from schools; but there are plenty of other problems. The staff responsible for work in main subjects must be well qualified specialists and this frequently means that they have been secondary school teachers. This in turn means that in nearly all colleges of education the proportion of students in training for primary teaching is much higher than the proportion of the staff who have had, at the time of their appointment, substantial experience of work in the primary schools. Many of these lecturers have to help with curriculum courses and with teaching practice, partly to relieve the burden which would otherwise fall on their colleagues, but even more to avoid a cleavage between the subject specialists and the members of the education staff which would defeat the purpose of concurrent training. Specialists in psychology and sociology may, like other specialists, know too little of the primary schools. The fact that the majority of the staff know more about secondary than primary schools may help to explain why students who have followed junior-secondary courses are over anxious to obtain posts in secondary schools. Other possible explanations are offered in Chapter 29.

976. Another problem faces the colleges in the appointment of education staff. Good practitioners with recent experience of teaching young children have an essential part to play, but some of them may lack the background of reading and the training in exact thought needed for successful work in college. In these related problems lies the cause of some of the criticism of college staffs by primary school teachers and others among our witnesses.

977. When the pace of expansion slows down these problems should be easier to solve. A larger proportion of subject specialists will be able to spend some time in primary school teaching before joining college staffs; primary school teachers will more frequently be able to take advanced diplomas before taking part in teacher training. In time there should be an inflow of recruits with a B.Ed. degree.

B.Ed. Courses

978. The universities are rightly anxious that high academic standards should be established in the B.Ed. degrees. We are equally concerned lest those who follow these courses should be less likely to enter primary schools and less well prepared to teach in them than if they had taken a teacher's certificate only. The degree put forward for consideration in the Robbins Report was envisaged as consisting of education and two other main subjects. This is well suited to the needs of students for secondary teaching who would be equipped with two strong teaching subjects and a limited range of curriculum courses in other subjects. But students training for primary teaching need a wider range of experience than they will be able to acquire if they have to concentrate on two main subjects and the theory of education. Another possible difficulty lies in the subjects acceptable for a B.Ed. degree course. Some of the main courses in colleges of education are not subjects for which universities have in the past granted degrees.

979. There is less anxiety than there was. A few universities have devised a scheme in which the education course is interwoven with subject studies and sufficient time left for curriculum courses. There is an encouraging trend for universities to accept for the B.Ed. course subjects such as art and craft, physical education and drama which prospective teachers in the primary schools may well wish to take. Some universities are allowing B.Ed. students to take education and one instead of two main subjects. Naturally there are still unsolved problems; and the plans of a few universities are deeply disturbing. In one university, education itself is not to figure in the fourth year course of a B.Ed. degree; in a few others the only subjects, other than education, to be allowed in the B.Ed. course, at any rate to begin with, are those normally examined by the universities. We hope that as universities, institutes of education and colleges come into closer contact, ways will be found of reconciling high academic standards in the B.Ed. course with relevance to primary education. We also hope that, as soon as possible, arrangements will be made for B.Ed. courses to be taken by established teachers.

Other Graduate Courses

980. The major problem of the post-graduate course for students preparing for primary education is that an academic year, nine months or less, allows too little time for the range of work which has to be covered or for developing

an understanding of education and child development. An interesting experimental scheme covering a two year period was introduced in one university department of education in 1963. A small group of graduate students embarked on a two year course (the first grant aided and the second salaried) in which training and teaching alternate, and the final assessment of practical teaching is postponed till the end of the second year. The scheme allows for a longer period in training without loss to the teaching force. If the results are favourable, this scheme might provide a useful alternative pattern for graduate training. It has also been suggested to us that particular help should be given to post graduate students in their probationary year. They should be able to go on learning after they complete training, especially if they are given sufficient guidance during their early years of teaching.

Some General Points about Students' Life and Work

981. The discipline in training colleges used often to be paternal and sometimes authoritarian. There has been a noteworthy movement in recent years towards treating students as adults, responsible for their personal lives and for the corporate life of the college. We welcome this trend which is exemplified by the agreement reached in 1964 by the A.T.C.D.E. and the National Union of Students on regulations for students who are in residence. It now remains for all colleges to follow the example of those which have accepted adjustments in discipline.

982. More emphasis is being placed in the three year course on independent study, which has been helped by great improvements in college libraries. A growth of seminar and tutorial methods, and a corresponding reduction in formal lectures, should help students develop active attitudes to learning and make it easier to meet their individual needs. When they become teachers, they are likely in turn to encourage a similar independence in their pupils. Some will teach in primary schools which already use modern methods; they will fit in naturally. Others will go to more traditional schools. We hope that those who do will neither flaunt their difference nor surrender to convention. They are more likely to succeed if they have been introduced during their training to the whole range of method and organisation in schools.

983. There are certain aspects of training both in colleges and departments of education which seem to us to be of especial importance. We should not want students to be overloaded with additional courses on these aspects, but rather that they should be emphasised in the education course. We recognise that many colleges are already taking into account the points mentioned below:

(i) An understanding of child development is of particular importance to those preparing for work in primary education. Students should be acquainted with the more important results of contemporary research, even when these are in dispute. They will then be more likely to interest themselves in similar debates when they become teachers.

(ii) Some acquaintance with the problems of handicapped children, and especially the slow learners, is essential for all students since these children are found in all schools.

(iii) One of the major findings of recent educational research—and of this Report—is that children's work and behaviour in school are profoundly influenced by their home circumstances. All students need to understand the effect of home and community on children. Special emphasis should be placed on the problems of children who are, in one or another way, gravely deprived by the circumstances of their homes and districts, and on the help that teachers can give to these children, in collaboration with other social services. Contacts with parents and others in the neighbour-hood should be organised in a positive fashion and should introduce students to situations to which they themselves can make a constructive contribution. Many young teachers feel anxious and inadequate when confronted by parents; they cannot be free from these anxieties unless meetings with parents are planned, and subsequently discussed with as much care as practice teaching itself.

(iv) Examination and other assessment of students should take account of these important aspects of training.

The Relationship between Schools and Teachers Training Institutions

984. The schools and colleges are yoked together. The purpose of training is to produce good teachers who will serve the schools. It cannot be achieved unless the staff of training institutions know what is happening in the schools and are sympathetic to their needs. Equally, schools will not provide good conditions for young teachers and students on teaching practice unless their staffs understand what the training institutions are trying to do. Evidence has already been quoted which suggests some failures in understanding and co-operation on both sides.

Teaching Practice

985. The purpose of teaching practice is to underpin and enliven theoretical studies in child development and education, and to provide sources from which theory can be derived. Teaching practice must also familiarise students with the problems and the daily round that will await them when they qualify. Through it, colleges and schools can learn about each other's new ideas.

986. Students have traditionally spent continuous periods of several weeks in a school. In 1964 most colleges were arranging three periods of "block practice"*, usually totalling 12 to 15 weeks, for students taking a three year course and fewer periods for those following shortened or post graduate courses. The recent request by the Secretary of State for a more intensive use of college premises has helped to stimulate proposals by colleges for some practices lasting a whole term, and amounting in a few instances to a year's practice in all.

987. Most lecturers are responsible for groups varying in size from two up to 12 or more students distributed among several schools. Lecturers in education act as general supervisors and consultants to groups of students and as consultants to their colleagues. In the present situation, when many subject specialists have come recently from secondary schools and know little about primary schools, some students may be visited by members of staff who cannot give them as much help as they need. But there is also evidence that students in some colleges receive too many visits and too much protection

---

*Block practice is practice undertaken over a substantial time.

from their supervisors. Several of the colleges which are experimenting with long periods of practice are proposing to associate schools more closely with the supervision and assessment of students. There have already been interesting experiments, notably in a university school of education, where practising teachers supervise students, take part in meetings with the university tutors and are paid small honoraria.

988. Periods of continuous work in schools are supplemented by intermittent visits. This type of visit is sometimes known as "group practice" because several students may work together in the same class. This often happens early in the course when students observe children and work with small groups rather than teach a whole class. In some colleges, students visit the same school and the same class for a day a week over a period which may last as long as six months or more. It is also not uncommon for teachers, college lecturers and students to work together with children, and this co-operative effort may be concentrated on a few weeks in the year or may take place at weekly intervals over a longer period. These types of practice interact usefully with the more theoretical aspects of the education course and provide valuable occasions for experimental work in the schools and collaboration between schools and colleges.

989. Films, closed circuit television and video tape recording can also enable students to observe children's behaviour and learning. They can reduce the number of occasions when students need to go into schools, and enable them to be differently spaced. They can depict schools from contrasting social areas, organised in different ways and using more varied educational methods than students can see at first hand. The camera and commentator can direct the attention of students to the behaviour of children in a way that is not possible in the classroom. Closed circuit television which at the moment is in its infancy has the advantage that students can help plan the work and can then see how children react.

990. The expansion of teacher training must influence the arrangements made for students. Its effects are already to be seen in some of the developments that have been described. Roughly 100,000 students are expected to require teaching practice in primary and secondary schools in 1971, three times as many as in 1961. The number of primary classes will not increase at anything like this rate. In addition, as the training of teachers' aides and nursery assistants begins, there will be a considerable further demand for practice places in primary schools. Students will have to travel further from their colleges than in the past. Most schools can expect to have one or more students on teaching practice in some part of every term. It has long been difficult to ensure that good schools were not over-used while others were used insufficiently or not at all. Co-ordination of teaching practice arrangements by Area Training Organisations and local education authorities is essential. This is already being done in some areas.

Our Views

991. Solutions to the problems of school practice must take account of local circumstances, but some general points should be made:

   (i) In planning teaching practice, colleges should help to meet the needs of the schools as well as those of their students. In areas where there is a grave shortage of teachers, colleges might collaborate to ensure that there are students in the schools in each term of the year. In making this recommendation we realize that all students, even those in their final year, make demands on the schools, as well as give relief, and that some students ask much more from the schools to which they are attached than they can contribute.

(ii) There are advantages for students and schools in a long practice especially when it takes place towards the end of a student's course. It is a useful bridge to the full responsibility of the probationary year. Many students are sufficiently effective by the time of their final practice to release teachers for periods of in-service training or experimental work. Some colleges now provide, or co-operate in providing, in-service training for practising teachers at times when teachers are freed by the presence of students in their schools.

(iii) The ultimate responsibility for students and for their courses, including teaching practice, rests with the college. To divorce teaching practice from the college course would separate theory from practice, to the impoverishment of both. Some students are in particular need of help from tutors who have watched their progress throughout their course, but day to day guidance could rest to a greater extent with the schools. In many colleges and universities the supervision of students on practice is being re-examined. The A.T.C.D.E. are also enquiring into the many problems of teaching practice. We hope that account will be taken of new ideas about the supervision of practical work which other professions have developed. For example it is usual for social workers who are helping to train students to be allowed reduced case loads. Despite the pressure under which primary school teachers are working we think that further experiments should be made in giving schools increased responsibility for the guidance of students. In the final section of this chapter we recommend that in large schools graded posts might be allocated to teachers with special responsibility for guiding probationer teachers. Holders of such posts might give advice to students on teaching practice. Those who give guidance to students, whether they are head teachers, graded post holders or class teachers ought to be in close contact with college tutors.

(iv) The interests of students and of the schools would be generally served by an extension of group practice arrangements.

(v) The partnership between college and school, and the close relationship often involved in group practice, would be especially helpful to schools in under privileged areas. Sometimes pupils are brought into college and given use of college facilities. As many colleges as possible should develop a partnership with schools which have a large proportion of slow learning pupils and of parents who, for whatever reason, do not encourage their children to learn, or which suffer from a rapid turnover of pupils and of staff. These schools would be in effect practising schools, though not attached to the college or subservient to its needs as such schools used to be. If schools with special difficulties were closely associated with colleges, students would be better prepared for the problems they are likely to meet when they begin to teach.

(vi) Closed circuit television, video tape recorders and films are not yet widely enough used in colleges for observation purposes. More films on child development and on teaching techniques should be available. But it is obvious that television and films can only substitute in a small degree for first hand contact with children.

(vii) As our final point, we should like to stress that all students following junior-secondary courses should undertake, at a relatively late stage in their course, a block practice in a primary school. Without it, students will almost certainly lack confidence and knowledge to teach in the primary schools where their services are most needed. Similarly students undertaking infant-junior courses should have practical experience with young children towards the end of their course.

Other Aspects of the Relationship between Schools and Teacher Training Institutions

992. Partnership between schools and teacher training institutions is the key to satisfactory arrangements for teaching practice and is worth almost any effort to achieve. Relations between colleges and the schools they use for teaching practice are usually cordial, but often restricted to the necessary arrangements and to the work of particular students. The suggestions we have made for school practice will of themselves widen and deepen the relationships between training institutions and the schools. But we have some further suggestions to make, which fall outside school practice, and almost all of which derive from arrangements which already exist in some parts of the country. Initiative for a closer relationship coming from the college or department of education is most likely to be welcomed if it is clear that its purpose is to seek ways in which the teachers' knowledge can contribute more fully to students' training, as well as means by which the college can be of greater service to the schools. We hope that schools will put forward their own suggestions for strengthening links with the colleges and schools of education in their district.

993. Some colleges offer teachers an opportunity to share their facilities. A college with a good collection of children's books may invite teachers to make use of the library and call upon the help of the librarian, in choosing books for their schools. Similarly some colleges invite teachers to try out their experimental material for work in mathematics and science. We know college which have established teachers' centres and have appointed members of staff to be in charge of in-service training for teaching.

994. Quite apart from group practice, an increasing number of lecturers in colleges and departments of education make arrangements to teach regularly in local schools. In this way lecturers can extend their experience with children of differing ages and try out new ideas. The schools may receive fresh stimulus.

995. Conversely, teachers could with advantage take a fuller share in the work of the colleges. Some teachers could make a contribution as visiting lecturers and talk to a large group of students. More often, perhaps, their most useful contribution would be in the intimate setting of a discussion group. It can be of great value to students to discuss their school problems with teachers and lecturers in such a context and to gain more precise ideas on the range of children's achievement by seeing and discussing work brought in by a teacher

from his own class. The colleges have sometimes been hesitant about asking for this help because they have felt it would be unfair to impose yet another burden on the hard pressed schools. Many teachers have said, however, that they would welcome an occasional invitation of this kind, and local authorities are usually co-operative in making it possible for teachers to visit colleges during school hours.

996. Joint appointments for work partly in school and partly in college are another useful form of collaboration. At present they are rare, but they should be much easier to arrange now that part-time teachers are becoming common in primary schools. There are some complications over salary arrangements and we recommend that the bodies responsible for negotiating salaries should consider the problems arising from full-time joint appointments. Similar problems have been solved in other professions. Secondment is another possibility. There are, of course, difficulties especially at present. Experienced lecturers and teachers have to help the many newcomers to college and school staffs, and often cannot be released. But both schools and colleges have much to gain from the exchange or renewal of experience.

997. There are many other possible useful contacts. Curriculum development, such as the new work in primary school mathematics, may provide an incentive for discussion and collaboration. Innumerable conferences are open to lecturers and teachers; they could with profit more frequently be focused on the problems of teacher training itself. The need for recruiting college lecturers with experience in primary school teaching was one reason for a recent series of courses for primary school teachers during which the teachers saw something of a college of education. Research projects could often be carried out jointly by institutes of education and schools. Some institutes publish journals which might, even more frequently than at present, provide opportunities for teachers to describe innovations which they have found to be successful.

998. The English system of teacher training, whi.h puts great store on the student's gradual growth in understanding of children and of the educational process, stands or falls on the degree of contact which there is between training institutions and schools.

The Probationary Year

999. On first entering teaching service in a maintained school the qualified teacher has to serve a probationary period, normally of one year. The Secretary of State may extend the period if the teacher has not proved sufficiently proficient or may declare him unsuitable. When a teacher is trained in the United Kingdom the local education authority acts as the agent of the Secretary of State in determining whether he is satisfactory, but in other cases the authority makes a recommendation to the Secretary of State which is considered, together with the opinion of H.M.I. Since it is difficult for all untrained teachers to be visited within a year by local authority advisers and H.M. Inspectors, we concur with the recommendation made by a Working Party of the A.T.C.D.E., the National Association of Inspectors and Organisers and the N.U.T. that the probationary period for teachers without a professional qualification should normally be two years. The analysis of extensions of probation of trained teachers in 1961/62[1] showed that up to

nine per cent were recommended for extension in counties and up to five per cent in county boroughs. Since the gravest shortage of teachers and the more difficult schools are in the boroughs, it is reasonable to suppose that the higher extension rate in the counties reflects more exacting standards and more thorough checks on efficiency rather than a poorer quality of teacher. The number whose probation is extended in different areas should be made known to all authorities. Differences in the standard required could be reduced if there were more advisers and advisory teachers to supervise probationers, and if head teachers were helped to understand what their responsibility is towards young teachers. The Department of Education and Science have begun to notify colleges and departments of education of former students whose probation has been extended. This should help colleges to assess the strengths and weaknesses of their training, and to recognise other students who are likely to fail or who need special help. Closer consultation between authorities and colleges of education about young teachers who are in danger of failure would be advantageous. Some young teachers, who are working in the area where they were trained, might be advised to return to their college for help, or tutors might be invited to visit young teachers in difficulty and see their problems at first hand.

1000. It is a small minority of teachers who fail to reach a minimum standard of proficiency in their first year. But it is doubtful if the majority of young teachers are given the conditions and guidance in their first posts which will reinforce their training and lead to rising standards in the profession as a whole.

1001. Most of our witnesses believe that insufficient care is taken in placing teachers in their first posts, though they realise that vacancies have to be filled and that some schools which are not really suitable for probationers because of their shortage of experienced teachers could not remain open unless some probationers were sent to them. There is dissatisfaction about the classes to which probationers are assigned, as well as with the schools to which they are posted. Similar dissatisfaction was expressed by the majority of the sample of teachers whose opinions were asked by the Council (Appendix 1, Table E.27). The young teachers were more discontented with the arrangements than those whose probationary period was further away. Witnesses suggested to the Council that insufficient guidance was available for young teachers who ought to receive more help from both local authority advisers and from colleges of education in the neighbourhood. The A.T.C.D.E. and the N.U.T. agree that the probationary year should be regarded as an extension of training rather than as a period when young teachers prove themselves.

1002. In the last five years various enquiries have been undertaken into the probationary year. The A.T.C.D.E. and the N.U.T. issued a joint pamphlet "Teachers in their First Posts"[2] in 1962. This was followed the next year by a Working Party of the A.T.C.D.E., the N.A.I.E.O. and the N.U.T. which has produced an interim report[3]. The Birmingham Institute of Education Training Colleges Research Group in 1962 sent a questionnaire to 2,000 teachers who had recently left their colleges. 58 per cent replied, including 604 primary teachers. As the report suggests, "if a considerable number of students indicate that they meet a particular problem, then whether the sample is representative or not it remains true that this is a problem worth investigation".[4]

In 1964–65 H.M. Inspectors made a small enquiry into the problems of 67 teachers in their probationary year.

1003. The Bristol University Institute of Education is now carrying out a systematic factual investigation into teachers' first year of service. Authorities are being asked about the arrangements which they make both for the introduction and supervision of beginners, and for judging their performance. Two questionnaires will be addressed to a national sample of probationers who will be asked about their problems and about the guidance they receive. This research will only establish facts. Further research, for example, into the circumstances of probationary teachers who fail, may then be necessary.

1004. The Birmingham enquiry provided little direct evidence on the question whether probationers were in schools that were suitable for their reception. About one third of the primary teachers were appointed to the service of the authority and not to a specific school, an arrangement which, however questionable in other ways, has the advantage that probationers who are unsuitably placed can be moved. Many of these teachers were probably used to fill vacancies for which teachers could not otherwise be found. We heard of one rural area where it is difficult to appoint assistant teachers to two teacher schools. In consequence, posts for assistants tend to be filled by a succession of probationers to whom the head teacher, because of his preoccupation with his own class, can give little help. Probationers are also found in schools with a bad history of staffing instability.

1005. The Birmingham enquiry showed that 70 per cent of the respondents who were in infant schools were given five year old pupils to teach, though it was not clear how many of these children were beginners at school. Nearly half of the women probationers in junior schools were teaching seven year olds. Colleges of education should take account, when preparing students, of the age groups in which young teachers are usually placed. The allocation of classes to probationers in streamed schools did not support the view that they are automatically given the lowest streams; in two stream schools they were much more likely to be with B classes than with A classes; in three stream schools, they tended to be given the B streams and about the same proportions were with A and C classes. But the H.M.I. enquiry into the cases of 67 probationers gives examples of what statistics may mean in practice. A teacher with one year's training after failing a degree course was teaching a C stream. Another was in charge of 46 pupils in a B class which had a 50 per cent changeover after the first term. A graduate in agriculture with a teaching diploma was taking first year juniors, and an untrained graduate was with a reception class. It seems inescapable that in a period of shortage and maldistribution of teachers, some probationers will be placed in unsuitable schools and unsuitably placed within them. But we endorse the recommendation of the joint Working Party of the A.T.C.D.E., N.A.I.O. and N.U.T. that Administrative Memorandum 4/59 should be revised to give greater emphasis to the need for careful placing and systematic guidance for teachers in their first posts. We also agree that the reports, sent by the colleges of education to employing authorities, should be made available to heads of schools to help them in their placings.

1006. During teaching practice the student has the support of the college staff and the relief of a time table which is usually less than full time. It has been rare for students to be in charge of the class for as long as a term though this length of practice is becoming more common, and will, we hope, become fairly general. The more thoroughly students are drawn into the life of the school, the less likely are they later to be worried, as many of the probationers in the Birmingham Survey were worried, by such problems as class organisation, backward children and correction of children's work. It is reasonable to expect more from probationers who have followed a three year course than from those in the Birmingham Survey who had spent only two years in college. Nevertheless we hope that with the help of part-time teachers and teachers' aides, probationers will be allowed some non-teaching time in which to visit schools and classes other than their own.

1007. Although the primary school probationers in the Birmingham Survey were more satisfied than the secondary teachers with the guidance they had been given, many would have liked more advice from their head teachers and experienced colleagues. Here again, if the schools take over more responsibility for the guidance of students, it will be natural to continue that guidance into the probationary year. It is disturbing to find that many young teachers have no contact before they start work with the school to which they are going. When further guidance is issued by the Department, it should stress the importance of a good beginning to the probationary year. It should ask local authorities to emphasise the responsibility of head teachers for seeing that probationers know in advance what work they will be undertaking. It should also ask training establishments to impress upon students the need for visiting the schools in which they will be working.

1008. It would be easier for probationers to make contact with the schools to which they are appointed if all authorities followed the example of those that reimburse the expenses of teachers who visit the schools where they are going to work. Some authorities sensibly arrange for students to start work in school as soon as their training has finished. Unfortunately they often do not go to the school in which they will spend their probationary year. If they do, they get to know the background of the school, their future colleagues and often their future pupils. They prepare for the work they will be doing during the following year, and help the schools at a time of great pressure. This applies with especial force to those who are to teach in poor neighbourhoods where schools are often chronically short of teachers, and a settling in period for probationary teachers is particularly useful. If it is desirable for young teachers to be at the school to which they will be appointed for the end of the summer term, it is essential that they should turn up in good time for the autumn term and attend preliminary staff conferences when these are held. Colleges of education can do much to put high professional standards before their students. Local education authorities should give early notification to young teachers of their appointments. Most do. Some do not.

1009. The number of probationers in large schools may mean that head teachers, with their many other duties, can give insufficient help to young teachers. In any case there will always be some young teachers who seek and take advice more easily from their equals than from anyone in authority over them. Though the ultimate responsibility for probationers within the school must rest with the head, detailed arrangements should vary according to individual circumstances. In some schools, the deputy head may be the right person to give advice; in others, the holder of a graded post might be responsible for probationers and students on teaching practice, and keep in touch with the colleges of education. Support can be given to a probationer by the skilful allocation of classes to teachers. If, for example, an experienced teacher and a probationer are placed with parallel age groups, a modest degree of team teaching, helpful to experienced teacher and probationer alike, can develop. The work to be done can be discussed, books and equipment shared, and there may be an occasional exchange of classes or joint teaching. These devices are particularly necessary in junior mixed and infant schools, where a head master may be unable to give much help to beginners who are teaching infants. Whoever gives the help needs to know, in general terms at least, what the probationer has been doing at college. Local education authorities might well organise small conferences or study groups, for head teachers and others who share their responsibility, at which the placing and guidance of young teachers can be discussed. Lecturers from colleges of education should also be invited to take part and the programme should include some guidance on the assessment of teaching skill.

1010. The local education authorities are rightly responsible for providing further guidance to probationers in addition to what is given by the school. Some authorities have no inspectors, organisers or advisers, and more are without inspectors with a special knowledge of primary education. Even when they have organisers, the demands on their time are usually heavy and help is sometimes confined to those probationers who are in danger of failure. The enquiry by H.M. Inspectors showed that in the areas examined, noteworthy help was given by only one authority, though in that instance the support from an advisory teachers' service was of the greatest possible value. All authorities need officers who are known to have the immediate responsibility for probationers and who are accessible to them and to head teachers. It must be for the authorities to decide whether to have separate advisers for probationers or whether to divide the responsibility among several organisers or advisers with other duties. The officer with special responsibility for probationers might maintain contact with colleges of education. In some large authorities a welfare officer is appointed to assist probationers in personal problems such as finding accommodation.

1011. It seems to us that some general supervision is needed, so that probationers can get advice on the problems that confront them in and out of school. It is sensible for all probationary teachers to be visited by an adviser in their first term, so that an unsuitable posting can be altered before too much damage is done. We have been impressed by what we have seen and heard of advisory teacher services. We wish to stress the need for advisory teachers who can work beside young teachers in the classroom. This help is particularly necessary in rural and deprived areas. Probationary teachers are visited for a half day, a full day or even several consecutive days if this is needed. There is time for discussion of books, materials and organisation and for letting head teachers know the advice that has been given. Help need not come to an end when probation is completed. Advisers or advisory teachers can arrange conferences, courses and visits for young teachers when they are sufficiently experienced to profit from them. Conferences and courses should be informal and provide opportunities for young teachers to meet one another to talk over common problems. We suggest that probationers should be provided with information about the educational services in their authority either by a booklet or conference or both.

1012. The teachers who replied to the Birmingham enquiry placed training colleges high among sources of help from outside the schools, though it was not certain that they referred to contacts during the first year of teaching. The enquiry by H.M. Inspectors also noted that some teachers had been helped by students' reunions at their former colleges and that others wished to go back for advice to their tutors. "Teachers in their First Posts" described an experimental group run by the Reading Institute of Education which offered young teachers guidance which came neither from "the employer, the inspector or training college tutor"[5]. There may be something in the argument that the institutes offer neutral ground from the point of view of the young teacher; but their geographical distribution is such that they can provide only a patchy contribution to the general problem. On the whole, the responsibility for organising conferences and other help for probationers should rest with the authorities who alone know all the probationers, trained or untrained. We assume that the authority will want to draw in the local institute and colleges of education. But the immediate, and therefore the greatest, responsibility for the welfare of young teachers must rest on their schools. It is for head teachers and colleagues in the staff room to look after them, to give favourable conditions and to set, mainly by example, high standards for them.

In-Service Training

1013. The unique freedom of the English schools is defensible only if teachers prove themselves equipped to meet demands which are increasingly exacting. The three year course is no more than a basis. In-service training provides a necessary superstructure. The Department of Education has recently issued a circular[6] which reviews the problems for in-service training created by the number of new teachers.

Present Provision of Courses and Plans for Expansion

1014. Our concern is primarily with the purpose of in-service training and the extent to which it succeeds. The National Association of Schoolmasters drew our attention to the difficulties which prevent teachers from taking subject degrees. Few authorities, they say, allow secondment for a first degree course because there is no pooling arrangement for the expenditure. This, we agree, is deplorable; but, as we have suggested, it is particularly important that experienced teachers, as well as new entrants, should be able to obtain a B.Ed. degree. As soon as the main outlines of the B.Ed. courses have been agreed, arrangements should be made for serving teachers, including those holding posts of responsibility to take these degrees, probably by a combination of part-time and full-time study.

1015. There are two types of one year course held in institutes of education, colleges of education and university departments of education. Supplementary courses are designed to give a year of further training to experienced teachers who have had only two year training college courses. For the most part they give additional experience in a special area of the curriculum, for example art and crafts, divinity, history and mathematics. These courses will increasingly be replaced by courses of advanced study for teachers with at least five years experience. They normally lead to a university diploma or certificate. Their original purpose was to deal with an aspect of education such as junior education. They have been extended to include study in depth of an area of the curriculum. Last year 625 teachers attended full-time advanced courses, a sixth of them on topics related exclusively to primary education. The corresponding part-time numbers were 1,753 and 135. At least 1,000 full-time students annually are expected by 1974. In addition last year there were 35 courses for teachers of handicapped children attended by 415 students.

1016. Advanced courses are intended to equip teachers for responsible posts in colleges, schools advisory services and remedial centres. Their status may be affected by the introduction of the B.Ed. degree and it has been suggested to us in evidence that they should be regarded as a qualifying examination for a higher degree in education. Since 1965, one year of full-time study for a higher degree has been possible under the regulations governing advanced courses. We think that the rapid expansion of these courses should continue. They can do much to meet the acute shortage of lecturers who combine specialised subject knowledge with insight into primary education. It is important too, that some teachers who have no intention of leaving the schools should follow these courses; their work is the spear head of advance.

1017. The expansion of one year courses should not be at the expense of the one term courses of which there are about a hundred a year. Their merit is that they provide a flexible means of meeting changing needs by giving teachers time to become familiar with new content and methods and to try out experiments, free from the day to day responsibility of teaching. They have played an important part in the revolution in the teaching of mathematics. They could be valuable in preparing teachers for work with children who are socially deprived, including immigrants, and could accelerate collaboration between school, home and community.

1018. Short courses, lasting for a day, a weekend, a week or longer, or taking place for one or more sessions weekly over a period in time are especially important now that the shortage of teachers makes secondment difficult. Residential short courses have been one of the main ways by which H.M. Inspectors have influenced the school curriculum and been brought into informal contact with teachers to their common benefit. In recent years teachers from colleges of education and schools and local inspectors have often joined the staff of these courses which have included also many who are not in a formal sense educationalists. Though there are often six times as many teachers applying for primary courses as there is room for, pressure on the inspectors' time prevents much further expansion. For this reason the policy of Circular 7/64 is timely. Courses are arranged which bring together successful and original teachers, head teachers, college of education lecturers and local authority advisers to discuss their work with H.M. Inspectors and to take their thinking and practice further. Those who attend these courses can then help on local courses and conferences in their home area. Some outstanding teachers hesitate to apply for this type of course out of modesty; there is a strong case for attendance at some courses to be by invitation. Certainly, the frontiersmen of education need opportunities to meet like-minded teachers, to test innovations by the practice of others, and to continue their personal education. There are occasions when it is better to confine a course to a group of people from the same area even if good candidates from elsewhere have to be turned down. As research and enquiry expose areas of primary education where change is called for, national courses can make the new findings known to those teachers who are most likely to act on them.

1019. Numerous short courses are also provided by local authorities, by professional associations, by informal groups of teachers and by institutes and colleges of education. The part played by these bodies in in-service training is vital. National and local courses are complementary. At local courses the findings of research and good practice can be made available in a way that will encourage teachers to think more deeply about their own methods, or take from new curricular materials and method whatever meets the need of their pupils, and to reject the irrelevant. In this way a base is established from which further advances can be made. Local courses are also invaluable in supporting the innovations introduced by individual teachers, the source of most educational progress. They ought to start from a knowledge of what local teachers are doing. They can provide opportunities for teachers to meet others who are a little ahead of themselves but whose practice is within their reach. Before the end of a course, all teachers can be playing an active part in discussion, in learning and in making, just as we hope that they will encourage all children to play an active part in the classroom. The work done on a course can be followed up in a teachers' group or in the schools. The diffident can be encouraged to break new ground, but not so hastily that disheartenment is the outcome. This slow building up of teachers, best done on small courses, is perhaps the most difficult and the most rewarding aspect of in-service training. We have seen its results in some of the most distinguished primary school work in the country. Local courses should be staffed by the same combination of people as national courses, though perhaps in different proportions.

1020. Residential courses, where talk can go on into the small hours, have a value of their own. In some areas a general adult education centre provides accommodation. Teachers gain from meeting adults from other occupations. We have seen for ourselves the value of a residential centre where teachers can feel at home and where there can be permanent displays of books and equipment useful to them. A network of residential centres throughout the country would be useful, but these teachers' centres ought to be available for courses for others than teachers. Residential centres or residential short courses will not meet the whole need. There is a case for more local centres some of which are being provided by colleges of education. In local centres, equipment and materials can be tried out and discussed and the ideas gained at residential courses can be appraised after being tested in the schools. These centres, for which some of the stimulus has come from the Nuffield projects, are excellent for courses of one session a week for several terms, a pattern which is of particular value when there is new subject matter which has to be mastered. In sparsely populated rural areas, the follow up of residential courses is best provided by meetings in different schools in turn, and by the help of advisory teachers and inspectors.

1021. Co-ordination of in-service training is needed at several levels nationally, regionally and locally. National responsibility for co-ordination should, it seems to us, rest with the Department of Education and Science. It will want to see that the character and extent of the national programme meet the needs which are created by the curriculum studies and other work commissioned by the Schools Council. The Department are in close contact with institutes of education, colleges of education, local authorities and above all with the schools. The inspectorate can serve as "eyes and ears" to report existing demand and to indicate where it is necessary to provide courses to make new work and ideas better known.

1022. There is also a need for regional planning. The final responsibility for local courses should rest with the local education authorities who are in contact with their teachers and able to know their needs. The authorities, however, will not necessarily be the sole agency through which in-service training takes place. Some are too small to make adequate provision; even in medium sized authorities in-service training may become too inbred. The resources of institutes and colleges of education and of colleges of further education ought to be used to the full. The institutes of education are particularly well placed for bringing universities, colleges of education and schools together for conferences and courses. They need staff and material resources to carry out this important role.

1023. Even so, some small authorities will be unable to provide in-service training for their teachers, and larger authorities may have difficulty in arranging sufficiently varied and balanced courses. The Schools Council has met this obstacle to the development of its projects by suggesting "ad hoc" groupings of authorities. We think that authorities should review their arrangements for in-service training and should be asked to submit plans to the Department for their areas, and that some form of regional planning should be devised. In this way authorities would be encouraged to run joint courses, or to make their courses available to teachers from other authorities within the region. Any regional body ought to include representatives of institutes and of teachers. It might need a small staff paid by the group of local authorities concerned.

1024. The primary teacher, who normally is responsible for all subjects and may teach children of all levels of ability, is in particular need of the refreshment of in-service training. We were glad to find from the National Survey that two-thirds of all primary teachers had followed a refresher course between September 1961 and June 1964, and that on average these teachers had spent 13 days on courses (Appendix 5, paragraphs 15 to 26)*. But most courses, particularly those organised by local authorities, are very short. We think that there should be more courses where teachers can study the problems of primary school teaching in some depth. It is excellent that many teachers (26 per cent) have attended courses in mathematics at this time of rapid change in the curriculum. It is less clear that provision of, and attendance at, other types of courses reflects the needs of the schools. For example, many teachers (21 per cent) attended courses in physical education. Is this because most authorities have advisers in physical education? Relatively few teachers (nine per cent) go to music courses despite the generally acknowledged shortage of teachers competent in this subject in the schools. The relatively small number of courses in science, though they have probably increased since our survey, and the almost complete absence of in-service training in history and geography are a matter for some concern. Some of

*This average is inflated by the small numbers attending one term and year courses. Other reservations about these figures appear in Appendix 5.

these aspects of the curriculum may be treated in general courses. But comparatively few teachers attend general courses. Only eight per cent of the total number of teachers in the National Survey had attended a general primary course, three per cent a junior course and nine per cent an infant course. It is doubtful whether there are enough general courses or teachers attending them, especially at this time of changing organisation and curriculum.

1025. From all sides we have heard of the inadequate provision of courses to prepare new and prospective head and deputy head teachers for their future duties. There are opportunities for them to increase their understanding of children and of the curriculum; but they need help about management and administration. They need to study social problems and their impact on children, and to understand the work of the family social services. This study should be in a local context and should include contact with workers in the social services.

Courses for Returning Teachers

1026. Married women who return to teaching either full or part-time after a lengthy break in service may lack confidence and be out of touch with recent developments in the schools. About a fifth of authorities are now providing courses to meet this special need. Some of these courses are also for secondary trained teachers who want to transfer to primary work and for graduates who have never taught. Some teachers coming back to the schools do not feel the need for any special help, although authorities have often found that when courses are known to be available the response is good. A small survey carried out by one authority showed that some returning teachers found a period of observation and teaching practice to be more valuable than formal courses. Most of the courses are divided between practical work, lectures and discussions. Some are full-time from two weeks to a term in length; others are part-time, often a day, half day or evening a week, supplemented by school visits and teaching practice. In one area courses of whole-day lectures are provided which teachers can join or leave at any time. Teachers who have no opportunity of following a course before returning should at least visit for observation other schools than that to which they are appointed. Two out of three authorities already arrange this. The more that authorities can help married women when they wish to return to teaching, the more effective will be their contribution to the schools.

1027. We think all teachers should have a substantial period of in-service training at least every five years. Some of the teachers who do attend courses are among the leaders of primary education; other would no doubt be less effective without the help which they get. But the review of in-service training ought to answer the question whether it reaches the teachers and areas most in need of it, as distinct from those who apply for it, and whether it is dealing with the right topics and in sufficient depth. An enquiry should be made into the expenses of teachers attending courses in order to ensure that no teacher is prevented for financial reasons from improving his efficiency as we suspect sometimes happens now. Should we go further and provide incentives as the U.S.A. does for those who attend courses? Teachers who successfully complete diploma and certain other courses already receive an addition under the Burnham scale. We think it would be impracticable to reward attendance at

N

short courses irrespective of the qualification to which they lead. Authorities and heads should use more freely the power they have (within a minimum obligatory number of sessions in the school year) to close schools in order to make possible in-service training. Closure of schools is particularly suitable for local conferences on such matters as continuity between stages of education when it is desirable that all members of school staffs should be present. It is bad when it leads to mammoth courses or forces teachers to unwilling attendance.

Recommendations

1028.   (i) There should be a full enquiry into the system of training teachers.

(ii) The number of courses in which future teachers are trained side by side with entrants to other social service professions should be increased.

(iii) The proportion of students admitted to colleges of education without an "O" level pass in mathematics is too high; the proportion of students who have specialised in the sixth form in mathematics and science subjects is too low. Efforts should be made to improve qualifications in these subjects.

(iv) More men teachers are needed in primary schools and the attention of the secondary schools should be drawn to this.

(v) Mature students have proved their value; the network of day colleges and outposts should be extended.

(vi) More graduates are required in primary schools, and more facilities should be provided for their training.

(vii) Arrangements should be made to inform schools of the record of their former pupils in colleges of education.

(viii) Graduates should be required to receive professional training if they are going to teach in primary schools.

(ix) There should be closer partnership and contact between schools and colleges.

(x) The agreement between the A.T.C.D.E. and the National Union of Students on college discipline is welcome: all colleges should put it into operation. Colleges of education should develop close associations with schools with special difficulties.

(xi) The arrangements for teaching practice should take account of the needs of the schools. Final responsibility for supervision of students should rest with the colleges, but schools can play a bigger part.

(xii) More joint appointments to college and school staffs should be made.

(xiii) In order to reduce variations in standards, local education authorities should be informed of the number of teachers, authority by authority, whose probation is extended or who are declared unsuitable.

(xiv) The normal period of probation for untrained graduates and for teachers trained outside the U.K. should be two years.

(xv) Local education authorities should pay the travelling expenses of students who visit the schools to which they are appointed before they take up work; more should start work in the summer as soon as the examinations are over.

(xvi) Graded posts should be available in large schools for teachers who supervise students and probationers and maintain contacts with colleges of education. All local education authorities should designate officers to deal with young teachers. In smaller schools teachers with graded posts should take responsibility for students and probationers.

(xvii) The B.Ed. degree courses should be made available to serving teachers.

(xviii) The expansion of one year advanced and one term full-time in-service courses should continue. Every teacher should have a substantial period of in-service training at least every five years.

(xix) A network of residential teachers' courses should be developed.

(xx) Local education authorities should be asked to submit plans for in-service training. Regional co-operation should be encouraged.

(xxi) Short courses should be arranged for new or prospective head teachers and deputies.

(xxii) Teachers should not be financially penalised for attending short courses.

REFERENCES

[1]'The Probationary Year', Interim Report of Joint Working Party of A.T.C.D.E., N.A.I.E.O. and N.U.T.
[2]'Teachers in their First Posts', A.T.C.D.E., 1962.
[3]See [2] above.
[4]'The Probationary Year', J. Cornwall, University of Birmingham Institute of Education, 1965.
[5]See [2] above.
[6]Department of Education and Science Circular 7/64, dated 25th May 1964.

Table 25

Qualifications of Students Admitted to General, Housecraft, P.E. and Shortened Courses in Colleges of Education in the years 1960-61, 1961-62 and 1965-66. (England and Wales)

I. Three Year General, Housecraft and P.E. Courses.

Qualifications	MEN 1960-61 No.	% of total	MEN 1961-62 No.	% of total	MEN 1965-66 No.	% of total	WOMEN 1960-61 No.	% of total	WOMEN 1961-62 No.	% of total	WOMEN 1965-66 No.	% of total	TOTAL 1960-61 No.	% of total	TOTAL 1961-62 No.	% of total	TOTAL 1965-66 No.	% of total
More than 1 'A' level	1,409	35	1,466	37	2,780	38	3,455	34	3,585	37	7,665	39	4,864	34	5,051	37	10,445	39
1 'A' level	1,085	27	1,035	26	2,001	28	2,510	25	2,378	24	5,138	26	3,595	25	3,413	25	7,139	27
5 or more 'O' levels but no 'A' level	1,371	34	1,260	31	2,017	28	3,819	38	3,301	34	5,284	27	5,190	37	4,561	33	7,301	27
School or Higher School Cert. or Matric	91	2	110	3	199	3	207	2	250	3	943	5	298	2	360	3	1,142	4
Other Quals. equiv. to 5 'O' levels	54	1	61	1	75	1	122	1	126	1	217	1	176	1	187	1	292	1
Exceptional admissions	48	1	67	2	176	2	54	0	83	1	321	2	102	1	150	1	497	2
TOTALS	4,058	100	3,999	100	7,248	100	10,167	100	9,723	100	19,568	100	14,225	100	13,722	100	26,816	100

II. Shortened General Courses.

Qualifications	MEN 1960-61 No.	% of total	MEN 1961-62 No.	% of total	MEN 1965-66 No.	% of total	WOMEN 1960-61 No.	% of total	WOMEN 1961-62 No.	% of total	WOMEN 1965-66 No.	% of total	TOTAL 1960-61 No.	% of total	TOTAL 1961-62 No.	% of total	TOTAL 1965-66 No.	% of total
More than 1 'A' level	219	28	143	36	134	25	113	14	63	14	168	20	332	21	206	24	302	22
1 'A' level	50	7	27	7	65	12	52	6	19	4	60	7	102	6	46	6	125	9
5 or more 'O' levels but no 'A' level	151	19	39	10	92	17	96	11	18	4	75	9	247	15	57	7	167	12
School or Higher School Cert. or Matric	244	31	118	30	144	27	429	51	265	59	406	49	673	42	383	45	550	40
Other Quals. equiv. to 5 'O' levels	40	5	25	6	29	6	62	7	29	7	45	5	102	6	54	6	74	6
Exceptional admissions	74	10	43	11	69	13	90	11	55	12	81	10	164	10	98	12	150	11
TOTALS	778	100	395	100	533	100	842	100	449	100	835	100	1,620	100	844	100	1,368	100

Table 25 (Continued)

III. Total of I and II Above.

Qualifications	MEN						WOMEN						TOTAL					
	1690-61		1961-62		1965-66		1960-61		1961-62		1965-66		1960-61		1961-62		1965-66	
	No.	% of total	No.	% of total	No.	% of total	No.	% of total	No.	% of total	No.	% of total	No.	% of total	No.	% of total	No.	% of total
More than 1 'A' level	1,628	34	1,609	37	2,914	38	3,568	32	3,648	36	7,833	38	5,196	33	5,257	36	10,747	38
1 "A" level	1,135	23	1,062	24	2,066	27	2,562	23	2,397	24	5,198	26	3,697	23	3,459	24	7,264	26
5 or more 'O' levels but no 'A' levels	1,522	31	1,299	30	2,109	27	3,915	36	3,319	33	5,359	26	5,437	34	4,618	32	7,468	27
School or Higher School Cert. or Matric.	335	7	228	5	343	4	636	6	515	5	1,349	7	971	6	743	5	1,692	6
Other Quals. equiv. to 5 'O' levels	94	2	86	2	104	1	184	2	155	1	262	1	278	2	241	1	366	1
Exceptional admissions	122	3	110	2	245	3	144	1	138	1	402	2	266	2	248	2	647	2
TOTAL	4,836	100	4,394	100	7,781	100	11,009	100	10,172	100	20,403	100	15,845	100	14,566	100	28,184	100

Table 26

Total Number of Students in Initial Non-Graduate Courses in Colleges of Education by Type of Course and Years
(England and Wales)

(1) Year	(2) Full length Course Specialist and General 3 Year			(3) Shortened Courses (A) General 1 Year Courses			(B) General and Specialist 2 Year Courses			(4) Total—Shortened Courses (3) (A) + (B)			Total: All Courses (2) + (3)		
	Men	Women	Total	Men	Women	Total	Men	Women	Total	Men	Women	Total	Men	Women	Total
1961-62	8,007	22,000	30,007	143	63	206	966	1,183	2,149	1,109	1,246	2,355	9,116	23,246	33,362
1962-63	12,090	31,697	43,787	69	36	105	633	897	1,530	702	933	1,635	12,792	32,630	45,422
1963-64	13,626	35,968	49,594	97	45	142	689	1,026	1,715	786	1,071	1,857	14,412	37,039	51,451
1964-65	15,560	39,310	54,870	96	50	146	798	1,181	1,979	894	1,231	2,125	16,454	40,541	56,995
1965-66	18,385	46,850	65,235	77	53	130	877	1,419	2,296	954	1,472	2,426	19,339	48,322	67,661

Table 27. *Number of General and Specialist Colleges*
offering Different Types of Courses.

(*1*) Type of Course	(*2*) No. of Colleges offering courses as in (*1*)	(*3*) Colleges offering Courses as in (*1*) expressed as a percentage of total number of colleges*
Nursery	6	4
Nursery/Infant	14	9
Infant	76	49
Infant/Junior	81	52
Junior	94	61
Junior/Secondary	105	68
Secondary—General	91	59
Secondary—Domestic Science	8	5
Secondary—Physical Education	10	6

*The total number of colleges of education in England and Wales including those offering specialist courses in Housecraft and Physical Education is 155. (1965–66).

Table 28. *Annual Intake of Students to Non-Graduate Courses in General Colleges of Education.* (*England andWales*).

	1963/64		1964/65		1965/66	
	Men	Women	Men	Women	Men	Women
(1) Nursery/Infant		305		332		451
(2) Infant		1,893		2,153	2	2,534
(3) Infant/Junior	59	3,292	155	4,469	268	6,539
(4) Junior	943	2,664	1,100	3,158	1,230	3,663
(5) Junior/Secondary	2,156	2,618	2,864	3,335	4,025	4,319
(6) Secondary	1,958	1,655	2,228	6,355	2,343	2,081
(7) Total: Men and women	5,113	12,427	6,347	19,802	7,868	19,587
(8) Men and Women as percentage of total	29	71	24	76	29	71
(9) Total men and women taking nursery, infant and junior courses (1, 2 and 3 above)	992	8,154	1,255	10,112	1,500	13,187
(10) Men and Women in (9) as percentage of all students	5	43	4	38	5	48
(11) Men and Women taking junior/secondary courses (5) as percentage of all students	12	15	10	11	15	16

CHAPTER 26

The Training of Nursery Assistants and Teachers' Aides

Existing Schemes of Training

1029. Well established schemes of work-based training leading to the Certificate of the National Nursery Examination Board already exist for nursery nurses and those in similar types of employment. These schemes are conducted in institutions approved for the purpose by the Department of Education and Science, and by the Home Office or the Ministry of Health. The National Nursery Examination Board lay down entry requirements to courses, administer the final examinations and provide an outline syllabus for the guidance of those conducting the courses. About 2,000 students qualify each year from over 60 establishments for further education, either in the colleges themselves or in nursery training centres, and there are also nine nursery nurses colleges. The minimum age of entry to a course is 16 years of age but many students enter at 17. Although no formal qualifications are required for entry to examinations many students have one or more passes in the Ordinary level of the General Certificate of Education. From the evidence that has reached us from individual establishments it seems that the number of candidates greatly exceeds the number of places. The courses generally last for two years although for some students who are at least 18 on entry into training and possess certain qualifications the course may be shortened to 18 months.

1030. Training is the joint responsibility of the training institution and the establishment in which the student is employed. N.N.E.B. regulations have recently been changed to include the care of children from birth to seven years instead of from birth to five years. In consequence infant schools have been recently added to establishments which may be used as centres for practical training. Under the new arrangements, each student's practical training is related to the age range of the establishment or establishments to which she is attached. Practical training may take place in either one or two institutions so that students can gain experience with children either in a day or residential nursery, or in a nursery school and in either nursery classes or infant schools.

1031. The courses are devised by each training establishment within broad outlines suggested by the N.N.E.B. About three-fifths of the training period is spent on active work with young children, and students follow the pattern of life in the institutions to which they are attached, often undertaking the same hours of duty as the staff. An important part of the training is observation of the growth and development of children and students are expected to keep records which they discuss with their tutors. The more theoretical parts of the course in the care of children cover the following topics:—

Young children in the community
Children's needs
Children's development
Special aspects of the care of children.
Services relating to the care of children.

Students are encouraged to develop their own creative abilities and to read widely. General studies form part of the course and provide opportunities for personal development and for education for parenthood and for good citizenship. Some of these courses, of which details have reached us, provide a vigorous cultural and social life. Many include a large number of visits of a general educational nature and draw on visiting lecturers for a wide range of subjects. Students are encouraged to extend their knowledge of children through holiday work in private homes and through many forms of service to the community.

1032. At least two centres have established a course for mature students aged 25 to 45 years. They take the two year course for the N.N.E.B. examination and certificate. For both courses the number of applications far exceeds the number of places. At another training establishment many applications from married women have been received for a N.N.E.B. course but it has not been possible to admit them because of the competition from girls leaving school. A one year course is at present under consideration.

1033. When trained, N.N.E.B. students work in a variety of establishments, including nursery schools and classes, day nurseries, residential nurseries, children's homes and children's wards of hospitals. They also work as welfare assistants in infant schools. Other enter various kinds of private employment. Details received from training establishments show that some trained students have gone on to colleges of education and to S.R.N. courses; in some instances the numbers doing this have been large.

Other Training Schemes

1034. An enquiry to local education authorities has shown that some ten authorities are running courses on a more modest scale for welfare assistants in infant schools. Two courses consisted of one session meetings each week for a year; two courses took the form of once weekly meetings for a term. One authority ran a concentrated course for a month which ancillary workers had to attend. Other courses varied in length from ten days to one day. In addition to local schemes, the Central Training Council in Child Care is about to launch a new type of training in colleges of further education. This will emphasise residential child care and general further education, to meet the needs of girls who do not wish to be committed at 16 to work with children of any particular age. Some eight or nine pilot two year courses of 12 to 20 students started in September 1966. It is already clear from the interest shown in these courses that a good many more may be expected to be set up in the future.

Our Proposal

1035. The N.N.E.B. courses have made a substantial contribution to the staffing of nursery schools and classes during the period when little encouragement has been forthcoming from the central government; those who provide them have a fund of experience on which any new scheme can be built. Our proposals must call for some changes in the existing arrangements because the scale of the new schemes will make a greater flexibility in organisation desirable. There will also be some change in purpose. Thus, because we are recommending large increases in the number to be trained and because of the need for greater stability of staffing, it is essential that many more older women should be trained. Only a small beginning has so far been made on this. We are also recommending that teachers' aides should be trained for employment throughout the primary stage of education, and that their training should equip them for wider functions in the schools than those of welfare assistants. These changes of scale and purpose may make it necessary to adjust the composition and the structure of the central examining body.

Similarities of Training and Recruitment

1036. Nursery assistants will work with children up to five or six; teachers' aides with children from 5 to nearly 13. Different emphases in their training will therefore be needed, just as different emphases are found in the training of primary and secondary school teachers. But there should be much in common, in their qualifications for entry to training, their status and the training itself. Their work will overlap since under our proposals children of the same age will be found in nursery groups and in reception classes. Young children in both types of institution need more opportunities for conversation with adults than children in admission classes usually have. In all respects, there ought to be continuity of method and aims between nursery and first school education. In some areas there might be vacancies for aides or assistants, but not for both. What is needed in fact is the development of a general class of helpers for an integrated nursery and primary system who will have a bias towards a part of the age range. They can assist hard pressed teachers and take over some of their lesser responsibilities.

1037. Recruitment will be determined both by the entry qualifications required and by the demand for women workers in other sectors of the economy. Although no hard and fast lines can be laid down, two main sources may be envisaged. There should be large numbers both of qualified school leavers and of older women, many of them married, who could be encouraged to train. Both types have a place both in the schools and the nursery groups. Their recruitment will, however, be determined by supply. Local authorities might also recruit older men whose special skills in crafts and the like could make them particularly useful in middle schools. The more that local authorities can recruit women and men from age groups still underemployed, the greater the chance of success and the less the strain that these educational advances will place on the nation's manpower. We examine the sources of recruitment further in the annexes to Chapter 31.

Entry Qualifications

1038. Entry qualifications should be the same for both services. The emphasis ought to be, as it is now in N.N.E.B. courses, on qualities of character, personality and interest, as identified through a study of the candidate's previous record and by interview. Candidates will need to be of an educational level enabling them to get a grasp of the purposes and functioning of nursery and primary education. With the younger candidates, evidence of a good general education, demonstrated perhaps, but not necessarily, by passes in some subjects of the Certificate of Secondary Education or General Certificate of Education might be expected. For the older women, many of whom may have left school at 14 or 15 years, evidence of one form or another of further education, or of relevant experience at work, would be sufficient if there was evidence from the interview, or other tests, of ability to understand and apply the more theoretical parts of the course.

1039. The importance of personal qualities cannot be overstated. Nursery assistants will carry immediate responsibility for a group of young children. Teachers' aides, too, will have direct contact with, and some responsibility for, children. It cannot be taken for granted that a mother's experience with her own children will of itself qualify her for the work. Neither type of work will be a "soft option" for a mother who wants an easy part-time job.

The Nature of the Courses

1040. Courses should be developed by each centre within the general lines laid down by a central examining body. What are given here are merely suggestions for the training institutions and the examining body to consider. Most of the time in N.N.E.B. courses is spent with children. This is the pattern that should be continued. For younger students, general and vocational education could take up one-third of the course and for the older women one-fifth.

1041. Both nursery assistants and teachers' aides need in their training some general education as well as courses on children's development, the educational services and the social services for children, though there might be differences in the treatment of these subjects according to the ages of children with whom the student intended to work. Teachers' aides will need to cover a wider age range in their study of children's development and to know more about the materials and equipment used in primary schools. Their courses ought often to be individually tailored so that they can see the place in a school context of any special skills and interests they may have. How much of the college training of nursery assistants and teachers' aides could be on a joint basis would vary with the number of students involved and the arrangements for distribution of college work and practical work. In the first year, at least, some teaching might be shared between these and other similar courses.

1042. Some N.N.E.B. courses have experimented successfully with alternating blocks of time spent in general work in college and practical work. When first year students are in college, second year students are in their nurseries or schools. In this way the college staff are fully occupied and nurseries and schools are not left without help. Some such arrangement would be desirable for mature students. They could begin with a course which would include films of children's growth and development and visits to different types of nursery institution and primary school to help them to observe children. They could then decide the age range on which they wished to concentrate. Students in nurseries and schools should not change institutions so rapidly that children cannot form stable relationships with them and the staff cannot make good use of them. Success will depend on close co-operation between the colleges of further education and nursery centres, and the nursery groups and schools where students will be working. There are some excellent models of this co-operation in existing N.N.E.B. courses. In one case, regular meetings are held of the staff at the training establishment and of the heads and matrons of institutions where students practise. Details of students' courses of study are sent to the schools and nurseries and their staff are welcome to attend lectures. Visits are paid each term by the full-time tutors of the course to the schools and nurseries. As the pace of expansion increases, the sense of responsibility should not diminish.

1043. At present the N.N.E.B. approve institutions for practical work. Schools and other establishments will, however, be hard pressed to make room for all who will need practical training. Course tutors will, therefore, need considerable freedom in selecting practice schools and groups. Within the present N.N.E.B. pattern, practice can take place in those types of institutions in which the student hopes eventually to work. Nursery students will practise in all types of nursery and primary schools. Teachers' aides will, we hope, spend most of their training in first or middle schools, although some introduction to the whole range of nursery and primary education should be available to both groups.

1044. Training schemes must start long before there are enough nursery groups in which practice can take place. Even when nursery groups have been generally established, there will be difficulties. The first schools will have to provide for teachers' aides and nursery assistants in training, and will also be under heavy pressure from colleges of education for practice places. Some schools with a nursery group—perhaps the more remote ones—may be less suitable than others for students because the teacher has other groups to visit. It seems inevitable that the schools will have to accept many more students of all kinds and that all types of training institutions may have to cast their net wider than they would wish. But students training for teaching should work alongside nursery assistants and teachers' aides whose help they must use when they become teachers.

Length of Courses

1045. Nursery assistants will have a definable responsibility for children, although working under supervision, but aides will work in closer contact with teachers. We have considered whether the course for teachers' aides should be as long as that for nursery assistants. We believe that girls who enter training shortly after they leave school should follow a two year course, whichever type of service they propose to enter. Those employed as teachers' aides will be in close contact with children, and with the teaching situation. They require a minimum of two years' training to reach a suitable educational standard. A course of this length will ensure that they are at least 18 before entry into full service—an important consideration because they may be working in middle schools where some pupils will be nearly 13 before transfer to secondary schools. Furthermore, interchange between aides and assistants will be permissible only if comparable training is given. A two year course agrees with the suggestions contained in the Newsom Report for combining education in schools with training for a specified job, and with the provisions of the 1944 Education Act for part-time release for attendance at county colleges. For teachers' aides, as for nursery assistants, the greater part of the two year course will be training on the job; the course will be the equivalent of a nine or ten month course of full time study.

1046. At present most N.N.E.B. students undertake a two year course. We are anxious, however, to attract older women and to bring them as rapidly as possible into full service in the nurseries and schools. We therefore recommend that suitable candidates of 21 years of age and over should be permitted to qualify after one year of training in which the equivalent of one day a week would be spent on course work. Although training institutions should be free to advise older students, in individual cases, to take a two year rather than a one year course, we hope mature students will normally be admitted to a one year course.

Status and Salaries of Trainees

1047. The status and pay of both aides and assistants should be the same and they should receive N.N.E.B. student salaries while they are in training. Whereas aides in training will work under the close supervision of a teacher and can, therefore, be regarded as part of the school staff, nursery students in the nursery groups ought not to be so regarded because a qualified teacher may not always be on the premises. Although students should participate fully in the work of a nursery group, they should not take responsibility for children, which must include responsibility for safety.

Part Time Training

1048. Because of family and other commitments, some older women may be able to work only part-time in schools or nursery groups, and may want to train part-time. Since much of the training will be practical, it should be possible to arrange for part-time training over a longer period. Some who already help with older children on such subjects as needlecraft and games could be encouraged to take the parts of the course which will help them to use their skills more effectively in the school.

Location and Staffing of Training

1049. N.N.E.B. courses are at present held in colleges of further education, training centres and nursery colleges. They are not provided by colleges of education, and with the continuing expansion of the number of students training to become teachers, it is unlikely that the colleges could find room for them. In any case, it is important that training for assistants and aides should be available in every area if women who cannot live away from home are to attend them. We envisage, therefore, a continuation of existing courses and a substantial increase in the number of institutions providing training, particularly since the present courses are concentrated largely in areas where there is a strong tradition of nursery provision. Both the central and local arrangements for training should provide for close contact between nursery training institutions and the colleges of further education. Additional accommodation may have to be found in some colleges of further education or their annexes, but no large building programme is envisaged. Whilst courses in colleges of further education should benefit from and contribute to the general activities of the college, including their social life, it is hoped that they will be able to establish an identity of their own and enjoy reasonable autonomy. Much of the work in general education could be undertaken by the present lecturers in colleges of further education. It may be difficult to recruit teachers, particularly nursery teachers, since so few have been trained in recent years.

Award of Qualifications

1050. Although certificates should be awarded by the institution responsible for training, there should be a central examining body who would moderate qualifications throughout the country. Examinations would be set and administered locally, but examination questions would be scrutinised by the central body who would also provide a panel of external examiners. Students would continue, as under the existing N.N.E.B. arrangements, to take a theoretical examination as well as being assessed on their practical training. It would be preferable for one body to cover the training of teachers' aides, nursery assistants and of workers in the other services at present within the N.N.E.B. field of interest. That body might well be the N.N.E.B. suitably re-constituted to take account of the wider functions it would be asked to perform. Alternatively, the N.N.E.B. might become part of a more broadly constituted body which would be concerned with teachers' aides as well as with the N.N.E.B's. present functions. The N.N.E.B. covers a wider field than that of nursery education, since their certificate is a recognised qualification for staff who look after young children in a variety of institutions. The additional responsibilities for training for work with older children must imply that the central body should include representatives of teachers, local authorities and those concerned with training teachers. Our proposals clearly have implications for the N.N.E.B. and for those other non-educational services in the nursery field which the present N.N.E.B. is designed to provide. Much good could come from the creation of a single body covering a wide range since services for young children ought to be integrated as far as possible. The government departments concerned, the N.N.E.B. and other such bodies as the Central Training Council in Child Care should consider these proposals.

Career Prospects

1051. Many nursery assistants and teachers' aides will acquire a great deal of experience of young children. It is important that they should not feel that they are in a job without hope of advancement. Career prospects might be offered to them in two ways. Experienced nursery assistants might receive a responsibility allowance for being in charge of an isolated nursery group or of two groups on the same site. Provision for such a post could be made under the Whitley salary structure. Teachers' aides will always work under the immediate guidance of qualified teachers so that it is difficult to envisage the creation of a supervisory grade. Nevertheless, they might move into nursery education and eventually assume responsibility for a pair or more of nursery groups. There should also be a route to teacher training for suitable assistants and aides. Few will possess the minimum educational qualifications but colleges and institutes of education should take into account their training and experience with children. In some instances admission to a shortened course might be justified. A number of students in some N.N.E.B. courses have already passed on to colleges of education and to training for S.R.N. qualifications. The proportion suitable for further training would not be large, but a substantial contribution might be made to professions in great need of recruits.

Probation

1052. At present, nursery staff trained by the N.N.E.B. do not have to complete a period of probation. We have considered whether, in view of the considerable expansion of the training system that is envisaged, and the fact that nursery assistants may well have to work without continuous supervision by a qualified teacher, they should be expected to work a probationary year. We think this unnecessary because nursery assistants are closely supervised by qualified teachers during their practical training. For a period after training, however, nursery assistants should not work alone in an isolated nursery group.

Build Up of Recruitment

1053. In Chapter 31 we have suggested that nursery assistants might be recruited so as to achieve a full build-up of the groups by the early 1980s and we give details of costing. We have assumed that teachers' aides should be recruited at a much faster rate. To recruit the full number in five years, over 12,000 students must be recruited in the early years. In the first year of the scheme the cost of training will be about £5m. and in the fifth year of the scheme training and employment will cost over £22m. After the fifth year, recruitment might vary to keep numbers stable.

1054. These training schemes may have effects beyond their immediate intention. Many of the women who take this training will in due course have families. They will be better able because of it to bring up their children sensibly and to give them the understanding and encouragement on which educational success depends. It is in the interests of the community that the general education of its members should be carried forward, and that understanding of the social services should be widely diffused. Those who provide the courses should be aware of these wider purposes. They should also be remembered when the cost is counted.

Recommendations

1055. (i) Entry qualifications should be the same for both services. Younger candidates should give evidence of a good general education, demonstrated, if possible, by passes in some subjects of the Certificate of Secondary Education or the General Certificate of Education. For the older women some evidence of further education or relevant experience at work supplemented by interviews or other tests would be necessary.

(ii) Younger students should undertake a two year course of training, three fifths of which would be spent on practical work. Suitable candidates of 21 years of age and over should be permitted to qualify after one year of training of which four fifths will be spent on practical work. Longer part-time training might be arranged for some students.

(iii) Courses should be developed by each training centre within the general lines laid down by a central examining body who would moderate qualifications throughout the country. The responsible government departments and other bodies concerned should consider the creation of a single body to cover the training of teachers aides, nursery assistants and of workers in other services at present within the N.N.E.B. field of interest. Local authority and teacher representatives as well as those concerned with teacher training should be members.

(iv) Aides and assistants during training should receive the rate at present paid to N.N.E.B. students. Aides should be regarded as part of the school staff during training. Nursery students in nursery groups ought not to be regarded as part of the staffing complement.

(v) Teacher training should be open to suitable assistants and aides, and colleges and institutes of education should take account of their training and experience with children where they lack the minimum educational qualifications.

(vi) The Whitley salary structure might make provision for experienced nursery assistants to receive a responsibility allowance for being in charge of isolated nursery groups.

Part Seven

Independent Schools

CHAPTER 27

Independent Primary Schools*

1056. Any discussion of independent primary schools soon comes up against questions which derive not so much from the nature of the education provided as from the fact that the schools exist at all. It has been urged, for example, that the existence of independent primary schools takes away from maintained schools the interest and support of some of the more articulate and intelligent parents; and that a society seeking to remove inequality in education and to create "one nation" ought not to allow children, least of all in their early years, to be taught in schools that are cut off from the common neighbourhood school.** Against this it is argued that society should not

*Independent schools cannot be classed into primary and secondary in the same way as maintained schools because they often cover different age ranges. We refer to those schools which do not provide at least a four year course after 11 (for example preparatory schools with a normal leaving age of 13) as primary schools. Those covering the primary age range and educating children to 16 or over are termed primary and secondary schools.

**Those who hold this view often quote a former Minister of Education, Sir David Eccles, who said:—

"Recently I repeated that ... it would be a good thing if all, or nearly all, parents sent their children to maintained primary schools. I never gave the slightest ground for thinking that the Government would use compulsion or that any form of legislation to achieve this was in our minds ...

... It has always been the confident expectation of the maintained system that in time more parents would choose, for their own reasons, to send their children to primary schools because they themselves were satisfied that that would be the best school for their child. We have always held that as our objective.

On the other hand, if parents feel—and some of them always will—that they can secure a better education in a private school, they are absolutely right to send their children to such a school. Of that I have no doubt, if they can get a better education. My experience, however, has led me to think that a good many parents do not know how excellent some of our primary schools are. I do not think they reckon them within their field of choice. That is a pity, because when a child can get a really good education at a primary school—and that is more often so than is realised—there are additional and valuable social advantages in sending him there. I said at Brighton that small children learn and play together without any sense of difference. They make friends very easily and that this should happen among children from all kinds of homes appears to be highly desirable. I do not think there is any real difference of opinion on that in any part of the House.

It is wrong to think, as some people, I believe, imagine, that if the established middle-class send their children to primary schools, that is something revolutionary, almost Socialist. It is not revolutionary at all. It is happening now and it is happening more each year. This is often, but not always, a matter of hard cash. The young salary-earner in the professions or in business who has no private means and two or three children simply cannot afford the fees of the independent boarding schools. I am glad to say that one begins to hear of other parents who could afford the fees but who choose a primary school for the reasons which appeal to me.

I have had in mind these two ideas. First, I should like to encourage, for educational and social reasons, a movement that is already taking place. Secondly, I would like to suggest to the public schools that they should give the primary school child as good a chance to pass his entrance examination as a child whose parents are able to pay fees. If the public schools can do this, then the choice of secondary school for many parents will become much wider, and that must be good for the public schools and very welcome to many parents and their children."

House of Commons, 3rd November 1961.

remove parents' rights to have their children educated as they think best, nor the right of teachers to create and run a school in which they can follow their own educational theories and practices.

1057. Because these arguments are largely political, we have not tried to draw the balance between them but only to describe briefly the general condition of independent primary education and ways in which it might be improved. Nor has time allowed us to study boarding education. Some of us see advantage in a form of education in which children learn early to be self-reliant members of a community: others are concerned at the separation brought about between the home and school life of children. We hope that the Public Schools Commission will be able to consider the arguments for and against boarding for children of primary age.

1058. Several questions are, however, raised in this chapter. How far have the independent primary schools kept pace with new developments in curriculum, method and knowledge of children's ways of learning? Ought the Department of Education's powers for the supervision of independent primary schools to be extended, or be administered more strictly? Can the central government and local education authorities help the independent schools to keep abreast of new developments? How far would such help divert manpower and other resources from the maintained system? And should staffing restrictions similar to those existing in primary schools be imposed on the independent schools?

1059. The Department of Education have shown an interest in independent education since the beginning of the century, although before the 1944 Act the Department's powers were minimal, and proprietors of a school not in receipt of grant were simply required to supply a brief description of the school in a prescribed form. Under Part III of the 1944 Act—which was not brought into force until 1957—all independent schools must be registered. In the first instance, provisional registration was accorded to all existing independent schools: this still happens when a new school is opened. A visit of inspection follows provisional registration and if H.M.I. is satisfied, registration is made substantive. If H.M.I. is not satisfied, he reports to that effect to the Secretary of State who may either allow a longer period of provisional registration in order that the school may improve or he may issue a Notice of Complaint on one of four grounds:

1. Unsuitability of the premises.
2. Deficiencies of accommodation, having regard to the number, ages and sex of the children.
3. Deficiencies of the instruction.
4. Unsuitability of the head teacher or staff to be in charge of children.

The Secretary of State can, subject to the opportunity of an appeal to a Tribunal, close the school if his requirements are not met.

1060. In addition to registration a school may also seek to be "recognised as efficient". Recognition, which has existed since 1906, is granted only after full inspection by H.M.I. Recognised schools are automatically deemed to be registered. Their higher status makes it easier for them to recruit staff, particularly as they are entitled, unlike the staff of other independent schools, to belong to the national superannuation scheme. Recognised schools which fall below the high standard required may lose recognition or their recognition may be made provisional for a stated period. The Incorporated Association of Preparatory Schools make possession of recognition a condition of membership. A list of recognised schools (List 70) is published by the Department. In January 1965 it showed that of the total of 2,762 independent primary and primary and secondary schools in England 1,188 were recognised or provisionally recognised as efficient. From now on, we shall follow normal practice by speaking of recognised schools and registered schools to distinguish registered schools which are recognised as efficient from those which are not.

1061. The number of independent schools has decreased progressively over the years. In 1861 the Newcastle Commission estimated that there were 860,000 pupils (of the whole school age range including secondary) in "private venture" schools. In 1931 it was estimated that there were approximately 10,000 private schools containing 400,000 pupils. In January 1965 there were 256,000 children under the age of 12 (about five per cent of the whole primary age group) in 2,762 primary and primary and secondary independent schools in England.

1062. There are many reasons for the fall off in the number of pupils and schools. Improvements in maintained primary schools often lead to the withdrawal of parental support from neighbouring independent schools, with the result that some of them are unable to continue. In general, independent schools are not now very profitable undertakings and some proprietors on retirement have had difficulty in finding successors. Yet there is an exception to this trend. The number of recognised schools increases each year. In recognised schools the number of children in a given age group becomes greater as the age advances: in registered schools it becomes smaller. Many parents will send their little children to a school near home whether it is recognised or not, but as the children grow older they are transferred to recognised schools. Boys often attend small unrecognised preparatory schools until they are about eight. They then enter recognised schools belonging to the Incorporated Association of Preparatory Schools.

1063. The Department of Education recognise a school as efficient when they are satisfied that it is at least of a standard equivalent to that expected in a maintained school. There may, however, be differences in what is expected in maintained and independent schools. For example, the premises of some independent schools may not be as good as those found in post-war maintained schools but there may be compensations in the smaller size of classes. Credit is given for the competence of teachers in specific situations whether they have qualifications or not. In fact, though there are more unqualified teachers in recognised schools than in maintained schools, the proportion of graduates is much higher. About one third of teachers in all independent schools are graduates. The corresponding figure for the maintained system is about one quarter.

1064. Recognised schools must, by the rules (Rules 16) governing recognition, be of a size to permit adequate staffing, have a reasonable range of subjects and have at least a three year course. They are expected to have positive merits in all or most respects and no really serious weaknesses. Registered schools vary from some which are just tolerable on the Department's present standards, to others approaching the standards of the recognised schools. It is often difficult to classify registered schools or to give advice for their improvement. Their fees are usually lower than those of the recognised schools, and the standard of premises is sometimes low. The proportion of qualified teachers is much smaller than in the recognised schools.

1065. Generalisations about independent primary schools are largely meaningless. Not only do the schools vary in quality but they have differing purposes. Some seem almost to exist only to preserve precarious social differences. Others are of quite a different calibre. They include the old established boys' preparatory schools which prepare boys for entrance to the public schools, and they include the preparatory departments of girls' public and direct grant schools. They include schools adopting new methods, some of which have been pioneers in educational thought and practice, and schools which make special provision for the maladjusted and handicapped or for children with special artistic gifts. In curriculum, method and handling of children they vary from the most conservative to the most advanced. Some are in beautiful and well adapted surroundings, others in poky private houses. A growing number are interested in innovation. The I.A.P.S., which has generally represented a conservative educational view has recently produced two reports which are full of constructive thinking. Many schools are particularly good in the activities and care they provide for their pupils out of school hours. Virtually all, of course, have the great advantage of small classes. The best of them are hard to beat. But the range is wide and many are backward in methods, poor in facilities and do not compare well with the maintained schools serving the same neighbourhood.

1066. Parents may wish to send their children to an independent school for such reasons as different methods of teaching, small classes or a desire or need for boarding education. Sometimes parents are anxious for children to attend an independent preparatory school to help ensure entry to an independent secondary school of their choice. But some parents may base their choice of school on the vaguest of reasons and on slender information and knowledge. Those who choose the independent schools simply because they are independent should realise their varying quality and, in particular, the significance of "recognition as efficient".

1067. To help parents decide between schools we should like to see all prospectuses state that it is open to schools to apply for recognition as efficient and what this implies. The prospectus should then state whether the school is recognised or simply registered. Legislation would be necessary to enforce this. We also think that the Department should reconsider the term "recognised" and "registered", and try to devise more informative ones.

1068. So far as we can judge, the Department of Education have used their powers of registration with the right degree of firmness in the eight years since Part III of the Education Act was put into force. They had to apply pressure to the worst schools while at the same time establishing standards for registration. The Independent Schools Tribunals which are appointed by the Lord Chancellor, and not by the Secretary of State for Education, who is an interested party in the proceedings, offer protection for individual schools against arbitary judgements of the Department. A tribunal has three members: the chairman, who is always a lawyer, and two members with educational experience. An appeal against Notice of Complaint is heard openly and the appellant may be represented by counsel. Of the 98 Notices of Complaint served between 1957 and 1964—mainly relating to physical conditions—only 11 have led to appeal and in all of them the Department have been upheld.

1069. The time has now come when standards should be improved and criteria for registration raised. Ultimately, the sanctions available to the Secretary of State are those specified in legislation, and the basis of any Notice of Complaint is defined with some precision in Section 71 of the Education Act. More stringent criteria might require fresh legislation to allow the Secretary of State to serve Notices of Complaint which will not merely exclude the obviously bad schools but which will demand a reasonable minimum standard of premises, equipment and education. We recommend that the construction of "objectionable" should be widened to include any conditions, physical or educational, in which children's welfare is not thought to be adequately safeguarded. It should include those schools in which the infliction of physical pain is a recognised form of punishment for children of primary school age, after the time when it is prohibited in maintained primary schools (see Chapter 19). We have even considered whether there is not a case for closing all schools which are not recognised* but this would be difficult for several reasons, not least because there are undoubtedly registered schools of higher quality than some maintained schools. Schools are constantly changing and there is a need to retain a grade for those schools which might in time become recognised. Moreover, some feel an objection in principle to extending the Secretary of State's powers in this way. We hope that more schools than at present will work towards recognition. In the meanwhile, the Department should continue to aim at the gradual elimination of poorer schools, and continue the efforts to improve the rest.

1070. As part of the move towards improvement we recommend that all head teachers of independent schools should by law have to be qualified teachers. After a date to be specified, only qualified teachers should be appointed as heads in new schools or where there is a change of head teacher. We are advised that this will have little effect on the supply of teachers for the maintained schools. For this purpose distinction will have to be made between head teachers and proprietors. This requirement, and any other specific requirements, will not themselves ensure quality; the recommendation is directed against the present situation in which any unqalified person, unless declared unsuitable, can run a school. In the longer term we look forward to the time when all teachers in independent schools have qualified teacher or equivalent status.

1071. The quality of education for the primary school child depends in the independent as in the maintained schools most of all on the quality of staff. This in turn is affected by their initial training and their success in seeking in-service training and contacts with institutes of education, H.M. Inspectors, local authority advisors and professional associations. The better independent schools have for a long time had contacts with those who can help them,

---

*One of our members, Professor A. J. Ayer, would like to see the establishment of a strictly enforced minimum standard below which schools would not be allowed to operate. Schools above the minimum standard could be graded accordingly to quality.

in particular through activities arranged by the Incorporated Association of Preparatory Schools. But the worst schools and teachers, as in the maintained system, are rarely concerned to improve themselves. The one certain and useful point of contact with the outside educational world for all independent schools is H.M. Inspectors who have the sole right and duty of access and have behind them the sanctions deriving from their power to recommend registration or recognition. H.M.Is' visits have over the years been increasingly directed towards informal and constructive discussion rather than inspection in the strict sense of the word. We have, however, to recognise that there is a limit to the number of visits that H.M.I.s can make and to the help that can be given by overburdened local education authorities.

1072. We thus return to a conclusion which appears constantly through the Report. There must be a major increase in in-service training if all schools are to keep abreast of new developments and if individual teachers are to get the professional and intellectual refreshment that they need. We hope that providers of courses, the Department, the local education authorities and the colleges and institutes of education, will do their best to find places for teachers from independent schools and that these schools will be ready to release their teachers to attend such courses. But the independent schools must develop and strengthen their own resources. We have been much impressed by what we have learned about the schemes of in-service training run by the I.A.P.S., but there is little work of this kind for independent schools outside this body. Many independent schools belong to no association. It is time that this isolation came to an end, and that all schools had access to the means of professional improvement.

1073. We would also like to see initiatives taken by individual teachers and schools to break down barriers between schools that often serve the same neighbourhoods. There should be regular interchanges and visits between pupils and staff of the different types of school, joint exhibitions of work, school plays and "friendly games". In one area, sports and games associations, a primary schools' choir, orchestra and brass band and many other activities are common to both kinds of schools, and teachers from independent schools attend courses organised by the authority. The local authorities might help independent schools, as the 1944 Education Act permits, by making the School Health Service more easily available to them.

1074. Some of our witnesses suggested that the Secretary of State should take powers to control the number of teachers employed in independent schools in order to align their staffing standards with those in comparable maintained schools. The aim would be to make more teachers available for the maintained schools, particularly scarce teachers of subjects like mathematics. We have considered carefully whether it would be practicable to devise such a scheme and what effect it would have.

1075. Any such scheme would need to take account of the main factors, such as the number and age range of its pupils, which influence the staffing standards of a maintained school. It would also need to allow for the residential responsibilities undertaken by teaching staff in boarding schools, including duty at weekends. Because of the wide variations among the independent schools, the scheme would need to be quite elaborate if it were to achieve what was intended. It is almost certain that schools would have to be compelled rather than persuaded into the scheme.

1076. If present staffing standards were aligned in the maintained and independent schools, both primary and secondary, we estimate that independent schools would be required to surrender about a quarter of their teachers—that is about 8,000. If they all found their way into the maintained schools, this would be a useful accession to their teacher force. But they would not all be acceptable for permanent employment in the maintained schools; for this purpose, a teacher needs to hold "qualified teacher" status, and it is estimated that at present about one-third of all teachers in the whole independent sector, that is, about 12,000, would not qualify for this status. There is another implication. The scheme might prescribe, in addition to a total staffing complement for each independent school, a limit to the number or proportion of qualified teachers which the school could employ within that complement. But any such rule would have quite different effects on individual schools some of which may have no qualified teachers at all while others may have as many as 90 per cent of their staff qualified. It could not be justified by reference to the principle of comparability with the maintained schools, where 97 per cent of the total teacher force is qualified. Nor can it be assumed that all teachers released from the independent schools would take posts in maintained schools even if they were qualified to do so.

1077. In short, while it is possible to envisage a scheme of the kind suggested, it would be administratively cumbersome, would generate much friction and, indeed, hostility between the maintained and independent sectors, and would jeopardise the continued existence of many independent schools—with no guarantee whatever of a substantial staffing benefit to the maintained schools. Such a measure would also be a negative one. The Secretary of State has a responsibility for improving all sectors of primary education and his aim should be to improve maintained schools and to encourage the less good independent schools to improve themselves rather than to establish measures that will merely harm the better independent schools.

1078. We have been conscious of the need to avoid a diversion of resources from the maintained system in order to improve the independent schools. This concern for the state system should not prevent us helping and persuading the independent schools to profit from the benefits of the recent thinking that has done so much to improve the curriculum of the best maintained schools. Our aim, simply, is better primary education, everywhere.

Summary of Conclusions and Recommendations

1079. (i) The Department of Education and Science should consider taking steps which would require all independent schools to state on their prospectuses whether the schools were recognised or registered and what this implies. The Department of Education and Science should reconsider the terms "recognised" and "registered" and try to devise more informative ones.

(ii) The Secretary of State's powers to serve Notices of Complaint on independent schools should be based on more stringent criteria. The construction of "objectionable" should be widened to include any conditions, physical or educational, in which children's welfare was not thought to be adequately safeguarded.

(iii) All head teachers of independent schools should be qualified teachers. After a date to be specified, only qualified teachers should be appointed as heads in new schools, or when there is a change of head teacher.

(iv) In-service courses should wherever possible allow some places for teachers from independent schools. The independent schools themselves should take steps through their professional organisations to increase the facilities for in-service training for teachers in independent schools.

Part Eight

Primary School Buildings and Equipment; Status;
and Research

CHAPTER 28

Primary School Buildings and Equipment

1080. The design of British school building since the war has deservedly won an international reputation. Much thought has been given to planning buildings which are in line with current educational trends. In spite of shortages of manpower and money, between one and two new primary and secondary schools are opened in England and Wales every day. Most of this new building has to house the expanding and shifting population. By contrast there remains a large backlog of bad old buildings in which far too many children spend their years of compulsory education. The thinking about the building itself has not been matched by work on the relationships between the school and its surrounding environment.

I. PRIMARY SCHOOL BUILDING

The Present State of Primary Buildings

1081. Surveys of the state of school buildings in 1962, one by the Department of Education and Science[1] and a second by the N.U.T.[2] have confirmed the existence of serious deficiencies. Although the N.U.T. survey was based on a relatively small sample, its results were similar to the Department's survey. As Table 29 shows, according to the Department's Survey nearly three quarters of a million primary school children in England were in schools of which the main buildings were built before 1875.

Table 29. Age of Primary and Secondary School Buildings (England 1962)

Age of Oldest Main Building	Primary Schools	Nos. of Pupils (Thousands)	Secondary Schools	Nos. of Pupils (Thousands)
1. Pre-1875	6,580	725·7	349	135·6
2. 1875 to 1902	5,986	972·0	818	326·0
3. 1903 to 1918	2,582	559·5	817	364·3
4. 1919 to 1944	2,483	675·3	1,619	789·5
5. 1945 to date	3,424	941·2	1,869	1,037·5
6. All schools and pupils	21,055	3,873·7	5,472	2,652·9

1082. The two 1962 surveys are now somewhat out of date. For example, the major building programmes for England and Wales* for 1965/66 to 1967/68 include 1,492 primary school projects at a total cost of £108 million. (In 1967/68 about £20 million were allowed for improvements in primary schools). Less than half of these were intended to improve or replace old buildings but the whole programme will have increased the proportion of new buildings. Authorities are allocated money for minor works to be used at their

*Apportionment of the most recent building programme between England and Wales is not yet complete.

discretion, and no apportionment between primary and secondary schools is available. The total amount spent on minor works in England from 1962/63 to 1965/66 was £59 million.

1083. Generalised statements of deficiencies and of building programmes give only part of the story. As new schools are opened, old ones are not necessarily closed. Children living in new houses often go to new schools. Yet children left behind in the decaying centres of large towns attend schools that often match their environment. This tendency is illustrated by figures supplied by the Inner London Education Authority[3]. They show that in the London area 67 per cent of county primary and 85 per cent of voluntary primary school buildings were erected before 1918. Both figures are near to the top of the range for the whole country which for county schools runs from 48 per cent in the most favoured authority to 70 per cent in the worst placed. The corresponding figures for voluntary schools are 76 per cent and 95 per cent. In London, 80 per cent of primary school buildings had outside sanitation whereas in other areas the range was from 48 to 80 per cent. Old schools are not necessarily unsuitable. Some can be brought up to modern standards. But cramped buildings make modern primary school methods more difficult and may add to the problems of recruiting teachers. Some schools have temporary annexes and this division between two buildings is awkward for both teachers and children. Old buildings are often on restricted sites, in neighbourhoods with little space for children to play, and near or on main roads.

School Building Since 1945: Number of Places and Costs

1084. The main effort in school building after 1945 was devoted to meeting the demands created by war damage, by the lack of building during the war years, by movements of population, by the raising of the school leaving age from 14 to 15 and the abnormally high numbers of births in the immediate post-war years, a birth rate which stabilised above that of the 1930s. In spite of all of the difficulties faced by the building industry between January 1946 and the end of 1965, nearly 5,000 new primary schools were completed, providing about 1,200,000 places. Another 800,000 new primary places were provided by extensions and remodelling. Some of these are in temporary accommodation which eventually must be taken out of use. In the past 20 years, about £1,000 million worth of building for primary and secondary schools has been completed, three quarters of it by major projects and a quarter by minor works. In addition, there is about £100 million worth of work under construction.

1085. Total school building programmes in England and Wales for the next few years are 1967/68* £120 million, 1968/69 £138 million and 1969/70 £138 million. New places will continue to be used mainly for shifts of population and for increases in the secondary school population resulting from larger age groups and the raising of the school leaving age. As a result the money available for improving primary schools is likely to be small. The capacity of local

---

*All the programme values are expressed in terms of costs in the first part of 1966. The money value of future programmes will depend, of course, on changes in building costs. An announcement made in July 1966 had the effect of raising the face value of future building programmes by nine per cent.

education authorities to carry out the increased work may also limit building. There is a shortage of professional staff in local authority offices that has already caused less work to be started than is authorised by the Department. Local education authorities will have to increase their capacity by 20 per cent in order to reach current authorised levels. In the 1970s, the schools will continue to make great demands on building. On present birth rate projecttions over 400,000 extra primary places are expected to be necessary from 1971/72 to 1976/77. It is estimated that in this five year period building worth more than £110 million a year will be needed, about £76 million to meet increased school population and about £34 million for new housing development.

The Improvement of Old Buildings

1086. The Department's Survey estimated that building work costing £588 million would be needed to bring all English primary schools up to standard. Of this, £491 million would be needed for improvements, the rest for the replacement of places in schools to be closed or reduced in size. In all, the cost of bringing all schools, primary and secondary, in England up to the standard required by current building regulations would be £1,268 million including provision for raising the leaving age and the complete elimination of overcrowding. These estimates are now out of date: even at the time they were made movements in population could not accurately be estimated and local education authorities had to make assumptions that will not all hold true when rebuilding actually takes place. Nonetheless, the surveys point to two main conclusions. The first is that many primary school children will long continue to attend schools in really poor buildings unless there can be a speeding up of programmes aimed at less ambitious schemes of improvement than are at present usual. The second is that primary schools are bound to make enormous and continuing demands for building resources. Since the total cost will be so high it becomes all the more necessary that new buildings must be adaptable to changes in the patterns of education, some of which can hardly be predicted now.

1087. We have seen for ourselves that outstanding primary school buildings can support teachers in their use of modern methods, raise the standard of children's behaviour and change their attitude to school, and win the enthusiasm of parents. As one mother said "it's worth a long walk to bring the children here". We are deeply concerned about the number of primary schools that must continue in old buildings for which there is no hope of replacement. Standards of school buildings often fall short of those of quite ordinary households. Children have to use cold, dark and sometimes even insanitary lavatories. In 65 per cent of schools they are outside the main building. We have heard from many sources of the dislike of school that can be created by the condition of school lavatories. This is supported by recent studies of the difficulties in adjusting to school experienced by a small sample of children[4]. Children cannot be encouraged in hygienic habits if there are no basins adjacent to the sanitation. Equally, they cannot be expected to keep themselves clean if there is no warm water or even no piped water at all. Serious problems are caused by small classrooms and lack of space for physical education.

1088. Table 30 gives the number of primary schools in the Department's survey with specified defects. We consider that an essential minimum is that all schools should have piped water, a warm water supply, water borne sanitation indoors, electricity and a staff room, although this is not to dismiss the other deficiencies as unimportant. Table 31* shows what the total cost of remedying these deficiencies might be. These estimates can only be a rough guide, and the number of schools involved has almost certainly decreased since the 1962 survey.

Table 30. Specified Defects in Primary School Accommodation (England 1962).

	No. of Schools	Nos. of Pupils (Thousands)
1. No piped water supply	166	6·8
2. No warm water supply for pupils	4,701	531·5
3. No water borne sanitation for pupils	1,280	52·2
4. Sanitation mainly out of doors	13,810	2,179·7
5. No central heating system	5,014	437·7
6. No electricity	135	8·8
7. No kitchen or scullery on school site	4,119	603·6
8. No staff room	7,463	653·5
9. Half or more of school in temporary premises (i)	524	119·7
10. Buildings on more than one site (ii)	1,598	381·8
11. Seriously sub-standard site (iii)	8,304	1,304·3
12. No hall (iv)	3,666	732·8
13. Dining in classrooms (unless designed for the purpose) (iv)	2,144	433·4
Schools with none of these defects	4,541	1,197·2
Schools with one or more of these defects	16,514	2,676·5
All schools	21,055	3,873·7

(i) Temporary premises include hired premises off the main site and buildings in temporary construction: in cases of doubt, a building was classed as temporary if the loan period was less than 30 years.

(ii) This covered schools which were using separate sets of premises on a temporary basis, not those whose buildings had been deliberately designed to be dispersed.

(iii) Excluding playing fields. A school's site was regarded as seriously sub-standard if it was two thirds or less of the minimum area prescribed in the Building Regulations for the school at its existing size.

(iv) Excluding primary schools for less than 100 pupils.

1089. The cost of remedying the worst defects, if all these schools remain open, may be as much as £70 million, and is unlikely to be less than £50 million. The improvement would not be a substitute for complete modernisation, but would provide better conditions in the worst primary schools which will have to remain in use. We recommend that the Government should an-

*The lack of piped water (166 schools) and electricity (135 schools) is often the result of a lack of a mains supply in the area. Since we could not envisage a pipeline or electricity pylon being built out of educational funds, we have not estimated the cost of providing these services.

nounce a building programme of minor works designed to get rid of these deficiencies within a period of seven years. At this rate the annual cost would be £7–10 million.

Table 31. Cost of Remedying Defects in School Accommodation.
(England only).

Specified Features	Average cost of improvement £	No. of Schools	Total Cost £ million
1. No warm water supply for pupils	400–500	4,701	2
2. No water borne sanitation for pupils	4,000	1,280 ⎫	
		⎬	35–55*
3. Sanitation mainly out of doors	2,000–4,000	13,810 ⎭	
4. No staff room	1,500	7,463	11·5

*(1) Nearly all schools without water borne sanitation also have outdoor lavatories. This estimate assumes schemes remedying both defects.

(2) The cost will vary according to whether the lavatories are modernised but left detached or brought into the main building.

1090. This will involve a new emphasis in building investment. We have been told by the local authority associations of the difficulties caused by what seems to them to be an artificial division between the major building programmes (projects costing more than £20,000) and the minor works programmes. An authority unable to begin a major project cannot transfer the money to a number of minor works projects no matter how urgent they are. At present money saved by skilful design cannot be used for work elsewhere. Many authorities find it hard to keep within the cost limits; those who do should be allowed to apply the savings elsewhere. We appreciate that flexibility may make government control of investment more difficult. Thus, a local authority that is able to fit in a series of small minor works is hardly likely to defer for long the major projects whose place they take. Minor works are completed more quickly so that the gross total of completed works over quite a short period might be larger than the country can afford. Yet the improvement of primary schools will depend on an increase in the money that can be spent on minor projects. We hope that the Department will make further changes in their controls so that small jobs that can be done easily will be carried out quickly. There should be greater flexibility in expenditure as between major and minor building projects and we hope that authorities will be allowed to spend the money saved in the completion of major projects on minor projects.

1091. The Department offered guidance to local education authorities on the problem of dealing with old schools in a building bulletin published in 1963[5]. It was suggested that a school should not have a minor capital building project unless it would be in use for more than ten years. It was assumed that old schools would be brought up to the same standards as a new school. Such projects can cost as much as 80 per cent of the cost of a new school and make a heavy, and disproportionate, demand on professional manpower. For these reasons, perhaps, few old schools have been completely remodelled and methods of making modest improvements in old schools with say, 10 to 20 years of life, have not so far been studied systematically. We, therefore, suggest that the Department of Education and Science should undertake detailed exercises on the relationship between costs and the provision of essential amenities. It may be that for relatively small sums large improvements can be made but that after a certain point the return from increased expenditure decreases. We also hope that one of the foundations might institute a competition somewhat on the lines of the Civic Trust awards for imaginative but inexpensive improvement to old schools. Understandably enough, architects prefer a clear site and a free hand with a new building. Yet old schools need schemes that for small cost will go straight for the essentials of opening up space, introducing more light and colour and remedying deficiencies in acoustics, heating and sanitation.

Developments in School Building Since 1945

1092. Most of the schools built immediately after 1945 were not dissimilar to pre-war schools. Architects concentrated on physical standards and in particular on lighting and ventilation. The kind of plan often produced was that known as "the Finger Plan". One storey classrooms were arranged in parallel rows, with a wide corridor on one side. Only about 40 per cent of the total floor area was to be found in the teaching spaces, though some teachers continue to appreciate the generous circulation and cloakroom areas that were characteristic of those buildings. Buildings sprawled over sites using up valuable land. Classes were dispersed, children were involved in long journeys to cloakroom, lavatories, hall and dining room. Most of the rooms were of similar size and character and their relationships were not determined by educational needs.

1093. In the late 1940s, two connected developments took place. The first was in design. From the end of the war, some architects had been observing children at work and consulting teachers about the sort of environment they wished to create for them. Up to 1949, primary schools were costing more than £200 a place and were taking a long time to build. It became clear that the necessary places could only be provided if there were a new approach to the cost of school building. As a result, in 1950, the cost limits were reduced from £200 a place to £140. Much more compact plans were designed in which the total floor area was reduced by rather more than a third although the amount of teaching space increased. Circulation space was reduced and such corridors as were necessary were often designed as part of the teaching space. It then became possible for some authorities to build classrooms exceeding 800 sq. ft. in area, in contrast to those of 520 sq. ft. which had previously been a regulation minimum. Buildings become more informal and domestic in character and likely to foster friendly, personal relationships. A greater variety of equipment and materials including more books led to new needs for display and storage, and for different types of working surfaces. Cost studies were also made so that by careful control of items the cost per square foot was kept down. Although some useful features may have been lost in the drive towards economy, inessentials were sacrificed to safeguard essentials, and the schools which emerged provide greater educational opportunities than their predecessors.

Developments Since 1956

1094. Many of the new trends began in local education authorities and were taken up by the Ministry. In 1956, the Ministry's Development Group made a detailed study of junior school requirements and the result was a new school for 320 built at Amersham in Buckinghamshire. This project included the design of all the furniture, and applied the results of new studies in lighting, colour and acoustics[6]. In this and previous investigations, the architects had observed a new relationship between teachers and children and a blurring of division between one subject and another, between theoretical and practical work and between one lesson period and the next. The "teaching area" was conceived as the whole school environment, rather than as a series of individual rooms. The design of class spaces offered opportunities for changing ways of learning as the children grew older. The Amersham school was followed by the Finmere village primary school for 50 children (see Diagram 8). This design followed a pattern well suited to the family character of the village community. "School" includes the buildings, garden, play area, and games space. Outside and inside provide an integrated learning environment. Inside, there are small working areas each with a degree of privacy and a character of its own, opening on to a larger space sufficiently uncluttered to allow children to climb and jump, dance and to engage in drama. Among the small working spaces is a sitting room, a library, two workshops with water available, a kitchen and three group study spaces. The 50 children can be divided into two working groups in separate spaces, if need be. Privacy can be secured by means of folding partitions. This design has been particularly successful and within its fluid arrangements many observers see the solution to some of the most pressing design problems.

1095. Can such arrangements be effective in much larger urban and suburban primary schools where classes are larger? The design of the Eveline Lowe Primary School, Southwark (see Diagram 9), for 320 children ranging in age from three and a half to nine years, and of Vittoria School, Islington has attempted to take account of many current educational and social problems. Elsewhere many other schools are being built on new designs. They are intended to help teachers to co-operate more easily in schools in which many may only be able to give part-time service, and to provide for flexibility of organisation and individual learning. In spite of great progress, there are still too many school buildings being erected which are poorly designed and unrelated to developing ideas about primary school education[7].

1096. At the same time new designs in fittings and furnishings are being tried out. There must be suitable surfaces for the many kinds of jobs to be done at appropriate heights for the children. Upright chairs, upholstered chairs, rocking chairs, stools, window seats and boxes can all find a place in the school. Even the walls providing space for the display of children's work and for exhibitions have a valuable educational function to perform. The relationship between furniture and buildings is now being studied by the consortia established by the local education authorities for co-operation and economy in building.

1097. Hundreds of new schools are built every year. Schools last longer than teachers so that it is necessary to design for trends rather than for current average practice, otherwise schools will become obsolete long before they are

Diagram 8*
A School for 50 Pupils Aged 5 to 11 Years at Finmere, Oxfordshire

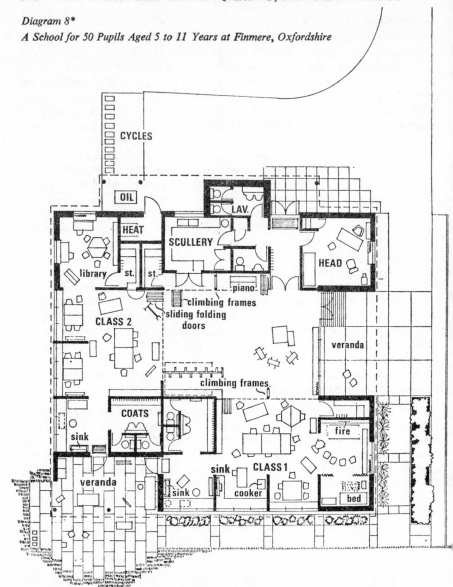

This village school was designed, in 1958, by the Ministry's Development Group in collaboration with the Oxfordshire local education authority. The essence of the plan is that the children mostly work in small groups or individually, the two teachers sharing their time between them. The accommodation consists, therefore, of a series of small working areas, all with a degree of seclusion, while still a part of the whole. One is a sitting room, with a curtained bed recess. Three are furnished as studies; two others as 'workshops', with access to a verandah. One is a 'kitchen' and one a library. These open on to somewhat larger areas which in turn are linked, by means of sliding-folding doors, to a space large enough for groups of children to move about more freely. If both sets of doors are open, the whole teaching area (approximately 1,800 sq. ft.) can become one space. By closing one or both sets of doors, it can become either two or three separate rooms.

*A fuller description of the design of this school can be found in Building Bulletin No. 3. Village Schools. H.M.S.O. 1961.

worn out. It is both an educational and an architectural responsibility to see that the shape of schools is determined by educational trends rather than by architectural fashion. To get good school buildings requires sensitive and sympathetic co-operation between the local education authorities, who own, pay for and have statutory responsibility for them, and architects and educationalists, including teachers. Local education authorities are sometimes, but not sufficiently often, as much concerned to commission first rate buildings as to keep within cost limits and build schools quickly. More architects need to spend more time in schools getting to understand their needs. Educationalists also should think about the type of physical provision which suits schools. When there is interplay between all concerned architects can interpret in terms of space and equipment the implications of what they have seen in action, instead of making a jigsaw puzzle of rooms of specific sizes and of structural grids. All this should be implied by the architect's brief. There must always be a spearhead in educational design. These advanced schools need to be evaluated individually before their designs are adopted by building consortia.

Some Design and Planning Implications of Our Report

1098. We now summarise some of the implications of our Report for the siting and building of schools:

(i) *Building Within the Environment*

In Part III we have referred to the need for establishing better contacts between schools, parents and the community. The architectural and town planning implications of such schemes as community schools and the extension of the school day have as yet been insufficiently studied—far less has been written on them than on school building itself. We are glad to learn that the Urban Planning Division of the Building Research Station will be publishing, at the same time as our Report appears, a study of factors affecting the location of primary schools. It considers amongst other things the effect of location on the extent to which children must be accompanied to school, their mode of travel, the convenience to mothers of nearby shopping centres, the number of children staying for lunch and the size of school. The following are aspects of these problems upon which further thought is needed:

(a) The creation of traffic-free, pedestrian ways and precincts linking schools to the surrounding neighbourhood—shops, library, parks and the like.

(b) Space for parents to meet and talk at the entrance, space to set up a bookstall, for example, showing good children's books—staffed by volunteers.

(c) Space within the school site to permit the kind of extensions that parent-teacher associations and neighbourhood groups may wish to provide—covered play space, or a garden, or swimming pool, or a parents' room.

(d) School playgrounds should be readily usable during holidays and evenings, with minimum of supervision, and safety for the school itself.

(e) At the same time, the school should be protected from traffic noise and danger, fumes, offensive industrial processes and the like.

These requirements call for a particularly difficult and challenging blend of protection from the surrounding urban environment, and exposure to neighbours and the community. Town planners must co-operate closely with teachers and local education authorities to solve these problems. The greatly enlarged slum clearance and redevelopment programmes of the next decade will offer enormous opportunities of progress (or lasting failure) on all these matters in the older cities. The enlarged programme for expanding towns and for new towns will provide similar opportunities.

(ii) *Nursery Education*

In Chapter 9 we have recommended a major expansion of nursery education, and have described the various ways in which it can be provided. Where new accommodation is needed, there should be a scrutiny of existing standards, especially since most children will not stay for lunch. We recommend that the Department should undertake a careful study of present requirements which may well be unnecessarily lavish in some respects. A building project by the Development Group would help local education authorities in designing for the expansion of nursery education.

(iii) *Changes in Organisation*

Proposals have been made in Chapter 10 for changes in the age of transfer from first to middle schools, and from middle to secondary schools. In the succeeding pages we reproduce design sketches of schools, or extensions to existing schools which illustrate ways in which new problems of organisation might be met:

*Diagram 9: Eveline Lowe Primary School, Camberwell, London (3½ to 9 years).

**Diagram 10: The Extension of an Infant School (5 to 7 years) to a First School (5 to 8 years).

**Diagram 11: The Extension of a Junior School (7 to 11 years) to a Middle School (8 to 12 years).

**Diagrams 12 A and B: A Middle School for Pupils of 8 to 12 years.

(iv) *School Playgrounds*

Playgrounds have been and are too often wasted. We think that working areas inside schools should be extended by covered space out of doors. Playgrounds should provide the opportunities for a similar range of activities out of doors to those allowed for by new types of school

These diagrams are taken from Department of Education and Science Building Bulletins to which reference should be made for fuller discussion, as follows :—
*Building Bulletin 36. Eveline Lowe Primary School, London. H.M.S.O. 1967.
**Building Bulletin 35. Middle Schools. New Problems in School Design: Implications of transfer at 12 or 13. H.M.S.O. 1966.

buildings **indoors**. There should be quiet corners where children can sit and read, parts left wild, and "dens" for group play: there should be challenges to physical activity as well as space for ball **games.** Imaginative use should be made of natural features, such as changes of level and trees.

(v) *Accommodation for Teachers*

Not enough thought has been given to accommodation for teachers, or to the numbers, including part-time teachers and students, who must use it. The head teacher's room needs to be a sitting room rather than an office if it is to be a satisfactory setting for meeting teachers, parents, children and visitors. Head teachers and staff need working surfaces and storage space, as well as somewhere to relax. Rarely is there sufficieni provision for their personal belongings, the shopping they often bring with them, or any arrangement for them to change their clothes.

Cost Limits

1099. As middle schools are created and other changes in organisation made, and as new trends in the curriculum affect design, the cost limits of school building must be reviewed. At present, regulations provide that children in large primary schools have a smaller minimum classroom area per head than children in smaller primary schools, in nursery schools or in secondary schools. Inevitably, they are more restricted. Since middle schools will be allowed higher cost limits because of the needs of older children, a little more flexibility in design will become possible. We cannot attempt here to make any analysis of what revisions are needed. But there is a case for examining the whole structure of cost limits and regulations to ensure that the best possible development of working areas can be achieved from nursery, through first and middle, to secondary schools. We think that cost limits for building, and the sharpness of variations between the different stages of education, may be based (like staffing ratios) partly, at least, on tradition. Continuing review is required. The heating, lighting and cleaning of schools, the cost results of using different qualities and kinds of finishing material in a situation in which labour is more scarce and expensive than even the dearest of materials, all need to be considered more fully. The wider use of industrialised building is beyond our terms of reference, but current achievements suggest that these techniques are logical means of combining higher standards with lower costs.

Educational Furniture and Equipment

1100. In the last few years the Department of Education and Science have become increasingly interested in the design of furniture and equipment. perhaps the most important single development has been the furniture programme in which the Department are collaborating with the Ministry of Public Building and Works and the CLASP Building Consortium. The Department of Education and Science are responsible for the basic design of the furniture while the Ministry of Public Building and Works have carried designs through the stage of working drawings and have invited tenders and placed contracts. The CLASP building programme of new schools has provided a market of sufficient size to make the operation economically practicable.

Diagram 9 (see also Plate 3)
School for 320 Pupils Aged 3½ to 9 Years
Eveline Lowe School. Rolls Road, London, S.E. 1

This school was designed by the Department's Development Group in collaboration with the Inner London Education Authority within the current cost limit. The accommodation was planned for the following groupings of the 320 pupils:

Two nursery groups of 30 children (A and C on plan)
Four "family" groups of 40 children, with an age range of about two years (B, D, E, & F)
Two groups of older children, one of 40 (G) and one of 60 (H).
The last group was, of course, to be looked after by more than one teacher.
The main features to emerge, in the interpretation of the educational requirements in terms of planning for each of these eight groups were:

(a) The need to sub-divide the available space to allow a number of small groups of individuals to pursue widely varying activities.
(b) The need to make a distinction in character (i.e. in finishes, scale, colour, lighting, furniture) between a small, quiet carpeted area; a general working area; and an area equipped for messier kinds of work.
(c) The importance of direct access to a sheltered verandah and to the ground outside.
(d) The need to take into account the use of sizes of furniture from an early stage in design process.

There is no hard and fast division between these group spaces and the rest of the school, for the whole environment (both inside and out) was conceived as potential 'teaching space', as opposed to a series of closed classrooms and 'non-teaching' areas. For example the arrangements for dining include a series of bays, furnished with tables and window seats, which look across to alternating display alcoves and window seats—an area designed not only for dining but as a small exhibition gallery and as working space for groups of individuals at other times of the day. The hall is equipped for a variety of large movement and drama work.

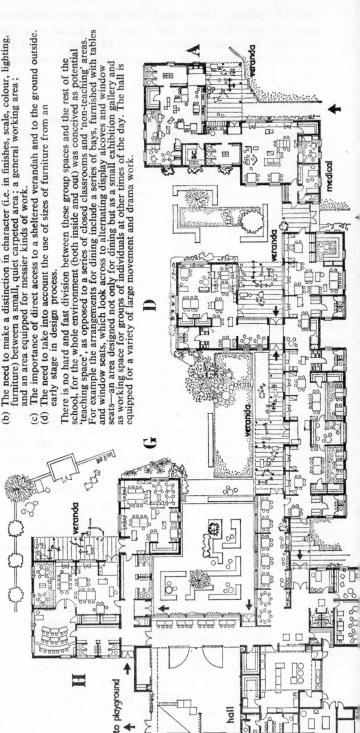

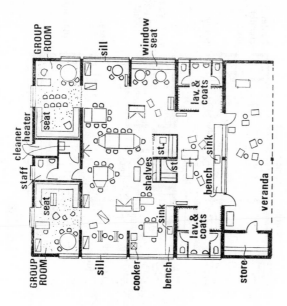

Diagram 10

Extension to Convert Existing Infants' School for 240 Pupils of 5 to 7 years into School for 320 Pupils of 5 to 8 years.

Diagram 10 shows one possible way of providing for an additional age group in the infants' schools within the current framework of cost allowances.

It is designed for a 'community' of 80 children and two teachers, with the aim of encouraging a flexible approach to the pattern of activity. In Diagram 10 the space can, if desired, be treated as two separate rooms, each with a small enclosed carpeted area with window seating, where up to 40 children can gather for story-telling and the like, or where a few individuals can read quietly. But there is also a shared area for the messier activities, equipped with benching, sink and tools, which opens on to the veranda. Quite a large central space could be cleared on occasions for impromptu drama, etc.

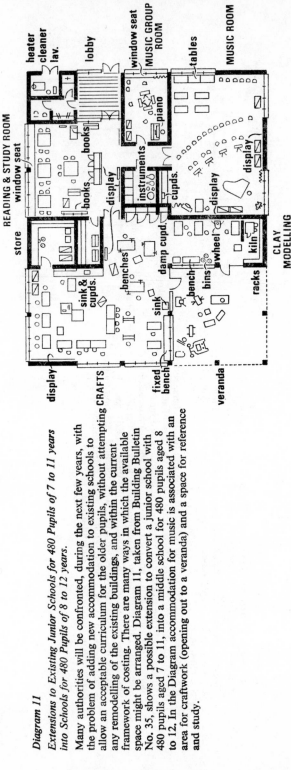

Diagram 11

Extensions to Existing Junior Schools for 480 Pupils of 7 to 11 years into Schools for 480 Pupils of 8 to 12 years.

Many authorities will be confronted, during the next few years, with the problem of adding new accommodation to existing schools to allow an acceptable curriculum for the older pupils, without attempting any remodelling of the existing buildings, and within the current framework of costing. There are many ways in which the available space might be arranged. Diagram 11, taken from Building Bulletin No. 35, shows a possible extension to convert a junior school with 480 pupils aged 7 to 11, into a middle school for 480 pupils aged 8 to 12. In the Diagram accommodation for music is associated with an area for craftwork (opening out to a veranda) and a space for reference and study.

Diagrams 12A and B
A Middle School for Pupils of 8 to 12 Years.

Annotation to Key Plan

One example of a school for 480 pupils of 8 to 12 years, designed within the current net cost limit. In the design it has been assumed that such a school will have much in common with those primary schools which have been most successful in giving opportunities for more advanced work for the older pupils, but that it should be possible to provide rather more facilities to encourage these to develop. The cost limit does not, however, allow the architect to go very far in this direction.

This particular example has been planned for an organisation of the school into three main groups, each the responsibility of a group of teachers. Each has its base in a centre. One of these, the base for 240 pupils, is planned round its own garden court; the other two, each for 120 pupils, are in a two-storey wing. The teaching area has been increased from the prescribed minimum of 12,240 sq. ft. to roughly 60% of the total area available. A yard-stick of about 20 sq. ft. per pupil has been taken as a basis for planning the working areas in each centre, whatever sizes of working groups they are designed for (i.e. a total of 9,600 sq. ft. for the 480 pupils). This leaves out of the total teaching area which can be provided, some 3,000 sq. ft. for spaces either to be shared by the whole school (e.g. for music, drama, physical education or crafts) or to supplement the teaching area in one or more of the centres.

Plan for School for Pupils of 8 to 12 Years

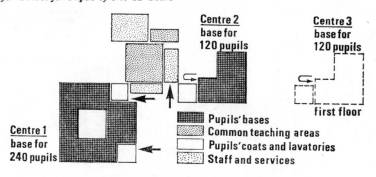

Net cost limit	£112,750
Area	21,600 sq. ft. (except porch and veranda: 504 sq. ft.)
Minimum Teaching Area	12,240 sq. ft.
Actual Teaching Area	12,852 sq. ft. (i.e. 59·5% of total area)

Diagram 12B

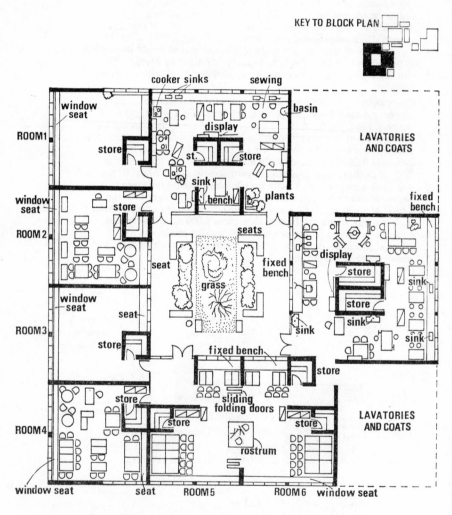

This arrangement of space for 240 pupils assumes close co-operation among the teachers concerned in the organisation of work and flexible groupings. The accommodation includes rooms with seating for up to 40 pupils, but equipped for working groups of 27 or 28. Two of these, with sliding-folding doors between them, can become one space for a larger group, or for small-scale drama work. There are also two spaces equipped for a variety of practical activities.

The first items were mobile and wall storage display units for primary schools. This furniture is now generally available. The second phase has been the design of tables, chairs and other items to provide a complete range of primary school furniture. By the beginning of 1967 it is hoped that a school in Manchester will be equipped with the complete range of new central supply primary school furniture. A research project has been commissioned from the Furniture Industry Research Association to provide design data based on direct measurement of children in action. Information about this furniture is to be included in a future Building Bulletin. We applaud these measures which seem an imaginative attempt by local authorities and central government to put furniture on the market which matches educational needs and yet is economical.

1101. School building has been a fine example of how a government department can, with its partners in the local authorities, produce good results through the exercise of imagination and effort.

II. EQUIPMENT ALLOWANCES FOR PRIMARY SCHOOLS

1102. We turn to a separate but related subject, equipment allowances. At the beginning of our study, we asked English local education authorities to supply details of the equipment allowances made to primary schools. They all responded and we are grateful to them for the detailed work that they must have put into their replies. The facts in this section of the chapter are based on the financial year 1963/64.

1103. Whilst many items of expenditure, including the largest such as staffing and accommodation, are not completely within the discretion of local education authorities, the supply of equipment is. Equipment allowances are one of the few areas of expenditure in which estimates can be cut and they are, therefore, particularly vulnerable to pressure to keep down the rates. We became aware in our visits to schools of the differences in quality, range and amount of equipment available to different schools.

1104. Returns made to us by the 129 local education authorities in 1963 showed a wide range of capitation allowances. For children in nursery schools and classes the capitation allowances range from 10s. 0d. to 69s. 0d. a head; for infant school children the range is from 16s. 5d. to 50s. 0d. and for junior schools from 19s. 0d. to 54s. 6d. These contrast with allowances for secondary modern schools which range from 30s. 0d. to 126s. 6d. and for grammar schools from 32s. 6d. to 126s. 6d. Table 32 shows the range and distribution of allowances.

1105. These figures cannot be taken at their face value. In some areas well known for work of outstanding quality, the allowances for some age groups appear low, but the methods by which local authorities finance the equipping of their schools are often complicated. In some areas extensive buying by bulk and large discounts enable allowances to go further. Expensive equipment may be supplied outside the allowance. Eighty-nine authorities, moreover, meet all or part of the cost of library books from a special allowance.

1106. Stationery, textbooks, small apparatus and equipment and most consumable materials come from the capitation allowances. The distinction made in some areas between books and library books may encourage spending on such items as books of English exercises, which are of little value, at the

Table 32 Equipment and Capitation Allowances: Numbers of L.E.As. and Amounts Available at Different Stages of Education (1963)

			Counties			
	Nursery	*Infant*	*Junior*		*Lower Secondary Modern*	*Lower Secondary Grammar*
Under 20/–	1	1	—	Under 40/–	4	2
21–30/–	6	15	8	41–50/–	3	4
31–40/–	3	22	30	51–60/–	5	3
Over 40/–	—	10	10	61–70/–	7	5
				71–80/–	16	12
				81–90/–	3	5
				91–100/–	3	2
				101–120/–	3	3

			County Boroughs			
	Nursery	*Infant*	*Junior*		*Lower Secondary Modern*	*Lower Secondary Grammar*
Under 20/–	1	1	1	Under 40/–	3	1
21–30/–	28	30	13	41–50/–	5	3
31–40/–	15	37	48	51–60/–	15	10
Over 40/–	3	6	16	61–70/–	20	22
				71–80/–	21	19
				81–90/–	5	8
				91–100/–	3	6
				101–120/–	3	5
				Over 120/–	—	1

expense of story books and books of information. In most areas, such expensive equipment as wireless and television sets, tape recorders, physical education equipment and large toys for infants are either wholly or in part additional to the allowance. We suggest that it is wrong for local education authorities to provide automatically such expensive items as apparatus for physical education, projectors or movable platforms for drama which may not suit the character or stage of development of a particular school and may be used infrequently or not at all. It would be better to increase allowances so that schools can buy for their current needs. Here and there, an element of paternalism is evident.

Choices Open to Schools

1107. The amount of freedom allowed to schools varies greatly. Four authorities give strict instructions on the amounts that may be spent on different classes of equipment. One hundred and four say they leave this decision to the schools and the rest exercise varying degrees of control. All except three authorities exercise some control over the firms with whom the money is spent. Schools are required to send all or some of their requisitions through the local authority who get a discount for large scale buying. Some authorities strongly recommend that the schools buy from certain prescribed firms. Others compile lists of recommended materials from several such firms. In about half of the areas, smaller amounts may be spent on urgent direct local purchase. In most cases, these amounts may not exceed ten per cent of the full allowance. Head teachers should be capable of making decisions on what proportions of the allowance should be spent on different kinds of equipment and on where materials should be bought. Some loss of discount on bulk purchase would be compensated for by the fact that schools can obtain what they need without delay. Abuse of freedom could be met through audit. There should be stated limits of discretion. As more freedom is given, teachers will need more advice on the choice of equipment both from their authorities and such bodies as the School Library Association and the Educational Foundation for Visual Aids.

1108. Not all schools are equally able to see new and interesting materials. In urban areas it is relatively easy to keep a permanent collection of materials from which schools can select, for teachers to visit showrooms and for exhibitions to be arranged. More isolated schools may have to rely on catalogues and on visits from travelling representatives of the suppliers. Lectures, courses and the work of county advisers should contribute more to bringing new materials to the notice of the schools.

1109. Several kinds of loan collection are kept and they supplement the resources of the school. Sixty-three authorities have circulating loan picture schemes. Sixty-seven have books available on loan for class and school libraries, sometimes as an alternative to the special library grant. In 57 areas, films, film strips and other visual aids may be borrowed. Twenty authorities have a record library and 27 provide a museum loan service.

1110. Enterprising head teachers often augment their schools' allowance. Expensive equipment or additions to outdoor amenities are often paid for by money raising activities, such as jumble sales, or by the work of parent-teacher associations. Parents help by buying learner swimming baths, pottery kilns, greenhouses, outside climbing apparatus and so on. They also help to make, maintain and repair equipment in the school. This is a powerful means of identifying them with the life of the school. But essentials must be provided by local education authorities.

Assistance for Schools in Special Need

1111. Small schools are generally at a disadvantage because they need large items but have fewer capitation allowances to pay for them. About half the local authorities go some way towards meeting the needs of small schools. Some allow as much as £50 annually to all schools with a roll of under 50. Other authorities increase the capitation allowance when the roll is small. Some give extra financial help for the purchase of expensive items of equipment while others are prepared to meet special requests. The failure of some authorities, however, to make allowance for small schools is a striking example of unfair treatment. Small schools which do not get special help are often penalised. Extra allowances are given in other circumstances. Twenty authorities make allowances for newly appointed head teachers. Newly opened classrooms, sharp increases in the number of children on roll, schools wishing to experiment with, for example, teaching machines, suggestions made after inspections, are examples of cases in which extra allowances are and should be given. Only nine authorities, however, say that special help is given to schools in difficult areas where wear and tear on all kinds of equipment are often particularly heavy. There is, we believe, a strong case for allowances to meet needs of these kinds.

Disparity in Local Practice

1112. There is wide disparity between local authorities. In some areas allowances are so low that the educational opportunities of the children are impoverished. In one area, for example, the capitation allowance for infant and nursery schools is 23s. 0d. from which consumable materials, books, including library books, apparatus and equipment must be bought. Help is given for the purchase of physical education equipment and large toys, but not automatically, and parents are not encouraged to help raise money. Not surprisingly, this authority in 1961/62 fell short by one third of what the Publishers' Association in their report on expenditure on books in maintained schools, which was endorsed by the A.E.C., considered to be a reasonable rather than a good level of expenditure on books. This is not an isolated example. Head teachers in such areas need to be exceptionally enterprising and skilled in improvisation, if their schools are to be even adequately equipped. Not all head teachers use their initiative in this way. Some in all areas persistently fail to spend their allowance even when the allowance is not generous, and may believe that there is merit in practising such an economy.

Recommendations

1113. In this chapter we have not attempted to cost the main demands on building resources apart from those needed for essential minimum improvements in primary achools. The total building cost implications of our Report are summarised in Chapter 31 and Tables 39 and 40.

Our recommendations on buildings are as follows:

(i) The Government should make the additional money available for a building programme of minor works over seven years starting in 1971 at an annual cost of £7–10 million designed to rid primary schools of the worst deficiencies.

(ii) More money should be available for minor projects. To enable small jobs to be carried out more quickly, more flexibility on expenditure as between major and minor building projects should be allowed. Authorities saving money on individual major projects should be permitted to spend it on minor projects.

(iii) The Department should undertake detailed exercises on the relationship between costs and the provision of essential amenities.

(iv) One of the Foundations might institute a competition on the lines of the Civic Trust Awards for imaginative but inexpensive improvement to old schools.

(v) The Department should undertake a careful study of present requirements for nursery education which may well be lavish in some respects. A building project by the Development Group would help local authorities in designing for the expansion of nursery education.

(vi) Continuing review is needed of the whole structure of cost limits and regulations particularly in view of the sharpness in variations between the different stages of education.

(vii) Teachers should be more directly involved in the design of schools.

(viii) Much further thought is needed on siting and planning schools so that they are more accessible to parents and the community, and free from traffic dangers and other nuisances.

Our recommendations on equipment allowances are as follows:

(i) Local education authorities should take steps to remove the inequalities described in this chapter. To bring up all allowances to the average figure without reducing the more generous allowances would cost between half a million pounds and one million pounds a year.

(ii) Schools with special difficulties should have extra allowances.

(iii) Although bulk buying of some items may be sensible head teachers should be given more freedom in spending.

REFERENCES

[1] The School Building Survey, 1962, Department of Education and Science, H.M.S.O., 1965.

[2] 'The State of Our Schools', Report of the National Survey of School Conditions, National Union of Teachers, 1962.

[3] Supplementary Evidence to the Council from the Inner London Education Authority.

[4] Moore, T., 'Difficulties of the Ordinary Child in Adjusting to Primary School', Journal of Child Psychology and Psychiatry, Vol. 7, No. 1, 1966.

[5] 'Remodelling of Old Schools', Building Bulletin No. 21, Ministry of Education, H.M.S.O., 1963.

[6] 'Development Projects: Junior School, Amersham', Building Bulletin No. 16, H.M.S.O., 1958.

[7] 'The Primary School: An Environment for Education', Edited by Manning, P., Results of a pilot survey by the Pilkington Research Unit, University of Liverpool, forthcoming 1967. This work contains some criticism of primary school design.

CHAPTER 29

The Status and Government of Primary Education

1114. Primary education is exacting in its demands on teachers' skill, training, intellectual ability and their concern for, and understanding of, children. The importance of the job matches its difficulty. Yet, in visits to schools and from evidence from associations and individual teachers, we have gained the strong impression that primary school teachers feel that their work does not receive the appreciation it deserves, and that their standing both in the educational system and in the community at large ought to be improved. In this country their status and working conditions have improved greatly since the war: the main source of discontent is their treatment compared with that of other professions.

1115. This feeling is not confined to English primary school teachers. In most western European countries, in the U.S.A. and indeed in most parts of the world, primary school and elementary teachers feel inferior to secondary teachers and to members of other professions. Primary education is sometimes regarded as a stepping stone to "promotion" to work in secondary education. Our own country is, indeed, unusual in having a uniform basic salary for all school teachers no matter in what type of school they teach. Elsewhere primary teachers are often recruited from different sources and trained by different methods for shorter periods of time. Salary scales are lower and emphasise a distinction which is always to the disadvantage of primary teachers.

Some of the Evidence

1116. Evidence from associations and from individual teachers has been confirmed by three larger scale enquiries. Sixty-five per cent of the head and assistant primary school teachers to whom we sent our questionnaire (Appendix 1, Table G.39) thought the status of primary education lower than that of secondary education. A study by the Social Survey of undergraduates' attitudes to school teaching as a career[1] showed that less than a third of those interviewed were able to think of anything attractive about infant or junior school teaching. While the largest factor was the belief that the standards of work would make insufficient intellectual demands on graduate teachers, some held such opinions as "you would be more like a nursemaid than a teacher with the five year olds"[2]. There was also a general under-estimation of the financial rewards of teaching. The great majority believed, inaccurately, that basic salaries as opposed to those actually earned, were different in primary, grammar and non-selective schools.

1117. We have tried to examine the strength of, and reasons for, this feeling amongst English teachers, which compares oddly with the good general reputation of primary education in this country. This has not proved easy but our attempts to answer four main questions may throw some light on the problem. The questions are:

(a) What is the standing of primary school teachers in the community at large?

(b) What is the standing of primary school teachers compared with that of teachers in secondary schools?

(c) Do primary school teachers have a proper standing in their dealings with local education authorities and managers?

(d) Do assistant teachers in primary schools have a proper standing and proper responsibilities in the school and in their relations with heads?

Standing of Teachers in the Community

1118. First, we believe that there ought to be improvement in the standing of teachers generally. We have undertaken no systematic enquiry in connection with this question, but we are clear that many teachers, particularly those in charge of younger children, think that their work is widely regarded as demanding meagre qualifications, or skill or application. The fact that teaching in maintained schools generally, with the possible exception of grammar schools, ranks lower socially than teaching in many independent schools or in universities and than many other professions, has effects which cannot be denied or ignored. Whether primary school teachers are particularly affected is difficult to say. There is a feeling that attendance at a university is socially as well as academically more desirable than at a college of education, and that to teach young children is less exacting than to teach older ones. Higher status may, indeed, go with membership of professions which are less accessible to the general public. This may in part be due to the generally higher esteem placed on more specialist work in the whole of society—irrespective of the level of skill and responsibility that the work itself involves.[3]

The Standing of Primary Teachers Compared with that of Secondary School Teachers

1119. Although there is no difference in formal status between those qualified for work in primary or secondary education and the same basic salary scale, primary teachers sometimes feel that they are regarded as poor relations. Some of the factors which create this impression can be quite easily identified.

1120. As we show in Chapter 28, school building programmes since the war have favoured the secondary schools. Although nearly a third of primary school children are being taught in buildings completed since 1945, there are large numbers of teachers in rural primary schools and in the older parts of towns who are very conscious of the sad difference between the conditions in which they work and those enjoyed by their colleagues in the new secondary schools nearby. This may be a transitional problem, although whether the transitional period will be further prolonged will depend on the ways in which extra buildings are provided for the extended period of compulsory education. Primary education has been universal for a long time, secondary education only since the war. More new secondary schools have been necessary to permit this revolutionary change. The design of new primary school building has often been superb. But a rapid programme of improvement is needed, as we argue earlier in our Report.

1121. Secondly, and perhaps most important of all, there is the size of classes, which we consider more generally in Chapter 20. Here we are concerned with the fact that the statutory figure above which classes are described as "oversize" is 30 for secondary schools and 40 for primary schools. This is deeply deplored by primary school teachers. The fact that if the maximum for primary classes were reduced by Regulation to 30 tomorrow, it would have no immediate consequence because of the shortage of primary school teachers is not the whole point. The Regulations are taken as an official confirmation of the view that teaching a class of secondary pupils is more exacting than teaching the same number of primary school children. No educational justification for the difference in maximum size has been or, in our view, could be advanced, and it appears in no other country of which we know.

1122. Thirdly, there are big differences between the capitation and equipment allowances made by local education authorities to primary and secondary schools. (See Chapter 28.) The range of capitation allowances varies widely between authorities but the differences in range between primary and secondary schools is what is significant. While some difference between the allowances for primary and secondary schools is to be expected, the order of the difference appears to us to be quite unreasonable and to be a cause of low morale. This kind of disparity could be removed with small cost and virtually at once.

1123. The distribution of teaching posts carrying higher salaries is a matter that keenly concerns primary teachers. While the basic scale is the same, the method of calculating unit totals (described in the Annex to this chapter) affects both the scales and the numbers of teachers holding posts above the basic scale in primary and secondary schools. For example, in most cases the head of a primary school has a lower salary than the head of a secondary school of identical size, and there will be more responsibility allowances in the latter, because children of primary school age count as one unit each and children over 13 as more than one unit.

1124. The career structure favours teachers in secondary schools. It is true that the chances of a headship are four times as great for primary as for secondary teachers, but other posts above the basic scale attract more pay in large schools: primary schools tend to be smaller than secondary, while many are so small that the head teacher has to take full charge of a class. The prospects for advancement to posts carrying the highest salaries are certainly brighter for teachers in secondary schools. While less than half of primary teachers receive a salary above the basic scale, in the secondary schools about three quarters have additions to salary. Differences in the number and value of allowances reduce the attraction of primary school teaching, particularly for men who might add more stability to the primary schools.

1125. There is an unquestionable difference of status, to which we have already referred, between a degree and a non-graduate teaching qualification. The former is associated mainly with secondary and the latter with primary schools. The teachers' associations made this point in their evidence. There is a danger that the gulf between primary and secondary teachers will be widened if secondary schools are increasingly staffed by graduates from universities, and primary schools by teachers from colleges of education. The institution of the Bachelor of Education degree may accentuate problems of status if only a minority of those taking it are training for primary education. The point is not that there is no academic difference between a degree and certificate, although as the three year course gets under way and larger numbers enter university courses the difference in standards may be reduced. But even a good degree is no measure of teaching ability; and a qualified non-graduate may be a more useful member of the profession than a graduate. Primary teachers need reasonable academic ability and must have a thorough knowledge of such subjects as child development. Other qualities such as perseverance, ingenuity, intuition and the ability to get on with people, are also needed. It is not easy, therefore, to see what differences in salary are justified.

1126. In a period of idealism at the time of the 1944 Education Act a unified salary structure was created. It was not the unified basis but the level of salaries which could be afforded if all had to have the same rate which affected the outcome. It proved difficult to recruit graduates with good honours degrees for advanced work in sixth forms, and although differentials have been gradually reintroduced in the form of allowances, they are still insufficient, many would think, to compete with scales offered in industry to those with similar qualifications. It is particularly difficult therefore to say where the right answer lies in the matter of salaries. But the present differences between primary and secondary schools in size of class, equipment allowances and expenditure per place on school buildings seem too large. They relate in part to differences in need, but also to differences in standing. The fact that such differences are far more marked in the foreign countries that our members visited than in England does not alter the need to narrow the gap here.

The Standing of Primary School Teachers in their Dealings with Local Education Authorities

1127. We made a brief survey of the status and responsibilities of teachers as interpreted by their employing authorities and exhibited by the rules made by these authorities. A straightforward analysis of the returns revealed relatively little variation between different areas, yet our observations have convinced us that substantial variation does exist. It is not so much the rules themselves that matter as the interpretation of them and, more subtly, the tone and quality of the relationship between local authorities and teachers. We are certain that these relationships have improved greatly in the last 20 years, but there is room for further improvement. We therefore put forward a number of propositions which ought to govern the relationship between authorities and their teachers.

1128. First, it is important that teachers should be represented on education committees and that primary school teachers specifically should be represented on sub-committees and advisory committees that concern primary education. Members of a committee who vote on expenditure of public money should not, of course, have a vested interest in the matter on which they are voting, but in practice it is unusual for teacher representatives to be full voting members. Apart from committee membership, it is desirable that consultation should take place whenever changes are made affecting the profession. Regular consultative machinery should be established for this.

1129. Officials of local education authorites, both administrative and advisory, should be easily accessible to head teachers and to assistants for the discussion of anything that may affect the life, work and morale of the schools. While most head teachers who answered our questionnaire on teacher opinion thought that officials were accessible to both head teachers and assistants, only half the assistants thought that they themselves had access to officials (Appendix 1, Table G.40).

1130. Authorities should use every means to bring the knowledge, experience and ability of the profession to bear on the work of their education committees. Many authorities already do this: representative committees are consulted, and not just as a matter of form, on all major issues of educational policy such as the reorganisation of secondary education. Teachers take a leading part in in-service courses and educational experiments. We should like to see these practices extended to all areas, particularly as our proposals, such as those for the establishment of middle schools, come into effect. To realise these principles it will be necessary to ensure that administrative and advisory staff are adequate in quality and quantity: in some parts of the country they are too overburdened to do more than keep the system going.

Management of Schools

1131. The whole subject of school management requires reconsideration. Great care should be exercised in the appointment of school managers who should be persons genuinely concerned with education and prepared to devote time and trouble to it. There is good reason to be disturbed when only 41 per cent of the head teachers and assistants think managing bodies helpful to primary schools, while nearly 30 per cent think they are not. The rest are undecided (Appendix 1, Table G.41). A study* still in progress shows that practice in the appointment of managers for county schools varies greatly between different authorities and between rural and city areas. In the succeeding paragraphs we refer only to county schools since the research study quoted did not cover voluntary schools. While it is reasonable for some managers to be appointed on a political basis, the first aim should be to find good managers irrespective of party allegiance. In at least one area recommendations for appointments are sent back if the education committee believes that insufficient regard is being paid to relevant experience. This is the right attitude to appointments. Most authorities appoint for a specified term of office, but these are too often renewed and care is needed to ensure that there is a reasonably good flow of new appointments.

1132. In 1944 the Parliamentary Secretary to the Board of Education expressed a strong hope that managers should be chosen so as to ensure at least some representation of parents of children attending the individual school. While the great majority of authorities believe that parents should be represented, most believe, particularly in the rural areas, that their present procedure allows for this. Only a small minority make specific provision for parent representation—usually of a parent-teacher association. The majority of chief education officers in county areas welcome the contribution which parents make. They tend to be younger than most managers, and more directly

*A study of school management and government in county schools is being undertaken by the Research Unit on School Management and Government, University of London Institute of Education. These paragraphs draw on their preliminary findings which are given in Appendix 13, Vol. 2 to this Report. The areas studied to date comprise of 25 county boroughs (including most of the larger ones), 27 counties and 18 Outer London Boroughs.

concerned with the issues discussed. We favour the appointment as managers of parents who have children at the school. The rules should make it clear that they must not vote on issues involving their own children. Two thirds of the managers of county schools in country areas are appointed by the local education authorities and one third on the nomination of minor authorities. Authorities at both levels should try to select managers representative of those who are most concerned with the schools.

1133. In most rural areas, individual primary schools have their own managing body. This should be the aim everywhere, although it may not always be easily achieved. In a minority of urban areas managers are appointed for a group of primary schools which may vary from 3 to 12 schools. This is permitted by Section 20 of the 1944 Education Act. We are clear that the needs of schools are best met when each has its own body of managers. But where large numbers of managers are needed, there may be a danger that many who have the time to serve will have retired from work and thus be too old to have direct experience of the problems confronting the school. There may be strong administrative arguments for grouping primary schools under a stronger body of managers than would be available to each individually. If so the groups should be as small as possible. The majority of urban areas (16 out of a sample of 25) make the primary sub-committee of the education committee the body of managers for all primary schools. This arrangement makes nonsense of the conception of school managers as friends and neighbours of a school who give it their constant interest and help, sometimes arguing on its behalf in dealings with the education authority. We deplore this practice which sometimes leads to a succession of head teachers having to wait outside the door of the room in which the managers are meeting. As a general rule, meetings of managers should take place on school premises, so as to ensure that the managers see the buildings regularly, and the condition for which they carry responsibility. Most parents, we are sure, have not the slightest idea who are the managers of their children's schools. Although the appointment of managers is a matter of public knowledge in as much as they must be confirmed by the education committee, few parents can have any idea as to their functions or of their right of access to them. The names of managers, and the nominating bodies, might be posted in a prominent place in each primary school, and also be published in the leaflets giving general information about the school which we suggest in Chapter 4.

1134. Articles of Government under which secondary schools function, have to be approved in the case of county schools and made in the case of voluntary schools by the Secretary of State, while the Rules of Management for primary schools are made by local authorities without reference to the Department. The formal powers of governors are in practice greater than those of managers. These differences are largely historical in origin[4]. Since the reasons for them no longer hold, authorities should give managers the same powers, and perhaps the same title, as governors. This last change would involve legislation. Enquiries show that there are considerable differences between the function of managers and governors in most cases. The appointment of head teachers is usually made on the recommendation of joint committees of governors and the education committee in the case of secondary schools. This is less often the case with primary schools, except where managing bodies are sub-committees of the education committee. Many governing bodies prepare annual estimates of expenditure for their secondary schools: few managing bodies do so, probably because there are many more primary schools and they are smaller. While governing bodies have the "general direction of the conduct and curriculum of the school" (a phrase appearing in the Department's model Instrument and Articles of Government), few managing bodies have the same status or power. This may not be a bad thing for the head teacher who is then freer in his control of the school. In most Rules of Management either the reference to curriculum or the entire clause is omitted.

1135. An active and knowledgeable body of managers can be a great support to a head teacher, and a useful interpreter of a school to the community it serves and vice versa. Their powers should not be exercised in such a way that they limit the professional judgement of the head teacher, and there are matters that must be left to the local authority. They can act usefully as a bridge between the Education Committee and the school, putting the case for the school where this is needed, explaining through its councillor members to the teachers and parents what the authority is getting at by some new line of policy. If local authority areas become bigger, some local representative body will be even more necessary. It will be even more important to appoint men and women of the right calibre—but, if they are to be found, more power will have to be given them. It is worth noting that none of the countries we visited have anything like our system of managers, though several—the U.S.A. and Denmark, for example—have other ways of enlisting community support.

1136. Most managers are given little or no guidance about their functions, the informal aspects of school management and the general work of the school. Some are not even given copies of the Instrument and Rules of Management. Some authorities, however, produce handbooks, and arrange conferences, and one even publishes a regular news letter for managers.

1137. It is laid down in the Instruments of Management produced by the Department of Education and Science for voluntary schools and by the local education authorities for county schools that a teacher may not be a member of the managing body of the school at which he teaches. This is reasonable as a head teacher could be placed in an intolerable situation if one of his assistant teachers was on the managing body of the school; but the head teacher should be fully conversant with the managers' views on the running of the school, and attend all their meetings, as he usually does in rural areas, unless he is himself the subject of discussion. The managers should consult him on all points, and should understand his views on the running of the school.

1138. There are a few areas where a joint governing body and managing body is established. In practice, while it might contribute to continuity between a secondary school and its contributing primary schools, the device might prove too cumbersome if there are a large number of contributing primary schools. It would be far better if these bodies had overlapping memberships.

Appointment of Staff

1139. In the case of county and voluntary controlled schools the appointment of head teachers is the responsibility of the local education authority, which may act on the advice of joint committees of managers and the education committee. The head teachers of voluntary aided schools are appointed by the managers. This is as it should be, but in both cases the merits of the candidates cannot be effectively assessed unless professional advice is sought from officials who are in a position to give it.

1140. The interviewing of candidates should not be a mere formality but a genuine part of the selection process. In one area, managers receive written guidance on the ways in which interviews should be conducted, and managers should be given some instruction in, or have some knowledge of, the techniques of interviewing. It is common practice for the chief education officer to give interviewing committees detailed advice on the appointment of a head or deputy head teacher. We do not believe that the promotion lists favoured by some authorities, on which the records and assessments of their own teachers are noted, result in the best applicants applying for posts or encourage the inter-change of ideas and good practice between different parts of the country. All posts should be freely open to talent wherever it is found.

1141. Every head teacher should be given the opportunity of saying what qualities and qualifications he wants in his staff and the specific duties attached to every post of special responsibility. He should also be shown, and be able to comment on, the list of applicants and should be present at all stages of the selective process. While there will be cases in which the head cannot have the applicant he wants, his wishes should always be seriously considered. He should also be able to recommend members of his staff for graded posts, though the final decision must remain with the authority who alone can consider the claims of all applicants. As far as probationary teachers are concerned, we recognise that the authority must have some control* over first postings. Supply problems apart, the authority are in a favourable position to know which school is best able to help teachers in their first post. But the basic principle of giving teachers choice of school should be followed wherever possible. Head teachers should be consulted before first appointments are made to make sure that the newcomer fits, as far as possible; and heads should have as much notice as possible of the appointment of a probationary teacher to their staff.

Powers of Head Teachers

1142. There is a good deal of evidence that heads are sometimes ignored or by-passed by authorities where they clearly ought to have a say. We give four instances. First, heads and their staff should always be consulted by local education authorities about major or minor capital works involving an alteration to the school, and be free to make comments and suggestions, not only about furniture and colour schemes, but also about basic design and layout. The most imaginative and exciting design has usually emerged when architects, with the help of the local authority, take great pains to discover how the teachers and children will use the building.

*Direct control applies to county schools and, to a large measure, controlled schools: voluntary aided schools appoint their own staff (subject to certain conditions laid down in sub-section 24(2) of the Education Act, 1944).

1143. Secondly, although it is not always possible for head teachers to have complete control over the use of their schools out of school hours, particularly when dual use is common and unavoidable, they should always be consulted and kept informed.

1144. Thirdly, head teachers should always have a fund at their disposal for the immediate purchase of small articles. We are unconvinced by the arguments put forward by some authorities against this practice, and convinced by the success of those authorities who have embarked on it.

1145. Fourthly, head teachers should be allowed proper discretion in deciding the circumstances in which they themselves and members of their staffs may be occasionally absent from school. The authority is justified in laying down the general limits of this discretion, but within those limits no unnecessary formalities should be required. Similarly, educational visits need not be restricted if insurance policies are taken out which allow reasonable discretion to heads. A man or woman who cannot be trusted to use discretion about visits should never have been appointed to a headship.

1146. We have already mentioned the need for secretarial help. Some such help, together with a telephone, a typewriter and duplicating equipment, should be available in every school so that the head can devote himself to the work for which he is being paid and not use valuable time on work which would be better done by someone else. Many authorities are generous in these respects. But occasionally restrictions are of a comic triviality. In at least one area a typewriter can only be used in an educational establishment on the approval of the Finance and General Purposes Committee, except in a college of further education or for teaching purposes in secondary schools.

Relationships of Heads and Assistant Staff

1147. Just as head teachers should be treated with proper respect by their employing authorities, assistant staff should be drawn as much as possible into the planning and organisation of school life. While the great majority of the head teachers and assistant teachers answering our questionnaire (Appendix 1: Table G.37) thought that assistant teachers were allowed sufficient freedom to organise work in their own classes, a substantially smaller number (though still the majority) of assistant teachers thought they were consulted sufficiently about the running of the school. The authority of English head teachers is considerable, yet there are many schools in which a free interchange of ideas exists between the head and his staff without his essential leadership being impaired. Assistant teachers should have access to managers and to local education authorities. But the important things cannot be achieved by regulations no matter how liberal. They depend on the trusting, charitable and decent human relations which characterise the majority of primary schools today.

1148. Most of what is here recommended will be taken for granted by local education authorities and teachers in areas where enlightened practices are already well established. But there are areas in which there is great room for improvement. We hope that here, too, the practices we recommend will be commonplace before long.

General

1149. Grievances about status are often strongly felt but ill defined. Many of the points discussed in this chapter, however, reveal inequitable or even downright shoddy treatment. Primary education seems always to get the worst treatment—the largest classes, the oldest buildings, poor career prospects and the most restricted professional autonomy. We want two changes. The first is the elimination of all unjustifiable differences in treatment between primary and secondary education. The second is to see the primary school take on a new status as a centre of community activity. This may not lead to an improvement in status in the conventional sense, but parents will appreciate more clearly that the education of their children is in the hands of people with professional training who need and welcome their help. The last thing we want is a status based on social distance and superiority. The status of the primary schools and their teachers should rest on the respect of those who know what they are achieving.

Recommendations

1150. (i) Primary school teachers should be represented on local education committees and on the sub-committee and advisory committees that specifically concern primary education. Machinery for consultation with teachers on policy changes affecting them is desirable.

(ii) Officials of local education authorities should be easily accessible to head and assistant teachers for the discussion of matters which might affect the life, work and morale of the schools.

(iii) School managers should be appointed on the basis of their genuine concern with education and readiness to devote time and trouble to their managerial duties irrespective of party allegiance. Authorities should ensure a reasonably good flow of new appointments.

(iv) Parents of children attending the schools should be represented on the managing body.

(v) As far as it compatible with effective management, all individual primary schools should have their own managing body.

(vi) Where several primary schools are grouped, the groups should be as small as possible.

(vii) Managers' meetings should take place on the school premises, and managers' names should be posted in a prominent position in each primary school together with the names of any nominating bodies.

(viii) Local authorities should bring the powers of managers in primary schools into line with those of governors of secondary schools.

(ix) Managers need to be more actively concerned in the school to further relations between school and community and to serve as a support for the head teacher.

(x) The responsibilities of managers must be increased if candidates of the right calibre care to be attracted.

(xi) The head teacher should be fully conversant with the managers' views on the running of the school and vice-versa. He should attend all managers' meetings unless he is himself the subject of discussion. The managers should consult him at all points.

(xii) Overlap in membership between governing bodies of secondary schools and the managing bodies of their contributory primary schools is preferable to the establishment of a joint governing and managing body.

(xiii) Managing bodies in considering the merit of candidates for headships and deputy headships should seek the expert advice of officials..

(xiv) The interviewing of candidates for headships and deputy headships should be a genuine part of the selection process and managers should have some knowledge of the techniques of interviewing. All posts for headships and deputy headships should be open to talent from all parts of the country.

(xv) Head teachers should be given the opportunity of saying what qualities and qualifications they want in their staff and take part in all stages of selection. They should also be able to give views on the specific duties attached to every post of special responsibility, and to recommend members of their staff for such posts. They should be consulted about the needs of their schools when the appointments of probationers are being considered.

(xvi) Head teachers and their staff should always be consulted by local education authorities about major or minor capital works involving their schools and be free to comment on and make suggestions on alterations at all stages.

(xvii) Heads should be consulted over the use of their schools in or out of school hours.

(xviii) Heads should be allowed discretion in deciding in what circumstances they or members of their staff should be allowed occasional absences from school. Regulations about taking children on educational visits should be restricted to those circumstances where insurance and legal liability make it necessary.

(xix) Secretarial help, a telephone, a typewriter and duplicating equipment should be available in all schools.

(xx) Assistant staff should play as large a part as possible in the planning and organisation of school life. Assistants should have access to managers and to local education authorities.

(xxi) All unnecessary and unjustified differences of treatment between primary and secondary education should be eliminated.

REFERENCES

[1] Undergraduate's Attitudes to School Teaching as a Career. The Social Survey. 1965. Section X.

[2] See [1] above. Section 12.21.

[3] "The Teacher's Role. A Sociological Analysis. Wilson B." Brit. Jnl. of Sociology. XII, p.p. 15-32.

[4] E. J. R. Eaglesham. "The Centenary of Sir Robert Morant". British Journal of Education. Vol. XII. November 1963.

Annex to Chapter 29

A NOTE ON THE METHOD OF CALCULATING UNIT TOTALS

1. The allowances for head teachers, deputy heads and holders of posts of special responsibility are determined on the basis of the school's or department's "unit total" or "review average", which is a figure assessed by reference, first, to the number of pupils on the roll of the school or department as on 1st January of the year concerned, and, secondly, to the ages of the pupils as at 31st March following. The unit total is calculated as follows:

For each pupil under 13 years of age (including children under 5)	1 unit
For each pupil aged 13 and under 15	2 units
For each pupil aged 15 and under 16	4 units
For each pupil aged 16 and under 17	6 units
For each pupil aged 17 and over	10 units

2. The review average of a school or department, which is calculated every three years, is the mean of the unit totals for the year of the review and the previous two years. Tables 33 and 34 show the amounts of allowances paid to holders in the different groups of primary and secondary schools.

Table 33

Since 1st April 1965 the following salary scales have operated for head teachers:

Salary Scales for Head Teachers

Group	Review Average or Unit Total	Minimum (£)	Annual Increment (£)	Maximum (£)
0	Up to 40	*	50	1600
1	41— 100	*	50	1700
2	101— 200	1650	50 (3)	1800
3	201— 300	1720	60 (3)	1900
4	301— 500	1810	60 (4)	2050
5	501— 700	1925	75 (4)	2225
6	701—1000	2125	75 (4)	2425
7	1001—1300	2325	75 (4)	2625
8	1301—1800	2525	75 (4)	2825
9	1801—2400	2750	75 (4)	3050
10	2401—3300	2950	75 (4)	3250
11	3301—4600	3150	75 (4)	3450
12	4601—6000	3350	100 (3)	3650
13	over 6000	3550	100 (3)	3850

Source: Burnham Primary and Secondary Schools Report, 1965, Section K.

*The commencing salary of a head teacher in Group 0 and 1 schools is the salary payable to him as an assistant teacher prior to his appointment including any allowance or additional payment in respect of a post of special responsibility, other than that of acting head teacher, but excluding London allowance to which, subject to the maximum of the new scale, a promotion increase of £200 where the appointment is to a Group 0 school and £250 where the appointment is to a Group 1 school shall be added.

Table 34. Deputy Head Teachers and Graded Posts.

Group	0	1	2	3	4	5	7	6	8	9	10	12	12	13
Review Average or Unit Total			101–200	201–300	301–500	501–700	701–1100	1001–1300	1301–1800	1801–2400	2401–3300	3301–4600	4601–6000	over 6000
Deputy head allowance			*	£140	£205	£275	£360	£455	£545	£635	£725	£815	£905	£1000
Score for Graded Posts				†	2	4	7	10	15	21	30	43	57	70

Source: Burnham Primary and Secondary Schools Report, 1965, Sections M and O.

*The l.e.a. must appoint a deputy head with an allowance of a £120 in a primary school or department in Group 2 where there are both infant and junior children.

†The l.e.a. may in its discretion establish a Scale I graded post in a Group 3 school or department.

Payments to holders of graded posts.

Scale I £120—one point
   II £200—two points
   III £300—three points

The number and grading of these posts in any school or department are determined by the local education authority in accordance with the "score" of points to which the school or department is entitled.

CHAPTER 30

Research, Innovation and the Dissemination of Information

1151. The willingness of teachers to experiment, to innovate and to change has been one of the mainsprings of progress in the primary schools. This source of improvements will continue so long as we have forward and inventive teachers. At the same time, in spite of the slender resources devoted to it, educational research has contributed much to progress since the turn of the century. One only has to recall the impact on the schools of the work of Burt, Schonell and their followers in the improvement of the teaching of reading and arithmetic and the treatment of backwardness, the influence of the studies of Susan Isaacs and D. E. M. Gardner on learning through activity and experience, the insights from studies of child development into the genesis of emotional disturbances to realise that there has long existed a considerable body of research-based knowledge and theory. It is doubtful however whether, with the exception of tests of ability and attainment, teachers were, or are, fully aware that their art has already a considerable technological base.

1152. Because education is an applied discipline, the relation between research and practice is and should be reciprocal. From studies of what individual teachers are doing, useful pointers can be obtained to fruitful directions for experiment and research: research in education or in such ancillary sciences as child development, social psychology, or learning theory will throw up ideas with which the innovating teacher can experiment. In this very important sense, research and practice are parts of a whole, and neither can flourish without the other.

1153. In recent years there has been a substantial growth in the resources devoted to educational research and development. The Department of Education and Science have been making grants for educational research on an increasing scale since 1962; by the end of 1965 £1¼ million had been committed to about 120 research projects. Independent trusts have provided generous support; in particular, the Nuffield Foundation has spent or committed over £2 million on development work much of it conducted in close association with the Schools Council. This itself sponsors development and research projects, and plans are on foot to spend under its auspices over £1 million a year, coming partly from the Department of Education and Science and partly from local education authorities. More recently still, the Social Science Research Council has been set up following the recommendations of the Heyworth Committee on Social Studies and is currently making grants for educational research projects. The universities support some research out of their general funds. Local education authorities and teachers' associations are also involved in other ways, for example by subscribing money to the National Foundation for Educational Research.

1154. This Foundation, which is the only body in England and Wales established specifically to conduct educational research, grew out of the Foundation for Educational Research which was set up in 1943 under the aegis of the University of London Institute of Education with the generous aid of various teachers' associations as well as the Carnegie and Leverhulme Trusts. In 1955, ten years after the National Foundation was established, its total budget was only £20,000; by 1964–65 it had risen to over £150,000. Apart from undertaking research the Foundation devotes considerable effort to disseminating the results of research.

1155. In addition to other independent bodies, the universities and the institutes of education conduct research projects, ranging from large scale, long term and sometimes inter-disciplinary studies to individual ones leading to higher degrees or diplomas. Research undertaken in many university departments, such as departments of medicine or psychology, often has a bearing on education. Medical and educational research on disturbed children has, for example, increased knowledge of the normal child. Local education authorities, teachers' associations or local groups of teachers sometimes carry out their own investigations.

1156. Despite the growth in the amount of research and in the interest taken in educational research by teachers and local education authorities, there are a number of problems to be solved as well as gaps in the subjects so far covered by research. We want to say something about four of these—the relationship between teachers and research, co-ordination, dissemination and training.

1157. Scepticism among teachers will only be removed when the value of research to classroom practice is demonstrated. In some parts of the country there is a proliferation of research workers in schools on projects of small apparent usefulness to classroom teachers. The range of useful research has yet to be clarified. Research is bound to involve subjective judgments which must depend on a thorough knowledge and understanding of the schools. Without this understanding the researcher cannot ask the right questions or check his findings.

1158. Closer co-ordination of research would reduce wasted effort, avoid unnecessary overlap and enable researchers to build more effectively on each other's work. But co-ordination can have different meanings and it is important to be clear which is intended. It could mean working out a master plan and expecting everybody to fit in with it. This would plainly not be right. Or it could mean the establishment of a clearing house of information from which anybody interested could discover what research had been, or was being, done. The N.F.E.R. already does much through its register of research in progress. Co-ordination on a voluntary rather than a compulsory basis is much to be preferred. We are glad to hear that the National Foundation for Educational Research has been giving some thought to the sort of machinery needed. The kind of result looked for is a closer relationship between highly specialised or fundamental research and studies undertaken within the school environment.

1159. Adequate communication of results is essential in the interests not only of other research workers but also of its interpreters, such as university and college teachers and the potential users of research, teachers and administrators. Present means of dissemination include: "Educational Research" and the other publications of the National Foundation; the main journals in education, psychology and sociology; the curriculum bulletins and working papers of the Schools Council; the Department's publications and those of institutes of education. In-service courses help to bring new work to the attention of teachers. All these means are valuable, but they are far from adequate. When we began our enquiry we had to commission a survey of research and development relevant to our field because no other was available. The time lag in getting research reports published in the professional journals can mean serious delay in reaching other research workers. Teachers often find reports incomprehensible, inconsistent and irrelevant. At the local level, schools in adjacent areas may be engaged in interesting innovation, the results of which are never made more generally known or evaluated. A more comprehensive service for disseminating the results of research at all levels seems to be required.

1160. Dissemination is important as a means of giving teachers confidence in the aims and methods of research workers. Many teachers have participated in the research programmes of the N.F.E.R., and the work of the Schools Council and the Nuffield Foundation has demonstrated the willingness of teachers to take part in development work. It is important that, if closer collaboration between research workers and practitioners is to be fruitful, teachers should be given some positive help and reassurance on the purpose of the research work, and that where teachers and researchers are engaged on the same project, the functions of both are clearly defined and understood.

1161. If teachers are to collaborate fruitfully in research projects, for example, by taking part in fieldwork and in controlled experiments, they need some training. In their initial courses of teacher training, they should be made familiar with some of the techniques, as well as the results, of research and development. Much the best way for students or young teachers to get the "feel" of research is to participate, even to a small extent, in a research project. For a student this will hardly be possible unless there is on the staff of the college or department of education a member who is himself or herself a trained research worker and carrying out a continuous programme of research.

1162. There is a most serious and general shortage of trained and competent research workers. Some people who have taken university courses in psychology, sociology, or statistics lack the teaching experience that is desirable for most educational research. We are glad to know that the Social Science Research Council is granting some studentships for graduates in such subjects to provide a year's training in research in a university department of education. There is need for parallel training in research for experienced teachers. We hope that firm proposals will be put forward in the near future and that the necessary funds will be forthcoming.

1163. In any additional work that is undertaken on these or any topics, one important principle should be borne in mind. Educational research which leaves the teacher out of account ignores a prime source of knowledge and experience. Not only should more teachers be actively involved in large research and development projects, but the continuing value of small scale enquiries and investigations by teachers and administrators at the local level should be recognised. Apart from their contribution to knowledge these investigations can foster liveliness of mind and an enquiring attitude to everyday problems and practices. For such studies some simple services of advice, consultation and data analysis should be provided, since without them much enthusiasm runs to waste in the sands of frustration.

P

1164. In spite of our reservations about the existing state of research, we have no doubt that well designed studies are needed. Those that have been commissioned for us have proved to be extremely valuable. There are, as we see it, several general needs. First, for carefully planned longitudinal cohort studies associated with special studies in depth. Cause and effect could then to some extent be unravelled and there might even be hope of answering Cyril Burt's classic question—"What happened to Lizzie?" Accounts of the progress of such studies should be available to other researchers. Such studies as those of Dr. J. W. B. Douglas' National Survey of Child Health and Development and of the National Child Development Study (see Appendix 10) have been of considerable value in providing data not available elsewhere. Such successive studies over a period of pupils' and schools achievements as the Department's Reading Surveys (1948, 1956, 1961 and 1964) have already proved their worth. We are glad to know that the N.F.E.R. are making continuing studies in reading and mathematics. We hope that the H.M.I. survey of the quality of primary schools (see Chapter 8) will be repeated at least at ten year intervals. But there are many useful forms of research other than surveys. We see particular value in creating experimental situations in schools and comparing results before and after change is made. Our proposals for educational priority areas should, if carried out, offer excellent opportunities for this kind of study.

Further Studies

1165. In the course of our enquiries we have found a number of gaps in existing knowledge which it might be possible to fill by means of research. The following list is not exhaustive, but brings together the points which, in our view, are most likely to repay further study:

(a) Whether early developers retain their superiority or lose their initial advantage. (Chapter 2.)

(b) The existence of critical periods in the development of children, i.e. stages after which it is markedly less easy to remedy deficiencies of development in education. (Chapter 2.)

(c) Further studies of the growth of the brain and the development of its mechanisms are necessary to complement fundamental work on children's intellectual and emotional development. (Chapter 2.)

(d) Research should be started to discover which of the developments in educational priority areas have the most constructive effects, to assist in planning the longer term programme, and, at the same time, to assess the usefulness of the criteria suggested. (Chapter 5.)

(e) The development of diagnostic and other tests for use by teachers in the context of the waning of selection procedures and the changing primary curriculum. (Chapters 11, 12, 16.)

(f) The construction and use of tests which sample such characteristics as inventiveness and originality. (Chapter 11.)

(g) The educational and economic characteristics of schools of different sizes. (Chapter 13.)

(h) Study of the long term impact of primary education, including nursery education, on subsequent educational history, to include study of the long term consequences of teaching by formal and informal methods, children's reactions to permissive and authoritarian attitudes within the school, and rewards and punishments and the ways differences in temperament affect learning. (Chapters 9 and 16.)

(i) There should also be recurring national surveys of attainment similar to those carried out by the N.F.E.R. and the Department in reading. (Chapter 16.)

(j) Investigation of the extent to which the school environment and guidance and teaching provided by teachers can accelerate the development of children's concepts. (Chapter 16.)

(k) Research into religious education related to children's concepts, their experience of life and their intellectual powers. More research is needed into the development of moral values. (Chapter 17.)

(l) Research into the types of primer and library books most effective with children from different backgrounds and of varying levels of ability. (Chapter 17).

(m) An enquiry into children's understanding of time and other concepts related to history. (Chapter 17.)

(n) Research into the development of creative powers in music. (Chapter 17.)

(o) Continuing research into the uses of audio-visual and other aids, with particular attention to programmed learning.

(p) Experiments should be made to test the effects of small classes and generous staffing. (Chapter 20.)

(q) Longitudinal research studies into the ways of dealing with handicapped children. (Chapter 21.)

(r) Long term studies should be made on the needs and achievements of gifted children. (Chapter 22.)

(s) Continuing study of the right ratio of teachers to pupils of different ages given modern equipment and the employment of ancillary staff. (Chapter 23.)

1166. Finally, we have suggested that a full scale enquiry, possibly by the Central Advisory Council for Education, into teacher training is needed. Such an enquiry should be backed by comprehensive research and surveys planned well in advance.

Part Nine

Conclusions and Recommendations

CHAPTER 31

The Costs and Priorities of Our Recommendations

"To my great-grandfather I am debtor in that he taught me that on education we must spend with an open hand."

1167. This is not the best time in our history to attempt to follow the advice given to Marcus Aurelius. Throughout the three years in which we have studied our subject it has been borne in on us that even in our sphere of enquiry, only one part of the educational system, more money, manpower and new buildings are needed; and this at a time when demands for all public services are on the increase. Accordingly we have tried to assess the costs as well as the benefits of our proposals; and to match our assessment of educational and social needs against the resources we think might be available. We have asked what demands our proposals make on overall resources, on specific resources like teachers and buildings, and we have looked at the time-scale over which costs have to be met. In trying to assess the resources of money, manpower and buildings required to achieve our objectives, we have adjusted the scale and timing of our proposals and fitted them into a pattern which reflects their relative importance and which we hope will be realistic in the light of available resources. Nevertheless our recommendations will cost both resources and money; although we have looked for improvements in the most economical ways, what we suggest will entail new priorities as between education and other services and within education itself.

The Present Position

1168. The first question to be asked is, indeed, not so much what more needs to be spent as whether what is being spent is being well spent. Our answer to this question, which might legitimately be posed by ratepayers and taxpayers, is that the primary schools are giving good value for the inadequate amount of money spent on them. Teachers, for example, who are the most costly element in expenditure, are not too many, but are too few and too unevenly distributed to do the job adequately.

1169. In none of our visits to schools did we see lavish provision of equipment, books, mechanical aids, tape recorders or film projectors. Nor was there sufficient secretarial or other ancillary assistance. On the contrary, we found an attitude of making do with the materials that were to hand. Far from there being unnecessary expense, increased provision of such aids would enable teachers to be more effective. As much as in any of the social services, the quality of the educational process depends on the nature and richness of the interaction between those who provide and those who receive the service. Those of our proposals which will improve the quality of the contact between teacher and pupil should be given high priority. It is for this reason that we stress the importance of recruiting large numbers of teachers' aides. For the same reason, we argue for better equipment and book allowances.

1170. There is a strong feeling that primary education, more than any other sector of education, is failing to secure its share of educational and of national expenditure. Some of the evidence is quoted in Chapter 28 where we have brought together facts concerning the relatively poor treatment of primary teachers and schools, in terms of cash and other resources. Here we need only note that the staffing ratios, the condition of school building in many primary schools, and the treatment of primary schools in respect of equipment and capitation allowances all combine to provide for primary education less than it needs to do the job properly.

The Economic Yield of Primary Education

1171. Before setting out the economic cost of our proposals we discuss the economic yields of primary education. We have noted the work which has been done, principally in the United States, to estimate the economic return to education[1,2]. Much of the work relates to education generally; data have been presented to show that the total amount of education received, and hence the stock of educated human capital, is growing faster than that of physical capital and estimates have been made of the contribution of education to economic growth. From this work it is clear that investment in education in Britain could make a substantial contribution to faster growth.

1172. It is difficult to quantify the educational benefits of primary education, and in the present state of knowledge it is also difficult to disentangle the economic contribution of primary from other stages of education. Primary education equips children to benefit from later schooling and further higher education. As the foundation laid in the primary schools is improved, more children will get on to more specific training after the school leaving age. The Robbins Report[3] argued that there is much untapped ability at present in this country. Improvements in primary education will begin the process of tapping it.

1173. We have noted American attempts to calculate a rate of return on successive years of primary and later education*[4,5]. This suggests returns for primary education as a whole which are no lower than those for later stages of education. But we do not consider that such calculations are appropriate for Britain. Here, where virtually all children complete primary education, what is of interest is the return on extra expenditure on children already being educated rather than the return on successive years of primary education. Further study of matters which might be helpful, such as the costs and benefits of reduced class size and of a relatively greater use of mechanical aids or other help in the classroom, is badly needed.

1174. Good primary education will help to equip children to live and work in a rapidly changing economy. Unlike the economy of the nineteenth century

*The technique used is that based on the rate of return, which attempts to evaluate the economic return of additional years of schooling. The additional life time earnings of those with additional years of schooling is expressed as a rate of return on the cost of the extra years of schooling. For the United States income data are available for people who left school before completing the primary stage and W. Lee Hansen has calculated incremental rates of return for all stages of education from the ages of six to 20. His results suggest that the average rate of return in the years up to 11 was as high as the average return up to the age of 20—in both cases 12 per cent. The highest returns are shown for education between the ages of 12 and 13. Very high economic returns for the later stages of elementary education—returns considerably in excess of those shown by college education—are also suggested by Schultz. The actual figures, 29 per cent and 35 per cent shown by Hansen and Schultz may well be over-estimates, as the differences in life time earnings underlying the results are not attributable to education alone.

our present society does not require a small number of highly qualified men supported by an army of workers with routine skills owing little to education. It requires a highly adaptable labour force, which is not only more skilled, but is better able to learn new skills, to tackle new jobs and face new problems. Workers change their job and their homes frequently**. The educational assumptions that were appropriate for the economy of the nineteenth century have been largely superseded.

1175. The qualities needed in a modern economy extend far beyond skills such as accurate spelling and arithmetic. They include greater curiosity and adaptability, a high level of aspiration, and others which are difficult to measure. To assess these yields from primary education would require long term study of the effects of different systems and different approaches to the education of younger children.

1176. There are, besides, the more specific economic yields which may follow from the improvement of education in the most deprived areas. Those who receive their education under the handicaps described in Chapter 5 are often ill suited to the complex society in which they must live, unable to acquire skills and adapt to industrial change, unable to manage their family financial affairs, unable to adjust to social changes, and unable to pass on to their children abilities they have never themselves acquired. The support that society must give them is costly. Delinquency, family breakdown and long term dependence on public services are among the economic losses they impose on society as well as on themselves. Research may show whether such expensive consequences of poor early upbringing can be diminished if the quality of primary education is improved.

II. THE AVAILABILITY OF RESOURCES

Overall Resources

1177. Present policies allow for some improvement in terms of overall resources. During the first half of the sixties expenditure per child in real terms for the primary schools was stagnant, largely because they were unable to secure enough teachers. In 1963 there were fewer qualified teachers in the primary schools than in 1960, but the same number of pupils. But the National Plan[7] assumed an increase of about 25 per cent in expenditure on primary education in England and Wales between 1964/65 and 1969/70. Taking into account the increase of 16 per cent in the number of children in this period, the estimated increase per child is small—only some one and a half per cent a year—but it is a substantial improvement on the recent past. This point is also brought out by our own projections of expenditure. (Table 44, Column 2). If we assume that teacher supply improves at the rate recently announced by the Secretary of State, and that non-teaching costs per child rise at the annual rate of two and a half per cent predicted by the National Plan, expenditure per child will rise by eight per cent in the four years from 1966.

1178. The raising of the school leaving age in 1971 may cause difficulties for the primary schools. It will preempt nearly a quarter of the total capital investment in primary and secondary schools in the years 1969–72 and, unless

**In a decade, a quarter of the labour force in a region like North West England may enter or leave the region*.

the positive steps we have advised in Chapter 23 are taken to stop the transfer of teachers, may retard the improvement of staffing standards in the primary schools. But the teacher supply programme in Chapter 23 implies that increased manpower and money will be needed at a growing rate by the middle of the decade. Our projections in Table 44 show an increase of 30 per cent in total current expenditure in primary schools between 1970/71 and 1978/79. This would be an increase of 17 per cent per child, or two per cent per child a year

Teachers

1179. The prospects for teacher supply have been set out in Chapter 23. Additions to staff will cause an increase of £118m. in the cost of teachers at constant prices, 58 per cent between 1966/7 and 1978/9 or an average increase a child of 12 per cent. The schools are already making heavy demands on highly qualified manpower. We are anxious that primary education, with its poor staffing ratios, should not be left behind other stages of education; but we are bound to remember that in a fully employed and growing economy highly trained manpower is likely to remain scarce, and that education will face continual competition from other parts of the economy. If so, teacher shortage may persist.

1180. Economic growth will normally lead to relative increases in the cost of teachers compared with other educational costs. Education is "labour intensive"—a large proportion of its costs are labour costs, and in the whole economy it will be labour that will become scarcer and dearer and physical goods that will become relatively more abundant and cheaper. As incomes rise, those of teachers can be expected to rise roughly in line*. Compared with this the cost of materials, equipment, books, mechanical aids and the like, can be expected to fall.

Aides and Assistants

1181. The scarcity of highly trained manpower, the poor staffing situation in primary education, and the virtual impossibility of expanding nursery education under present staffing policies have led us to see whether trained workers can be found who would serve as aides in the primary schools and could, as nursery assistants, provide the main staffing of the nursery groups. More than half of them will be married women. The National Plan has already called attention to this untapped source of labour supply. We are reporting in advance of the Ministry of Labour's Survey of married women which should produce fuller and up to date data, but there is already evidence that more of these women want to work. In Annex A to this chapter we argue that our recruitment proposals are not unreasonable. Although the employment of these married women will lead to an increase in public expenditure, their resource cost will be less than the money cost implies. Many of them will be additional to the labour force, and will not be diverted from other jobs. The provision of nursery groups will of itself provide some of the supply of aides and assistants by releasing the time of mothers. There is a further offset to be made because nursery provision will release married women with

*The Robbins Report (Appendix 4, Pt. IV) estimated the effect of this by increasing the salary component in its expenditure projections by 3¼ per cent a year.

small children to work outside the educational sector. They will be an important addition to the labour force at a time when an attempt to increase the pace of economic growth is producing the labour shortage forecast in the National Plan. We argue in Annex B to this chapter that the sum of these offsets may be of the order of £16–22 million a year by 1974. When the full number of nursery places is provided it will be greater. This will offset a significant proportion of the cost of employing married women as aides and nursery assistants.

1182. We also suggest recruiting girl school leavers whose ability level is largely, but not exclusively, represented by one to four "O" level passes or the equivalent in C.S.E. If our argument for expansion of the educational service by using less expensively trained manpower is accepted, it will mean cutting into a tranche likely to be increasingly needed for such jobs as nursing, the social and welfare services and other services, trades and professions. In the late sixties recruitment may be particularly difficult as numbers in this group will not increase for the years 1968–71, at a time when demand for such labour is rising. But from 1971, the number will grow, especially during the second half of the seventies. We discuss the chance of recruiting these girls in Annex A to this chapter; the evidence presented there suggests that it should be possible to recruit the numbers needed.

1183. The rise in the number of pupils in the primary schools, as predicted by the Registrar-General and the Department of Education and Science, and the consequence of shifts in population in the near future will require considerable new building. To meet this a programme for primary schools in England and Wales of £44–£45 million a year at June 1966 prices is scheduled for the three years 1967/68–1969/70*. In the first half of the seventies, on the assumption that the pattern of provision for the increase in the primary school population and for population shift remains much as at present, primary school building for these basic needs is expected to run at a rate of about £40 million a year. But secondary school building for basic needs, which will run at between £40 and £50 million a year in the late sixties (excluding provision for raising of the school leaving age), is estimated to rise to about £70 million in the first half of the seventies. Thus, simply to meet basic needs, a rise in the building programme from about £90 million a year in the late 60s to over £110 million in the first half of the seventies can be foreseen. Programmes are expected to fall in the late seventies when the school population is estimated to increase less rapidly. In the 1967/68 programme, about one quarter of the resources allocated to approved projects at the end of June 1966 (over £20 million) was for the improvement of existing schools, mainly the replacement of primary schools. It cannot be assumed that such substantial allocations for improvement will be possible in the programmes for the two subsequent years. However, in the 1970s, elimination of some of the bottlenecks in the construction industry may remove one of the obstacles in the way of allocating more resources to the improvement of existing schools. Moreover, requirements of other sectors of the economy, notably house building, may ease as the rate of new household formation falls off in the seventies.

*All figures relate to starts. Actual expenditure which includes the cost of land, fees and equipment will be about 35 to 40 per cent above this level.

Priorities

1184. Although the word "priority" can mean both to have a stronger claim and to have a first claim in point of time, most of our proposals need not conflict with each other. There are several criteria by which priorities can be assessed. The first criterion is based on our judgements of educational and social needs. The second criterion is the measurable costs and benefits which can be balanced against each other. In making our recommendations on priorities we have asked ourselves the following questions about each proposal. What demands do they make on the overall resources of money or manpower? How far do they create demands on specific and limited resources and hence conflict directly with other schemes? Are there differences in the time scale over which costs have to be met and benefits felt? These are the main economic criteria. But economic costs must be set against educational and social objectives; educational and social objectives may still have priority even if they prove costly.

III. OUR PRINCIPAL PROPOSALS, THEIR PRIORITY AND TIMING

1185. We have taken account of the criteria and the constraints on additional expenditure discussed in earlier paragraphs in deciding the priorities that should be given to our main proposals. Otherwise we have fitted them into a pattern partly dictated by the available resources. We have given absolute priority to only one of our proposals—the creation of educational priority areas.

Our Proposals in More Detail

Educational Priority Areas

1186. Our first priority is the creation of the educational priority areas defined in Chapter 5. We assume, as a maximum, that ten per cent of the child population will be in educational priority areas by 1972/3 with a steady build up from perhaps two per cent of the child population over five years from 1968. By 1973, surveys should show whether further extensions will be necessary. The following specific points affect costings:

Manpower: Teachers (Tables 35 and 36)

(a) To reduce all oversize classes in educational priority areas to 40 would require about an additional 400* teachers in those areas in 1968 and 1,000 in 1972.

(b) On the same assumptions as in (a) to reduce classes in the educational priority areas to 30s would require about a total of 1,500 extra teachers in those areas in 1968 and 7,300 in 1972. This is a reasonable general aim although individual schools, of course, might have some classes smaller or larger than 30.

Inducements to Teacher Recruitment (Table 40)

(a) Additions to pay (£120) should be awarded at the rate of one for every teacher in educational priority areas. The cost will be about £½ million in 1968 and about £3 million in 1972.

---

*Throughout this chapter we have given our figures with some precision to enable us to cost our proposals. They are, of course, open to error.

Manpower: Teachers' Aides (Table 36)

(d) Teachers' aides for the whole country can be recruited in six years. But we propose that there should be a somewhat more generous recruitment of them in the educational priority areas—one to each two classes in the first and middle schools. The numbers required above those for recruiting aides at the rate to be adopted for the whole country will be 700 in 1968, rising to 3,700 in 1972, an additional cost of over £3 million in 1972.

Nursery Education (Table 36).

(e) In the first five years, we propose that the full scale nursery provision suggested in Chapter 9 should be made at least for the four to five year olds. In these areas we assume that 40 per cent would require part-time places and 50 per cent full-time places. This might, at peak, create a demand for an additional 1,400 teachers, some of whom might be diverted from elsewhere, while others might be diverted from the infant classes when admission arrangements are changed. These changes might, however, take place at different times in different areas. This provision would not be additional to what we propose for the country as a whole. We have had the needs of children in educational priority areas in mind when assessing the total number of children who might need full-time nursery provision. That is to say, the staff required for nurseries in the priority areas do not constitute an addition to the numbers we have assumed for the whole country.

Buildings (Table 39).

(f) Special minor works allocations for the rapid improvement of schools are proposed. If it is assumed, arbitrarily, that every primary school in an area (although some will be new) will need a minor works job of, say, £5,000, and that 2,100 primary schools (that is one tenth of the total of all primary schools) will be in educational priority areas, the cost will total £10·5 million by 1972, or £2·1 million each year between 1968 and 1972.

1187. Three main points need to be made about the proposals discussed in paragraph 1186. First, the money and other resources needed for the creation of the educational priority areas will not all be net additions to the total cost of primary education even though more teachers' aides will be needed than elsewhere. Many of our proposals represent either a diversion of resources or an acceleration of the improvements called for elsewhere. Secondly, we have not tried to estimate the rate of development beyond 1972/3. A further review will be called for after the completion of the first five years. Thirdly, what we propose will inevitably and rightly have chain effects on secondary education. The proposals which were made in the report of our predecessors have so far hardly been implemented. Plainly, children in depressed areas should continue to benefit from improvements when they leave the primary schools. The more detailed working out of proposals for secondary education are not, however, within our province.

Improvement of Staffing Elsewhere: Teachers (Table 24 and 35)

1188. We assume here that teachers will be recruited at the rate stated by the Secretary of State in his speech at Eastbourne in April 1966, and that the secondary schools will face the raising of the school leaving age with the additions of staff that can be recruited up to the autumn of 1971. As we prepare this Report, recent figures of births suggest that the child population may not become as great as is currently forecast. It is too early to be certain and all our calculations and costings are based on figures available in July 1966. On these assumptions our proposals are as follows:—

(a) as Column 3 of Table 35 shows, there will be a steady improvement in the numbers of qualified teachers reaching the primary schools from now on and through the 1970s. If no primary teachers are diverted to the secondary schools, and if recruitment to the schools generally continues as we hope, classes with more than 40 pupils could be abolished by 1974/75 over the country as a whole and steady progress made with the elimination of classes over 30 from then onwards;

(b) but our proposals for the educational priority areas (see paragraph 1186) will certainly affect the rate at which general staffing can be improved and, since other resources are limited, may affect the rate of other improvements. Thus Table 35 shows that the abolition of classes over 30 in the E.P.As. will slow down the improvement of staffing standards elsewhere and will delay the elimination of classes over 40 for two years, until 1976. In effect, our proposals accelerate in some selected areas the improvements desired for all schools.

(c) the 3,700 additional aides required for the educational priority areas will slow down the expansion of nursery education. Had they been used as nursery assistants, an extra 34,000 full-time equivalent nursery places could have been provided. This would, on our assumptions on the build up of aides and assistants, have enabled an additional eight per cent of the three year olds in the late seventies to have part-time nursery education.

Staffing: Aides and Assistants (Table 37)

1189. We think it is more important to concentrate first on the recruitment of teachers' aides for primary schools than to recruit nursery assistants. Our reasons are threefold. First, the schools need help to cope with large classes as soon as it can be given to them. It will be right to help them before adding substantially to the school system by introducing nursery groups. Secondly, the employment of teachers' aides will provide substantial benefits quickly and at a relatively low cost. Thirdly, although we believe that a start should be made immediately on expanding nursery education, it is unlikely that a large scale expansion can take place in the near future. Therefore, we suggest that 70 per cent of the older women recruited from 1968 to 1972 should train as teachers' aides. This proportion should fall to 25 per cent by 1975 and continue at this figure. Initially, 80 per cent of the girls recruited will train as teachers' aides, but this proportion will fall to 37 per cent in 1975 when the targets for the primary schools are achieved, and to 26 per cent by 1979 by which time the number of qualified school leavers will have risen by 40 per cent over the 1968 figure. These calculations relate to the country as a whole. There will however, be variations throughout the country as in, for example, educational priority areas.

Building (Table 39)

1190. Our proposals will involve a great deal of building. Our first priority outside the educational priority areas is a programme of minor improvements to primary school buildings which lack essentials. The proposals detailed in Chapter 28 will cost £50–£70 million to be phased over a period of seven years. The total size of building programme up to 1969/70 has been announced and in any case we do not imagine that additional resources will be forthcoming during the next few years. Thus our proposed programme would begin in 1970/71.

1191. We cannot say how much building will be needed for our proposals on the ages and stages of primary education. A full exercise proved impossible because we were advised that many local education authorities would be too busy on secondary reorganisation to be able to help us. We attempted an exercise of our own which with its many imperfections tended to show that our proposed transfer ages might make better use of the stock of existing primary school buildings than a later age of transfer. We were not able to extend our exercise to secondary buildings, and so could not work out the relative costs of different ages of transfer. Moreover, the costs are in any case unpredictable because Circular 13/66 (May, 1966) allows for a degree of local option for the age of transfer to secondary education.

1192. We link our proposals for a change in transfer ages to a single date of entry and nursery provision; we think that it will be difficult to achieve sufficient nursery provision to put our changes in transfer ages into operation until the second half of the seventies. Table 38 suggests that it would be possible, if an early enough start were made on recruiting nursery assistants, to introduce the single date of entry nationally by around 1977. In some areas it may be possible to achieve this earlier. But the prospect of finding class spaces is less certain. It will depend on the disposition of buildings and of the school population using them, as well as on the school building which takes place in the first half of the seventies. It is impossible for us to make useful estimates of these factors.

1193. Our nursery proposals will involve much building. In Chapter 9, we have estimated that, of the 776,000 places which will be needed, between 175,000 and 250,000 places can be found in existing buildings. For purposes of calculation we assume that 200,000 places will be available. In Table 38 we show the likely pattern and possible scale of building. These figures are however speculative; ten years ahead, other uncertainties will replace present uncertainties about the extent to which we can use the present stock of places. We have no firm cost figures for nursery places. As we have said in Chapter 28, we consider that the standards now set should be reconsidered. Some nursery groups could be housed in existing non-educational building, for example, in adequately converted houses. The full number of places in nurseries for all children of three and four cannot be provided until the early 1980s, a time for which the population figures are uncertain. For these reasons it is impossible for us to cost them accurately. We propose there should be a build up of the equivalent of 650,000 full-time places by 1979 which might involve new building of over 400,000 places, or a total building programme of about £110 million. In Table 39 we assume that 50 per cent of the new places will be provided in groups detached from existing primary schools, and that these places will cost £300 each. The rest will be housed, we have assumed, in buildings added to existing schools at a cost of £242 a place.

1194. Because of the shortage of teachers, our scheme for the expansion of nursery education is based largely on the use of teachers set free from the primary schools when, first, the rising fives are excluded and then a single term of entry is adopted. Just as the introduction of the single term of entry depends on the provision of nursery education for at least one year before children reach the age of entry to the infant school, so the provision of nursery education depends on the release of teachers and buildings by the later entry to the primary school. They are interdependent.

1195. The critical path we have chosen, therefore, for our nursery build-up is the supply of nursery assistants. (See Table 37). As we have given priority to teachers' aides, the supply of nursery assistants does not become substantial until the middle 1970s. There should be enough nursery assistants by 1972 to provide for the 15 per cent of four to five year olds who need full-time nursery education. By 1977 it will be possible to provide nursery education for a further 75 per cent of the four year olds part-time, and by 1979 for 15 per cent of the three year olds full-time. Not until the 1980s will it be possible to provide for the full proportion of the three and four year olds who should have nursery education. The relative proportions of older women and school leavers determine the numbers of aides and assistants actually in the schools and nursery groups because they will have different wastage rates.

1196. If the main expansion of nursery education is to take place in the middle and late seventies. it will be less difficult to divert teachers to nursery groups than if it took place earlier; by then the worst shortages of teachers should have been eliminated.

Other Proposals

1197. So far, we have discussed those proposals which might create large demands on resources and where there might be conflict between different priorities. Our Report also contains proposals which, whilst not easy to cost, will undoubtedly lead to increased expenditure.

1198. We have not attempted to cost all of these proposals in detail: indeed, it would not be possible to gauge the response to some of them so that costings would be artificial. We have instead noted in Chapter 32, where we summarise our conclusions and recommendations, those proposals which will create additional expenditure. Here we mention briefly other proposals which deserve to be singled out.

1199. They are as follows:—

(a) In Chapter 7 we have suggested ways of strengthening the social and welfare services that affect school children. We cannot cost our recommendations although additional costs will be inevitable if staffing is brought up to the necessary standards. We have also suggested that multiple teams should be established experimentally in areas of special difficulty. These proposals do not involve expenditure that is exclusively educational or attributable to primary education alone.

(b) In Chapter 24 we have discussed the need for strengthening advisory services to teachers. Although a large expansion is necessary the difficulty of recruiting advisers of the quality needed is likely to restrict costs.

c) Other recommendations in the Report need not be expensive in themselves, but cumulatively might be costly. These include (Chapter 24) the employment of part-time teachers to enable head and deputy head teachers to exercise their functions more fruitfully, and the employment of adequate secretarial assistance in the schools.

(d) In Chapter 24 and 25 we have suggested a more flexible use of allowances additional to basic scales, including special responsibility allowances. The amount of additional expenditure is uncertain but it is unlikely to be large.

(e) Improvements in in-service training of teachers. We propose, as a minimum, that every teacher should have a substantial period of further training every five years. This will lead to additional demands on the teaching force, and extra tuition and other costs. We cannot, however, estimate these additions since our proposals in Chapter 25 also lay emphasis on weekend and vacation courses, and the balance between them and one year and one term courses cannot be assessed.

(f) In Chapter 28, we have estimated that additional expenditure of between £½ million and £1 million each year would enable all primary schools to be adequately equipped.

1200. It will be seen that our Report calls for additional money and labour at almost every point. Such additions are inevitable if a service of the size and complexity of primary education is to reach maximum efficiency and effectiveness.

The Order of Priorities

1201. In this chapter we have tried to consider educational and social objectives within the restrictions that will be imposed by money and other resource costs. For all of the reasons given in this chapter and throughout the rest of the Report we here state the order of priorities that should result:

(a) The first priority should be the establishment of educational priority areas. *Timing* 1968/9—72/3 (first phase)

(b) Secondly, the recruitment of teachers' aides will be an immediate and essential source of help to the schools everywhere. 1968/9—72/3

(c) Thirdly, the essential improvement of bad primary school building should be undertaken as soon as possible everywhere. 1971/2—77/8

(d) The extension of nursery education ought to take place as soon as staff and buildings make it possible. To begin in 1968 and to be available for all 4s—5s

(e) Finally, of our major recommendations, planning should begin on changes in the national dates of entry and on the ages of transfer between the different stages of primary education. Some authorities should be able to introduce them sooner than others. Chapter 10 contains short term suggestions for those authorities who must delay the major changes. by 1977, subject to introduction of single date of entry.

1202. We have listed the main new policies that we wish to see adopted and the order in which they should be tackled. Nothing that we say diminishes the need for continued advances throughout the system. School building programmes must continue to be large enough to ensure that all children have a place in school. The improvement of staffing in all primary schools ought to proceed steadily throughout the 1970s until classes with more than 40 children are eliminated and a start thus made on achieving parity between primary and lower secondary school class sizes. These are the continuing policies which we have discussed fully in earlier chapters but have not considered in detail here. Existing policies and the new policies suggested in this Report ought to be considered together as soon as possible so that plans can be laid down for them, even though their fulfilment must in some cases lie in the future.

Costs and Benefits

1203. In this chapter, we have been more ambitious than our predecessors in trying to cost our recommendations. We have not, however, been able, for the most part, to quantify the economic benefits of primary education. Such issues as the extent to which delinquency will diminish as primary education improves are beyond our ability to discuss since the long term studies required to inform such a discussion have not been undertaken. We hope that future studies of primary education will be able to explore these issues further.

The Total Costs

1204. In Tables 39 and 40 we estimate the total additional costs of our proposals. By 1979 the additional running cost which would result from the adoption of our proposals is £74 million. Additional capital expenditure rises to a peak of £40 million by 1974 and then falls to a much lower figure by 1979. In order to show the scale of our proposals we have made our own projections (Table 43) of the cost of primary education on present policies. We recognise that such long range projections are hazardous, but we hope they will be helpful. Table 44 shows that our proposals for the primary schools, excluding our nursery proposals, will raise current expenditure by £5 a child or by nearly six per cent by 1978/79. This increase is modest compared with the increase of £18 a child between 1966/67 and 1978/79 which we estimate will take place on present policies. When our nursery proposals are included, as Table 45 shows, our proposals will result in an increase in the total current costs of primary and nursery education of eight per cent by 1972/73 and 14 per cent by 1978/79.

REFERENCES

[1]Assessing the Economic Contribution of Education: The Appraisal of Alternative Approaches, W. G. Bowen. Report of the Committee on Higher Education, 1963. Cmnd. 2154. Appendix 4, pp. 73-96.

[2]The Economic Value of Education, T. W. Schultz, New York, 1963, Chapter 3.

[3]Robbins Report (see [1] above). Appendix One, page 89.

[4]Total and Private Rates of Return to Investment in Schooling, W. Lee Hansen, Journal of Political Economy, 1963.

[5]Education and Economic Growth, T. W. Schultz in 'Social Forces Influencing American Education', ed. N. B. Henry.

[6]The North West: A Regional Study, H.M.S.O. 1965.

[7]The National Plan, 1965, Cmnd. 2764.

[8]'Half Our Future', Paragraphs 68-74.

Table 35

The Effects on Overall Staffing Standards of More Favourable Staffing Ratios in Educational Priority Areas

Thousands

(1) YEAR (SEPT.)	(2) Supply of teachers (including full-time equivalent of part-time teachers)	(3) Deficiency or surplus of teachers for reducing over-size classes to 40 (i) and 30 (ii)	(4) Pupil-teacher ratio	(5) Number of teachers diverted to E.P.As to reduce classes to 30 and to provide nursery education for 90% of 4s–5s (50% full-time 40% part-time)	(6) Deficiency or surplus of teachers for reducing classes to 40 (i) and 30 (ii)** elsewhere if classes reduced to 30 in E.P.As and nursery education provided for 4s–5s	(7) Effect on pupil-teacher ratio elsewhere if teachers in (5) diverted to E.P.A.s
1966	135·8	—20·2 (i)	30·2		—20·2 (i)	30·2
1967	140·7	—20·5 (i)	30·1		—20·5 (i)	30·1
1968	147·3	—19·3 (i)	29·8	1·7	—21·0 (i)	30·1
1969	154·8	—16·9 (i)	29·2	3·5	—20·4 (i)	29·9
1970	162·4	—14·3 (i)	28·6	5·2	—19·5 (i)	29·6
1971	170·4	—11·4 (i)	28·1	6·9	—18·3 (i)	29·3
1972	177·9	— 9·6 (i)	27·7	8·7	—18·3 (i)	29·3
1973	185·1	— 5·2 (i)	27·0		—13·9 (i)	28·5
1974	192·5	— 0·8 (i)	26·4		— 9·5 (i)	27·8
1975	199·9	+ 3·1 (i)* —62·8 (ii)	25·9		— 5·6 (i)	27·2
1976	207·3	—59·1 (ii)	25·3		— 0·9 (i)	26·5
1977	213·4	—56·3 (ii)	24·9		+ 2·7 (i)* —57·7 (ii)	26·1
1978	219·0	—53·7 (ii)	24·5		—55·1 (ii)	25·7
1979	226·9	—48·7 (ii)	23·9		—50·1 (ii)	25·0

*Classes over 40 eliminated everywhere.

**The pupil-teacher ratio necessary to reduce classes to 30 everywhere is 19·7.

In this and subsequent tables in this chapter figures are given for statistical convenience with an apparent precision which is not justified by the margins of error inherent in them.

Table 36

Educational Priority Areas: Teachers, Teachers' Aides and Nursery Assistants

Thousands

(1) YEAR (SEPT.)	(2) Maintained school population in E.P.As.	(3) Number of teachers provided if no special measures taken for E.P.As.	(4) Additional number of teachers needed to eliminate classes over 30 in E.P.As.	(5) Number of aides provided if no special measures taken for E.P.As.	(6) Aides additional to (5) needed for ratio of 1 to 60 children	(7) Number of children aged 4 – 5 in E.P.As.	(8) Number of nursery places to be provided (50% full-time and 40% part-time) (full-time equivalent)	(9) Number of nursery assistants needed for (8)	(10) Number of teachers required for (8)	(11) Number of new nursery places to be built in E.P.As.
1968	87·6	2·9	1·5	0·8	0·7	15·7	11·0	1·2	0·2	10·0*
1969	180·6	6·2	3·0	1·7	1·3	32·1	22·5	2·5	0·5	10·5*
1970	278·8	9·7	4·4	2·6	2·1	47·7	33·4	3·8	0·8	10·0*
1971	382·6	13·6	5·8	3·5	2·9	64·5	45·2	5·0	1·1	10·0*
1972	493·2	17·8	7·3	4·6	3·7	82·3	57·6	6·3	1·4	11·0*

* Assumes that 20 per cent of existing places are in educational priority areas.

Table 37

Build-up of Recruitment of Nursery Assistants and Teachers' Aides (Including Those Needed for Educational Priority Areas)

Thousands

	(1)	(2)	(3)	(4)	(5)	(6)	(7)	(8)
YEAR	Numbers in service resulting from recruitment of school leavers. (Details of annual intake in Annex A, Chapter (SEPT 31)	Number of full-time older married women in service recruited direct at rate of 10,000 full-time equivalents a year	Numbers in training available for service in primary schools (full-time equivalents)	Existing N.N.E.B. and others available	Total of aides & assistants available for service ((1) + (2) + (3) + (4) = (6) + (7))	Number of nursery assistants available for nursery	Number of aides available for primary schools	Numbers of children (full-time equivalents) who can be accommodated in nurseries
1967	—	—	—	2·9	2·9	2·9	—	26
1968	—	—	8·9	2·9	11·8	2·9	8·9	26
1969	—	9·5	11·9	2·7	24·1	5·6	18·5	51
1970	5·6	18·5	11·6	2·6	38·4	9·3	29·0	85
1971	10·6	27·1	11·0	2·4	51·4	12·7	38·4	116
1972	15·2	35·3	8·7	2·3	61·9	16·4	45·1	149
1973	19·0	43·0	7·8	2·2	72·9	22·1	49·9	201
1974	22·6	50·5	5·1	2·1	81·5	29·5	50·8	268
1975	25·8	57·5	4·9	2·0	91·7	38·6	51·6	351
1976	28·7	64·1	4·9	1·9	101·5	47·3	52·3	430
1977	31·5	70·5	4·9	1·8	110·9	55·8	52·9	508
1978	34·2	76·5	4·9	1·7	119·8	63·9	53·4	581
1979	37·0	82·2	4·9	1·6	128·4	71·7	54·0	652

Notes:

Column (1) Assumes 10% wastage in training and first two years service; then assumes non-graduate women's wastage rates and re-entry rates following entry into service. (N.A.C. 9th Report, page 84).

Column (2) Assumes 5% wastage a year in training and subsequently.

Column (3) Initially, most entrants will train as teachers' aides till sufficient are in service in primary schools. Details of recruitment are explained in Annex A. Of those training for teachers' aides, the school leavers will spend 3/5ths of training time in accountable service and the older women 4/5ths.

Column (4) 2,850 nursery assistants at present. We assume this number will continue in service with a wastage of 5% per annum.

Column (6) Aides and assistants in service less those required for primary schools.

Column (7) Total in service on assumption that initially the majority of those trained enter the primary schools, plus those available for accountable service (see note to Column 3) during training.

Column (8) Column (6) multiplied by assistant/child ratio of 1 to 9·1.

Table 38

Chart Illustrating Possible Expansion of Nursery Provision in the Non-Educational Priority Areas and Introduction of Single Date of Entry

(1) YEAR (SEPT.)	(2) Nursery assistants to be available (Thousands)	(3) Teachers required (Thousands)	(4) Teachers available	(5) Places that can be supervised by nursery assistants in (2) (full-time equiv.) (Thousands)	(6) Number of places for Non E.P.As. (4 – 5s) (full-time equiv.) (Thousands)	(7) Building supply: places available	(8) New places needed (Thousands)
1966	—	—	Increasing Exclusion of non-statutory fives. More teachers available	—	—	Places available increased by changes in entry, but numbers uncertain	—
1967	—	—		—	—		—
1968	1·7	0·3		15	399		—
1969	3·1	0·3		29	398		9
1970	5·6	0·6		51	380		22
1971	8·0	0·9		71	374		20
1972	10·5	1·2		91	371		20
1973	21·5	2·1		143	378	50 thousand places available. (Exclusion of non-statutory fives)	2
1974	29·3	3·3		210	385		67
1975	38·7	4·7		293	392		83
1976	47·8	6·1		372	399		79
1977	56·6	7·4	8,000 more teachers with single date of entry—possibly 10,000 in all	450	405	125–200 thousand places available (single date of entry)	—
1978	65·0	8·7		523	410		1
1979	73·0	9·9		594	407		71
							full nursery provision in early 1980s

Table 39

Additional Capital Building Costs of Recommendations in the Report (Excluding Additions for Increased Numbers, Rehousing and Replacements)

£ million

	Educational Priority Areas				Other Areas			All Areas
(1)	(2)	(3)	(4)	(5)	(6)	(7)	(8)	(9)
YEAR	Extra classrooms to reduce all classes to 30	Minor works	Nursery building required	Total additional capital costs in E.P.As.	Nursery education (excluding E.P.As.)	Essential improvements to all primary schools (excluding replacements & building for extra numbers)	Total additional capital costs in other areas	Total additional capital costs over country as a whole (5) + (8)
(SEPT)								
1967	2·7		3·4	6·1	0·4		0·4	6·5
1968	2·5	2·1	3·9	8·5	3·6		3·6	12·1
1969	2·9	2·1	3·8	8·8	7·7		7·7	16·5
1970	3·1	2·1	4·1	9·3	7·5		7·5	16·8
1971	3·3	2·1	3·6	9·0	6·6	7·9	14·5	23·5
1972	0·3	2·1	0·4	2·8	4·3	7·9	12·2	15·0
1973					23·5	10·0	33·5	33·5
1974					30·2	10·0	40·2	40·2
1975					25·8	10·0	35·8	35·8
1976					2·6	10·0	12·6	12·6
1977					3·6	10·0	13·6	13·6
1978					20·8		20·8	20·8
1979					2·3		2·3	2·3

Column (2): Assumes the maximum number of extra classrooms needed if all classes in E.P.As. reduced to 30 (830 rooms in 1968, rising to 4,110 in 1972). Also assumes that cost of each additional classroom is £3,000, that "starts" are made in the previous year and appropriate additions for fees and equipment are included.

Column (3): Assumes minor works of £5,000 in each school.

Columns (4) and (6): Places needed are shown in Column (11) of Table 36 and Column (8) of Table 38. It is assumed that 50% of new places will be in isolated nursery groups at a cost of £300 per place. The rest will be housed in additions to existing buildings at a cost of £242 per place. "Starts" will be made in the previous year and additions for land, fees and equipment are included. Since children excluded from infant schools by single date of entry will be in nursery groups, it is assumed that costs of adaptation will be small and none are included.

Column (7): Assumes a programme of minor works over seven years of £10m. a year to make essential improvements in all primary schools and eliminate the following defects: (a) no warm water supply, (b) no water-borne sanitation, (c) sanitation mainly out of doors, (d) no staff room.

Table 40

Additional Running Costs of Recommendations in the Report

£ million

(1)	Educational Priority Areas					Non-Priority Areas					All areas		
Year (SEPT.)	(2) Additional allowances of £120 for teachers in E.P.As*	(3) Teachers' aides: salaries**	(4) Nursery assistants: salaries**	(5) Extra building maintenance and capitation***	(6) Total additional running costs in E.P.As.	(7) Teachers' aides: salaries**	(8) Nursery assistants: salaries**	(9) Extra building maintenance and capitation***	(10) Additional running costs in non-E.P.As	(11) Additional equipment allowances	(12) Total Training Costs Teachers' aides****	(13) Total Training Costs Nursery Assistants****	(14) Total Additional Running Costs (6) + (10) + (11 to 13)
1966													
1967	0·6												0·5
1968	1·2	1·5	0·7	0·1	1·4	1·7	0·9		0·9	0·5	5·4	0·9	9·1
1969	1·8	2·3	1·3	·2	4·2	6·4	1·5		3·2	0·5	7·9	2·5	18·3
1970	2·4	3·2	1·9	·4	6·4	10·7	2·8	·05	9·4	0·5	7·6	3·8	27·7
1971	3·2	4·1	2·5	·5	8·6	14·1	3·8	·2	14·8	0·5	7·1	3·3	34·3
1972	3·2	4·1	3·1	·7	11·1	17·1	5·1	·3	19·6	0·5	5·8	4·9	41·9
1973	3·2	4·1	3·1	·7	11·1	18·9	8·0	·4	25·5	0·5	5·1	6·0	48·2
1974	3·2	4·1	3·1	·7	11·1	19·5	11·8	·4	31·4	0·5	3·5	7·7	54·2
1975	3·2	4·1	3·1	·7	11·1	19·8	15·3	·7	35·9	0·5	3·3	8·2	59·0
1976	3·2	4·1	3·1	·7	11·1	20·1	20·8	1·1	42·1	0·5	3·3	8·5	65·5
1977	3·2	4·1	3·1	·7	11·1	20·3	25·1	1·5	46·7	0·5	3·3	8·9	70·5
1978	3·2	4·1	3·1	·7	11·1	20·6	29·0	1·5	50·8	0·5	3·3	9·2	74·9
1979	3·2	4·1	3·1	·7	11·1		32·6	1·8	55·0	0·5	3·3	9·5	79·4

* Assumes that all teachers in E.P.As. receive an additional allowance of £120.

** Assumes that teachers' aides and nursery assistants are paid the same rate. The salaries shown assume an average of £460 per annum, that is, the average of the Class 1 Nursery Assistant scale of £330–£590 per annum. Additions are included for National Insurance and employers' superannuation contributions.

*** Assumes maintenance costs per 1,000 sq. ft. In nursery groups and primary classes of £150 per annum. This figure represents an annual average cost over several years covering the building maintenance, fuel and light, cost of interior and exterior decoration and cleaning. Also assumes an annual capitation allowance of 30/- per head. The maintenance costs of existing nursery and primary places which would be used for nursery groups are offset against the total maintenance costs resulting from our proposals, as are the capitation allowances for children in existing nursery schools and those who would be excluded from primary schools by changes in admission arrangements.

**** Assumes that tuition costs for training aides and assistants will be at the intermediate further education ratio. Tuition for school leavers will cost about £200 per annum and for older women about £100 per annum. During training, aides and assistants will be paid the equivalent of the N.N.E.B. student salary rate of £290 per annum. It is not possible to divide the training costs for aides and assistants between E.P.As. and non-priority areas.

Table 41
The Financial Cost of Proposed Nursery Provision

A. *Cost per full-time equivalent place of proposed provision*

	£
Teachers	20
Assistants	55
Cleaning, maintenance, heating capitation allowances	6
Imputed rents*	29
Total	110

B. *Cost per full-time equivalent place of provision for children under five years to five years 11 months.*

	£
(i) Infant Schools	80
(ii) Nursery Schools	156
(iii) Day Nurseries	187

* Measured by loan charges. An interest ratio of 7% is assumed on loans of 35 years for buildings, 60 years for land and 15 years for equipment.

By 1977, when single date of entry is introduced, annual financial cost will be £56** million, rising to £72** million by 1979, and to £85 million when full provision is achieved in the 1980s. The cost now of providing for 3s–5s in the infant and nursery schools is £36 million. Additional expenditure will thus be only £20** million a year by 1977, £36** million by 1979 and £49** million by the time full provision is achieved.

** These additional costs exclude the cost of training nursery assistants as do the cost of provision for the threes to fives on present policies. These training costs will be particularly heavy during the period of build up (see Table 40, Column (13)).

Table 42
Public Authorities' Expenditure on Maintained Primary and Nursery Schools: England*

£ million (current prices)

(1) Financial Year	(2) Teaching Costs	(3) Other Running Expenses	(4) Loan Charges	(5) Total Current Costs	(6) Capital Expenditure	(7) Total Expenditure
1955/56	90	40	8	138	16	154
1957/58	113	49	11	173	18	191
1959/60	124	53	14	191	15	206
1961/62	136	60	17	213	21	234
1963/64	166	68	19	253	27	280
1964/65	172	69	21	262	39	301

*Figures for England have been estimated from returns for England and Wales.

Notes to Table 43

There is no accurate method of expressing the expenditure on primary education in terms of constant prices, because no price indices are available which properly correspond to the individual components of it. But adjustments for price changes have been made by using such information as is available.

Teaching Costs (Column (2))

1. Salaries are at constant 1966 actual prices. The average salary per teacher was very slightly (1·5 per cent) in excess of that which would have been predicted by extrapolating the exponential trend of average salaries for primary school teachers in England for the years 1955/56 to 1964/65. The 1966 figure was applied to the projections of qualified teachers given in Table 24, after the addition of some unqualified teachers. We assume, we hope wrongly, that the number of unqualified teachers will remain at about 5,000.

2. Our estimate assumes that there are no changes in the age structure and qualifications of teachers, and therefore no change in the average salary per teacher. This assumption will not be precisely fulfilled in practice, but the possible error is not large compared with the margin of error in the supply assumptions.

3. We have not assumed, as did the Robbins Report, that teachers' salaries will rise in real terms as the economy grows. Such an assumption would have added substantially to teaching costs by the late seventies. Had we made such an assumption we probably ought to have assumed a fall in real terms in other running costs, and possibly some increase in imputed rents as building standards rise—as they probably will. We have decided to avoid these complications.

Other Running Costs (Column (3))

4. We assume, as did the National Plan, that other running costs will rise by 2½ per cent per child each year and project this increase through the seventies. It is based on an extrapolation of past trends and not on any sophisticated assessment of future needs.

Imputed Rents (Column (4))

5. Any estimate of imputed rents is necessarily arbitrary, since school buildings are not

Table 43

Past and Projected Costs of Maintained Primary Schools on Present Policies, 1960/61–1978/79: England

£ million at June 1966 prices

(1)	(2)	(3)	(4)	(5)	(6)	(7)
				Total Current Costs	Capital Expenditure for Basic Needs	Total Costs
Financial Year	Teaching Costs	Other Running Costs	Imputed Rents			
1960/61	185	58	9	252	21	273
1962/63	185	67	11	263	27	290
1964/65	194	68	12	274	39	313
1966/67	202	79	13	294	38	332
1968/69	221	88	14	323	48	371
1970/71	242	98	16	356	54	410
1972/73	262	108	17	387	51	438
1974/75	283	116	19	418	45	463
1976/77	302	126	20	448	42	490
1978/79	320	134	21	475	39	514

normally sold or rented. But these buildings do have alternative uses, and it is appropriate to attempt to quantify this.

6. In Statistics of Education loan charges are taken as a measure of imputed rents. But in the *National Income and Expenditure* Blue Books for 1964 and 5 and in the *National Plan*, imputed rental income and payments in respect of local authority fixed assets employed in education were charged on to a basis related to rateable values. This practice has been adopted here.

7. These imputed rents are considerably lower than loan charges. An alternative method would have been one similar to that adopted by the *Robbins Report*, Appendix 4, Annex E, paragraph 8, where the stock of university buildings was valued and rents imputed on the basis of a 60 year life at an interest rate of 6 per cent. We attempted a valuation of the

stock of primary school buildings from the 1962 School Building Survey, and carried this forward by new places built since and our estimates of future buildings for basic needs. We assumed a life of 60 years and valued this stock at June 1966 cost limits with additions for land etc. We took a higher interest rate (8 per cent) to reflect the fact that the Government borrowing rate does not reflect the scarcity of capital in the economy. Our results exceeded those which we published in Table 43 by a factor of 3·3 in 1960/61 rising to 3·6 in 1978/79. This difference is large though the Robbins estimate of imputed rents was also very considerably in excess of the rateable value of buildings in higher education. By adopting the rateable value method we are probably underestimating the real cost to the economy of primary education by perhaps £6 per pupil a year in 1964/65 and £10 in 1978/79.

8. The rateable value method has also been applied to the additional capital expenditure resulting from the adoption of our proposals. However, the use of different methods of evaluating imputed rents makes only a small difference to the percentage addition in costs which would result from the adoption of our proposals (Table 45).

Capital Expenditure for Basic Needs (Column (6))

9. Our projections are of capital expenditure for basic needs only. Basic needs are the increase in the child population in the relevant age groups which will attend maintained schools, and an allowance for population shift. This latter has been found to be closely related to public sector house building, and we have assumed a continuation of this relationship. The public sector housing programmes for the late sixties have been derived from the policies set out in Cmnd. 2838 *The Housing Programme, 1965–70* (November 1965). For the seventies no public housing programmes have been announced. We have assumed, arbitrarily, that the 1969/70 figure will continue throughout the seventies.

10. June 1966 cost limits have been used. Thus no allowance has been made for rising standards.

11. Adjustments have been made to convert the figures from programme terms (Chapter 28) into projected expenditure for financial years.

Table 44

Projected Costs of Maintained Primary Schools and Additional Costs Resulting from the Adoption of Our Proposals: England

1966 prices

(1) Financial Year	(2) Past and projected current costs (Table 43, Col. (5))		(3) Proposed additional current costs for primary schools (excluding nursery proposals)*		(4) Past and projected capital expenditure for basic needs (Table 43, Col. (6))	(5) Proposed additional capital expenditure for primary schools (excluding nursery proposals)
	Total £m	£ per child	Total £m	£ per child	£m	£m
1960/61	252	66			21	
1962/63	263	68			27	
1964/65	274	68			39	
1966/67	294	69			38	
1968/69	323	72	1		48	4
1970/71	356	74	9	2	54	5
1972/73	387	77	21	4	51	11
1974/75	418	81	27	5	45	10
1976/77	448	84	29	5	42	10
1978/79	475	88	29	5	39	3

*Training costs for teachers' aides are excluded from the column as teacher training is from Column (2). Imputed rents on additional capital expenditure are included.

Table 45

Projected Costs of Maintained Primary and Nursery Schools and the Additional Costs of Our Proposals: England

£ million at 1966 prices

(1)	(2)	(3)	(4)	(5)	(6)
Financial year	Projected current costs on present policies*	Our proposals for additional current expenditure**	Percentage increase in current costs as a result of adoption of our proposals %	Projected capital expenditure for basic needs	The capital costs of our proposals
1964/65	277			39	
1966/67	297			38	
1968/69	326	3	1	48	10
1970/71	359	14	4	54	17
1972/73	390	31	8	51	18
1974/75	421	43	10	45	38
1976/77	451	55	12	42	21
1978/79	478	65	14	39	18

* Includes £3 million a year for nursery schools.

** Excludes training costs and includes imputed rents on cost of proposals for extra capital expenditure.

ANNEX A TO CHAPTER 31

FACTORS AFFECTING RECRUITMENT OF ASSISTANTS AND AIDES

1205. Nursery assistants and teachers' aides will be drawn from the same groups of girl leavers and older married women; here we discuss the size of the group from which they will be recruited.

1206. We have suggested that school leavers who begin training should have between one and four passes in the ordinary level of the General Certificate of Education, or the equivalent in Group I and II of C.S.E. The number of girls leaving school with five or more "O" level passes will rise substantially. The Department's projections show a rise in the number of girls leaving school with five or more "O" level passes from 15 per cent in 1962/63 to 20 per cent in 1970/71 and 24 per cent in 1979/80[1]. The 1963/64 number of girls leaving with one to four "O" level passes was less than the number leaving with five "O" level passes and above. For the period after 1968 we made one projection of the numbers of girls with one to four "O" level passes or equivalent ability by assuming that they were equal to the number of girls with five or more "O" level passes. This is in accordance with the assumption made in the Seventh Report of the Secondary School Examinations Council[2] and is consistent with the basic hypothesis that as school opportunities increase, the stock of qualified school leavers will increase pari passu. Another projection was based on the assumption that the relevant ability range comprised roughly 20 per cent of the 16 year old girl school leavers. This second projection gave slightly higher numbers than the first up to about 1972/73, and then rather lower numbers. The two projections were averaged.

1207. The proportion of these school leavers who could be recruited for work in the schools is more difficult to estimate. Nursing provides strong competition. In 1962/63 the number of new entrants to nursing courses leading to the qualifications of State Registered Nurse and State Enrolled Nurse were together over 25,000 for England and Wales. The minimum qualifications for these courses were either two "O" level passes or success in the G.N.C.'s suitability test, approximately the ability range from which nursery assistants might be recruited. Competition between the two groups is thus inevitable although if the Platt Committee's[3] recommendations are accepted that all entrants to nursing should have a minimum of five "O" level passes the competition will be much reduced. However, office employment, which will also compete heavily for these girls, is growing rapidly. Service employment will overlap with office employment in demanding their labour; the Ministry of Labour estimates that service employment, which rose from 44 per cent of employees in 1953 to 48 per cent in 1963, will rise to 49 per cent by 1968. This increase can be expected to persist. Forecasts of local authorities' staffing needs in the health and welfare services in the next ten years show a substantial rise in the demand for the employment of women[4]. The trend to earlier marriage will reduce the supply of single women, and will lead to a strong demand for the services of girls leaving school.

1208. In 1964/65 there were over 4,000 candidates for N.N.E.B. courses. The figure is considerably greater than the number of girls accepted for these courses even though it may contain some duplicate applications. There would probably be more applications if the chance of acceptance were greater. In 1962/63, 36,350, and 1963/64, 38,000 girls with one to four "O" level passes left school to enter employment (not further forms of full-time education or training). With an expansion of nursery education, some girls would transfer from other forms of further education.

1209. From these admittedly rather speculative calculations, we think that recruitment of around 7,500 a year in the early seventies would be possible. The recruitment figure we use throughout the period is 11 per cent of the mean of the projections described above. These are set out in Table 46.

Table 46

Assumed Annual Recruitment of School Leavers for Training as Nursery Assistants and Teachers' Aides

	Thousands
1968	6·9
1969	6·9
1970	7·0
1971	6·9
1972	7·4
1973	7·6
1974	7·9
1975	8·2
1976	8·5
1977	8·9
1978	9·2
1979	9·5

1210. The wastage rates of these girls will be high; we assume ten per cent a year during training during the first two years of service, the rates assumed for non-graduate women teachers in the years immediately following the completion of their training[5]. Thus we are tacitly assuming that they would leave to get married roughly two years before non-graduate women teachers do. We assume also that they would return into service two years before the women non-graduate teachers, but otherwise at the same re-entry rate[6]. With this rate of recruitment wastage and re-entry, the build up of aides and assistants in service will be slow; ten years after the beginning of the scheme only 34,000 aides and assistants will be in service from this source.

1211. The build up of aides and assistants, especially in the early years, is heavily dependent on the recruitment of older married women, who we assume will stay longer than the school leavers. When girl entrants begin to re-enter after marriage a much smaller number of new recruits will be needed from among the older married women. But this stage will not come until some 15 years from the beginning of the scheme.

1212. It is more difficult to estimate the recruitment of mature women than of girls. We know that there are many married women not at present employed. The National Plan states that there are 3,000,000 married women over the age of 45 not in employment[7]. Surveys have suggested considerable willingness among married women to enter employment; if sufficient opportunities are available for part time employment, the number which could be recruited might be very considerable. One survey[8] gave an overall estimate of 700,000 women who if they had the choice would work full time and $4\frac{1}{2}$ million who would like to work part-time. If as many married as single women in 1960 had worked, there would have been an additional two and a half million workers under 35 and three and a quarter million between 35 and 60. Most of the younger women might only be prepared to work part-time but many of the elder ones might work full-time.

1213. It would be unrealistic to conclude too much from the absolute numbers of women not employed at the moment. However, it is clear that there is increasing employment of married women. As homes become mechanised women wish to spend less time in them. There are strong reasons for supposing that the rising propensity for married women to work will continue.

1214. The National Institute of Economic and Social Research has projected the number of married women who are likely to work up to 1975[9]. They calculate that there will be a yearly increase of 70,000 married women seeking work between 1967 and 1975. These figures are based on long term trends and may underestimate the growth of the married women labour force, as there may be an acceleration in the willingness of married women to return to work.

1215. The educational system is in a favourable position to recruit married women. The total number of hours worked by nursery assistants or teachers' aides would be considerably less than the hours worked by other full-time employees. Part-time employment would be fairly easy to arrange both in the primary schools, and in the nurseries. It would be conveniently close to their homes. The expansion of nursery education will create some of its own supply of assistants insofar as these are drawn from married women with young families. Surveys show that the proportion of married women working is particularly low where there are children below school age in the family. For these reasons we conclude that the N.I.E.S.R. estimates of the increase in the supply of married women workers is an underestimate of the pool of women workers which the schools might draw on for nursery assistants and aides.

1216. We hope to recruit the equivalent of 10,000 older women a year. At the moment roughly half the married women in employment work part-time; if this proportion were applied to the new teachers' aides and nursery assistants this would involve a recruitment of 13,340 per annum. Many women who would only take part-time jobs outside the schools may be persuaded to take full-time ones in schools so that less than this number may be required. Although recruitment of 11 to 12,000 married women a year may look large compared with the probable increase of the married women labour force over this period it looks very much smaller when it is remembered that much of the demand will be for nursery assistants who will release women for this and other work.

1217. We assume that these older married women would have a wastage rate of ten per cent during training and five per cent per annum thereafter. This wastage rate is higher than the wastage rate for non-graduate women teachers in comparable age ranges; but much depends on the age at which these married women are recruited. In ten years there would, on these assumptions, be 77,000 married women aides and assistants in the schools (not counting any of the girls who may by now have returned).

1218. Only experience with the scheme will show whether the assumptions about the relative numbers of girls and older married women who can be recruited and their wastage are reasonably correct. But the build-up of the scheme is in many ways more critical than the continuation of it.

References

[1]Statistics of Education, 1963, Part 3, Table 21. H.M.S.O. 1964.

[2]Seventh Report of the Secondary School Examinations Council. H.M.S.O. 1963.,

[3]Report of the Joint Working Party on the Medical Staffing Structure in the Hospital Service, 1961, H.M.S.O. and Royal College of Nursing. A Reform of Nursing Education. Journal of Royal College Nursing and National Council of Nurses of the United Kingdom, 1964, Volume 8, Page 57.

[4]'Health and Welfare: The Development of Community Care', Cmnd. 3022, paragraph 94-7.

[5]The Ninth Report of the National Advisory Council for the Training and Supply of Teachers, H.M.S.O., 1965, page 84.

[6]See [5] above.

[7]The National Plan, 1965, Cmnd. 2764, page 39.

[8]New Society, 28th March, 1963.

[9]W. Beckerman and Associates, 'The British Economy in 1975', National Institute of Economic and Social Research, Cambridge University Press, 1965.

ANNEX B TO CHAPTER 31

OFFSETS TO THE COSTS OF NURSERY PROVISION
AND THE USE OF TEACHERS' AIDES:
AN ESTIMATE OF THE OUTPUT OF MOTHERS WHO RETURN TO WORK

1219. An important offset to the cost of the additional resources required for our proposed expansion of nursery education and the recruitment of married women as teachers' aides is the increased production which we expect will take place as some of the mothers of the three and four year olds return to work, either as assistants or aides, or to other jobs. The recruitment of married women as aides and assistants will lead to an increase in the numbers of mothers with children of school age who will work as well as some diversion from other jobs. Much as we may deplore the increasing tendency of mothers of young children to work, it would be unrealistic not to count its economic yields. We have already quoted evidence showing the increased willingness of successive generations of married women to return to work: there are important economic trends underlying this movement, and we expect them to continue. Thus our proposals will tap unused reserves of labour.

1220. Expenditure on labour saving devices will increase more rapidly than household income, and the total stock of them will be substantially higher in the seventies than it is now [1, 2]. In other ways housewives are able to run their homes more easily at a somewhat higher money cost. Even more important than household appliances may be the purchase of the services of factories, shops and restaurants who now undertake much of the preparation of clothing and partial preparation of food which once took place at home. The declining size of family has also substantially reduced housework*.

1221. These changes reduce the amount of housework; they produce the social problem of under employment, and bored housewives. The housewife has both the time and the need to take up some outside work, and herself provides some of the paid labour which reduces the need for housework. At the same time there has been a substantial increase in the demand for labour traditionally performed by women**[4].

1222. There are now more small families with less support than in the past from the extended family. This produces economic strains during periods of sickness and temporary low earnings for other reasons, as well as demands for help from outside the family for child minding, baby sitting and the like. It makes it more necessary for housewives to work for money.

*It is not easy to quantify these factors. We note the work of C. D. Long in the United States. He estimates that changes in technology (increases in the number of household appliances and the switch to buying food and clothing outside the home) may have 'saved' eight per cent of the work of women above 14 between 1890 and 1940, and that by 1950 a further three per cent was thus 'saved'. Reductions in family size similarly 'saved' a further eight per cent between 1890 and 1940, and two per cent from 1940 to 1950. Not all this work was actually saved and available for employment; some of it no doubt went into higher standards of housework.[3]

**U.S. studies of female employment have shown that while there are many instances of women moving into occupations formerly thought to be exclusively men's, most of the increase in the employment of women has been due to the rapid increase in the jobs traditionally held by women.[6]

457

Q

1223. More married women are working. On the figures given in paragraph 1214 it seems possible that the figure will rise to 38 per cent by 1975[5]. The big increase is expected in the age groups over 35. Because of the continuing trend to early child bearing a slight fall in participation rates is forecast for married women between 25 and 35.*

1224. The provision of nursery education will enable some younger mothers of children aged three to five to undertake part-time, and in some cases full-time, work but their ability to do so may be complicated by school holidays. It will also depend on the availability of part-time work and the extent to which the short periods of nursery attendance can be used, that is, on mothers being able to make arrangements for work near home or for their children to be taken to and from school by other mothers. In an important sense the demand for the women's work is there; the attempt to force the pace of growth has produced a forecast "labour shortage". Increasingly employers are making arrangements for part-time employment. Between 1960 and 1965 the number of part-time employees has increased by 22 per cent[12]. But official policies may need to be changed if full use is to be made of this labour reserve.

1225. Given the poor information at our disposal on this vital part of the labour force, and the dependence of the outcome on a number of factors in the labour market outside the field of educational policy, we can only make a tentative estimate of the size of this important offset to the resource cost of nursery provision.

1226. Many of the older women who become nursery assistants or teachers' aides may have children in nursery groups or for other reasons will enter the labour force. In our hypothetical build-up we assume that there will be some 82,000 full-time equivalent older women in service as aides and assistants by 1979**. We assume that 25 to 35 thousand full-time equivalents of these will be mothers of children in the nursery groups, or women with older school children who are not already at work. Their earnings will be £506 a year (including superannuation) on 1966 prices making a total of £13–£18 million a year.

1227. There will be many mothers of children attending full or part-time who do not become teachers' aides or nursery assistants. We assume that the

*The presence of young children is an important deterrent to a married woman working. Kelsall and Mitchell, working on 1949 data, show that only 12 per cent of women with a child under school age worked, while 26 per cent of those with a child of school age did. Thirty-seven per cent of married women without children were at work[7]. Klein reaches a similar conclusion[8]. An American study which attempted to quantify some of the reasons for married women working concluded that the existence of a child under six in the family was the most important determinant of whether the housewife worked or not, when factors related to the secular rise in participation rates are held constant[9]. U.S. data show that the participation rate for mothers with children under five is a quarter to a third of that of mothers of children over five[10]. In Britain there are substantial differences between the participation rates of women aged 25–30 and those 35–40, ages when there are substantially different probabilities of having children below and above five. Allowing for the upward trend in participation rates generally, comparison of the N.I.E.S.R's projected participation rates for married women age 35–40 in 1967, 1972 and 1977 with the actual and projected ones for the age group 25 -30 in 1957, 1962 and 1967 reveals a difference of 11–13 percentage points[11]. This is an underestimate of the difference resulting from the presence or not of children below school age in the family.

**During the 1980s the recruitment of married women may fall off, but there will be substantial re-entry of those initially recruited as girls returning after child bearing.

proportion who work will rise to nearly that of mothers with children of school age, a rise of between ten and 15 percentage points. Perhaps a third of mothers with children aged three to five will have other children below school age. Klein[13] has shown that often married women returners take less skilled jobs than they held previously. There will be important exceptions and in some cases professional women will be able to return to fill posts where there are severe shortages. In addition, as the economy becomes geared to the employment of women part-time, they will be used more in skilled jobs. Thus in taking the average earnings of women manual workers (five shillings an hour in 1965)[14] as the appropriate value of their time we are being cautious. We also assume that they are only employed for 200 days a year—full-time workers for five hours and part-time workers for two hours. On this basis 50—70,000 additional women may be released for full or part-time work as a consequence of nursery provision. Of these, perhaps 5,000 will work as nursery assistants or teachers' aides. On all these assumptions the value of the extra production of women who begin work outside the educational sector (50–70,000 less 5,000) may be of the order of £3–4 million a year by 1979. This figure is small because some children are giving up full-time school to be provided with part-time nursery education.

1228. Adding this to the range estimated in paragraph 1226 we have a full offset which may be between £16 and 22 million per annum by 1979.

LIST OF REFERENCES

[1]Needleman, L., 'The Demand for Domestic Appliances', National Institute Economic Review, 1960.

[2]Beckerman, W., and Associates, 'The British Economy in 1975', National Institute of Economic and Social Research, p. 192–3, Cambridge University Press, 1965.

[3]Long, C. D., 'The Labour Force under Changing Incomes and Employment', Princeton, 1958, Chapter 7.

[4]Routh, G., 'Occupation and Pay in Great Britain', Cambridge, 1965.

[5]See [2] above.

[6]Long, C. D., op. cit. page 268. National Manpower Council. Women Power, N.W., 1957. Woytinskly, N. S. et al, 'Employment and Wages in the United States', N.Y., 1953. 'Changes in Women's Occupations 1940–50', Women's Bureau Bulletin 253, U.S. Department of Labour, 1953.

[7]Kelsall and Mitchell, 'Married Women and Employment', Population Studies, Vol. XIII, 1959–60, page 28.

[8]Klein, V., 'Working Wives', Institute of Personal Management, page 41, 1959.

[9]Rossett, R. N., 'Working Wives: An Econometric Study' in Dernburg, T. F., Rossett, R. N. and Watts, H. W., Studies in Household Behaviour, New Haven, 1958.

[10]U.S. Bureau of Labour Statistics, Table of Working Life for Women 1950, Bulletin 1204, Washington, 1957.

[11]See [2] above, page 91.

[12]From 1960 to 1965 Ministry of Labour statistics.

[13]See [8] above.

[14]Average of April and October 1965 figures, Ministry of Labour Statistics on Prices, Incomes, Production and Employment.

CHAPTER 32

Recommendations and Conclusions
I. The Changing Direction

1229. Our terms of reference, "primary education in all its aspects and the transition to secondary education" were wide ranging. Our interpretation has been correspondingly wide. We conceived it as our duty to see the primary school not only in its strictly educational context but also as a part of society and of the economy.

1230. The cost of the proposals we have made is large. This is in part the cost of bringing a system designed for "other people's children" up to the standard which "a good and wise parent" would accept for his own children. Neither in our staffing proposals, nor in our demand for buildings and equipment, have we been luxurious or extravagant. What we propose does not go beyond what is needed to provide a perfectly ordinary, well staffed school. Yet in the present difficult economic circumstances it is not a programme capable of being carried out in the next five years.

1231. Since the war there has been a great increase in secondary education and in further and higher education. These developments were necessary if we were to hold our own with other advanced industrial countries. We are certainly not leading an advance party. This progress, however, has been in part at the expense of primary education. We think that a higher priority in the total educational budget ought now to be given to primary education. It is desirable in its own right: nobody ought to be satisfied with the conditions under which many of the four million primary school children are educated. It is also desirable in the interests of secondary and further education. A good deal of the money spent on older children will be wasted if more is not spent on them during their primary school years. Yet not everything costs money. Some of our recommendations call mainly for changes of attitude, understanding and knowledge in individual teachers.

1232. In the introduction to our Report we posed certain questions. Now we attempt to answer them. We found that the Hadow reports understated rather than over estimated the differences between children. They are too great for children to be tidily assigned to streams or types of schools. Children are unequal in their endowment and in their rates of development. Their achievements are the result of the interaction of nature and of nurture. We conclude that the Hadow emphasis on the individual was right though we would wish to take it further. Whatever form of organisation is adopted, teachers will have to adapt their methods to individuals within a class or school. Only in this way can the needs of gifted and slow learning children and all those between the extremes be met.

1233. The appraisal we have made of the curriculum, and of the methods which have proved to be the most fruitful, confirm many or most of the suggestions that our predecessors made. Their insights have been justified and refined by experience. "Finding out" has proved to be better for children than "being told". Children's capacity to create in words, pictorially and through many other forms of expression, is astonishing. The third of the three R'S is no longer mere mechanical arithmetic, French has made its way into the primary school, nature study is becoming science. There has been dramatic and continuing advance in standards of reading. The gloomy forebodings of the decline of knowledge which would follow progressive methods have been discredited. Our review is a report of progress and a spur to more.

1234. This may sound complacent. We are not. The more dismal corners of primary education produce plenty of evidence of parochialism, lack of understanding of the needs of children and of the differing homes from which they come, lack of continued training of teachers and lack of opportunities for professional contact. Had we ignored these facts, we should have ignored what is well known to teachers and, increasingly, to parents. If all or most teachers are to approach the standards of the best, far more effort must be put into their in-service training.

There may be a good school without good buildings, though this is no excuse for the deplorable conditions in which many children are educated. There cannot be a good school without good teachers. Even one or two can leaven a whole staff. But there are staffs without leaven. We set these facts down here lest we should be accused of wilful ignorance because in the Report we have for the most part described English primary education at its best. That in our belief is very good indeed. Only rarely is it very bad. The average is good.

1235. We hope we have described in the Report what good primary education is, and how robust, imaginative, sensitive and skilful the work of a good primary school pupil can be. Much of our thinking, however, has been given to considering those children to whose work none of these epithets could be applied. We know that in almost every primary school there are some such children. We know that in some districts almost every child is at a disadvantage that can only be removed by unusual excellence in the school. An outstanding trend in recent years has been the growing awareness of the importance for the individual of his family and social background. The last three reports by the Council and the Robbins report on higher education produced evidence that shows how closely associated are social circumstances and academic achievement. We have been able to set on foot research which has suggested that the most vital factor in a child's home is the attitude to school, and all that goes on there, of his mother and father. The interested parent has the interested child. In contrast we have been conscious of the unfairness that dogs many boys and girls through life. The loss to them, the loss to the community that arises because of the inequality of educational opportunity, is avoidable and in consequence intolerable. We have, therefore, deliberately given their needs the first priority among our recommendations even though this may delay for a while long overdue benefits for the greater number of children. Our proposal for the introduction of educational priority areas, a detailed plan for dealing with a situation to which the Council's last report also drew attention, is sufficiently urgent to be put forward for immediate action even in the present economic difficulties.

1236. We think of primary education as something that ought to start gradually without a sudden transition from whole time home to whole time school, from the day with mother to the day with teacher. This lies behind our recommendation for half time education in nursery groups for nearly all four year olds and for a good many three year olds. That is why we have advocated a slightly later start than now to school, and why we have suggested that it may sometimes be right for a mother to be with her child in the class-room until he has settled down. Were this to happen, it would be a symbol of the partnership between schools and parents that we hope will persist in different forms through the whole length of education.

1237. We have recommended a single term of intake to first schools and a complete three year course in them for all children. Perhaps the greatest bene-fit that time in the infant school gives is confidence in what has been learned. The child's own satisfaction in having really mastered something—whether it be riding a bicycle or telling the time—is important. If the beginnings of school work are only half learned and anxiety ridden, the effects may persist throughout school days. Confidence in the power to learn is vital.

1238. The middle school will start and finish a year later than the junior school. Its staff will need to be drawn from secondary schools as well as primary. Both have a contribution to make. If the middle school is simply thought of as providing an "extra year" to the junior school, many children will be working well below their capacity and become bored. If the middle school is thought of as a junior secondary school to be organised and taught in the ways that secondary schools are run, there is an equal risk that we may lose too soon the enquiring spirit which drives a child to follow through an interest without respect to subject frontiers. We cannot give a description of a good middle school because such schools do not yet exist. They will have to work out their own pattern. We can only say that their work must be carried further than that of junior schools, their ways of learning be less stereotyped than those of secondary schools. In a world where secondary schools have increasingly to adapt their style to the needs of older adolescents and near adults, the middle school ought to provide the right environment for the last years of childhood as it passes over into adolescence.

1239. No report on primary education today could be realistic if it did not attempt to deal with the revolutionary change that has come over the com-position of the body of teachers. Before the war the schools could count on most teachers giving 40 years of service. A school staff was a body of ex-perienced professionals in which a newcomer could easily learn to find his feet. Today the proportions are often reversed. A small body of experienced teachers is surrounded by a rapidly changing group of young women who expect to marry soon after they leave college and in many cases to leave within a few years, at least for the time being, in order to start their own families. Some return to teaching; more should. When they return they are the richer because they are themselves mothers, the poorer because they have often not had long enough to reach professional competence before they gave up teaching. Some can teach full-time; some part-time. The schools have to accustom themselves to being staffed in a novel way at the same time as they are developing new methods of individual and group work which demand greater competence and co-operation from teachers.

1240. In these circumstances we make recommendations on the staffing of the schools on which we lay special emphasis. The first has only temporary application. It is that those who are planning now for the raising of the school leaving age should not reckon on any transfers from the primary schools to carry out the operation. The place for trained primary school teachers is in the primary schools. The second recommendation is that the work of teachers should be lightened by the provision of aides, who should be given one or two years training. The more individual the methods of teaching, the stronger the case for teachers' aides. The scheme will be expensive; we are sure the teachers deserve the relief it will provide.

1241. The favourable judgment we have formed of English primary education as a whole, and the confidence with which we have made far reaching recommendations for its development, reflect the devoted and perceptive service of the vast majority of the 140,000 primary school teachers. Most of what is best in English schools has come straight from individual teachers. We could wish no child a happier fate than to encounter, as many do, a good teacher.

II. RECOMMENDATIONS AND CONCLUSIONS

1242. We have summarised our main recommendations and conclusions at the end of the chapters to which they apply. Chapter 30 contains recommendations on further studies and research and Chapter 31 discusses the main priorities which should be adopted. In this chapter we draw together our main recommendations and indicate the agency from which action on them is required. We also indicate those recommendations which will result in markedly increased expenditure or a change in law. Many of our lesser recommendations and suggestions are not summarised here and must be found in the main body of the Report.

1243. The following are our main recommendations. Those calling for extra expenditure are marked (£). Those requiring changes of law or of the Department's Regulations are marked (*).

Chapter 4

Participation by Parents

Agency mainly responsible for putting recommendations into effect.

1. All schools should have a programme for contact with children's homes to include:

(a) A regular system for the head and class teacher to meet parents before the child enters.

(b) Arrangements for more formal private talks, preferably twice a year.

(c) Open days to be held at times chosen to enable parents to attend.

(d) Parents to be given booklets prepared by the schools to enable them to choose their children's schools and to know how they are being educated.

(e) Written reports on children to be made at least once a year. The child's work to be seen by parents.

(f) Special efforts are needed to make contact with parents who do not visit the schools.

SCHOOLS
L.E.As.

2. The Department of Education and Science should issue a booklet containing examples of good practices in parent-teacher relations. The Department should inform themselves of the steps taken by authorities to encourage schools to foster good relations.

D.E.S.

3. Parents should be allowed to choose their children's primary school whenever this is possible. Authorities should take steps to improve schools which are shown to be consistently unpopular with parents.

L.E.As.

4. Primary schools should be used as fully as possible out of ordinary hours.

L.E.As.

5. Parents and other adults should be invited to help the school with its out of school activities. Parents might **(£)** contribute towards the cost of out of school activities, to supplement the costs borne by the local education authority.

SCHOOLS

L.E.As.

6. Heads should have a say in the evening use of their buildings. When buildings are heavily used two deputy **(£)** head teachers should be appointed, one responsible for out of school activities. This would involve a modification of the Burnham provisions.

L.E.As.

BURNHAM

(£) 7. Community schools should be developed in all areas but especially in educational priority areas.

L.E.As.

Chapter 5

Educational Priority Areas

8. As a matter of national policy, "positive discrimination" should favour schools in neighbourhoods where

(£)(*) children are most severely handicapped by home conditions. The programme should be phased to make schools in the most deprived areas as good as the best of the country. For this it may be necessary that their greater claim on resources should be maintained.   L.E.As.

9. A start should be made as soon as possible by giving   D.E.S.
priority to the most severely deprived pupils, starting with two per cent of the pupils and building up to ten per cent over five years. The purpose of the short term programme would be partly to discover which measures best compensate for educational deprivation. In the longer term, the programme may be expanded to cover a larger proportion of the population.

10. Every local education authority having schools in which children's educational handicaps are reinforced by social deprivation should be asked to adopt the measures suggested below and to report from time to time on the progress made. Local authorities should be encouraged to select schools within their areas for special attention even though they are not eligible for extra help from national resources.

11. A wide variety of criteria should be employed initially. Experience will show which of these criteria are most useful.

12. Authorities should be asked to assess which of their schools should qualify for extra help from national resources. The Department of Education should formally designate those schools and areas in most need as educational priority areas. Priority areas and the progress made in them should be reappraised regularly by local education authorities and the Department of Education and Science.

13. Authorities and the Department of Education and Science should ensure that the needs of other educationally deprived groups, such as gypsies, which will not be picked out by the general criteria laid down, are not overlooked.

Steps to be Taken: 1968 to 1972

14. (a) Measures should be taken to improve the ratio of teachers to children in educational priority areas   L.E.As.
to a point at which no class in these areas exceeds

(£)   `   30. Additions to salary amounting in total to £120   D.E.S.
for every teacher in the priority areas should be paid. It should be open to authorities to award increases according to any plan approved by the   BURNHAM
Department of Education and Science as being likely to improve education in these areas.

(£)   (b) Teachers' aides should be provided in the priority schools at a ratio of one to every two infant and junior classes.

(c) In building programmes, priority should be given to these areas for the replacement or improvement of schools with old or out of date premises. The element of the total school building programme reserved for minor works should be increased specifically for their benefit. Approximately £5,000 should be allocated for minor works in each school.　L.E.As.

(£)

(d) Extra books and equipment should be given for schools in priority areas.

(£)

(e) The expansion of nursery education should begin in the priority areas.

15. The Department of Education and Science should modify its quota arrangements so that they take into account the varying resources of immobile teachers available in each area. Authorities with large numbers of qualified married women willing to teach but unable to work in other areas should gradually be persuaded to employ all of them before drawing on mobile teachers who might be available for priority areas.　D.E.S.

16. Colleges of education should, wherever possible, establish a continuing link with priority schools. Students should do part of their teaching practice in these schools.　COLLEGES of EDUCATION

17. Teacher centres should be set up for in-service training. They might run longer courses with the co-operation of local colleges of education. Such courses might be recognised for salary purposes.　L.E.As. COLLEGES of EDUCATION BURNHAM

(£)

18. The development of social work in conjunction with schools should begin in priority areas and be more heavily concentrated there subsequently.　L.E.As. D.E.S. H. OFFICE M. of H.L.G.

(£) 19. Community schools should be tried out first in priority areas.　L.E.A.s.

20. Sustained efforts should be made to diversify the social composition of the districts where priority schools are so that teachers and others who make an essential contribution to the life and public services of the neighbourhood are not excluded from them. Co-ordinated action will be necessary on the part of authorities responsible for employment, industrial training, housing and town planning if educational deprivation is to be rapidly reduced.　M. of H.L.G. L. HOUSING & PLANNING AUTHORITIES L.E.As.

21. Research should be started to discover which of the developments in educational priority areas have the most constructive effects, so as to assist in planning the longer term programme to follow.　D.E.S. & RESEARCH BODIES

22. Exchequer grants to local authorities with educational priority areas should be increased and the necessary changes in the grant making system made.　D.E.S. M. of H.L.G.

(£)(*)

Chapter 6

Children of Immigrants

23. Colleges, institutes of education and local education authorities should expand opportunities through initial and in-service courses for some teachers to train in teaching English to immigrants and to increase their knowledge of the background from which children come.

(£)

COLLEGES **and** INSTITUTES OF EDUCATION

L.E.As.

24. Work already started on the development of suitable materials and methods for teaching English to immigrants should continue and be expanded.

(£)

25. Dispersal may be necessary but language and other difficulties should be the criteria employed.

L.E.As.
D.E.S.

26. There should be an expansion of remedial courses in spoken English for immigrant teachers.

(£)

D.E.S.
INSTITUTES

27. Schools with special language problems and others of the kind referred to in this chapter should be generously staffed: further experiments might be made in the use of student volunteers.

L.E.As.

Chapter 7

The Health and Social Services and the School Child

28. All children should be examined before entry to school for the purpose of assessing their developmental and medical needs.

29. Selective but more intensive medical examinations should become the normal practice in later school life.

30. Particular attention should be paid to the development of "observation registers" starting with perinatal information, developmental tests and other procedures for identifying children showing tendencies to disorders. Social information should appear in these registers. Social workers collaborating with the School Health Services should be informed in confidence of needs and problems which concern them, subject to parental consent.

D.E.S.
L.H.As.
L.C.As.
M. of H.
H. O.

31. Co-operation between family doctors, school and public health services and hospitals should be closer.

32. More staff is needed in almost all branches of the School Health Service.

33. Closer collaboration between social workers and medical and nursing staff is necessary.

34. There is a need for adequately trained social workers who would collaborate closely with schools, would be capable of assuming responsibility for cases beyond the competence, time or training of the head or class teacher, and capable of securing local authorities' help quickly from more specialised social services. The principal need is for

a grouping of existing organisations within a comprehensive plan of action which will enable these functions to be fulfilled.

(£)   35. In those areas where help is most urgently needed, teams should be established to include experienced workers from the relevant fields including social workers largely responsible for school social work. Such experiments should be started as soon as possible, particularly in some of the educational priority areas, and linked with research designed to test their value.

36. Social workers should always work in the schools with the consent of the head teacher and be immediately responsible to him in much of their work. Their administrative responsibility should normally be to a team leader located in a service having broader social work functions.

37. A new grade of welfare assistant working with social workers might take over much of the routine work carried out by education welfare officers. Some of the work at present carried out by E.W.Os. could more appropriately be undertaken by clerical workers.

38. Medical and social workers should inform the schools of action being taken in respect of their pupils whenever this information would help teachers in their work with children. Such information should be treated as confidential and its use should be subject to the consent of parents.

Training

(£)   39. Education welfare officers could be trained to carry out wider social work functions. Two year training should be established for selected education welfare officers.

TRAINING BODIES

40. The training of teachers should take more account of the social factors that affect school performance and of the structure and functions of the social services. Such training is particularly necessary for head teachers and deputies.

41. There should be experimental schemes for the joint training of social workers and teachers. Social work courses should contain adequate instruction about educational aspects of their work.

COLLEGES of EDUCATION D.E.S.

Chapter 8

Primary Education in the 1960s: Its Organisation and Effectiveness

42. Surveys similar to that carried out by H.M. Inspectorate to assess the quality of primary education for the Council should be undertaken at ten year intervals.

H.M.Is.

Chapter 9

Providing for Children Before Compulsory Education

43. There should be a large expansion of nursery education and a start should be made as soon as possible.

(£)

44. Nursery education should be available to children at any time after the beginning of the school year after they reach the age of three until they reach the age of compulsory schooling.

L.E.As.

45. Nursery education should be available either for a morning or afternoon session for five days a week so that over the country as a whole provision should be made for 15 per cent of children to attend both a morning and afternoon session.

46. The take up of nursery places by children in special need should be carefully watched by local education authorities and by the Department of Education and Science so that further methods of persuasion can be used to bring in all children who are in need of nursery education.

47. Low priority should be given to full-time nursery education for children whose mothers cannot satisfy the authorities that they have exceptionally good reasons for working.

D.E.S.

48. Children should be introduced gradually to nursery education.

49. Nursery education should be provided in nursery groups of up to 20 places. More than one and up to three groups might form a unit to be called a nursery centre or be combined with day nurseries or clinics in children's centres.

L.H.As.
M. of H.
L.E.As.
D.E.S.

50. The education of children over three in day nurseries should be the responsibility of the education rather than health departments.

51. All nursery groups should be under the ultimate supervision of a qualified teacher in the ratio of one qualified teacher to 60 places. The main day to day work of the groups will be undertaken by two year trained nursery assistants in the ratio of a minimum of one to every ten children. There should be at least one experienced nursery assistant in each group and, where no teacher is always on the premises, one assistant able to cope with accidents and safety risks. Experienced assistants should be able to qualify on merit for a responsibility allowance.

L.E.As.
D.E.S.

52. Nursery groups which are under the supervision of a teacher or head teacher of an adjoining primary school will be part of that school. Groups not attached to a school should form a single nursery centre with the other groups, which are supervised by the same qualified teacher.

D.E.S.

53. Until enough maintained places are available, local education authorities should be given power and be encouraged to give financial or other assistance to nursery groups run by non-profit making associations which in (£)(*) their opinion fill a need which they cannot meet. Voluntary groups, with or without help from public funds, should be subject to inspection by local education authorities and H.M. Inspectorate similar to that of the maintained nurseries.

L.E.As.
D.E.S.

54. Ideally, all services, including nursery, for the care of young children should be grouped together and placed near the children's homes and the primary schools. The planning of new areas and the rebuilding of old should take account of nursery education.

L.E.As.
D.E.S.
M.H.L.G.
LOCAL
PLANNING
AUTHORITIES

55. Local authorities should undertake local surveys at an appropriate time to assess the net cost of extra accommodation needed to establish nursery provision in their area and to see how many qualified teachers will be available following changes in the age of entry to the first school.

L.E.As.
D.E.S.

Chapter 10

The Ages and Stages of Primary Education
Long-Term Recommendations

56. As soon as there is nursery provision for all children whose parents wish it, for a year before starting school, (*) the normal time by which a child should go to school should be defined as the September term following his fifth birthday. This would require legislation. Schools should be allowed to space admissions over the first half-term of the school year.

D.E.S.

57. There should be a three year course in the first (at present the infant) school.

58. This should be followed by a four year course in the middle (at present the junior) school.

L.E.As.

59. There should be flexibility in entry to school and in transfer between the stages of education to allow for the circumstances of individual pupils.

60. Children should be allowed for the first term after the normal time of entry to attend a nursery group, if the parents wish, and to attend school for half a day only for the term or until their sixth birthday, if this is later than the end of the term, at the request of the parents.

61. The Department should announce as soon as possible (*) a national policy on the structure of nursery and primary education and on the ages of transfer from stage to stage and should fix a date by which these should become binding.

D.E.S.

Interim Recommendations

62. Until this date, children should begin whole-day attendance at school twice a year, those reaching the age of five between February 1st and August 31st in the following September, and those reaching five between September 1st and January 31st in the following April. This would also require legislation which should permit staggered admission over half a term.

(*)

D.E.S.

63. Part-time attendance should be available at a morning or afternoon session for up to two terms before full-time entry. Exceptionally, a child should be allowed to attend part-time at the request of his parents until he reaches the age of six.

(*)

Chapter 11

Selection for Secondary Education

64. Authorities who for an interim period continue to need selection procedures should cease to rely on externally imposed intelligence and attainment tests.

L.E.As.

65. Further work is needed on tests for use by teachers in the context of the changing curriculum.

Chapter 12

Continuity and Consistency Between the Stages of Education

66. Mothers and children should spend some time in the reception class before admission, and mothers stay with children when necessary during the first few days at school. Meetings between staff and parents should be arranged.

SCHOOLS

67. The most suitable organisation of primary education is in separate first and middle schools, though combined schools may be necessary in rural areas and for some voluntary schools.

L.E.As.
D.E.S.

68. The initial and in-service training of teachers should overlap more than one stage of education.

L.E.As.
COLLS, DEPTS.
& INSTS. OF ED.

69. There should be a variety of contacts between teachers in successive stages of education.

70. Local education authorities should close schools for one day to arrange conferences for all teachers, when there is evidence of lack of contact.

L.E.As.

71. Authorities should call area conferences of teachers to consider the information passed on within the primary stage and from primary to secondary schools, and the use made of it.

72. There should be a detailed folder on each child which could provide a basis for a regular review with children's parents of their progress. The folders should accompany the child into the middle and secondary schools and should

be available to the child's class or form teacher. Information about former pupils should be sent back from secondary to primary schools.

73. All children should make at least one visit to their new school in the term before they transfer.   L.E.As.
SCHOOLS

74. Authorities should send parents a leaflet explaining the choice of secondary schools available and the courses provided within them.

75. All secondary schools should make arrangements to meet the parents of new entrants.

76. There should be no sharp break between infant or first and junior or middle school methods. In allocating staff, heads should try to avoid giving to a weak member of staff responsibility for children who are adjusting to a new school.

77. Discussions should be held between primary and secondary teachers to avoid overlap in such matters as text books and to discuss pupils' records.

Chapter 13

The Size of Primary Schools

78. The most satisfactory size for new reorganised first schools will normally be two form entry (240 children) and for middle schools two to three form entry (300 to 450). When class sizes are reduced, the same number of children   L.E.As.
can be retained on roll but schools should be organised on   D.E.S.
the basis of three form entry first and middle schools, or two form entry first schools and four form entry middle schools.

79. With the exception of small schools in rural areas and voluntary schools, combined first and middle schools are undesirable.

80. Further study should be made of the educational characteristics of schools of different sizes, and the economic data should be analysed on well matched samples of   D.E.S.
schools.

Chapter 14

Education in Rural Areas

81. Schools with an age range of 5 to 11 should usually have at least three classes, each covering two age groups.

82. If the age range is extended to 12, further teaching help may be needed to provide adequately for the older children.

83. A two tier system of primary education is preferable in the country as in the towns. Greater flexibility will be needed in the age of transfer to meet local circumstances and to fit the needs of individual children.

84. One or two class first schools or annexes should be provided for younger children who would otherwise have a long journey to school.   L.E.As.

85. Teachers' aides should be employed in small rural schools.

86. Teachers in rural schools need help from advisers and advisory teachers, and opportunities for regular association with other teachers and schools.

Chapter 16

Children Learning in School

87. There should be recurring national surveys of attainment similar to that undertaken in reading by the Department of Education, and those carried out by the N.F.E.R. in reading and mathematics.   D.E.S. N.F.E.R.

88. Primary schools should hear from secondary schools how their children compare over a period with children from other schools.   SCHOOLS

Chapter 17

A. Religious Education

89. Parents should be told when their children are admitted to school of their rights of excusal from the Act of Worship and from religious education.

90. There should be more freedom in the interpretation of the law on the Act of Worship and it should not necessarily be conducted by the head teacher.   SCHOOLS

91. Further enquiry should be made into the aspects of religious faith which can be presented to young children.

92. Further in-service training should be provided to familiarise teachers with modern thinking on religious education.

Chapter 19

The Child in the School Community

93. Decisions on punishment should generally be left to the professional judgement of the individual teacher acting within the policy of the school.   SCHOOLS

94. The infliction of physical pain as a method of punishment in primary schools should be forbidden. Schools
(*) Regulations, which apply only to maintained schools, should be amended accordingly.   D.E.S.

(*) 95. The Secretary of State should be given power to deny registration to any independent school in which the infliction of physical pain is a recognised method of punishment. Until such time as change in the law can be made, no   D.E.S. INDEPENDENT SCHOOL ASSOCIATIONS

independent school in which this practice obtains should be recognised as efficient, and the professional associations of the independent schools should endeavour to ensure its discontinuance in non-recognised schools.

Chapter 20

How Primary Schools are Organised

96. We recommend a combination of individual group and class work and welcome the trend towards individual learning.

97. The class should remain the basic unit of school organisation, particularly for the younger children; even so, children should have access to more than one teacher and teachers should work in close association.   TEACHERS

98. Experiments should be tried in associating two or three classes of the older children—up to about 100 children in the care of three teachers. Some experiments might treat the large group as a social unit.

99. The maximum size of primary school classes should be reduced. Experiments to test the effects of small classes and generous staffing should be established.   D.E.S.

100. We welcome unstreaming in the infant school and hope that it will continue to spread through the age groups of the junior school.   TEACHERS

101. Flexibility in the length of the school day and the spacing of the school year should be encouraged.   L.E.As. D.E.S.

Chapter 21

Handicapped Children in Ordinary Schools

102. Early and accurate identification of handicapped children from birth onwards is essential. Teachers need to be alert to children showing difficulty and to arrange for them to have expert examination without delay.   L.E.As. L.H.As. SCHOOLS

103. Assessment of handicap should be a continuing process in which teachers, doctors, psychologists and parents must co-operate as a team.

104. A counselling service is needed for the parents of handicapped children.   L.E.As. L.H.As.

105. A detailed enquiry should be made into the needs of handicapped children including slow learners and the provision made for them.   D.E.S.

106. The term "slow learner" should be substituted for "educationally subnormal".   D.E.S.

107. Teachers in training should be equipped to help handicapped children as far as they can.   COLLEGES of EDUCATION

Chapter 22

The Education of Gifted Children

RESEARCH BODIES

108. Long term studies should be made on the needs and achievements of gifted children.

Chapter 23

The Staffing of the School

COLLEGES of EDUCATION

109. Those who are concerned with appointing teachers should do their utmost to persuade all those who have been trained for primary work not to transfer to secondary schools.

L.E.As.

(£) 110. A larger number of training courses for teachers of children from three to nine should be provided, and students persuaded into them; colleges of education should emphasise work with young children more heavily in infant-junior and junior-secondary courses. In-service training for married women returners should stress work with young children.

D.E.S.

COLLEGES of EDUCATION

111. If this persuasion is not sufficiently effective, it may be necessary to rely on a selective quota system.

112. Continuing study should be undertaken of the right proportion of teachers to pupils of different ages.

D.E.S.

113. As a general rule, the maximum size of primary classes should be the same as that in the first two or three years of the secondary school, this principle to be taken into account as teachers are recruited for the raising of the school leaving age.

L.E.As.
D.E.S.

Chapter 24

The Deployment of Staff

114. More men are needed in first schools. Prospective men head teachers or deputies of first or combined schools should have had direct experience or in-service training in infant as well as junior work. A sufficient number of women heads and deputies should continue to be appointed.

L.E.As.

115. Neither class size nor the pupil-teacher ratio gives a sufficient picture of the state of a school. Both should be used in reporting conditions and defining objectives. Separate returns should be made for schools of different sizes. Head teachers should be included in the ratio.

D.E.S.

(£) 116. More generous staffing should be given to schools satisfying certain requirements which we specify.

117. Satisfactory conditions of part-time service need to be negotiated, and local registers of "immobile" teachers should be compiled.

L.E.As.
D.E.S.

118. Part-time teachers should serve in well staffed as well as understaffed schools to release full-time teachers for more difficult areas. L.E.As.

119. More profitable use should be made of meals assistants, secretaries and welfare assistants and in smaller schools their duties might be combined.

(£) 120. Trained teachers' aides in ratio of one full-time aide to 60–80 children (two infant classes) and one aide to 120–160 children (four junior classes) (except in educational priority areas) should be employed in primary schools under supervision of qualified teachers to provide them L.E.As. with help within the classroom. The condition of service D.E.S. of aides should be regulated by local education authorities but discretion in the matter of their duties should be left to head teachers. A national scheme for the employment of aides should be accompanied by an assurance that objectives in teacher-pupil ratios will not be adversely affected. Authorities which are well staffed should be encouraged to experiment with different ways of using ancillary help.

(£) 121. Nursery assistants and teachers' aides should be on a higher salary scale than welfare and meals assistants.

(£) 122. In exceptional circumstances qualified teachers and L.E.As. teachers' aides should be associated for the supervision of larger groups of children than those laid down by Regulations and the additional responsibility of the teachers should be recognised by the payment of an allowance.

123. Schools should enlist the voluntary help of parents and other members of the community both in school and SCHOOLS for out of school activities, provided such help is at the invitation and under the strict control of the head teacher.

(£) 124. Head teachers ought to teach. Those in charge of a class should be given part-time teaching and secretarial help.

(£) 125. In bigger schools part-time teaching help should be provided for deputy heads and holders of graded posts so that they may assist the head with guidance of probationers and students, interviews with parents and in other ways.

126. The planning of schemes of work should increasingly be undertaken by assistant teachers. L.E.As.

127. The present review of the points system should pay D.E.S. attention to the need for reducing the turnover in school staffs.

128. Authorities should consult head teachers about the filling of staff vacancies to ensure a proper balance in the staff as far as possible.

(£) 129. Authorities should use more the powers they have to appoint deputy heads in schools with less than 200 on roll.

130. Schools need inspection as well as advice.

(£) 131. There is need for a greater number of local authority advisers with special knowledge of primary education. Some authorities may need to combine for this.

132. There should be a general review of advisory services.

133. Advisory posts should be established for such developing subjects as mathematics, science and drama, and in English and religious education. Experiments should be tried in appointing advisers who combine knowledge in two or three subjects with interest in primary education.

Chapter 25

The Training of Primary School Teachers

134. There should be a full enquiry into the system of training teachers.

135. The number of courses in which future teachers are D.E.S. trained side by side with entrants to other social science professions should be increased.

136. The proportion of students admitted to colleges of education without an "O" level pass in mathematics is too high: the proportion of students who have specialised in the sixth form in mathematics and science is too low. Efforts should be made to improve qualifications in these SCHOOLS subjects.

137. More men teachers are needed in primary schools and the attention of the secondary schools should be drawn to this.

138. Mature students have proved their value; the net- D.E.S. work of day colleges and "outposts" should be extended.

139. More graduates are required in primary schools, and COLLS, DEPTs. & more facilities should be provided for their training. INSTS. of ED.

140. Arrangements should be made to inform schools of COLLEGES of the record of their former pupils in colleges of education. EDUCATION

141. Graduates should be required to receive professional D.E.S. training if they are going to teach in primary schools.

142. There should be closer partnership and contact COLLS. of ED. between schools and colleges. SCHOOLS

143. The agreement between the A.T.C.D.E. and the National Union of Students on college discipline is welcome: all colleges should put it into operation. Colleges of education should develop close associations with schools with special difficulties. COLLS. of ED.

144. The arrangements for teaching practice should take account of the needs of the schools. Final responsibility for supervision of students should rest with the colleges, but schools can play a bigger part.

145. More joint appointments to college and school staffs should be made. **L.E.As.**
COLLEGES OF EDUCATION

146. In order to reduce variations in standards local education authorities should be informed of the number of teachers, authority by authority, whose probation is extended or who are declared unsuitable. **BURNHAM PELHAM**

D.E.S.

147. The normal period of probation for untrained graduates and for teachers trained outside the U.K. should be two years. **L.E.As.**
D.E.S.

148. Local education authorities should pay the travelling expenses of students who visit the schools to which they are appointed before they take up work; more should start work in the summer as soon as the examinations are over.

149. Graded posts should be available in large schools for teachers who supervise students and probationers and maintain contacts with colleges of education. All local education authorities should designate officers to deal with young teachers. In smaller schools holders of graded posts should have responsibility for students and probationers. **L.E.As.**

150. The B.Ed. degree courses should be made available to serving teachers. **COLLEGES of EDUCATION**

151. The expansion of one year advanced and one term full-time courses should continue. Every teacher should have a substantial period of in-service training at least every five years. **L.E.As.**
D.E.S.

(£) 152. A network of residential teachers' courses should be developed. **D.E.S.**

153. Local education authorities should be asked to submit plans for in-service training. Regional co-operation should be encouraged. **L.E.As.**
D.E.S.

154. Short courses should be arranged for new or prospective head teachers and deputies.

(£) 155. Teachers should not be financially penalised for attending short courses. **L.E.As.**

Chapter 26

The Training of Nursery Assistants and Teachers' Aides

156. Entry qualifications to training should be the same for both services. Younger candidates should give evidence of a good general education. For the older women some evidence of further education or relevant experience is necessary. **D.E.S.**
M.O.H.
HOME OFFICE

157. Younger students should undertake a two year course of training, three fifths of which would be spent on practical work. Suitable candidates of 21 years of age and

over should be permitted to qualify after one year of training of which four fifths will be spent on practical work. Longer part-time training might be arranged for some students.

158. Courses should be developed by each training centre within the general lines laid down by a central examining body who would moderate qualifications throughout the country. The responsible government departments and other bodies concerned should consider the creation of a single body to cover the training of teachers' aides, nursery assistants and of workers in other services at present within the N.N.E.B. field of interest. Local authority and teacher representatives as well as those concerned with teacher training should be members.

D.E.S.

159. Aides and assistants during training should receive the rate at present paid to N.N.E.B. students. Aides should be regarded as part of the school staff during training. Nursery students in nursery groups ought not to be regarded as part of the staffing complement.

(£)

160. Teacher training should be open to suitable assistants and aides, and colleges and institutes of education should take account of their training and experience with children where they lack the minimum educational qualifications.

INSTITUTES of EDUCATION

161. The Whitley salary structure might make provision for experienced nursery assistants to receive a responsibility allowance for being in charge of isolated nursery groups.

(£)

D.E.S.

Chapter 27

Independent Primary Schools

(*) 162. The Department of Education and Science should consider taking steps which would require all independent schools to state on their prospectuses whether the schools were recognised or registered and what this implies. The Department of Education and Science should reconsider the terms "recognised" and "registered" and try to devise more informative ones.

D.E.S.

163. The Secretary of State's powers to serve Notices of Complaint on independent schools should be based on more stringent criteria. The construction of "objectionable" should be widened to include any conditions, physical or educational, in which children's welfare was not thought to be adequately safeguarded.

(*)

164. All head teachers of independent schools should be qualified teachers. After a date to be specified, only qualified teachers should be appointed as heads in new schools, or when there is a change of head teacher.

(*)

165. In-service courses should wherever possible allow some places for teachers from independent schools. The independent schools themselves should take steps through their professional organisations to increase the facilities for in-service training for teachers in independent schools.

L.E.As.
D.E.S.
PROFESSIONAL
ASSOCIATIONS
of
INDEPENDENT
SCHOOLS

Chapter 28

Primary School Buildings and Equipment

(£)
166. The Government should make additional money available for a building programme of minor works over seven years starting in 1971 at an annual cost of £7–10 million designed to rid primary schools of the worst deficiencies.

D.E.S.

(£)
167. More money should be available for minor projects. To enable small jobs to be carried out more quickly, more flexibility on expenditure as between major and minor building projects should be allowed. Authorities saving money on individual major projects should be permitted to spend it on minor projects.

168. The Department should undertake detailed exercises on the relationship between costs and the provision of essential amenities.

D.E.S.

169. One of the Foundations might institute a competition on the lines of the Civic Trust Awards for imaginative but inexpensive improvements to old schools.

170. The Department should undertake a careful study of present requirements for nursery education which may well be lavish in some respects. A building project by the Development Group would help local authorities in designing for the expansion of nursery education.

D.E.S.

171. Continuing review is needed of the whole structure of cost limits and regulations particularly in view of the sharpness in variations between the different stages.

172. Teachers should be more directly involved in the design of schools.

L.E.As.

173. Much further thought is needed on siting and planning schools so that they are more accessible to parents and the community, and free from traffic dangers and other nuisances.

L.E.As.
L.H.As. & L.P.As.

(£)
174. Local education authorities should take steps to remove the inequalities in allowances to schools. To bring up all allowances to the average figure without reducing the more generous allowances would cost between half a million pounds and one million pounds a year.

L.E.As.

175. Schools with special difficulties should have extra allowances.

176. Although bulk buying of some items may be sensible head teachers should be given more freedom in spending.

Chapter 29

The Status and Government of Primary Education

177. Primary school teachers should be represented on local education committees and on the sub-committees L.E.As and advisory committees that specifically concern primary education. Machinery for consultation with teachers on policy changes affecting them is desirable.

178. Officials of local education authorities should be easily accessible to head and assistant teachers for the discussion of matters which might affect the life, work and morale of the schools.

179. School managers should be appointed on the basis of their genuine concern with education and readiness to devote time and trouble to their managerial duties irrespective of party allegiance. Authorities should ensure a reasonably good flow of new appointments.

180. There should be representatives on the managing body of parents of children attending the school.

181. As far as it is compatible with effective management, all individual primary schools should have their own managing bodies.

182. Where several primary schools are grouped, the L.E.As. groups should be as small as possible.

183. Managers' meetings should take place on the school premises, and managers' names should be posted in a prominent position in each primary school together with the names of any nominating bodies.

184. Local authorities should bring the powers of managers in primary schools into line with those of governors of secondary schools.

185. Managers need to be more actively concerned in the school to further relations between school and community and to serve as a support for the head teachers.

186. The responsibilities of managers must be increased if candidates of the right calibre are to be attracted.

187. The head teacher should be fully conversant with the managers' views on the running of the school and vice versa. He should attend all managers' meetings unless he MANAGERS is himself the subject of discussion. The managers should consult him at all points.

188. Overlap in membership between governing bodies of secondary schools and the managing bodies of their L.E.As. contributory primary schools is preferable to the establishment of joint governing and managing bodies.

189. Managing bodies in considering the merit of candidates for headships and deputy headships should seek the expert advice of officials.

190. The interviewing of candidates for headships and deputy headships should be a genuine part of the selection process and managers should have some knowledge of the techniques of interviewing. All posts for headships and deputy headships should be open to talent from all parts of the country.

L.E.As.
MANAGERS

191. Head teachers should be given the opportunity of saying what qualities and qualifications they want in their staff and take part in all stages of selection. They should also be able to give views on the specific duties attached to every post of special responsibility, and to recommend members of their staff for such posts. They should be consulted about the needs of their schools when the appointments of probationers are being considered.

192. Head teachers and their staff should always be consulted by local education authorities about major or minor capital works involving their schools and be free to comment on and make suggestions on alterations at all stages.

193. Heads should be consulted over the use of their schools in or out of school hours.

L.E.As.

194. Heads should be allowed discretion in deciding in what circumstances they or members of their staff should be allowed occasional absences from school. Regulations about taking children on educational visits should be restricted to those circumstances where insurance and legal liability makes it necessary.

(£) 195. Secretarial help, a telephone, a typewriter and duplicating equipment should be available in all schools.

196. Assistant staff should play as large a part as possible in the planning and organisation of school life. Assistants should have access to managers and to local education authorities.

L.E.As.
SCHOOLS

197. All unnecessary and unjustified differences of treatment between primary and secondary education should be eliminated.

L.E.As.
D.E.S.

III. A NOTE ON OUR METHODS OF WORK, AND ACKNOWLEDGEMENTS

1244. The Council were asked in August 1963 "to consider primary education in all its aspects and the transition to secondary education".

1245. Our terms of reference were wide and we must begin by acknowledging our debt to all who have helped us. The fact that we cannot mention them all individually does not lessen our gratitude. The list of witnesses alone which follows in Annex C is some measure of the response that met our request for information and statements of views. Their written evidence, in many cases supplemented by oral evidence, went deeply into the questions at issue and gave us much information on current practice all over the country. Copies of written evidence received have been lodged in the Department of Education and Science Library. In addition we were helped on many issues by the response of the 2,500 teachers who answered our questionnaire (Appendix 1, Volume 2).

1246. We could not adequately have covered the many aspects involved had we worked only as a full Council. We began our first year by dividing into two study groups and visited nurseries, infant and junior schools, and the lower forms of secondary schools. We also formed eight working parties and groups to study different aspects of our work in depth. These working parties, too, visited schools, colleges of education and some university departments of education. As the enquiry went forward further visits were made in the course of which more specific and detailed issues were discussed. Many of the judgements reached in our Report have been tested and affected by what we saw and heard as we visited schools about the country. In all we visited 267 schools and 11 colleges of education in England and in Scotland. To the children and individual teachers who received us into their classrooms, to the members and officials of local education committees who welcomed us, we are indeed grateful. They answered our questions willingly and our informal meetings with them were most valuable. The Council, the Working Parties, the Working Groups and Study Groups between them met 107 times and all of their meetings occupied the equivalent of 116 days. Four hundred and sixty-five papers on different subjects were received, leaving aside the evidence submitted by outside bodies.

1247. We wished to know something of the current thinking about primary education in some other countries. We were fortunate in being able to visit some Scottish schools and schools and other establishments in countries outside the United Kingdom. For arranging these visits and for the hospitality received during them we are grateful to the Royal Danish Ministry of Education, the French Ministry of Education and L'Institut Pedagogique Nationale, the Polish Ministry of Education, the Royal Swedish Board of Education, the Ministries of Education of the U.S.S.R. and Russian Soviet Federative Socialist Republic (R.S.F.S.R.) and to many universities, schools and school districts in the U.S.A. Our visits were necessarily brief and we have not thought it right to produce accounts of them because we could not do justice to the structure and content of primary education in each of these countries in the short time at our disposal. The visits served, however, to put our own problems and achievements into perspective and to make us examine more closely some of our own assumptions.

1248. In Annex C we list the names of those who received us so kindly in our own country and abroad and hope that they will take this as further evidence of our gratitude to them. It was interesting to find how, despite the different philosophies of the various countries, we were all concerned with many of the same issues. We are indebted to our hosts and to the numerous officials of the Foreign Office, the British Council and the Department of Education and Science who made these visits possible.

1249. At the beginning of our work, we commissioned various studies and research, reports and full acknowledgements of which will be found in Volume 2. We must thank here Mr. G. F. Peaker, C.B.E., the architect of the multiple regression analyses in the National Survey which has so greatly influenced our thinking. We were fortunate in having a ready response from all of those whom we asked to make research studies of which we have been able to make use at many points of our enquiry.

1250. We should not have been able to make our study "in all its aspects" without the help of those who administer and those who are expert in primary education. Our thanks are due particularly to those members of the Department of Education and Science who have given us so freely of their time and knowledge. Equally we have been helped by individual members and by the accumulated experience of the whole of H.M. Inspectorate. The disinterested advice which was given to us was of great value and fundamental to our thinking. We wish to record our special debt to Mr. D. G. Ayerst, C.B.E., the late Miss V. L. Gray, H.M.I., Dr. K. Whitmore and to Dr. G. A. V. Morgan, H.M.I., Secretary to the Welsh Central Advisory Council. Mr. J. E. H. Blackie, C.B., H.M.I., Mr. D. H. Leadbetter, C.B., Miss E. M. McDougall, H.M.I. and Miss M. E. Nicholls, H.M.I., acted as our assessors. Their wide knowledge of the complicated structure and pattern of education in this country, and of primary education in particular, was of the greatest help to our deliberations and in guiding us through difficulties. We were fortunate in having for the larger part of our enquiries the wise counsel of Miss N. Goddard, Inspector of Schools, I.L.E.A. Her imaginative guidance on the education of the younger children contributed greatly to our studies. For a shorter time we were greatly helped by Mr. D. T. Jones, O.B.E., H.M.I.

1251. We owe a large debt to Miss S. M. C. Duncan, H.M.I., who has been associated with our work from the beginning. Her deep understanding of the problems under discussion was a great strength to us and she was our main source of educational advice. The burden of the organisation of our work fell on our Secretary, Mr. M. Kogan. His clarity of thought made a major contribution to our work and, in particular, he took the responsibility for advising us on the economic aspects of our investigation. To him and to Miss Duncan we wish to record our deep obligation. They initiated and handled a vast volume of material and worked under pressure for over three years. Our enquiry has been so many sided that we could never have dealt with it adequately without their far-sightedness, their energy and their knowledge. Our discussions with them have stimulated our thought and warned us of pitfalls.

1252. We were fortunate in having as Assistant Secretaries, Mr. N. Summers from 1963 to 1965 and Miss C. K. Burke from 1964 to 1966 who met the heavy demands made on them with great competence. The Secretariat were

ANMCE

supported by an industrious and efficient team, to whom we are most grateful; Mr. R. G. Ross, Mr. R. H. Sinclair, Miss S. A. Swinburne, Mr. D. Dobbie, Mr. D. W. Brown, Miss M. T. McFall and Mrs. A. Reich. Skilled assistance from many people was provided by the Department of Education and Science for dealing with all the necessary paperwork.

(Signed)

Bridget Plowden (*Chairman*)

John Newsom (*Deputy Chairman*)

H. G. Armstrong

A. J. Ayer

M. F. M. Bailey

Moyra Bannister

M. Brearley

I. C. R. Byatt

J. P. Campbell

D. V. Donnison

Z. E. Dix

Charles Gittins

S. Ena Grey

E. W. Hawkins

E. M. Parry

Alan Puckey

T. H. F. Raison

E. V. Smith

R. T. Smith

J. M. Tanner

L. L. Thwaytes

T. Harold Tunn

H. Martin Wilson

F. M. White

Michael Young

M. Kogan (*Secretary*)

NOTE OF RESERVATION ON NURSERY EDUCATION (CHAPTER 9)

BY MRS. M. BANNISTER

1. Instead of a nation-wide extension of nursery education as proposed by the Council, I suggest that all efforts should be made to provide play centres and encourage play groups, except in "educational priority areas" where nursery schools are justified. These play centres should be open all day and all year and should cater for a much wider age range. Mothers should play a full part in helping to run them on a pattern similar to the 600 already in successful existence.

2. If harm comes to a child it is too late to rescue him at three. Play centres and groups where much younger children could be brought together would go some way towards mitigating such ill effects so that they could all enjoy a rich play life. I would hope that these groups might have the help eventually of a peripatetic and highly trained teacher so that the mothers could benefit from her expertise and the children come earlier under her benevolent eye.

3. Nursery education as proposed by the Council tends to disrupt the mother, child and sibling relationship.

4. It is unlikely that the scheme as proposed would produce a stable staff of real quality. An earlier and higher marriage rate will lead to a reduction in the number of experienced single women who at the moment make such a valuable contribution and help to form a stable framework.

5. The nursery assistants will be drawn from the same source as the nursing profession, which is already gravely understaffed, and cannot afford the loss of any potential nurses. Nor does it seem wise to divert any teachers from the primary schools to effect nursery education.

6. The expansion of nursery education will make for an increase in working mothers and it will be difficult for the mothers to care for their children in the holidays unless special arrangements are made by industry and the professional bodies. Any such arrangement must introduce another element of instability.

7. I am convinced by the evidence concerning the harm that may come to pre-school children of working mothers. Therefore the present increase in working mothers seems to me undesirable on educational grounds and, except where economic necessities are paramount, it should be discouraged.

8. The scheme as proposed by the Council does little to enable mothers to participate actively in the early school experiences of their children. The mothers' loneliness and boredom are also major social problems which play centres and groups might help to solve.

9. Even if fees were charged they would cover only a small fraction of the real cost.

10. It is an open question whether the money which it is proposed to spend on nursery education in "educational priority areas" might not be better spent on housing. Since all our evidence suggests the quality of the home has the decisive influence on the child's educational future, the money might be better spent on improved housing and means directed towards improving maternal care.

NOTE OF RESERVATION ON THE ORGANISATION OF SERVICES FOR UNDER FIVES (CHAPTER 9) BY PROFESSOR D. V. DONNISON, SIR JOHN NEWSOM AND DR. M. YOUNG.

Day nurseries should be as much within the educational service as nursery schools, and responsible to education authorities. The problems that will arise through confining the under threes to day nurseries and providing all day nursery schools for the over threes will be formidable enough anyway, but less so if the responsibility for the reorganisation rests with one authority rather than two. Any joint authority is liable to have more joint than authority about it. Moreover, the trend of modern thinking is to emphasise the educational needs rather than the purely physical health of children, including the under threes; and in accordance with this trend it would be appropriate for nurseries, whatever the age of their children, to be part of the educational rather than of the health service.

NOTE OF RESERVATION ON PARENTAL CONTRIBUTION TO THE COSTS OF NURSERY EDUCATION (CHAPTER 9). BY PROFESSOR A. J. AYER, DR. I. C. R. BYATT, PROFESSOR D. V. DONNISON, MR. E. W. HAWKINS, LADY PLOWDEN, MR. T. H. F. RAISON, BRIGADIER L. L. THWAYTES AND DR. M. YOUNG.

1. Chapter 9 notes that the Hadow Report recommended nursery schools in 1933 and that the Education Act of 1944 gave them the blessing of Parliament; yet it does not draw what seems to us the obvious lesson. Why has nothing effective been done? Quite simply, there have not been enough resources, in teachers or buildings. If that is true of the past it certainly remains true of the present. Resources are relatively as scarce as ever. The prospects of nurseries are not therefore that much better than they were in 1944, and will not become so without the crucial further proposal we make here. Extra resources are needed, and (apart perhaps from some voluntary and private nurseries which will charge anyway) will not be forthcoming on a large scale unless the amount of money being spent on education is substantially increased. The necessity for this is shown in Chapter 31. The answer we suggest is a parental contribution. If nurseries were the Council's over-riding priority the situation would perhaps be different. They are not.

2. Our suggestion is advanced as much in the interests of children whose parents cannot afford to pay as it is of others. Without a parental contribution we fear that nursery education will not be extended at all and such children be no better off than they are today. With it, we can be more optimistic, and, if the hopes are realised, there will be nursery schools which can be attended by the children of poorer parents, in and out of educational priority areas. They are often just the ones who could benefit most. Charging the richer will be a means of helping the poorer. Charging those with smaller families will be a means of helping those with larger.

3. What other sources of finance are there? We cannot be confident that, of the public money available for social services, less should necessarily be spent on housing or old age pensions so that more could be spent on nursery schools. Rates and taxes cannot be raised expressly for the purpose. We

recognise that in public services benefits and contribution to cost cannot, and should not, be precisely equated. Public services exist where one cannot, and should not, try to. But the resistance of people to pay higher taxes is still an important consideration. Pensioners and others would scarcely welcome such an impost just for the purpose of financing nurseries. This is all the more so because a few of the mothers who will send their children to nursery schools will be able in consequence to go out to work part-time and add to the income of themselves and their families, and a great deal could be made of those few by the opponents of nursery schools.

Facing up to affluence

4. To the majority of the Council a principle that should be sacrosanct appears to be at stake. Maintained schools have always been free, and therefore should always remain so. But the principle crystallised at a time when incomes were a good deal lower. Parents are now more affluent; they are more interested in education. Today they are for the most part able and willing to contribute, and their willingness to do so could be used as a lever for getting a more general service. Particular proposals for educational improvement should surely be considered to see if on their merits it would be right or not to ask parents to contribute.

5. If this be the approach, contributions for nursery schools recommend themselves. Where the community makes education compulsory it is in general right that the community at large should pay. But this is not proposed for nursery education. It is not to be compulsory. Not to charge would therefore be to create injustice as between parents who do not choose to make use of nursery schools and those who do. The parents who do not would be paying, through their rates or taxes, for a service to other parents, sometimes wealthier parents, who take advantage of the new schools. Nor is nursery education to be universal for many years. It will develop in some districts more rapidly than in others. Not to charge would be to create further injustice between people in one district, who do not yet have nursery schools but have to pay for them through taxes, and people in other districts who do have them. In these two ways nursery schools will be different from most other maintained schools, and, if they differ, so should their finance.

6. Another argument is that payment—up to 13s. 6d a day—is already made for children attending day nurseries, and for much private baby-minding as well. Day nurseries constitute a precedent on which we lean. The majority do not suggest that charges for day nurseries should cease. The consequence would be that parents would pay for children up to three but at this age, though the service would be much the same, charges would be dropped. To act as we propose on this and to bring nursery schools into line with day nurseries would be more sensible, and should lead to more of the children who are at present privately minded for a charge being given an educational experience in a nursery school. It is also worth noting that in nearly all other countries visited by members of the C.A.C., including Denmark, France, Poland, Sweden and the U.S.S.R., there were charges for nurseries. We cannot see that Britain should on this stand apart.

Remission of fees

7. We are naturally in favour of remissions of charges for those who cannot afford to pay. For our main purpose in proposing charges at all for those who

can afford them is, as we have said, to secure nursery schools which would not otherwise be there at all for those who cannot. The suggestion is that the standard charge should be the 5s. per half day which is reckoned as the full cost (see Table 41), but if some l.e.a.'s could get the cost down to less the charges would also be less. Such a sum would clearly be beyond the means of families with low incomes or several children, and these should get free places. The larger the number of children, the higher the level of income that should qualify a family for remission. We further recommend that as soon as charges and remissions are introduced (even experimentally) steps should be taken by means of research to find out whether children who should be in nursery schools are not there because their parents are being deterred by the charges. The system for remission should be revised if necessary in the light of the results of the research. Whatever happens, all nursery schools in educational priority areas should be free to begin with in order to make sure that the children who need them most are not kept out. We propose that fees should be introduced as soon as possible in some other areas so that the size of demand (given charges and remissions) could be estimated as a basis for general national planning.

8. Nursery education needs definition. We do not think it would be right to charge fees for schools given the label of nursery, and not to children of the same age in schools called infant. Age should be the criterion, not type of school. We recommend that fees should therefore be charged for all children under five, irrespective of which sort of school they are in. It also follows that children of over five in nursery schools, who will be plentiful once the single date of entry is introduced, should not be charged.

9. If resources were more plentiful we would not favour charges. This is particularly because some parents who cannot afford to pay may be too proud to accept remission and therefore keep their children away. But new traditions can be created. Few parents are now too proud to accept State support for the education of their children in universities. If in universities, why not in nursery schools?

NOTE OF RESERVATION ON RELIGIOUS EDUCATION (SECTION A OF CHAPTER 17), BY PROFESSOR A. J. AYER, DR. I. C. R. BYATT, PROFESSOR D. V. DONNISON, MRS. E. V. SMITH, PROFESSOR J. M. TANNER AND DR. M. YOUNG

1. *The Teaching of Theology*

1. We share the view of our colleagues that the present state of religious education in primary schools is not satisfactory, but do not think that their proposals go far enough in the way of reform. In our view the root of the trouble is that religious education, if it is taken at all seriously, is bound to involve theology; and theology is both too recondite and too controversial a subject to be suitable for inclusion in the curriculum of primary schools. It cannot be properly adapted either to the understanding of children of this age or to the methods by which we are proposing that they should be taught.

R

2. This does not mean that we wish children to grow up in ignorance of the content of Christian beliefs. Whether they end by accepting or rejecting Christian theology, they ought to be given the opportunity to acquire an adequate knowledge of all that it implies. They should be presented with the arguments in its favour and the arguments against it and allowed to decide whether they find it credible. It is, however, absurd to suppose that the average, or even the very gifted child, is capable of appreciating these arguments before he is 12 years old.

II. *The Cultural Factor.*

3. There is, indeed, more to the study of Christianity than its theology. We believe that, apart from its theological implications, the Bible ought to be studied as literature both on its own account and on account of the literature and art which it has inspired. But the English of the Authorized Version is not easy reading for a modern child, and it is doubtful whether its literary quality can be appreciated until the child's mastery of English has at least attained the secondary level. There is of course no reason why younger children should not be told Bible stories, just as, for very much the same cultural motives, they should be told the stories and legends of classical antiquity

III. *Religion and Morals.*

4. It may be argued that the main function of religious education in primary schools is to supply the children with a moral basis which they may not all be able to derive from their home life. What is true in this argument is that the school has a considerable part to play in inducing the children to accept an adequate set of moral, social and aesthetic values: and, independently of their religious outlook, both parents and teachers are likely to agree very largely as to what at least the moral values ought to be. On the other hand, we doubt if it is either necessary or desirable to insist on tying this aspect of education to theology. We do not deny that religious belief has served as a means of enforcing compliance with a moral code; but all too often the motive to which it has mainly appealed in this connection has been the motive of fear.

5. If religious belief is to serve moral education otherwise than as a weapon of terror, it can only be through its providing children with models for them to imitate, and the idea of a superior guide whom they will freely choose to follow. In this connection the force of the moral example which the story of Christ can be used to furnish is certainly not to be discounted. But no story is likely to have so strong effect upon children's conduct as the examples which they personally encounter. The moral benefit which a young child derives from his schooling will be a function rather of the whole atmosphere of the school, and of the personalities of the teachers, than of any form of homiletics. Even so it is reasonable to assume that something is gained by giving him examples from history or legend. But from this point of view, the theological content of the Christian story is of minimal importance. On the contrary, since the point of such examples is that the child is encouraged to identify himself with the hero, the lesson is more likely to have its intended appeal if it represents Christ as an exceptional human being, rather than as an incarnate deity.

IV. THE POSITION OF TEACHERS

6. We have been told that most primary school teachers do not have any objection to giving religious instruction. Nevertheless there is a minority of teachers, both male and female, who would prefer not to give it, whether because they are agnostics, or because they disapprove of the type of religious instruction which they would be expected to give, or because, while they themselves are Christians, they think that religious instruction ought not to be given in primary schools or that they are not fit to give it. Such persons have the legal right to opt out, but we have reason to believe that some of them do not exercise this right because they fear that to do so would prejudice their careers. In particular it is believed, apparently with some justification, that teachers who are known not to be willing to give religious instruction are less likely to be appointed to headships, partly on the ground that they will be unfitted to conduct the morning assembly which is legally required to constitute an Act of Worship. Now it is surely wrong that teachers of this kind should be put in a position where they are either denied access to the posts to which their talents and service entitle them or forced into hypocrisy.

V. MINORITY GROUPS

7. While the inference to be drawn from public opinion surveys is that most people wish the present provisions for compulsory religious instruction in schools to remain in force, there is a minority of parents who for one reason or another, but most often because of their own religious beliefs or disbeliefs, would prefer their children not to receive the kind of religious teaching which the primary schools now give. These parents have the right to withdraw their children from religious instruction, but in many cases do not exercise it either because they do not know that they possess it or because they fear that it will prejudice the children's standing in the school. Moreover the children themselves do not like to be put in a position which sets them apart from their fellows. It is, indeed, arguable that it is beneficial for the children of Mahommedan, Jewish or agnostic parents to be obliged to learn something about Christianity; but again this is an argument that applies better to the stage of secondary education. For younger children, the effects of the conflict between the ostensible views of their teachers and the views of their parents may not be altogether healthy.

VI. A SUGGESTED ALTERNATIVE

8. It has been suggested by one of our members that our conflicting views on the subject of religious instruction, could be very largely reconciled if we adopted the proposal that parents should be given the option of enrolling their children for religious instruction or for a secular course in moral and social education. It would also be open to teachers to choose which of those forms of instruction they wished to give. We agree that if religious instruction is to remain a subject in primary schools it should be left to the parents to enrol their children for it and left also to the teachers to volunteer to give it; or, in other words, that opting in should be substituted for the present system of opting out. On the other hand, though the idea of there being a second alternative is attractive to some of us, we have yet to be convinced that it is viable. It is not easy to see what form the syllabus of moral and social

s

education could take. We are far from wishing to deny the importance of this branch of education but we think that it should arise out of the general life of the school.

VII. CONCLUSIONS

9. (a) As we see it, the balance of argument strongly favours the conclusion that religious instruction is not a suitable subject to be taken in primary schools. We therefore wish to see legislation enacted by which it would cease to be an obligatory part of the curriculum. We are aware that public opinion may not be on our side, but in this instance, as in that of corporal punishment, we do not believe that this consideration should debar us from advocating what we think is right.

(b) If religious instruction is to remain obligatory, we support our colleagues in recommending that the moral element should predominate over the theological. We agree that the examples given should not be exclusively Christian. They should be drawn also from the lives and teaching of other religious teachers, like Buddha, and of outstandingly good men from Socrates onwards.

(c) Whether or not religious instruction remains a compulsory subject Assembly should be legally dissociated from the Act of Worship, for the reasons which we have given under headings IV or V. We are aware that in many schools Assembly is so conducted as to be almost devoid of any religious content, but the fact that the provisions of the law are successfully avoided does not appear to us to be a sufficient reason for maintaining it.

(d) If the children raise metaphysical questions about the origin of the Universe, as even very young children are likely quite to do, the teacher should give them his own opinion, honestly and undogmatically. He would not be failing in his duty if he told them that the answers to these questions were not known.

NOTE OF RESERVATION ON RELIGIOUS EDUCATION (SECTION A OF CHAPTER 17) BY MR. E. W. HAWKINS AND MR. M. WILSON

While not dissenting from a lot of this chapter and with great respect for much of the thoughtful R.E. work in schools, we are concerned about the difficulty which at present faces parents who wish to exercise their right under the Act of 1944 to withdraw their children from religious education. The difficulty is that withdrawal generally means withdrawal into an empty room or corridor. No alternative programme of moral or ethical education exists for such parents to choose for their children. The admittedly difficult problem of drawing up such a programme should surely be faced. One would welcome the setting up of committees of interested teachers, lecturers (and parents) within local education authorities and institutes of education to devise an alternative "Agreed Syllabus" of ethical teaching which does not rely on the sanction of religious belief. It is probable that as the work of devising such a syllabus progressed (and hitherto almost nothing at all has been attempted along these lines) what may now seem to be immense difficulties would come to assume reasonable proportions. At the infant stage the programme might not be much more than a series of well considered answers to the questions children ask and the kind of learning by example that we have outlined in paragraph 568. For older children one would hope that university and college staffs and teachers, and parents, working together, would be able to isolate those strands of experience, including children's own experience, and truth that would weave into a discipline of ethics for children that some would consider a worthwhile alternative to the traditional R.E. lessons. Even though immensely difficult, the attempt should surely be made to determine precisely what it is that we wish our children to learn of ethics in a society which is increasingly rejecting the sanction of supernatural revelation.

NOTE OF RESERVATION ON CORPORAL PUNISHMENT (CHAPTER 19) BY MISS M. F. M. BAILEY

I do not agree with the recommendation that corporal punishment should be abolished in primary schools. I believe that the practice is in any case dying out. While I deplore the use of corporal punishment and wish it to be strongly discouraged I believe that compulsory abolition will add to the difficulties experienced by the teachers coping with over-large classes in unsuitable buildings. In particular, teachers in difficult areas will be placed in an impossible position if they are forbidden to use a reasonable amount of force by way of correction, and if the children know that they are forbidden to do so.

A SUGGESTION ON THE SUPPLY AND TRAINING OF TEACHERS (CHAPTERS 23 AND 25) BY PROFESSOR A. J. AYER, DR. I. C. R. BYATT MR. E. W. HAWKINS, SIR JOHN NEWSOM, LADY PLOWDEN AND MR. T. H. F. RAISON

1. A group of us feel that, despite the value of, and the need for, a three year training course as a preparation for teaching, consideration should be given to making some adjustment in the training which could, we believe, make a very substantial contribution to improving staffing standards in the primary schools and thus to improving the quality of primary education. We put forward our suggestions with some reluctance, because the majority of the Council strongly disagree with them. We are also conscious that we have not made a full study of the system of teacher training, and we know that similar proposals have been considered before and rejected.

2. Nevertheless, we are concerned with the effect on the size of primary school classes, particularly infants classes, of the rapid and increasing wastage of young women teachers. We can expect that of every 100 women who enter the training colleges, only 47 will be in the schools after three years service and after six years only 30.*

3. During the first half of the sixties staffing standards in the primary schools scarcely improved despite an increase in the number of unqualified teachers. This lack of improvement was associated with the lengthening of the training

*National Advisory Council for the Supply and Training of Teachers, 9th Report 1965.

college course. We think it of great importance that staffing standards should be rapidly improved. But we are bound to ask whether it is justifiable to expand the colleges of education even faster than is planned only to achieve a diminishing return in women teachers staying on in the schools. We also believe that with the changing pattern of the lives of women—their early marriage and child-bearing, their subsequent length of life and increasing tendency to want to work—there is a need to look critically at the most effective way of giving them professional training so that they may be enabled to use it most productively.

4. For these reasons we suggest that the three years of teacher training, might, for some students, be divided into a basic two years with a third year further training to be taken after a few years in the schools. Thus the third year would only be taken by those who intended to stay in teaching, and the spaces released in the training colleges could be used to increase the number of teachers entering the schools or eventually for in-service training. The present courses of advanced study for teachers with at least five years experience might be the foundation for the third year's course, but there is a variety of patterns it could take. It would rarely be residential.

5. To show the effect of such a scheme we have estimated the extra teachers who might be in service if it were started in 1968 as an alternative to the present three year scheme. It provides a "short service commission" of five years for those with only two years training. We assume for purposes of calculation that two thirds of the women opt for it. We then assume that half of these opt for a third year's training and the rest leave the schools. All re-entrants with only two years basic training would take the third year. All the men and one third of the women opt for three years initial training. What all these proportions would be in practice would depend on the details of particular schemes and particularly on any changes in salary structure as a consequence of adopting any of them.

6. The scheme would provide ten thousand more teachers in the schools during the first half of the seventies. It would provide help at a time when the staffing situation will be difficult with rising numbers of children and advances the elimination of classes over 40 by three years. The additional numbers might be rather less in the second half of the seventies, but would continue to make a significant contribution to staffing standards.

7. We are confident that these extra numbers can be recruited without risking any significant deterioration in the standards of students entering the colleges of education. As the scheme would be using existing capacity we are not suggesting any addition to training costs. The present expansion of the colleges of education has created problems for the grammar schools as a significant number of their teachers have left to become training college lecturers. To take teachers from hard pressed schools in order to train students who will not make careers in teaching raises questions about the economy of the operation.

8. Many will feel that the educational disadvantages of such a scheme outweigh the benefits of more teachers. We do not agree. Indeed there are educational arguments in its favour. The two years basic course would provide a sound basis for work in the schools. Those who found, after being in the schools, that they wanted to work towards a B.Ed. would return to a third

and fourth year. They, and the other third year returners, would be able go back to theoretical study after five years experience; they would be able to reflect on and analyse their experience in school and bring mature understanding to developments in the curriculum and in teaching methods. Because of the opportunity to experience a long period of teaching and then go back to theoretical work the "sandwich" three year trained teacher might well be a better one than the continuous three year trained teacher. The two year trained teachers would only be in the schools for up to five years—which is as long as most of them would stay in any case. Especially with the greater flexibility in classroom organisation suggested in Chapter 20, they would have a valuable contribution to make in that time.

9. It is relevant to point out that nearly all the teachers whose work we commend in this report have had only two years training.

10. This note contains only suggestions; we know that there are a number of practical problems which would have to be solved before definite proposals could be made. There would be problems of salary differentials, the question of whether the third year should be at full rates of pay or on a student's grant and the question as to whether teachers would be seconded for a third year or whether they would be obliged to resign. Nevertheless we think that such a scheme deserves serious consideration by the teachers, the colleges of education, and the Secretary of State.

Annexes, Glossary and Index

ANNEX A

We were greatly helped by the evidence submitted to us by the teacher and local authority associations and by several hundred individual witnesses. Those who gave evidence are listed in Annex B. At the beginning of our enquiry we prepared a questionnaire which was sent to all witnesses as a guide to the main issues that the Council were to consider. The questionnaire is reproduced below. We also decided to send a questionnaire to a random sample of some 2,500 primary and secondary school teachers in the hope of getting their views on some of the major issues. Many of their replies proved illuminating and have been referred to in the Report. We reproduce as Appendix 1, (Volume 2) the questionnaire sent to them and the tables of their replies that proved to be of most interest.

ANNEX A

CENTRAL ADVISORY COUNCIL FOR EDUCATION (ENGLAND)

Replies to the
Secretary Central
Advisory Council
HYDe Park 7070
C.A.C. Letter No. 1.

CURZON STREET HOUSE
CURZON STREET
LONDON W.1

12th November, 1963.

I am writing to invite your Association/Union/Council/you/to give evidence to the Central Advisory Council for Education (England). As you know, the Council was reconstituted on 7th August, 1963, under the chairmanship of Lady Plowden with the following terms of reference:—

"To consider primary education in all its aspects and the
transition to secondary education."

The Council will be grateful for a statement of your views on any matters pertinent to their enquiry. They have, however, prepared a list of questions which seem, at this early stage in their work, to be particularly relevant and upon which you may care to base evidence. The Council ask me to emphasise, however, that they will be most happy to receive evidence in any form which you consider convenient, and that either part or the whole of the questionnaire can be ignored if you so wish. Some of those receiving this letter may wish to concentrate on one or two questions only; detailed evidence on any single question will be welcomed.

In order that a full range of teacher opinion can be taken into account by the Council copies of this questionnaire* are also to be sent to a large number of teachers, mainly chosen on a random sample basis. At the same time the Council will make it known that they will be willing to receive evidence from members of the general public.

It will be helpful if evidence can be submitted in writing so that the taking of oral evidence can be directed towards issues of special importance.

I should be most grateful if 40 copies of your reply can be sent to me not later than 1st May, 1964. It will be helpful if some replies can be sent well before that. Obviously, you will wish to have a reasonable period in which to consider your reply but we should be glad to know when it will be ready so that the Council's programme of work can be planned.

I am enclosing 12 copies of this letter and its Appendix. Further copies can be supplied on request.

Yours sincerely,

M. KOGAN

Secretary

* in an abbreviated version.

QUESTIONNAIRE UPON WHICH EVIDENCE MIGHT BE BASED

1. *The stages of primary education*

(a) How far do you think chronological age is a satisfactory criterion for entry and transfer within and from primary education? How much flexibility should there be at various stages? In particular, how far does lack of flexibility in entry and promotion prejudice the future of children born in the spring and summer?

(b) At what age should nursery or infant education become *available*, and its provision an obligation on the L.E.A., for children other than those with very exceptional problems?

(c) At what age should education, whether part-time or full-time, be made *compulsory*?

(d) From what age should full-time (morning and afternoon) education be:
 (i) available
 (ii) compulsory?

(e) How long should the school day be at various stages, and should any changes be made in the arrangement of the school holidays?

(f) Are breaks desirable within primary education and if so at what ages?

(g) What is the balance of gain and loss in:
 (i) separate nursery and infant schools as compared with infant schools with nursery classes or nursery/infant schools.
 (ii) separate infant and junior schools as compared with junior/infant schools?

(h) Is there sufficient contact and consistency between:
 (i) infant schools and contributory nursery schools.
 (ii) junior schools and contributory infant schools?

(i) What suggestions, if any, would you make for strengthening contacts and continuing development at:
 (i) the nursery/infant transition.
 (ii) the infant/junior transition?

2. *The transition from primary to secondary education*

(a) At what age should children transfer from primary to secondary education?

(b) What are the effects of present methods of selection on the work and organisation of:
 (i) the primary schools.
 (ii) the secondary schools?

(c) Assuming the continued existence of selective secondary education, what are the most desirable methods of selection from the point of view of the placing of children in appropriate courses, possible strain on children and parents, and the effects on the schools?

(d) Is selective secondary education desirable at all? If not, how should pupils be guided into the secondary school courses most suitable for them?

(e) Should more transfer between the maintained and independent schools be encouraged and provided for? If so, are there any special implications for the age of transfer from primary to secondary education?

(f) Is there sufficient contact and continuity of development between primary and secondary schools? If not, what suggestions might be made for improvement?

3. *The work of the primary schools*

(a) What do you consider should be the main aims of primary education and how ought they to be distinguished from those of secondary education?

(b) Do the life and work of the primary schools favour the achievement of these aims?

(c) Are the content of the curriculum and teaching methods which are commonly found well suited to present needs?

(d) Are satisfactory standards of attainment being reached with children of varying levels of ability?

(e) Are the needs of children of exceptional ability satisfactorily met?

(f) Do present teaching and discipline in primary schools prepare children adequately for secondary education and lay the right foundations for life and work increasingly requiring high degrees of skill?

(g) What influence has the emphasis on active learning in the 1931 Hadow Report had on schools, and how far has it been beneficial?

(h) Have there been significant improvements in primary education since the publication of the Hadow reports (1931 and 1933)? If so, what are the most striking advances you would wish to bring to the attention of the Council?

4. *Size and organisation of primary schools*

(a) What is the smallest and largest suitable size of school for various age groups and in urban and rural settings?

(b) What size of class for various ages should be adopted as an aim to be achieved over the next 20 year period? For what teaching purposes and in what circumstances would (i) larger groups (ii) smaller groups be profitable?

(c) What age-range within a class is:
(i) desirable
(ii) tolerable
for various ages? Are different age-ranges appropriate according to the subject matter that is being treated and the manner in which it is taught?

(d) To what extent is:
(i) classification by ability
(ii) cross-setting for ability in specific subjects
desirable in primary schools?

(e) How far should the organisation of the primary school at various stages be based on the class and the class teacher?

(f) Is there any advantage in linking classes and regrouping children possibly in units of different size, for various activities and according to teachers' strengths? (One example is the American concept of "team teaching").

(g) What use can be made of teachers' specialist knowledge and skill in the primary school?

(h) Are the present rates of turnover of teachers harmful to pupils and, if so, how can the ill effects be reduced?

(i) How far are the answers to the questions in this section applicable to the first two years of the secondary school?

5. *Teachers and their training*

(a) How well do:
(i) training courses
(ii) a combination of graduate and professional courses, whether consecutive or integrated
(iii) graduate courses without professional training
equip teachers for work in primary schools?

(b) How adequate are in-service training arrangements, and how adequate are the other opportunities and facilities for teachers to reappraise their professional work? How far do teachers take advantage of them?

(c) Do teachers receive too little help, or conversely too much guidance from sources outside the school such as Institutes of Education, teacher training colleges, inspectors, advisers, administrators, professional organisations and educational publishers?

(d) Is enough care taken in placing teachers in their first posts and is sufficient guidance available to them? To what extent do young teachers leave the profession because their special needs are not met?

(e) Is the present staffing structure of head, deputy head and holders of posts of responsibility helpful to the primary school?

(f) What proportion of men to women teachers is appropriate at various stages in the primary school? Should more men be encouraged to teach infants?

(g) What use can be made of part-time trained teachers and full-time and part-time helpers at various stages in the primary school? If helpers are to be used what training or qualifications should they have? Have you any further suggestions for meeting the present deficiency of teachers in the primary schools?

6. *Handicapped children*

(a) To what extent is it in the interest of:
    (i) the children concerned
    (ii) the general good of the school
    for children in some of the categories which need special educational treatment to be taught in ordinary primary schools?

(b) If these children are taught in ordinary primary schools should special provision be made for them by:
    (i) concentrating a group of children with a special handicap in a particular school
    (ii) grouping handicapped children in special classes
    (iii) providing specially trained or supernumerary help?

7. *The relationship of home, school and community*

(a) How far are present contacts between home, school and community effective, and what improvements to them could be suggested?

(b) Is collaboration between home and school best achieved by formal means (for example, parent-teacher associations) or by informal means?

(c) Should parents have more freedom than they do at present in their choice of schools for their children, and is sufficient information and guidance available to them about educational facilities?

(d) Does educational planning take enough into account, particularly in policy on buildings, equipment and supply of teachers, existing inequalities in primary provision and the special needs of children from poor backgrounds?

(e) Is residential experience valuable or necessary for children of primary school age, and is there adequate boarding provision?

(f) How effective is existing machinery in dealing with such social and educational problems as truancy?

8. *General questions*

(a) Do (i) head teachers, (ii) assistant teachers enjoy too much freedom or too little in organising their work? Is the traditional freedom of the schools appropriate in modern circumstances?

(b) Are there any issues not sufficiently covered by the questions above on which you wish to state your views?

(e) What major problems remain to be solved, and in what order of priority should they be placed in relation to each other and the needs of the educational service as a whole?

ANNEX B

A. List of Witnesses who gave Oral (and in most cases Written) Evidence

(i) Associations of local authorities and of education committees

Association of Education Committees

Alderman J. Wood, Past President.
Sir William Alexander, Secretary of the Association.
Mr. B. S. Braithwaite, Chief Education Officer, East Sussex.
Mr. S. W. Hobson, Chief Education Officer, Kingston upon Hull.
Dr. F. Lincoln Ralphs, Chief Education Officer, Norfolk.
Sir Lionel Russell, Chief Education Officer, Birmingham.
Mr. W. G. Stone, Director of Education, Brighton.

Association of Municipal Corporations

Alderman A. Ballard, Vice-Chairman of the Education Committee of the Association.
Mr. L. J. Drew, Director of Education, Swansea.
Councillor J. E. Evans, Maidstone.
Alderman M. A. Lower, Oxford.
Mr. K. P. Poole, Assistant Secretary of the Association.
Sir Lionel Russell, Chief Education Officer, Birmingham.
Alderman Mrs. M. E. Sutton, South Shields.

County Councils Association

Sir Alan Lubbock, Vice-Chairman, Executive Council, Chairman of the Education Committee of the Association.
Mr. S. T. Broad, County Education Officer, Hertfordshire.
Mr. L. W. K. Brown, Deputy Secretary.
Mr. J. R. Coxon, Vice-Chairman of the Education Committee of the Association.
Mr. Mansel Williams, Director of Education, Caernarvonshire.

London County Council

Mr. James Young, Chairman of the Education Committee.
Mrs. Helen C. Bentwich, Chairman of the Primary and Secondary Schools Sub-Committee.
Dr. E. W. H. Briault, Deputy Education Officer.
Mrs. Irene Chaplin, Vice-Chairman of the General Purposes Sub-Committee.
Mr. W. F. Houghton, Education Officer.
Lady Nathan, Vice-Chairman of the Education Committee and Chairman of the General Purposes Sub-Committee.
Dr. L. W. H. Payling, Chief Inspector.

(ii) ASSOCIATIONS OF EDUCATION OFFICERS

Association of Chief Education Officers

The late Mr. H. Oldman, President, Chief Education Officer, York.
Dr. J. J. B. Dempster, Honorary Secretary of the Association. Chief Education Officer, Southampton.
Mr. W. E. Philip, Chief Education Officer, Devon.

Association of Education Officers

Mr. C. L. Mellowes, President. Director of Education, Northumberland.
Mr. J. C. Brooke, Honorary Secretary of the Association. County Education Officer, Worcestershire.
Mr. A. L. Hutchinson, County Education Officer, Isle of Wight.
Mr. E. M. Littlecott, Deputy County Education Officer, Hampshire.

(iii) ORGANISATIONS REPRESENTING TEACHERS

Association of Teachers in Colleges and Departments of Education

Miss A. M. Dawson, Principal, Newton Park College of Education, Chairman of the Committee of the Association which prepared evidence for the C.A.C.
Dr. A. M. Ross, Institute of Education, University of Exeter.
Mr. L. W. G. Sealey, Principal, North Bucks College of Education.
Miss H. M. Simpson, Honorary Secretary of the Association.

Conference of Institute Directors

Professor W. A. C. Stewart, Chairman of the Conference of Institute Directors, Professor of Education, Institute of Education, University of Keele.
Professor W. R. Niblett, Director, Institute of Education, University of London.
Professor J. W. Tibble, Director, Institute of Education, University of Leicester.

Conservative and Unionist Teachers' Association

Mr. W. Higgins, Chairman of the Association. Headmaster, South Charwood Secondary School.
Councillor K. Double, Deputy Head, North Ealing Primary School.
Miss P. Hookey, Vice-Chairman of the Association. Headmistress of Williams' Junior School.
Miss M. Jackson, Past President, Nursery Schools Association. Supervisor of Nursery Education, City of Manchester.
Miss J. Phillips, Deputy Head, Addison Primary School, London.

The Joint Four Secondary Associations

Miss M. R. Price, Chairman. Headmistress, Milham Ford School, Oxford.

Mr. R. R. Pedley, Vice-Chairman. Headmaster, Chislehurst & Sidcup Grammar School, Sidcup, Kent.

Mr. A. W. S. Hutchings, Joint Honorary Secretary, Association of Assistant Masters.

Miss S. D. Wood, Joint Honorary Secretary, Association of Assistant Mistresses.

Association of Assistant Masters

Mr. J. W. Gray, County Grammar School, Woking, Surrey.

Mr. J. W. B. Ruffle, Bishop Wordsworth's School, Salisbury, Wiltshire.

Association of Assistant Mistresses

Miss V. M. Richardson, North Kesteven Grammar School, North Hykeham, Lincoln.

Miss M. A. Richmond, The High School for Girls, Worthing Road, Horsham, Sussex.

Association of Head Masters

Mr. T. W. H. Holland, Reigate Grammar School, Reigate, Surrey.

Mr. N. H. Evans, Senacre Secondary School, Maidstone, Kent.

Association of Head Mistresses

Miss R. E. Scargill, Girls' High School, Wolverhampton.

Miss J. R. Glover, Sutton High School, Sutton.

National Association of Schoolmasters

Mr. A. J. Smyth, President.

Mr. T. A. Casey, General Secretary.

Mr. R. B. Cooking, Vice-Chairman, Education Committee.

Mr. L. G. Harris, Vice-President.

Mr. J. D. Marsh, Assistant Secretary.

Mr. B. Morton, Member of Executive.

Mr. A. C. E. Waston, Chairman of Education Committee.

National Union of Teachers

Miss M. Stewart, President.

Mr. N. Bagnall, Editor, The Teacher.

Mr. M. J. C. Clarke, Chairman of the Special School Advisory Committee.

Miss M. G. Fazey, Member of the Executive.

Mr. D. Gilbert, Chairman of the Education Committee.

Sir Ronald Gould, General Secretary.

Mr. E. Powell, Vice-Chairman of the Education Committee.

Mr. M. G. Powell-Davies, Secretary of the Education Committee.

Mr. R. W. E. Wilkinson, Chairman of Primary Schools Advisory Committee.

Nursery School Association of Great Britain and Northern Ireland

Miss D. E. M. Gardner, Chairman, Nursery School Association. Head of Department of Child Development, Institute of Education, University of London.

Miss A. A. Babb, Head Teacher, Curzon Crescent Nursery School, Willesden.

Mrs. N. Britton, General Inspector of Infant and Nursery Education, Surrey.

Mr. D. K. Daniels, Honorary Treasurer. Headmaster, Ulverley Junior School, Solihull.

Mr. K. Pickett, Chairman of Working Party which prepared the Association's evidence to the Council. Head of Department of Social Studies, North Western Polytechnic, London.

Socialist Education Association

Mr. G. Heaven.
Mr. P. Ibbotson.
Mr. S. C. Lubin, General Secretary.

(iv) OTHER INSTITUTIONS AND ORGANISATIONS

Confederation for the Advancement of State Education

Mrs. S. Caston.
Mrs. M. Gowing.
Mrs. D. Higgin.

Council for Training in Social Work

Miss G. M. Aves, Formerly Chief Welfare Officer to the Ministry of Health. Governor of the National Institute for Training in Social Work.

Mr. R. C. Wright, Chief Professional Adviser to the Council.

Educational Foundation for Visual Aids

Dr. J. A. Harrison, Director.

Education Welfare Officers National Association

Mr. R. H. Potter, President.
Mr. F. F. Coombes, Honorary General Secretary.
Mr. A. R. Millington, Treasurer.

English New Education Fellowship

Dr. M. Johnson, Chairman of the Fellowship, Research Fellow, Institute of Education, University of London.

Dr. J. Hemming, Author, Broadcaster, Educational Psychologist.

Miss J. M. Horsburgh, Head, Sherwood Primary School, Mitcham, Surrey.

Mr. J. F. Porter, Past Chairman of the Fellowship, Vice-Principal, Coventry College of Education.

Miss G. M. Sharman, Head, Intake County Infants' School, Doncaster.

Fabian Society

Mr. J. Hall.
Mrs. P. Jay.
Mr. N. Morris.
Mr. T. Ponsonby, General Secretary.
Mrs. S. Williams, M.P.

Forum Editorial Board

Mr. G. C. Freeland, Head Teacher, Mowacre Junior School, Leicester.
Mr. E. Linfield, Senior Lecturer in Education, Newton Park College of Education,
Dr. B. Simon, Editor "Forum," Reader in Education, School of Education, University of Leicester.

Home Tuition Scheme for Backward Readers

Mrs. P. Jay.
Mrs. M. Kamm.
Mrs. M. Spencer.

Independent Television Authority

Mr. J. Weltman, Education Officer.

National Association of Chief Education Welfare Officers

Mr. C. Wood, President.
Mr. C. M. Tordoff, Honorary Secretary.
Mr. H. A. White.

Standing Conference of Organisations of Social Workers

Mr. D. Jones, Chairman of the Standing Conference, Lecturer at the National Institute for Social Work Training.
Miss M. Barnes, Honorary Secretary of the Standing Conference. General Secretary of the Association of Psychiatric Social Workers.
Miss P. Hammond, Lecturer at the National Institute of Social Workers at the Denbigh Hospital for Nervous Cases.
Miss S. Himmel, Member of the General Purposes Committee of the Standing Conference. Probation Officer.

School Broadcasting Council for the United Kingdom

Mr. R. C. Steele, Secretary.
Mrs. E. C. Mee, Consultant on Primary Education.
Mr. K. V. Bailey, Senior Education Officer.
Miss B. Crispin, Assistant Senior Education Officer.

Trades Union Congress

Mr. C. T. H. Plant, Member of the T.U.C. General Council and General Education Committee.
Mr. R. Milsom, Assistant, Education Department.
Mrs. C. M. Patterson, Member of the T.U.C. General Council and General Education Committee.
Mr. D. Winnard, Secretary, Education Committee.

(V). INDIVIDUALS WHO GAVE ORAL EVIDENCE TO THE COUNCIL
(SOME ALSO SUBMITTED PAPERS).

Miss G. E. Allen, Lecturer in Education, Froebel Educational Institute.

Miss P. J. Ault, Assistant Teacher, Applecroft Primary School, Welwyn Garden City, Hertfordshire.

Mr. D. G. O. Ayerst, Formerly Her Majesty's Inspector of Schools.

Mr. G. R. Baines, Head Teacher, Brize Norton Primary School, Oxfordshire.

Mr. A. Beales, Head Teacher, Yarborough County Primary School, Grimsby.

Mr. B. Bernstein, Institute of Education, University of London.

Mr. E. Blishen, Author and Broadcaster. Lecturer in Education, University of York.

Sir Alec Clegg, Education Officer, West Riding of Yorkshire.

Mr. A. T. Collis, Faculty of Commerce and Social Science, University of Birmingham.

Mr. J. A. Cutforth, Basil Blackwell and Mott Ltd.

Mr. T. Derrick, Lecturer in Education, Edgehill College of Education.

Miss A. Dixon, Former Assistant Primary School Teacher.

Dr. J. W. B. Douglas, Medical Research Unit, London School of Economics and Political Science.

Mr. J. A. Downing, Director, Reading Research Unit, Institute of Education, University of London.

Professor B. M. Foss, Professor of Educational Psychology, Institute of Education, University of London.

Miss D. E. M. Gardner, Reader in Child Development, Institute of Education, University of London.

Miss J. R. Glover, Headmistress, Sutton High School.

Mrs. D. M. Glynn, Senior Lecturer in Education, Nottingham Training College of Education.

Dr. R. J. Goldman, Senior Lecturer in Educational Psychology, University of Reading.

Miss D. Gould, Dartington College of Arts.

Mr. J. W. Gray, Assistant Master, Woking Grammar School.

Miss J. A. Grimsley, Head Teacher, Four Oaks County Junior School, Sutton Coldfield.

Dr. J. Hemming, Author, Broadcaster and Educational Psychologist.

Mr. D. G. E. Hurd, Headmaster, John Mason High School, Abingdon, Berkshire.

Mr. N. Isaacs, Author.

Mrs. M. Jeffreys, London School of Hygiene and Tropical Medicine.

Mr. D. King, Modern Languages Adviser, East Riding of Yorkshire.

Dr. K. Lovell, Lecturer, Institute of Education, University of Leeds.

Mrs. J. Lunn, Research Officer, National Foundation for Educational Research.

Mr. G. W. Miller, London School of Economics and Political Science.

Mr. P. K. C. Millins, Principal, Edge Hill College of Education.

Mrs. O. M. Milnes, Head Teacher, Swansdowne Infants School, Nottingham.

Miss B. Mogford, Nuffield Foundation.

Professor Ben Morris, Director, Institute of Education, University of Bristol.

Dr. J. M. Morris, Head of Reading Department, National Foundation for Educational Research.

Miss R. Morton-Williams, Social Survey, Central Office of Information.

Mr. L. Moss, Social Survey, Central Office of Information.

Mr. G. Palmer, Head Teacher, Highbury Quadrant Junior School, London.

Mrs. J. Parker, Department of Social and Administrative Studies, University of Oxford.

Mr. F. L. Penty, Head Teacher, Beeston Primary School, Leeds.

Professor R. Peters, Professor of Philosophy of Education, Institute of Education, University of London.

Mr. D. A. Pidgeon, Deputy Director, National Foundation for Educational Research.

Mr. T. C. Powell, Head Teacher, Gig Mill County Junior School, Stourbridge Worcestershire.

Miss V. M. Richardson, Assistant Mistress, North Kesteven Grammar School.

Mr. J. S. Robinson, Headmaster, Hemel Hempstead Grammar School.

Miss M. M. Robson, Head Teacher, Hugh Myddleton Infant School, London.

Miss J. M. Ross, Medical Research Unit, London School of Economics and Political Science.

Dr. W. Roy, Headmaster, Stopeley Secondary School, Luton.

Miss R. E. Scargill, Girls' High School, Wolverhampton.

Mr. A. Spicer, Nuffield Foundation.

Dr. D. H. Stott, Lecturer in Psychology, University of Glasgow.

Mrs. A. Swain, Architect, Ministry of Housing and Local Government.

Mr. R. F. A. Tanner, Formerly Her Majesty's Inspector of Schools.

Professor J. W. Tibble, Director, School of Education, University of Leicester.

Mr. N. C. Tyack, Headmaster, Willenhall Comprehensive School, Staffordshire.

Mr. J. Vaizey, Fellow, Worcester College, Oxford.

Professor P. E. Vernon, Professor, Institute of Education, University of London.

Dr. W. D. Wall, Director, National Foundation for Educational Research.

Professor F. W. Warburton, Professor, School of Education, University of Manchester.

Mr. F. R. Wastnedge, Nuffield Foundation.

Mr. W. L. White, Head Teacher, Connaught Junior Boys' School, Bristol.

Mrs. D. E. Whittaker Advisory Teacher for Mathematics, Nottingham.

Mr. R. E. Williams, Institute of Education, University of London. Formerly Chief Inspector for Teaching Training, Ministry of Education.

Professor S. Wiseman, Director, School of Education, University of Manchester.

Religious Education in Primary Schools

The Council also wishes to record its gratitude to:

The Most Reverend G. A. Beck, Roman Catholic Archbishop of Liverpool.

The Right Reverend R. P. Wilson, Bishop of Chichester.

Dr. K. Bliss, General Secretary, Church of England Board of Education.

The Reverend J. Huxtable, Secretary, Congregational Union of Great Britain.

who joined them for a discussion on Religious Education.

(VI). DEPARTMENT OF EDUCATION AND SCIENCE

The members of the Department of Education and Science and H.M. Inspectors listed below gave oral evidence. Some also submitted papers. Other government departments, notably the Ministry of Health, the Home Office and the Ministry of Housing and Local Government provided information at our request.

Miss E. E. Biggs, H.M.I.

Mr. J. D. Brierley.

Mr. P. Burns, H.M.I.

Mr. L. J. Burrows, H.M.I.

Mr. C. E. Cave, H.M.I.

Miss D. Clark, H.M.I.

Mr. L. Clark, H.M.I.

Miss M. B. Crowley.

Mr. H. O. Dovey.

Mr. H. J. Edwards, H.M.I.

Mr. W. R. Elliott, H.M.I.

Mr. J. F. E. Embling.

Mr. L. F. Ennever, H.M.I.

Miss R. Foster, formerly Her Majesty's Inspector of Schools.

Mr. C. J. Gill, H.M.I.

Mr. J. H. Goldsmith, H.M.I.

The late Miss V. L. Gray, H.M.I.

Miss J. M. Grinham.

Miss W. P. Harte.

Mr. M. J. G. Hearley, H.M.I.

Mr. D. A. C. Heigham.

Dr. J. N. Horne.

Mr. J. W. Horton, H.M.I.
Mr. R. Howlett.
Mr. J. A. Hudson.
Mr. J. R. Jameson.
Miss M. E. Johnston, H.M.I.
Mr. A. R. M. Maxwell-Hyslop.
Mr. D. L. Medd.
Mr. D. H. Morrell.
Mr. J. W. Morris, H.M.I.
Mr. P. R. Odgers.
Mr. G. F. Peaker, formerly Her Majesty's Inspector of Schools.
Mr. E. Pearson, H.M.I.
Mr. B. C. Peatey.
Mr. W. D. Pile.
Mr. O. J. E. Pullen, H.M.I
Mr. D. C. Riddy, H.M.I.
Mr. H. Sagar, H.M.I.
Miss E. M. Sharman, H.M.I.
Mr. E. H. Simpson.
Mr. P. Sloman.
Mr. P. H. Taylor.
Mr. W. B. Tudhope, H.M.I.
Mr. A. H. Williams, H.M.I.
Mr. E. W. Wilkinson, H.M.I.
Mr. J. W. Withrington, H.M.I.

We also wish to acknowledge gratefully the expert help given by the staff of the Department of Education Library.

B. List of Organisations and Persons Who Submitted Written Evidence

(i) Bodies who submitted written evidence
(some also gave evidence orally)

Association of Chief Education Officers.
Association of Children's Officers.
Association of Education Committees.
Association of Education Officers.
Association of Educational Psychologists.
Association of Headmistresses of Preparatory Schools.
Association of Municipal Corporations.
Association for Special Education.
Association of Teachers in Colleges and Departments of Education.

British Association of Lecturers and Organisers of Physical Education.
British Council of Churches.
British Employers' Confederation.
British Federation of University Women.
British Humanist Association.
British Psychological Society.
Catholic Education Council.
Catholic Teacher Federation.
Child Development Society.
Church of England Board of Education.
College of Speech Therapists.
Communist Party of Great Britain.
Community Service Volunteers.
Confederation for the Advancement of State Education.
Conference of Institute Directors.
Conservative and Unionist Teachers' Association.
Co-operative College.
Co-operative Women's Guild.
Council for Children's Welfare.
Council for Training in Social Work.
Council for the Training of Health Visitors.
County Councils' Association.
Durham County Council.
Ealing Head Teachers' Association.
Education Welfare Officers' National Association.
English Association.
English New Education Fellowship.
Fabian Society.
Federation of British Industries.
Federation of Soroptimist Clubs of Great Britain and Northern Ireland.
Geographical Association.
Headmasters' Conference.
Health Visitors' Association.
Historical Association.
Incorporated Association of Preparatory Schools.
Incorporated Society of Musicians.
Independent Schools Association.
Independent Television Authority.
Joint Four Secondary Associations.
Kesteven College of Education Science Teachers' Conference.
Kettering and District Association, National Union of Teachers.
Kettering and District Head Teachers' Association.
London County Council.
London and Greater London Playing Fields Association.

London Head Teachers' Association.
Mathematical Association.
Medical Commission on Accident Prevention. Royal College of Surgeons.
Medical Women's Federation (Cambridge Branch).
Montgomeryshire Education Committee.
National Association for Mental Health.
National Association for the Teaching of English.
National Association of Chief Education Welfare Officers.
National Association of Divisional Executives for Education.
National Association of Governing Bodies of Aided Grammar Schools.
National Association of Head Teachers.
National Association of Inspectors of Schools and Educational Organisers.
National Association of Labour Student Organisations.
National Association of Schoolmasters.
National Association of Tutors in Education and Health.
National Board of Catholic Women.
National Farmers' Union.
National Federation of Parent/Teacher Associations.
National Federation of Women's Institutes.
National Froebel Foundation.
National Marriage Guidance Council.
National Playing Fields Association.
National Rural Studies Association.
National Secular Society.
National Union of Students.
National Union of Teachers.
Nuffield Foundation.
Nursery School Association.
Physical Education Association.
Pre-School Play Groups Association.
Preston Education Committee.
Publishers' Association.
Rediffusion: Education Advisory Council.
Research and Development Panel, Association of Teachers of Mathematics.
Royal College of Nursing.
Royal Institute of Chemistry.
Royal Society for the Prevention of Accidents.
St. Gabriel's College of Education, Camberwell.
Salford Head Teachers' Association.
Save the Children Fund.
School Broadcasting Council for the United Kingdom.
School Library Association.
School Natural Science Society.
Sheffield Head Teachers' Association.

Socialist Education Association.
Socialist Party of Great Britain.
Society for Education through Art.
Society for Italic Handwriting.
Society of Assistants Teaching in Preparatory Schools.
Society of British Esperantist Teachers.
Society of Medical Officers of Health.
Southwark Diocesan Catholic Parents' and Electors' Association.
Standing Conference of Organisations of Social Workers.
Standing Conference of Women's Organisations, York Branch.
Tavistock Institute of Human Relations.
Trades Union Congress.
University of Leicester School of Education.
University of Nottingham.
Women's Group on Public Welfare.
Workers' Educational Association.

(ii) INDIVIDUALS WHO SUBMITTED WRITTEN EVIDENCE
(some also submitted oral evidence)

Mr. M. A. Ascher, Senior Lecturer in Education, Avery Hill College of Education.

Miss M. Atkinson, Principal, St. Gabriel's College of Education.

Miss J. B. Bailey, Head Teacher, Chelwood Nursery School, London.

Dr. R. G. Bannister, Consultant Neurologist.

Mr. H. R. Bass, B.E.M., Assistant Teacher, Carlton Central Junior Mixed and Infant School, Nottingham.

Miss F. D. Batstone, Principal, Gipsy Hill College of Education.

Mr. L. G. Bewsher, Senior Lecturer in Education, Trent Park College of Education.

Mrs. M. Blend, Parent and School Manager.

Miss D. Bloor, Head Teacher, Blacon Infants School, Blacon, Cheshire.

Miss M. Boydell, Inspector of Schools, Salford.

Mrs. D. R. Bradbury, Head Teacher, Comberback Infants School, Northwich, Chester.

Mr. F. W. Bramley, Head Teacher, Hessle C.E. Junior School, East Riding of Yorkshire.

Mr. C. Broad, Head Teacher, Durants School, Enfield.

Mr. J. B. Brocklehurst, Lecturer in Education, University of Birmingham.

Mr. G. W. Brown, Inspector of Schools, Cheshire.

Miss A. Bullen, Head Teacher, Beech Nursery School, Aylesbury, Bucks.

Mr. T. Burgess, Educational Journalist.

Mr. E. T. Butcher, Head Teacher, Colne Valley Comprehensive School, West Riding of Yorkshire.

Miss N. M. Caine, Nursery Adviser, Birmingham.

Mr. F. C. A. Cammaerts, Principal, City of Leicester College of Education.

Mrs. S. W. Cheetham, Lecturer, Poulton-le-Fylde College of Education.

Mr. V. Clark, Chief Education Officer, East Riding of Yorkshire.

Miss M. Clark, Schools Adviser, Devon.

Miss J. M. Claxton, Head Teacher, Gifford Infants School, Middlesex.

Sir Alec Clegg, Chief Education Officer, West Riding of Yorkshire.

Professor Nevill Coghill, Merton Professor of English Literature, University of Oxford.

Miss M. C. Cockayne, Head Teacher, Chorlton Park Junior School, Manchester.

Mr. J. A. Coe, Head Teacher, Lawford Mead Junior Mixed School, Chelmsford.

Dr. W. A. L. Collier, Medical Practitioner, Halstead, Essex.

Dr. M. Collis, Inspector of Schools, Kent.

Dr. J. B. Coltham, Lecturer, Department of Education, University of Manchester.

Dr. D. Cook, Deputy Chief Education Officer, Devon.

Mr. B. Cousin, Retired Primary School Teacher.

Very Rev. K. Cronin, Principal, St. Mary's R.C. College of Education.

Mr. J. Cutforth, Basil Blackwell & Mott Ltd.

Miss F. Digby, Head Teacher, Elizabeth Lansbury Nursery School, London.

Professor C. H. Dobinson, Department of Education, University of Leeds.

Mr. H. H. Dorrell, Parent, Maidenhead, Berks.

Mr. J. A. Downing, Reading Research Unit, Institute of Education, University of London.

Mrs. A. Drabble, Head Teacher, Vauxhall Junior School, London.

Professor E. J. R. Eaglesham, Director, Department of Education, University of Durham.

Miss H. M. Edwards, Principal Lecturer, Margaret McMillan College of Education, Bradford.

Miss M. Ellison, Primary Schools Adviser, Shropshire.

Sister M. Eucharia, Head Teacher, St. Aelred's R.C. Primary School, York.

Mr. J. J. Fairbairn, Senior Lecturer in Education, St. John's College of Education, York.

Mrs. W. Fawcus, Senior Staff Tutor, Institute of Education, King's College, Newcastle.

Miss D. O. Fawell, Head Teacher, Pikes Lane Nursery School, Bolton, Lancashire.

Miss J. G. V. Finch, Primary Schools Adviser, Shropshire.

Miss A. E. FitzJohn, Assistant Education Officer (Primary), East Suffolk.

Dr. N. France, Chief Educational Psychologist, Kent.

Miss B. N. Furneaux, Head Teacher, Kintore Way Nursery School, London.

Miss D. E. M. Gardner, Reader in Child Development, Institute of Education, University of London.

Miss M. A. Gibbs, Vice-Principal, Southlands College of Education.

Miss D. R. Gilbert, Head Teacher, Cambridge Road Junior School, Ellesmere Port, Cheshire.

Miss M. Glasgow, Director, Mary Glasgow Ltd.

Mrs. D. M. Glynn, Senior Lecturer, Nottingham College of Education.

Miss M. L. Glynn Jones, Head Teacher, Ibstock Place School, Roehampton.

Dr. R. J. Goldman, Lecturer in Educational Psychology, University of Reading.

Miss I. E. Gregory, Primary Schools Inspector, Essex.

Miss G. Greiner, Senior Lecturer in Education, Goldsmiths' College of Education.

Miss J. A. Grimsley, Head Teacher, Four Oaks Junior School, Sutton Coldfield.

Mr. R. M. Groom, Head Teacher, John Hampden Junior Mixed & Infant School, Thame, Oxfordshire.

Miss E. M. Groves, Head Teacher, Springwell Junior School, Heston, Middlesex.

Mr. D. Hanff, Lecturer, Newton Park College of Education.

Mr. J. Haynes, Chief Education Officer, Kent.

Miss M. Hennessy, St. John the Evangelist School, London.

Mrs. V. R. Hewitt, Assistant Teacher, Essex.

Mr. P. Heywood, Head Teacher, Morganwalk Junior Mixed and Infant School, Hertford.

Mr. L. Hinds, Stafford County Junior School, Eastbourne.

Miss E. M. Hitchfield, Lecturer, Froebel Educational Institute.

Mr. R. E. Hodd, Chief Education Officer, Blackpool.

Miss D. K. Horsley, Head Teacher, Greenacres Junior School, London.

Miss F. H. Horsley, Head Teacher, Denby Free Junior Mixed & Infant School, Derbyshire.

Mr. E. L. Hughes, Head Teacher, Upton Junior Mixed and Infant School, Upton, Chester.

Mr. J. W. Hunt, Head Teacher, Trosnant Junior School, Havant, Hampshire.

Lady Allen of Hurtwood, Chairman, London Adventure Playground Association.

Mrs. M. Hynds, Head Teacher, Vauxhall Infant School, London.

The late Mr. N. Isaacs, Author.

Mr. A. James, Lecturer, Margaret McMillan College of Education, Bradford.

Mr. J. Jeffery, Assistant Masters' Association, Methodist College, Belfast.

Mr. T. W. John, Head Teacher, Tower Hill Junior Mixed School, Witney.

Mr. J. Johnston, Southall, Middlesex.

Mr. H. C. Jones, Head Teacher, Cottingham Croxby County Primary School, East Riding of Yorkshire.

Dr. M. L. Kellmer Pringle, Director, The National Bureau for Co-operation in Child Care.

Mrs. N. H. Kemp, Nursery Schools Organiser, Berkshire.

Miss K. M. Kinder, Head Teacher, Cracoe-in-Rylstone, C. of E. Primary School, Yorkshire.

Mr. D. King, Modern Languages Adviser, East Riding of Yorkshire.

Mr. J. C. Kingsland, Headmaster, Cray Valley Technical High School, St. Mary's Cray, Kent.

Mr. R. M. T. Kneebone, Headmaster, Beckfield Secondary Modern School, York.

Mrs. E. M. Lawson, Lecturer, Nottingham College of Education.

Dr. E. Lawrence, Formerly Director, The National Froebel Foundation.

Mr. J. F. Leedham, Head Teacher, South Wigton Junior School, Leicester.

Mr. S. P. Leigh, Head Teacher, Henry Whipple Junior School, Nottingham.

Mr. H. K. Lewenhak, Head of Production, Westward Television.

Miss E. G. Linecar, Headmistress, Four Dwellings Secondary Girls' School, Birmingham.

Mr. G. Long, Head Teacher, Stradbrooke Junior Mixed School, Nottingham.

Dr. K. Lovell, Lecturer, Institute of Education, University of Leeds.

Mr. N. Loverdo, Inventor of a new alphabet.

Miss R. E. Maguire, Public Health Nursery Officer, Ministry of Health.

Mr. C. Malden, Headmaster, Windlesham House School, Washington, Sussex.

Mrs. S. M. Marshall, Lecturer in Primary Education, Institute of Education, University of Sheffield.

Mr. S. C. Mason, Director of Education, Leicestershire.

Mrs. E. C. Mee, Formerly Chief Inspector of Primary Education, Ministry of Education.

Mr. R. J. O. Meyer, Headmaster, Millfield School, Street, Somerset.

Mr. J. G. Millward, Headmaster, Ullenhall Junior Mixed School, Warks.

Miss E. Moorhouse, Primary Schools Adviser, Oxfordshire County Council.

Dr. J. M. Morris, Head of the Reading Department, National Foundation for Educational Research.

Mrs. D. Munday, Parent.

Miss M. A. Mycock, Vice Principal, Manchester Day College of Education.

Mr. D. J. MacIntyre, Assistant Education Officer, Cambridge (evidence submitted jointly with Mrs. D. J. MacIntyre).

Mr. V. G. McCandless, Head Teacher, Mill Street Junior School, Crewe, Cheshire.

Mr. J. McCann, Parent.

Miss F. J. C. McInnes, Inspector of Schools, Worcestershire.

Dr. K. H. Nahapiet, Principal, St. Katherine's College of Education.

Mr. K. O'Brien, Head Teacher, Hilderthorpe County Junior School, Bridlington, East Riding of Yorkshire.

Mr. W. J. Osborne, Head of the Department of History, Newland Park College of Education.

Mr. R. M. Parker, Deputy Director of Education, West Sussex.

Dr. H. J. Peake, Headmaster, Bilborough Grammar School, Nottingham.

Mrs. C. W. Peneycad, Head Teacher, Colstons Junior Mixed School, Bristol

Mrs. M. Perraton, Chairman, Havant and Waterloo Excepted District Education Committee.

Sir James Pitman, Director, Pitman's Publishing Company.

Mrs. E. B. Pitt, Head Teacher, Bishopstoke Infant School, Eastleigh, Hampshire.

Mr. T. C. Powell, Head Teacher, Gig Mill Junior Mixed School, Stourbridge, Worcestershire.

Mr. G. Price, Senior Lecturer in Education, Chorley Day College of Education.

Mr. H. H. Pryce, Head Teacher, Deepdale Junior School, Preston.

Miss E. M. Puddephat, Principal, Rachel McMillan College of Education, London.

Mr. A. G. Razzell, Head Teacher, De Lucy Junior School, London.

Mr. W. J. Reed, Head Teacher, Broadstairs C.E. Primary Boys School, Broadstairs.

Mrs. E. Reid, Head Teacher, Hilderthorpe County Infant School, Bridlington, East Riding of Yorkshire.

Miss B. E. Robbins, Head Teacher, Charles Lamb Infant School, London.

Miss M. J. Roberts, Senior Lecturer in Education, Hobart Teachers' College, Tasmania.

Sister Rose, Headmistress, St. Thomas More R.C. Secondary Modern School, Wigan, Lancashire.

Mr. L. C. Schiller, Formerly Her Majesty's Inspector of Schools.

Mr. S. S. Segal, Chairman, Guild of Teachers of Backward Children.

Mr. M. Sheldon, Schools Music Adviser, Oxfordshire.

Mr. P. Slade, Drama Adviser, Birmingham.

Miss M. M. Smith, Lecturer, Institute of Education, University of Leeds.

Mr. S. J. W. Smith, Head Teacher, Broadstone Junior Mixed and Infant School, Poole, Dorset.

Miss M. E. Southam, Senior Tutor, Head of Department of Primary Education, University of London, Goldsmiths' College, New Cross, London.

Mr. A. E. Sparrow, Assistant Teacher, Millfield School, Street, Somerset.

Mrs. A. Stallibrass, Superintendent of a Pre-School Playgroup, Croydon.

Mr. P. K. Steel, Assistant Teacher, Fairlawn Primary School, London.

Professor W. A. C. Stewart, Director, Institute of Education, University of Keele.

Mr. W. R. Stirling, Headmaster, Burnt Mill Comprehensive School, Harlow, Essex.

Mr. R. W. Stockdale, Lecturer, Darlington College of Education.

Dr. D. H. Stott, Lecturer in Psychology, University of Glasgow.

Mr. C. H. Stowasser, Teacher in Charge, Adjustment Class, Bassett Road, Camborne, Cornwall.

Mrs. M. H. Stripe, Head Teacher, Wyborne Infant School, London.

Lady Stross, Inspector, Children's Department, Home Office.

Mr. G. H. Sylvester, Chief Education Officer, Bristol.

Mr. S. Taylor, Lecturer in Modern Language Method, University of Reading.

Mr. W. T. Telfer-Davey, Head Teacher, Galton and Lake Junior Mixed and Infant School, Shanklin, Isle of Wight.

Mr. R. H. Thompson, Head Teacher, Penshurst County Primary School, Hessle, East Riding of Yorkshire.

Miss J. Tinton, Principal Lecturer in Education, Bordesley Day College of Education, Birmingham.

Professor J. P. Tuck, Department of Education, University of Newcastle.

Mr. P. R. Unwin, Assistant Master, Yeovil School, Somerset.

Mr. J. Vaizey, Fellow, Worcester College, Oxford.

Professor P. E. Vernon, Professor of Educational Psychology, University of London Institute of Education.

Mr. C. B. Viney, Head Teacher, Hawne County Primary Junior Mixed School, Halesowen.

Miss M. Waddington, Lecturer, Institute of Education, University of London.

Professor F. W. Wagner, Director, Institute of Education, University of Southampton.

Miss M. Walton, Head Teacher, Turncroft Nursery School, Darwen, Lancashire.

Mr. R. Wesley, Principal, Cheshire County College of Education.

Mr. R. H. West, Principal Lecturer, Cheltenham St. Paul's College of Education.

Mr. J. A. Wheldon, Head Teacher, Huntington Junior Mixed and Infant School, Huntington, Chester.

Miss M. Whitley, Principal, Neville's Cross College of Education, Durham.

Mrs. D. E. Whittaker, Advisory Teacher for Mathematics, Nottingham.

Mr. A. M. Wilkinson, Lecturer in Education, University of Birmingham.

Dr. M. D. Wilson, Inspector, Special Education, Inner London Education Authority.

Mr. W. Wilson, Deputy Head Teacher, St. Mary's R.C. Junior Boys' School, London.

Miss M. M. Withers, Formerly Her Majesty's Inspector of Schools.

Mr. J. L. Womersley, Architect.

Mr. F. Woolaghan, Head Teacher, Elaine Junior Mixed and Infant School, Rochester, Kent.

Miss M. Woollett, Headmistress, Doncaster Technical Grammar School for Girls.

Mr. A. Wright, Principal Lecturer, Department of History, College of St. Matthias.

The Council was greatly helped by those who willingly provided manuscripts in advance of publication, or other material based on enquiry, in response to specific requests from the Council. We gratefully acknowledge help of this kind from the following: Dr. Basil Bernstein, Professor W. L. Blyth, Miss I. E. Caspari, Mr. C. P. R. Clarke (Director of Education, Liverpool), Dr. J. W. B. Douglas (who produced data on several occasions), Dr. G. Hawkins, Dr. P. H. Levin (Building Research Station), Dr. Terence Moore, Mr. J. E. Nesbitt, Professor J. D. Nisbet, Dr. D. Odlum, Professor R. S. Peters, members of the Pilkington Research Unit, University of Liverpool,

Mr. H. W. Pitt, Mrs. J. Tamburrini, Miss M. Waddington, Dr. W. Warren, Mrs. J. Parris, Dr. W. D. Wall and his colleagues at the National Foundation for Educational Research, who helped us in several ways, Dr. J. Grey Walter and Professor S. Wiseman. Other research undertaken for the Council is acknowledged and reported in Volume 2 or at the appropriate place in the main Report. We also sought and received advice on visits to be made abroad from Mr. Nigel Grant, Mr. Wright Miller and Miss M. Waddington.

ANNEX C

Visits Made

In this Annex we list the names of those who received us so kindly in our own country and abroad and hope that they will take this as further evidence of our gratitude to them.

I. Visits the Council made in the U.K.

Schools visited in the United Kingdom:

(i) *Schools In England.* (Schools are listed according to their local authority areas).

School	Head Teacher
Birmingham	
Follett Osler County Primary School	Miss M. E. Ray
Four Dwellings Girls' Secondary School	Miss E. G. M. Linecar
Great Barr Comprehensive School	Mr. O. Beynon
Highfield County Primary School	Miss M. J. Wise
Sheldon Heath Comprehensive School	Mr. J. E. Smith
Bournemouth	
The Drama Centre, Boscombe	Mr. L. Williams
St. John's Church of England Primary School	Mr. G. Williams
Winton and Moordown Junior School	Miss A. M. Watton
Bradford	
Drummond High School	Mr. C. Styles
	Miss M. J. Sampson
Frizinghall Junior High School	Mr. J. V. Walker
Green Lane Junior School	Mr. H. Dawson
Swain House Junior School	Mr. J. Nicholson
Undercliffe Junior High School	Miss J. W. Brown
Whetley Lane Junior High School	Mr. G. F. Watson
Bristol	
Badminton School, Westbury on Trym	Miss B. Sanderson
Bannerman Nursery School	Miss M. Ausch
Burnbush Junior Mixed and Infant School	Mr. N. Griffiths
Colston's Primary School	Mrs. C. W. Peneycad
Connaught Junior Boys' School	Mr. W. L. White
Filton Avenue Infant School	Mrs. W. Griffiths
Filton Avenue Junior Mixed School	Mr. K. G. Chivers
Filton Avenue Nursery School	Miss I. Bugden

School	*Head Teacher*
Four Acres Junior School	Mr. J. Wayborn
Henleaze Infant School, Westbury on Trym	Mrs. K. M. Rostron
Henleaze Play Group, Henleaze	Mrs. R. Andrews
Hillfields Park Infant School, Fishponds	Miss B. M. Tarr
Holymead Infant School	Mrs. E. French
Novers Lane Infant School	Miss R. Pryce
Sea Mills Infant School, Sea Mills	Miss M. Nash
Sea Mills Junior School, Sea Mills	Mr. J. Edwards
St. Christopher's Play Group	Mrs. M. Taylor
St. Mary Redcliffe Nursery School	Miss C. Hoare
Teyfant Infant School	Mrs. K. Blackwell
Teyfant Junior School	Miss H. Vear
Weston Park Infant School, Lawrence Weston	Miss M. Davidson
West Town Lane Junior School	Mrs. G. Bolhovener
Whitehall Day Nursery	Miss C. Lambert

Cambridgeshire

St. Faith's, Cambridge	Mr. F. M. White

Buckinghamshire

Eton College, Windsor	Mr. A. Chenevix-Trench

Durham

Bishopston Church of England Primary School, Hurworth	Mr. J. Kirkbride
Blackhall Mill County Primary School, Chopwell	Mr. J. H. Ross
Chopwell Junior School	Miss K. Fairburn
Chopwell Secondary Modern School	Mr. W. Low
Croft Terrace Secondary Modern School, Jarrow	Mr. R. W. Purvis
Grange Junior School, Jarrow	Mr. S. Scott
Hookergate Grammar School, Chopwell	Mr. E. Fawcett
Hurworth County Primary School	Mr. G. E. Addison
Hurworth Secondary Modern School	Mr. R. Copperthwaite
Jarrow Grammar Technical School, Jarrow	Mr. A. Masterman
Marlow Hall Secondary Modern School, Newton Aycliffe	Mr. J. H. Pearson
Marsden Primary School, Whitburn	Mr. F. C. Burn
Ryhope Grammar School, Whitburn	Mr. S. B. Graham
Sadberge Church of England Primary School, Hurworth	Mr. N. Brookes
Sugar Hill Junior School, Newton Aycliffe	Mr. D. H. Swan
Valley View Junior School, Jarrow	Mr. J. H. Jones
Vane Road Junior School, Newton Aycliffe	Mr. G. W. Ridley
Whitburn Junior School	Mr. B. Peart
Whitburn Secondary Modern School	Mr. R. Muncaster

School   *Head Teacher*

Essex

Beacontree Heath County Junior School, Dagenham	Mr. G. Bateman
Cleveland Junior Girls' School, Ilford	Miss M. A. E. Blake
Great Dunmow Junior Mixed and Infant School	Mr. V. Farthing
Great Sampford Junior and Infant School, Saffron Walden	Mr. G. Cuthbert
Hare Street County Junior School, Harlow	Mr. C. H. Kreling
John Bunyan County Infant School, Braintree	Miss E. Jenkins
King's Road County Junior School, Chelmsford	Mr. J. M. Jones
Lawford Mead County Junior School, Chelmsford	Mr. R. A. White
Maldon County Primary School, Maldon	Mr. D. J. R. Ferriby
Maldon Court Independent Preparatory School	Miss I. G. Carter
Marksgate County Infant School, Romford	Miss A. M. Woodiwiss
Mead County Infant School, Romford	Mrs. J. Lonsdale
Pitsea County Infant School, Basildon	Mrs. V. Telfer
The Spinney County Infant School, Harlow	Miss M. R. Killon
St. Cedd's Independent School, Chelmsford	Miss J. Ticken-Smith
St. Edward's Church of England Primary School, Romford	Mr. J. A. Davis
St. Mary's Roman Catholic Junior School	Sister Emanuel
St. Peter's Church of England Primary School, Brentwood	Mrs. M. Rogerson
Uphall County Primary School, Ilford	Mr. D. P. Griffiths
Wickford County Junior School, Basildon	Mr. R. E. Cole
Woodford Green County Primary School, Walthamstow	Mr. D. B. Spelman

Grimsby

Yarborough County Primary School	Mr. A. Beales

Hampshire

Ampfield Church of England Controlled Primary School, Romsey	Mr. N. D. Loader
Ashley Remedial Unit, New Milton	Mr. A. G. E. Sach
Botley Church of England Controlled Primary School, Southampton	Mr. J. Cresswell
Broughton County Primary School, Stockbridge	Miss M. M. Edwards
Cheriton County Primary School, Alresford	Miss M. G. Norman
Crampmoor Church of England Controlled Infant School, Winchester	Mrs. M. E. Barrington
East Boldre Controlled Primary School, Brockenhurst	Mrs. K. Harris
East Stratton County Primary School, Winchester	Mrs. R. J. Peachey
Hamble County Primary School, Southampton	Mr. H. J. Probert
Herriard Church of England Aided Primary School, Basingstoke	Mr. E. C. McCombie
Holybourne Andrew's Endowed Primary School, Alton	Mrs. D. M. Southeard

School	Head Teacher
Hursley The Keble Memorial Primary School, Winchester	Mrs. E. M. A. Warr
King's Sombourne Church of England Controlled Primary School, Stockbridge	Mr. D. W. Jones
Laverstoke County Primary School	Mr. G. Martin
Meonstroke Controlled Infant School, Southampton	Mrs. C. V. A. Ware
Micheldever County Primary School, Winchester	Mr. G. A. Brown
New Alresford County Primary School, Alresford	Mr. R. Whitaker
Nursling Controlled Primary School, Southampton	Miss J. E. Johnson
Old Alresford Controlled Primary School, Alresford	Mr. F. W. A. Lavis
Otterbourne Church of England Controlled Primary School, Winchester	Mrs. I. Livingstone
Overton Church of England Controlled Primary School	Mr. R. F. Hammond
Rownhams Controlled Primary School, Southampton	Miss M. E. Young
Steep Controlled Primary School, Petersfield	Mrs. M. M. Fletcher
Upham Aided Primary School, Southampton	Mr. M. C. Gladwell

Hertfordshire

Applecroft Junior School, Welwyn Garden City	Mr. R. G. Dawe
Bandley Hill Infant School, Stevenage	Mrs. J. K. Thomas
Howe Dell School, Hatfield	Miss B. Matthews
Howlands Primary School, Welwyn Garden City	Mrs. E. M. Cann
Strathmore Primary School, Hitchin	Miss K. Robinson

Kent

Lower Hardres Church of England Primary School, Canterbury	Miss M. I. Clough
Petham County Primary School, Canterbury	Mr. P. P. Squirrel
Waltham County Primary School, Canterbury	Mr. E. G. Hollick

Leicestershire

Abington High School, Wigston	Mr. T. Milner
Bushloe High School, Wigston	Mr. J. A. Blackhurst
Gartree High School, Oadby	Mr. E. S. Coggins
Glenmere County Primary School, Wigston	Mr. W. E. Looker
Launde Junior School, Oadby	Mr. G. R. Tipton
Ravenhurst County Junior School, Braunstone	Mr. W. G. Hazel
Stonehill High School, Birstall	Mr. I. S. Gaylon

London

Bellenden Infant School, S.E.15	Miss G. M. Clemens
Bellenden Junior School, S.E.15	Mr. A. D. Woodfield
Bessemer Grange Infant School, S.E.5	Mrs. D. F. Rankin
Bessemer Grange Junior School, S.E.5	Mr. L. A. Holden
Charles Lamb Infant School, N.1	Miss B. E. Robbins
Charles Lamb Junior School, N.1	Mr. A. D. Thake

T

School	Head Teacher
Duncombe Infant School, N.1	Miss I. Ofstein
Duncombe Junior Boys' School, N.1	Mr. G. E. Lynn-wood
Duncombe Play Centre, N.1	Mrs. M. Lonsdale
Edith Cavell Comprehensive School, E.6	Mr. R. Hase
Elizabeth Lansbury Nursery School, E.14	Miss F. Digby
Gilliatt Comprehensive School, S.W.6	Miss M. L. Kindred
Haggerston Park Play Park, E.2	Mr. J. D. Dennis
Hanover Primary School, N.1	Mr. G. J. H. Wakeman
Harmood Secondary School, N.W.1	Mr. S. S. Segal
Heathbrook Primary School, S.W.8	Mr. M. H. Evans
Henry Fawcett Infant School, S.E.11	Miss A. M. Johns
Highbury Quadrant Junior School, N.5	Mr. G. Palmer
Hungerford Infant School, N.7	Mrs. E. James
John Milton Primary School, S.W.8	Mr. E. J. Norfield
Langbourne Infant School, S.E.21	Mrs. J. Holden
Langbourne Junior School, S.E.21	Miss M. M. H. Stevens
Mayfield Comprehensive School, S.W.15	Miss M. Miles
New End Primary School, N.W.3	Mrs. C. V. Deslandes
Offord Primary School, N.7	Mrs. V. G. Klinger
Parliament Hill Comprehensive School, N.W.5	Mrs. F. R. Alvarez
Sherington Junior Boys' School, S.E.7	Mr. J. J. Harris
Sherington Junior Girls' School, S.E.7	Miss E. Diffey
Swaffield Junior Girls' School, Wandsworth, S.W.18	Miss E. Tonks
Susan Lawrence Infant School, E.14	Mrs. E. Abrahams
Tachbrook Nursery School, S.W.1	Miss I. Perlmutter
Tidemill Infant School, S.E.8	Miss D. I. Faithful
Vauxhall Adventure Playground, S.E.11	Mr. F. Nash
Vauxhall Infant School, S.E.11	Mrs. M. Hynds
Vauxhall Junior School, S.E.11	Mrs. A. Drabble
Watling Primary School, S.E.15	Mrs. V. Brennan
Wyborne Infant School, S.E.9	Mrs. M. H. Stripe

Manchester

Chorlton Park County Primary School	Miss M. C. Cockayne
King David Infant School	Mrs. B. Linton
Parkside School, Prestwich	Mr. R. J. Pitcomb
Poundswick County Infant School	Mrs. J. Butterworth
Princess Road Primary School	Mrs. B. Wigley (Infant)
	Miss D. Beavan (Junior)
Ross Place County Infant School	Mrs. E. M. Morris
Shakespeare Street Nursery	Miss E. Evanson
St. Aloysius Roman Catholic Infant School	Mrs. E. Secretan
St. Francis Gorton Roman Catholic Infant School	Miss H. Holt

Nottinghamshire

Bramcote Hills Primary School, Beeston	Mr. D. W. Wing
Ladybrook Junior School, Mansfield	Mr. G. Wilkinson

School   *Head Teacher*

Nottingham

School	Head Teacher
Arkwright Infant School	Mrs. N. Brooks
Blenheim Secondary Modern Girls' School, Bulwell	Miss E. M. Gutteridge
Blue Bell Junior Mixed and Infant School	Mr. J. Lowe
Brinkhill Junior Mixed School, Clifton Estate	Mr. M. Leishman
Fernwood Junior Mixed School, Woolaton	Mr. F. Whittaker
Glade Hill Infant School, Bulwell	Miss M. Cree
Glade Hill Junior School, Bulwell	Mr. D. A. Griffiths
Glaisdale Secondary Modern Mixed School, Bilborough	Mr. M. Unwin
Glapton Infant School, Clifton Estate	Mrs. E. Carrington
Glapton Junior Mixed School, Clifton Estate	Mr. E. A. Denman
Glenbrook Junior Boys' School, Bilborough	Mr. T. G. Cooper
Glenbrook Junior Girls' School, Bilborough	Miss I. Swindell
Middleton Junior Mixed and Infant School, Wollaton Park	Miss M. G. Walker
Nottingham Girls' School	Miss F. M. Milford
Robert Shaw Junior Mixed and Infant School	Mr. A. Smith
Robin Hood Infant School, Bulwell	Miss B. E. Standeven
Robin Hood Junior Mixed and Infant School, Bulwell	Mr. J. K. Crookes
St. Joseph's Preparatory School	Sister Augustine
Swansdowne Infant School, Clifton Estate	Mrs. O. M. Milnes

Oldham

School	Head Teacher
Ault County Infant School	Miss V. M. Sykes
Fitton Hill County Infant School	Miss P. O. Bennett
Limeside County Infant School	Mrs. E. Hall
Parish Church of England Junior Mixed and Infant School	Mr. J. N. Sharrocks
St. Anne's Roman Catholic School	Miss A. Walsh (Infant) Mr. T. McGrail (Junior)
St. Martin's Church of England School	Mr. J. A. Chapman

Oxfordshire

School	Head Teacher
Aston Bampton Church of England Primary School	Miss D. W. Pope
Brize Norton County Primary School	Mr. G. R. Baines
Cottisford County Primary School	Miss G. Broughton
Cropredy Church of England Primary School	Mrs. E. J. Samuels
Dr. South Primary School, Islip	Mr. W. J. Sydenham
Dragon School	Mr. J. H. R. Lynam
Filkins Church of England Primary School	Mr. E. F. Haycroft
Finmere Church of England Primary School, Finmere	Miss O. Bates

School	Head Teacher
Freeland Church of England Primary School	Mrs. W. G. E. Williams
Goring Church of England Primary School	Mr. D. L. Williams
Great Rollright Church of England Primary School	Miss B. W. Smith
Grey's Green Church of England Primary School	Mrs. F. Brain
Headington School for Girls	Miss P. A. Dunn
Hornton County Primary School	Mr. F. Blackhouse
John Hampden County Primary School, Thame	Mr. R. M. Groom
St. Christopher's Church of England Primary School, Langford	Mr. D. Evans
Mapledurham Church of England Primary School	Miss M. Kift
Mollington Church of England Primary School	Mrs. G. T. O'Brien
Mongewell County Primary School	Mrs. E. E. Hardman
Nuffield County Primary School	Mr. R. J. Horth
Our Lady of Lourdes Roman Catholic Primary School, Witney	Miss M. Maher
Sibford Gowe Church of England Primary School	Mr. J. Walpole
Speedwell County Infant School	Miss M. P. H. Medhurst
St. Christopher's Church of England Primary School, Langford	Mr. D. H. Evans
Stoke Row Church of England Primary School	Mr. C. B. Smith
The Manor County Primary School, Long Hanborough	Mr. J. W. Davidson
Tower Hill County Primary School, Witney	Mr. T. W. John
West Kidlington County Primary School	Mr. D. Clarke
Wroxton Church of England Primary School	Miss E. M. Hussey

Rochdale

Castleton Junior Mixed and Infant School	Mr. R. Redfern
Cronkeyshaw Junior Mixed and Infant School	Miss E. Wilkinson
Sacred Heart Roman Catholic School	Mr. K. A. Oakley
St. Gabriel's Roman Catholic Infant School	Miss B. M. Cleary

Salford

Brindle Heath Controlled School	Mr. J. L. Wilson
Great Clowes Nursery	Miss M. G. Edwards
North Grecian Street Infant School	Miss M. K. Chisholm
Tootal Drive Junior Mixed School	Mr. N. F. Clarke

Sheffield

Hucklow Junior Mixed School	Mr. V. Bradley
Stradbrooke Junior Mixed School	Mr. G. Long

West Sussex

Birdham School, Chichester	Mr. F. Morgan
Bishop's Bell Infant School, Crawley	Mrs. B. Toman

School	Head Teacher
Bishop's Bell Junior School, Crawley	Mr. D. Oakley
Bury Church of England Aided School, Arundel	Mr. J. W. M. Hamilton
Coldwaltham Church of England Controlled School, Pulborough	Mr. P. H. Horner
Findon Church of England Aided School, Worthing	Mrs. H. M. Powell
Gossops Green Infant School, Crawley	Miss E. Morgan
Gossops Green Junior School, Crawley	Mr. R. W. Needle
Ifield County Infant School, Crawley	Miss V. F. Beale
Ifield Junior School, Crawley	Mr. A. Worthy
Nuthurst Church of England Aided School, Horsham	Mr. A. G. Tittensor
Pound Hill County Infant School, Crawley	Miss D. M. Gutteridge
Pound Hill County Junior School, Crawley	Mr. C. W. Wragg
Rogate Church of England Controlled School, Petersfield	Mr. J. F. Rowe
Southgate County Infant School (with unit for physically handicapped), Crawley	Mrs. L. M. Catterick
Southgate County Junior School, Crawley	Mr. R. R. Greenwood
Washington Church of England Controlled School	Mr. L. Birch

Yorkshire (West Riding)

School	Head Teacher
Airedale Junior School, Castleford	Mrs. C. Pyrah
Ashton Junior School, Castleford	Mr. G. Neal
Castle School (Educationally Sub-Normal), Castleford	Mr. J. Shillitoe
Colne Valley High School, Huddersfield	Mr. E. T. Butcher
Darton Infant School, Kexborough	Mrs. L. Wraith
Girnhill Infant School, Featherstone	Miss M. S. Mackie
Lady Hastings Junior Mixed and Infant School, Ledsham	Mr. G. Murray
Lilly Hall Junior School, Maltby	Mr. F. T. Scholey
Loxley Junior School, Bradfield	Mr. C. Round
Netherton Junior Mixed and Infant School, Sitlington	Miss N. Smith
Orchard Head Junior Mixed and Infant School, Pontefract	Mr. L. Pritchard
Oyster Park Junior School, Castleford	Mr. J. Blackhouse
Redhill Infant School, Castleford	Miss M. G. Sanderson
Redhill Junior School, Castleford	Miss M. Walker
Regent Street Infant School, Featherstone	Miss M. A. Canning
Rossington Junior Boys' School, Doncaster	Mr. L. Tattersall
Thurcroft Infant School, Rotherham	Miss J. Marshall
Thurnscoe Infant School, Dearne	Miss M. Clarkson
Wath Central Junior School, Wath-on-Dearne	Mr. D. N. Hubbard
Wheldon Lane Junior Mixed and Infant School, Castleford	Mr. L. Harrison
Woodlands Infant School, Ardwick-le-Street	Miss J. Hairsine

(ii) *Schools in Scotland*

Bernard Street Secondary School	Mr. W. Wyatt
Copeland Road Secondary School	Mr. M. Buchanan
Glenwood Secondary School	Mr. M. Gardner
Kinning Park Secondary School	Mr. H. McKay
Mosspark Primary School	Mr. R. Brough
St. Columba's Secondary Roman Catholic School	Mr. J. McEwan

(iii) *Visits to Colleges of Education, University Departments, University Institutes of Education and other Institutions in England and Scotland*

Institution	*Principal or Director*
Avery Hill Training College, London, S.E.9	Mrs. K. E. Jones
Bletchley Park Training College, Buckinghamshire	Miss D. G. Cohen
College of St. Mark and St. John, London S.W.10	Mr. A. A. Evans
College of the Venerable Bede, Durham	Mr. K. G. Collier
Darlington College of Education	Miss P. M. Steele
Didsbury College of Education	Mr. A. H. Body
Langside College of Further Education	Mr. H. C. Allan
Manchester College of Education	Miss M. S. Valentine
Neville's Cross College of Education, Durham	Miss M. Whitley
Padgate College of Education, Fearnhead, Warrington	Dr. J. L. Dobson
St. Mary's College of Education, Newcastle upon Tyne	Madame P. M. Baker
University of Manchester, Department of Education	Director: Professor R. A. C. Oliver
University of Manchester, School of Education	Director: Professor S. Wiseman
Victoria University of Manchester	Vice Chancellor: Sir William Mansfield Cooper, and members of the University School and Department of Education

Members of the Council met and conferred with Dr. J. J. Grant, Director, University of Durham, Institute of Education and Professor B. Stanley, Director, University of Newcastle upon Tyne, Institute of Education. They also met and conferred with Professor J. D. Nisbet, Director, University of Aberdeen, Department of Education.

(iv) *Discussions with Members and Officials of Local Education Authorities*

In the course of their visits to local authority areas, members of the Council held conferences with members and officials of local education authorities. In this way evidence was received informally from the following authorities:—
Bradford, Bristol, Durham, Essex, Hampshire, Leicestershire, London, Manchester, Nottingham, Oldham, Oxfordshire, Rochdale, Salford, West Riding and West Sussex.

II. List of Visits the Council made Outside the U.K.

DENMARK

The Royal Ministry of Education, Copenhagen	Head of the Department for International Relations of the Ministry of Education: Mr. E. Drostby
	Government Adviser of the Ministry of Education: Mr. V. Baltzer
Skolen Ved Sundet, Copenhagen	Headmaster: Mr. Chr. Borgwardt Christensen
Voldparkins Skole, Copenhagen	Asst. Headmaster: Mr. L. Smith
Nyboder Skole, Copenhagen	Headmaster: Mr. R. Mejlasing
Oehlenschlaegersgades Skol, Copenhagen	Headmaster: Mr. Bruno Jørgensen
Børnegården I Utterslev, Utterslev	
Saxogården, Copenhagen	
Oehlenschlaegersgades Børnehave, Copenhagen	
Jonstrup Statsseminarium, Lyngby	Rector: Mr. Mogens Hansen
Primary School Lyngby	
Skaevinge Primary and Reale School	Headmaster: Mr. Becker Gassen
Police Youth Club, Baldersgade	

FRANCE

Discussions were held at the Institut Pédagogique National with officials of the Insitut and the Ministry of Education	M. M. Leherpeux, Chef du Service d'Accueil et de Liaison
Visit to the Municipality of Sarcelles, Écoles Maternelles, Primary Schools and Maison des Jeunes et de la Culture	
Visits to:—	
L'École Normale d'Instituteurs, Rue Molitor	
L'École Normale d'Institutrices, Rue Anizan Cavillon	
Centre National d'Education de Plein Air	
L'École Departementale d'Asnières, Seine	
Classes de Mi-temps Pédagogiques de Vandes	
Centre International d'Études Pédagogiques de Sèvres	
Maison des Enfants, Meudon, Sèvres	

POLAND

Discussions at Ministry of Education of the Polish People's Republic with Vice Minister of Education, Mr. Ferdynand Herok and others. Discussions at Polish Institute of Pedagogy with Dr. Okon and others.
Visits to:—

Kindergarten 12, Warsaw	
Kindergarten 165, Warsaw	
Kindergarten 185, Warsaw	
Hospital School, Ul. Ozakowslia 75a, Konstancin	Headmaster: Dr. Weiss
Experimental School No. 4, Warsaw	Headmaster: Dr. Fleming
Muriana Buczku Primary School, Ottarzewie	Headmistress: Mrs. Maria Lopatkova
Pedagogical Lyceum, Obozowa, Warsaw	Headmistress: Mrs. Kocanowa
Nauczycielskie School, Warsaw	
Primary School No. 234, Warsaw	Headmistress: Mrs. Bogusz
Palace of Youth	

SWEDEN

Conferences with senior officials, Royal Swedish Board of Education, Stockholm.
Meetings with Professor T. Husen and other members of Faculty of the Teacher Training University at Stockholm.
Visits in Stockholm area to:—

St. Görans day nursery	Mrs. Adler
Visits to children's playgrounds	
Aspuddens comprehensive school	Headmaster: Mr. S. Munknäs
Tallkrogens comprehensive school	Headmaster: Mr. H. Ekman
Kungsklippans kindergarten	Miss B. Schlyter
Training Institution for nursery school teachers, Kungsholmsgatan	Headmistress: Miss B. Schill
National Federation of Parent-Teacher Associations	Mrs Edgård
Gubbängens comprehensive school	Headmaster: Mr. S. Forsberg

Visits to the County of Västmanland and the town of Västerås. The group were received by members and officials of the Provincial Board of Education and by the Västerås City Authorities.
Visits were made to:—

Centralskolan Fjärhundra	Headmaster: Mr. Torsten Esemark
Persboskolan Skultuna	Headmaster: Mr. David Hallsman
Kristiansborgssskolan, Västerås	Director: Mr. Per Thorsell
Centralskolan, Kolbäck	Senior Headmaster: Mr. Einar Andersson
Lillängsskolan, Västerås	Headmaster: Mr. L. Petterson
Hagaskolan, Västerås	Headmaster: Mr. N. Källbäck

U.S.S.R.

Discussions were held at the Ministry of Education for the R.S.F.S.R. (Mr. Ivanov and others): Academy of Pedagogical Sciences (Mr. A. I. Marcoushievich, First Vice-President): State Educational Publishing House (Mr. Terekhov): Ministry of Education, Mme. M. V. Tarasova (Head, preschool directorate).
Visits were paid to:—

Moscow

The Pioneers' Palace	
Kindergarten No. 1301	Headmistress: Mme. Budarina
Secondary School No. 1 English	Headmistress: Mme. I. L. Shipova
Boarding School No. 15	Headmaster: Dr. Shervindi
V.I. Lenin Moscow Pedagogical Institute	Headmaster: Mr. Gherasin
Academy of Pedagogic Sciences	

Gorki

Leniniski Gorki School, Lenin Hills

U.S.A.

Visits were paid to a large number of schools, universities and colleges throughout the U.S.A. The following visits were made:—

New York

Visits to:

P-33-M School	Principal: Dr. Martin Silverman
P-161-M School	Principal: Dr. Bernard Friedman
P-92-Q School	Principal: Miss Ellen M. Maguire
P-149-Q School	Principal: Mr. David Price
P-89-Q School	Principal: Mrs. Reba Mayer
P-196-Q School	Principal: Mr. Fred H. Morris
P-129-M School	Principal: Mrs. Martha Froelich
P-187-M School	Principal: Mrs. Sarah L. Mandel
P-123-M School	Principal: Mr. Erwin C. Kaufman
P-152-M School	Principal: Miss Veronica A. Myers
Bank Street Training College	Mrs. Charlotte B. Winsor, Chairman, Graduate Program in Education
Education Division, The Ford Foundation	Mr. Frank Bowles, Program Director, Education Division
Institute of Developmental Studies	Dr. Martin Deutsch Mrs. Caroline Saxe

The Centre for Programmed Instruction of the Institute of Educational Technology — Mr. P. Kenneth Komoski, Associate Executive Officer

Horace Mann-Lincoln Institute of School Experimentation, Teachers College, Columbia University — Professor Arthur Foshay

Experimental Teaching Centre, New York University School of Education — Dr. Glen Heathers, Co-ordinator for the Dual Progress Plan

Centre for Urban Education — Dr. A. H. Bowker

Conference with Association of Social Workers — Miss Barbara M. Moore, Associate Director, Department of Social Work and Practice.

Centre for Urban Education, City University of New York — Albert H. Bowker, Chancellor, City University of New York, Professor Robert Dentler, Chairman of Centre's Planning Committee. Professor Miriam Goldberg Mr. K. Komoski, Center for Programmed Instruction of the Institute of Educational Technology Teachers College, Columbia University

Syracuse, New York

Visit to Syracuse University School of Education — Professor Don Adams

Ford Foundation Programme — Dr. Ernest Milner

Pre-school group in campus school — Mrs. Betty Robinson

Discussions with officials of Madison School Project — Mr. Gerry Weinstein and others

New Haven, Connecticut

Visit to C.P.I. and associated schools and the Ford Foundation Project — Mr. Sviridoff

Dwight Community School — Miss May White

Henry Conte Community School — Mr. Jack Doyle

Winchester Community School — Mr. Barbarissi

Mr. O'Hare

Hagerstown, Maryland

Visit to Schools Television Project — Dr. William M. Brish, Superintendent of Schools, Washington County

Washington

Conference with Mr. Francis Keppel, U.S. Commissioner of Education

Visit to National Education Association — Dr. Ashby and Mr. Childs

Atlanta

Visit to the Faculty of Teacher Education at Emory University	Professor T. Ladd, Director, Division of Teacher Education
	Dr. Ralph D. Schmid, Associate Director, Division of Teacher Education

Wesley Avenue School
Tull Waters School
Meeting with Atlanta City school workers

Los Angeles

Visit to University Demonstration School, University College, Los Angeles (University of California)	Professor John Goodlad, Director, University Elementary School, School of Education

Santa Monica

Visits to schools and nurseries to see parent education. Mrs. Avanot, Parent Education Department.

San Francisco Area

Conference with Dean Quillen, Professors Robert Bush and Dwight Allen, Stanford University School of Education.

Visit to Center for Advanced Study of the Behavioral Sciences	Dr. Preston Cutler, Associate Director
Stanford Elementary School	Principal: Dr. H. W. Dohemann

Visits to Schools in Stanford and San Francisco areas.

University Elementary Education Department, Berkely University	Dr. Lloyd Scott and Dr. Enoch Dumas

Chicago

Conferences with Dean R. Campbell and members of faculty.

Visits to University Laboratory School.	Principal: Dr. Lloyd.
Florence Addams School of Social Work	Professor Florence Poole
	Professor June Wille

Madison

Visit to University of Wisconsin, Madison	Dean, School of Education; Dr. Lindley Stiles
Multimedia Instructional Laboratory	Dr. J. Guy Foulkes

Demonstration, Computer Based Program Instruction
Visit to Wisconsin Improvement Program 1965 Spring Conference
Visits to schools in City of Madison

School of the Air, Radio Hall	Dr. Arlene McKeller
Elementary School Program in Madison Schools	Mr. Arthur Mennes, Director of Curriculum and Instruction for Elementary Schools
Pre-School Laboratory, University of Wisconsin	Dr. Helen C. Dawe

Conferences with:—

Dr. Russell T. Gregg, Professor of Educational Administration
Dr. Arthur P. Miles, Professor of Social Work
Mr. Angus Rothwell, State Superintendent of Public Instruction, State of
  Wisconsin

Harvard Graduate School of Education: Dean Theodore Sizer and
                                                  Dr. J. Anderson.

Visits to:—

Franklin School, Lexington   Mrs. Bears
Estabrook School   Mr. Cummings
Horace Mann School, Newton   Mr. Danielson
Hamilton School   Mrs. Chadwick

Conferences with:—

Dr. Edward Landy, Professor of Education and Assistant Superintendent,
  Department of Special Education and Pupil Personnel, Newton Public
  Schools
Dr. Edwin E. Moise, James Bryant Conant Professor of Education and
  Mathematics
Dr. Joseph Grannis, Assistant Professor of Education
Dr. Douglas Porter, Assistant Professor of Education and Research Associate
  in the University Committee on Programmed Instruction
Dr. Charles Brown, Superintendent of Schools, Newton, Mass.
Dr. Maurice Belanger, Assistant Professor of Education
Dr. David Purpel, Assistant Professor of Education, Director of Secondary
  School Student Teaching and Acting Director of the Master of Arts in
  Teaching Program
Dr. James G. Holland, Lecturer of Education, Research Associate in the
  University Committee on Programmed Instruction and Executive Secretary
  of the University Committee on Programmed Instruction
Dr. Benjamin Nichols, Director Elementary Science Study
Mr. Michael Katz and other doctoral students

Advanced Course: Course in a university or university department of education leading usually to a higher degree, or diploma designed to equip experienced teachers for more responsible posts.

Adviser: A specialist employed by a local education authority to advise the authority and teachers on the organisation and teaching of a special subject or stage of education.

Advisory Teachers: Peripatetic advisers employed by some local education authorities to work beside teachers in the classroom.

A.E.C.: Association of Education Committees.

Agreed Syllabus: Syllabus of religious instruction agreed between representatives of a local education authority, religious denominations and teachers.

Aided School: A voluntary school whose managers are responsible for repairs to the exterior of the building, and for capital expenditure for alterations required by the local education authority to bring the premises up to the standards of the Building Regulations. All running costs are met by the authority; capital costs of improvement and repair to external fabric are eligible for 75 per cent Exchequer grant. The managers have substantial rights in the appointment and dismissal of teachers and in the giving of denominational religious education. One third of the managers are appointed by the local education authority.

Aides, Teachers: Trained ancillaries who it is suggested will give substantial help to teachers inside and outside the classroom.

All-Age School: A school containing pupils of both primary and secondary ages.

A.M.C.: Association of Municipal Corporations.

Ancillary: Auxiliary: A paid worker who is not a qualified teacher and who assists in the school in any capacity.

A.T.C.D.E.: Association of Teachers in Colleges and Departments of Education.

A.T.O.: Area Training Organisation. A grouping of colleges and departments of education, usually called an institute of education, but sometimes a school of education. All but one are part of a university. They vary in structure but all are concerned to integrate the facilities in their area for training teachers; to oversee the academic content of the training course: to examine all candidates for the initial qualification for teaching (teachers' certificate or teachers' diploma) and to recommend them to the Department of Education and Science for the status of qualified teacher. They provide courses and conferences for serving teachers, organise research and bring together for various purposes the staffs and students of the institutions included in the organisation.

B.Ed.: Degree of Bachelor of Education. A degree in education proposed by the Committee on Higher Education to be awarded after a four year course. (See paragraph 978).

Building Programme: A list of projects on which the Department will allow building to start in a particular financial year. The total value of the programme is determined in advance according to the predicted educational demands and the capital investment available, and allocations are made to local education authorities as far in advance as possible, to enable them to begin planning.

Burnham Committee: (properly the Burnham Primary and Secondary Committee). A committee consisting of representatives of teachers, local education authorities and the Secretary of State for Education and Science, which negotiates teachers' salaries.

Capitation Allowance: Annual allowance allocated by local education authorities in respect of each pupil for expenditure by schools on consumable materials, equipment, books and the like.

Child Guidance Clinic: Centre run by local authority or other agency to treat maladjustment and allied handicaps in children.

Children's Centre: A grouping of nursery groups with day nurseries or clinics. (See paragraph 311).

C.L.A.S.P.: A consortium of local education authorities co-operating in the design and building of schools and in the design and marketing of school furniture and equipment.

Community School: (See paragraph 121).

Comprehensive School: A secondary school intended to cater for the secondary education of all the pupils in an area, organised as a whole and not in clearly defined grammar, modern and technical sides. Following Circular 10/65, local education authorities are reorganising secondary education in their areas on comprehensive lines.

Concurrent Course: Teacher training course in which academic and professional studies are followed at the same time.

Consecutive Course: Courses of professional education which follow academic studies for graduates and holders of other specified qualifications.

Controlled School: A voluntary school for which the local education authority is financially responsible. The authority appoints two-thirds of the managers as compared with one third in aided schools. Although controlled schools follow the Agreed Syllabus (q.v.) parents may opt for not more than two periods a week of denominational instruction. Teachers necessary to give this denominational instruction—"reserved teachers"—may be appointed for the purpose.

Cost Limit: The upper limit of costs for a building project, calculated from published standard formulae (which take account of the requirements of the different sizes and types of school) and prescribed for the project before it is included in a building programme.

C.C.A.: County Councils' Association.

County School: School which is built, maintained and staffed by the local education authority. Its full cost falls on public funds.

Critical Periods: (See paragraph 25).

C.S.E.: Certificate of Secondary Education. A subject examination taken at the end of a five year course of secondary education.

Day Nursery: Establishment under the control of health authorities where children under five can be left while parents are at work and for attendance at which fees may be paid.

D.E.S.: Department of Education and Science. (Originally the Board of Education, until 1945, and Ministry of Education, 1945 to 1964).

Direct Grant School: School receiving maintenance grants directly from the Exchequer in return for which 25 per cent of its places are offered free mainly through the local education authority to pupils who have attended a maintained school for not less than two years. The remainder of the places may be available for fee payers, except that a further 25 per cent must be made available to the authority if they wish to take them up.

Educational Priority Areas (E.P.As.)*:* Areas to be designated by the Secretary of State as in need of special provision because of a high incidence of educational deprivation (see paragraph 151).

Eleven Plus (11 +): The conventional term used to cover the techniques (e.g. attainment or intelligence tests) which a local education authority may use to allocate pupils leaving primary schools at or about the age of 11 to different types of secondary education.

E.S.N.: Educationally subnormal. Slow learning (see paragraph 849).

E.W.O.: Education Welfare Officer. An officer employed by local education authority on school attendance and welfare work (see paragraph 217).

Family Grouping: (see Vertical Classification).

First School: Term to be used for a school for the five to eight year age group.

Form Entry: The number of classes admitted in a year.

G.C.E.: General Certificate of Education. A subject examination normally taken at the end of a five year course of secondary education ('Ordinary level') and at the end of a seven year course ('Advanced level').

Government, Articles of: Regulations covering the conduct of a secondary school.

Governors: Members of a governing body of a secondary school.

Graded Post: A post of responsibility which carries an allowance additional to the basic salary scale.

Graduate Teacher: A teacher holding a university degree. Teachers holding certain other professional qualifications are recognised for salary purposes as 'graduate equivalent'. Graduate teachers may or may not have received a year's professional training, for which they receive a diploma or certificate in education.

Hadow Reports: Reports of the Consultative Committee under the Chairmanship of Sir Henry Hadow. They were: The Education of the Adolescent (1926), the Primary School (1931) and Infant and Nursery Schools (1933).

Handicapped: Child suffering from mental or physical handicap and in need of special educational treatment.

Health Service, School: The service through which a local education authority meet their statutory obligation to arrange for the medical examination and medical treatment where necessary, of children in school.

Health Visitor: State Registered Nurse with obstetrical experience who takes an additional year of study leading to the Certificate of the Council for the Training of Health Visitors. (See paragraph 204).

Helper: See Ancillary.

H.M.I.: Her Majesty's Inspector of Schools.

I.A.P.S.: Incorporated Association of Preparatory Schools. An association of schools consisting of preparatory schools recognised as efficient.

I.L.E.A.: Inner London Education Authority.

Independent School: A school which is not supported out of public funds, providing primary or secondary education or both. (See also Registered and Recognised).

Infant: Literally, a child who cannot speak. Child between 5 and 7 or 8 years receiving education. In health service a child over six months. At common law, a person who has not reached the day before his 21st birthday.

Infant School: School or department for children from five to seven or eight (see First School).

In-Service Training: Courses of further training which teachers undertake while in service, provided by the D.E.S., local education authorities, colleges, institutes or departments of education and which vary in length from one day to a year or more.

Institute of Education: See A.T.O.

I.Q.: Intelligence Quotient. (see paragraph 56).

I.T.A.: Independent Television Authority.

i.t.a.: Initial Teaching Alphabet. Alphabet invented by Sir James Pitman designed to help children more quickly over the first stages of learning to read (see paragraph 589).

Joint Four: The Joint Four Secondary Associations (the Incorporated Associations of Head Masters, the Association of Head Mistresses, Assistant Masters Association, Association of Assistant Mistresses).

Junior School: School for children from seven to twelve.

J.M.I.: Junior Mixed and Infant School. A co-educational school for children from five to twelve.

Junior-Secondary: Initial course which provides training for teachers in either junior or secondary schools.

L.C.C.: London County Council.

L.E.A.: County or County Borough Council with responsibility for education in its area.

L.H.A.: Local Health Authority.

L.H.A.: Local Housing Authority.

L.P.A.: Local Planning Authority.

Main Course: Part of the teacher training course reserved for the students' personal education, in which one or two subjects are studied in depth.

Maintained School: A county or voluntary school maintained by a local education authority.

Major Work: A building project costing more than £20,000.

Management, Rules of: Rules made by a L.E.A. for the conduct of primary schools, maintained or voluntary. Rules are administered by a Managing Body of not less than six members who are representative of the various interests concerned with the school and appointed according to the terms of an Instrument of Management.

Managers: Members of the managing body of a primary school.

Mature Students: Late entrants to teacher training who are 25 and over.

Middle School: A school for children aged 8 to 12 (or 9 to 13).

Minor Work: Building project costing less than £20,000.

M.O.H.: Ministry of Health.

M.H.L.G.: Ministry of Housing and Local Government.

N.A.I.E.O.: National Association of Inspectors and Educational Organisers.

N.A.S.: National Association of School Masters.

National Survey: 1964 National Survey of Parental Attitudes and Circumstances Related to School and Pupil Characteristics, 1966. Survey commissioned by the Council and reported in Appendices 3, 4, 5, 6 and 7 and Chapters 3 and 4.

National Survey of Child Health and Development: Longitudinal study of 5,000 children born in March 1946 and followed up through their school career and beyond.

N.C.D.S.: National Child Development Study (1958 Cohort). Multi-disciplinary follow-up study of a group of children in the 1958 Perinatal Mortality Survey which studied 17,000 babies born during a week in March in 1958. Reported in Appendix 10.

N.F.E.R.: National Foundation for Educational Research (see paragraph 1154).

N.N.E.B.: National Nursery Examination Board. A central examining body which grants certificates for nursery nurse work and similar types of employment.

Norm: Mean or median score for an age group of a representative population in an intelligence or attainment test.

Nuffield Foundation: An independent trust which has sponsored research and development in various fields. Currently sponsoring projects in French, mathematics and science in primary schools in collaboration with the Schools Council.

Nursery Assistant: Trained person assisting qualified teachers in nursery school, class or group holding a certificate of N.N.E.B. (q.v.).

Nursery Centre: A unit comprising two or three nursery groups.

Nursery Class: Class attached to primary school for children aged three to five with up to a maximum of 30 places.

Nursery Group: A unit, not exceeding 20 places, to provide nursery education for children from three to five.

Nursery School: School providing education for children from two to five.

N.U.S.: National Union of Students.

N.U.T.: National Union of Teachers.

Observation Register: (See paragraph 215).

Occasional Teacher: A teacher for whom no qualifications are prescribed and who may be employed only in an emergency, or part-time to meet some special need.

Oversized Classes: Classes containing more pupils than laid down in the Department's Regulations, that is 30 for nursery classes in primary schools or for senior pupils in all-age schools, 40 in other primary schools and 30 in secondary schools.

Pre-School Play Groups: Voluntary part-time play groups for children under five.

Primary School: School at present catering for children under 12.

Probationary Year: First year of service in a maintained school during which a teacher is required to prove his practical efficiency on which depends the grant of recognition as a qualified teacher. The period of probation may be extended.

P.T.A.: Parent-Teacher Association. Voluntary association of the parents and teachers of a school.

Pupil-Teacher Ratio: Average number of pupils to a teacher in a school or an area or the country as a whole.

Qualified Teacher: Teacher who has successfully completed a course of training in a college of education or university department of education, has been awarded a teacher's certificate and granted qualified teacher (Q.T.) status by the D.E.S. A graduate without professional training can be granted Q.T. status.

Quota: A system designed to alleviate maldistribution of teachers. L.E.As. are assigned by the D.E.S. a total number of full-time teachers for staffing their schools which they are not expected to exceed.

R.E.: Religious Education. (Called 'Religious Instruction' (R.I.) in Education Act, 1944).

Recognised as Efficient: All independent schools must be registered by the D.E.S. which lays down certain minimum standards. Schools can apply to be 'recognised as efficient' under the Department's Rules 16. Such recognition is only granted to schools achieving much more stringent standards.

Registered: See Recognised as Efficient.

Rising Fives: Children who start school at the beginning of the term in which they reach the age of five. The statutory age of entry to schools is the beginning of the term after the child's fifth birthday.

Schools Council for the Curriculum and Examinations: A body set up in 1964 jointly by local authority and teacher associations and the Department of Education and Science.

School Leaving Age: Date at which compulsory education ends, at present the Easter or Summer after a pupil's 15th birthday. The leaving age is to be raised to 16 in 1970–71.

Secondary School: School at present catering for children over eleven.

Selective School: School for which pupils can be selected, usually at 11 plus, on the grounds that they would benefit from a more academic education than is provided in non-selective schools.

Setting: Division of an age group into different groups or sets for some subjects according to ability.

Short Courses: Residential courses from 4 to 14 days duration for serving teachers organised by the D.E.S.

Shortened Courses: In specially approved cases students in training for teaching may, by virtue of age, education or experience, be allowed to complete their course in less than the normal three years.

Special Educational Treatment: Educational treatment provided for handicapped children in special schools, or classes or ordinary classes as appropriate.

S.S.R.C.: Social Science Research Council. A body set up in 1966 following the recommendations of the Heyworth Committee on Social Studies.

Streaming: Grouping of children in an age group according to ability.

S.R.N.: State Registered Nurse.

Supplementary Courses: Courses designed to give a year of further training to experienced teachers who have had a two-year course of initial training only.

Teaching Practice: Periods of practical teaching in schools undertaken by students during their training. Can be either 'block practice' in which a substantial period of time is spent in the school or 'group practice' in which students make intermittent visits to schools during the college course and usually work with small groups of children rather than the whole class.

Team Teaching: Method of teaching developed in the U.S.A. by which teams of teachers of varying skills and experience are organised within a school with responsibility for groups of children up to two hundred.

Temporary Teacher: Unqualified teacher with at least five G.C.E. 'O' levels or equivalent whose employment has to be approved by the Secretary of State. Approval is normally given for two years and then renewed, if necessary, at yearly intervals.

U.D.E.: University Department of Education. Department of a university providing postgraduate course of professional teacher training.

Unit Totals: A figure determined by the number of pupils in different age groups in a school, which is used to calculate allowances for heads, deputy heads and other holders of posts of responsibility.

Vertical Classification: Form of grouping found mainly in infant schools in which a class extends over two or three age groups.

Voluntary School: A school which can be built by a voluntary body, for example, a denomination, but which is maintained by an L.E.A. (see Aided and Controlled Schools).

Index

Index

Unless otherwise stated, references are to paragraph numbers. Printed sources are indexed only if referred to directly in text. References to other printed texts are placed at the end of the appropriate chapter. References are made to both Volumes of the Report although Volume 2 has not been indexed in detail. There are several references in the text to the National Survey (Appendices 3, 4, 5, 6 and 7) and to the questionnaire to a sample of teachers (Appendix 1) which are not given in the Index.

Abel-Smith, B. 36
Ability
  Differences between children in rates of attaining, 16
  Pool of (Crowther Report), 83
Act of Worship, 561, 562, 571, 572
  Excusal from, 570
Adams, B. and Smith, D.M., App. 12
Advisory Services, 941–947
  And religious education, 577
  For probationers, 1010
  Cost of expansion, 1199, 1112
  Need for expansion, 947
  Need for general review, 947
A.E.C. Study of ancillary help in schools, 891, Table 23
Age
  Changes in transfer ages and buildings, 396–398
  Compulsory attendance at school, 345–346, Table 11,
  Developmental, 15–20, 352, 370, 389
  Joining nursery groups, 316
  National policy on transfer ages, 393–396
  Of menarche, changes in, 39–41, Diagram 2
  Raising of school leaving age, 365–387, 1178
  Transfer to middle school, 360–364
  Transfer to secondary school, 365–387
Agreed Syllabuses, 562, 563, 567, 574–576
Aides
  Awards of qualifications, 1050
  Career prospects, 1051
  Comparability with nursery assistants, 1036
  Costs of, 1219–1228
  Entry qualifications, 1038
  Expansion of training, 1049
  N.A.S. views, 924
  Nature and length of courses, 1040–1046, 1048
  Numbers and recruitment, 924, 1037, 1053, 1181–1182, Table 37, 1205–1218
  Status and Salary, 922, 923, 1047
  Functions, 918, 922–925
  Training, 922, 1035–1037, 1040–1046

Aids To learning and teaching, 637, 722–73
  (see also *Books, Equipment, Films, Radio T.V.*)
Aims of primary education, 493–507
All-Age Schools (see *Reorganisation of Schools*)
Ancillary Helpers
  Association of Education Committees Report, 891, Table 23
  Definition, 918 (and F.)
  Employment in primary schools, 890–893, Table 23, 918–921
  N.U.T. Survey, 891–918
  Voluntary helpers, 927
Art and Craft, 676–685
Assessment
  At 11 (see *Selection for Secondary Education*), 418
  Teachers, 414, 416, 419
Assistant Teachers (see *Teachers*)
A.T.C.D.E., 981, 982
  Joint report and evidence on probation of teachers, 999, 1001, 1002
A.T.Os. (see *Institute of Education*)
Attainment
  And different educational methods, 508–555
  And streaming, 791, 803, App. 4, App. 9 App. 11
  In rural areas, 478
  Relationship with class size, 780–788
  Relationship to size of child, 38
  Relationship with home conditions (see also National Survey) 76–101, Table 1, App. 4
  Tests of, 414–415
  Possibilities of error in testing, 420

Baldwin, J., 521
B.Ed., 595, 966, 978–79
Behaviour
  Discipline within school, (*see also Punishment*), 734–742
  Factors in development of, 42–52
  Social, stages of, 72–74
Behaviourists, 519–20
Belgium, 798
Bernstein, B., 302

545

Birmingham Survey (1962) into teachers' first posts, 1002–5, 1007
Birthrate, 328 (and F) 879
Books (see also Reading)
  Allowances for, 1106
  Collections, 591, App. 5
  For Immigrant Children, 187
  Numbers in homes, 97, App. 3
  Provision of, 591
  Report by A.E.C., 1112
  Report by Publishers' Association, 1112
  Space for, 1093
  Use of, 591–96, 722
Bowlby, J., 70
Boyle, Sir Edward, 85
Boys
  Differences in rates of development from girls, 13, 14, 34, Diagrams 1A & B, App. 10, 362
  Predominance in child guidance clinics, 34, App. 10
  Proneness to disabilities, 34
  Streaming, disadvantages of, for, 814
  Test biases, 420
Bristol Adjustment Guide, 848
Bristol Institute of Education
  Enquiry into probationary year, 1003
British Broadcasting Corporation
  Science programmes, 663
British Psychological Society
  Enquiry into 11+, 411
  Survey of children in hospitals for the subnormal, 841 (and F)
Bruner, J., 521
Buildings
  Building Bulletins, 1080–1103, Diagrams 8–13
  Building Research Station Study of location of schools, 1098 (i)
  Costs of, Table 39
  C.L.A.S.P., 1100
  Cost Limits, 458, Table 13, 1093, 1094
  Department of Education Building Survey (1962), 1081, Tables 29–31
  Design for new age structure of education, 1098 (iii), Diagrams 9–13
  Educational innovation and, 1087, 1092–98
  In educational priority areas, 164
  Major building programmes, 1082, 1085, 1120, 1190–3
  Minor building programmes, 1082, 1089, 1120, 1190–3
  N.U.T. Building Survey (1962) 'State of Our Schools', 1081
  Of nurseries, 326, 339, 340, 1098 (iii), Diagram 9
  Playgrounds, 1098 (iv)
  Remodelling old schools, 1086–91, Tables 30, 31
  Sanitation, 1083
  Shortages of and needs for, 133, 164,

Buildings (cont.)
  1081–3, Tables 29–31
  Size of school and cost of, 458
  The environment, 162, 326, 1098 (i)
Burnham Scale Allowances
  Additions for, 1027
  Deputy Heads, 939, Table 34
  E.P.As. 159, 170 (ii)
  Graded posts, 936, 939–40, Table 34
  Head of department, 939–40
  Head teachers, Table 33
  Points system, method of calculation, 940, Annex to Ch. 29
  Rural areas, 475
  Special responsibility, 1151
Burt, Cyril, 59, 153 (e), 1164

C.A.C. (England) Reports
  Crowther, 83, 138
  Early Leaving, 82
  Newsom, 82, 85, 138, 457, 894, 899
  Out of School, 122
C.A.C. (Wales), Ch. 14 (and F.), 483
Canal Boat Families, 155, 159, App. 12
Care Committee, 241, 927
Central Council for Training in Child Care, 234, 246, 1034
Certificate, Council for the Training of Health Visitors, 204
Certificate in Education Welfare, 220
Certificate of Secondary Education (C.S.E.), 1038
Child Care Officres, Children's Officers and Children's Departments, 221–27, 229, 230, App. 8
Child Guidance Clinics, 211–14
Child Minders, 293, 299
'The Child, The Family and the Young Offender' (White Paper), 221
Children and Young Persons, Act 1963, 221
Children in Care, 221, Table 5
Coeducation, 259, Diagram 4
CLASP, 1100
Classes (see Streaming, Vertical Classification, Team Teaching)
  Admission 345–346
  Class spaces, 761, 1092–95, Diagrams 8–13
  Class teachers, 769, 772
  Different class sizes at different stages, 894, 895, 898–900
  Division of groups, 757–60, 775
  Grouping of (see Team Teaching), 773
  Instruction in, 752, 757, 772
  Interchange of, 763, 764, 766
  Size (see Size of Class)
  Special, for handicapped children, 859
Colleges of Education (see also B.Ed., Courses for Teachers, Graduates and *Teacher Training)*
  Admission policies, 861, 962
  Discipline (agreement between A.T.C.D.E. and N.U.S.), 981, 982

Colleges of Education (cont.)
Expansion programmes and number of places, 950–952
In E.P.As., 163
Men and women students, 963
Mature students and shortened courses, 952, 954, 964
Qualifications of students, 953
Relations with schools, 984–998
Staffing, 975–977
Combined Schools (*see J. M. and I. Schools*)
Community Schools
Appointment of heads and deputy heads, 126
Cambridgeshire Village Colleges, 122
Extended hours, 122
Findings of N.U.T. Survey, 124
In E.P.As., 126
In other countries, 123
L.C.C. play centres, 122
Out of school clubs, 125
Payment of staff by parents, 126
Recommendation, 126
Comprehensive Education, 418
Conel, J. L., 22
Consultative Committee Reports (*see Hadow Reports*)
Continuity, 431–437
Contacts between teachers, 424–435
Of curriculum and organisation, 442–447
Pupils' records, 435–437
Conversation, 535
Costs of Primary Education, 1167–1204, Tables 39, 40, 43, 44 and 45
And yield, 1171–1176
Running costs, Table 40
Council for Training in Social Work, 234, 246
Courses for Teachers (*see also B.Ed., Colleges of Education, Graduates, Teacher Training* and *In-service Training*)
B.Ed., 978–979
Concurrent, 959
Consecutive, 958
Content of, 970, 971
Curriculum, 974
Description of, 970–974, 982
Education, 973
Junior-secondary, 382, 429
Main, 972
Nursery, 950
Three year, 950
Critical Periods (Sensitive periods), 24–29
Curriculum (for references to subjects see separate headings)
Developments since beginning of century, 508–571
For immigrant children, 187–192
Flexibility in, 538–542
Recommendations of Hadow Report (1931), 529

Dance and Movement 1933 Syllabus, 702–4, 705
Davies, B. P., 150, 227, App. 14
Day Nurseries
Age range, 314
Co-operation with nursery schools, 314
Departmental control, 313
Note of Reservation on Organisation By Professor D. V. Donnison, Sir John Newsom and Dr. M. Young, page 487.
Reasons for admission, 313
Denmark
Length of day, 827
Recreation for school children, 123
Sizes of schools, 462
Dental Service, School, 211
Department of Education and Science
List of recommendations in Chapter 32 gives references to Department of Education
Development Group, 473, 1094
1962 School Building Survey, 1081, 1082, 1084, 1086, 1088, Table 30, 31
Deprivation (*see also Educational Priority Areas*)
Emotional, 70
Language development of deprived children (*see Language*)
Proportion of handicapped in deprived areas, 153 (f)
School and teachers in deprived areas, 131–146
Specially deprived groups: gypsies and service children, 155–157
Deputy Heads, 935
Training for, 1025
Deutsch, M., 7, 302
Development
Age (*see Age, Developmental*)
Behaviour, 42–52
Economic and social development and primary education, 140, 143, 145
Emotional, 65–75
In communication, 53–55
Intellectual, 50 (and F.), 51, 56–64
Late development, 17, 390, 391
Moral, 73
Social, 71, 72
Variations in, 14–20, 47
Dewey, J., 510
Discipline, 734–750
Discovery Methods, 549, 550
In Science, 669
Doctors, School, 205
Dossier Scolaire, 436 (f)
Douglas, J. W. B., 84, 1164, (and J. M. Ross) 302
Drama, 600
Dyslexia, 590

'*Early Leaving*' (1954) (*see* C.A.C.)
Education Acts
  1944, Provision for primary education, provisions for age of transfer to secondary education, 257
  1964, Provisions for different ages of transfer, 257 (b)
Education Welfare Officers
  Number and qualifications, 216, App. 8
  Organisation, 228
  Role and status, 217–219, 245–246
  Training (Certificate in Education Welfare), 220
Educational Priority Areas, 131–173
  Additions to teachers' pay, 171 (ii), 1186
  Colleges of education, 163
  Community schools, 167
  Criteria, 147–157
  Government expenditure (*see also Grants*) 170 (vi)
  Housing, 162
  Nursery assistants, Table 36
  Nursery education, 165, 170 (iv)–173, 319, 1186
  Parents, 136
  School building, 164, 1186
  Schools, 131–135
  Social work, 166, 248
  Special groups, 155–157
  Steps to be taken for improvement, 168–173
  Teachers, 158–162, 170 (i), 1186, Table 35, Table 36
  Teachers' Aides, 170 (iii)
Educational Foundation for Visual Aids, 1107
Elementary Code, 1918, 508
  Abolition, 1944, 508
Eleven Plus (*see Selection for Secondary Education*)
Emotional Development
  Anthropological aspects, 65
  Freudian interpretation, 65
  Sequence of, 65–74
  Social aspects, 65
English, 578–613
  Project English, 612, 613
Entry to School
  Age of, 357–359
  Part-time, 354, 355
  Staggered, 355
  Termly, 347–351
Environment
  Effect on physical growth, 33–38
  Environmental studies, 626–628
  Interaction with genetic factors, 29–32
  Relationships with educational attainment (*see Attainment*)
  Use of, 543–548
Equipment
  Allowances, 1102–1112, 1122
  Cost of, 1199
  Design of new furniture, 1100

Equipment (cont.)
  Local authority variations, 1104, 1105, Table 32, 1112
Evaluation of primary education, 551–553
Examinations
  Developmental, 215 (iii), 352
  Medical, 208–210, 215 (i)–(iii)
  Eleven plus (*see Selection for Secondary Education*)
Expenses, Enquiry into, 1027

Families
  Age of puberty, 36
  Extended families, 297
  Family Service Units, 318
  Incomplete, 154(g)
  Size of, 153(b)
    correlated with class, 153(b)
      housing, 153(b)
      income, 153(b)
      intelligence, 90
      nutrition, 153(b)
      physical growth, 36
Fathers
  Role in children's education, 108, 109
  Visits to schools, 112(ii)–(iii)
Films and Hand Viewers, 637, 725, 726
First Schools (*see Infant Schools*)
Floud, J., 93
Fraser, E., 93
Froebel, 510, 511, 753
French, teaching of, 614–619

Gardner, D.E.M., 1151
Genes
  And environment, 29–32
  "sleeper effect", 32
Geography, 634–636
Gifted Children, Education of, 861–872
Girls (*see also Boys*)
  Age of menarche, 39–41
Glasgow
  School welfare officers, 249
Grading
  By ability, 806
  By age, 793, 798, 805, App. 11
Graduates (*see also B.Ed.*)
  Probation of, 999
  Training of, 955, 956, 959, 965, 980
  Untrained, 999
Grammar, 612
Grants
  From central government to local authorities, 147–150
Groups
  Group instruction, 755–770
  Size of, 757
  Team teaching, 761–770
  Vertical grouping, (*see Vertical Classification*)

Growth
And family size, 36
Economic, and primary edn., 1171–1176
Of brain, 21–23
Physical, 12–20, Diagram 1A, 1B
Relationship to environment, 33–38
Sex differences in, 34
Gypsies, 155, 157, App. 12

Hadow, Sir Henry (*see Hadow Reports*)
Hadow Reports (Reports of the Consultative Committee)
1926, 1, 258, 263
1931, 1, 6, 77, 263, 512, 513, 529, 621, 753, 778, 791, 898
1933, 1, 262, 306, 320–322, 345, 753
Half-Day Attendance (*see also Nursery Education*)
First school, 353–359
Halsey, A. H., 93
Handbook for Teachers (*1905*), 508
Handicapped Children, 834–859
Advisory Committee on, 835
And parents, 843, 844
Assessment and ascertainment of, 836–842
Categories of, 840, Table 17
Children unsuitable for education in schools, 841
In educational priority areas, 153(f)
In the ordinary school, 845–848
Junior training centres, 841
Need for study of, 859
Provision for, 836, 840, Table 17
Relationship between handicapped and other children, 845, 852
The Handicapped Pupils Regulations, 1959, 840 (and F.)
Training of Teachers for, 854–856
Slow learners, 849–853
Head Teachers
And welfare work, 932
Freedom of head teachers, 929
Functions, 931, 934, 938, 1141–6
Head teachers and staffing ratios, 460, 907–908
In-service training, 1025
Numbers of men and women, 882
Relations with parents, 932, 938
Relationship with managing body, 1137–1139
Relationship with other staff, 933, 935, 1147
Health of School Child, 202, 206, 210, Table 3, App. 2
Health Services (*see also Appendix 2*)
Care of children before school, 203
Developmental examinations, 209
Health Visitors, 203, 204, 232, 319
Improvement in children's health, 202–206

Health Services (*see also Appendix 2*) (cont.)
Links between school health and other health services, 207, 313
Medical examinations, 208–210
School dental services, 210
School doctors, 204, 205
Schools Health Service and the Handicapped Pupils, 1953, 208
School nurses, 204
Selective medical examinations, 209
Hebb, D. O., 64
Height
Rate of growth (height velocity), 12
Relationship to educational performance, 38
Relationship to size of family, 36
Relationship to social class, 35, 37
Sex differences, 13, Diagram 1A
Trend towards greater height, Diagram 1B
Heredity and Environment, 29–32
Heyworth Committee on Social Studies, 1153
Hindley, C. B., 84
History, 620–634
In junior schools, 622
H.M.Is.
Advice on size of school, 455
Complementary roles with local inspectors, 943–944
Enquiries by, teachers' first year, 1002 continuity, 442
National Survey, 88
Quality of primary education, 267–276, 290
Functions, 509, 552, 943
Inspection of nurseries, 325
National Survey, assessment of schools, 88, App. 5, 267–276
Work on primary school mathematics, 650
Holidays, 829, 830, 832
Home Circumstances
Visits by teachers (*see also Parents*), 113
Homework, 112(iv), App. 3
Home Office, 201, 223, 293, 1029
Hubel, D. H., 24
Hull, C. L., 519
Hungary
Musical education, 693
Hunt, J. McV., 302
Husen, T., 59
Howell, D., App. 13

I.A.P.S., 1060, 1062, 1065
Immigrant Children, 178–198
Contacts with homes, 188–189
Curriculum for, 187–192
Dispersal policies, 193–195
In educational priority areas, 153(h)
Language difficulties, 190–192
Numbers, 181, 182, Table 2
Special provision for, 195, 196

Immigrant Children (cont.)
  Teacher training, 197
Income, Family, 79
Independent Primary Schools, 1056–1078
  Contacts with maintained schools, 1069–1073
    Improvements in, 1065, 1069–1073
  Independent Schools Tribunal, 1068
  Notices of Complaint, 1059, 1068, 1069
  Numbers of pupils and schools, 1060, 1062
  Recognition under Rules 16, 1060, 1063, 1064
  Registration under Part III of Act, 1059, 1069
  Staffing of, 1070–1072
Individual Differences, 47
Infant Schools (First Schools)
  Age of entry and transfer, 344–364, 388–390, 392(a)–(e)
  Age range, 261–263, 360–364
  Emergency plan for, 399–405, Table 12
  Length of course, 360–364
  Optional part-time education, 355–356
  Reading in, 583–589
  Short-term proposals for entry arrangements, 399–405, Table 12
  Size of, 463, 464
  Staggered entry, 355
  Teachers' aides, 924
  Termly and annual entry, 357–359
Ingleby Report, 201(F), 221, 239
Inhelder, B., 23
In-Service Training, 1013–1027
  Advanced courses, 1016
  Closure of schools, 1027
  Cost of, 1199
  Department circular, 1013, 1018
  For continuity, 430
  For heads, 1025
  Mathematics, 650, 651
  N.A.S. views, 1014
  One term courses, 1017
  Organisation and co-ordination of, 1014–1024
  Recommendations, 1023, 1027
  Residential and local centres, 1018, 1020
  Returners, 1026
  Secondment for, 1014
  Short courses: local, 1019
    national, 1018
  Supplementary courses, 1015
Institute of Community Studies, 115–117
Institutes of Education, 957, 990
Intelligence (Measured)
  And children's size, 38
  Correlation with parental occupation, 56, 57, 62, 63
  Genetic and environmental factors, 56, 57, 62
  Group intelligence tests, 61, 422, 811
  Inconstancy of I.Q., 58–61

Intelligence (measured) (cont.)
  Individual intelligence tests, 61, 811
  Intelligence quotient, 56
  Testing of, 59–61, 64, 413–416, 796, 811, 817–819
  Wechsler Intelligence Scale test, 64
Isaacs, Nathan, 521
Isaacs, Susan, 309(a), 513, 1151
I.T.A. (*see Reading*)

Joint Four Secondary Associations, 898
J.M. & I. Schools (Combined Schools)
  For and against, 426, 428
Junior Schools (Middle Schools)
  Ages of entry and transfer, 360–387
  Origin and progress, 263
  Size, 463–465
  Streaming, 806–825

Kilbrandon Committee, 201 (F.), 239

Language
  Attempts to improve poor use of, 302
  Deprived children, 136, 301, 302
  Development of, 53–55, 672, 675
  Immigrant children, 190–194
  Second Language (*see Modern Languages*)
  Teachers of immigrants, 197, 198
  Vocabulary counts, 55, 639
Learning
  Behaviourists (*see Behaviourists*)
  Learning theories, 67, 518, 535
  Piaget (*see Piaget J.*)
  Relation with other development, 16–20
  Role of play, 523–539
Legal Position of Primary Education, 257
Length of Day, 826–828
Length of Term, 829–832
Linguistics, 611
Local Authority Inspectors
  Complementary to H.M.Is., 943–944
  Creation of outstanding schools, 945
Local Government Bill (1966), 195
Local Options, 368, 395–398, 1192, 1201 (e)
London County Council
  Evidence on buildings, 1083
  Evidence on size of school, 456
  Play centres, 122
Longitudinal Studies, 1164
Lorenz, K., 27
Luria, A. R., 521

Management of Schools, 1131–1138, App. 13
  Appointment of parents as, 1132
  Differences between functions of managers and governors, 1134
  Managers, 1131
  Managing Bodies, 1131
Manchester Survey, 93, 144, 454, App. 9, 781, 817

Married Women
  As nursery assistants and teachers' aides, 305, 1037, 1211–1218, 1219, 1228
  Register of married women teachers, 160, 161, 912
  Returners, 883
  Training for, 1026
Martin, F. M., 93
Mathematics (see also National Foundation for Educational Research), 647–662
  Curriculum Bulletin No. 1 (Schools Council), 651, 654
Mathematical Association 'The Teaching of Mathematics', 649
Maturation
  Individual differences in rates, 14–20
  Secular trend towards earlier maturation, 39–41, Diagram 2
Mays, J. B., 113
Macmillan, Margaret and Rachel, 264, 510
Meals Assistants, 919
Medical Examinations, 208–210, App. 2
Men Teachers, 903–905
  In infant schools, 904, 905
  Quality of, 904
Middle School (see Junior Schools)
Milner Holland Committee Reports (1964), 141
Ministry of Health, 201, 293, 313, 1029
Ministry of Housing and Local Government, 201
  Sociological Research Unit, App. 12
Ministry of Labour
  Statistics on Mobility, 394
  Survey of Married Women, 1181
Ministry of Public Building and Works, 1100
Modern Languages, 614–619
Montessori, 510, 753
Moral Development, 73
Mothers
  Child Mother relationship, 70, 307
  Disadvantages of over separation, 307
  Correlation between social background and interest in education, App. 3
  Economic benefits, 1219–1228
  Mothers and nursery groups, 320–322
  Mothers at work, 305, 330
Music, 686–696

National Advisory Council for the Supply and Training of Teachers (N.A.C.)
  Ninth Report, 799, 894, 901, 907
National Assistance, 200
  Indicator of deprivation, 153(c)
National Association of Inspectors and Educational Organisers (N.A.I.E.O.)
  Evidence on advisory services, 947
  Joint report on Probation, 999, 1002
National Census, 153(a)
National Child Development Study

(N.C.D.S.)
  (1964 Cohort), 34, 302, 305, 351, 355, 362, 549, 851, 1164
National Food Surveys, 36
National Foundation for Educational Research (N.F.E.R.), 1153–1160
  Analysis of Pupils' Allocation to secondary schools (1964), 408
  Enquiry in Twickenham, 1956, 415
  'Educational Research', 1159–1160
  Register of research, 1158
  Survey of junior school organisation and streaming (1962 and 1966), 443, 610, 763, 783, 793, 795–797, 803, 806, 810, 812, 814, App. 11, 816, 817
  Survey of mathematics, 552
  Survey of Reading, 362, 454, 552
National Institute for Economic and Social Research (prediction of married women workers), 305, 1214, 1223
National Institute for Social Work Training, 234
N.N.E.B. (National Nursery Examination Board)
  Arrangements for practical training, 1030
  Courses, 922, 1050
  Functions, 1030–1033
National Plan, 1177, 1181
National Society, 473
National Survey of Parental Attitudes and Circumstances Related to School and Pupil Characteristics (1966), 76 (and F), Apps. 3, 4, 5, 6
  Summary of Findings, 90–101
National Union of Students (N.U.S.), 981
National Union of Teachers
  Survey of Nursery Education (1964), 294, 297
  'State of Our Schools', (1962), 124, 468, 470, 881, 885, 891, 918, 1081
  Joint Report on Probation, 999, 1002
Newcastle Commission, 1061
Newsom Report (see C.A.C. (England) Reports)
Nuffield Foundation, 1153, 1160
  Projects, 517, 615, 651, 652, 667
Nursery Assistants, 311, 1195
  Career prospects, 1051
  Costs, 1181
  Entry qualifications, 1038
  Expansion of training, 1049
  Final qualifications, 1050
  Functions, 323, 333
  Interchangeability with teachers' aides, 1047
  Nature and length of courses, 1040–1046, 1048
  Numbers, 336–338
  Recruitment, 1036–1039, 1053, 1182–1183, 1189, Table 37, 1205–1218
  Status in salary, 1047, 1051
  Training, 1030, 1035–1037

Nursery Education
  Age range, 316
  Buildings needed (*see Buildings*)
  Case for and against, 296–308
  Circular 8/60, 295
  Control of nursery education, 295
  Cost, 342, Table 41
  Council's proposals, 309, 311, Table 38, 1219–1228
  Employment of teachers, 310, 312, 333–335, 338, 1195
  Factories, 326
  Fees for, Note of reservation by Dr. M. Young and others, page 487
  History, 264, Table 4
  In E.P.As. (*See Educational Priority Areas*)
  Nursery centres, 311
  Nursery classes, 264, 295, Tables 4, 5
  Nursery nurses, 1029
  Nursery schools, 264, Tables 4, 5
  N.U.T. Survey, (*see National Union of Teachers*)
  Part-time and full-time places, 317, 328(a), 329, 330
  Places needed, 328, 331, Table 10
  Present provision, 292–294, Table 5
  Requirement of compulsory education, 358
  Research, 297, 301–303, 305, 307, 309
  Residential nurseries, 293, Table 5
  Siting of nurseries, 326
  Social handicaps, 295, 302
  Status of nurseries, 312
  Voluntary groups, L.E.A. grants, 323
  Working Mothers (*see Mothers at work*)
  Note of reservation by Mrs. M. Bannister, page 486
Nursery Schools Association, Evidence, 298
Nurses, School, 204, App. 2

Orff, C., 688
Out of School Activities (*see Community Schools*)
Owen, R., 753

Parents, 102–129
  Advice to, 112–118
  Anxiety about selection (*see Selection for Secondary Education*)
  As managers (*see Management of Schools*)
  Choice of school, 120
  Immigrants, 181, 188, 189
  Information on education, 112(iv)
  Nursery education, 320
  Occupation and children's intelligence, 62, 63, 78, 85, 86, 89, Table 1, 94
  Unco-operative parents, 113
  Pamphlets, 112 (iv), 119
  Parental attitudes (*see also Social Survey Study of Parental Attitudes*), 92–101, App. 3, 4
  Parent teacher relations, 107–110

Parents (cont.)
  Parent teacher association, 110, 111
  Policy for local education authority, 119, 120
  Policy for schools, 112, 118
  Providing voluntary help in schools, 126
  Relationships in rural areas, 491
Part-time Attendants (*see half-time attendants and nursery education*)
Part-time Teachers, 883, 912–917
  Burnham Committee study of salaries, 912
  Cost of, 1199
  Department of Education information, 883, 912, 913
  Employment of, 912–917
  For handicapped children, 857
  Help to head teachers, 914(c), 389
  Superannuation scheme, 912
Pavlov, I. P., 519
Peaker, G. F., App. 4, 7
Perinatal Mortality Survey (*1958*) 141,
Pestalozzi, J. H., 510
Physical Education, 697–713
  1933 Syllabus, 697–698
Piaget, J., 23, 50, (and F), 371, 521, 522, 530, 649
Play
  Centres, 122
  Importance in learning, 523–528
  In infant schools, 523
  In nurseries, 523
Poetry, 597, 598
Poland
  Extended hours, 123
Pre-School children
  Social differences in ability, 84
Pre-School Play Groups Association, 323
'*Primary Education*' (*1959*), 615
Priorities, 1184–1202
Probationary Period, 999–1012
  Associations' reports on probation, 999, 1002–1005, 1012
  Length of probation for graduates, 999
  Numbers of extensions, 1000
  Placing Probationers, 1001
  Probationers and advisers, 1011
  Role of L.E.A.s., 1010, 1011
Probation Service, 221–227, App. 8, 230
Programmed Learning, 519, 728, 731, 853
Project Work, 540–542
Psychologists Educational (and School Psychological Services), 211, 212, App. 2
Psychiatric Social Workers, 211, 229
Public Schools Commission, 1058
Punishment, 743–750
  Corporal Punishment, 744–750
  In independent schools, 749
  Note of reservation on corporal punishment by Miss M. F. M. Bailey page 493

Pupil-Teacher Ratios
Present ratios, 886, 887, Tables 18–22, 889, Table 24
Differences between primary and secondary, 894, 895, 898–901, 1121
Recommendations, 910, 911
Qualified Teachers (see also Graduates)
Numbers, 878–889, Tables 18–22, 24, 894, 901
Award of status, 957
Quota, Teachers, 881, 889, 897

Radio, 637, 725–727
Reading
Ability, 583–588
C.A.C. Survey of Reading Ability, 583, App. 7, 553, 585
N.F.E.R. Survey of, 586
I.T.A., 362, 454, 553, 588–589
Reading aloud, 599
Related to size of class, 587
Related to size of school, 454
Relations to social class, 586
Social class bias, 587
Teaching of, 583, 584
Transfer to middle (junior) school, 586
'Readiness', 534
Reading Institute Study of Probation, 1012
Recommendations and Conclusions, 1219–1243
Religious Education, 559–576
1944 Act, provisions of, 560–563
H.M.I. survey of, 564
Note of Reservation by Professor A. J. Ayer and others, page 489
by Mr. E. W. Hawkins, page 492
Reorganisation of Schools, 258, Diagram 3, 259, 261, 263
Reports on Children, Annex to Part III, Volume 1, 112 (v)
Research
On children's learning, 1151–1166
Studies needed, 1165
Richardson, M., 677
Robbins Report
Handicaps of children of manual workers, 84
Imputed rents, Table 43 (and F.)
Structure of teacher training (*see also* B.Ed.), 949
Roberts, Dame Jean
Dame Jean Roberts Committee Report (Scotland, 1966), 159
Rousseau, J. J., 510
Rural Schools
Age range, 463, 480–483
Closures, 469, 470
Developments in design, 1094
Experimental schemes, 484, 485
Help for, 484–491
Lack of facilities, 473, 474
Numbers, 468, 470

Rural Schools (cont.)
Sizes, 470, Table 15, 480
Staffing, 475–477, 486–490
Save the Children Fund, 318, 323
Schemes of Work, 934
School Broadcasting Council for the United Kingdom, 688
School Library Association, 1107
School Secretaries
Fuctions, 919, 920
Schools Council for the Curriculum and Examinations, 516, 517, 612, 651, 654, 667, 1153, 1159, 1160
Schonell, F. J., 1151
Science
Department pamphlet (1957), 667
Physical sciences, 666
Study of living things, 663–666, 670
Scottish Council for Research in Education: Report on Age of Transfer, 384 (and F.)
Secondary Modern Schools
G.C.E. courses, 411
Secondary Schools (Education)
Age of transfer, 365–387
Continuity between primary and secondary education, 429, 431–439, 441
Earlier intakes to, 391, 392 (e)–(g)
One and two tier schools, 375, 376
Selection for (*see Selection for Secondary Education*)
Staffing ratios (*see Size of Class*)
Transfer—special cases, 388–392,
Seebohm Committee, 201, 221, 242
Selection for Secondary Education
H.M.I. assessment of effects, 412
Impact on primary education, 409, 411, 412
Methods of, 414–422
N.F.E.R. analysis (1964), 408
Parents' anxiety and complaints, 412
Sensory Motor Skills, 46
Sex Education, 714–721
Size of Class, 778–788
And pupil-teacher ratio, 907, 908
Conclusions, 786–788
Differences in sizes, 780, 1121
Facts, Diagram 7, Table 16, 779, Table 22
Hadow (1931) recommendations, 778
In infant schools, 788, 792
Manchester Survey, 781
Oversize, 897
Relationship with attainment, 781–784
Research on, 780–785
Scottish Research Council's views, 785
Statutory maximum, 778, 898
Size of School
Building and maintenance costs, 457–459
Educational characteristics, 454
Changes in sizes, 260
In rural areas, 480–483
L.C.C. evidence, 456
Optimum size, 451–456, 463–466

Size of School (cont.)
Present sizes (1965), 480, Table 8, Table 15
Staffing costs, 460, Table 14
Skinner, B. F., 519
Sleeper Effect, 32
Slow Learners (see Handicapped Children)
Smiling Response, 43
Social and Welfare Services, 200–254, App. 8
Cost of, 1199
In E.P.A.s., 248
In Scotland, 249, 253
Integration of, 244
Local studies in three areas, 225, 227, 232, 237, App. 8
Organisation and deployment of, 228–233
Recommendations, 242–254
Relationship with schools, 235–241
Relationship with teachers, 238
Training and recruitment for, 234, 246, 247, 253
Voluntary Organisations, 224
Social Science Research Council, 1153, 1162
Social Survey Study of Parental Attitudes (see National Survey of Parental Attitudes . . .)
Southampton School Mathematics Project, 661
Special Schools (see Handicapped Children)
Specialists and Specialisation, 538
In primary schools, 370, 934, 947
Transition to secondary education, 381
Speech (see also Language)
Development of speech, 580–582
Therapists, 213, App. 2
Staff Meetings, 933
Staffrooms, 1088, Table 31
Standards
Assessment of standards of primary education, 267–276
Assessment of standards of pupils, 552–554
Reading (see Reading)
Status of Primary Education, 1114–1149
Comparisons with secondary teachers, 1119
Differences between primary and secondary qualifications, 1125–1126
Salary scales, 1115, 1123, 1124
Social Survey study of undergraduate attitudes to teaching, 1116
Streaming (see also Grading)
Conclusion, 818–825
Effect on children, 815–817
Favourable to girls, 814
Hadow recommendations (1931), 791
Jackson Study (1962), 806, 807
N.F.E.R. Survey, 795–797, 803, 806, 810, 812, 814, App. 11
Other Research, 806–817
Parents' opinions, 808

Streaming (see also Grading) (cont.)
Relationship to achievement, 817
Social background, 815
Teachers' opinions, 807
Students (see Teacher Training)
Summer Born Children, 347–350
Sweden
Contact with parents, 113
Location of schools, 462
Royal Swedish Board of Education, 462
Size of class, 780
Size of schools, 462

Teachers (see also Nursery Education)
Advisory, *(see Advisers)*
Balance between men and women, 881, 882, 903–905
Costs of, 1179–1180
Distribution of, 160, 161, 889
Full-time and part-time, 883
Occasional, 926
Peripatetic, 333, 857
Qualified, *(see Qualified Teachers)*
Representation on committees, 1128–1130
Role of, 873–878
Salaries *(see Burnham Scale of Allowances* and *Status of Primary Education Salary Scales)*
Shortage of, 878–880, 1188
Shortage of infant teachers, 896, App. 5,
Supplementary, 476
Supply and training of, a suggestion by Dr. I. C. R. Byatt and others, page 493
Teachers' Aides, *(see Aides)*
Temporary, 926
Unqualified, 476, 884, 885, 893
Wastage, 880, 881
Teachers' Centres, 674
Residential courses, 1020
Teacher Training
Day colleges and outposts, 960, 980
For handicapped children, 854–856
For immigrants, 197
For P.E., 713
For R.E., 577
Graduates *(see Graduates)*
In technical colleges, 960
Need for enquiry into, 949, 1166
Teaching practice, 973, 985–991
Team Teaching, 761–770
Television, 724, 725
Termly Entry, 347–351
Testing (see Intelligence, Measured and Selection for Secondary Education, Methods of)
Thorndike, R. L., 519
Thorne Scheme, 417
Time-Table, 536–537, 640
Townsend, P., 36